FIX-IT
and
FORGET-IT®
BIG COOKBOOK

FIX-IT and FORGET-IT®

BIG COOKBOOK

1400 Best Slow Cooker Recipes!

By *The New York Times*
bestselling author
Phyllis Pellman Good

Good ❖ Books®

Intercourse, PA 17534
800/762-7171
www.GoodBooks.com

Although the analysts and editors have attempted full accuracy in the nutritional data and analyses included with the "Light" recipes in this cookbook, many variables (including variations related to particular brands, to the refinement of products, and to the exact amounts of ingredients, as well as whether they are cooked or raw) could result in the analyses being approximate.

Because many factors influence your health, please check with your health-care expert before making substantial changes in what you eat.

Cover illustrations and illustrations throughout the book by Cheryl Benner.

Photographs at bottom of front cover, photograph on back cover, and photographs on pages 29, 97, 233, 301, 401, 501, 601, and 699 by Jason Varney.

Photographs on pages 30–32, 98–100, 165–168, 234–236, 302–304, 402–404, 502–504, and 602–604 © by Oxmoor House.

Design by Cliff Snyder

FIX-IT AND FORGET-IT!® BIG COOKBOOK

Copyright © 2008 by Good Books, Intercourse, PA 17534

International Standard Book Number: 978-1-56148-640-3
Library of Congress Catalog Card Number: 2008030360

Library of Congress Cataloging-in-Publication Data

Good, Phyllis Pellman
  Fix-it and forget-it big cookbook : 1400 best slow cooker recipes! / Phyllis Pellman Good.
      p. cm.
  Includes index.
  ISBN 978-1-56148-640-3 (hardcover : alk. paper) 1. Electric cookery, Slow. 2. Quick and easy cookery. I. Title.
  TX827.G6324 2008
  641.5'55--dc22   2008030360

Table of Contents

About
Fix-It and Forget-It Big Cookbook

This grand treasury of the best "make-it-again" slow-cooker dishes is ready to be your steady kitchen companion.

I selected these 1400 favorite recipes from our five beloved *Fix-It and Forget-It* cookbook series. They are gathered here in one handsome, meant-to-be-used volume!

THE BIG SOLUTION

Fix-It and Forget-It BIG COOKBOOK offers tasty cooking solutions every day.

- Too little time to cook?
- Worried about your skills in the kitchen?
- Scared of a flop?

Note the Prep Time at the head of each recipe. Most are happily short.

Each recipe's instructions spells out every step so you won't get stranded along the way. This book makes cooking manageable, even though you might feel inexperienced. (I first fell in love with the "peepy-step" approach to cookbook instructions when I was a completely novice cook.)

And all of these recipes come from home cooks. These are their favorite dishes, loved by families and households across the country. So get out your slow cooker—or cookers—and choose from these flexible, forgiving, and absolutely scrumptious recipes.

There's tempting variety among the recipes, and many differ only by a tantalizing ingredient or two. So pick the particular recipe that suits your mood, pleases those who eat at your table, or matches the ingredients you have on hand.

You'll find helpful Tips spread among the recipes—the kind of pointers that you usually learn only after a long acquaintance with a slow cooker, or with cooking in general. Think of them as the voices of your favorite aunt or grandmother, standing at your elbow with their cooking wisdom.

A WORD ABOUT SLOW COOKERS

Slow cookers have proven to be the efficient friend of those cooks who are gone all day, or who don't want to be occupied in the kitchen for hours, but want to offer substantial home-cooked food to their households.

You can prepare a dish one evening, store the filled "lift-out" vessel in the fridge overnight, and then place it into its electric component in the morning as you do your dash to the door. Or you can tote the whole works to a buffet or carry-in meal, doing no damage to the quality of its contents.

These great little appliances can vary considerably in their heat intensity and speed of cooking. Older models often require more cooking time than newer ones. That's why I give a range of cooking times for many of the recipes. Experiment by using the shorter cooking time first. Then make a note right on the recipe page itself about what you discovered works best for your cooker. Personalize this cookbook.

IDEAL SLOW-COOKER SIZES

The ideal slow-cooker size given with each recipe is just a suggestion. I went big in most cases so that you aren't faced with a pot that's running over. (On the other hand, be aware of the fact that your food may get too dry if your pot is less than half full.)

Some raw vegetables stand up and take a lot of room. As they cook, they quiet down and sink together. So some recipes with an abundance of uncooked vegetables suggest a larger cooker than other recipes which yield the same number of servings.

Slow cookers are great for carry-in meals and pot-lucks.

But who wants an overflowing pot in the back of a vehicle? So, again, I tilted toward the larger size.

VARIABLES TO KEEP IN MIND

Ideally, you should fill your slow cooker about ⅔ full. You may need to increase the cooking time if you've exceeded that amount, or reduce it if you've put in less than that.

- The fuller your slow cooker, the longer it will take its contents to cook.
- The more densely packed the cooker's contents are, the longer they will take to cook.
- The larger the chunks of meat or vegetables, the longer they will take to cook.

If you put ingredients into the cooker straight out of the refrigerator, you may need to add 20–30 minutes to the suggested cooking time.

If you put frozen meat into the cooker, you should add 4–6 hours of cooking time on Low, or 2 hours on High.

If you're using a slow cooker at an altitude over 3,500 feet, you will need to cook its contents somewhat longer than the recipe states. Allow time to experiment, and then write what worked next to the recipe.

If you want to check that the meat in your slow cooker is fully cooked, use a food thermometer:

- Beef should reach an internal temperature of 155°–160° F.

About Fix-It and Forget-It Big Cookbook

- Pork should reach an internal temperature of 155°–160° F.
- Poultry breasts should reach an internal temperature of 160° F; poultry thighs 175° F.

CONVERTING RECIPES FOR SLOW-COOKER USE

Many stove-top and oven recipes can be adapted for a slow cooker. If you want to experiment, use these conversion factors:
- Low (in a slow cooker) = 200°, approximately (in an oven).
- High (in a slow cooker) = 300°, approximately (in an oven).
- In a slow cooker, 2 hours on Low = 1 hour, approximately, on High.

CONSIDER THE WONDER OF OWNING SLOW COOKERS OF VARYING SIZES

Slow cookers do their job famously well, whatever their size—1-quart, 3-quart, 6-quart, or in between. Little ones work well for singles or doubles, or they cook the vegetables while the beef burbles away in a bigger cooker, sharing the same counter-space. In fact, you can do a whole meal in slow cookers, thereby multiplying the pleasure without significantly increasing the work. Just be alert to the lesser amount of cooking time needed by the small cookers. (Check the instruction manuals to get the cooking time right.)

"LIGHT" RECIPES

You'll notice that some of the recipes in this book include nutritional analyses. These are the dishes to prepare when you're looking for light and healthy eating.

CALCULATING THE NUTRITIONAL ANALYSES

The recipe analyses for these recipes are based on the lesser amount of an ingredient when a range of amounts is given. Optional ingredients are not included in the analyses. Only those items on a recipe's list of ingredients are part of that recipe's analysis. (If a recipe's procedure or notes suggest serving it with pasta or potatoes, for example, those foods are not calculated in the analysis.) The serving sizes are quite modest in these recipes, all in an effort to assist with portion control.

THE PASS-IT-ON TRADITION

Good cooks love to share their recipes. They don't possess them; they pass them on. This collection is rich because of all the home cooks who generously offered their favorite recipes, so that all of us could fix satisfyingly delicious food at home. Thanks to each of you who has shared your gems. This books holds your precious food traditions, and we are all grateful.

Thank you, too, to the cooks who tested and evaluated these recipes. Your comments, as well as those from the family and friends around your dinner tables, were invaluable.

This champion collection of recipes came together with the superb assistance of many staff members at Good Books through the years, especially Esther Becker, Tony Gehman, Cliff Snyder, Jamie Schwankl, Dawn Ranck, Delphine Martin, Norma Gehman, and Melissa Horst, as well as Jan Mast, Dean Mast, Peggy High, Kate Good, and Rebecca Fennimore. And always Merle. Thank you. Thank you.

WHY IS THE *FIX-IT AND FORGET-IT BIG COOKBOOK* SUCH A RELIABLE FRIEND?

- Its pages are packed with recipes.
- Many of its recipes call for just a few ingredients—and they're readily available.
- Lots of the recipes are offered in multiple variations. Find the one that suits your taste—and the ingredients you have on hand.
- Preparations are easy; the ingredients are reasonably priced.
- Everybody eats well—without the cook being under pressure.
- Little fuss. Lots of flavor!

You'll love cooking, hosting, and eating from this treasure of good food. *Fix-It and Forget-It BIG COOKBOOK* makes it possible for you to sit at the table together with your family and friends, around absolutely tasty food, no matter how wild and crazy your day.

Phyllis Pellman Good

Appetizers, Snacks, and Spreads

Spicy Cheese Dip with Ground Beef

Susan Tjon   Austin, TX

MAKES: **12–15 SERVINGS**
PREP. TIME: **25 MINUTES**
COOKING TIME: **2½ HOURS**
IDEAL SLOW COOKER SIZE: **2–3-QUART**

1 lb. lean ground beef
¼ cup onions, finely chopped
half a large onion, finely chopped
1½ lbs. Velveeta cheese, cubed
15-oz. can Rotel tomatoes with green chili peppers

1. Brown ground beef and ¼ cup onions in a large nonstick skillet. Break beef apart as needed. Drain.
2. Combine beef with remaining ingredients in slow cooker.
3. Cook on Low 2½ hours, or until cheese is melted.
4. Serve from slow cooker with scoop-shaped tortilla chips.

Tip: *The smaller the Velveeta chunks, the faster they will melt.*

Variation: *Instead of the ¼ cup onions, use ¾ tsp. garlic powder.*

Tierra Woods   Duenweg, MO

Mexican Chip Dip Olé

Joy Sutter   Iowa City, IA

MAKES: **10–12 SERVINGS**
PREP. TIME: **15 MINUTES**
COOKING TIME: **2–4 HOURS**
IDEAL SLOW COOKER SIZE: **3-QUART**

2 lbs. ground turkey

1 large onion, chopped

15-oz. can tomato sauce

4-oz. can green chilies, chopped

3-oz. can jalapeño peppers, chopped

2 lbs. Velveeta cheese, cubed

1. Brown turkey and onion. Drain.
2. Add tomato sauce, chilies, jalapeño peppers, and cheese. Pour into slow cooker.
3. Cover. Cook on Low 4 hours, or on High 2 hours.
4. Serve warm with tortilla chips.

Chili-Cheese and Beef Dip

Barbara Shie   Colorado Springs, CO

MAKES: **8–10 SERVINGS**
PREP. TIME: **15 MINUTES**
COOKING TIME: **1 HOUR**
IDEAL SLOW COOKER SIZE: **1-QUART**

1 lb. ground beef

1 lb. Velveeta cheese, cubed

8-oz. can green chilies and tomato sauce

2 tsp. Worcestershire sauce

½ tsp., or more, chili powder

¼ cup salsa with jalapeño peppers

1. Brown ground beef, crumble fine, and drain.
2. Combine all ingredients in slow cooker. Stir well.

3. Cover. Cook on High 1 hour, stirring until cheese is melted. Serve immediately, or turn on Low for serving up to 6 hours later.
4. Serve with tortilla or corn chips.

Tip: *Serve over rice, noodles, or baked potatoes as a main dish, making 4–5 servings.*

Ground Beef Pizza Fondue

Lisa Warren   Parkesburg, PA

MAKES: **8–12 SERVINGS**
PREP. TIME: **10 MINUTES**
COOKING TIME: **2–3 HOURS**
IDEAL SLOW COOKER SIZE: **3-QUART**

1 lb. ground beef

2 cans pizza sauce with cheese

8 oz. cheddar cheese, shredded

8 oz. mozzarella cheese, shredded

1 tsp. dried oregano

½ tsp. fennel seed, *optional*

1 Tbsp. cornstarch

1. Brown beef, crumble fine, and drain.
2. Combine all ingredients in slow cooker.
3. Cover. Heat on Low 2–3 hours.
4. Serve with tortilla chips.

Buy dried herbs and spices in small amounts because they lose their flavor over time.

Tomato-Beef Dip

Cynthia Morris Grottoes, VA

MAKES: **20–30 SERVINGS**
PREP. TIME: **20–30 MINUTES**
COOKING TIME: **45 MINUTES TO 1 HOUR**
IDEAL SLOW COOKER SIZE: **6-QUART**

1 lb. lean ground beef
2 lbs. Velveeta cheese, cubed
2 10¾-oz. cans tomato soup
2 10¾-oz. cans cream of celery soup
chopped green pepper, *optional*
chopped onion, *optional*

1. Brown ground beef in large nonstick skillet. Drain.
2. Return drained beef to skillet. Turn heat to low. Stir cubed cheese into beef in skillet. Heat gently until cheese melts, stirring occasionally.
3. Place browned beef and melted cheese in slow cooker. Add remaining ingredients and stir well.
4. Cook on High 45–60 minutes, or until heated through.
5. Serve with nacho chips.

Creamy Ground Beef Cheese Dip

Carol Eberly Harrisonburg, VA

MAKES: **ABOUT 6 CUPS DIP**
PREP. TIME: **20 MINUTES**
COOKING TIME: **2 HOURS**
IDEAL SLOW COOKER SIZE: **2-QUART**

2-lb. box Velveeta cheese, cubed
1 lb. ground beef
1 onion, chopped
10¾-oz. can cream of mushroom soup
14½-oz. can diced tomatoes with green chilies

1. While cutting up cheese, brown beef and onions in skillet. Drain meat mixture and place in slow cooker.
2. Place all remaining ingredients in slow cooker and combine.
3. Cover. Cook on Low 2 hours, or until cheese is melted, stirring occasionally.
4. Serve over baked potatoes or with tortilla chips.

Variation: *For more snap, add 4¼-oz. can green chilies in Step 2.*

Cheesy Ground Beef Salsa Dip

Mary Jane Musser Manheim, PA • *Colleen Heatwole* Burton, MI

MAKES: **20 SERVINGS**
PREP. TIME: **15 MINUTES**
COOKING TIME: **1 HOUR**
IDEAL SLOW COOKER SIZE: **3–4-QUART**

2 lbs. ground beef

2 lbs. Velveeta cheese, cubed

16-, or 32-oz., jar salsa, your choice of heat

1. Brown beef in nonstick skillet. Drain.
2. Place beef in cooker while hot. Stir in cheese until melted.
3. Add salsa.
4. Turn slow cooker to High for 1 hour. Turn to Low and serve with tortilla chips for dipping.

Variations:

1. Add ¼ cup milk for a creamier consistency.

Ruth Ann Bender Cochranville, PA

2. Add a 4-oz. can of green chilies.

Norma Grieser Clarksville, MI

Tip: *You can make this ahead of time and refrigerate it, then reheat it in the slow cooker for an hour or two before you're ready to serve it.*

Wrapped-in-Salsa Ground Beef Dip

Karen Stoltzfus Alto, MI

MAKES: **10–12 SERVINGS**
PREP. TIME: **10 MINUTES**
COOKING TIME: **1 HOUR**
IDEAL SLOW COOKER SIZE: **3-QUART**

1 lb. ground beef

2 lbs. American cheese, cubed

16-oz. jar salsa, your choice of heat

1 Tbsp. Worcestershire sauce

1. Brown beef, crumble into small pieces, and drain.
2. Combine beef, cheese, salsa, and Worcestershire sauce in slow cooker.
3. Cover. Cook on High 1 hour, stirring occasionally until cheese is fully melted.
4. Serve immediately, with tortilla or corn chips, or turn to Low for serving up to 6 hours later.

Taco Salsa Dip

Barbara Smith Bedford, PA

MAKES: **20 SERVINGS**
PREP. TIME: **20 MINUTES**
COOKING TIME: **4 HOURS**
IDEAL SLOW COOKER SIZE: **3–4-QUART**

½ lb. lean ground beef

1 lb. Velveeta cheese, cubed

3-oz. pkg. cream cheese

half an envelope dry taco seasoning

14-oz. jar salsa, your choice of heat

1. Brown ground beef in a nonstick skillet. Drain.
2. Place in slow cooker. Add remaining ingredients. Stir well.
3. Cover and cook on Low 4 hours.
4. Stir, and then serve with taco chips.

Mexican Ground Beef Cheese Dip

Liz Rugg Wayland, IA

MAKES: **10 SERVINGS**
PREP. TIME: **15 MINUTES**
COOKING TIME: **4–5 HOURS**
IDEAL SLOW COOKER SIZE: **2-QUART**

1 lb. ground beef

15-oz. can enchilada sauce

1 lb. Velveeta cheese, cubed

1. Brown ground beef in nonstick skillet. Drain.
2. Place in slow cooker. Add sauce and cubed cheese. Stir well.
3. Cover and cook on Low 4–5 hours.
4. When heated through, serve with your favorite taco chips.

Taco Pizza Dip

Arlene Snyder Millerstown, PA

MAKES: **8–10 SERVINGS**
PREP. TIME: **15 MINUTES**
COOKING TIME: **1½–2 HOURS**
IDEAL SLOW COOKER SIZE: **2–3-QUART**

2 8-oz. pkgs. cream cheese, softened

8–12-oz. container French onion dip

1 lb. ground beef

half an envelope dry taco seasoning mix

1 cup shredded cheddar cheese

green pepper, diced, *optional*

mushrooms, sliced, *optional*

1. Combine cream cheese and onion dip. Spread in slow cooker.
2. Brown ground beef in a skillet. Drain. Stir taco seasoning into meat.
3. Place seasoned meat on top of cream cheese mixture.

4. Sprinkle cheddar cheese on top of meat. Top with peppers and mushrooms, if you wish.
5. Cover and cook on Low 1½–2 hours. Serve with white corn chips.

Hamburger Hot Dip

Janice Martins Fairbank, IA

MAKES: **6 CUPS DIP**
PREP. TIME: **15 MINUTES**
COOKING TIME: **4 HOURS**
IDEAL SLOW COOKER SIZE: **1-QUART**

1 lb. ground beef

1 medium onion, chopped fine

½ tsp. salt

¼ tsp. pepper

8-oz. jar salsa

14-oz. can nacho cheese soup

8 slices Velveeta cheese

1. Brown ground beef and onions in saucepan. Drain. Season with salt and pepper.
2. Combine all ingredients in slow cooker.
3. Cover. Cook on Low 4 hours. Stir occasionally.
4. Serve with nacho chips.

Wet your knife when cubing cheese to keep it from sticking.

Chili con Queso Cheese Dip

Melanie Thrower McPherson, KS

MAKES: **8 SERVINGS**
PREP. TIME: **15 MINUTES**
COOKING TIME: **1–2 HOURS**
IDEAL SLOW COOKER SIZE: **1-QUART**

1 lb. ground beef

½ cup chopped onion

1 cup Velveeta cheese, cubed

10-oz. can diced tomatoes and green chilies

1 can evaporated milk

2 Tbsp. chili powder

1. Brown ground beef and onion. Crumble beef into fine pieces. Drain.
2. Combine all ingredients in slow cooker.
3. Cover. Heat on Low 1–2 hours, until cheese is melted.
4. Serve with tortilla chips.

TNT Dip

Sheila Plock Boalsburg, PA

MAKES: **8 CUPS**
PREP. TIME: **15 MINUTES**
COOKING TIME: **1–1¼ HOURS**
IDEAL SLOW COOKER SIZE: **3-QUART**

1½ lbs. ground beef, browned

10¾-oz. can cream of mushroom soup

¼ cup butter, melted

1 lb. Velveeta cheese, cubed

1 cup salsa

2 Tbsp. chili powder

1. Combine all ingredients in slow cooker.
2. Cover. Cook on High 1–1¼ hours, or until cheese is melted, stirring occasionally.
3. Serve with tortilla chips, corn chips, or party rye bread.

Note: *My son has hosted a Super Bowl party for his college friends at our house the past two years. He served this dip the first year, and the second year it was requested. His friends claim it's the best dip they've ever eaten. With a bunch of college kids it disappears quickly.*

Variation: *To change the balance of flavors, use 1 lb. browned ground beef and 1½ cups salsa.*

Creamy Taco Dip

Elaine Rineer Lancaster, PA

MAKES: **10–12 SERVINGS**
PREP. TIME: **15 MINUTES**
COOKING TIME: **2–3 HOURS**
IDEAL SLOW COOKER SIZE: **2-3-QUART**

1½ lbs. ground beef

1 envelope dry taco seasoning mix

16-oz. jar of salsa

2 cups sour cream

1 cup shredded cheddar cheese

1. Brown ground beef in nonstick skillet. Drain.
2. Return beef to skillet. Add taco seasoning and salsa.
3. Remove from stove and add sour cream and cheese. Pour mixture into slow cooker.
4. Cover and cook on Low 2–3 hours, or until hot.
5. Serve with tortilla chips.

You can freeze cheese and use it later in cooking or baking.

Appetizers, Snacks, and Spreads

Hearty Broccoli-Beef Dip

Renee Baum   Chambersburg, PA

MAKES: **24 SERVINGS**
PREP. TIME: **15–20 MINUTES**
COOKING TIME: **2–3 HOURS**
IDEAL SLOW COOKER SIZE: **3-QUART**

1 lb. ground beef

1 lb. American cheese, cubed

10¾-oz. can cream of mushroom soup

10-oz. pkg. frozen chopped broccoli, thawed

2 Tbsp. salsa, your choice of heat

1. Brown ground beef in nonstick skillet. Drain.
2. Combine all ingredients in slow cooker. Mix well.
3. Cover and cook on Low 2–3 hours, or until heated through, stirring after 1 hour.
4. Serve with tortilla chips.

Tip: *Serve as a main dish over baked potatoes or cooked rice.*

Cindy Harney   Lowville, NY

Hot Chip Dip

Sharon Wantland   Menomonee Falls, WI

MAKES: **8 SERVINGS**
PREP. TIME: **15 MINUTES**
COOKING TIME: **1½ HOURS**
IDEAL SLOW COOKER SIZE: **4-QUART**

1 lb. ground beef

1-lb. can chili without beans

1 bunch green onions, chopped

4¼-oz. can green chilies, chopped

1 lb. Velveeta cheese, cubed

1. Brown beef in nonstick skillet until crumbly. Drain.

2. Place in slow cooker and add all other ingredients. Mix together well.
3. Cover and cook on High 1½ hours.
4. Turn cooker to Low and serve dip with large tortilla chips.

Hot Hamburger Dip

Kristi See   Weskan, KS

MAKES: **12 SERVINGS**
PREP. TIME: **20 MINUTES**
COOKING TIME: **2 HOURS**
IDEAL SLOW COOKER SIZE: **4–5-QUART**

½ lb. lean ground beef

2 small onions, chopped

½ lb. Velveeta Light cheese, cubed

10-oz. can green chilies and tomatoes

2 tsp. Worcestershire sauce

½ tsp. chili powder

1 tsp. garlic powder

½ tsp. black pepper

10¾-oz. can low-sodium tomato soup

10¾-oz. can 98% fat-free mushroom soup

1. Brown beef and onions in a nonstick skillet. Place in slow cooker.
2. Add remaining ingredients and stir well.
3. Cover. Cook on Low until cheese is melted, about 2 hours.

Per Serving: 110 calories (40 calories from fat), 4.5g total fat (2.5g saturated, 1g trans), 15mg cholesterol, 620mg sodium, 9g total carbohydrate (0g fiber, 3g sugar), 8g protein, 6%DV vitamin A, 6%DV vitamin C, 15%DV calcium, 4%DV iron.

Tomatoes and Chili Cheese Dip

Dorothy Lingerfelt Stonyford, CA • *Gertrude Dutcher* Hartville, OH
Corinna Herr Stevens, PA

MAKES: **10–12 SERVINGS**
PREP. TIME: **10 MINUTES**
COOKING TIME: **1 HOUR**
IDEAL SLOW COOKER SIZE: **4-QUART**

1 lb. lean ground beef

1 lb. American cheese, cubed

8–10-oz. can tomatoes and green chilies

2 tsp. Worcestershire sauce

½ tsp. chili powder

1. Brown ground beef in nonstick skillet. Drain.
2. Place browned beef in slow cooker. Add all remaining ingredients. Stir well.
3. Cover and cook on High 1 hour, stirring occasionally until cheese is fully melted.
4. Serve immediately or turn to Low for serving up to 6 hours later.
5. Serve with tortilla or corn chips.

Variation: *For a thicker dip, stir 2 Tbsp. flour and 3 Tbsp. water together in a small bowl until smooth. When dip is hot and cheese is melted, stir paste into slow cooker. Continue to stir until thoroughly blended.*

Heated-Up Nacho Dip

Gladys M. High Ephrata, PA

MAKES: **10–12 SERVINGS**
PREP. TIME: **15 MINUTES**
COOKING TIME: **1 HOUR**
IDEAL SLOW COOKER SIZE: **5–6-QUART**

1 lb. ground beef

2 lbs. American cheese, cubed

16-oz. jar salsa, your choice of heat

1 Tbsp. Worcestershire sauce

1. Brown ground beef in nonstick skillet. Drain.
2. Place beef in slow cooker. Add all other ingredients and blend well.
3. Cover and cook on High for 1 hour. Stir occasionally until cheese is fully melted.
4. Serve immediately, or turn to Low for serving up to 6 hours later.
5. Serve with tortilla or corn chips.

Easy Pizza Appetizers

Sharon Wantland Menomonee Falls, WI

MAKES: **8 SERVINGS**
PREP. TIME: **15 MINUTES**
COOKING TIME: **1 HOUR**
IDEAL SLOW COOKER SIZE: **4-QUART**

1 lb. ground beef

1 lb. bulk Italian sausage

1 lb. Velveeta cheese, cubed

4 tsp. pizza seasoning

½ tsp. Worcestershire sauce

1. In a large nonstick skillet, brown beef and sausage until crumbly. Drain.
2. Add remaining ingredients and place mixture in slow cooker.
3. Cover and heat on Low for 1 hour.
4. When thoroughly warmed, offer a small spoon or knife for spreading and serve with party rye bread.

Mexican Meat Dip

Deborah Swartz Grottoes, VA

MAKES: **20 SERVINGS**
PREP. TIME: **20 MINUTES**
COOKING TIME: **¾–1½ HOURS**
IDEAL SLOW COOKER SIZE: **3-QUART**

1 lb. ground beef
¾–1 cup chopped onions
15-oz. can refried beans
1 pkg. dry taco seasoning mix
1 cup sour cream
1½ cups shredded mozzarella cheese

1. Brown ground beef and onions in skillet. Drain. Place meat and onions in slow cooker.
2. Add beans and taco seasoning mix. Mix together well.
3. Spread sour cream over mixture. Sprinkle cheese over top.
4. Cover. Cook on Low 1½ hours, or on High ¾ hour.
5. Serve warm from the cooker with tortilla chips.

Quick and Easy Nacho Dip

Kristina Shull Timberville, VA

MAKES: **10–15 SERVINGS**
PREP. TIME: **15 MINUTES**
COOKING TIME: **2 HOURS**
IDEAL SLOW COOKER SIZE: **3-QUART**

1 lb. ground beef
dash of salt
dash of pepper
dash of onion powder
2 garlic cloves, minced, *optional*
2 16-oz. jars salsa, your choice of heat
15-oz. can refried beans
1½ cups sour cream
3 cups shredded cheddar cheese, *divided*

1. Brown ground beef. Drain. Add salt, pepper, onion powder, and minced garlic.
2. Combine beef, salsa, beans, sour cream, and 2 cups cheese in slow cooker.
3. Cover. Heat on Low 2 hours. Just before serving sprinkle with 1 cup cheese.
4. Serve with tortilla chips.

Southwest Hot Chip Dip

Annabelle Unternahrer Shipshewana, IN

MAKES: **15–20 SERVINGS**
PREP. TIME: **15 MINUTES**
COOKING TIME: **1½–4 HOURS**
IDEAL SLOW COOKER SIZE: **3-QUART**

1 lb. ground beef, browned, crumbled fine, and drained
2 15-oz. cans refried beans
2 10-oz. cans diced tomatoes and chilies
1 pkg. taco seasoning
1 lb. Velveeta cheese, cubed

1. Combine ground beef, beans, tomatoes, and taco seasoning in slow cooker.
2. Cover. Cook on Low 3-4 hours, or on High 1½ hours.
3. Add cheese. Stir occasionally. Heat until cheese is melted.
4. Serve with tortilla chips.

Tip: *Serve as a main dish alongside a soup.*

Always have ingredients for simple recipes on hand.

Hot Refried-Bean Dip

Sharon Anders Alburtis, PA

MAKES: **1½ QUARTS, OR 12–20 SERVINGS**
PREP. TIME: **15 MINUTES**
COOKING TIME: **45 MINUTES**
IDEAL SLOW COOKER SIZE: **3-QUART**

15-oz. can refried beans, drained and mashed
½ lb. ground beef
3 Tbsp. bacon drippings
1 lb. American cheese, cubed
1–3 Tbsp. taco sauce
1 Tbsp. taco seasoning
dash garlic salt

1. In skillet, brown beans and ground beef in bacon drippings. Pour into slow cooker.
2. Stir in cheese, taco sauce, taco seasoning, and garlic salt.
3. Cover. Cook on High 45 minutes, or until cheese is melted, stirring occasionally. Or turn to Low until ready to serve, up to 6 hours.
4. Serve warm with tortilla chips.

Chili-Cheese Taco Dip

Kim Stoltzfus New Holland, PA

MAKES: **10–12 SERVINGS**
PREP. TIME: **15 MINUTES**
COOKING TIME: **1–1½ HOURS**
IDEAL SLOW COOKER SIZE: **1-QUART**

1 lb. ground beef
1 can chili, without beans
1 lb. mild Mexican cheese
Velveeta cheese, cubed

1. Brown beef, crumble into small pieces, and drain.

2. Combine beef, chili, and cheese in slow cooker.
3. Cover. Cook on Low 1–1½ hours, or until cheese is melted, stirring occasionally to blend ingredients.
4. Serve warm with taco or tortilla chips.

Hamburger-Cheese Dip

Julia Lapp New Holland, PA

MAKES: **8–10 SERVINGS**
PREP. TIME: **20 MINUTES**
COOKING TIME: **2–3 HOURS**
IDEAL SLOW COOKER SIZE: **1-QUART**

1 lb. ground beef, browned and crumbled into small pieces
½ tsp. salt
½ cup chopped green peppers
¾ cup chopped onion
8-oz. can tomato sauce
4-oz. can green chilies, chopped
1 Tbsp. Worcestershire sauce
1 Tbsp. brown sugar
1 lb. Velveeta cheese, cubed
1 Tbsp. paprika
red pepper to taste

1. Combine beef, salt, green peppers, onion, tomato sauce, green chilies, Worcestershire sauce, and brown sugar in slow cooker.
2. Cover. Cook on Low 2–3 hours. During the last hour stir in cheese, paprika, and red pepper.
3. Serve with tortilla chips.

Variation: *Prepare recipe using only ⅓–½ lb. ground beef.*

Appetizers, Snacks, and Spreads

Super-Bowl Dip

Liz Rugg   Wayland, IA

MAKES: **30 SERVINGS**
PREP. TIME: **15 MINUTES**
COOKING TIME: **2–3 HOURS**
IDEAL SLOW COOKER SIZE: **3–4-QUART**

2 lbs. ground beef

1 envelope dry taco seasoning mix

24-oz. jar salsa, your choice of heat

1 lb. Velveeta cheese, cubed

16-oz. can refried beans

1. Brown beef in nonstick skillet. Drain.
2. Place beef in slow cooker. Stir in remaining ingredients.
3. Cover and cook on Low 2–3 hours, or until cheese is melted.
4. Serve with tortilla chips.

Hot Dried-Beef Dip

Sarah Miller   Harrisonburg, VA

MAKES: **12–15 SERVINGS**
PREP. TIME: **30 MINUTES**
COOKING TIME: **2–3 HOURS**
IDEAL SLOW COOKER SIZE: **1–2-QUART**

2 8-oz. pkgs. cream cheese, softened

8 ozs. cheddar cheese, shredded

1 green pepper, chopped fine

1 small onion, chopped fine

¼ lb. dried beef, shredded

1. In a medium-sized mixing bowl, combine cream cheese and shredded cheese.
2. Fold in peppers, onions, and dried beef. Place stiff mixture in slow cooker.
3. Cover and cook on Low 2–3 hours. Stir occasionally.
4. Serve hot with crackers.

Variation: *Use only one pkg. cream cheese. Drop cheddar cheese. Add 1 cup sour cream to Step 1. Serve with toasted bread tips for dipping.*

Judith A. Govotsos   Frederick, MD

Meaty Queso Dip

Janie Steele   Moore, OK

MAKES: **15 APPETIZER SERVINGS**
PREP. TIME: **50 MINUTES**
COOKING TIME: **30–60 MINUTES**
IDEAL SLOW COOKER SIZE: **3–4-QUART**

1 lb. ground beef

1 lb. bulk hot Italian sausage

1 lb. jalapeño Velveeta cheese, cubed

10¾-oz. can golden mushroom soup

1. Brown ground beef in nonstick skillet. Drain. Place in slow cooker.
2. Brown loose sausage in skillet. Drain. Add to slow cooker.
3. Add all remaining ingredients to slow cooker. Mix together well.
4. Cook on High for 30–60 minutes, stirring frequently until cheese is melted.
5. Turn to Low, stirring occasionally to prevent scorching. Serve with tortilla chips.

To grate cheese neatly, place the grater in a plastic bag and insert a wedge of cheese in the bag. Grasp the cheese through the bag. No mess.

Hearty Pizza Dip

Natalia Showalter Mt. Solon, VA

MAKES: **18 SERVINGS**
PREP. TIME: **30 MINUTES**
COOKING TIME: **3 HOURS**
IDEAL SLOW COOKER SIZE: **3-QUART**

1 lb. bulk smoked sausage

2 8-oz. pkgs. cream cheese, cubed

2 cups pizza sauce

2 cups shredded mozzarella cheese

1 cup shredded cheddar cheese

1. Brown the sausage in a skillet, breaking it up into small pieces with a spoon as it browns. Drain.
2. Place sausage in slow cooker. Stir in all remaining ingredients.
3. Cover and cook on High for 1 hour. Stir.
4. Cook on Low until heated through, about 2 more hours.
5. Serve with corn chips.

Variation: *For a stick-to-the-ribs breakfast, stir 2 Tbsp. of the finished dip into 3 eggs while scrambling them. Serve the mixture open-faced on toasted English muffins.*

Elaine Patton West Middletown, PA

Beef 'n Sausage Nacho Dip

Beth Maurer Harrisonburg, VA

MAKES: **10–12 SERVINGS**
PREP. TIME: **20 MINUTES**
COOKING TIME: **4–5 HOURS**
IDEAL SLOW COOKER SIZE: **5-QUART**

2 lbs. ground beef, browned

1 lb. sausage, browned

16-oz. jar salsa, medium or hot

1 pkg. dry taco seasoning mix

2-lb. box Velveeta cheese, cubed

10¾-oz. can cream of mushroom soup

1. Stir salsa and seasoning mix into meat. Then spread in bottom of slow cooker.
2. Cover and cook on High 1 hour.
3. Stir in cheese and soup.
4. Cover. Cook on Low 3–4 hours, until ingredients are hot and cheese and soup are melted.
5. Serve with unsalted chips, tortilla or nacho chips, pita wedges, chopped tomatoes, refried beans, onions, and sour cream.

Note: *This is a delight at any party or get-together. We serve it at every Christmas party.*

Good 'n Hot Dip

Joyce B. Suiter   Garysburg, NC

MAKES: **30–50 SERVINGS**
PREP. TIME: **15 MINUTES**
COOKING TIME: **1 HOUR**
IDEAL SLOW COOKER SIZE: **3-QUART**

1 lb. ground beef

1 lb. bulk sausage

10¾-oz. can cream of chicken soup

10¾-oz. can cream of celery soup

24-oz. jar salsa (use hot for some zing)

1 lb. Velveeta cheese, cubed

chips

1. Brown beef and sausage, crumbling into small pieces. Drain.
2. Combine meat, soups, salsa, and cheese in slow cooker.
3. Cover. Cook on High 1 hour. Stir. Cook on Low until ready to serve.
4. Serve with chips.

Make-Mine-Sausage Queso Dip

Janie Steele   Moore, OK

MAKES: **ABOUT 2 QUARTS DIP**
PREP. TIME: **10 MINUTES**
COOKING TIME: **1–2 HOURS**
IDEAL SLOW COOKER SIZE: **2-QUART**

2-lbs. Velveeta cheese, cubed

10-oz. can diced tomatoes and chilies

1 lb. bulk sausage, browned, crumbled fine, and drained

1. Combine all ingredients in slow cooker.
2. Cover. Heat on Low 1–2 hours.
3. Serve with tortilla chips.

Hot Cheese and Bacon Dip

Lee Ann Hazlett   Freeport, IL

MAKES: **6–8 SERVINGS**
PREP. TIME: **15 MINUTES**
COOKING TIME: **1 HOUR**
IDEAL SLOW COOKER SIZE: **1-QUART**

16 slices bacon, diced

2 8-oz. pkgs. cream cheese, cubed and softened

4 cups shredded mild cheddar cheese

1 cup half-and-half

2 tsp. Worcestershire sauce

1 tsp. dried minced onion

½ tsp. dry mustard

½ tsp. salt

2–3 drops Tabasco

1. Brown and drain bacon. Set aside.
2. Mix remaining ingredients in slow cooker.
3. Cover. Cook on Low 1 hour, stirring occasionally until cheese melts.
4. Stir in bacon.
5. Serve with fruit slices or French bread slices. (Dip fruit in lemon juice to prevent browning.)

For convenient and economically priced bacon, buy bacon ends and pieces. Chop into small pieces in a food processor and sauté until crisp. Drain well in a sieve, then freeze. The bacon is handy for seasoning many dishes, baked potatoes, salads, and omelets.

Zippy Sausage Cheese Dip

Reita Yoder   Carlsbad, NM

MAKES: **12 SERVINGS**
PREP. TIME: **15 MINUTES**
COOKING TIME: **1–2 HOURS**
IDEAL SLOW COOKER SIZE: **1-QUART**

1 lb. pork sausage, thinly sliced, or squeezed out of casing and crumbled

2 lbs. Velveeta cheese, cubed

2 10¾-oz. cans Rotel tomatoes with chilies, undrained

1. Brown sausage in large nonstick skillet. Drain.
2. Return browned sausage to skillet and stir in cubed Velveeta cheese.
3. Cook over low heat until cheese melts. Stir occasionally.
4. Place pork and melted cheese in slow cooker. Stir in tomatoes.
5. Cover and cook on Low 1–2 hours until heated through.
6. Serve warm with raw, cut-up veggies or chips.

Tips:

1. If the dip gets too dry, add ¼–½ cup warm water.

2. If the cheese looks curdled, stir the mixture and reduce the heat, or turn off the cooker.

Variation: *For a creamier dish, add 2 10¾-oz. cans cream of mushroom soup to Step 4, stirring the soup in with the tomatoes.*

Edna Mae Herschberger   Arthur, IL

Creamy Salsa-Sausage Dip

Reba Rhodes   Bridgewater, VA

MAKES: **12–14 SERVINGS**
PREP. TIME: **10–15 MINUTES**
COOKING TIME: **1½–2 HOURS**
IDEAL SLOW COOKER SIZE: **3-QUART**

1 lb. smoked sausage, chopped

1 lb. Velveeta cheese, cubed

1¼ cups salsa

1. Brown sausage in skillet. Drain and place in slow cooker.
2. Add cheese. Pour salsa over top.
3. Cover. Cook on Low 1½–2 hours.
4. Serve with tortilla chips or party rye bread.

Sausage-Cheese Dip

Fannie Miller   Hutchinson, KS

MAKES: **20 SERVINGS**
PREP. TIME: **20 MINUTES**
COOKING TIME: **4–5 HOURS**
IDEAL SLOW COOKER SIZE: **4-QUART**

1 lb. sausage, either thinly sliced, or with casings removed and crumbled

1 medium onion, chopped

1 green pepper, chopped

2 lbs. Velveeta *or* American cheese, cubed

16-oz. jar medium salsa

1. Brown sausage and onions in skillet. Drain off drippings and transfer meat and onions to slow cooker.
2. Add remaining ingredients to slow cooker and stir well.
3. Cover. Cook on Low 4–5 hours.
4. Serve warm from cooker with tortilla chips.

Bacon Cheddar Dip

Arlene Snyder   Millerstown, PA

MAKES: **15 SERVINGS**
PREP. TIME: **10–15 MINUTES**
COOKING TIME: **1½–2 HOURS**
IDEAL SLOW COOKER SIZE: **4-QUART**

2 8-oz. pkgs. cream cheese, softened

2 cups sour cream

1 lb. bacon, fried and crumbled

4 cups shredded cheddar cheese, *divided*

1. In a mixing bowl, beat cream cheese and sour cream until smooth.
2. Fold in bacon and 3 cups cheddar cheese.
3. Place mixture in slow cooker and sprinkle with remaining cheese.
4. Cover and cook on Low 1½–2 hours, or until heated through.
5. Serve with white corn chips.

Tip: *Save a few bacon crumbs to sprinkle on top.*

Variation: *For a spicier version, stir some fresh herbs, or some chopped chilies, into Step 2.*

Hot Cheese Melt

Tierra Woods   Duenweg, MO

MAKES: **9–10 SERVINGS**
PREP. TIME: **5–10 MINUTES**
COOKING TIME: **1½–2 HOURS**
IDEAL SLOW COOKER SIZE: **3–4-QUART**

12-oz. can whole or chopped jalapeño peppers, drained

15-oz. can Mexican stewed *or* Rotel tomatoes, undrained

2 lbs. Velveeta cheese, cubed

4 slices bacon, cooked crisp and crumbled

1. Put chopped jalapeños in bottom of slow cooker. Spoon in tomatoes and then top with chunks of cheese.
2. Cover and cook on Low for 1½ hours, or until cheese is melted.
3. When ready to serve, sprinkle bacon on top.
4. Keep cooker turned to Low and serve Melt with tortilla chips, bread chunks, or fresh, cut-up vegetables.

Swiss Cheese Dip

Jennifer Yoder Sommers   Harrisonburg, VA

MAKES: **12 SERVINGS**
PREP. TIME: **5 MINUTES**
COOKING TIME: **1–2 HOURS**
IDEAL SLOW COOKER SIZE: **1½-QUART**

2 cups (8 ozs.) shredded Swiss cheese

1 cup mayonnaise

½ cup bacon bits

2 Tbsp. chopped onion

½ cup snack cracker crumbs

1. Combine cheese, mayonnaise, bacon bits, and onion in slow cooker.
2. Sprinkle cracker crumbs over top.
3. Cover and cook on Low 1–2 hours.
4. Serve with a variety of snack crackers or cut-up, fresh vegetables.

Pepperoni Pizza Dip

Annabelle Unternahrer Shipshewana, IN

MAKES: **10–15 SERVINGS**
PREP. TIME: **10 MINUTES**
COOKING TIME: **2 HOURS**
IDEAL SLOW COOKER SIZE: **3-QUART**

2 8-oz. pkgs. cream cheese, cubed

14-oz. can pizza sauce

8-oz. pkg. sliced pepperoni, chopped

1 small can sliced ripe olives, drained

2 cups (8 ozs.) shredded mozzarella cheese

1. Place the cream cheese in your slow cooker.
2. In a small bowl, combine the pizza sauce, pepperoni, and olives. Pour over the cream cheese.
3. Sprinkle mozzarella cheese over the top.
4. Cover and cook on Low 2 hours, or until the cheese is melted.
5. Stir and serve with tortilla chips, bagel chips, or little garlic toasts.

Lotsa-Olives Pizza Dip

Barbara Jean Fabel Wausau, WI

MAKES: **8–10 SERVINGS**
PREP. TIME: **10 MINUTES**
COOKING TIME: **2 HOURS**
IDEAL SLOW COOKER SIZE: **2-QUART**

4 ozs. mozzarella cheese, shredded

4 ozs. cheddar cheese, shredded

1 green pepper, minced

5-oz. can sliced black olives

5-oz. jar sliced stuffed green olives

4 ozs. sliced mushrooms

1 cup mayonnaise

pepperoni slices, cut up

1. Combine all ingredients except pepperoni in slow cooker.
2. Top with pepperoni.
3. Cover. Cook on Low 2 hours.
4. Stir well before bringing to the buffet or table.
5. Serve with snack crackers, or pour over steamed cauliflower and broccoli.

Spray a little cooking spray on your cheese grater before grating cheese. It keeps the grater free of gummed up cheese and cleanup is a breeze.

Appetizers, Snacks, and Spreads

Slow Cooker Reuben Dip

Allison Ingels Maynard, IA

MAKES: **8–12 SERVINGS**
PREP. TIME: **10 MINUTES**
COOKING TIME: **3–4 HOURS**
IDEAL SLOW COOKER SIZE: **3-QUART**

8-oz. carton sour cream

2 8-oz. pkgs. cream cheese, softened

8-oz. can sauerkraut, drained

3 2½-oz. pkgs. dried corned beef, finely chopped

6-oz. pkg. shredded Swiss cheese

1. Combine ingredients in slow cooker.
2. Cover. Heat on Low 3–4 hours, or until cheeses are melted.
3. Serve from cooker with rye crackers or rye party bread.

Reuben Spread

Clarice Williams Fairbank, IA • *Julie McKenzie* Punxsutawney, PA

MAKES: **5 CUPS SPREAD**
PREP. TIME: **10 MINUTES**
COOKING TIME: **1–2 HOURS**
IDEAL SLOW COOKER SIZE: **3-QUART**

½ lb. corned beef, shredded or chopped

16-oz. can sauerkraut, well drained

1–2 cups shredded Swiss cheese*

1–2 cups shredded cheddar cheese*

1 cup mayonnaise*

Thousand Island dressing, *optional*

1. Combine all ingredients except Thousand Island dressing in slow cooker. Mix well.
2. Cover. Cook on High 1–2 hours until heated through, stirring occasionally.
3. Turn to Low and keep warm in cooker while serving. Put spread on rye party bread.

Top individual servings with Thousand Island dressing, if desired.

* *Low-fat cheese and mayonnaise are not recommended for this spread.*

Variation: *Use dried beef instead of corned beef.*

Mexican Dip with Refried Beans

Marla Folkerts Holland, OH

MAKES: **15 SERVINGS**
PREP. TIME: **10 MINUTES**
WARMING TIME: **UNTIL THE COOKER IS EMPTY!**
IDEAL SLOW COOKER SIZE: **3-QUART**

1 lb. low-fat ground beef *or* turkey

8-oz. pkg. no-fat Mexican cheese, shredded

16-oz. jar mild, thick and chunky picante salsa, *or* thick and chunky salsa

16-oz. can vegetarian refried beans

1. Brown meat. Do not drain.
2. Add remaining ingredients. Stir until mixed and hot.
3. Keep warm in slow cooker. Serve with low-fat tortilla chips.

Per Serving: 110 calories (25 calories from fat), 3g total fat (1g saturated, 0g trans), 15mg cholesterol, 400mg sodium, 7g total carbohydrate (2g fiber, 1g sugar), 12g protein, 6%DV vitamin A, 8%DV vitamin C, 25%DV calcium, 8%DV iron.

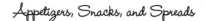

Chicken-Cheese Dip

Sheridy Steele   Ardmore, OK

MAKES: **10 SERVINGS**
PREP. TIME: **15 MINUTES**
COOKING TIME: **1–2 HOURS**
IDEAL SLOW COOKER SIZE: **1–1½-QUART**

½ lb. Velveeta cheese

12-oz. can tomatoes with chilies

1 cup cooked skinless chicken breast, diced and shredded

½ cup bell peppers, chopped

1. Cube cheese. Melt.
2. Combine cheese, tomatoes, chicken, and peppers in slow cooker.
3. Cook on Low 1–2 hours.
4. Serve with baked chips.

_____

Per Serving: 270 calories (45 calories from fat), 5g total fat (2g saturated, 0g trans), 30mg cholesterol, 830mg sodium, 43g total carbohydrate (4g fiber, 2g sugar), 15g protein, 8%DV vitamin A, 10%DV vitamin C, 20%DV calcium, 6%DV iron.

Mexican Chicken Dip

Barb Yoder   Angola, IN

MAKES: **12 SERVINGS**
PREP. TIME: **20 MINUTES**
COOKING TIME: **5–6 HOURS**
IDEAL SLOW COOKER SIZE: **3-QUART**

15-oz. can fat-free chicken breast, roasted

1½ cups fat-free sour cream

10-oz. can cut-up tomatoes and green chilies

10¾-oz. can condensed cream of chicken soup

10¾-oz. can 98% fat-free cream of mushroom soup

¾ lb. Velveeta Light cheese, cubed, *divided*

10-oz. pkg. fat-free flour tortillas

1. In a large bowl, mix together chicken, sour cream, tomatoes and chilies, soups and about half of the cheese cubes.
2. With a kitchen shears, cut tortillas into 1–1½-inch squares.
3. Place a thin layer of sauce mixture on bottom of slow cooker sprayed with non-fat cooking spray.
4. Add a thick layer of tortilla squares. Then add a thick layer of sauce.
5. Repeat layers.
6. Pour remaining cheese cubes over all.
7. Cover. Cook on Low 5–6 hours. Do not stir for first 3 hours.
8. Stir about ½ hour before serving. Stir again just before serving.

_____

Per Serving: 230 calories (60 calories from fat), 7g total fat (3g saturated, 1.5g trans), 35mg cholesterol, 1540mg sodium, 26g total carbohydrate (0.5g fiber, 6g sugar), 16g protein, 10%DV vitamin A, 2%DV vitamin C, 25%DV calcium, 8%DV iron.

Mexican Bean and Cheese Dip

Mary Sommerfeld   Lancaster, PA

MAKES: **ABOUT 5 CUPS DIP**
PREP. TIME: **5 MINUTES**
COOKING TIME: **2–3 HOURS**
IDEAL SLOW COOKER SIZE: **2-QUART**

15-oz. can refried beans
8-oz. jar taco sauce
1 lb. Velveeta cheese, cubed
1 pkg. dry taco seasoning

1. Combine ingredients in slow cooker.
2. Cover. Cook on Low 2–3 hours, or until cheese is melted.
3. Serve warm from the cooker with tortilla chips.

   Tip: *If you're cautious about salt, choose minimally salted chips.*

Prairie Fire Dip

Cheri Jantzen   Houston, TX

MAKES: **10 SERVINGS (ABOUT 1¼ CUPS TOTAL)**
PREP. TIME: **5 MINUTES**
COOKING TIME: **1–3 HOURS**
IDEAL SLOW COOKER SIZE: **2-QUART**

1 cup fat-free refried beans (half of a 15-oz. can)
½ cup shredded fat-free Monterey Jack cheese
¼ cup water
1 Tbsp. minced onion
1 clove garlic, minced
2 tsp. chili powder
hot sauce as desired

1. Combine all ingredients in slow cooker.
2. Cover. Cook on High 1 hour, or on Low 2–3 hours. Serve with baked tortilla chips

---

Per Serving: 45 calories (0 calories from fat), 0g total fat (0g saturated, 0g trans), 0mg cholesterol, 190mg sodium, 6g total carbohydrate (2g fiber, 0g sugar), 5g protein, 6%DV vitamin A, 0%DV vitamin C, 15%DV calcium, 4%DV iron.

   Tip: *This recipe can easily be doubled.*

Make an alphabetical list of all the spices in your cupboard and tape it inside your cupboard door for easy reference. Arrange your spices in alphabetical order so you can easily locate them.

Chili-Cheese with Salsa Dip

Vicki Dinkel   Sharon Springs, KS

MAKES: **8 SERVINGS**
PREP. TIME: **10 MINUTES**
COOKING TIME: **4 HOURS**
IDEAL SLOW COOKER SIZE: **2-QUART**

1 onion, diced

8-oz. pkg. fat-free cream cheese, cubed

2 15-oz. cans low-fat vegetarian chili without beans

2 tsp. garlic salt

1½ cups salsa

1. Lightly brown onion in skillet sprayed with non-fat cooking spray. Transfer to slow cooker.
2. Stir in cream cheese, chili, garlic salt, and salsa.
3. Cover. Cook on Low 4 hours, stirring occasionally.
4. Serve with baked tortilla chips.

Per Serving: 230 calories (15 calories from fat), 2g total fat (0g saturated, 0g trans), 0mg cholesterol, 1420mg sodium, 40g total carbohydrate (8g fiber, 2g sugar), 15g protein, 10%DV vitamin A, 4%DV vitamin C, 10%DV calcium, 10%DV iron.

Chili con Queso Dip

Janie Steele   Moore, OK

MAKES: **12–15 SERVINGS**
PREP. TIME: **5–10 MINUTES**
COOKING TIME: **1–2 HOURS**
IDEAL SLOW COOKER SIZE: **4-QUART**

1 lb. Velveeta cheese, cubed

15-oz. can of chili with beans

4-oz. can chopped green chilies

1 medium onion, chopped

1. Combine all ingredients in slow cooker.
2. Cover and cook on High for 30 minutes, stirring frequently until cheese is melted.
3. Turn to Low, keeping the cooker covered, for 30–60 minutes. Stir occasionally to prevent scorching.
4. Serve with chips.

Creamy Chili-Cheese Dip

Maryann Westerberg   Rosamond, CA

MAKES: **ABOUT 10 SERVINGS**
PREP. TIME: **10 MINUTES**
COOKING TIME: **2 HOURS**
IDEAL SLOW COOKER SIZE: **3-QUART**

2 lbs. Velveeta cheese, cubed

16-oz. can chili without beans

10-oz. can diced tomatoes with chilies, drained

10¾-oz. can cream of mushroom soup

1. Combine cheese and chili in slow cooker. Heat on Low until cheese melts, stirring occasionally.
2. Add tomatoes and soup.
3. Cover. Cook on Low 2 hours. Stir before serving.
4. Serve with tortilla chips.

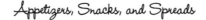

Revved-Up Chili Dip

Renee Baum Chambersburg, PA • *Shirley Sears* Sarasota, FL
Mary Lynn Miller Reinholds, PA

MAKES: **15 SERVINGS**
PREP. TIME: **5–10 MINUTES**
COOKING TIME: **2 HOURS**
IDEAL SLOW COOKER SIZE: **2–3-QUART**

24-oz. jar salsa

15-oz. can chili with beans

2 2¼-oz. cans sliced ripe olives, drained

12 ozs. American cheese, cubed

1. In slow cooker, combine salsa, chili, and olives. Stir in cheese.
2. Cover and cook on Low 2 hours, or until cheese is melted, stirring halfway through.
3. Serve with sturdy tortilla chips.

Easy Refried Bean Dip

Katrina Eberly Stevens, PA

MAKES: **12 SERVINGS**
PREP. TIME: **10 MINUTES**
COOKING TIME: **1½ HOURS**
IDEAL SLOW COOKER SIZE: **2-QUART**

2 15-oz. cans refried beans

1 envelope taco seasoning mix (use all, or ¾, depending on your taste preference)

½ cup chopped onions

2 cups shredded Monterey Jack *or* Mexican Blend cheese

chopped jalapeños *or* mild chilies, to taste

2–4 drops Tabasco sauce, *optional*

1. Place beans, taco seasoning, onions, and cheese in your slow cooker. Stir well to blend.
2. Stir in jalapeños or chilies and Tabasco sauce.
3. Cook on Low until cheese is melted, about 1½ hours.
4. Add a little water if the dip seems too thick.

Tip: *If you have leftovers (unlikely!), wrap the remaining dip in a flour tortilla and top with some sour cream for a light lunch or dinner.*

Joleen Albrecht Gladstone, MI

Cheesy Bean Dip

Deborah Heatwole Waynesboro, GA

MAKES: **18–20 SERVINGS**
PREP. TIME: **5–10 MINUTES**
COOKING TIME: **1½–3 HOURS**
IDEAL SLOW COOKER SIZE: **2-QUART**

16-oz. can refried beans

2 8-oz. pkgs. cream cheese, cubed

2 cups salsa, your choice of heat

2 cups shredded cheddar cheese

1 envelope dry taco seasoning mix

1. Mix all ingredients in slow cooker. Stir to combine well.
2. Cover and heat on High for 1½ hours, or on Low for 3 hours, stirring occasionally.
3. Serve with corn chips.

Tip: *A potato masher works well for blending the ingredients together.*

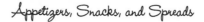

Appetizers, Snacks, and Spreads

Fiesta Dip

Melissa Warner Broad Top, PA

MAKES: **8 SERVINGS**
PREP. TIME: **10 MINUTES**
COOKING TIME: **30–60 MINUTES**
IDEAL SLOW COOKER SIZE: **1-QUART**

16-oz. can refried beans

1 cup shredded cheddar cheese

½ cup Mexican salsa

1 green chili pepper, chopped, *optional*

1. Combine all ingredients and place in slow cooker.
2. Cover and heat 30–60 minutes, or until cheese is melted.
3. Serve with tortilla chips or corn chips.

Championship Bean Dip

Renee Shirk Mt. Joy, PA • *Ada Miller* Sugarcreek, OH

MAKES: **4½ CUPS DIP**
PREP. TIME: **10 MINUTES**
COOKING TIME: **2 HOURS**
IDEAL SLOW COOKER SIZE: **3-QUART**

15-oz. can refried beans

1 cup picante sauce

1 cup (4 oz.) shredded Monterey Jack cheese

1 cup (4 oz.) shredded cheddar cheese

¾ cup sour cream

3-oz. pkg. cream cheese, softened

1 Tbsp. chili powder

¼ tsp. ground cumin

1. In a bowl, combine all ingredients and transfer to slow cooker.
2. Cover. Cook on High 2 hours, or until heated through, stirring once or twice.
3. Serve with tortilla chips and salsa.

Mile-High Chili con Queso

Jeanne Allen Rye, CO

MAKES: **15–20 SERVINGS**
PREP. TIME: **10 MINUTES**
COOKING TIME: **1–2 HOURS**
IDEAL SLOW COOKER SIZE: **3-QUART**

40-oz. can chili without beans

2-lbs. Velveeta cheese, cubed

16-oz. jar picante sauce, your choice of heat

1. Combine all ingredients except chips in slow cooker.
2. Cover. Cook on Low 1–2 hours, until cheese is melted. Stir.
3. Serve with tortilla chips.

Wide-Awake Refried Bean Dip

Mabel Shirk Mount Crawford, VA • *Wilma Haberkamp* Fairbank, IA

MAKES: **8–10 SERVINGS**
PREP. TIME: **5–10 MINUTES**
COOKING TIME: **2–2½ HOURS**
IDEAL SLOW COOKER SIZE: **1–2-QUART**

20-oz. can refried beans

1 cup shredded cheddar *or* **hot pepper cheese**

½ cup chopped green onions

¼ tsp. salt

2–4 Tbsp. bottled taco sauce (depending on your taste preference)

1. In slow cooker, combine beans with cheese, onions, salt, and taco sauce.
2. Cover and cook on Low 2 to 2½ hours.
3. Serve hot from the pot with tortilla chips.

Blueberry Fancy, page 73

Roasted Pepper and Artichoke Spread,
  page 40

30

Carmeled Pears 'n Wine, page 623

31

Meatballs and Spaghetti Sauce,
  page 308

Irresistible Cheesy Hot-Bean Dip

John D. Allen   Rye, CO

MAKES: **4–5 CUPS DIP**
PREP. TIME: **10 MINUTES**
COOKING TIME: **2 HOURS**
IDEAL SLOW COOKER SIZE: **2-QUART**

16-oz. can refried beans

1 cup salsa

2 cups (8 ozs.) shredded Monterey Jack and cheddar cheeses, mixed

1 cup sour cream

3-oz. pkg. cream cheese, cubed

1 Tbsp. chili powder

¼ tsp. ground cumin

1. Combine all ingredients in slow cooker.
2. Cover. Cook on High 2 hours. Stir 2–3 times during cooking.
3. Serve warm from the cooker with tortilla chips.

Note: *This bean dip is a favorite. Once you start on it, it's hard to leave it alone. We have been known to dip into it even when it's cold.*

Any-Time-of-Day Cheese Dip

Tina Houk   Clinton, MO

MAKES: **12 SERVINGS**
PREP. TIME: **5–10 MINUTES**
COOKING TIME: **1–1½ HOURS**
IDEAL SLOW COOKER SIZE: **3-QUART**

2 8-oz. pkgs. cream cheese, softened

3 15½-oz. cans chili

2 cups shredded cheddar *or* mozzarella cheese

1. Spread cream cheese in bottom of slow cooker.
2. Spread chili on top of cream cheese.
3. Top with shredded cheese.
4. Cover. Cook on Low 1–1½ hours, until shredded cheese is melted. Stir.
5. Serve with tortilla chips.

Soft Cheese Spread

Barbara Kuhns   Millersburg, OH

MAKES: **APPROXIMATELY 12–15 SERVINGS**
PREP. TIME: **5 MINUTES**
COOKING TIME: **2 HOURS**
IDEAL SLOW COOKER SIZE: **1-QUART**

1 lb. white American cheese, cubed

1½ cups milk

1. Combine cheese and milk in slow cooker.
2. Cover. Cook on Low about 2 hours, or until cheese is melted, stirring occasionally.
3. Serve on crackers.

Mexicana Dip

Julia B. Boyd   Memphis, TN   •   *Sue Williams*   Gulfport, MS

MAKES: **10–12 SERVINGS**
PREP. TIME: **10 MINUTES**
COOKING TIME: **2–3 HOURS**
IDEAL SLOW COOKER SIZE: **3-QUART**

2 lbs. American *or* Velveeta cheese, cubed
10-oz. can tomatoes with green chilies
tortilla chips, corn chips, *or* potato chips

1. Combine cheese and tomatoes in slow cooker.
2. Cover. Cook on Low 2–3 hours, stirring until cheese is melted. If mixture is too thick, add a little milk.
3. Serve as a dip, or pour over a platter of your favorite chips.

Variation: *Stir in ½ lb. browned bulk sausage, crumbled into small pieces.*

Jane Steele   Moore, OK

Cheddary con Queso Dip

Bonita Ensenberger   Albuquerque, NM

MAKES: **8–10 SERVINGS (1 QUART)**
PREP. TIME: **5 MINUTES**
COOKING TIME: **1–1½ HOURS**
IDEAL SLOW COOKER SIZE: **1-QUART**

2 10¾-oz. cans cheddar cheese soup
7-oz. can chopped green chilies
1 garlic clove, minced
½ tsp. dried cilantro leaves
½ tsp. ground cumin

1. Mix together all ingredients in slow cooker.
2. Cover. Cook on Low 1–1½ hours. Stir well. Cook an additional 1½ hours.
3. Serve with corn chips.

Tip: *Make this a main dish by serving over baked potatoes.*

Hint-of-Chicken Nacho Dip

Lilli Peters   Dodge City, KS

MAKES: **10 SERVINGS**
PREP. TIME: **10 MINUTES**
COOKING TIME: **1–2 HOURS**
IDEAL SLOW COOKER SIZE: **3-QUART**

3-lbs. Velveeta cheese, cubed
10¾-oz. can cream of chicken soup
2 4-oz. cans chopped green chilies and juice
tortilla chips

1. Place cheese in slow cooker. Cook on Low until cheese melts, stirring occasionally.
2. Add soup and chilies. Stir. Heat on Low 1 hour.
3. Pour over tortilla chips just before serving.

Variations:

1. If you want to speed up the process, melt the cheese in the microwave. Heat on High for 1½ minutes, stir, and continue heating at 1½-minute intervals as long as needed.

2. Instead of using 2 4-oz. cans chilies, use 10-oz. can tomatoes and chilies.

3. For a heartier dip, add ½–1 lb. bulk sausage, browned, crumbled into small pieces, and drained.

Vegetable Chili con Queso

Marilyn Mowry   Irving, TX

MAKES: **2 CUPS DIP**
PREP. TIME: **10–15 MINUTES**
COOKING TIME: **1–2 HOURS**
IDEAL SLOW COOKER SIZE: **1-QUART**

1 Tbsp. chopped green peppers
1 Tbsp. chopped celery
1 Tbsp. chopped onions
2 Tbsp. diced tomatoes
2 tsp. chopped jalapeño pepper
½ cup water
¾ cup heavy cream
8 oz. Velveeta cheese, cubed
2 oz. cheddar cheese, shredded

1. Place first 5 ingredients in slow cooker. Add water.
2. Cover. Cook on High 1 hour, or until vegetables are tender.
3. Stir in cream and cheeses.
4. Reduce heat to Low. Cook until cheese is melted. Serve immediately, or keep warm on Low for hours.
5. Serve with tortilla chips.

Sour Cream con Queso Dip

Jenny R. Unternahrer   Wayland, IA

MAKES: **APPROXIMATELY 12 SERVINGS**
PREP. TIME: **5 MINUTES**
COOKING TIME: **1–1½ HOURS**
IDEAL SLOW COOKER SIZE: **1-QUART**

1 lb. Velveeta cheese, cubed
1 cup salsa, your choice of heat
1 cup sour cream

1. Combine cheese, salsa, and sour cream in slow cooker.
2. Cover. Heat on Low, stirring occasionally until cheese melts and dip is well blended, about 1–1½ hours.
3. Serve with tortilla chips.

Short-Cut Fondue Dip

Jean Butzer   Batavia, NY

MAKES: **8–10 SERVINGS**
PREP. TIME: **10 MINUTES**
COOKING TIME: **2–2½ HOURS**
IDEAL SLOW COOKER SIZE: **1-QUART**

2 10¾-oz. cans condensed cheese soup
2 cups shredded sharp cheddar cheese
1 Tbsp. Worcestershire sauce
1 tsp. lemon juice
2 Tbsp. dried chopped chives

1. Combine all ingredients in slow cooker.
2. Cover. Heat on Low 2–2½ hours. Stir until smooth and well blended.
3. Serve warm dip with celery sticks, cauliflower, and corn chips.

Chunky-Cheesy Salsa Dip

Susan Tjon   Austin, TX

Light

MAKES: **8 SERVINGS**
PREP. TIME: **10 MINUTES**
COOKING TIME: **2 HOURS**
IDEAL SLOW COOKER SIZE: **3-QUART**

8 ozs. fat-free cream cheese

1 cup shredded reduced-fat cheddar cheese

½ cup mild or medium chunky salsa

¼ cup fat-free or 2% milk

8-oz. bag baked tortilla chips *or* assorted fresh
   vegetables

1. Cut cream cheese into chunks.
2. Combine cream cheese, cheddar cheese,
   salsa, and milk in slow cooker.
3. Cook on Low 2 hours. Stir to blend.
4. When smooth and hot, serve with baked
   tortilla chips or assorted fresh vegetables.

Per Serving: 170 calories (25 calories from fat), 2.5 total fat (1g
saturated, 0g trans), 5mg cholesterol, 430mg sodium, 27g total
carbohydrate (2g fiber, 1g sugar), 10g protein, 8%DV vitamin A, 4%DV
vitamin C, 20%DV calcium, 4%DV iron.

Tip: *You may double this recipe successfully.*
Just be sure to allow extra cooking time.

South-of-the-Border Cheese Dip

Dale Peterson   Rapid City, SD

MAKES: **12 SERVINGS**
PREP. TIME: **10 MINUTES**
COOKING TIME: **2–3 HOURS**
IDEAL SLOW COOKER SIZE: **3-QUART**

2 lbs. Velveeta cheese, cubed

2 tsp. taco seasoning

10-oz. can tomatoes and green chilies, undrained

1. Place cubed cheese in slow cooker.
2. Cover and cook on Low 1–1½ hours, or
   until cheese is melted.
3. Stir in seasoning and tomatoes with green
   chilies.
4. Cover and cook on Low another 1–1½
   hours. Stir occasionally to keep cheese from
   sticking to the bottom of the cooker.
5. Serve with your favorite sturdy chips.

Garden Chili con Queso

Arlene Leaman Kliewer   Lakewood, CO

MAKES: **12–16 SERVINGS**
PREP. TIME: **15 MINUTES**
COOKING TIME: **2 HOURS**
IDEAL SLOW COOKER SIZE: **2-QUART**

2 Tbsp. oil

1 medium onion, chopped

2 4¼-oz. cans chopped green chilies

14½-oz. can Mexican-style stewed tomatoes, drained

1 lb. Velveeta cheese, cubed

1. In skillet, sauté onion in oil until transparent.
   Add chilies and tomatoes. Bring to boil.
2. Add cheese. Pour into slow cooker on Low.
   Cook for 2 hours.
3. Keep warm in slow cooker, stirring occasionally.
4. Serve with tortilla chips.

Chili Rellanos

Andrea Cunningham   Arlington, KS

MAKES: **8 SERVINGS**
PREP. TIME: **15 MINUTES**
COOKING TIME: **6–8 HOURS**
IDEAL SLOW COOKER SIZE: **4-QUART**

1¼ cups milk

4 eggs, beaten

3 Tbsp. flour

12-oz. can chopped green chilies

2 cups shredded cheddar cheese

1. Combine all ingredients in slow cooker until well blended.
2. Cover and cook on Low for 6–8 hours.
3. Serve with tortilla chips and salsa

Variation: *Serve as a burrito filling.*

Peppy Chip Dip

Penny Blosser   Beavercreek, OH

MAKES: **18–24 SERVINGS**
PREP. TIME: **15 MINUTES**
COOKING TIME: **1 HOUR**
IDEAL SLOW COOKER SIZE: **3-QUART**

2 pounds Velveeta cheese, cubed

¼ cup milk

1 cup shredded sharp cheddar cheese

2 2¾-oz. cans green chilies

1 small jar pimentos

1. Combine all ingredients in slow cooker.
2. Cover and cook on High 1 hour, or until cheese melts. Stir frequently.
3. Turn cooker to Low and serve with chips of your choice.

Variation: *Add chopped jalapeño peppers if you want a spicier dip.*

Cheesy Tomato Pizza Fondue

Bonnie Whaling   Clearfield, PA

MAKES: **4–6 SERVINGS**
PREP. TIME: **15 MINUTES**
COOKING TIME: **1 HOUR**
IDEAL SLOW COOKER SIZE: **3½-QUART**

1-lb. block of cheese, your choice of good melting cheese(s), cut in ½-inch cubes

2 cups shredded mozzarella cheese

19-oz. can Italian-style stewed tomatoes with juice

loaf of Italian bread, slices toasted and then cut into 1-inch cubes

1. Place cheese cubes, shredded mozzarella cheese, and tomatoes in a lightly greased slow cooker.
2. Cover and cook on High 45–60 minutes, or until cheese is melted.
3. Stir occasionally and scrape down sides of slow cooker with rubber spatula to prevent scorching.
4. Reduce heat to Low and serve. (Fondue will keep a smooth consistency for up to 4 hours.)
5. Serve with toasted bread cubes for dipping.

Variation: *Add ¼ lb. thinly sliced pepperoni to Step 1.*

The Warm setting on a slow cooker holds food at a temperature between 145° and 165° F.

Cider Cheese Fondue—
for a Buffet Table

Ruth Ann Bender   Cochranville, PA

MAKES: **4 SERVINGS**
PREP. TIME: **15 MINUTES**
WARMING TIME: **UNTIL THE COOKER IS EMPTY!**
IDEAL SLOW COOKER SIZE: **1-QUART**

¾ **cup apple juice or cider**

2 **cups (8–10 ozs.) shredded cheddar cheese**

1 **cup (4–5 ozs.) shredded Swiss cheese**

1 **Tbsp. cornstarch**

⅛ **tsp. pepper**

1 **lb. loaf French bread, cut into chunks**

1. In a large saucepan, bring cider to a boil. Reduce heat to medium low.
2. In a large mixing bowl, toss together the cheeses with cornstarch and pepper.
3. Stir mixture into cider. Cook and stir for 3–4 minutes, or until cheese is melted.
4. Transfer to a 1-quart slow cooker to keep warm. Stir occasionally
5. Serve with bread cubes or apple wedges for dipping.

"Baked" Brie with
Cranberry Chutney

Amymariene Jensen   Fountain, CO

MAKES: **8–10 SERVINGS**
PREP. TIME: **5–10 MINUTES**
COOKING TIME: **4 HOURS**
IDEAL SLOW COOKER SIZE: **1-QUART**

1 **cup fresh or dried cranberries**

½ **cup brown sugar**

⅓ **cup cider vinegar**

2 **Tbsp. water *or* orange juice**

2 **tsp. minced crystallized ginger**

¼ **tsp. cinnamon**

⅛ **tsp. ground cloves**

oil

8-**oz. round of Brie cheese**

1 **Tbsp. sliced almonds, toasted**

crackers

1. Mix together cranberries, brown sugar, vinegar, water or juice, ginger, cinnamon, and cloves in slow cooker.
2. Cover. Cook on Low 4 hours. Stir once near the end to see if it is thickening. If not, remove lid, turn heat to High and cook 30 minutes without lid.
3. Put cranberry chutney in covered container and chill for up to 2 weeks. When ready to serve, bring to room temperature.
4. Brush ovenproof plate with vegetable oil, place unpeeled Brie on plate, and bake uncovered at 350° for 9 minutes, until cheese is soft and partially melted. Remove from oven.
5. Top with at least half the chutney and garnish with almonds. Serve with crackers.

Appetizers, Snacks, and Spreads

Hearty Beef Dip Fondue

Ann Bender Ft. Defiance, VA • *Charlotte Shaffer* East Earl, PA

MAKES: **2½ CUPS DIP**
PREP. TIME: **20–30 MINUTES**
COOKING TIME: **UP TO 6 HOURS**
IDEAL SLOW COOKER SIZE: **1½-QUART**

1¾ cups milk

2 8-oz. pkgs. cream cheese, cubed

2 tsp. dry mustard

¼ cup chopped green onions

2½ ozs. sliced dried beef, shredded or torn into small
     pieces

French bread, cut into bite-sized pieces, each having a
     side of crust

1. Heat milk in slow cooker on High.
2. Add cheese. Stir until melted.
3. Add mustard, green onions, and dried beef.
   Stir well.
4. Cover. Cook on Low for up to 6 hours.
5. Serve by dipping bread pieces on long forks
   into mixture.

Note: *I make this on cold winter evenings, and
we sit around the table playing games.*

Variation: *Add ½ cup chopped pecans, 2 Tbsp.
chopped olives, or 1 tsp. minced onion in Step 3.*

Curried Cheese Dip

Susan Kasting Jenks, OK

MAKES: **9–10 SERVINGS**
PREP. TIME: **10 MINUTES**
COOKING TIME: **45 MINUTES–1 HOUR**
IDEAL SLOW COOKER SIZE: **1–2-QUART**

2 cups shredded cheddar cheese

8-oz. pkg. cream cheese, softened

½ cup milk

¼ cup chopped scallions

1½ tsp. curry powder

1. Mix ingredients together in slow cooker.
2. Cover and heat on High 45 minutes to
   1 hour, or until cheeses are melted and
   dip is heated through. Stir occasionally.
3. Turn cooker to Low and serve dip with
   crackers or veggies.

Red Pepper Cheese Dip

Ann Bender Ft. Defiance, VA

MAKES: **12–15 SERVINGS**
PREP. TIME: **10 MINUTES**
COOKING TIME: **2 HOURS**
IDEAL SLOW COOKER SIZE: **3-QUART**

2 Tbsp. olive oil

4–6 large red peppers, cut into 1-inch squares

½ lb. feta cheese

crackers *or* pita bread

1. Pour oil into slow cooker. Stir in peppers.
2. Cover. Cook on Low 2 hours.
3. Serve with feta cheese on crackers.

Roasted Pepper and Artichoke Spread

Sherril Bieberly   Sauna, KS

PICTURED ON PAGE 30

MAKES: **3 CUPS, OR ABOUT 12 SERVINGS**
PREP. TIME: **10 MINUTES**
COOKING TIME: **1 HOUR**
IDEAL SLOW COOKER SIZE: **1-QUART**

1 cup grated Parmesan cheese

½ cup mayonnaise

8-oz. pkg. cream cheese, softened

1 garlic clove, minced

14-oz. can artichoke hearts, drained and chopped finely

⅓ cup finely chopped roasted red bell peppers
   (from 7¼-oz. jar)

1. Combine Parmesan cheese, mayonnaise, cream cheese, and garlic in food processor. Process until smooth. Place mixture in slow cooker.
2. Add artichoke hearts and red bell pepper. Stir well.
3. Cover. Cook on Low 1 hour. Stir again.
4. Use as spread for crackers, cut-up fresh vegetables, or snack-bread slices.

Party-Time Artichokes

Dorothy Lingerfelt   Stonyford, CA

MAKES: **4 SERVINGS**
PREP. TIME: **10 MINUTES**
COOKING TIME: **2½–4 HOURS**
IDEAL SLOW COOKER SIZE: **4-QUART**

4 whole, fresh artichokes

1 tsp. salt

4 Tbsp. lemon juice, *divided*

2 Tbsp. butter, melted

1. Wash and trim off the tough outer leaves and around the bottom of the artichokes. Cut off about 1 inch from the tops of each, and trim off the tips of the leaves. Spread the top leaves apart and use a long-handled spoon to pull out the fuzzy chokes in their centers.
2. Stand the prepared artichokes upright in the slow cooker. Sprinkle each with ¼ tsp. salt.
3. Spoon 2 Tbsp. lemon juice over the artichokes. Pour in enough water to cover the bottom half of the artichokes.
4. Cover and cook on High for 2½–4 hours.
5. Serve with melted butter and remaining lemon juice for dipping.

Write in your cookbook the date when you tried a particular recipe and whether or not you liked it. Develop a rating system for each recipe you try (Excellent, Good, Yummy, Okay). Write notes about what might be a good addition or deletion the next time you make it.

Artichoke Dip

Maryann Markano   Wilmington, DE

MAKES: **6–10 SERVINGS**
PREP. TIME: **10 MINUTES**
COOKING TIME: **1½ HOURS**
IDEAL SLOW COOKER SIZE: **2½–3-QUART**

14-oz. can non-marinated artichoke hearts, chopped

10¾-oz. can cream of mushroom/roasted garlic condensed soup

1 cup fat-free cream cheese, broken into small pieces

¼ tsp. black pepper

⅛ tsp. crushed red pepper flakes, *optional*

dash of salt

½ cup fat-free shredded Parmesan cheese

½ cup fat-free shredded mozzarella cheese

½ cup sliced green onions

½ cup roasted red peppers, chopped

baked pita *or* **bagel chips (for dipping)**

1. Spray inside of slow cooker with fat-free vegetable spray.
2. Combine all ingredients except chips in slow cooker. Mix well.
3. Cook on High 1½ hours. Reduce to Low and keep warm for serving.
4. Stir just before serving.

Per Serving: 170 calories (10 calories from fat), 1.5g total fat (0.5g saturated, 0g trans), 5mg cholesterol, 600mg sodium, 25g total carbohydrate (3g fiber, 2g sugar), 12g protein, 10%DV vitamin A, 10%DV vitamin C, 30%DV calcium, 8%DV iron.

Hot Artichoke Dip

Mary E. Wheatley   Mashpee, MA

MAKES: **7–8 CUPS, OR 28 2-OZ. SERVINGS**
PREP. TIME: **10 MINUTES**
COOKING TIME: **1–4 HOURS**
IDEAL SLOW COOKER SIZE: **3-QUART**

2 14¾-oz. jars marinated artichoke hearts, drained

1½ cups fat-free mayonnaise

1½ cups fat-free sour cream

1 cup water chestnuts, chopped

¼ cup grated Parmesan cheese

¼ cup finely chopped scallions

1. Cut artichoke hearts into small pieces. Add mayonnaise, sour cream, water chestnuts, cheese, and scallions. Pour into slow cooker.
2. Cover. Cook on High 1–2 hours, or on Low 3–4 hours.
3. Serve with crackers or crusty French bread.

Per Serving: 60 calories (20 calories from fat), 2.5g total fat (0g saturated, 0g trans), 5mg cholesterol, 240mg sodium, 8g total carbohydrate (2g fiber, 2g sugar), 2g protein, 0%DV vitamin A, 10%DV vitamin C, 4%DV calcium, 0%DV iron.

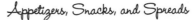

Black-Eyed Pea Dip

Audrey Romonosky   Austin, TX

MAKES: **12 APPETIZER SERVINGS**
PREP. TIME: **5–10 MINUTES**
COOKING TIME: **2–2½ HOURS**
IDEAL SLOW COOKER SIZE: **2-QUART**

8 ozs. Velveeta cheese, cubed

15½-oz. can black-eyed peas, drained

4½-oz. can chopped green chilies

½ cup (1 stick) butter, melted

4 chopped green onions

1. Combine all ingredients in slow cooker.
2. Cover. Cook on Low, stirring occasionally, until cheese melts. Cook an additional 1½ hours on Low.
3. Serve warm from cooker with tortilla chips.

Slim Dunk

Vera Smucker   Goshen, IN

MAKES: **3 CUPS OR 12 SERVINGS**
PREP. TIME: **10 MINUTES**
COOKING TIME: **1 HOUR**
IDEAL SLOW COOKER SIZE: **1½-QUART**

2 cups fat-free sour cream

¼ cup fat-free miracle whip salad dressing

10-oz. pkg. frozen chopped spinach, squeezed dry and chopped

1.8-oz. envelope dry leek soup mix

¼ cup red bell pepper, minced

1. Combine all ingredients in slow cooker. Mix well.
2. Cover. Cook on High 1 hour.
3. Serve with fat-free baked tortilla chips.

Per Serving: 70 calories (10 calories from fat), 1 total fat (0.5g saturated, 0g trans), 5mg cholesterol, 310mg sodium, 11g total carbohydrate (0.5g fiber, 4g sugar), 3g protein, 25%DV vitamin A, 10%DV vitamin C, 10%DV calcium, 4%DV iron.

Broccoli-Cheese Dip

Carla Koslowsky   Hillsboro, KS

MAKES: **6 CUPS DIP, OR ABOUT 23 2-OZ. SERVINGS**
PREP. TIME: **15 MINUTES**
COOKING TIME: **2 HOURS**
IDEAL SLOW COOKER SIZE: **3–4-QUART**

1 cup chopped celery

½ cup chopped onions

10-oz. pkg. frozen chopped broccoli, cooked

1 cup rice, cooked

10¾-oz. can fat-free, sodium-free cream of mushroom
    soup

16-oz. jar fat-free cheese spread

1. Combine all ingredients in slow cooker.
2. Cover. Heat on Low 2 hours.
3. Serve with snack breads or crackers.

Per Serving: 60 calories (15 calories from fat), 1.5g total fat (1g saturated, 0g trans), 5mg cholesterol, 110mg sodium, 7g total carbohydrate (0g fiber, 1g sugar), 6g protein, 0%DV vitamin A, 0%DV vitamin C, 15%DV calcium, 2%DV iron.

Variations:

1. If you're an onion-lover, you may want to increase the chopped onions to ¾ cup.

2. If you prefer your vegetables soft rather than crunchy, you may want to cook the onions and celery before adding them to the cooker.

Cheese and Broccoli Dip

Maryann Markano   Wilmington, DE

MAKES: **24 SERVINGS**
PREP. TIME: **20–25 MINUTES**
COOKING TIME: **1½–2 HOURS**
IDEAL SLOW COOKER SIZE: **3–4-QUART**

2 10-oz. pkgs. frozen chopped broccoli

1 lb. cubed Mexican Velveeta cheese, *or* plain Velveeta,
    or a combination of the two

2 10¾-oz. cans cream of mushroom soup

¼ cup sour cream

1 tsp. garlic powder

1. Cook broccoli until just-tender in a saucepan. Drain.
2. Melt cheese in slow cooker on Low for about 1½–2 hours. (You can jumpstart things by melting the cheese in the microwave—30 seconds on High. Stir. Continue heating on High for 15-second increments, followed by stirring each time, until cheese is melted).
3. In a large mixing bowl, mix together the soup, sour cream, broccoli, and garlic powder. Stir in melted cheese.
4. Spoon into slow cooker. Keep slow cooker on warm while serving with tortilla chips. Stir occasionally.

Hot Broccoli Dip

Brenda Hochstedler   East Earl, PA

MAKES: **24 SERVINGS**
PREP. TIME: **20 MINUTES**
COOKING TIME: **1 HOUR**
IDEAL SLOW COOKER SIZE: **2-QUART**

2 cups fresh *or* frozen broccoli, chopped

4 Tbsp. chopped red bell pepper

2 8-oz. containers ranch dip

½ cup grated Parmesan cheese

2 cups shredded cheddar cheese

1. Mix together all ingredients in your slow cooker.
2. Cook on Low for 1 hour.
3. Serve with pita chips, veggie chips, or raw, cut-up vegetables.

Hot Mushroom Dip

Carol L. Stroh   Akron, NY

MAKES: **6–8 SERVINGS**
PREP. TIME: **30 MINUTES**
COOKING TIME: **3–4 HOURS**
IDEAL SLOW COOKER SIZE: **1½–2-QUART**

8-oz. pkg. cream cheese

10¾-oz. can cream of mushroom soup

4-oz. can mushrooms, chopped and drained

⅔ cup chopped shrimp, crab, *or* ham

½ cup milk

1. Cut cream cheese into small pieces and place in slow cooker with remaining ingredients. Stir to mix.
2. Heat on Low 3–4 hours, stirring occasionally during first hour.
3. Serve with your choice of dippers—French bread, veggies, or crackers.

Salsa

Wilma J. Haberkamp   Fairbank, IA

MAKES: **6–7 PINTS, OR 48 OR MORE 4-TBSP.-SIZE SERVINGS**
PREP. TIME: **30 MINUTES**
COOKING TIME: **3 HOURS**
IDEAL SLOW COOKER SIZE: **6-QUART OR LARGER**

13 tomatoes, peeled and seeded

1 tsp. salt

4 tsp. white vinegar

2 6½-oz. cans tomato paste

⅔ cup Louisiana Pure Hot Sauce

1 large yellow onion, chopped

1 large red onion, chopped

1 green bell pepper, seeded and chopped

1 red bell pepper, seeded and chopped

1 yellow bell pepper, seeded and chopped

1 or 2 hot peppers, seeded

3 banana peppers, seeded and chopped

1. Combine all ingredients in large bowl and mix well. Ladle into 6-quart, or larger, slow cooker.
2. Cook on High 1 hour, and then reduce to Low for 2 hours.
3. Pour into sterilized jars and follow directions from your canner for sealing and preserving.

Per Serving: 25 calories (0 calories from fat), 0g total fat (0g saturated, 0g trans), 0mg cholesterol, 140mg sodium, 6g total carbohydrate (1g fiber, 2g sugar), 1g protein, 15%DV vitamin A, 40%DV vitamin C, 0%DV calcium, 2%DV iron.

A note from the tester: *When I served the salsa, I stirred in some fresh chopped cilantro to add taste and lively green color. I served it as an appetizer and 8 people almost finished a pint jar!*

Slow Cooker Salsa

Joyce Shackelford   Green Bay, WI

MAKES: **2 CUPS OR 8 SERVINGS**
PREP. TIME: **20 MINUTES**
COOKING TIME: **2½–3 HOURS**
IDEAL SLOW COOKER SIZE: **1–2 QUART**

10 plum tomatoes, cored

2 garlic cloves

1 medium onion, cut in wedges

2 or 3 jalapeño peppers

half a medium green bell pepper, chopped

¼ cup cilantro *or* parsley leaves

½ tsp. salt

¼ tsp. black pepper

1. Cut a small slit in two tomatoes. Insert a garlic clove in each slit. Place tomatoes and onions in slow cooker.
2. Cut stems off jalapeños. Remove seeds for a milder salsa. Place jalapeños in slow cooker. Add chopped bell pepper.
3. Cover. Cook on High 2½–3 hours. Cool.
4. In a blender, combine the tomato mixture, cilantro, and salt. Process until smooth.
5. Refrigerate leftovers.

Per Serving: 25 calories (0 calories from fat), 0 total fat (0g saturated, 0g trans), 0mg cholesterol, 150mg sodium, 5g total carbohydrate (1g fiber, 3g sugar), 1g protein, 10%DV vitamin A, 20%DV vitamin C, 0%DV calcium, 2%DV iron.

Tip: *Use rubber gloves when cutting hot peppers.*

Fruit Salsa

Joyce Shackelford   Green Bay, WI

MAKES: **4 CUPS OR 16 SERVINGS**
PREP. TIME: **15 MINUTES**
COOKING TIME: **2 HOURS**
IDEAL SLOW COOKER SIZE: **2–3-QUART**

11-oz. can mandarin oranges

8½-oz. can unsweetened sliced peaches, undrained

8-oz. can unsweetened pineapple tidbits, undrained

1 medium onion, chopped

half a medium green bell pepper, chopped

half a medium red bell pepper, chopped

half a medium yellow bell pepper, chopped

3 garlic cloves, minced

3 Tbsp. cornstarch

4 tsp. vinegar

1. Combine all ingredients in slow cooker.
2. Cover. Cook on High 2 hours, stirring occasionally.
3. Serve with baked tortilla chips.

Per Serving: 35 calories (0 calories from fat), 0 total fat (0g saturated, 0g trans), 0mg cholesterol, 5mg sodium, 8g total carbohydrate (0.5g fiber, 6g sugar), 0g protein, 10%DV vitamin A, 20%DV vitamin C, 0%DV calcium, 2%DV iron.

Crab Spread

Jeanette Oberholtzer Manheim, PA

MAKES: **8 SERVINGS**
PREP. TIME: **20 MINUTES**
COOKING TIME: **4 HOURS**
IDEAL SLOW COOKER SIZE: **1–3-QUART**

½ cup mayonnaise

8 ozs. cream cheese, softened

2 Tbsp. apple juice

1 onion, minced

1 lb. lump crabmeat, picked over to remove cartilage
and shell bits

1. Mix mayonnaise, cheese, and juice in medium-sized bowl until blended.
2. Stir in onions, mixing well. Gently stir in crabmeat.
3. Place in slow cooker, cover, and cook on Low for 4 hours.
4. Dip will hold for 2 hours. Stir occasionally. Serve with snack crackers, snack bread, or crudites.

Hot Crab Dip

Karen Waggoner Joplin, MO

MAKES: **5 CUPS**
PREP. TIME: **15 MINUTES**
COOKING TIME: **3–4 HOURS**
IDEAL SLOW COOKER SIZE: **2-QUART**

⅓ cup salsa

½ cup fat-free milk

2 8-oz. pkgs. imitation crabmeat, flaked finely

¾ cup green onions, thinly sliced

4-oz. can chopped green chilies

3 8-oz. pkgs. fat-free cream cheese, cubed

10 ozs. stone wheat crackers

1. Spray slow cooker with fat-free cooking spray.
2. Mix salsa and milk.
3. Stir in all remaining ingredients except crackers.
4. Cover. Cook on Low 3–4 hours.
5. Stir approximately every half hour.
6. Serve with crackers or raw vegetables.

Per Serving: 520 calories (110 calories from fat), 12g total fat (3g saturated, 0g trans), 55mg cholesterol, 1410mg sodium, 65g total carbohydrate (8g fiber, 4g sugar), 38g protein, 20%DV vitamin A, 10%DV vitamin C, 35%DV calcium, 15%DV iron.

Seafood Dip

Joan Rosenberger   Stephens City, VA

MAKES: **24 SERVINGS OF 2 TBSP. EACH**
PREP. TIME: **10 MINUTES**
COOKING TIME: **3 HOURS**
IDEAL SLOW COOKER SIZE: **3½-QUART**

PICTURED
ON PAGE
99

8-oz. pkg. fat-free cream cheese

8-oz. pkg. imitation crab strands, freeze-dried

2 Tbsp. onion, finely chopped

4–5 drops hot sauce

¼ cup walnuts, finely chopped

1 tsp. paprika

1. Blend all ingredients except nuts and paprika until well mixed.
2. Spread in slow cooker. Sprinkle with nuts and paprika.
3. Cook on Low 3 hours.

Per Serving: 70 calories (10 calories from fat), 1.5g total fat (0g saturated, 0g trans), 5mg cholesterol, 370mg sodium, 7g total carbohydrate (0g fiber, 3g sugar), 7g protein, 6%DV vitamin A, 0%DV vitamin C, 4%DV calcium, 0%DV iron.

Tip: *Serve with crackers.*

Crab Dip

Rebecca Plank Leichty   Harrisonburg, VA

MAKES: **8–10 SERVINGS**
PREP. TIME: **10 MINUTES**
COOKING TIME: **3 HOURS**
IDEAL SLOW COOKER SIZE: **2-QUART**

2 eggs, beaten

1 green pepper, diced

2 Tbsp. diced pimento

½ tsp. ground mustard

⅛ tsp. pepper

1 tsp. salt

10¾-oz. can cream of celery soup

1-lb. can white crabmeat *or* imitation crabmeat

1. Beat eggs with whisk in greased slow cooker.
2. Add green pepper, pimento, seasonings, and soup. Mix well.
3. Fold in crabmeat.
4. Cover. Cook on High 3 hours.
5. Serve with toasted bread crisps for dipping.

Tip: *To make bread crisps, cut crusts off bread slices. Cut remaining bread into triangles. Toast on baking sheet in 350° oven. Turn once to brown evenly.*
This is an easy way to serve an appetizer before a meal.

Don't measure ingredients over the bowl in which you are mixing or baking the recipe, in case more than you need comes tumbling out.

Cheese, Crab, and Shrimp Dip

Donna Lantgen Rapid City, SD

MAKES: **10–12 SERVINGS**
PREP. TIME: **10 MINUTES**
COOKING TIME: **2 HOURS**
IDEAL SLOW COOKER SIZE: **2-QUART**

3 8-oz. pkgs. cream cheese, at room temperature
2 6-oz. cans crabmeat, drained
1 can broken shrimp, drained
6 Tbsp. finely chopped onions
1 tsp. horseradish
½ cup toasted almonds, broken

1. Combine all ingredients in slow cooker.
2. Cover. Cook on Low 2 hours.
3. Serve with crackers or bread cubes.

Cheesy New Orleans Shrimp Dip

Kelly Evenson Pittsboro, NC

MAKES: **3–4 CUPS DIP, OR 24 SERVINGS**
PREP. TIME: **20 MINUTES**
COOKING TIME: **1 HOUR**
IDEAL SLOW COOKER SIZE: **2-QUART**

1 slice lean turkey bacon
3 medium onions, chopped
1 garlic clove, minced
4 jumbo shrimp, peeled and deveined
1 medium tomato, peeled and chopped
3 cups low-fat Monterey Jack cheese, shredded
4 drops Tabasco sauce
⅛ tsp. cayenne pepper
dash of black pepper

1. Cook bacon until crisp. Drain on paper towel. Crumble.
2. Sauté onion and garlic in bacon drippings. Drain on paper towel.
3. Coarsely chop shrimp.
4. Combine all ingredients in slow cooker.
5. Cover. Cook on Low 1 hour, or until cheese melts. Thin with milk if too thick.
6. Serve with chips.

Per Serving: 130 calories (5 calories from fat), 0.5g total fat (0g saturated, 0g trans), 10mg cholesterol, 520mg sodium, 12g total carbohydrate (1g fiber, 4g sugar), 18g protein, 10%DV vitamin A, 0%DV vitamin C, 60%DV calcium, 2%DV iron.

Pickled Whiting

Sue Hamilton Minooka, IL

MAKES: **24 SERVINGS**
PREP. TIME: **10 MINUTES**
COOKING TIME: **3–4 HOURS**
IDEAL SLOW COOKER SIZE: **6-QUART**

2 onions, sliced

1 cup white vinegar

¾ cup Splenda

1 tsp. salt

1 Tbsp. allspice

2 lbs. frozen individual whiting with skin

1. Combine onions, vinegar, Splenda, salt, and allspice in bottom of slow cooker.
2. Slice frozen whiting into 2-inch slices, each with skin on. Place fish in slow cooker, pushing it down into the liquid as much as possible.
3. Cook on Low 3–4 hours.
4. Pour cooking liquid over fish, cover, and refrigerate. Serve when well chilled.

Per Serving: 45 calories (5 calories from fat), 0.5 total fat (0g saturated, 0g trans), 25mg cholesterol, 125mg sodium, 2g total carbohydrate (0g fiber, 1g sugar), 7g protein, 0%DV vitamin A, 0%DV vitamin C, 2%DV calcium, 0%DV iron.

Simmered Smoked Sausages

Jonice Crist Quinter, KS • *Mary Lynn Miller* Reinholds, PA
Joette Droz Kalona, IA • *Renee Baum* Chambersburg, PA

MAKES: **16–20 SERVINGS**
PREP. TIME: **15 MINUTES**
COOKING TIME: **4 HOURS**
IDEAL SLOW COOKER SIZE: **2-QUART**

2 16-oz. pkgs. miniature smoked sausage links

1 cup brown sugar, packed

½ cup ketchup

¼ cup prepared horseradish

1. Place sausages in slow cooker.
2. Combine remaining ingredients in a bowl and pour over sausages.
3. Cover and cook on Low for 4 hours.

Slow-Cooked Smokies

Renee Baum Chambersburg, PA

MAKES: **12–16 SERVINGS**
PREP. TIME: **5 MINUTES**
COOKING TIME: **6–7 HOURS**
IDEAL SLOW COOKER SIZE: **3–4-QUART**

2 lbs. miniature smoked sausage links

28-oz. bottle barbecue sauce

1¼ cups water

3 Tbsp. Worcestershire sauce

3 Tbsp. steak sauce

½ tsp. pepper

1. In a slow cooker, combine all ingredients. Mix well.
2. Cover and cook on Low 6–7 hours.

Barbecued Lil' Smokies

Jena Hammond   Traverse City, MI

MAKES: **48–60 APPETIZER SERVINGS**
PREP. TIME: **5 MINUTES**
COOKING TIME: **4 HOURS**
IDEAL SLOW COOKER SIZE: **4-QUART**

4 16-oz. pkgs. little smokies
18-oz. bottle barbecue sauce

1. Mix ingredients together in slow cooker.
2. Cover and cook on Low for 4 hours.

Apple-y Kielbasa

Jeanette Oberholtzer   Manheim, PA

MAKES: **12 SERVINGS**
PREP. TIME: **15 MINUTES**
COOKING TIME: **6–8 HOURS**
IDEAL SLOW COOKER SIZE: **3-QUART**

2 lbs. fully cooked kielbasa sausage, cut into 1-inch
   pieces
¾ cup brown sugar
1 cup chunky applesauce
2 cloves garlic, minced

1. Combine all ingredients in slow cooker.
2. Cover and cook on Low 6–8 hours until
   thoroughly heated.

Easy Barbecue Smokies

Ruth Ann Bender   Cochranville, PA

MAKES: **12–16 SERVINGS**
PREP. TIME: **5 MINUTES**
COOKING TIME: **2 HOURS**
IDEAL SLOW COOKER SIZE: **3½-QUART**

18-oz. bottle barbecue sauce
8 ozs. salsa
2 16-oz. pkgs. little smokies

1. Mix barbecue sauce and salsa in slow cooker.
2. Add the little smokies.
3. Heat on High for 2 hours.
4. Stir. Turn to Low to serve.

Mustard-Lovers' Party Dogs

Barb Harvey   Quarryville, PA

MAKES: **12 SERVINGS**
PREP. TIME: **15 MINUTES**
COOKING TIME: **1–2 HOURS**
IDEAL SLOW COOKER SIZE: **3-QUART**

12 hot dogs cut into bite-size pieces
1 cup grape jelly
1 cup prepared mustard

1. Place all ingredients in slow cooker. Stir well.
2. Turn on High until mixture boils. Stir.
3. Turn to Low and bring to the buffet table.

Mini Hot Dogs

Carolyn Fultz Angola, IN

MAKES: **20–30 APPETIZER SERVINGS**
PREP. TIME: **5 MINUTES**
COOKING TIME: **4–5 HOURS**
IDEAL SLOW COOKER SIZE: **4-QUART**

2 cups brown sugar

1 Tbsp. Worcestershire sauce

14-oz. bottle ketchup

2 or 3 lbs. mini-hot dogs

1. In slow cooker, mix together brown sugar, Worcestershire sauce, and ketchup.
2. Stir in hot dogs.
3. Cover and cook on High 1 hour. Turn to Low and cook 3–4 hours.
4. Serve from the cooker while turned to Low.

Tangy Cocktail Franks

Linda Sluiter Schererville, IN

MAKES: **12 SERVINGS**
PREP. TIME: **10 MINUTES**
COOKING TIME: **1–2 HOURS**
IDEAL SLOW COOKER SIZE: **3-QUART**

14-oz. jar currant jelly

¼ cup prepared mustard

3 Tbsp. dry sherry

¼ tsp. ground allspice

30-oz. can unsweetened pineapple chunks

6-oz. pkg. low-sodium cocktail franks

1. Melt jelly in slow cooker turned on High. Stir in seasonings until blended.
2. Drain pineapple chunks and any liquid in cocktail franks package. Discard juice. Gently stir pineapple and franks into slow cooker.
3. Cover. Cook on Low 1–2 hours.
4. Serve and enjoy.

Per Serving: 160 calories (40 calories from fat), 4g total fat (2g saturated, 0g trans), 10mg cholesterol, 170mg sodium, 28g total carbohydrate (0.5g fiber, 25g sugar), 2g protein, 0%DV vitamin A, 0%DV vitamin C, 2%DV calcium, 4%DV iron.

Leave the lid on while the slow cooker cooks. The steam that condenses on the lid helps cook the food from the top. Every time you take the lid off, the cooker loses steam. After you put the lid back on, it takes up to 20 minutes to regain the lost steam and temperature. That means it takes longer for the food to cook.

Sausages in Wine

Mary E. Wheatley   Mashpee, MA

MAKES: **6 SERVINGS, OR 24 APPETIZERS**
PREP. TIME: **15 MINUTES**
COOKING TIME: **45 MINUTES–1 HOUR**
IDEAL SLOW COOKER SIZE: **3-QUART**

1 cup dry red wine
2 Tbsp. currant jelly
6–8 mild Italian sausages *or* **Polish sausages**

1. Place wine and jelly in slow cooker. Heat until jelly is dissolved and sauce begins to simmer. Add sausages.
2. Cover and cook on High 45 minutes to 1 hour, or until sausages are cooked through and lightly glazed.
3. Transfer sausages to a cutting board and slice. Serve with juices spooned over.

Mini Hot Dogs and Meatballs

Mary Kay Nolt   Newmanstown, PA

MAKES: **15 SERVINGS**
PREP. TIME: **5 MINUTES**
COOKING TIME: **2–3 HOURS**
IDEAL SLOW COOKER SIZE: **5–6-QUART**

36 frozen cooked Italian meatballs (½-oz. each)
16-oz. pkg. miniature hot dogs *or* **little smoked sausages**
26-oz. jar meatless spaghetti sauce
18-oz. bottle barbecue sauce
12-oz. bottle chili sauce

1. Combine all ingredients in slow cooker.
2. Cover and cook on High 2 hours, or on Low 3 hours, until heated through.

Variation: *Add 3½-oz. pkg. sliced pepperoni to Step 1.*

Meaty Buffet Favorites

Judy A. Wantland   Menomonee Falls, WI

MAKES: **24 SERVINGS**
PREP. TIME: **5 MINUTES**
COOKING TIME: **2 HOURS**
IDEAL SLOW COOKER SIZE: **2–3-QUART**

1 cup tomato sauce
1 tsp. Worcestershire sauce
½ tsp. prepared mustard
2 Tbsp. brown sugar
1 lb. prepared meatballs *or* **mini-wieners**

1. Mix first four ingredients in slow cooker.
2. Add meatballs or mini-wieners.
3. Cover and cook on High for 2 hours. Turn to Low and serve as an appetizer from the slow cooker.

Variations:
1. Double the sauce and add both wieners and meatballs.
2. Add ¼–½ cup onion for extra flavor and texture.

Tangy Meatballs

Penny Blosser Beavercreek, OH

MAKES: **50–60 MEATBALLS**
PREP. TIME: **15 MINUTES**
COOKING TIME: **2–4 HOURS**
IDEAL SLOW COOKER SIZE: **4-QUART**

2 lbs. pre-cooked meatballs
16-oz. bottle barbecue sauce
8 ozs. grape jelly

1. Place meatballs in slow cooker.
2. Combine barbecue sauce and jelly in medium-sized mixing bowl.
3. Pour over meatballs and stir well.
4. Cover and cook on High 2 hours, or on Low 4 hours.
5. Turn to Low and serve.

Sweet 'n Sour Meatballs

Valerie Drobel Carlisle, PA • *Sharon Hannaby* Frederick, MD

MAKES: **15–20 SERVINGS**
PREP. TIME: **10 MINUTES**
COOKING TIME: **2–4 HOURS**
IDEAL SLOW COOKER SIZE: **3–4-QUART**

12-oz. jar grape jelly
12-oz. jar chili sauce
2 1-lb. bags prepared frozen meatballs, thawed

1. Combine jelly and sauce in slow cooker. Stir well.
2. Add meatballs. Stir to coat.
3. Cover and heat on Low 4 hours, or on High 2 hours. Keep slow cooker on Low while serving.

Tip: *If your meatballs are frozen, add another hour to the cooking time.*

Variation: *Instead of meatballs, use 2 1-lb. pkgs. little smokies.*

Krista Hershberger Elverson, PA

Liver Paté

Barbara Walker   Sturgis, SD

MAKES: **1½ CUPS PATÉ**
PREP. TIME: **10–15 MINUTES**
COOKING TIME: **4–5 HOURS**
IDEAL SLOW COOKER SIZE: **1½-QUART**

1 lb. chicken livers

½ cup dry wine

1 tsp. instant chicken bouillon

1 tsp. minced parsley

1 Tbsp. instant minced onion

¼ tsp. ground ginger

½ tsp. seasoned salt

1 Tbsp. soy sauce

¼ tsp. dry mustard

¼ cup soft butter

1 Tbsp. brandy

1. In slow cooker, combine all ingredients except butter and brandy.
2. Cover. Cook on Low 4–5 hours. Let stand in liquid until cool.
3. Drain. Place in blender or food grinder. Add butter and brandy. Process until smooth.
4. Serve with crackers or toast.

Try out a recipe you've never had before. It is fun to see the family react to it.

Apple Butter — for Your Toast

Alix Nancy Botsford   Seminole, OK

PICTURED
ON PAGE
165

MAKES: **9 CUPS**
PREP. TIME: **5 MINUTES**
COOKING TIME: **4–5 HOURS**
IDEAL SLOW COOKER SIZE: **5–6-QUART**

108-oz. can (#8 size) unsweetened applesauce

2 cups cider

1 Tbsp. ground cinnamon

1 tsp. ground ginger

½ tsp. ground cloves, *or* 1 tsp. ground nutmeg, *optional*

1. Combine applesauce and cider in slow cooker.
2. Cover. Cook on High 3–4 hours.
3. Add spices.
4. Cover. Cook 1 hour more.
5. Sterilize cup- or pint-size jars. Heat lids.
6. Fill jars with apple butter. Clean rim with damp paper towel. Put on lids.
7. Place in canner and cook according to manufacturer's instructions.

Per Serving: 180 calories (0 calories from fat), 0g total fat (0g saturated, 0g trans), 0mg cholesterol, 15mg sodium, 46g total carbohydrate (5g fiber, 38g sugar), 1g protein, 0%DV vitamin A, 60%DV vitamin C, 2%DV calcium, 4%DV iron.

Note: *This is better than any air freshener. When anyone comes home I receive a hug and then a question: "Where's the toast?" It also tastes wonderful on plain yogurt!*

Applesauce Apple Butter

Dolores Metzler Mechanicsburg, PA

MAKES: **3 QUARTS APPLE BUTTER**
PREP. TIME: **5 MINUTES**
COOKING TIME: **8–10 HOURS**
IDEAL SLOW COOKER SIZE: **4-QUART**

3 quarts unsweetened applesauce

3 cups sugar or sweeten to taste

2 tsp. cinnamon

1 tsp., or less, ground cloves

1. Combine all ingredients in large slow cooker.
2. Cover. Cook on High 8–10 hours. Remove lid during last 4 hours. Stir occasionally.

Spicy Apple Butter

Ann Bender Ft. Defiance, VA

MAKES: **2 PINTS APPLE BUTTER**
PREP. TIME: **5 MINUTES**
COOKING TIME: **8–10 HOURS**
IDEAL SLOW COOKER SIZE: **3-QUART**

7 cups unsweetened applesauce

2–3 cups sugar, depending upon the sweetness of the applesauce and your own preference

2 tsp. cinnamon

1 tsp. ground nutmeg

¼ tsp. allspice

1. Combine all ingredients in slow cooker.
2. Put a layer of paper towels under lid to prevent condensation from dripping into apple butter. Cook on High 8–10 hours. Remove lid during last hour. Stir occasionally.

Variation: *Use canned peaches, pears, or apricots in place of applesauce.*

Satisfying Slow Cooker Apple Butter

Anna Musser Manheim, PA

MAKES: **6 PINTS APPLE BUTTER**
PREP. TIME: **10 MINUTES**
COOKING TIME: **12–16 HOURS**
IDEAL SLOW COOKER SIZE: **4–5-QUART**

1 cup cider *or* apple juice

2½ quarts unsweetened applesauce

2–3 cups sugar, depending upon the sweetness of the applesauce and your own preference

1 tsp. vinegar

1 tsp. cinnamon

½ tsp. allspice

1. Boil cider until ½ cup remains.
2. Combine all ingredients in slow cooker.
3. Cover. Cook on High 12-16 hours, until apple butter has cooked down to half the original amount. Put in containers and freeze.

Red-Hots Slow Cooker Apple Butter

Marilyn Yoder   Archbold, OH

MAKES: **80 SERVINGS**
PREP. TIME: **5 MINUTES**
COOKING TIME: **8–10 HOURS**
IDEAL SLOW COOKER SIZE: **3–4-QUART**

2 quarts unsweetened applesauce

2–4 cups sugar, depending upon sweetness of applesauce and your preference

½ tsp. ground cloves

2 Tbsp. lemon juice

¼ heaping cup red hot candies

1. Combine all ingredients in slow cooker.
2. Vent lid. Cook on Low 8–10 hours, stirring about every hour. Apple butter thickens as it cooks, so cook longer to make it thicker.

Traditional Apple Butter

Wilma Haberkamp   Fairbank, IA • *Vera Martin*   East Earl, PA

MAKES: **8 CUPS**
PREP. TIME: **15 MINUTES**
COOKING TIME: **10–13 HOURS**
IDEAL SLOW COOKER SIZE: **3-QUART**

12–14 medium, tart cooking apples (about 16 cups chopped)

2 cups cider or apple juice

2 cups sugar

1 tsp. ground cinnamon

⅛–¼ tsp. ground cloves (add ⅛ tsp. cloves first; taste about halfway through the cooking time to decide if you want to add the other ⅛ tsp.)

1. Core and chop the apples. Do not peel them. Combine apples and cider in your slow cooker.

2. Cover and cook on Low 9–12 hours, or until apples turn mushy and then thicken.
3. Puree apples in a food mill or sieve.
4. Return pureed mixture to your slow cooker.
5. Add sugar, cinnamon, and cloves and mix together well.
6. Cover and cook on Low 1 hour.

Tips:
1. This will keep several weeks in your refrigerator. You may also can or freeze it.

2. This is good on bread or toast. Or use it as a topping over ice cream. Or try it as a filling for apple turnovers.

Variation: *For a thicker finished product, drop Step 6 and do this instead:*

1. Cover and cook on High 6–8 hours, stirring about every 2 hours.

2. Remove the cover after 3 hours so that the fruit and juice can cook down and become thicker and more concentrated.

3. Spoon into hot sterilized jars and process according to standard canning methods.

Dorothy VanDeest   Memphis, TN

Hint-of-Anise Apple Butter

Charlotte Fry   St. Charles, MO

MAKES: **5 PINTS APPLE BUTTER**
PREP. TIME: **15 MINUTES**
COOKING TIME: **14–18 HOURS**
IDEAL SLOW COOKER SIZE: **3–4-QUART**

3 quarts Jonathan *or* Winesap apples

2 cups apple cider

2½ cups sugar

1 tsp. star anise, *optional*

2 Tbsp. lemon juice

2 sticks cinnamon

1. Peel, core, and chop apples. Combine with apple cider in large slow cooker.
2. Cover. Cook on Low 10–12 hours.
3. Stir in sugar, star anise, lemon juice, and stick cinnamon.
4. Cover. Cook on High 2 hours. Stir. Remove lid and cook on High 2–4 hours more, until thickened.
5. Pour into sterilized jars and seal.

Honey Apple Butter

Dianna Milhizer   Springfield, VA

MAKES: **6 PINTS APPLE BUTTER**
PREP. TIME: **30–40 HOUR**
COOKING TIME: **16 HOURS**
IDEAL SLOW COOKER SIZE: **4–5-QUART**

1 bushel tart red apples (Winesap, Rome, *or* Macintosh)

1 quart "raw" honey or least-processed honey available

½ cup cinnamon sticks

1 Tbsp. salt

1. Peel, core, and slice apples.
2. Combine all ingredients in large slow cooker. If apples don't fit, continue to add them as butter cooks down.
3. Cover. Cook on High 8 hours. Stir. Remove lid and let butter cook down on Low 8 additional hours. Consistency should be thick and creamy.
4. Freeze, or pack into sterilized jars and seal.

Apple Butter with Help from the Bees

Lilli Peters   Dodge City, KS

MAKES: **ABOUT 2 PINTS APPLE BUTTER**
PREP. TIME: **5 MINUTES**
COOKING TIME: **14–15 HOURS**
IDEAL SLOW COOKER SIZE: **3-QUART**

7 cups unsweetened applesauce

2 cups apple cider

1½ cups honey

1 tsp. cinnamon

½ tsp. ground cloves

½ tsp. allspice

1. Combine all ingredients in slow cooker. Mix well with whisk.
2. Cook on Low 14–15 hours.

Peach or Apricot Butter

Charlotte Shaffer East Earl. PA

MAKES: **6 8-OZ. JARS BUTTER**
PREP. TIME: **10 MINUTES**
COOKING TIME: **8–10 HOURS**
IDEAL SLOW COOKER SIZE: **4-QUART**

4 1-lb. 13-oz. cans peaches *or* apricots

2¾–3 cups sugar

2 tsp. cinnamon

1 tsp. ground cloves

1. Drain fruit. Remove pits. Puree in blender. Pour into slow cooker.
2. Stir in remaining ingredients.
3. Cover. Cook on High 8–10 hours. Remove cover during last half of cooking. Stir occasionally.

Tip: *Spread on bread, or use as a topping for ice cream or toasted pound cake.*

Buy fruits and vegetables when they are in season. They will be cheaper, and their quality will be greater than those that are out of season and have been shipped long distances.

Citrus Pear Butter

Betty Moore Plano, Il

MAKES: **2 PINTS**
PREP. TIME: **30 MINUTES**
COOKING TIME: **13 HOURS**
COOLING TIME: **24 HOURS**
IDEAL SLOW COOKER SIZE: **5-QUART**

10 large, well-ripened pears (4 lbs.)

2 Tbsp. frozen orange juice concentrate

2 cups sugar

1 tsp. ground cinnamon

1 tsp. ground cloves

½ tsp. ground allspice

1. Peel and quarter pears. Place in slow cooker.
2. Cover. Cook on Low 12 hours. Drain thoroughly and then discard liquid.
3. Mash or puree pears. Add remaining ingredients. Mix well and return to slow cooker.
4. Cover. Cook on High 1 hour.
5. Place in hot sterile jars and seal. Process in hot water bath for 10 minutes. Allow to cool undisturbed for 24 hours.

Per Serving: 100 calories (0 calories from fat), 0g total fat (0g saturated, 0g trans), 0mg cholesterol, 0mg sodium, 26g total carbohydrate (2g fiber, 23g sugar), 0g protein, 0%DV vitamin A, 0%DV vitamin C, 0%DV calcium, 0%DV iron.

Tip: *If the butter is too soupy after cooking on Low 12 hours, you may want to cook it uncovered during Step 4 in order to create a stiffer consistency.*

Appetizers, Snacks, and Spreads

Brown-Sugar Pear Butter

Dorothy Miller   Gulfport, MI

MAKES: **6 PINTS**
PREP. TIME: **5 MINUTES**
COOKING TIME: **10–12 HOURS**
IDEAL SLOW COOKER SIZE: **5-QUART**

8 cups pear sauce
3 cups brown sugar
1 Tbsp. lemon juice
1 Tbsp. cinnamon

1. Combine all ingredients in slow cooker.
2. Cover. Cook on High 10–12 hours.

Per Serving: 40 calories (0 calories from fat), 0g total fat (0g saturated, 0g trans), 0mg cholesterol, 0mg sodium, 10g total carbohydrate (0g fiber, 10g sugar), 0g protein, 0%DV vitamin A, 0%DV vitamin C, 0%DV calcium, 0%DV iron.

Tip: *To make pear sauce, peel, core, and slice 12 large, well-ripened pears. Place in slow cooker with ¾ cup water. Cover and cook on Low 8–10 hours, or until very soft. Stir to blend.*

Apple Dip

Leticia A. Zehr   Lowville, NY

MAKES: **24 SERVINGS**
PREP. TIME: **15 MINUTES**
COOKING TIME: **20 MINUTES**
IDEAL SLOW COOKER SIZE: **2–3-QUART**

2 sticks (1 cup) butter
2 cups brown sugar, packed
2 14-oz. cans sweetened, condensed milk
1 cup corn syrup
1 cup peanut butter, *optional*
apple slices to dip

1. Combine all ingredients except apple slices in a saucepan until smooth. Heat until scalding, watching to make sure it doesn't stick to the bottom of the pan.
2. Transfer dip to slow cooker.
3. Cover and cook on Low 20 minutes.
4. While the dip is warming, slice the apples and place on a serving plate.
5. Serve the dip from the cooker, while turned on Low to keep it creamy.

Butterscotch Dip

Renee Baum   Chambersburg, PA

MAKES: **10–15 SERVINGS**
PREP. TIME: **5–10 MINUTES**
COOKING TIME: **45–50 MINUTES**
IDEAL SLOW COOKER SIZE: **1-QUART**

2 10–11-oz. pkgs. butterscotch chips
5-oz. can evaporated milk
⅔ cup chopped pecans
1 Tbsp. rum extract, *optional*
apple and pear wedges

1. Combine butterscotch chips and milk in slow cooker.
2. Cover and cook on Low 45–50 minutes, or until chips are softened. Stir until smooth.
3. Stir in pecans and extract.
4. Serve warm with fruit wedges for dipping.

Slow Cooker Candy

Eileen M. Landis Lebanon, PA • *Sarah Miller* Harrisonburg, VA
Janet Oberholtzer Ephrata, PA

MAKES: **80–100 PIECES**
PREP. TIME: **5–10 MINUTES**
COOKING TIME: **2 HOURS**
CHILLING TIME: **45 MINUTES**
IDEAL SLOW COOKER SIZE: **2–3-QUART**

1½ lbs. almond bark, broken

4-oz. Baker's Brand German sweet chocolate bar, broken

8 ozs. chocolate chips

8 ozs. peanut butter chips

2 lbs. lightly salted *or* unsalted peanuts

1. Spray inside of cooker with nonstick cooking spray.
2. Layer ingredients into slow cooker in the order given above.
3. Cook on Low 2 hours. Do not stir or lift the lid during the cooking time.
4. After 2 hours, mix well.
5. Drop by teaspoonsfuls onto waxed paper. Refrigerate for approximately 45 minutes before serving or storing.

Peanut Clusters

Jeannine Janzen Elbing, KS • *Marcia Parker* Lansdale, PA

MAKES: **3½–4 DOZEN PIECES**
PREP. TIME: **20 MINUTES**
COOKING TIME: **3 HOURS**
COOLING TIME: **30 MINUTES**
IDEAL SLOW COOKER SIZE: **4-QUART**

2 lbs. white candy coating, chopped

12-oz. pkg. semi-sweet chocolate chips

4-oz. milk chocolate bar, *or* 4-oz. pkg. German sweet chocolate, chopped

24-oz. jar dry roasted peanuts

1. Spray inside of slow cooker with nonstick cooking spray.
2. In slow cooker, combine white candy coating, chocolate chips, and milk chocolate.
3. Cover and cook on Low 3 hours. Stir every 15 minutes.
4. Add peanuts to melted chocolate. Mix well.
5. Drop by tablespoonsfuls onto waxed paper. Cool until set. Serve immediately, or store in a tightly covered container, separating layers with waxed paper. Keep cool and dry.

Tips:

1. This rich mixture can be lumpy as it melts. Stir often, using a wooden spoon to flatten out the lumps.

2. This makes great holiday gifts. And the taste improves a day after it's been made.

Butterscotch Haystacks

Cathy Boshart Lebanon, PA

MAKES: **3 DOZEN PIECES**
PREP. TIME: **15 MINUTES**
COOKING TIME: **15 MINUTES**
COOLING TIME: **30 MINUTES**
IDEAL SLOW COOKER SIZE: **2-QUART**

2 6-oz. pkgs. butterscotch chips

¾ cup chopped almonds

5-oz. can chow mein noodles

1. Turn cooker to High. Place chips in slow cooker. Stir every few minutes until they're melted.
2. When the chips are completely melted, gently stir in almonds and noodles.
3. When well mixed, drop by teaspoonsfuls onto waxed paper.

4. Let stand until haystacks are set, or speed things up by placing them in the fridge until set.

5. Serve, or store in a covered container, placing waxed paper between layers of candy. Keep in a cool, dry place.

All-American Snack

Doris M. Coyle-Zipp South Ozone Park, NY • *Nanci Keatley* Salem, OR
Ada Miller Sugarcreek, OH • *Melissa Raber* Millersburg, OH

MAKES: **3 QUARTS SNACK MIX**
PREP. TIME: **10 MINUTES**
COOKING TIME: **3 HOURS**
IDEAL SLOW COOKER SIZE: **4-QUART**

3 cups thin pretzel sticks

4 cups Wheat Chex

4 cups Cheerios

12-oz. can salted peanuts

¼ cup butter, melted

1 tsp. garlic powder

1 tsp. celery salt

½ tsp. seasoned salt

2 Tbsp. grated Parmesan cheese

1. Combine pretzels, cereal, and peanuts in large bowl.

2. Melt butter. Stir in garlic powder, celery salt, seasoned salt, and Parmesan cheese. Pour over pretzels and cereal. Toss until well mixed.

3. Pour into large slow cooker. Cover. Cook on Low 2½ hours, stirring every 30 minutes. Remove lid and cook another 30 minutes on Low.

4. Serve warm or at room temperature. Store in tightly covered container.

Variations:

1. Use 3 cups Wheat Chex (instead of 4 cups) and 3 cups Cheerios (instead of 4 cups). Add 3 cups Corn Chex.

Marcia S. Myer Manheim, PA

2. Alter the amounts of pretzels, cereal, and peanuts to reflect your preferences.

Snack Mix

Yvonne Boettger Harrisonburg, VA

PICTURED
ON PAGE
302

MAKES: **10–14 SERVINGS**
PREP. TIME: **10 MINUTES**
COOKING TIME: **2 HOURS**
IDEAL SLOW COOKER SIZE: **5-QUART**

8 cups Chex cereal, of any combination

6 cups from the following: pretzels, snack crackers, goldfish, Cheerios, nuts, bagel chips, toasted corn

6 Tbsp. butter, melted

2 Tbsp. Worcestershire sauce

1 tsp. seasoned salt

½ tsp. garlic powder

½ tsp. onion salt

½ tsp. onion powder

1. Combine first two ingredients in slow cooker.

2. Combine butter and seasonings. Pour over dry mixture. Toss until well mixed.

3. Cover. Cook on Low 2 hours, stirring every 30 minutes.

Appetizers, Snacks, and Spreads

Curried Almonds

Barbara Aston   Ashdown, AR

MAKES: **4 CUPS NUTS**
PREP. TIME: **5 MINUTES**
COOKING TIME: **3–4½ HOURS**
IDEAL SLOW COOKER SIZE: **3-QUART**

2 Tbsp. butter, melted
1 Tbsp. curry powder
½ tsp. seasoned salt
1 lb. blanched almonds

1. Combine butter with curry powder and seasoned salt.
2. Pour over almonds in slow cooker. Mix to coat well.
3. Cover. Cook on Low 2–3 hours. Turn to High. Uncover cooker and cook 1–1½ hours.
4. Serve hot or cold.

Chili Nuts

Barbara Aston   Ashdown, AR

MAKES: **5 CUPS NUTS**
PREP. TIME: **5 MINUTES**
COOKING TIME: **2–2½ HOURS**
IDEAL SLOW COOKER SIZE: **3-QUART**

¼ cup butter, melted
2 12-oz. cans cocktail peanuts
1⅝-oz. pkg. chili seasoning mix

1. Pour butter over nuts in slow cooker. Sprinkle in dry chili mix. Toss together.
2. Cover. Heat on Low 2–2½ hours. Turn to High. Remove lid and cook 10–15 minutes.
3. Serve warm or cool.

Old-Fashioned Hot Chocolate Syrup

Jennie Martin   Richfield, PA

MAKES: **18 SERVINGS**
PREP. TIME: **10 MINUTES**
WARMING TIME: **4 HOURS, OR UNTIL THE COOKER IS EMPTY!**
IDEAL SLOW COOKER SIZE: **5-QUART**

1 cup dry cocoa powder
2 cups sugar
1½ cups hot water
½ tsp. vanilla
3 quarts milk

1. Mix first three ingredients together with a whisk in a 2-quart saucepan. Bring to a boil and boil for 2 minutes.
2. Remove from heat and stir in vanilla.
3. Add this syrup to approximately 3 quarts milk. You can heat the milk in a 5-quart saucepan, stir the syrup into it, and then pour the hot chocolate into your slow cooker. Or you can heat the milk in your slow cooker and add the syrup to it.
4. Either way, you can maintain the hot chocolate in the slow cooker throughout an evening party.

Breakfasts and Brunches

Breakfast Sausage Casserole

Kendra Dreps Liberty, PA

MAKES: **8 SERVINGS**
PREP. TIME: **15 MINUTES**
CHILLING TIME: **8 HOURS, OR OVERNIGHT**
COOKING TIME: **4 HOURS**
IDEAL SLOW COOKER SIZE: **3-QUART**

1 lb. loose sausage

6 eggs

2 cups milk

8 slices bread, cubed

2 cups shredded cheddar cheese

1. In a nonstick skillet, brown and drain sausage.
2. Mix together eggs and milk in a large bowl.
3. Stir in bread cubes, cheese, and sausage.
4. Place in greased slow cooker.
5. Refrigerate overnight.
6. Cook on Low 4 hours.

Variation: *Use cubed cooked ham instead of sausage.*

Easy Egg and Sausage Puff

Sara Kinsinger Stuarts Draft, VA

MAKES: **6 SERVINGS**
PREP. TIME: **10–15 MINUTES**
COOKING TIME: **2–2½ HOURS**
IDEAL SLOW COOKER SIZE: **2–4-QUART**

1 lb. loose sausage

6 eggs

1 cup all-purpose baking mix

1 cup shredded cheddar cheese

2 cups milk

¼ tsp. dry mustard, *optional*

1. Brown sausage in nonstick skillet. Break up chunks of meat as it cooks. Drain.
2. Meanwhile, spray interior of slow cooker with nonstick cooking spray.
3. Mix all ingredients in slow cooker.
4. Cover and cook on High 1 hour. Turn to Low and cook 1–1½ hours, or until the dish is fully cooked in the center.

Layered Breakfast Casserole

Cathy Boshart Lebanon, PA

MAKES: **8–10 SERVINGS**
PREP. TIME: **30 MINUTES**
CHILLING TIME: **4–8 HOURS**
COOKING TIME: **1 HOUR**
IDEAL SLOW COOKER SIZE: **6-QUART**

6 medium potatoes

2 dozen eggs

1 lb. chopped ham

12 ozs. Velveeta cheese, shredded

1. The day before you want to serve the dish, boil the potatoes in their skins until soft. Chill. When thoroughly chilled, grate. Spread in bottom of greased slow cooker.
2. Scramble and cook eggs in a nonstick skillet. When just set, spoon cooked eggs over top of potatoes.
3. Layer ham evenly over eggs. Sprinkle with cheese.
4. Bake on Low for 1 hour or until cheese melts.

Tips:

1. Toasted English muffins and fresh fruit are great go-alongs.

2. This is a perfect dish to serve on a buffet.

Variations:

1. You can make half, or even one-fourth, of this recipe if this quantity is too large. And you don't need to scramble the eggs before placing them in the cooker. Simply mix the cooked potatoes, ham, and cheese together in the slow cooker. Beat the eggs in a separate bowl, along with salt and pepper to taste. Then pour them over the other ingredients and cook on Low for 2–4 hours.

Kendra Dreps Liberty, PA

2. Prepare through the first instruction in Step 3 a day ahead (chill in the fridge overnight), but sprinkle the cheese over top just before cooking.

If you've refrigerated the slow cooker overnight, allow it to reach room temperature before turning it on and reheating the dish.

Breakfast Bake

Kristi See Weskan, KS

MAKES: **10 SERVINGS**
PREP. TIME: **15 MINUTES**
COOKING TIME: **3–4 HOURS**
IDEAL SLOW COOKER SIZE: **4–5-QUART**

12 eggs

1½–2 cups shredded cheese, your choice

1 cup diced cooked ham

1 cup milk

1 tsp. salt

½ tsp. pepper

1. Beat eggs. Pour into slow cooker.
2. Mix in remaining ingredients.
3. Cover and cook on Low 3–4 hours.

Breakfast Skillet

Sue Hamilton   Minooka, IL

MAKES: **4–5 SERVINGS**
PREP. TIME: **15 MINUTES**
COOKING TIME: **2½–3 HOURS**
IDEAL SLOW COOKER SIZE: **3½-QUART**

3 cups milk

5½ oz. box au gratin potatoes

1 tsp. hot sauce

5 eggs, lightly beaten

1 Tbsp. prepared mustard

4-oz. can sliced mushrooms

8 slices bacon, fried and crumbled

1 cup cheddar cheese, shredded

1. Combine milk, au gratin-sauce packet, hot sauce, eggs, and mustard.
2. Stir in dried potatoes, mushrooms, and bacon.
3. Cover. Cook on High 2½–3 hours, or on Low 5–6 hours.
4. Sprinkle cheese over top. Cover until melted.

Western Omelet Casserole

Mary Louise Martin   Boyd, WI

MAKES: **10 SERVINGS**
PREP. TIME: **15 MINUTES**
COOKING TIME: **8–9 HOURS**
IDEAL SLOW COOKER SIZE: **5-QUART**

32-oz. bag frozen hash brown potatoes

1 lb. cooked ham, cubed

1 medium onion, diced

1½ cups shredded cheddar cheese

12 eggs

1 cup milk

1 tsp. salt

1 tsp. pepper

1. Layer one-third each of frozen potatoes, ham, onions, and cheese in bottom of slow cooker. Repeat 2 times.
2. Beat together eggs, milk, salt, and pepper. Pour over mixture in slow cooker.
3. Cover. Cook on Low 8–9 hours.
4. Serve with orange juice and fresh fruit.

Cheese and Ham Soufflé Casserole

Iva Schmidt   Fergus Falls, MN

MAKES: **6 SERVINGS**
PREP. TIME: **15 MINUTES**
COOKING TIME: **3–4 HOURS**
IDEAL SLOW COOKER SIZE: **3–4-QUART**

8 slices bread (crusts removed), cubed or torn into squares

2 cups (8 oz.) shredded cheddar, Swiss, *or* American cheese

1 cup cooked, chopped ham

4 eggs

1 cup light cream *or* milk

1 cup evaporated milk

¼ tsp. salt

1 Tbsp. parsley

paprika

1. Lightly grease slow cooker. Alternate layers of bread and cheese and ham.
2. Beat together eggs, milk, salt, and parsley. Pour over bread in slow cooker.
3. Sprinkle with paprika.
4. Cover and cook on Low 3–4 hours. (The longer cooking time yields a firmer, dryer dish.)

Smoky Breakfast Casserole

Shirley Hinh   Wayland, IA

MAKES: **8–10 SERVINGS**
PREP. TIME: **15 MINUTES**
COOKING TIME: **3 HOURS**
IDEAL SLOW COOKER SIZE: **4-QUART**

6 eggs, beaten
1 lb. little smokies (cocktail wieners), or 1½ lbs. bulk
    sausage, browned and drained
1½ cups milk
1 cup shredded cheddar cheese
8 slices bread, torn into pieces
1 tsp. salt
½ tsp. dry mustard
1 cup shredded mozzarella cheese

1. Mix together all ingredients except mozzarella cheese. Pour into greased slow cooker.
2. Sprinkle mozzarella cheese over top.
3. Cover and cook 2 hours on High, and then 1 hour on Low.

Egg and Cheese Bake

Evie Hershey   Atglen, PA

MAKES: **6 SERVINGS**
PREP. TIME: **15 MINUTES**
COOKING TIME: **4–6 HOURS**
IDEAL SLOW COOKER SIZE: **4-QUART**

3 cups toasted bread cubes
1½ cups shredded cheese
fried, crumbled bacon *or* ham chunks, *optional*
6 eggs, beaten
3 cups milk
¾ tsp. salt
¼ tsp. pepper

1. Combine bread cubes, cheese, and meat in greased slow cooker.

2. Mix together eggs, milk, salt, and pepper. Pour over bread.
3. Cook on Low 4–6 hours.

Welsh Rarebit

Sharon Timpe   Mequon, WI

PICTURED ON PAGE 403

MAKES: **6–8 SERVINGS**
PREP. TIME: **10 MINUTES**
COOKING TIME: **1½–2½ HOURS**
IDEAL SLOW COOKER SIZE: **3–4-QUART**

12-oz. can beer
1 Tbsp. dry mustard
1 tsp. Worcestershire sauce
½ tsp. salt
⅛ tsp. black *or* white pepper
1 lb. American cheese, cubed
1 lb. sharp cheddar cheese, cubed
English muffins *or* toast
tomato slices
bacon, cooked until crisp
fresh steamed asparagus spears

1. In slow cooker, combine beer, mustard, Worcestershire sauce, salt, and pepper.
2. Cover and cook on High 1–2 hours, until mixture boils.
3. Add cheese, a little at a time, stirring constantly until all the cheese melts.
4. Heat on High 20–30 minutes with cover off, stirring frequently.
5. Serve hot over toasted English muffins or over toasted bread cut into triangles. Garnish with tomato slices, strips of crisp bacon and steamed asparagus spears.

Tip: *This is a good dish for brunch with fresh fruit, juice, and coffee. Also makes a great lunch or late-night light supper. Serve with a tossed* *green salad, especially fresh spinach and orange slices with a vinaigrette dressing.*

Egg and Broccoli Casserole

Joette Droz   Kalona, IA

MAKES: **6 SERVINGS**
PREP. TIME: **15 MINUTES**
COOKING TIME: **2½–3 HOURS**
IDEAL SLOW COOKER SIZE: **4-QUART**

24-oz. carton small-curd cottage cheese

10-oz. pkg. frozen chopped broccoli, thawed and drained

2 cups (8 oz.) shredded cheddar cheese

6 eggs, beaten

⅓ cup flour

¼ cup butter, melted

3 Tbsp. finely chopped onion

½ tsp. salt

shredded cheese, *optional*

1. Combine first 8 ingredients. Pour into greased slow cooker.
2. Cover and cook on High 1 hour. Stir. Reduce heat to Low. Cover and cook 2½–3 hours, or until temperature reaches 160° and eggs are set.
3. Sprinkle with cheese and serve.

Creamy Old-Fashioned Oatmeal

Mary Wheatley   Mashpee, MA

MAKES: **4 SERVINGS**
PREP. TIME: **5 MINUTES**
COOKING TIME: **6 HOURS**
IDEAL SLOW COOKER SIZE: **3-QUART**

1⅓ cups dry old-fashioned rolled oats

2½ cups, plus 1 Tbsp., water

dash of salt

1. Mix together cereal, water, and salt in slow cooker.
2. Cook on Low 6 hours.

Tip: *The formula is this: for one serving, use ⅓ cup dry oats and ⅔ cup water, plus a few grains salt. Multiply by the number of servings you need.*

Variation: *Before cooking, stir in a few chopped dates or raisins for each serving, if you wish.*

Cathy Boshart   Lebanon, PA

"Baked" Oatmeal

Ellen Ranck   Gap, PA

MAKES: **4–6 SERVINGS**
PREP. TIME: **10 MINUTES**
COOKING TIME: **2½–3 HOURS**
IDEAL SLOW COOKER SIZE: **3-QUART**

⅓ cup oil

½ cup sugar

1 large egg, beaten

2 cups dry quick oats

1½ tsp. baking powder

½ tsp. salt

¾ cup milk

1. Pour the oil into the slow cooker to grease bottom and sides.
2. Add remaining ingredients. Mix well.
3. Bake on Low 2½–3 hours.

A word of caution — it is a common mistake to add too much liquid when cooking in your slow cooker.

Almond-Date Oatmeal

Darla Sathre Baxter, MN

MAKES: **8 SERVINGS**
PREP. TIME: **5 MINUTES**
COOKING TIME: **4–6 HOURS**
IDEAL SLOW COOKER SIZE: **3-QUART**

2 cups dry rolled oats

½ cup dry Grape-Nuts cereal

½ cup almonds, slivered

¼ cup dates, chopped

4 cups water

1. Combine all ingredients in slow cooker.
2. Cook on Low 4–6 hours.
3. Serve with fat-free milk.

Per Serving: 160 calories (45 calories from fat), 5g total fat (0g saturated, 0g trans), 0mg cholesterol, 50mg sodium, 26g total carbohydrate (4g fiber, 5g sugar), 5g protein, 2%DV vitamin A, 0%DV vitamin C, 2%DV calcium, 15%DV iron.

Overnight Apple Oatmeal

Frances Musser Newmanstown, PA • *John D. Allen* Rye, CO

MAKES: **4 SERVINGS**
PREP. TIME: **10 MINUTES**
COOKING TIME: **6–8 HOURS, OR OVERNIGHT**
IDEAL SLOW COOKER SIZE: **2-QUART**

2 cups skim *or* 2% milk

2 Tbsp. honey, *or* ¼ cup brown sugar

1 Tbsp. margarine

¼ tsp. salt

½ tsp. ground cinnamon

1 cup dry rolled oats

1 cup apples, chopped

½ cup raisins, *optional*

¼ cup walnuts, chopped

½ cup fat-free half-and-half

1. Spray inside of slow cooker with non-fat cooking spray.
2. In a mixing bowl, combine all ingredients except half-and-half. Pour into cooker.
3. Cover and cook on Low overnight, ideally 6–8 hours. The oatmeal is ready to eat in the morning.
4. Stir in the half-and-half just before serving.

Per Serving: 240 calories (60 calories from fat), 6g total fat (1g saturated, 0g trans), 0mg cholesterol, 240mg sodium, 37g total carbohydrate (4g fiber, 21g sugar), 10g protein, 8%DV vitamin A, 6%DV vitamin C, 20%DV calcium, 8%DV iron.

Slow Cooker Oatmeal

Martha Bender New Paris, IN

MAKES: **7–8 SERVINGS**
PREP. TIME: **10–15 MINUTES**
COOKING TIME: **8–9 HOURS, OR OVERNIGHT**
IDEAL SLOW COOKER SIZE: **4–5-QUART**

2 cups dry rolled oats

4 cups water

1 large apple, peeled and chopped

1 cup raisins

1 tsp. cinnamon

1–2 Tbsp. orange zest

1. Combine all ingredients in your slow cooker.
2. Cover and cook on Low 8–9 hours.
3. Serve topped with brown sugar, if you wish, and milk.

Fill the cooker no more than ⅔ full and no less than half-full.

Breakfasts and Brunches

Breakfast Oatmeal

Donna Conto   Saylorsburg, PA

MAKES: **6 SERVINGS**
PREP. TIME: **5 MINUTES**
COOKING TIME: **8 HOURS, OR OVERNIGHT**
IDEAL SLOW COOKER SIZE: **4-QUART**

2 cups dry rolled oats

4 cups water

1 tsp. salt

½–1 cup chopped dates, or raisins, or cranberries, or a mixture of any of these fruits

1. Combine all ingredients in slow cooker.
2. Cover and cook on Low overnight, or for 8 hours.

Tip: *This is a great dish when you have company for breakfast. No last-minute preparation needed!*

Pineapple "Baked" Oatmeal

Sandra Haverstraw   Hummelstown, PA

MAKES: **5–6 SERVINGS**
PREP. TIME: **5 MINUTES**
COOKING TIME: **1½–2½ HOURS**
IDEAL SLOW COOKER SIZE: **2–3½-QUART**

1 box of 8 instant oatmeal packets (approx. a 12- to 14-oz. box), any flavor

1½ tsp. baking powder

2 eggs, beaten

½ cup milk

8-oz. can crushed pineapple in juice, undrained

1. Spray inside of slow cooker with nonstick cooking spray.
2. Empty packets of oatmeal into a large bowl. Add baking powder and mix.

3. Stir in eggs, milk, and undrained pineapple. Mix well. Pour mixture into slow cooker.
4. Cover and cook on High 1½ hours, or on Low 2½ hours.

Tips:

1. Serve warm as is, or with milk, for breakfast.

2. This is also a good, hearty, not-too-sweet dessert served with ice cream.

3. Individual servings reheat well in the microwave for a quick breakfast.

Overnight Steel-Cut Oats

Jody Moore   Pendleton, IN

MAKES: **4–5 SERVINGS**
PREP. TIME: **5 MINUTES**
COOKING TIME: **8 HOURS, OR OVERNIGHT**
IDEAL SLOW COOKER SIZE: **3-QUART**

1 cup dry steel-cut oats

4 cups water

1. Combine ingredients in slow cooker.
2. Cover and cook on Low overnight, or for 8 hours.
3. Stir before serving. Serve with brown sugar, ground cinnamon, fruit preserves, jam, jelly, pumpkin pie spice, fresh fruit, maple syrup, or your other favorite toppings.

Tip: *Please note that steel-cut oats are called for. They are different—with more texture, requiring a longer cooking time—than old-fashioned or rolled oatmeal.*

Breakfast Apple Cobbler

Virginia Graybill Hershey, PA

MAKES: **8–10 SERVINGS**
PREP. TIME: **20 MINUTES**
COOKING TIME: **2–6 HOURS**
IDEAL SLOW COOKER SIZE: **5–6-QUART**

8 medium, tart apples

½ cup sugar

2 Tbsp. fresh lemon juice

1–2 tsp. grated lemon rind

dash of ground cinnamon

¼ cup butter, melted

1½ cups natural fat-free cereal mixed with fruit and nuts

1. Spray interior of cooker lightly with nonfat cooking spray.
2. Core, peel, and slice apples into slow cooker.
3. Add sugar, lemon juice, rind, and cinnamon.
4. Mix cereal and melted butter together.
5. Add to ingredients in slow cooker. Mix thoroughly.
6. Cover. Cook on Low 6 hours, or on High 2–3 hours.

Per Serving: 210 calories (45 calories from fat), 5g total fat (3g saturated, 0g trans), 10mg cholesterol, 105mg sodium, 43g total carbohydrate (6g fiber, 25g sugar), 2g protein, 6%DV vitamin A, 10%DV vitamin C, 2%DV calcium, 30%DV iron.

Tip: *You can serve this with fat-free milk for breakfast. If diets permit, you can also serve it as a dessert with fat-free frozen yogurt instead.*

Hot Wheatberry Cereal

Rosemarie Fitzgerald Gibsonia, PA

MAKES: **4 SERVINGS**
PREP. TIME: **5 MINUTES**
SOAKING TIME: **8 HOURS**
COOKING TIME: **10 HOURS, OR OVERNIGHT**
IDEAL SLOW COOKER SIZE: **3-QUART**

1 cup wheatberries

5 cups water

1. Rinse and sort berries. Cover with water and soak all day (or 8 hours) in slow cooker.
2. Cover. Cook on Low overnight (or 10 hours).
3. Drain, if needed. Serve hot with honey, milk, and butter.

Tips:

1. Eat your hot wheatberries with raisins and maple syrup as a variation.

2. Wheatberries can also be used in pilafs or grain salads. Cook as indicated, drain, and cool.

Peanut Butter Granola

Dawn Ranck   Harrisonburg, VA

MAKES: **16–20 SERVINGS**
PREP. TIME: **10–15 MINUTES**
COOKING TIME: **1½ HOURS**
IDEAL SLOW COOKER SIZE: **5-QUART**

6 cups dry oatmeal
½ cup wheat germ
½ cup toasted coconut
½ cup sunflower seeds
½ cup raisins
1 cup butter
1 cup peanut butter
1 cup brown sugar

1. Combine oatmeal, wheat germ, coconut, sunflower seeds, and raisins in large slow cooker.
2. Melt together butter, peanut butter, and brown sugar. Pour over oatmeal in cooker. Mix well.
3. Cover. Cook on Low 1½ hours, stirring every 15 minutes.
4. Allow to cool in cooker, stirring every 30 minutes or so, or spread onto cookie sheet. When thoroughly cooled, break into chunks and store in airtight container.

Mexican-Style Grits

Mary Sommerfeld   Lancaster, PA

MAKES: **10–12 SERVINGS**
PREP. TIME: **10 MINUTES**
COOKING TIME: **2–6 HOURS**
IDEAL SLOW COOKER SIZE: **3-QUART**

1½ cups instant grits
1 lb. Velveeta cheese, cubed
½ tsp. garlic powder
2 4-oz. cans diced chilies
½ cup (1 stick) butter

1. Prepare grits according to package directions.
2. Stir in cheese, garlic powder, and chilies, until cheese melts.
3. Stir in butter. Pour into greased slow cooker.
4. Cover. Cook on High 2–3 hours, or on Low 4–6 hours.

Cornmeal Mush

Betty Hostetler   Allensville, PA

MAKES: **15–18 SERVINGS**
PREP. TIME: **5–10 MINUTES**
COOKING TIME: **4–6 HOURS**
IDEAL SLOW COOKER SIZE: **4-QUART**

2 cups cornmeal

2 tsp. salt

2 cups cold water

6 cups hot water

1. Combine cornmeal, salt, and cold water.
2. Stir in hot water. Pour into greased slow cooker.
3. Cover. Cook on High 1 hour, then stir again and cook on Low 3–4 hours. Or cook on Low 5–6 hours, stirring once every hour during the first 2 hours.
4. Serve hot with butter as a side dish.

Note: *When we lived on the farm, Mother would prepare boiled mush for the evening meal. The rest she poured into pans and fried for supper the next evening. I adapted this recipe for the slow cooker several years ago when Mother was living with us and I needed to go to work.*

Tips:

1. Serve warm with milk, butter, and syrup or chili.

2. Serve slices for breakfast with maple syrup, bacon, sausage, or ham and eggs.

Variation: *Pour cooked cornmeal mush into loaf pans. Chill until set. Cut into ½-inch slices. Coat with flour and fry in butter.*

Polenta or Cornmeal Mush

Dorothy VanDeest   Memphis, TN

MAKES: **8–10 SERVINGS**
PREP. TIME: **10 MINUTES**
COOKING TIME: **2–9 HOURS**
CHILLING TIME: **8 HOURS, OR OVERNIGHT**
IDEAL SLOW COOKER SIZE: **1½-QUART**

4 Tbsp. butter, melted, *divided*

¼ tsp. paprika and/or dash of cayenne pepper

6 cups boiling water

2 cups dry cornmeal

2 tsp. salt

1. Use 1 Tbsp. butter to lightly grease the inside of the slow cooker. Sprinkle in paprika/cayenne. Turn to High setting.
2. Add remaining ingredients to slow cooker in the order listed, including 1 Tbsp. butter. Stir well.
3. Cover and cook on High 2–3 hours, or on Low 6–9 hours. Stir occasionally.
4. Pour hot cooked polenta/mush into 2 lightly greased loaf pans. Chill 8 hours or overnight.
5. To serve, cut into ¼-inch-thick slices. Melt 2 Tbsp. butter in large nonstick skillet, then lay in slices and cook until browned. Turn to brown other side.
6. For breakfast, serve with maple syrup, honey, or your choice of sweetener.

Tip: *Serve as a main course topped with sausage gravy, or as a side dish topped with a pat of butter.*

Sara Kinsinger   Stuarts Draft, VA

Beginner cooks should always measure carefully. With more experience you learn to adjust recipes.

Breakfast Hominy

Bonnie Goering   Bridgewater, VA

MAKES: **5 SERVINGS**
PREP. TIME: **5 MINUTES**
COOKING TIME: **8 HOURS, OR OVERNIGHT**
IDEAL SLOW COOKER SIZE: **2-QUART**

1 cup dry cracked hominy

1 tsp. salt

black pepper, *optional*

3 cups water

2 Tbsp. butter

1. Stir all ingredients together in a greased slow cooker.
2. Cover and cook on Low 8 hours, or overnight.
3. Serve warm for breakfast.

Variation: *You can make cheesy hominy by decreasing the salt to ¾ tsp. and adding 1 cup shredded cheese to Step 1.*

Quick-to-Fix Cheesy Hominy

Deborah Heatwole   Waynesboro, GA

MAKES: **6–8 SERVINGS**
PREP. TIME: **5 MINUTES**
COOKING TIME: **2½ HOURS**
IDEAL SLOW COOKER SIZE: **2-QUART**

1 29-oz., or 2 15½-oz., cans hominy, drained

1 cup diced cheese (cheddar or Velveeta work well)

½ tsp. salt

dash pepper

8 saltine crackers, crumbled

½ cup milk

butter, *optional*

1. Spray slow cooker with nonstick cooking spray. Add hominy, cheese, salt, pepper, and saltines. Stir to mix.

2. Pour milk over all. Dot with butter, if you wish.
3. Cover and cook on High 2½ hours.

Tip: *Serve for breakfast with sausage and fruit, or for a main meal with a meat and green vegetable.*

Blueberry Fancy

Leticia A. Zehr   Lowville, NY

MAKES: **12 SERVINGS**
PREP. TIME: **10–15 MINUTES**
COOKING TIME: **3–4 HOURS**
IDEAL SLOW COOKER SIZE: **5-QUART**

PICTURED ON PAGE 29

1 loaf Italian bread, cubed, *divided*

1 pint blueberries, *divided*

8 ozs. cream cheese, cubed, *divided*

6 eggs

1½ cups milk

1. Place half the bread cubes in the slow cooker.
2. Drop half the blueberries over top the bread.
3. Sprinkle half the cream cheese cubes over the blueberries.
4. Repeat all 3 layers.
5. In a mixing bowl, whisk together eggs and milk. Pour over all ingredients.
6. Cover and cook on Low until the dish is custardy and set.
7. Serve with maple syrup or blueberry sauce.

Variation: *Add 1 tsp. vanilla to Step 5.*

Streusel Cake

Jean Butzer Batavia, NY

MAKES: **8–10 SERVINGS**
PREP. TIME: **10 MINUTES**
COOKING TIME: **3–4 HOURS**
IDEAL SLOW COOKER SIZE: **3-QUART**

16-oz. pkg. pound cake mix, prepared according to
**   package directions**
¼ cup packed brown sugar
1 Tbsp. flour
¼ cup chopped nuts
1 tsp. cinnamon

1. Liberally grease and flour a 2-lb. coffee can, or slow cooker baking insert, that fits into your slow cooker. (See Tip on page 611.) Pour prepared cake mix into coffee can or baking insert.
2. In a small bowl, mix brown sugar, flour, nuts, and cinnamon together. Sprinkle over top of cake mix.
3. Place coffee tin or baking insert in slow cooker. Cover top of tin or insert with several layers of paper towels.
4. Cover cooker itself and cook on High 3–4 hours, or until toothpick inserted in center of cake comes out clean.
5. Remove baking tin from slow cooker and allow to cool for 30 minutes before cutting into wedges to serve.

Breakfast Fruit Compote

Betty K. Drescher Quakertown, PA

MAKES: **8–9 SERVINGS**
PREP. TIME: **5 MINUTES**
COOKING TIME: **2–7 HOURS**
IDEAL SLOW COOKER SIZE: **3–4-QUART**

12-oz. pkg. dried apricots
12-oz. pkg. pitted dried plums

11-oz. can mandarin oranges in light syrup, undrained
29-oz. can sliced peaches in light syrup, undrained
¼ cup white raisins
10 maraschino cherries

1. Combine all ingredients in slow cooker. Mix well.
2. Cover. Cook on Low 6–7 hours, or on High 2–3 hours.

Per Serving: 300 calories (0 calories from fat), 0g total fat (0g saturated, 0g trans), 0mg cholesterol, 40mg sodium, 74g total carbohydrate (5g fiber, 42g sugar), 3g protein, 30%DV vitamin A, 10%DV vitamin C, 4%DV calcium, 15%DV iron.

Tip: *If the fruit seems to be drying out as it cooks, you may want to add up to 1 cup water.*

Blueberry-Apple Waffle Topping

Willard E. Roth Elkhart, IN

MAKES: **10–12 SERVINGS**
PREP. TIME: **10 MINUTES**
COOKING TIME: **3 HOURS**
IDEAL SLOW COOKER SIZE: **3½–4-QUART**

1 quart natural applesauce, unsweetened
2 Granny Smith apples, unpeeled, cored, and sliced
1 pint fresh *or* frozen blueberries
½ Tbsp. ground cinnamon
½ cup pure maple syrup
1 tsp. almond flavoring
½ cup walnuts, chopped

1. Stir together applesauce, apples, and blueberries in slow cooker sprayed with non-fat cooking spray.
2. Add cinnamon and maple syrup.
3. Cover. Cook on Low 3 hours.

4. Add almond flavoring and walnuts just before serving.

Per Serving: 130 calories (35 calories from fat), 3.5g total fat (0g saturated, 0g trans), 0mg cholesterol, 0mg sodium, 25g total carbohydrate (3g fiber, 20g sugar), 2g protein, 0%DV vitamin A, 20%DV vitamin C, 2%DV calcium, 4%DV iron.

Tip: *If your diet allows, this is also delicious served over cake or fat-free frozen yogurt.*

Hot Applesauce Breakfast

Colleen Konetzni   Rio Rancho, NM

MAKES: **8 SERVINGS**
PREP. TIME: **15 MINUTES**
COOKING TIME: **8–10 HOURS, OR OVERNIGHT**
IDEAL SLOW COOKER SIZE: **3½-QUART**

10 apples, peeled and sliced
½–1 cup sugar
1 Tbsp. ground cinnamon
¼ tsp. ground nutmeg

1. Combine ingredients in slow cooker.
2. Cover. Cook on Low 8–10 hours.

Tips:
1. Also yummy over oatmeal or with vanilla yogurt. Or serve it over pancakes or waffles.
2. Add chopped nuts for an extra treat.

Breakfast Prunes

Jo Haberkamp   Fairbank, IA

MAKES: **6 SERVINGS**
PREP. TIME: **10 MINUTES**
COOKING TIME: **8-10 HOURS, OR OVERNIGHT**
IDEAL SLOW COOKER SIZE: **2-QUART**

2 cups orange juice
¼ cup orange marmalade
1 tsp. ground cinnamon
¼ tsp. ground cloves
¼ tsp. ground nutmeg
1 cup water
12-oz. pkg. pitted dried prunes (1¾ cups)
2 thin lemon slices

1. Combine orange juice, marmalade, cinnamon, cloves, nutmeg, and water in slow cooker.
2. Stir in prunes and lemon slices.
3. Cover. Cook on Low 8–10 hours, or overnight.
4. Serve warm as a breakfast food, or warm or chilled as a side dish with a meal later in the day.

Variation: *If you prefer more citrus flavor, eliminate the ground cloves and reduce the cinnamon to ½ tsp. and the nutmeg to ⅛ tsp.*

We like to freeze blueberries when they are in season for use throughout the year. Simply wash them, drain well, and place in freezer boxes. When needed, simply "squish" the sides of the box (with lid on) and they easily separate into individual berries. Pour out the amount you need for baking.

Dulce Leche (Sweet Milk)

Dorothy Horst Tiskilwa, IL

MAKES: **2½ CUPS**
PREP. TIME: **5 MINUTES**
COOKING TIME: **2 HOURS**
IDEAL SLOW COOKER SIZE: **LARGE ENOUGH TO HOLD TWO CANS**

2 14-oz. cans sweetened condensed milk

1. Place unopened cans of milk in slow cooker. Fill cooker with warm water so that it comes above the cans by 1½–2 inches.
2. Cover cooker. Cook on High 2 hours.
3. Cool unopened cans.
4. When opened, the contents should be thick and spreadable. Use as a filling between 2 cookies or crackers.

Note: *When on a tour in Argentina, we were served this at breakfast time as a spread on toast or thick slices of bread. We were also presented with a container of prepared Dulce Leche as a parting gift to take home. This dish also sometimes appears on Mexican menus.*

Breakfast Wassail

Lori Berezovsky Salina, KS

MAKES: **4 QUARTS**
PREP. TIME: **5–10 MINUTES**
COOKING TIME: **3 HOURS**
IDEAL SLOW COOKER SIZE: **6-QUART**

64-oz. bottle cranberry juice
32-oz. bottle apple juice
12-oz. can frozen pineapple juice concentrate
12-oz. can frozen lemonade concentrate
3–4 cinnamon sticks
1 quart water, *optional*

1. Combine all ingredients except water in slow cooker. Add water if mixture is too sweet.
2. Cover. Cook on Low 3 hours.

Note: *Even though the name of this recipe conjures up thoughts of Christmas, it is the perfect breakfast substitute for juice, especially when entertaining a houseful of overnight guests.*

Breads

Healthy Whole Wheat Bread

Esther Becker Gordonville, PA

MAKES: **8 SERVINGS**
PREP. TIME: **20 MINUTES**
COOKING TIME: **2½–3 HOURS**
IDEAL SLOW COOKER SIZE: **5–6-QUART**

2 cups warm reconstituted powdered milk
2 Tbsp. vegetable oil
¼ cup honey *or* brown sugar
¾ tsp. salt
1 pkg. yeast
2½ cups whole wheat flour
1¼ cups white flour

1. Mix together milk, oil, honey or brown sugar, salt, yeast, and half the flour in electric mixer bowl. Beat with mixer for 2 minutes. Add remaining flour. Mix well.

2. Place dough in well-greased bread or cake pan that will fit into your cooker. Cover with greased foil. Let stand for 5 minutes. Place in slow cooker.

3. Cover cooker and bake on High 2½–3 hours. Remove pan and uncover. Let stand for 5 minutes. Serve warm.

A slow cooker provides enough warmth to raise dough.

Cornbread from Scratch

Dorothy M. Van Deest   Memphis, TN

MAKES: **6 SERVINGS**
PREP. TIME: **15 MINUTES**
COOKING TIME: **2–3 HOURS**
IDEAL SLOW COOKER SIZE: **6-QUART**

1¼ cups flour
¾ cup yellow cornmeal
¼ cup sugar
4½ tsp. baking powder
1 tsp. salt
1 egg, slightly beaten
1 cup milk
⅓ cup butter, melted, *or* oil

1. In mixing bowl sift together flour, cornmeal, sugar, baking powder, and salt. Make a well in the center.
2. Pour egg, milk, and butter into well. Mix into the dry mixture until just moistened.
3. Pour mixture into a greased 2-quart mold. Cover with a plate. Place on a trivet or rack in the bottom of slow cooker.
4. Cover. Cook on High 2–3 hours.

Boston Brown Bread

Jean Butzer   Batavia, NY

PICTURED
ON PAGE
168

MAKES: **3 LOAVES**
PREP. TIME: **15–20 MINUTES**
COOKING TIME: **4 HOURS**
IDEAL SLOW COOKER SIZE: **LARGE ENOUGH TO HOLD YOUR BAKING INSERT**

3 16-oz. vegetable cans, cleaned and emptied
½ cup rye flour
½ cup yellow cornmeal
½ cup whole wheat flour
3 Tbsp. sugar
1 tsp. baking soda
¾ tsp. salt
½ cup chopped walnuts
½ cup raisins
1 cup buttermilk*
⅓ cup molasses

1. Spray insides of vegetable cans, and one side of 3 6-inch-square pieces of foil, with nonstick cooking spray. Set aside.
2. Combine rye flour, cornmeal, whole wheat flour, sugar, baking soda, and salt in a large bowl.
3. Stir in walnuts and raisins.
4. Whisk together buttermilk and molasses. Add to dry ingredients. Stir until well mixed. Spoon into prepared cans.
5. Place one piece of foil, greased side down, on top of each can. Secure foil with rubberbands or cotton string. Place upright in slow cooker.
6. Pour boiling water into slow cooker to come halfway up sides of cans. (Make sure foil tops do not touch boiling water).
7. Cover cooker. Cook on Low 4 hours, or until skewer inserted in center of bread comes out clean.
8. To remove bread, lay cans on their sides. Roll and tap gently on all sides until bread releases. Cool completely on wire racks.
9. Serve with butter or cream cheese, and bowls of soup.

* *To substitute for buttermilk, pour 1 Tbsp. lemon juice into 1-cup measure. Add enough milk to fill the cup. Let stand 5 minutes before mixing with molasses.*

Read the whole recipe before beginning to cook.

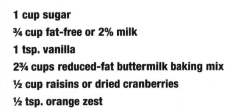

Parmesan-Garlic Quick Bread

Leona Miller   Millersburg, OH

MAKES: **8 SERVINGS**
PREP. TIME: **5 MINUTES**
COOKING TIME: **1 HOUR**
IDEAL SLOW COOKER SIZE: **2–3-QUART**

1½ cups reduced-fat buttermilk baking mix
2 egg whites
½ cup skim milk
1 Tbsp. minced onions
1 Tbsp. sugar
1½ tsp. garlic powder
¼ cup reduced-fat Parmesan cheese

1. Combine baking mix, egg whites, milk, onions, sugar, and garlic powder in a mixing bowl.
2. Spray slow cooker with cooking spray. Spoon dough into cooker.
3. Sprinkle dough with Parmesan cheese.
4. Cook on High 1 hour.

Per Serving: 120 calories (20 calories from fat), 2g total fat (1g saturated, 0g trans), 0mg cholesterol, 330mg sodium, 19g total carbohydrate (0g fiber, 4g sugar), 4g protein, 0%DV vitamin A, 0%DV vitamin C, 4%DV calcium, 4%DV iron.

Tip: *This bread is great with hot soup, Italian dishes, or salads.*

Cottage Cheese Bread

Leona Miller   Millersburg, OH

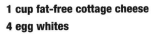

MAKES: **8 SERVINGS**
PREP. TIME: **5 MINUTES**
COOKING TIME: **2 HOURS**
IDEAL SLOW COOKER SIZE: **3-QUART**

PICTURED
ON PAGE
402

1 cup fat-free cottage cheese
4 egg whites

1 cup sugar
¾ cup fat-free or 2% milk
1 tsp. vanilla
2¾ cups reduced-fat buttermilk baking mix
½ cup raisins or dried cranberries
½ tsp. orange zest

1. Combine all ingredients in a mixing bowl.
2. Pour into greased slow cooker.
3. Cook on High 2 hours.

Per Serving: 320 calories (25 calories from fat), 3g total fat (0.5g saturated, 0g trans), 0mg cholesterol, 510mg sodium, 63g total carbohydrate (0.5g fiber, 34g sugar), 10g protein, 0%DV vitamin A, 0%DV vitamin C, 6%DV calcium, 10%DV iron.

Broccoli Cornbread

Winifred Ewy   Newton, KS

MAKES: **8 SERVINGS**
PREP. TIME: **15 MINUTES**
COOKING TIME: **6 HOURS**
IDEAL SLOW COOKER SIZE: **3–4-QUART**

1 stick butter, melted
10-oz. pkg. chopped broccoli, cooked and drained
1 onion, chopped
1 box cornbread mix
4 eggs, well beaten
8 oz. cottage cheese
1¼ tsp. salt

1. Combine all ingredients. Mix well.
2. Pour into greased slow cooker. Cook on Low 6 hours, or until toothpick inserted in center comes out clean.
3. Serve like spoon bread, or invert the pot, remove bread, and cut into wedges.

Lemon Bread

Ruth Ann Gingrich New Holland, PA

MAKES: **6 SERVINGS**
PREP. TIME: **15 MINUTES**
COOKING TIME: **2–2¼ HOURS**
IDEAL SLOW COOKER SIZE: **4-QUART**

½ cup shortening
¾ cup sugar
2 eggs, beaten
1⅔ cups flour
1⅔ tsp. baking powder
½ tsp. salt
½ cup milk
½ cup chopped nuts
grated peel from 1 lemon

Glaze:
¼ cup powdered sugar
juice of 1 lemon

1. Cream together shortening and sugar. Add eggs. Mix well.
2. Sift together flour, baking powder, and salt. Add flour mixture and milk alternately to shortening mixture.
3. Stir in nuts and lemon peel.
4. Spoon batter into well-greased 2-pound coffee can and cover with well-greased tin foil. Place in cooker set on High for 2–2¼ hours, or until done. Remove bread from coffee can.
5. Mix together powdered sugar and lemon juice. Pour over loaf.
6. Serve plain or with cream cheese.

Date and Nut Loaf

Jean Butzer Batavia, NY

MAKES: **16 SERVINGS**
PREP. TIME: **20 MINUTES**
COOKING TIME: **3½–4 HOURS**
IDEAL SLOW COOKER SIZE: **LARGE ENOUGH TO HOLD YOUR BAKING INSERT**

1½ cups boiling water
1½ cups chopped dates
1¼ cups sugar
1 egg
2 tsp. baking soda
½ tsp. salt
1 tsp. vanilla
1 Tbsp. butter, melted
2½ cups flour
1 cup walnuts, chopped
2 cups hot water

1. Pour 1½ cups boiling water over dates. Let stand 5–10 minutes.
2. Stir in sugar, egg, baking soda, salt, vanilla, and butter.
3. In separate bowl, combine flour and nuts. Stir into date mixture.
4. Pour into 2 greased 11½-oz. coffee cans or one 8-cup baking insert. If using coffee cans, cover with foil and tie. (See Tip on page 611.) If using baking insert, cover with its lid. Place cans or insert on rack in slow cooker. (If you don't have a rack, use rubber jar rings instead.)
5. Pour hot water around cans, up to half their height.
6. Cover slow cooker tightly. Cook on High 3½–4 hours.
7. Remove cans or insert from cooker. Let bread stand in coffee cans or baking insert 10 minutes. Turn out onto cooling rack. Slice. Spread with butter, cream cheese, or peanut butter.

Breads

Banana Loaf

Sue Hamilton Minooka, IL

MAKES: **6–8 SERVINGS**
PREP. TIME: **5–10 MINUTES**
COOKING TIME: **2–2½ HOURS**
IDEAL SLOW COOKER SIZE: **LARGE ENOUGH TO HOLD YOUR BAKING INSERT**

3 very ripe bananas

½ cup butter, softened

2 eggs

1 tsp. vanilla

1 cup sugar

1 cup flour

1 tsp. baking soda

1. Combine all ingredients in an electric mixing bowl. Beat 2 minutes or until well blended. Pour into well greased 2-lb. coffee can.
2. Place can in slow cooker. Cover can with 6 layers of paper towels between cooker lid and bread.
3. Cover cooker. Bake on High 2–2½ hours, or until toothpick inserted in center comes out clean. Cool 15 minutes before removing from pan.

Cheery Cherry Bread

Shirley Sears Tiskilwa, IL

MAKES: **6–8 SERVINGS**
PREP. TIME: **10–15 MINUTES**
COOKING TIME: **2–3 HOURS**
IDEAL SLOW COOKER SIZE: **LARGE ENOUGH TO HOLD YOUR BAKING INSERT**

6-oz. jar maraschino cherries

1½ cups flour

1½ tsp. baking powder

¼ tsp. salt

2 eggs

¾ cup sugar

¾ cup coarsely chopped pecans

1. Drain cherries, reserving ⅓ cup syrup. Cut cherries in pieces. Set aside.
2. Combine flour, baking powder, and salt.
3. Beat eggs and sugar together until thickened.
4. Alternately add flour mixture and cherry syrup to egg mixture, mixing until well blended after each addition.
5. Fold in cherries and pecans. Spread in well greased and floured baking insert or 2-lb. coffee can. (See Tip on page 611.) If using baking insert, cover with its lid; if using a coffee can, cover with 6 layers of paper towels. Set in slow cooker.
6. Cover cooker. Cook on High 2–3 hours.
7. Remove from slow cooker. Let stand 10 minutes before removing from pan.
8. Cool before slicing.

Breads

Gingerbread with Lemon Sauce

Jean Butzer Batavia, NY • *Marie Shank* Harrisonburg, VA

MAKES: **8 SERVINGS**
PREP. TIME: **15 MINUTES**
COOKING TIME: **1¾–4**
IDEAL SLOW COOKER SIZE: **LARGE ENOUGH TO HOLD YOUR BAKING INSERT**

½ cup butter, softened

½ cup sugar

1 egg, lightly beaten

1 cup sorghum molasses

2½ cups flour

1½ tsp. baking soda

1 tsp. cinnamon

2 tsp. ground ginger

½ tsp. ground cloves

½ tsp. salt

1 cup hot coffee *or* hot water

½ cup powdered sugar

2 tsp. cornstarch

pinch of salt

juice of 2 lemons

½ cup water

1 Tbsp. butter

powdered sugar for garnish

1. Cream together ½ cup butter and sugar.
2. Add egg. Mix well.
3. Add molasses. Mix well.
4. Sift together flour, baking soda, cinnamon, ginger, cloves, and salt. Stir into creamed mixture.
5. Add coffee or water. Beat well.
6. There are two ways to bake the gingerbread:
   a. If you have a baking insert, or a 2-lb. coffee can, grease and flour the inside of it. Pour in batter. Place in slow cooker. Pour water around insert or coffee can. Cover insert with its lid, or cover coffee can with 6–8 paper towels. (See Tip on page 611.)
   b. Cut waxed paper or parchment paper to fit bottom of slow cooker. Place in bottom of cooker. Spray paper and sides of cooker's interior with nonstick cooking spray. Pour batter into preheated slow cooker.
7. Cover cooker with its lid slightly ajar to allow excess moisture to escape. Cook on High 1¾–2 hours, or on Low 3–4 hours, or until edges are golden and knife inserted in center comes out clean.
8. If you used a baking insert or coffee can, remove from cooker. Cool on cake rack. Let stand 5 minutes before running knife around outer edge of cake and inverting onto serving plate. If you baked the gingerbread directly in the cooker, cut the cake into wedges after allowing it to cool for 30 minutes, and carefully lift the wedges out of the cooker onto serving plates.
9. In saucepan, mix together ½ cup powdered sugar, cornstarch, and salt. Add lemon juice and water, stirring with each addition. Cook over medium heat until thick and bubbly, about 1 minute. Remove from heat. Stir in butter.
10. If gingerbread has been cooling on a rack, cut it into wedges. To serve, top with sauce and sprinkle with powdered sugar.

Use the paper from inside cereal boxes instead of waxed paper.

Soups, Stews, and Chilis

Nancy's Vegetable-Beef Soup

Nancy Graves   Manhattan, KS

MAKES: **6–8 SERVINGS**
PREP. TIME: **10 MINUTES**
COOKING TIME: **8 HOURS**
IDEAL SLOW COOKER SIZE: **5–6-QUART**

2-lb. roast cut into bite-sized pieces, *or* 2 lbs. stewing meat

15-oz. can corn

15-oz. can green beans

1-lb. bag frozen peas

40-oz. can stewed tomatoes

5 beef bouillon cubes

Tabasco to taste

2 tsp. salt

1. Combine all ingredients in slow cooker. Do not drain vegetables.
2. Add water to fill slow cooker to within 3 inches of top
3. Cover. Cook on Low 8 hours, or until meat is tender and vegetables are soft.

Variation: *Add 1 large onion, sliced, 2 cups sliced carrots, and ¾ cup pearl barley to mixture before cooking.*

Lilli's Vegetable-Beef Soup

Lilli Peters   Dodge City, KS

MAKES: **10–12 SERVINGS**
PREP. TIME: **20–25 MINUTES**
COOKING TIME: **8–10 HOURS**
IDEAL SLOW COOKER SIZE: **4–5-QUART**

3 lbs. stewing meat, cut in 1-inch pieces

2 Tbsp. oil

4 potatoes, cubed

4 carrots, sliced

3 ribs celery, sliced

14-oz. can diced tomatoes

14-oz. can Italian tomatoes, crushed

2 medium onions, chopped

2 wedges cabbage, sliced thinly

2 beef bouillon cubes

2 Tbsp. fresh parsley

1 tsp. seasoned salt

1 tsp. garlic salt

½ tsp. pepper

water

1. Brown meat in oil in skillet. Drain.
2. Combine all ingredients except water in large slow cooker. Cover with water.
3. Cover. Cook on Low 8–10 hours.

Jeanne's Vegetable-Beef Borscht

Jeanne Heyerly   Chenoa, IL

MAKES: **8 SERVINGS**
PREP. TIME: **20 MINUTES**
COOKING TIME: **8–10 HOURS**
IDEAL SLOW COOKER SIZE: **5-QUART**

1 lb. beef roast, cooked and cubed

half a head of cabbage, sliced thinly

3 medium potatoes, diced

4 carrots, sliced

1 large onion, diced

1 cup tomatoes, diced

1 cup corn

1 cup green beans

2 cups beef broth

2 cups tomato juice

¼ tsp. garlic powder

¼ tsp. dill seed

2 tsp. salt

½ tsp. pepper

water

sour cream

1. Mix together all ingredients except water and sour cream. Add water to fill slow cooker three-quarters full.
2. Cover. Cook on Low 8–10 hours.
3. Top individual servings with sour cream.

Variation: *Add 1 cup diced cooked red beets during the last half hour of cooking.*

Remember to use leftover cooked vegetables from your refrigerator when making soup.

Winter's Night Beef Soup

Kimberly Jensen Bailey, CO

MAKES: **8–12 SERVINGS**
PREP. TIME: **25 MINUTES**
COOKING TIME: **6½ HOURS**
IDEAL SLOW COOKER SIZE: **5-QUART**

1 lb. boneless chuck, cut in ½-inch cubes

1–2 Tbsp. oil

28-oz. can tomatoes

2 tsp. garlic powder

2 carrots, sliced

2 ribs celery, sliced

4 cups water

½ cup red wine

1 small onion, coarsely chopped

4 beef bouillon cubes

1 tsp. pepper

1 tsp. dry oregano

½ tsp. dry thyme

1 bay leaf

¼-½ cup couscous

1. Brown beef cubes in oil in skillet.
2. Place vegetables in bottom of slow cooker. Add beef.
3. Combine all other ingredients in separate bowl except couscous. Pour over ingredients in slow cooker.
4. Cover. Cook on Low 6 hours. Stir in couscous. Cover and cook 30 minutes.

Variation: *Add zucchini or mushrooms to the rest of the vegetables before cooking.*

Browning meat in another pan means an extra step, but it adds a lot to a recipe's appearance and flavor.

Old-Fashioned Vegetable Beef Soup

Pam Hochstedler Kalona, IA

MAKES: **8–10 SERVINGS**
PREP. TIME: **25 MINUTES**
COOKING TIME: **6–9 HOURS**
IDEAL SLOW COOKER SIZE: **4-QUART**

1–2 lbs. beef short ribs

2 quarts water

1 tsp. salt

1 tsp. celery salt

1 small onion, chopped

1 cup diced carrots

½ cup diced celery

2 cups diced potatoes

1-lb. can whole-kernel corn, undrained

1-lb. can diced tomatoes and juice

1. Combine meat, water, salt, celery salt, onion, carrots, and celery in slow cooker.
2. Cover. Cook on Low 4–6 hours.
3. Debone meat, cut into bite-sized pieces, and return to pot.
4. Add potatoes, corn, and tomatoes.
5. Cover and cook on High 2–3 hours.

Hearty Alphabet Soup

Maryann Markano Wilmington, DE

MAKES: **5–6 SERVINGS**
PREP. TIME: **10 MINUTES**
COOKING TIME: **6½–8½ HOURS**
IDEAL SLOW COOKER SIZE: **4-QUART**

½ lb. beef stewing meat *or* round steak, cubed

14½-oz. can stewed tomatoes

8-oz. can tomato sauce

1 cup water

1 envelope dry onion soup mix

10-oz. pkg. frozen vegetables, partially thawed

½ cup alphabet noodles, uncooked

1. Combine meat, tomatoes, tomato sauce, water, and soup mix in slow cooker.
2. Cover. Cook on Low 6–8 hours. Turn to High.
3. Stir in vegetables and noodles. Add more water if mixture is too dry and thick.
4. Cover. Cook on High 30 minutes, or until vegetables are tender.

Busy Cook's Stew

Denise Nickel Goessel, KS

MAKES: **4–6 SERVINGS**
PREP. TIME: **30–40 MINUTES**
COOKING TIME: **6–8 HOURS**
IDEAL SLOW COOKER SIZE: **3-QUART**

1 lb. boneless stew meat, cut up

10¾-oz. can cream of mushroom soup

2 cups water

3 potatoes, cubed

3 carrots, diced

1 onion, chopped

1. Brown meat in large nonstick skillet. Don't crowd the skillet so the meat browns on all sides. (If your skillet is 10 inches or smaller, brown the beef in 2 batches.)
2. Place meat in slow cooker. Add remaining ingredients in the order listed. Stir well after each addition.
3. Cover and cook on Low 6–8 hours, or until meat and vegetables are tender but not mushy. Stir occasionally.

Variation: *If you wish, add salt and pepper to taste.*

Beef and Black-Eyed Pea Soup

Jeanette Oberholtzer Manheim, PA

MAKES: **6 SERVINGS**
PREP. TIME: **25 MINUTES**
COOKING TIME: **8–10 HOURS**
IDEAL SLOW COOKER SIZE: **6 QUART**

16-oz. pkg. dried black-eyed peas

10-oz. can condensed bean and bacon soup

3–4 cups water

4 large carrots, peeled and sliced

3-lb. beef chuck roast, cut into 2-inch cubes

½ tsp. *each* salt and pepper

1. Rinse and drain the peas.
2. Combine all ingredients in slow cooker.
3. Cook on Low 8–10 hours, or until peas and beef are tender.

Variation: *For added flavor, add chopped onion and minced garlic, or a 14½-oz. can chopped tomatoes, to Step 2.*

Beef Barley Soup

Stacie Skelly   Millersville, PA

MAKES: **8–10 SERVINGS**
PREP. TIME: **15 MINUTES**
COOKING TIME: **9¼–11½ HOURS**
IDEAL SLOW COOKER SIZE: **6-QUART**

3–4 lb. chuck roast

2 cups carrots, chopped

6 cups vegetable *or* tomato juice, *divided*

2 cups quick-cook barley

water, to desired consistency

salt and pepper to taste, *optional*

1. Place roast, carrots, and 4 cups juice in slow cooker.
2. Cover and cook on Low 8–10 hours.
3. Remove roast. Place on platter and cover with foil to keep warm.
4. Meanwhile, add barley to slow cooker. Stir well. Turn heat to High and cook 45 minutes to 1 hour, until barley is tender.
5. While barley is cooking, cut meat into bite-sized pieces.
6. When barley is tender, return chopped beef to slow cooker. Add 2 cups juice, water if you wish, and salt and pepper, if you want. Cook for 30 minutes on High, or until soup is heated through.

Beef Barley Lentil Soup

Janie Steele   Moore, OK

MAKES: **10 SERVINGS**
PREP. TIME: **20 MINUTES**
COOKING TIME: **8 HOURS**
IDEAL SLOW COOKER SIZE: **5–6-QUART**

1 lb. extra-lean ground beef

1 medium onion, chopped

2 cups cubed potatoes

1 cup chopped celery

1 cup diced carrots

1 cup dry lentils, rinsed

½ cup medium-sized pearl barley

8 cups water

2 tsp. beef bouillon granules

½ tsp. salt

½ tsp. lemon pepper seasoning

2 14½-oz. cans low-sodium stewed tomatoes, undrained

1. Brown ground beef with onions in a skillet. Drain.
2. Combine all ingredients except tomatoes in slow cooker.
3. Cook on Low 6 hours, or until tender.
4. Add tomatoes. Cook on Low 2 more hours.

Per Serving: 250 calories (40 calories from fat), 4.5g total fat (1.5g saturated, 0g trans), 15mg cholesterol, 680mg sodium, 35g total carbohydrate (9g fiber, 7g sugar), 17g protein, 60%DV vitamin A, 40%DV vitamin C, 6%DV calcium, 25%DV iron.

Variation: *For added zest, you may want to increase the lemon pepper seasoning to 1 tsp. You may also want to add ½ tsp. dried basil and ½ tsp. dried thyme to Step 2.*

Vegetable Beef Barley Soup

Mary Rogers Waseca, MN

MAKES: **12 SERVINGS**
PREP. TIME: **10 MINUTES**
COOKING TIME: **5-7 HOURS**
IDEAL SLOW COOKER SIZE: **5-6-QUART**

1 lb. lean stewing meat, cut into bite-sized pieces

½ cup onions, chopped

½ cup cut green beans, fresh *or* frozen

½ cup corn, fresh *or* frozen

4 cups fat-free, low-sodium beef broth

2 14½-oz. cans low-sodium stewed tomatoes

12-oz. can low-sodium V-8 juice

⅔ cup pearl barley, uncooked

1 cup water

1. Combine all ingredients in slow cooker.
2. Cover. Cook on High 5-7 hours, until vegetables are cooked to your liking.

Per Serving: 130 calories (20 calories from fat), 2g total fat (0.5g saturated, 0g trans), 25mg cholesterol, 65mg sodium, 15g total carbohydrate (4g fiber, 5g sugar), 12g protein, 4%DV vitamin A, 10%DV vitamin C, 4%DV calcium, 10%DV iron.

Vegetable Beef Soup

Doris Perkins Mashpee, MA

MAKES: **8 SERVINGS**
PREP. TIME: **15 MINUTES**
COOKING TIME: **4-6 HOURS**
IDEAL SLOW COOKER SIZE: **4-QUART**

1 lb. extra-lean ground beef

14½-oz. can low-sodium, stewed tomatoes

10¾-oz. can low-sodium tomato soup

1 onion, chopped

2 cups water

15½-oz. can garbanzo beans, drained

15¼-oz. can corn, drained

14½-oz. can sliced carrots, drained

1 cup diced potatoes

1 cup chopped celery

½ tsp. salt

¼ tsp. black pepper

chopped garlic to taste, *optional*

1. Sauté ground beef in nonstick skillet.
2. Combine all ingredients in slow cooker.
3. Cook on Low 4-6 hours.

Per Serving: 220 calories (50 calories from fat), 6g total fat (2g saturated, 0g trans), 20mg cholesterol, 590mg sodium, 28g total carbohydrate (5g fiber, 7g sugar), 15g protein, 100%DV vitamin A, 20%DV vitamin C, 8%DV calcium, 15%DV iron.

Tips:

1. You may use green beans and turnips, or any other combination of vegetables you wish.

2. If your diet allows, you may want to top individual servings with a spoonful of low-fat shredded cheddar cheese.

Ground Beef Minestrone Soup

Kathy Moyer   Ottsville, PA

MAKES: **12 SERVINGS**
PREP. TIME: **15 MINUTES**
COOKING TIME: **6 HOURS**
IDEAL SLOW COOKER SIZE: **4-QUART**

1 lb. extra-lean ground beef

1 large onion, chopped

1 clove garlic, minced

2 15½-oz. cans low-sodium stewed tomatoes

15-oz. can kidney beans, drained

10-oz. pkg. frozen corn

2 ribs celery, sliced

2 small zucchini, sliced

1 cup macaroni, uncooked

2½ cups hot water

2 beef bouillon cubes

½ tsp. salt

2 tsp. Italian seasoning

1. Brown ground beef in nonstick skillet.
2. Combine browned ground beef, onion, garlic, stewed tomatoes, kidney beans, corn, celery, zucchini, and macaroni in slow cooker.
3. Dissolve bouillon cubes in hot water. Combine with salt and Italian seasoning. Add to slow cooker.
4. Cover. Cook on Low 6 hours.

Per Serving: 180 calories (35 calories from fat), 4g total fat (1.5g saturated, 0g trans), 15mg cholesterol, 430mg sodium, 24g total carbohydrate (4g fiber, 6g sugar), 13g protein, 4%DV vitamin A, 10%DV vitamin C, 4%DV calcium, 15%DV iron.

Hamburger Soup

Betty Moore   Plano, IL

MAKES: **6 SERVINGS**
PREP. TIME: **10 MINUTES**
COOKING TIME: **6¼–8¼ HOURS**
IDEAL SLOW COOKER SIZE: **4-QUART**

1 lb. extra-lean ground beef

¼ tsp. black pepper

¼ tsp. dried oregano

¼ tsp. seasoned salt

1 envelope dry onion soup mix

3 cups hot water

8-oz. can tomato sauce

1 Tbsp. low-sodium soy sauce

1 cup carrots, sliced

1 cup celery, sliced

1 cup macaroni, cooked

¼ cup grated Parmesan cheese

1. Combine all ingredients except macaroni and Parmesan cheese in slow cooker.
2. Cook on Low 6–8 hours.
3. Turn to High. Add macaroni and Parmesan cheese.
4. Cook for another 15–20 minutes.

Per Serving: 160 calories (60 calories from fat), 6g total fat (2.5g saturated, 0g trans), 25mg cholesterol, 440mg sodium, 12g total carbohydrate (2g fiber, 4g sugar), 15g protein, 120%DV vitamin A, 10%DV vitamin C, 6%DV calcium, 10%DV iron.

Beef Dumpling Soup

Barbara Walker Sturgis, SD

MAKES: **5–6 SERVINGS**
PREP. TIME: **10–15 MINUTES**
COOKING TIME: **4½–6½ HOURS**
IDEAL SLOW COOKER SIZE: **4-QUART**

1 lb. beef stewing meat, cubed

1 envelope dry onion soup mix

6 cups hot water

2 carrots, peeled and shredded

1 celery rib, finely chopped

1 tomato, peeled and chopped

1 cup buttermilk biscuit mix

1 Tbsp. finely chopped parsley

6 Tbsp. milk

1. Place meat in slow cooker. Sprinkle with onion soup mix. Pour water over meat.
2. Add carrots, celery, and tomato.
3. Cover. Cook on Low 4–6 hours, or until meat is tender.
4. Combine biscuit mix and parsley. Stir in milk with fork until moistened. Drop dumplings by teaspoonfuls into pot.
5. Cover. Cook on High 30 minutes.

Variation: *Increase the flavor of the broth by adding 2 cloves garlic, ½ tsp. dried basil, and ¼ tsp. dill weed to Step 2.*

Don't have enough time? A lot of dishes can be made in less time by increasing the temperature to High and cooking the dish for about half the time as is necessary on Low.

Easy Vegetable Soup

Winifred Paul Scottdale, PA

MAKES: **8–10 SERVINGS**
PREP. TIME: **20 MINUTES**
COOKING TIME: **8–10 HOURS**
IDEAL SLOW COOKER SIZE: **5-QUART**

1 lb. ground beef, browned

1 cup chopped onions

15-oz. can kidney beans *or* butter beans, undrained

1 cup sliced carrots

¼ cup rice, uncooked

1 quart stewed tomatoes

3½ cups water

5 beef bouillon cubes

1 Tbsp. parsley flakes

1 tsp. salt

⅛ tsp. pepper

¼ tsp. dried basil

1 bay leaf

1. Combine all ingredients in slow cooker.
2. Cover. Cook on Low 8–10 hours.

Tip: *Add more herbs and additional seasonings for zestier flavor.*

Ground Beef Vegetable Soup

Renee Baum Chambersburg, PA • *Janet Oberholtzer* Ephrata, PA

MAKES: **10 SERVINGS**
PREP. TIME: **15 MINUTES**
COOKING TIME: **8–9 HOURS**
IDEAL SLOW COOKER SIZE: **5-QUART**

1 lb. ground beef

46-oz. can tomato, *or* V-8, juice

16-oz. pkg. frozen mixed vegetables, thawed

2 cups frozen cubed hash browns, thawed

1 envelope dry onion soup mix

1. Brown beef in nonstick skillet on stovetop. Drain.
2. Place beef in slow cooker. Stir in remaining ingredients.
3. Cover and cook on Low 8–9 hours, or until vegetables are cooked through.

Variations:

1. Instead of hash browns, use 2 cups cubed cooked potatoes.

Elsie Schlabach   Millersburg, OH

2. Instead of tomato or V-8 juice, use 2 beef bouillon cubes dissolved in 2 cups boiling water. And instead of dry onion soup mix, use salt and pepper to taste.

Sharon Wantland   Menomonee Falls, WI

Hamburger-Lentil Soup

Juanita Marner   Shipshewana, IN

MAKES: **8 SERVINGS**
PREP. TIME: **20 MINUTES**
COOKING TIME: **4–10 HOURS**
IDEAL SLOW COOKER SIZE: **4-QUART**

1 lb. ground beef

½ cup chopped onions

4 carrots, diced

3 ribs celery, diced

1 garlic clove, minced, *or* 1 tsp. garlic powder

1 quart tomato juice

1 Tbsp. salt

2 cups dry lentils, washed with stones removed

1 quart water

½ tsp. dried marjoram

1 Tbsp. brown sugar

1. Brown ground beef and onion in skillet. Drain.
2. Combine all ingredients in slow cooker.
3. Cover. Cook on Low 8–10 hours, or on High 4–6 hours.

Vegetable Soup with Noodles

Glenda S. Weaver   New Holland, PA

MAKES: **6 SERVINGS**
PREP. TIME: **15 MINUTES**
COOKING TIME: **2–6 HOURS**
IDEAL SLOW COOKER SIZE: **4-QUART**

1 pint water

2 beef bouillon cubes

1 onion, chopped

1 lb. ground beef

¼ cup ketchup

1 tsp. salt

⅛ tsp. celery salt

½ cup noodles, uncooked

12–16-oz. pkg. frozen mixed vegetables, *or* vegetables of your choice

1 pint tomato juice

1. Dissolve bouillon cubes in water.
2. Brown onion and beef in skillet. Drain.
3. Combine all ingredients in slow cooker.
4. Cover. Cook on Low 6 hours, or on High 2–3 hours, until vegetables are tender.

Steak Soup

Ilene Bontrager Arlington, KS • *Deb Unternahrer* Wayland, IA

MAKES: **10–12 SERVINGS**
PREP. TIME: **20 MINUTES**
COOKING TIME: **4–12 HOURS**
IDEAL SLOW COOKER SIZE: **4–5-QUART**

2 lbs. coarsely ground chuck, browned and drained

5 cups water

1 large onion, chopped

4 ribs celery, chopped

3 carrots, sliced

2 14½-oz. cans diced tomatoes

10-oz. pkg. frozen mixed vegetables

5 Tbsp. beef-based granules, *or* 5 beef bouillon cubes

½ tsp. pepper

½ cup butter, melted

½ cup flour

2 tsp. salt

1. Combine chuck, water, onion, celery, carrots, tomatoes, mixed vegetables, beef granules, and pepper in slow cooker.
2. Cover. Cook on Low 8–12 hours, or on High 4–6 hours.
3. One hour before serving, turn to High. Make a paste of melted butter and flour. Stir until smooth. Pour into slow cooker and stir until well blended. Add salt.
4. Cover. Continue cooking on High until thickened.

Dottie's Creamy Steak Soup

Debbie Zeida Mashpee, MA

MAKES: **4–6 SERVINGS**
PREP. TIME: **15 MINUTES**
COOKING TIME: **8–10 HOURS**
IDEAL SLOW COOKER SIZE: **4-QUART**

1 lb. ground beef

half a large onion, chopped

12-oz. can V-8 vegetable juice

2–3 medium potatoes, diced

10¾-oz. can cream of mushroom soup

10¾-oz. can cream of celery soup

16-oz. pkg. frozen mixed vegetables, *or* your choice of frozen vegetables

2 tsp. salt

½–¾ tsp. pepper

1. Sauté beef and onions in skillet. Drain.
2. Combine all ingredients in slow cooker.
3. Cover. Cook on Low 8–10 hours.

Easy Veggie-Beef Soup

Rebecca Plank Leichty   Harrisonburg, VA

MAKES: **6–8 SERVINGS**
PREP. TIME: **20 MINUTES**
COOKING TIME: **4–8 HOURS**
IDEAL SLOW COOKER SIZE: **5-QUART**

1 lb. browned ground beef, *or* 2 cups stewing beef

2 cups sliced carrots

1 lb. frozen green beans, thawed

14½-oz. can corn, drained, *or* 16-oz. bag frozen corn, thawed

28-oz. can diced tomatoes

3 cups beef *or* vegetable broth

3 tsp. instant beef bouillon

2 tsp. Worcestershire sauce

1 Tbsp. sugar

1 Tbsp. minced onion

10¾-oz. can cream of celery soup

1. Place meat in bottom of slow cooker.
2. Add remaining ingredients except celery soup. Mix well.
3. Stir in soup.
4. Cover. Cook on Low 7–8 hours, or on High 4 hours.
5. If using stewing meat, shred and mix through soup just before serving.
6. Serve with freshly baked bread and homemade jam.

The great thing about using a slow cooker in hot weather is that it doesn't heat up your kitchen like an oven does.

Hamburger Vegetable Soup

Joyce Shackelford   Green Bay, WI

MAKES: **8–10 SERVINGS**
PREP. TIME: **20 MINUTES**
COOKING TIME: **8–9 HOURS**
IDEAL SLOW COOKER SIZE: **5-QUART**

1 lb. ground chuck

1 onion, chopped

2 garlic cloves, minced

4 cups V-8 juice

14½-oz. can stewed tomatoes

2 cups cole slaw mix

2 cups frozen green beans

2 cups frozen corn

2 Tbsp. Worcestershire sauce

1 tsp. dried basil

½ tsp. salt

¼ tsp. pepper

1. Brown beef, onion, and garlic in skillet. Drain and transfer to slow cooker.
2. Add remaining ingredients to slow cooker and combine.
3. Cover. Cook on Low 8–9 hours.

Zesty Taco Soup

Suzanne Slagel Midway, OH

MAKES: **6–8 SERVINGS**
PREP. TIME: **15 MINUTES**
COOKING TIME: **4–6 HOURS**
IDEAL SLOW COOKER SIZE: **5–6-QUART**

1 lb. ground beef
1 large onion, chopped
16-oz. can Mexican-style tomatoes
16-oz. can ranch-style beans
16-oz. can whole-kernel corn, undrained
16-oz. can kidney beans, undrained
16-oz. can black beans, undrained
16-oz. jar picante sauce
corn *or* tortilla chips
sour cream
shredded cheddar cheese

1. Brown meat and onions in skillet. Drain.
2. Combine with all other vegetables and picante sauce in slow cooker.
3. Cover. Cook on Low 4–6 hours.
4. Serve with corn or tortilla chips, sour cream, and shredded cheese as toppings.

Taco Soup with Pizza Sauce

Barbara Kuhns Millersburg, OH

MAKES: **8–10 SERVINGS**
PREP. TIME: **15 MINUTES**
COOKING TIME: **3–4 HOURS**
IDEAL SLOW COOKER SIZE: **6-QUART**

2 lbs. ground beef, browned
1 small onion, chopped and sautéed in ground beef drippings
¾ tsp. salt
½ tsp. pepper
1½ pkgs. dry taco seasoning
1 quart pizza sauce
1 quart water
tortilla chips
shredded mozzarella cheese
sour cream

1. Combine ground beef, onion, salt, pepper, taco seasoning, pizza sauce, and water in 5-quart, or larger, slow cooker.
2. Cover. Cook on Low 3–4 hours.
3. Top individual servings with tortilla chips, cheese, and sour cream.

Variation: *Add 15-oz. can black beans and 4-oz. can chilies to mixture before cooking. (Be sure to use one very large cooker, or two medium-sized cookers.)*

Fresh lemon juice will remove onion scent from your hands.

Soups, Stews, and Chilis

Light Taco Soup

Sara Kinsinger   Stuarts Draft, VA

MAKES: **6 SERVINGS**
PREP. TIME: **10 MINUTES**
COOKING TIME: **4 HOURS**
IDEAL SLOW COOKER SIZE: **6-QUART**

1 large onion, chopped
1 lb. extra-lean ground beef
1 envelope dry taco seasoning
16-oz. can kidney beans, drained
16-oz. can corn, drained
2 quarts tomato juice
¼ cup sugar
½ tsp. salt
¼–½ tsp. black pepper, according to taste
7 ozs. baked corn chips, *optional*
reduced fat shredded cheese, *optional*
fat-free sour cream, *optional*

1. Brown the hamburger and chopped onion in a nonstick skillet. Drain.
2. Combine ground beef, onions, taco seasoning, kidney beans, corn, tomato juice, sugar, salt, and pepper in slow cooker.
3. Cook on Low 4 hours or until heated through.
4. Top individual servings with corn chips, cheese, and sour cream, if you wish.

Per Serving: 650 calories (210 calories from fat), 23g total fat (7g saturated, 0g trans), 40mg cholesterol, 2200mg sodium, 81g total carbohydrate (9g fiber, 25g sugar), 32g protein, 40%DV vitamin A, 40%DV vitamin C, 30%DV calcium, 30%DV iron.

Tip: *If you prefer a less juicy stew, remove the lid during the last hour of cooking.*

A note from the recipe's tester: *"Our son, Quincy, who would prefer to live on bread and chocolate alone, initially turned up his nose in disgust at the Soup. I explained that I wanted him to try this recipe and give his opinion because that's why I had made the Soup. So...3 good-sized servings later...we determined it was a rave review."*

Taco Soup with Hominy

Sue Tjon   Austin, TX

MAKES: **8 SERVINGS**
PREP. TIME: **15 MINUTES**
COOKING TIME: **4 HOURS**
IDEAL SLOW COOKER SIZE: **6-QUART**

1 lb. ground beef
1 envelope dry ranch dressing mix
1 envelope dry taco seasoning mix
3 12-oz. cans Rotel tomatoes, undrained
2 24-oz. cans pinto beans, undrained
24-oz. can hominy, undrained
14½-oz. can stewed tomatoes, undrained
1 onion, chopped
2 cups water

1. Brown meat in skillet. Pour into slow cooker.
2. Add remaining ingredients. Mix well.
3. Cover. Cook on Low 4 hours.

Tips:
1. Increase or decrease the amount of water you add to make the dish either stew-like or soup-like.

2. A serving suggestion is to line each individual soup bowl with tortilla chips, ladle taco soup on top, and sprinkle with shredded cheese.

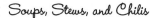

Taco Soup Plus

Marla Folkerts Holland, OH

MAKES: **6 SERVINGS**
PREP. TIME: **15 MINUTES**
COOKING TIME: **6–8 HOURS**
IDEAL SLOW COOKER SIZE: **3½–4-QUART**

Soup:

1 lb. extra-lean ground beef *or* ground turkey

1 medium onion, chopped

1 medium green bell pepper, chopped

1 envelope dry reduced-sodium taco seasoning

½ cup water

4 cups reduced-sodium vegetable juice

1 cup chunky salsa

Toppings:

¾ cup shredded lettuce

6 Tbsp. fresh tomato, chopped

6 Tbsp. reduced-fat cheddar cheese, shredded

¼ cup green onions *or* chives, chopped

¼ cup fat-free sour cream *or* fat-free plain yogurt

baked tortilla *or* corn chips

1. Brown meat with onion in nonstick skillet. Drain.
2. Combine all soup ingredients in slow cooker.
3. Cover. Cook on Low 6–8 hours.
4. Serve with your choice of toppings.

Per Serving: 260 calories (60 calories from fat), 7g total fat (2.5g saturated, 0g trans), 30mg cholesterol, 2190mg sodium, 29g total carbohydrate (2g fiber, 9g sugar), 17g protein, 50%DV vitamin A, 50%DV vitamin C, 4%DV calcium, 15%DV iron.

Chili-Taco Soup

Frances L. Kruba Dundalk, MD

MAKES: **8 SERVINGS**
PREP. TIME: **25–30 MINUTES**
COOKING TIME: **5–7 HOURS**
IDEAL SLOW COOKER SIZE: **1–2-QUART**

2 lbs. lean stew meat

2 15-oz. cans stewed tomatoes, Mexican or regular

1 envelope dry taco seasoning mix

2 15-oz. cans pinto beans

15-oz. can whole-kernel corn

¾ cup water

1. Cut large pieces of stew meat in half and brown in large nonstick skillet.
2. Combine all ingredients in slow cooker.
3. Cover and cook on Low 5–7 hours.

Sante Fe Soup with Melted Cheese

Carla Koslowsky Hillsboro, KS

MAKES: **8 SERVINGS**
PREP. TIME: **15 MINUTES**
COOKING TIME: **3 HOURS**
IDEAL SLOW COOKER SIZE: **4-QUART**

1 lb. Velveeta cheese, cubed

1 lb. ground beef, browned and drained

15¼-oz. can corn, undrained

15-oz. can kidney beans, undrained

14½-oz. can diced tomatoes with green chilies

14½-oz. can stewed tomatoes

2 Tbsp. dry taco seasoning

corn chips *or* soft tortillas

1. Combine all ingredients except chips or tortillas in slow cooker.
2. Cover. Cook on High 3 hours.
3. Serve with corn chips as a side, or dip soft tortillas in individual servings in soup bowls.

Soups, Stews, and Chilis

Golden Carrots, page 531

Turkey Meat Loaf, page 410

Seafood Dip, page 47

Manhattan Clam Chowder,
  page 159

Pizza in a Bowl

Laurie Sylvester Ridgely, MD

MAKES: **6 SERVINGS**
PREP. TIME: **10 MINUTES**
COOKING TIME: **5–6 HOURS**
IDEAL SLOW COOKER SIZE: **3½-QUART**

26-oz. jar fat-free, low-sodium marinara sauce

14½-oz. can low-sodium diced tomatoes

4 ozs. low-fat pepperoni, diced or sliced

1½ cups fresh mushrooms, sliced

1 large bell pepper, diced

1 large red onion, chopped

1 cup water

1 Tbsp. Italian seasoning

1 cup dry macaroni

low-fat shredded mozzarella cheese

1. Combine all ingredients, except cheese, in cooker.
2. Cover. Cook on Low 5–6 hours.
3. Ladle into soup bowls. Sprinkle with cheese.

Per Serving: 280 calories (100 calories from fat), 12g total fat (3.5g saturated, 0g trans), 15mg cholesterol, 1270mg sodium, 34g total carbohydrate (5g fiber, 12g sugar), 11g protein, 10%DV vitamin A, 30%DV vitamin C, 10%DV calcium, 15%DV iron.

Everyone's Hungry Soup

Janie Steele Moore, OK

MAKES: **20–25 SERVINGS**
PREP. TIME: **45 MINUTES**
COOKING TIME: **8–10 HOURS**
IDEAL SLOW COOKER SIZE: **6-QUART OR 2 LARGE**

6 thick slices bacon

3 lbs. boneless beef stewing meat, cubed

1 lb. boneless pork, cubed

3 14½-oz. cans tomatoes

10-oz. can Rotel tomatoes and chilies

3 celery ribs, chopped

3 large onions, chopped

garlic to taste

salt to taste

pepper to taste

½ cup Worcestershire sauce

2 Tbsp. chili powder

2 cups water

6–8 medium potatoes, peeled and cubed

1 lb. carrots, sliced

15-oz. can English peas, undrained

14½-oz. can green beans, undrained

15¼-oz. can corn, undrained

1 lb. cut-up okra, *optional*

1. Fry bacon in skillet until crisp. Remove bacon, but reserve drippings. Crumble bacon and divide between 2 large (6-quart or larger) slow cookers.
2. Brown stewing beef and pork in skillet in bacon drippings.
3. Combine all ingredients and divide between slow cookers.
4. Cover. Cook on Low 8–10 hours.
5. Serve with loaves of homemade bread or pans of cornbread.

Hamburger-Sausage Soup

Esther Becker Gordonville, PA

MAKES: **4–6 SERVINGS**
PREP. TIME: **20–25 MINUTES**
COOKING TIME: **8–10 HOURS**
IDEAL SLOW COOKER SIZE: **5-QUART**

1 lb. ground beef
1 lb. Polish sausage, sliced
½ tsp. seasoned salt
¼ tsp. dried oregano
¼ tsp. dried basil
1 pkg. dry onion soup mix
6 cups boiling water
16-oz. can diced tomatoes
1 Tbsp. soy sauce
½ cup sliced celery
¼ cup chopped celery leaves
1 cup pared, sliced carrots
1 cup macaroni, uncooked

1. Brown ground beef and sausage in skillet. Drain. Place in slow cooker.
2. Add seasoned salt, oregano, basil, and onion soup mix to cooker.
3. Stir in boiling water, tomatoes, and soy sauce.
4. Add celery, celery leaves, and carrots. Stir well.
5. Cover. Cook on Low 8–10 hours.
6. One hour before end of cooking time, stir in dry macaroni.
7. Serve with cornbread or corn muffins.

Delicious Sausage Soup

Karen Waggoner Joplin, MO

MAKES: **4 SERVINGS**
PREP. TIME: **15–20 MINUTES**
COOKING TIME: **4–5 HOURS**
IDEAL SLOW COOKER SIZE: **5-QUART**

5½ cups chicken broth
½ cup heavy cream
3 carrots, grated
4 potatoes, sliced or cubed
4 cups kale, chopped
1 lb. spicy Italian sausage, browned
½ tsp. salt
½ tsp. crushed red pepper flakes

1. Combine broth and cream in slow cooker. Turn on High.
2. Add carrots, potatoes, kale, and sausage.
3. Sprinkle spices over top.
4. Cover. Cook on High 4–5 hours, stirring occasionally.

Soups, Stews, and Chilis

Spicy Sausage Soup

Janie Steele   Moore, OK

MAKES: **8–10 SERVINGS**
PREP. TIME: **25 MINUTES**
COOKING TIME: **6–8 HOURS**
IDEAL SLOW COOKER SIZE: **5–6 QUART**

1 lb. ground beef

1 lb. bulk spicy sausage (casings removed)

half a large onion, chopped

2 cups chopped carrots

2 cups chopped celery

1 green *or* red bell pepper, chopped, *optional*

2 tsp. salt, or to taste

¼ tsp. pepper, or to taste

1 tsp. dried oregano, or to taste

2 or 3 garlic cloves, minced

14½-oz. can stewed tomatoes with chilies

14½-oz. can green beans

¼ tsp. chili powder

1 cup instant rice, uncooked

1. Combine beef, sausage, and onions. Form into balls. Place in slow cooker.
2. Add all remaining ingredients, except rice. Stir gently so as not to break up the meatballs.
3. Cover. Cook on Low 6–8 hours. Stir in rice 20 minutes before serving.
4. Serve with rolls or cornbread.

Put your cooker meal together the night before you want to cook it. The following morning put the mixture in the slow cooker, cover, and turn it on.

Toscano Soup

Sheila Soldner   Lititz, PA

MAKES: **4–6 SERVINGS**
PREP. TIME: **20–25 MINUTES**
COOKING TIME: **6–8 HOURS**
IDEAL SLOW COOKER SIZE: **4-QUART**

2 medium russet potatoes

1 lb. spicy Italian sausage

5½ cups chicken stock *or* low-sodium chicken broth

2 cups chopped kale

½ tsp. crushed red pepper flakes, *optional*

½ cup cream *or* evaporated milk

1. Cut potatoes into ½-inch cubes. Place in slow cooker.
2. Grill, broil, or brown sausage in a nonstick skillet. When cool enough to handle, cut into ½-inch-thick slices.
3. Add sliced sausage to slow cooker. Stir in all remaining ingredients, except cream.
4. Cover and cook on Low 6–8 hours.
5. Fifteen to 20 minutes before serving, add cream or evaporated milk and cook until soup is heated through.

Variation: *If you don't want the soup to be too spicy, use ½ lb. sweet sausage and ½ lb. spicy sausage.*

Chet's Trucker Stew

Janice Muller   Derwood, MD

MAKES: **8 SERVINGS**
PREP. TIME: **15 MINUTES**
COOKING TIME: **2–3 HOURS**
IDEAL SLOW COOKER SIZE: **4–5-QUART**

1 lb. bulk pork sausage, cooked and drained

1 lb. ground beef, cooked and drained

31-oz. can pork and beans

16-oz. can light kidney beans

16-oz. can dark kidney beans

14½-oz. can waxed beans, drained

14½-oz. can lima beans, drained

1 cup ketchup

1 cup brown sugar

1 Tbsp. spicy prepared mustard

1. Combine all ingredients in slow cooker.
2. Cover. Simmer on High 2–3 hours.

Hearty Lentil and Sausage Stew

Cindy Krestynick   Glen Lyon, PA

MAKES: **6 SERVINGS**
PREP. TIME: **5–10 MINUTES**
COOKING TIME: **4–6 HOURS**
IDEAL SLOW COOKER SIZE: **6-QUART**

2 cups dry lentils, picked over and rinsed

14½-oz. can diced tomatoes

8 cups canned chicken broth *or* water

1 Tbsp. salt

½–1 lb. pork *or* beef sausage, cut into 2-inch pieces

1. Place lentils, tomatoes, chicken broth, and salt in slow cooker. Stir to combine. Place sausage pieces on top.
2. Cover and cook on Low 4–6 hours, or until lentils are tender but not dry or mushy.

Bean and Bacon Soup

Jeanette Oberholtzer   Manheim, PA

MAKES: **6 SERVINGS**
PREP. TIME: **25 MINUTES**
COOKING TIME: **11–13½ HOURS**
IDEAL SLOW COOKER SIZE: **4-QUART**

1¼ cups dried bean soup mix, *or* any combination of mixed dried beans

5 cups water

1 onion, chopped

3 cups water

4 slices fried bacon (precooked bacon works well), crumbled

1 envelope taco seasoning

2 14-oz. cans diced tomatoes, undrained

1. Place dried beans in large stockpot. Cover with 5 cups water. Cover pot and bring to a boil. Cook 2 minutes over high heat.
2. Remove pot from heat and allow to stand, covered, for 1 hour. Return pot to stovetop and cook covered for 2½–3 hours, or until beans are tender. Drain.
3. Combine cooked beans, onion, 3 cups water, bacon, and taco seasoning in slow cooker. Mix well.
4. Cook on Low 8–10 hours.
5. Add tomatoes. Stir well. Cook another 30 minutes.

Tip: *If you like a thickened soup, mash some of the beans before adding the tomatoes.*

Bean and Herb Soup

LaVerne A. Olson   Willow Street, PA

MAKES: **6–8 SERVINGS**
PREP. TIME: **45–60 MINUTES**
STANDING TIME: **1 HOUR**
COOKING TIME: **4 HOURS**
IDEAL SLOW COOKER SIZE: **6–7-QUART**

1½ cups dry mixed beans

5 cups water

1 ham hock

1 cup chopped onions

1 cup chopped celery

1 cup chopped carrots

2-3 cups water

1 tsp. salt

¼–½ tsp. pepper

1–2 tsp. fresh basil, *or* ½ tsp. dried basil

1–2 tsp. fresh oregano, *or* ½ tsp. dried oregano

1–2 tsp. fresh thyme, *or* ½ tsp. dried thyme

2 cups fresh tomatoes, crushed, *or* 14½-oz. can crushed tomatoes

1. Combine beans, water, and ham in saucepan. Bring to boil. Turn off heat and let stand 1 hour.
2. Combine onions, celery, and carrots in 2–3 cups water in another saucepan. Cook until soft. Mash slightly.
3. Combine all ingredients in slow cooker.
4. Cover. Cook on High 2 hours, and then on Low 2 hours.

When using fresh herbs you may want to experiment with the amounts to use, because their strength is enhanced in the slow cooker, rather than becoming weaker.

Taco Bean Soup

Karen Waggoner   Joplin, MO

MAKES: **12 SERVINGS**
PREP. TIME: **10 MINUTES**
COOKING TIME: **1½ HOURS**
IDEAL SLOW COOKER SIZE: **6-QUART**

¾ lb. lean pork sausage

1 lb. extra-lean ground beef

1 envelope dry low-sodium taco seasoning

4 cups water

2 16-oz. cans kidney beans, rinsed and drained

2 14½-oz. cans low-sodium stewed tomatoes

2 14½-oz. cans diced Mexican tomatoes with juice

16-oz. jar chunky salsa

1. Cook sausage and beef in a nonstick skillet over medium heat until no longer pink. Spoon into slow cooker.
2. Add taco seasoning and mix well.
3. Stir in water, beans, tomatoes, and salsa.
4. Cover. Cook on High 1 hour.
5. Uncover. Cook another 30 minutes. Stir occasionally. Serve.

Per Serving: 320 calories (130 calories from fat), 14g total fat (5g saturated, 0g trans), 40mg cholesterol, 1830mg sodium, 27g total carbohydrate (7g fiber, 8g sugar), 20g protein, 20%DV vitamin A, 10%DV vitamin C, 10%DV calcium, 20%DV iron.

Tip: *If your diet allows, you may want to garnish individual servings with low-fat sour cream, shredded low-fat cheddar cheese, and a sprinkling of sliced ripe olives.*

Bean and Ham Soup

Dolores Kratz   Souderton, PA

Light

MAKES: **10 SERVINGS**
PREP. TIME: **30 MINUTES**
SOAKING TIME: **8 HOURS, OR OVERNIGHT**
COOKING TIME: **9–11 HOURS**
IDEAL SLOW COOKER SIZE: **7-QUART, OR 2 4-QUART COOKERS**

1 lb. mixed dry beans

ham bone from half a ham butt

1½ cups ham, cubed

1 large chopped onion

¾ cup chopped celery

¾ cup sliced or chopped carrots

15-oz. can low-sodium diced tomatoes

2 Tbsp. chopped parsley

1 cup low-sodium tomato juice

5 cups water

2 Tbsp. Worcestershire sauce

1 bay leaf

1 tsp. prepared mustard

½ tsp. chili powder

juice of 1 lemon

1 tsp. salt

½ tsp. black pepper

1. Place beans in saucepan. Cover with water and soak overnight. Drain.
2. Cover beans with fresh water and cook in saucepan 30 minutes uncovered. Drain again. Discard water.
3. Combine beans with remaining ingredients in slow cooker.
4. Cover. Cook on Low 9–11 hours.
5. Remove bay leaf and ham bone before serving.

Per Serving: 220 calories (30 calories from fat), 3g total fat (0.5g saturated, 0g trans), 20mg cholesterol, 200mg sodium, 34g total carbohydrate (11g fiber, 7g sugar), 17g protein, 50%DV vitamin A, 10%DV vitamin C, 10%DV calcium, 25%DV iron.

Note: *I chop the vegetables and mix the other ingredients together in the evening and then refrigerate them overnight. I have less work in the morning. A wonderful aroma greets the family as they come home for the evening meal. And it's healthy, too!*

French Market Soup

Ethel Mumaw   Berlin, OH

MAKES: **8 SERVINGS (2½ QUARTS)**
PREP. TIME: **10 MINUTES**
COOKING TIME: **10 HOURS**
IDEAL SLOW COOKER SIZE: **4-QUART**

2 cups dry bean mix, washed with stones removed

2 quarts water

1 ham hock

1 tsp. salt

¼ tsp. pepper

16-oz. can tomatoes

1 large onion, chopped

1 garlic clove, minced

1 chili pepper, chopped, *or* 1 tsp. chili powder

¼ cup lemon juice

1. Combine all ingredients in slow cooker.
2. Cover. Cook on Low 8 hours. Turn to High and cook an additional 2 hours, or until beans are tender.
3. Debone ham, cut meat into bite-sized pieces, and stir back into soup.

To chop onions painlessly, place your cutting board on a front unheated burner. Turn on the rear burner and chop the onions. The heat from the back burner will pull the "teary" oils away from you.

Black Bean and Ham Soup

Janie Steele   Moore, OK

MAKES: **18 SERVINGS (5–6 QUARTS)**
PREP. TIME: **20 MINUTES**
SOAKING TIME: **8 HOURS, OR OVERNIGHT**
COOKING TIME: **7½–10 HOURS**
IDEAL SLOW COOKER SIZE: **6-QUART OR 2 4–5-QUART**

4 cups dry black beans

5 quarts water

ham bone, ham pieces, *or* **ham hocks**

3 bunches of green onions, thinly sliced

4 bay leaves

1 Tbsp. salt

¼–½ tsp. pepper

3 cloves minced garlic

4 celery ribs, chopped

3 large onions, chopped

10½-oz. can consomme

½ cup butter

2½ Tbsp. flour

½ cup minced parsley

1 cup Madeira wine, *optional*

chopped parsley

1. In 6-quart slow cooker, soak beans in 5 quarts water for 8 hours. Rinse. Drain. Pour beans back into slow cooker, or divide between 2 4–5-quart cookers.
2. Add ham, green onions, bay, salt, pepper, garlic, celery, and onions. Pour in consomme. Add water to cover vegetables and meat.
3. Cover. Cook on High 1½–2 hours. Reduce heat to Low and cook for 6–8 hours.
4. Remove ham bones and bay leaves. Cut ham off bones and set meat aside.
5. Force vegetable mixture through sieve, if you wish.
6. Taste and adjust seasonings, adding more salt and pepper if needed. Return cooked ingredients and cut-up ham to cooker.
7. In saucepan, melt ½ cup butter. Stir in flour until smooth. Stir into soup to thicken and enrich.
8. Prior to serving, add wine to heated soup mixture. Garnish with chopped parsley.

Northern Bean Soup

Patricia Howard   Albuquerque, NM

MAKES: **6–8 SERVINGS**
PREP. TIME: **15 MINUTES**
SOAKING TIME: **8 HOURS, OR OVERNIGHT**
COOKING TIME: **12–14 HOURS**
IDEAL SLOW COOKER SIZE: **4-QUART**

1 lb. dry Northern beans

1 lb. ham

2 medium onions, chopped

half a green pepper, chopped

1 cup chopped celery

16-oz. can diced tomatoes

4 carrots, peeled and chopped

4-oz. can green chili peppers

1 tsp. garlic powder

1–2 quarts water

2–3 tsp. salt

1. Wash beans. Cover with water and soak overnight. Drain. Pour into slow cooker.
2. Dice ham into 1-inch pieces. Add to beans.
3. Stir in remaining ingredients.
4. Cover. Cook on High 2 hours, then on Low 10–12 hours, or until beans are tender.

Caribbean-Style Black Bean Soup

Sheryl Shenk   Harrisonburg, VA

MAKES: **8–10 SERVINGS**
PREP. TIME: **10 MINUTES**
SOAKING TIME: **8 HOURS, OR OVERNIGHT**
COOKING TIME: **4–10 HOURS**
IDEAL SLOW COOKER SIZE: **4-QUART**

1 lb. dried black beans, washed and stones removed

3 onions, chopped

1 green pepper, chopped

4 coves garlic, minced

1 ham hock, *or* ¾ cup cubed ham

1 Tbsp. oil

1 Tbsp. ground cumin

2 tsp. dried oregano

1 tsp. dried thyme

1 Tbsp. salt

½ tsp. pepper

3 cups water

2 Tbsp. vinegar

sour cream

fresh chopped cilantro

1. Soak beans overnight in 4 quarts water. Drain.
2. Combine beans, onions, green pepper, garlic, ham, oil, cumin, oregano, thyme, salt, pepper, and 3 cups fresh water. Stir well.
3. Cover. Cook on Low 8–10 hours, or on High 4–5 hours.
4. For a thick soup, remove half of cooked bean mixture and puree until smooth in blender or mash with potato masher. Return to cooker. If you like a thinner soup, leave as is.
5. Add vinegar and stir well. Debone ham, cut into bite-sized pieces, and return to soup.
6. Serve in soup bowls with a dollop of sour cream in the middle of each individual serving, topped with fresh cilantro.

Slow Cooker Black Bean Chili

Mary Seielstad   Sparks, NV

MAKES: **8 SERVINGS**
PREP. TIME: **10 MINUTES**
COOKING TIME: **6–8 HOURS**
IDEAL SLOW COOKER SIZE: **4-QUART**

1 lb. pork tenderloin, cut into 1-inch chunks

16-oz. jar thick chunky salsa

3 15-oz. cans black beans, rinsed and drained

½ cup chicken broth

1 medium red bell pepper, chopped

1 medium onion, chopped

1 tsp. ground cumin

2–3 tsp. chili powder

1–1½ tsp. dried oregano

¼ cup sour cream

1. Combine all ingredients except sour cream in slow cooker.
2. Cover. Cook on Low 6–8 hours, or until pork is tender.
3. Garnish individual servings with sour cream.

Pinto Beans and Ham

Barbara Walker Sturgis, SD

MAKES: **10 SERVINGS**
PREP. TIME: **10 MINUTES**
SOAKING TIME: **6–8 HOURS, OR OVERNIGHT**
COOKING TIME: **10 HOURS**
IDEAL SLOW COOKER SIZE: **5-QUART**

1 lb. dried pinto beans

5½ cups water

¼ lb. cooked ham, chopped

1 clove garlic, minced

1 Tbsp. chili powder

1 tsp. salt

1 tsp. black pepper

¼ tsp. dried oregano

¼ tsp. ground cumin

1. Cover bean with water and soak overnight, or 6–8 hours.
2. In the morning, drain and rinse beans, discard soaking water, and put beans in slow cooker.
3. Add remaining ingredients, including 5½ cups fresh water.
4. Cover. Cook on Low 10 hours.
5. Stir once or twice if possible during cooking time.

Per Serving: 60 calories (10 calories from fat), 1g total fat (0g saturated, 0g trans), 5mg cholesterol, 520mg sodium, 8g total carbohydrate (2g fiber, 1g sugar), 4g protein, 6%DV vitamin A, 2%DV vitamin C, 2%DV calcium, 6%DV iron.

Overnight Bean Soup

Marie Morucci Glen Lyon, PA

MAKES: **6–8 SERVINGS**
PREP. TIME: **10 MINUTES**
SOAKING TIME: **1 HOUR, OR OVERNIGHT**
COOKING TIME: **5¼–11¼ HOURS**
IDEAL SLOW COOKER SIZE: **5-QUART**

1 lb. dry small white beans

6 cups water

2 cups boiling water

2 large carrots, diced

3 ribs celery, diced

2 tsp. chicken bouillon granules, *or* 2 chicken bouillon cubes

1 bay leaf

½ tsp. dried thyme

½ tsp. salt

¼ tsp. pepper

¼ cup chopped fresh parsley

1 envelope dry onion soup mix

crispy, crumbled bacon, *optional*

1. Rinse beans. Combine beans and 6 cups water in saucepan. Bring to boil. Reduce heat to low and simmer 2 minutes. Remove from heat. Cover and let stand 1 hour or overnight.
2. Place beans and soaking water in slow cooker. Add 2 cups boiling water, carrots, celery, bouillon, bay leaf, thyme, salt, and pepper.
3. Cover. Cook on High 5-5½ hours, or on Low 10-11 hours, until beans are tender.
4. Stir in parsley and soup mix. Cover. Cook on High 10-15 minutes.
5. Remove bay leaf. Garnish individual servings with bacon.

Navy Bean and Bacon Chowder

Ruth A. Feister Narvon, PA

MAKES: **6 SERVINGS**
PREP. TIME: **15 MINUTES**
SOAKING TIME: **8 HOURS, OR OVERNIGHT**
COOKING TIME: **7¼–9¼ HOURS**
IDEAL SLOW COOKER SIZE: **5-QUART**

1½ cups dried navy beans

2 cups cold water

8 slices bacon, cooked and crumbled

2 medium carrots, sliced

1 rib celery, sliced

1 medium onion, chopped

1 tsp. dried Italian seasoning

⅛ tsp. pepper

46-oz. can chicken broth

1 cup milk

1. Soak beans in 2 cups cold water for 8 hours or overnight.
2. After beans have soaked, drain, if necessary, and place in slow cooker.
3. Add all remaining ingredients, except milk, to slow cooker.
4. Cover. Cook on Low 7–9 hours, or until beans are crisp-tender.
5. Place 2 cups cooked bean mixture into blender. Process until smooth. Return to slow cooker.
6. Add milk. Cover and heat on High 10 minutes.
7. Serve with crusty French bread and additional herbs and seasonings for diners to add as they wish.

Beans with Kielbasa

Colleen Heatwole Burton, MI

MAKES: **8 SERVINGS**
PREP. TIME: **10 MINUTES**
COOKING TIME: **6–8 HOURS**
IDEAL SLOW COOKER SIZE: **4-QUART**

1 medium green bell pepper, chopped

15½-oz. can Great Northern beans

15½-oz. can pinto beans

14½-oz. can low-sodium stewed tomatoes, *or* diced tomatoes with green chilies

8-oz. can low-sodium tomato sauce

1 large onion, chopped

1 lb. reduced-fat smoked turkey kielbasa, cut in 1-inch pieces

1 clove garlic, minced

¼ tsp. black pepper

1. Combine all ingredients in slow cooker.
2. Cover. Cook on Low 6–8 hours.

Per Serving: 210 calories (45 calories from fat), 5g total fat (1.5g saturated, 0g trans), 35mg cholesterol, 1010mg sodium, 25g total carbohydrate (7g fiber, 6g sugar), 15g protein, 10%DV vitamin A, 20%DV vitamin C, 8%DV calcium, 15%DV iron.

Tip: *This is juicy enough to serve over rice, mashed potatoes, or your favorite pasta.*

Sauerkraut-Sausage Bean Soup

Bonnie Goering   Bridgewater, VA

MAKES: **8–10 SERVINGS**
PREP. TIME: **10 MINUTES**
COOKING TIME: **2–3 HOURS**
IDEAL SLOW COOKER SIZE: **3–4-QUART**

3 15-oz. cans white beans, undrained

16-oz. can sauerkraut, drained and rinsed

1 lb. link sausage, sliced

¼ cup brown sugar

½ cup ketchup

1. Combine all ingredients in slow cooker.
2. Cover. Cook on High 2–3 hours.
3. Serve with cornbread, applesauce, or coleslaw.

Variation: *You may add tomato juice or water if you prefer a thinner soup.*

Sausage and Black Bean Stew

John D. Allen   Rye, CO

MAKES: **6 SERVINGS**
PREP. TIME: **20 MINUTES**
COOKING TIME: **5½–7½ HOURS**
IDEAL SLOW COOKER SIZE: **6-QUART**

3 15-oz. cans black beans, drained and rinsed

14½-oz. can fat-free, reduced-sodium chicken broth

1 cup celery, sliced

2 4-oz. cans green chilies, chopped

3 cloves garlic, minced

1½ tsp. dried oregano

¾ tsp. coriander, ground

½ tsp. ground cumin

¼ tsp. ground red pepper (not cayenne)

1 lb. link turkey sausage, thinly sliced and cooked

1. Combine all ingredients in slow cooker except sausage.
2. Cover. Cook on Low 5–7 hours.
3. Remove 1½ cups of the bean mixture and puree in blender. Return to slow cooker.
4. Add sliced sausage.
5. Cover. Cook on Low 30 minutes.

Per Serving: 310 calories (80 calories from fat), 9g total fat (2g saturated, 0g trans), 55mg cholesterol, 1580mg sodium, 36g total carbohydrate (13g fiber, 2g sugar), 28g protein, 2%DV vitamin A, 2%DV vitamin C, 15%DV calcium, 25%DV iron.

Variation: *If your diet permits, you may want to add ¾ tsp. salt to Step 1.*

Football Bean Serve

Dianna R. Milhizer   Brighton, MI

MAKES: **12 SERVINGS**
PREP. TIME: **20 MINUTES**
COOKING TIME: **6–8 HOURS**
IDEAL SLOW COOKER SIZE: **4-QUART**

1 lb. ground turkey

1 cup minced onions

2 cups diced celery

2 cups diced carrots

2 15-oz. cans kidney beans, drained and rinsed

2 15-oz. cans pinto beans, drained and rinsed

2 15-oz. cans diced tomatoes

2 cups water

1 Tbsp. garlic powder

1 Tbsp. parsley flakes

1 Tbsp. dried oregano

1 Tbsp. ground cumin

1 Tbsp. salt

1. Brown turkey with onions in a nonstick skillet over medium heat. Add celery and carrots and cook until just wilted. Place in slow cooker.
2. Add remaining ingredients. Stir to combine.
3. Cover. Cook on Low 6–8 hours.
4. Serve over brown rice. If you wish, sprinkle baked tortilla chips over top.

Per Serving: 200 calories (15 calories from fat), 1.5g total fat (0g saturated, 0g trans), 15mg cholesterol, 1280mg sodium, 29g total carbohydrate (8g fiber, 6g sugar), 18g protein, 100%DV vitamin A, 10%DV vitamin C, 10%DV calcium, 20%DV iron.

Tips:

1. This is a perfect dish to serve after an afternoon of football games.

2. This is a high-fiber meal. I usually cook dried beans from scratch the night before making the soup. You can adjust the spices, adding more or less to suit your taste.

3. If you start with dried beans, you can cook them whenever it's convenient for you and keep them in the freezer until you need them. You can then use them for soups or stews, or puree them for tacos or sandwiches.

Beef 'n Black Bean Soup

Deborah Santiago   Lancaster, PA

MAKES: **10 SERVINGS (2½ QUARTS)**
PREP. TIME: **30 MINUTES**
COOKING TIME: **5–7 HOURS**
IDEAL SLOW COOKER SIZE: **4–5-QUART**

1 lb. extra-lean ground beef

2 14½-oz. cans fat-free, low-sodium chicken broth

14½-oz. can low-sodium, diced tomatoes, undrained

8 green onions, thinly sliced

3 medium carrots, thinly sliced

2 celery ribs, thinly sliced

2 garlic cloves, minced

1 Tbsp. sugar

1½ tsp. dried basil

½ tsp. salt

½ tsp. dried oregano

½ tsp. ground cumin

½ tsp. chili powder

2 15-oz. cans black beans, rinsed and drained

1½ cups rice, cooked

1. In a nonstick skillet over medium heat, cook beef until no longer pink. Drain.
2. Place beef in slow cooker.
3. Add remaining ingredients except black beans and rice.
4. Cover. Cook on High 1 hour.
5. Reduce to Low. Cook 4–5 hours, or until vegetables are tender.
6. Add beans and rice.
7. Cook 1 hour longer on Low, or until heated through.

Per Serving: 200 calories (40 calories from fat), 4.5g total fat (1.5g saturated, 0g trans), 15mg cholesterol, 640mg sodium, 23g total carbohydrate (6g fiber, 4g sugar), 17g protein, 6%DV vitamin A, 10%DV vitamin C, 8%DV calcium, 20%DV iron.

Variation: *If you enjoy tomatoes, you can brighten the flavor by adding a second 14½-oz. can of diced tomatoes, undrained.*

Mexican Rice and Bean Soup

Esther J. Mast   East Petersburg, PA

MAKES: **6 SERVINGS**
PREP. TIME: **15–20 MINUTES**
COOKING TIME: **6 HOURS**
IDEAL SLOW COOKER SIZE: **4–5-QUART**

½ cup chopped onions
⅓ cup chopped green peppers
1 garlic clove, minced
1 Tbsp. oil
4-oz. pkg. sliced or chipped dried beef
18-oz. can tomato juice
15½-oz. can red kidney beans, undrained
1½ cups water
½ cup long-grain rice, uncooked
1 tsp. paprika
½–1 tsp. chili powder
½ tsp. salt
dash of pepper

1. Cook onions, green peppers, and garlic in oil in skillet until vegetables are tender but not brown. Transfer to slow cooker.
2. Tear beef into small pieces and add to slow cooker.
3. Add remaining ingredients. Mix well.
4. Cover. Cook on Low 6 hours. Stir before serving.

5. Serve with relish tray and cornbread, home-canned fruit, and cookies.

Note: *This is a recipe I fixed often when our sons were growing up. We have all enjoyed it in any season of the year.*

Turkey-Sausage Stew

Sheridy Steele   Ardmore, OK

MAKES: **6 SERVINGS**
PREP. TIME: **20 MINUTES**
COOKING TIME: **8–9 HOURS**
IDEAL SLOW COOKER SIZE: **3½–4-QUART**

½ lb. turkey sausage, removed from casing
1 large onion, chopped
2 garlic cloves, minced
¾ cup chopped carrots
1 fennel bulb, chopped
½ cup chopped celery
10¾-oz. can fat-free, reduced-sodium chicken broth
3 medium tomatoes, peeled, seeded, and chopped
1 tsp. dried basil
1 tsp. dried oregano
¼ tsp. salt
1 cup shell pasta, uncooked
15-oz. can navy beans, drained and rinsed
½ cup low-fat Parmesan cheese

1. In nonstick skillet, brown turkey sausage, onion, and garlic. Drain well.
2. Combine all ingredients except cheese in slow cooker.
3. Cook on Low 8–9 hours.
4. Sprinkle with cheese to serve.

Per Serving: 280 calories (60 calories from fat), 7 total fat (2.5g saturated, 0g trans), 35mg cholesterol, 930mg sodium, 36g total carbohydrate (7g fiber, 6g sugar), 20g protein, 80%DV vitamin A, 20%DV vitamin C, 20%DV calcium, 20%DV iron.

White Bean Fennel Soup

Janie Steele Moore, OK

MAKES: **6 SERVINGS**
PREP. TIME: **15 MINUTES**
COOKING TIME: **1–3 HOURS**
IDEAL SLOW COOKER SIZE: **5-QUART**

1 Tbsp. olive *or* canola oil
1 large onion, chopped
1 small fennel bulb, thinly sliced
5 cups fat-free chicken broth
15-oz. can white kidney *or* cannellini beans, rinsed and
   drained
14½-oz. can diced tomatoes, undrained
1 tsp. dried thyme
¼ tsp. black pepper
1 bay leaf
3 cups chopped fresh spinach

1. Sauté onions and fennel in oil in skillet until brown.
2. Combine onions, fennel, broth, beans, tomatoes, thyme, pepper, and bay leaf.
3. Cook on Low for several hours, or on High for 1 hour, until fennel and onions are tender.
4. Remove bay leaf.
5. Add spinach about 10 minutes before serving.

Per Serving: 160 calories (25 calories from fat), 3g total fat (0g saturated, 0g trans), 0mg cholesterol, 690mg sodium, 22g total carbohydrate (8g fiber, 4g sugar), 13g protein, 100%DV vitamin A, 40%DV vitamin C, 20%DV calcium, 35%DV iron.

Crockpot Bean Soup

Betty B. Dennison Grove City, PA

MAKES: **6 SERVINGS**
PREP. TIME: **30 MINUTES**
COOKING TIME: **4–5 HOURS**
IDEAL SLOW COOKER SIZE: **6-QUART**

3 15-oz. cans pinto beans, undrained
3 15-oz. cans Great Northern beans, undrained
4 cups chicken *or* vegetable broth
3 potatoes, peeled and chopped
4 carrots, sliced
2 celery ribs, sliced
1 large onion, chopped
1 green pepper, chopped
1 sweet red pepper, chopped, *optional*
2 garlic cloves, minced
1 tsp. salt, or to taste
¼ tsp. pepper, or to taste
1 bay leaf, *optional*
½ tsp. liquid barbecue smoke, *optional*

1. Empty beans into 6-quart slow cooker, or divide ingredients between 2 4–5-quart cookers.
2. Cover. Cook on Low while preparing vegetables.
3. Cook broth and vegetables in stockpot until vegetables are tender-crisp. Transfer to slow cooker.
4. Add remaining ingredients and mix well.
5. Cover. Cook on Low 4–5 hours.
6. Serve with tossed salad, Italian bread, or cornbread.

Tips:

1. You can add the broth and vegetables to the cooker without cooking them in advance. Simply extend the slow-cooker cooking time to 8 hours on Low.

2. This is a stress-free recipe when you're expecting guests, but you're not sure of their arrival time. Crockpot Bean Soup can burble on Low heat for longer than its appointed cooking time without being damaged.

3. Make a tossed salad and have the dressing ready to go. Add dressing to salad as your guests make their way to the table.

Southwestern Bean Soup with Cornmeal Dumplings

Melba Eshleman Manheim, PA

MAKES: **4 SERVINGS**
PREP. TIME: **20 MINUTES**
COOKING TIME: **4½–12½ HOURS**
IDEAL SLOW COOKER SIZE: **5-QUART**

15½-oz. can red kidney beans, rinsed and drained

15½-oz. can black beans, pinto beans, *or* Great Northern beans, rinsed and drained

3 cups water

14½-oz. can Mexican-style stewed tomatoes

10-oz. pkg. frozen whole-kernel corn, thawed

1 cup sliced carrots

1 cup chopped onions

4-oz. can chopped green chilies

2 Tbsp. instant beef, chicken, *or* vegetable bouillon granules

1–2 tsp. chili powder

2 cloves garlic, minced

Dumplings:

⅓ cup flour

¼ cup yellow cornmeal

1 tsp. baking powder

dash of salt

dash of pepper

1 egg white, beaten

2 Tbsp. milk

1 Tbsp. oil

1. Combine 11 soup ingredients in slow cooker.
2. Cover. Cook on Low 10–12 hours, or on High 4–5 hours.
3. Make dumplings by mixing together flour, cornmeal, baking powder, salt, and pepper.
4. Combine egg white, milk, and oil. Add to flour mixture. Stir with fork until just combined.
5. At the end of the soup's cooking time, turn slow cooker to High. Drop dumpling

mixture by rounded teaspoonfuls to make 8 mounds atop the soup.
6. Cover. Cook for 30 minutes (do not lift cover).

Garbanzo Souper

Willard E. Roth Elkhart, IN

MAKES: **6 SERVINGS**
PREP. TIME: **20 MINUTES**
SOAKING TIME: **8 HOURS, OR OVERNIGHT**
COOKING TIME: **6 HOURS**
IDEAL SLOW COOKER SIZE: **4-QUART**

1 lb. dry garbanzo beans

4 ozs. raw baby carrots, cut in halves

1 large onion, diced

3 ribs celery, cut in 1-inch pieces

1 large green pepper, diced

½ tsp. dried basil

½ tsp. dried oregano

½ tsp. dried rosemary

½ tsp. dried thyme

2 28-oz. cans vegetable broth

1 broth can of water

8-oz. can tomato sauce

8 ozs. prepared hummus

½ tsp. sea salt

1. Soak beans overnight. Drain. Place in bottom of slow cooker.
2. Add carrots, onion, celery, and green pepper.
3. Sprinkle with basil, oregano, rosemary, and thyme.
4. Cover with broth and water.
5. Cover. Cook on High 6 hours.
6. Half an hour before serving, stir in tomato sauce, hummus, and salt. Cook until hot.
7. Serve with Irish soda bread and lemon curd.

Note: *A fine meal for vegetarians on St. Patrick's Day!*

Black Bean and Tomato Soup

Sue Tjon   Austin, TX

MAKES: **6 SERVINGS**
PREP. TIME: **10–15 MINUTES**
SOAKING TIME: **8 HOURS, OR OVERNIGHT**
COOKING TIME: **8 HOURS**
IDEAL SLOW COOKER SIZE: **4-QUART**

1-lb. bag black beans
2 10-oz. cans Rotel tomatoes
1 medium onion, chopped
1 medium green bell pepper, chopped
1 Tbsp. minced garlic
14½-oz. can chicken *or* vegetable broth
water
Cajun seasoning to taste

1. Cover beans with water and soak for 8 hours or overnight. Drain well. Place beans in slow cooker.
2. Add tomatoes, onions, pepper, garlic, and chicken or vegetable broth. Add water just to cover beans. Add Cajun seasoning.
3. Cover. Cook on High 8 hours. Mash some of the beans before serving for a thicker consistency.
4. Serve over rice or in black bean tacos.

Tip: *Leftovers freeze well.*

Hearty Bean and Vegetable Soup

Jewel Showalter   Landisville, PA

MAKES: **6–8 SERVINGS**
PREP. TIME: **20–25 MINUTES**
COOKING TIME: **6–8 HOURS**
IDEAL SLOW COOKER SIZE: **5-QUART**

2 medium onions, sliced
2 garlic cloves, minced
2 Tbsp. olive oil
8 cups chicken *or* vegetable broth
1 small head cabbage, chopped
2 large red potatoes, chopped
2 cups chopped celery
2 cups chopped carrots
4 cups corn
2 tsp. dried basil
1 tsp. dried marjoram
¼ tsp. dried oregano
1 tsp. salt
½ tsp. pepper
2 15-oz. cans navy beans

1. Sauté onions and garlic in oil. Transfer to large slow cooker.
2. Add remaining ingredients, mixing together well.
3. Cover. Cook on Low 6–8 hours.

Note: *I discovered this recipe after my husband's heart attack. It's a great nutritious soup using only a little fat.*

Variation: *Add 2–3 cups cooked and cut-up chicken 30 minutes before serving if you wish.*

Wintertime Vegetable Chili

Maricarol Magill Freehold, NJ

MAKES: **6 SERVINGS**
PREP. TIME: **20 MINUTES**
COOKING TIME: **6–8 HOURS**
IDEAL SLOW COOKER SIZE: **6-QUART**

1 medium butternut squash, peeled and cubed

2 medium carrots, peeled and diced

1 medium onion, diced

3 tsp.–3 Tbsp. chili powder, depending upon how hot you like your chili

2 14-oz. cans diced tomatoes

4-oz. can chopped mild green chilies

1 tsp. salt, *optional*

1 cup vegetable broth

2 16-oz. cans black beans, drained and rinsed

sour cream, *optional*

1. In slow cooker, layer ingredients in order given—except sour cream.
2. Cover. Cook on Low 6–8 hours, or until vegetables are tender.
3. Stir before serving.
4. Top individual servings with dollops of sour cream.
5. Serve with crusty French bread.

Norma's Vegetarian Chili

Kathy Hertzler Lancaster, PA

MAKES: **8–10 SERVINGS**
PREP. TIME: **20 MINUTES**
COOKING TIME: **8½ HOURS**
IDEAL SLOW COOKER SIZE: **5-QUART**

2 Tbsp. oil

2 cups minced celery

1½ cups chopped green pepper

1 cup minced onions

4 garlic cloves, minced

5½ cups stewed tomatoes

2 1-lb. cans kidney beans, undrained

1½–2 cups raisins

¼ cup wine vinegar

1 Tbsp. chopped parsley

2 tsp. salt

1½ tsp. dried oregano

1½ tsp. cumin

¼ tsp. pepper

¼ tsp. Tabasco sauce

1 bay leaf

¾ cup cashews

1 cup shredded cheese, *optional*

1. Combine all ingredients except cashews and cheese in slow cooker.
2. Cover. Simmer on Low for 8 hours. Add cashews and simmer 30 minutes.
3. Garnish individual servings with shredded cheese.

Use freshly ground black pepper and freshly picked herbs to add an extra pop of flavor.

Black-Eyed Pea and Vegetable Chili

Julie Weaver Reinholds, PA

MAKES: **4–6 SERVINGS**
PREP. TIME: **20 MINUTES**
COOKING TIME: **4–8 HOURS**
IDEAL SLOW COOKER SIZE: **4-QUART**

MEATLESS

1 cup finely chopped onions

1 cup finely chopped carrots

1 cup finely chopped red *or* green pepper, *or* mixture of two

1 garlic clove, minced

4 tsp. chili powder

1 tsp. ground cumin

2 Tbsp. chopped cilantro

14½-oz. can diced tomatoes

3 cups black-eyed peas, cooked *or* 2 15-oz. cans black-eyed peas, drained

4-oz. can chopped green chilies

¾ cup orange juice

¾ cup water *or* broth

1 Tbsp. cornstarch

2 Tbsp. water

½ cup shredded cheddar cheese

2 Tbsp. chopped cilantro

1. Combine all ingredients except cornstarch, 2 Tbsp. water, cheese, and cilantro.
2. Cover. Cook on Low 6–8 hours, or High 4 hours.
3. Dissolve cornstarch in water. Stir into soup mixture 30 minutes before serving.
4. Garnish individual servings with cheese and cilantro.

Taco Twist Soup

Janie Steele Moore, OK

MAKES: **6–8 SERVINGS**
PREP. TIME: **10 MINUTES**
COOKING TIME: **4–6 HOURS**
IDEAL SLOW COOKER SIZE: **3–4-QUART**

Light MEATLESS

1 medium onion, chopped

2 garlic cloves, minced

2 Tbsp. canola *or* olive oil

3 cups reduced-sodium beef broth *or* vegetable broth

15-oz. can black beans, rinsed and drained

14½-oz. can diced tomatoes, undrained

1½ cups picante sauce

1 cup spiral pasta, uncooked

1 small green bell pepper, chopped

2 tsp. chili powder

1 tsp. ground cumin

½ cup shredded reduced-fat cheese

fat-free sour cream, *optional*

1. Sauté onions and garlic in oil in skillet.
2. Combine all ingredients except cheese and sour cream.
3. Cook on Low 4–6 hours, or just until pasta is tender.
4. Add cheese and sour cream as desired when serving.

Per Serving: 220 calories (60 calories from fat), 6g total fat (1g saturated, 0g trans), 0mg cholesterol, 1060mg sodium, 31g total carbohydrate (6g fiber, 6g sugar), 11g protein, 10%DV vitamin A, 20%DV vitamin C, 10%DV calcium, 10%DV iron.

Variation: *An alternative method is to cook the pasta in 3 cups broth on the top of the stove in a saucepan, and then add it (along with the broth in which it cooked) during the last 15 minutes of the Soup's cooking time. That would allow the Soup to cook longer without risking mushy noodles, if that better fits your schedule.*

White Bean and Barley Soup

Sharon Miller Holmesville, OH

MAKES: **12 SERVINGS**
PREP. TIME: **15 MINUTES**
COOKING TIME: **8–10 HOURS**
IDEAL SLOW COOKER SIZE: **6-QUART**

1 large onion, chopped
2 garlic cloves, minced
1 Tbsp. olive *or* canola oil
2 24-oz. cans Great Northern beans (or equal amount prepared from dried beans), undrained
4 cups no-fat, low-sodium chicken broth
4 cups water
2 large carrots, chunked
2 medium green *or* red bell peppers, chunked
2 celery ribs, chunked
½ cup quick-cooking barley
¼ cup chopped fresh parsley
2 bay leaves
½ tsp. dried thyme
¼ tsp. black pepper
28-oz. can diced tomatoes, undrained

1. Sauté onion and garlic in oil in skillet until just wilted.
2. Combine all ingredients in slow cooker.
3. Cook on Low 8–10 hours.
4. Discard bay leaves before serving.

Per Serving: 210 calories (15 calories from fat), 2g total fat (0g saturated, 0g trans), 0mg cholesterol, 260mg sodium, 36g total carbohydrate (9g fiber, 6g sugar), 12g protein, 50%DV vitamin A, 20%DV vitamin C, 15%DV calcium, 20%DV iron.

Variations:

1. If you wish, use pearl barley instead of quick-cooking, but cook it on the stove and add it halfway through the cooking cycle.

2. If you want, and your diet allows, you may want to add ½–¾ tsp. salt in Step 2.

Pasta and Bean Stew

Dale Peterson Rapid City, SD

MAKES: **6 SERVINGS**
PREP. TIME: **10 MINUTES**
COOKING TIME: **5–6 HOURS**
IDEAL SLOW COOKER SIZE: **3½-QUART**

1 cup chopped tomatoes
¾ cup macaroni shells, uncooked
¼ cup chopped onions
¼ cup chopped green bell peppers
1 tsp. dried basil leaves
1 tsp. Worcestershire sauce
1 clove garlic, chopped
15-oz. can kidney beans, drained
8-oz. can garbanzo beans, drained
14½-oz. can fat-free chicken broth

1. Combine all ingredients in slow cooker.
2. Cook on Low 5–6 hours.

Per Serving: 200 calories (10 calories from fat), 1g total fat (0g saturated, 0g trans), 0mg cholesterol, 510mg sodium, 37g total carbohydrate (6g fiber, 5g sugar), 11g protein, 6%DV vitamin A, 15%DV vitamin C, 6%DV calcium, 20%DV iron.

Variation: *To add some zing, stir in ⅓ cup salsa during last 15 minutes of cooking time.*

If you can read a recipe and follow directions, you can cook.

Black Bean and Corn Soup

Joy Sutter   Iowa City, IA

MAKES: **6–8 SERVINGS**
PREP. TIME: **10 MINUTES**
COOKING TIME: **5–6 HOURS**
IDEAL SLOW COOKER SIZE: **4-QUART**

2 15-oz. cans black beans, drained and rinsed

14½-oz. can Mexican stewed tomatoes, undrained

14½-oz. can diced tomatoes, undrained

11-oz. can whole-kernel corn, drained

4 green onions, sliced

2–3 Tbsp. chili powder

1 tsp. ground cumin

½ tsp. dried minced garlic

1. Combine all ingredients in slow cooker.
2. Cover. Cook on High 5–6 hours.

Variations:

1. Use 2 cloves fresh garlic, minced, instead of dried garlic.

2. Add 1 large rib celery, sliced thinly, and 1 small green pepper, chopped.

Mexican Black Bean Soup

Becky Harder   Monument, CO

MAKES: **8 SERVINGS**
PREP. TIME: **10 MINUTES**
COOKING TIME: **6–8 HOURS**
IDEAL SLOW COOKER SIZE: **4-QUART**

28-oz. can fat-free low-sodium chicken broth

1 cup chopped onions

2 tsp. minced garlic

3 cups fat-free black beans

2 tsp. chili powder

¾ tsp. ground cumin

28-oz. can Mexican tomatoes with green chilies *or* jalapeños

¾ tsp. lemon juice

1 bunch green onions

fat-free sour cream

1. Combine all ingredients except green onions and sour cream in slow cooker.
2. Cover. Cook on Low 6–8 hours.
3. Top each individual serving with sliced green onions sprinkled over a spoonful of sour cream.

Per Serving: 130 calories (10 calories from fat), 1g total fat (0g saturated, 0g trans), 0mg cholesterol, 830mg sodium, 24g total carbohydrate (7g fiber, 4g sugar), 10g protein, 10%DV vitamin A, 4%DV vitamin C, 10%DV calcium, 15%DV iron.

Bean Soup

Joyce Cox   Port Angeles, WA

MAKES: **10–12 SERVINGS**
PREP. TIME: **10 MINUTES**
COOKING TIME: **5½–13 HOURS**
IDEAL SLOW COOKER SIZE: **4-QUART**

1 cup dry Great Northern beans

1 cup dry red beans *or* pinto beans

4 cups water

28-oz. can diced tomatoes

1 medium onion, chopped

2 Tbsp. vegetable bouillon granules, *or* 4 bouillon cubes

2 garlic cloves, minced

2 tsp. Italian seasoning, crushed

9-oz. pkg. frozen green beans, thawed

1. Soak and rinse dried beans.
2. Combine all ingredients except green beans in slow cooker.
3. Cover. Cook on High 5½–6½ hours, or on Low 11–13 hours.
4. Stir green beans into soup during last 2 hours.

Veggie Stew

Ernestine Schrepfer   Trenton, MO

MEATLESS

MAKES: **10–15 SERVINGS**
PREP. TIME: **15 MINUTES**
COOKING TIME: **9–11 HOURS**
IDEAL SLOW COOKER SIZE: **7-QUART**

5–6 potatoes, cubed

3 carrots, cubed

1 onion, chopped

½ cup chopped celery

2 cups canned diced or stewed tomatoes

3 chicken bouillon cubes dissolved in 3 cups water

1½ tsp. dried thyme

½ tsp. dried parsley

½ cup brown rice, uncooked

1 lb. frozen green beans

1 lb. frozen corn

15-oz. can butter beans

46-oz. can V-8 juice

1. Combine potatoes, carrots, onion, celery, tomatoes, chicken stock, thyme, parsley, and rice in 5-quart cooker, or two medium-sized cookers.
2. Cover. Cook on High 2 hours. Puree one cup of mixture and add back to slow cooker to thicken the soup.
3. Stir in beans, corn, butter beans, and juice.
4. Cover. Cook on High 1 more hour, then reduce to Low and cook 6–8 more hours.

Hearty Bean and Vegetable Stew

Jeanette Oberholtzer   Manheim, PA

Light MEATLESS

MAKES: **12 SERVINGS**
PREP. TIME: **20 MINUTES**
COOKING TIME: **3–7 HOURS**
IDEAL SLOW COOKER SIZE: **5-QUART**

1 lb. dry beans, assorted

2 cups fat-free vegetable broth

½ cup white wine

⅓ cup soy sauce

⅓ cup apple *or* pineapple juice, unsweetened

vegetable stock *or* water

½ cup diced celery

½ cup diced parsnips

½ cup diced carrots

½ cup sliced mushrooms

1 onion, sliced

1 tsp. dried basil

1 tsp. parsley flakes

1 bay leaf

3 cloves garlic, minced

1 tsp. black pepper

1 cup rice *or* pasta, cooked

1. Sort and rinse beans and soak overnight in water. Drain. Place in slow cooker.
2. Add vegetable juice, wine, soy sauce, and apple or pineapple juice.
3. Cover with vegetable stock or water.
4. Cover. Cook on High 2 hours.
5. Add vegetables, herbs, and spices.
6. Cover cooker. Cook on Low 5–6 hours, or until carrots and parsnips are tender.
7. Add cooked rice or pasta.
8. Cover. Cook 1 hour more.

Per Serving: 180 calories (5 calories from fat), 0.5g total fat (0g saturated, 0g trans), 0mg cholesterol, 370mg sodium, 34g total carbohydrate (9g fiber, 6g sugar), 10g protein, 35%DV vitamin A, 10%DV vitamin C, 6%DV calcium, 20%DV iron.

Variation: *Use 3 or 4 kinds of beans such as black, kidney, pinto, baby lima, lentils, or split peas.*

Garden Chili

Stacy Schmucker Stoltzfus   Enola, PA

MAKES: **10 SERVINGS**
PREP. TIME: **15 MINUTES**
COOKING TIME: **6–8 HOURS**
IDEAL SLOW COOKER SIZE: **3½–4-QUART**

¾ lb. onions, chopped

1 tsp. garlic, minced

1 Tbsp. olive oil

¾ cup chopped celery

1 large carrot, peeled and thinly sliced

1 large green bell pepper, chopped

1 small zucchini, sliced

¼ lb. fresh mushrooms, sliced

1¼ cups water

14-oz. can kidney beans, drained

14-oz. can low-sodium diced tomatoes with juice

1 tsp. lemon juice

⅛ tsp. dried oregano

1 tsp. ground cumin

1 tsp. chili powder

1 tsp. salt

1 tsp. black pepper

1. Sauté onions and garlic in olive oil in a large skillet over medium heat until tender.
2. Add remaining fresh veggies. Sauté 2-3 minutes. Transfer to slow cooker.
3. Add remaining ingredients.
4. Cover. Cook on Low 6–8 hours.

Per Serving: 80 calories (15 calories from fat), 2g total fat (0g saturated, 0g trans), 0mg cholesterol, 500mg sodium, 14g total carbohydrate (4g fiber, 5g sugar), 4g protein, 30%DV vitamin A, 20%DV vitamin C, 6%DV calcium, 6%DV iron.

Tip: *This is good served over rice.*

Vegetarian Chili with Mushrooms

Leona Yoder   Hartville, OH

MAKES: **8 SERVINGS**
PREP. TIME: **1 HOUR**
COOKING TIME: **2–6 HOURS**
IDEAL SLOW COOKER SIZE: **4-QUART**

1 cup dried pinto *or* kidney beans

3 cups water

1 Tbsp. vegetable oil

2 cups chopped onions

1 green bell pepper, seeded and chopped

2 heaping cups sliced fresh mushrooms (about 10 ozs.)

1 cup thinly sliced carrots

2 cups fresh or canned unsalted tomatoes, chopped

6-oz. can unsalted tomato paste

¾ cup water

2 Tbsp. chili powder

1 large dried bay leaf

1 Tbsp. vinegar

1–2 tsp. finely minced garlic

1. Place beans and 3 cups water in a saucepan. Bring to a boil and cook 2 minutes. Do not drain. Let sit 1 hour.
2. Pour beans into slow cooker. If water does not cover beans, add additional water to cover them.
3. Cover cooker. Cook on High 2 hours.
4. Heat oil in skillet. Add onion and green pepper. Cook until onions are transparent. Drain. Add to slow cooker.
5. Add remaining ingredients.
6. Cover. Cook on Low 4–6 hours.
7. Remove bay leaf before serving.
8. Serve over brown rice or potatoes.

Per Serving: 100 calories (25 calories from fat), 2.5g total fat (0g saturated, 0g trans), 0mg cholesterol, 170mg sodium, 19g total carbohydrate (5g fiber, 6g sugar), 4g protein, 180%DV vitamin A, 20%DV vitamin C, 4%DV calcium, 10%DV iron.

Variations:

1. Add the onions and green peppers to the cooker without cooking them in the skillet if you like.

2. If your diet allows, you may want to add 1 tsp. salt to Step 5. You can also increase the amount of chili powder and add ¼–½ tsp. black pepper.

Vegetarian Chili Soup

Rosemarie Fitzgerald   Gibsonia, PA

MAKES: **8 SERVINGS**
PREP. TIME: **10 MINUTES**
COOKING TIME: **4–9½ HOURS**
IDEAL SLOW COOKER SIZE: **5-QUART**

1 large onion, chopped

1 Tbsp. margarine

1 clove garlic, finely chopped

2 tsp. chili powder

½ tsp. dried oregano, crumbled

2 14½-oz. cans vegetable broth

14½-oz. can no-salt-added stewed or diced tomatoes

5 cups water

½ tsp. salt

¼ tsp. black pepper

¾ lb. fresh kale

⅓ cup white long-grain rice

19-oz. can cannellini beans, drained and rinsed

1. Sauté onion in skillet with margarine until tender.
2. Add garlic, chili powder, and oregano. Cook for 30 seconds. Pour into slow cooker.
3. Add remaining ingredients except kale, rice, and beans.
4. Cover. Cook on Low 7 hours, or on High 3–4 hours.
5. Cut kale stalks into small pieces and chop leaves coarsely.
6. Add to soup with rice and beans.

7. Cover. Cook on High 1–2½ hours more, or until rice is tender and kale is done to your liking.

Per Serving: 120 calories (15 calories from fat), 1.5g total fat (0g saturated, 0g trans), 0mg cholesterol, 790mg sodium, 24g total carbohydrate (6g fiber, 6g sugar), 6g protein, 80%DV vitamin A, 20%DV vitamin C, 10%DV calcium, 15%DV iron.

Ground Beef Bean Soup

Dale Peterson   Rapid City, SD

MAKES: **8 SERVINGS**
PREP. TIME: **25 MINUTES**
COOKING TIME: **3–4 HOURS**
IDEAL SLOW COOKER SIZE: **6-QUART**

2 lbs. ground beef

3 15-oz. cans pinto beans, drained

2 10¾-oz. cans tomato soup

10¾-oz. can cheddar cheese soup

salt and pepper to taste

1. Brown beef in large nonstick skillet. Drain.
2. Place browned beef in slow cooker. Add remaining ingredients and mix well.
3. Cover and cook on Low 3–4 hours, or until soup is hot and until flavors have blended.

Tip: *Serve this as a topping over rice or baked potatoes.*

Carol Eveleth   Wellman, IA

Cook enough for two meals — and you can have a break from meal preparation.

Brown-Sugar Chili

Alma Weaver   Ephrata, PA

MAKES: **8 SERVINGS**
PREP. TIME: **15 MINUTES**
COOKING TIME: **2 HOURS**
IDEAL SLOW COOKER SIZE: **3½-QUART**

1 lb. extra-lean ground beef

½ cup brown sugar

2 Tbsp. prepared mustard

1 medium onion, chopped

2 14-oz. cans kidney beans, drained

1 pint low-sodium tomato juice

½ tsp. salt

¼ tsp. black pepper

1 tsp. chili powder

1. Brown lean ground beef and onion in a nonstick skillet over medium heat. Stir brown sugar and mustard into meat.
2. Combine all ingredients in slow cooker.
3. Cover. Cook on High 2 hours. If it's convenient, stir several times during cooking.

Per Serving: 240 calories (50 calories from fat), 6g total fat (2g saturated, 0g trans), 20mg cholesterol, 590mg sodium, 32g total carbohydrate (4g fiber, 18g sugar), 17g protein, 6%DV vitamin A, 10%DV vitamin C, 6%DV calcium, 20%DV iron.

Classic Beef Chili

Esther S. Martin   Ephrata, PA

MAKES: **6 SERVINGS**
PREP. TIME: **15 MINUTES**
COOKING TIME: **4–5 HOURS**
IDEAL SLOW COOKER SIZE: **4-QUART**

1 lb. extra-lean ground beef

2 cloves garlic, chopped finely

2 Tbsp. chili powder

1 tsp. ground cumin

28-oz. can crushed tomatoes

15-oz. can red kidney beans, rinsed and drained

1 onion, chopped

4-oz. can diced chilies, undrained

2 Tbsp. tomato paste

fresh oregano sprigs for garnish

1. In a large nonstick skillet, brown beef and garlic over medium heat. Stir to break up meat. Add chili powder and cumin. Stir to combine.
2. Mix together tomatoes, beans, onion, chilies, and tomato paste in slow cooker. Add beef mixture and mix thoroughly.
3. Cook on High 4–5 hours, or until flavors are well blended.
4. Garnish with oregano to serve.

Per Serving: 280 calories (70 calories from fat), 8g total fat (3g saturated, 0g trans), 30mg cholesterol, 300mg sodium, 30g total carbohydrate (11g fiber, 3g sugar), 24g protein, 40%DV vitamin A, 20%DV vitamin C, 8%DV calcium, 20%DV iron.

Chili Bake

Michele Rubola   Selden, NY

MAKES: **6 SERVINGS**
PREP. TIME: **15 MINUTES**
COOKING TIME: **4–5 HOURS**
IDEAL SLOW COOKER SIZE: **4-QUART**

3 turkey bacon slices

½ lb. extra-lean ground round

15½-oz. can lima beans, undrained

15-oz. can pork and beans, undrained

15-oz. can red kidney beans, drained

½ cup ketchup

½ cup barbecue sauce

¼ cup firmly packed brown sugar

1 tsp. dry mustard

1. Brown bacon until crisp in nonstick skillet. Crumble and set aside.
2. Cook beef in nonstick skillet over medium heat until beef is brown, stirring to crumble beef.
3. Combine all ingredients in slow cooker. Stir well.
4. Cover and cook on High for 1 hour; then reduce to Low and cook for 3–4 hours.

Per Serving: 380 calories (60 calories from fat), 7g total fat (2g saturated, 0g trans), 25mg cholesterol, 1200mg sodium, 59g total carbohydrate (11g fiber, 24g sugar), 22g protein, 10%DV vitamin A, 10%DV vitamin C, 10%DV calcium, 25%DV iron.

Keep it simple! Use prepared foods if you need to. Grandma had more time at home to cook even though she was busy with other housework.

Mexican Casserole

Janie Steele   Moore, OK

MAKES: **8 SERVINGS**
PREP. TIME: **15 MINUTES**
COOKING TIME: **8–9 HOURS**
IDEAL SLOW COOKER SIZE: **4–5-QUART**

1 lb. extra-lean ground beef

1 medium onion, chopped

1 small green bell pepper, chopped

16-oz. can kidney beans, rinsed and drained

14½-oz. can diced tomatoes, undrained

8-oz. can tomato sauce

¼ cup water

1 envelope reduced-sodium taco seasoning

1 Tbsp. chili powder

1⅓ cups instant rice, uncooked

1 cup low-fat cheddar cheese

1. Brown ground beef and onion in nonstick skillet.
2. Combine all ingredients in slow cooker except rice and cheese.
3. Cook on Low 8–9 hours.
4. Stir in rice, cover, and cook until tender.
5. Sprinkle with cheese. Cover and cook until cheese is melted. Serve.

Per Serving: 270 calories (60 calories from fat), 7g total fat (3g saturated, 0g trans), 25mg cholesterol, 820mg sodium, 32g total carbohydrate (5g fiber, 3g sugar), 21g protein, 25%DV vitamin A, 20%DV vitamin C, 15%DV calcium, 20%DV iron.

Many-Beans Chili

Rosann Zeiset   Stevens, PA

MAKES: **12 SERVINGS**
PREP. TIME: **15 MINUTES**
COOKING TIME: **8–10 HOURS**
IDEAL SLOW COOKER SIZE: **4-QUART**

½ lb. lean hamburger *or* ground turkey

½ lb. sausage

1 onion, chopped

15-oz. can kidney beans *or* chili beans, undrained

15-oz. can ranch-style beans, undrained

15-oz. can pinto beans, undrained

14½-oz. can stewed tomatoes, undrained

15-oz. can tomato sauce

1 envelope dry chili seasoning mix

3 Tbsp. brown sugar

3 Tbsp. chili powder

1. Brown hamburger, sausage, and onion together in nonstick skillet.
2. Combine all ingredients in large slow cooker. Mix well.
3. Cook on Low 8–10 hours.

Per Serving: 240 calories (60 calories from fat), 7g total fat (2g saturated, 0g trans), 15mg cholesterol, 1570mg sodium, 34g total carbohydrate (8g fiber, 11g sugar), 14g protein, 35%DV vitamin A, 10%DV vitamin C, 8%DV calcium, 25%DV iron.

Ed's Chili

Marie Miller   Scotia, NY

MAKES: **4–6 SERVINGS**
PREP. TIME: **15 MINUTES**
COOKING TIME: **2–2½ HOURS**
IDEAL SLOW COOKER SIZE: **4-QUART**

1 lb. ground beef

1 pkg. dry taco seasoning mix

half a 12-oz. jar salsa

16-oz. can kidney beans, undrained

15-oz. can black beans, undrained

14½-oz. can diced tomatoes, undrained

pinch of sugar

shredded cheese

chopped onions

sour cream

diced fresh tomatoes

guacamole

sliced black olives

1. Brown ground beef in skillet. Drain.
2. Combine first 7 ingredients in slow cooker.
3. Cover. Heat on High until mixture comes to boil. Reduce heat to Low. Simmer 1½ hours.
4. To reduce liquids, continue cooking uncovered.
5. Top individual servings with choice of shredded cheese, onions, a dollop of sour cream, fresh diced tomatoes, guacamole, and sliced olives.

Pirate Stew

Nancy Graves   Manhattan, KS

MAKES: **4–6 SERVINGS**
PREP. TIME: **15 MINUTES**
COOKING TIME: **6 HOURS**
IDEAL SLOW COOKER SIZE: **4-QUART**

¾ cup sliced onion

1 lb. ground beef

¼ cup long-grain rice, uncooked

3 cups diced raw potatoes

1 cup diced celery

2 cups canned kidney beans, drained

1 tsp. salt

⅛ tsp. pepper

¼ tsp. chili powder

¼ tsp. Worcestershire sauce

1 cup tomato sauce

½ cup water

1. Brown onions and ground beef in skillet. Drain.
2. Layer ingredients in slow cooker in order given.
3. Cover. Cook on Low 6 hours, or until potatoes and rice are cooked.

Variation: *Add a layer of 2 cups sliced carrots between potatoes and celery.*

Katrine Rose   Woodbridge, VA

Corn Chili

Gladys Longacre   Susquehanna, PA

MAKES: **4–6 SERVINGS**
PREP. TIME: **15 MINUTES**
COOKING TIME: **5–6 HOURS**
IDEAL SLOW COOKER SIZE: **4-QUART**

1 lb. ground beef

½ cup chopped onions

½ cup chopped green peppers

½ tsp. salt

⅛ tsp. pepper

¼ tsp. dried thyme

14½-oz. can diced tomatoes with Italian herbs

6-oz. can tomato paste, diluted with 1 can water

2 cups frozen whole-kernel corn

16-oz. can kidney beans

1 Tbsp. chili powder

sour cream

shredded cheese

1. Sauté ground beef, onions, and green peppers in deep saucepan. Drain and season with salt, pepper, and thyme.
2. Stir in tomatoes, tomato paste, and corn. Heat until corn is thawed. Add kidney beans and chili powder. Pour into slow cooker.
3. Cover. Cook on Low 5–6 hours.
4. Top individual servings with dollops of sour cream, or sprinkle with shredded cheese.

When sautéing or frying, turn a metal colander or strainer upside down over the skillet. This allows steam to escape and keeps fat from spattering.

Lotsa-Beans Chili

Jean Weller State College, PA

MAKES: **12–15 SERVINGS**
PREP. TIME: **25 MINUTES**
COOKING TIME: **8–9 HOURS**
IDEAL SLOW COOKER SIZE: **5-QUART**

1 lb. ground beef

1 lb. bacon, diced

½ cup chopped onions

½ cup brown sugar

½ cup sugar

½ cup ketchup

2 tsp. dry mustard

1 tsp. salt

½ tsp. pepper

2 15-oz. cans green beans, drained

2 14½-oz. cans baked beans

2 15-oz. cans butter beans, drained

2 16-oz. cans kidney beans, rinsed and drained

1. Brown ground beef and bacon in slow cooker. Drain.
2. Combine all ingredients in slow cooker.
3. Cover. Cook on High 1 hour. Reduce heat to Low and cook 7–8 hours.

So-Easy Chili

Sue Graber Eureka, IL

MAKES: **4 SERVINGS**
PREP. TIME: **15 MINUTES**
COOKING TIME: **4–6 HOURS**
IDEAL SLOW COOKER SIZE: **3½-QUART**

1 lb. ground beef

1 onion, chopped

15-oz. can chili, with or without beans

14½-oz. can diced tomatoes with green chilies, *or* with basil, garlic, and oregano

1 cup tomato juice

chopped onion

shredded cheddar cheese

1. Brown ground beef and onion in skillet. Drain and put in slow cooker.
2. Add chili, diced tomatoes, and tomato juice.
3. Cover. Cook on Low 4–6 hours.
4. Serve with onion and cheese on top of each individual serving.

Variation: *This chili is of a good consistency for serving over rice. For a thicker chili, add 4–6 ozs. tomato paste 20 minutes before end of cooking time.*

Grandma's Chili

Beverly (Flatt) Getz   Warriors Mark, PA

MAKES: **8 SERVINGS**
PREP. TIME: **20 MINUTES**
COOKING TIME: **4 HOURS**
IDEAL SLOW COOKER SIZE: **5-QUART**

1 large onion, chopped

2 lbs. ground beef

28-oz. can stewed tomatoes

16-oz. can dark kidney beans, undrained

15-oz. can Hormel chili with beans

10¾-oz. can tomato soup

1 tsp. K.C. Masterpiece BBQ sauce

¼ tsp. garlic salt

¼ tsp. garlic powder

¼ tsp. onion salt

¼ tsp. chili powder

pinch of sugar

1. Brown onion and beef in skillet, leaving meat in larger chunks. Place in slow cooker.
2. Add remaining ingredients. Stir.
3. Cover. Cook on High 4 hours.
4. Serve with crackers, rolls, butter, and apple crisp with whipped topping.

Note: *When the grandchildren come to visit from five different states, they always ask for Grandma's Chili. I just made up the recipe. Now I'm afraid to change it!*

When I want to warm rolls to go with a slow-cooker stew, I wrap them in foil and lay them on top of the stew until they're warm.

Our Favorite Chili

Ruth Shank   Gridley, IL

MAKES: **10–12 SERVINGS**
PREP. TIME: **20 MINUTES**
COOKING TIME: **4–10 HOURS**
IDEAL SLOW COOKER SIZE: **5-QUART**

1½ lbs. ground beef

¼ cup chopped onions

1 rib celery, chopped

29-oz. can stewed tomatoes

2 15½-oz. cans red kidney beans, undrained

2 16-oz. cans chili beans, undrained

½ cup ketchup

1½ tsp. lemon juice

2 tsp. vinegar

1½ tsp. brown sugar

1½ tsp. salt

1 tsp. Worcestershire sauce

½ tsp. garlic powder

½ tsp. dry mustard powder

1 Tbsp. chili powder

2 6-oz. cans tomato paste

1. Brown ground beef, onions, and celery in skillet. Drain. Place in slow cooker.
2. Add remaining ingredients. Mix well.
3. Cover. Cook on Low 8–10 hours, or on High 4–5 hours.
4. Serve with fresh warm cornbread and slices of Colby or Monterey Jack cheese.

Hearty Potato Chili

Janice Muller Derwood, MD

MAKES: **8 SERVINGS**
PREP. TIME: **20–25 MINUTES**
COOKING TIME: **4 HOURS**
IDEAL SLOW COOKER SIZE: **5-QUART**

1 lb. ground beef
½ cup chopped onions, *or* 2 Tbsp. dried minced onions
½ cup chopped green peppers
1 Tbsp. poppy seeds, *optional*
1 tsp. salt
½ tsp. chili powder
1 pkg. au gratin *or* scalloped potato mix
1 cup hot water
15-oz. can kidney beans, undrained
16-oz. can stewed tomatoes
4-oz. can mushroom pieces, undrained

1. Brown ground beef in skillet. Remove meat and place in slow cooker. Sauté onions and green peppers in drippings until softened.
2. Combine all ingredients in slow cooker.
3. Cover. Cook on High 4 hours, or until liquid is absorbed and potatoes are tender.

Slow Cooker Chili

Kay Magruder Seminole, OK

MAKES: **8–10 SERVINGS**
PREP. TIME: **25 MINUTES**
COOKING TIME: **6–12 HOURS**
IDEAL SLOW COOKER SIZE: **6-QUART**

3 lbs. stewing meat, browned
2 cloves garlic, minced
¼ tsp. pepper
½ tsp. cumin
¼ tsp. dry mustard
7½-oz. can jalapeño relish
1 cup beef broth

1–1½ onions, chopped, according to your taste preference
½ tsp. salt
½ tsp. dried oregano
1 Tbsp. chili powder
7-oz. can green chilies, chopped
14½-oz. can stewed tomatoes, chopped
15-oz. can tomato sauce
2 15-oz. cans red kidney beans, rinsed and drained
2 15-oz. cans pinto beans, rinsed and drained

1. Combine all ingredients except kidney and pinto beans in slow cooker.
2. Cover. Cook on Low 10–12 hours, or on High 6–7 hours. Add beans halfway through cooking time.
3. Serve with Mexican cornbread.

Texican Chili

Becky Oswald Broadway, VA

MAKES: **15 SERVINGS**
PREP. TIME: **20 MINUTES**
COOKING TIME: **9–10 HOURS**
IDEAL SLOW COOKER SIZE: **5–6-QUART**

8 bacon strips, diced
2½ lbs. beef stewing meat, cubed
28-oz. can stewed tomatoes
14½-oz. can stewed tomatoes
2 8-oz. cans tomato sauce
16-oz. can kidney beans, rinsed and drained
2 cups sliced carrots
1 medium onion, chopped
1 cup chopped celery
½ cup chopped green pepper
¼ cup minced fresh parsley
1 Tbsp. chili powder
1 tsp. salt
½ tsp. ground cumin
¼ tsp. pepper

Soups, Stews, and Chilis

1. Cook bacon in skillet until crisp. Drain on paper towel.
2. Brown beef in bacon drippings in skillet.
3. Combine all ingredients in slow cooker.
4. Cover. Cook on Low 9–10 hours, or until meat is tender. Stir occasionally.

Variations: *Add any or all of the following to Step 2:*

1 tsp. chili powder

1 tsp. ground cumin

15-oz. can black beans, undrained

15-oz. can whole-kernel corn, undrained

Spicy Chili

Deborah Swartz   Grottoes, VA

MAKES: **4–6 SERVINGS**
PREP. TIME: **20 MINUTES**
COOKING TIME: **2–3 HOURS**
IDEAL SLOW COOKER SIZE: **3½-QUART**

½ lb. sausage, either cut in thin slices or removed from casings

½ lb. ground beef

½ cup chopped onions

½ lb. fresh mushrooms, sliced

⅛ cup chopped celery

⅛ cup chopped green peppers

1 cup salsa

16-oz. can tomato juice

6-oz. can tomato paste

½ tsp. sugar

½ tsp. salt

½ tsp. dried oregano

½ tsp. Worcestershire sauce

¼ tsp. dried basil

¼ tsp. pepper

1. Brown sausage, ground beef, and onion in skillet. During last 3 minutes of browning, add mushrooms, celery, and green peppers. Continue cooking; then drain.
2. Add remaining ingredients. Pour into slow cooker.
3. Cover. Cook on High 2–3 hours.

Extra Easy Chili

Jennifer Gehman   Harrisburg, PA

MAKES: **4–6 SERVINGS**
PREP. TIME: **10 MINUTES**
COOKING TIME: **4–8 HOURS**
IDEAL SLOW COOKER SIZE: **4-QUART**

1 lb. ground beef *or* turkey, uncooked

1 envelope dry chili seasoning mix

16-oz. can chili beans in sauce

2 28-oz. cans crushed or diced tomatoes seasoned with garlic and onion

1. Crumble meat in bottom of slow cooker.
2. Add remaining ingredients. Stir.
3. Cover. Cook on High 4–6 hours, or on Low 6–8 hours. Stir halfway through cooking time.
4. Serve over white rice, topped with shredded cheddar cheese and chopped raw onions.

Note: *I decided to make this chili recipe one year for Christmas. Our family was hosting other family members—and we had had guests for about a week prior to Christmas. Needless to say, I was tired of cooking so this seemed easy enough. It was so nice to put the ingredients in the slow cooker and let it cook all day long. Not only did the chili warm us up on a cold day, but it was a welcomed change from the traditional Christmas meal. It has been my tradition ever since!*

Mexican Chili Mix and Fritos

Melanie Thrower McPherson, KS

MAKES: **4–6 SERVINGS**
PREP. TIME: **10–15 MINUTES**
COOKING TIME: **4 HOURS**
IDEAL SLOW COOKER SIZE: **2–3-QUART**

1 lb. ground beef

14¾–16-oz. can cream-style corn, drained

½ cup chunky picante sauce

16-oz. can pinto *or* black beans, drained

half an envelope dry taco seasoning

corn chips

shredded cheese, *optional*

chopped olives, *optional*

sour cream, *optional*

salsa, *optional*

1. Brown ground beef in a large nonstick skillet. Drain.
2. Mix beef, corn, picante sauce, beans, and taco seasoning in slow cooker.
3. Cover and cook on Low 4 hours.
4. Serve over corn chips with optional garnishes of shredded cheese, chopped olives, sour cream, and salsa.

Variation: *I like to substitute ground elk or venison for the beef in this recipe.*

Trail Chili

Jeanne Allen Rye, CO

MAKES: **8–10 SERVINGS**
PREP. TIME: **15 MINUTES**
COOKING TIME: **4½–6½ HOURS**
IDEAL SLOW COOKER SIZE: **4–5-QUART**

2 lbs. ground beef

1 large onion, diced

28-oz. can diced tomatoes

2 8-oz. cans tomato puree

1, or 2, 16-oz. cans kidney beans, undrained

4-oz. can diced green chilies

1 cup water

2 garlic cloves, minced

2 Tbsp. mild chili powder

2 tsp. salt

2 tsp. ground cumin

1 tsp. pepper

1. Brown beef and onion in skillet. Drain. Place in slow cooker on High.
2. Stir in remaining ingredients. Cook on High 30 minutes.
3. Reduce heat to Low. Cook 4–6 hours.

Tip: *Top individual servings with shredded cheese. Serve with taco chips.*

Chili con Carne

Donna Conto Saylorsburg, PA

MAKES: **8 SERVINGS**
PREP. TIME: **15 MINUTES**
COOKING TIME: **5–6 HOURS**
IDEAL SLOW COOKER SIZE: **4-QUART**

1 lb. ground beef
1 cup chopped onions
¾ cup chopped green peppers
1 garlic clove, minced
14½-oz. can tomatoes, cut up
16-oz. can kidney beans, drained
8-oz. can tomato sauce
2 tsp. chili powder
½ tsp. dried basil

1. Brown beef, onion, green pepper, and garlic in saucepan. Drain.
2. Combine all ingredients in slow cooker.
3. Cover. Cook on Low 5–6 hours.
4. Serve in bread bowl.

Variation: *Add 16-oz. can pinto beans, ¼ tsp. salt, and ¼ tsp. pepper in Step 2.*

Alexa Slonin Harrisonburg, VA

Quick and Easy Chili

Nan Decker Albuquerque, NM

MAKES: **4 SERVINGS**
PREP. TIME: **20 MINUTES**
COOKING TIME: **4–5 HOURS**
IDEAL SLOW COOKER SIZE: **3–4-QUART**

1 lb. ground beef
1 onion, chopped
16-oz. can stewed tomatoes
11½-oz. can Hot V-8 juice
2 15-oz. cans pinto beans
¼ tsp. cayenne pepper
½ tsp. salt
1 Tbsp. chili powder
sour cream
chopped green onions
shredded cheese
sliced ripe olives

1. Crumble ground beef in microwave-safe casserole. Add onion. Microwave, covered, on High 15 minutes. Drain. Break meat into pieces.
2. Combine all ingredients in slow cooker.
3. Cook on Low 4–5 hours.
4. Garnish with sour cream, chopped green onions, shredded cheese, and sliced ripe olives.

If there is too much liquid in your cooker, stick a toothpick under the edge of the lid to tilt it slightly and to allow the steam to escape.

Hot Chili

Kristen Allen   Houston, TX

MAKES: **8 SERVINGS**
PREP. TIME: **15 MINUTES**
COOKING TIME: **6–8 HOURS**
IDEAL SLOW COOKER SIZE: **5-QUART**

2 lbs. 99% fat-free ground turkey

2 medium onions, diced

2 garlic cloves, minced

1 green bell pepper, diced

⅔ Tbsp. chili powder

1 tsp. salt

1 tsp. black pepper

1 tsp. ground cumin

16-oz. can low-sodium stewed or diced tomatoes

2 12-oz. cans low-sodium tomato sauce

2 16-oz. cans Mexican chili beans

1. Brown turkey with onions, garlic, and green pepper in a nonstick skillet. Drain.
2. Combine all ingredients in slow cooker.
3. Cover. Cook on Low 6–8 hours.

Per Serving: 320 calories (40 calories from fat), 4.5g total fat (1g saturated, 0g trans), 45mg cholesterol, 1400mg sodium, 36g total carbohydrate (12g fiber, 8g sugar), 37g protein, 80%DV vitamin A, 30%DV vitamin C, 8%DV calcium, 30%DV iron.

Asian Turkey Chili

Kimberly Jensen   Bailey, CO

MAKES: **6 SERVINGS**
PREP. TIME: **20 MINUTES**
COOKING TIME: **6 HOURS**
IDEAL SLOW COOKER SIZE: **4-QUART**

2 cups yellow onions, diced

1 small red bell pepper, diced

1 lb. ground turkey, browned

2 Tbsp. minced gingerroot

3 cloves garlic, minced

¼ cup dry sherry

¼ cup hoisin sauce

2 Tbsp. chili powder

1 Tbsp. corn oil

2 Tbsp. soy sauce

1 tsp. sugar

2 cups canned whole tomatoes

16 oz. can dark red kidney beans, undrained

1. Combine all ingredients in slow cooker.
2. Cover. Cook on Low 6 hours.
3. Serve topped with chow mein noodles or over cooked white rice.

Tip: *If you serve this chili over rice, this recipe will yield 10–12 servings.*

Pumpkin Black Bean Turkey Chili

Rhoda Atzeff   Harrisburg, PA

MAKES: **10–12 SERVINGS**
PREP. TIME: **20 MINUTES**
COOKING TIME: **7–8 HOURS**
IDEAL SLOW COOKER SIZE: **5-QUART**

1 cup chopped onions

1 cup chopped yellow bell pepper

3 garlic cloves, minced

2 Tbsp. oil

1½ tsp. dried oregano

1½–2 tsp. ground cumin

2 tsp. chili powder

2 15-oz. cans black beans, rinsed and drained

2½ cups cooked turkey, chopped

16-oz. can pumpkin

14½-oz. can diced tomatoes

3 cups chicken broth

1. Sauté onions, yellow pepper, and garlic in oil for 8 minutes, or until soft.
2. Stir in oregano, cumin, and chili powder. Cook 1 minute. Transfer to slow cooker.
3. Add remaining ingredients.
4. Cover. Cook on Low 7–8 hours.

White Chili

Esther Martin   Ephrata, PA

MAKES: **8 SERVINGS**
PREP. TIME: **15 MINUTES**
COOKING TIME: **4–10 HOURS**
IDEAL SLOW COOKER SIZE: **5-QUART**

3 15-oz. cans Great Northern beans, drained
8 oz. cooked chicken breasts, shredded
1 cup chopped onions
1½ cups chopped yellow, red, *or* green bell peppers
2 jalapeño chili peppers, stemmed, seeded, and chopped, *optional*
2 garlic cloves, minced
2 tsp. ground cumin
½ tsp. salt
½ tsp. dried oregano
3½ cups chicken broth
sour cream
shredded cheddar cheese
tortilla chips

1. Combine all ingredients except sour cream, cheddar cheese, and chips in slow cooker.
2. Cover. Cook on Low 8–10 hours, or on High 4–5 hours.
3. Ladle into bowls and top individual servings with sour cream, cheddar cheese, and chips.

Chicken Tortilla Soup

Becky Harder   Monument, CO

MAKES: **6–8 SERVINGS**
PREP. TIME: **5–10 MINUTES**
COOKING TIME: **8 HOURS**
IDEAL SLOW COOKER SIZE: **4–5-QUART**

4 chicken breast halves
2 15-oz. cans black beans, undrained
2 15-oz. cans Mexican stewed tomatoes, *or* Rotel tomatoes
1 cup salsa, your choice of heat
4-oz. can chopped green chilies
14½-oz. can tomato sauce
tortilla chips
2 cups shredded cheese

1. Combine all ingredients except chips and cheese in large slow cooker.
2. Cover. Cook on Low 8 hours.
3. Just before serving, remove chicken breasts and slice into bite-sized pieces. Stir into soup.
4. To serve, put a handful of chips in each individual soup bowl. Ladle soup over chips. Top with cheese.

White Chicken Chili

Jewel Showalter   Landisville, PA

MAKES: **6–8 SERVINGS**
PREP. TIME: **25 MINUTES**
COOKING TIME: **3½–5 HOURS**
IDEAL SLOW COOKER SIZE: **5-QUART**

2 whole skinless chicken breasts
6 cups water
2 chopped onions
2 garlic cloves, minced
1 Tbsp. oil
2–4 4-oz. cans chopped green chilies
1–2 diced jalapeño peppers
2 tsp. ground cumin
1½ tsp. dried oregano
¼ tsp. cayenne pepper
½ tsp. salt
3-lb. can navy beans, undrained
1–2 cups shredded cheese
sour cream
salsa

1. Place chicken in slow cooker. Add 6 cups water.
2. Cover. Cook on Low 3-4 hours, or until tender.
3. Remove chicken from slow cooker. Cube and set aside.
4. Sauté onions and garlic in oil in skillet. Add chilies, jalapeño peppers, cumin, oregano, pepper, and salt. Sauté 2 minutes. Transfer to broth in slow cooker.
5. Add navy beans.
6. Cover. Cook on Low 30-60 minutes.
7. Right before serving add chicken and cheese.
8. Serve topped with sour cream and salsa. Cornbread or corn chips are good go-alongs with this chili.

Variation: *If you want to use dried beans, use 3 cups navy beans and cover with water in saucepan, soaking overnight. In the morning,* *drain and cover with fresh water. Cook in saucepan on low 7–8 hours, or until tender. Drain of excess moisture and stir into chicken and broth.*

Chicken Chili with Pesto

Light

Marilyn Mowry   Irving, TX

MAKES: **4 SERVINGS**
PREP. TIME: **20 MINUTES**
COOKING TIME: **6–8 HOURS**
IDEAL SLOW COOKER SIZE: **5-QUART**

¾ lb. boneless, skinless chicken breast, cut into bite-sized pieces
2 tsp. vegetable oil, *optional*
¾ cup finely chopped onion
1½ cups finely chopped carrots
¾ cup finely chopped red bell pepper
¾ cup thinly sliced celery
¼ cup canned chopped green chilies
¾ tsp. dried oregano
½ tsp. ground cumin
¼ tsp. salt
⅛ tsp. black pepper
16-oz. can cannellini beans *or* other white beans, rinsed and drained
14½-oz. can fat-free, low-sodium chicken broth
3 Tbsp. classic pesto sauce (recipe below)

1. Sauté chicken in a nonstick skillet, or in a traditional skillet with oil.
2. Combine all ingredients except pesto sauce in slow cooker.
3. Cook on Low 6-8 hours.
4. Stir in pesto just before serving.

Per Serving: 370 calories (110 calories from fat), 12 total fat (2.5g saturated, 0g trans), 50mg cholesterol, 820mg sodium, 36g total carbohydrate (9g fiber, 10g sugar), 29g protein, 200%DV vitamin A, 40%DV vitamin C, 15%DV calcium, 20%DV iron.

Pesto

MAKES: ¾ CUP

2 Tbsp. walnuts *or* pine nuts, coarsely chopped

2 garlic cloves, peeled

3 Tbsp. extra-virgin olive oil

4 cups fresh basil leaves (about 4 ozs.)

½ cup grated Parmesan cheese

¼ tsp. salt

1. Mince nuts and garlic in food processor.
2. Add oil, and pulse 3 times.
3. Add basil, cheese, and salt. Process until finely minced, scraping sides of bowl.

Taco Chicken Soup

Colleen Heatwole   Burton, MI

Janie Steele   Moore, OK

MAKES: 4–6 SERVINGS
PREP. TIME: 10 MINUTES
COOKING TIME: 5–7 HOURS
IDEAL SLOW COOKER SIZE: 4–5-QUART

1 envelope dry reduced-sodium taco seasoning

32-oz. can low-sodium V-8 juice

16-oz. jar salsa

15-oz. can black beans

1 cup frozen corn

1 cup frozen peas

2 whole chicken breasts, cooked and shredded

1. Combine all ingredients except corn, peas, and chicken in slow cooker.
2. Cover. Cook on Low 4–6 hours. Add remaining vegetables and chicken 1 hour before serving.

Per Serving: 210 calories (15 calories from fat), 2g total fat (0g saturated, 0g trans), 25mg cholesterol, 970mg sodium, 35g total carbohydrate (8g fiber, 9g sugar), 17g protein, 40%DV vitamin A, 40%DV vitamin C, 8%DV calcium, 20%DV iron.

Tip: *Garnish individual servings with chopped fresh cilantro, and, if diets allow, with chunks of avocado.*

Tortilla Soup

Janie Steele   Moore, OK

MAKES: 7 SERVINGS
PREP. TIME: 10 MINUTES
COOKING TIME: 3–4 HOURS
IDEAL SLOW COOKER SIZE: 3½–4-QUART

16-oz. can fat-free refried beans

15-oz. can black beans, rinsed and drained

14-oz. can fat-free chicken broth

1½ cups frozen corn

¾ cup chunky salsa

¾ cup boneless, skinless cooked chicken, cubed

¼ cup water

2 cups reduced-fat shredded cheese, *divided*

1 bag baked tortilla chips

1. Combine all ingredients except cheese and chips.
2. Cook on Low 3–4 hours, or until heated through.
3. Add half of cheese. Stir until melted
4. Crush chips in bowls. Add soup. Top with sour cream and more crushed chips.

Per Serving: 370 calories (40 calories from fat), 4.5g total fat (1.5g saturated, 0g trans), 20mg cholesterol, 1130mg sodium, 60g total carbohydrate (10g fiber, 3g sugar), 25g protein, 4%DV vitamin A, 4%DV vitamin C, 25%DV calcium, 20%DV iron.

Tex-Mex Chicken Chowder

Janie Steele Moore, OK

MAKES: **8–10 SERVINGS**
PREP. TIME: **20 MINUTES**
COOKING TIME: **4½–6½ HOURS**
IDEAL SLOW COOKER SIZE: **5-QUART**

1 cup chopped onions

1 cup thinly sliced celery

2 garlic cloves, minced

1 Tbsp. oil

1½ lbs. boneless, skinless chicken breasts, cubed

32-oz. can chicken broth

1 pkg. country gravy mix

2 cups milk

16-oz. jar chunky salsa

32-oz. bag frozen hash brown potatoes

4½-oz. can chopped green chilies

8 oz. Velveeta cheese, cubed

1. Combine onions, celery, garlic, oil, chicken, and broth in 5-quart or larger slow cooker.
2. Cover. Cook on Low 2½ hours, until chicken is no longer pink.
3. In separate bowl, dissolve gravy mix in milk. Stir into chicken mixture. Add salsa, potatoes, chilies, and cheese and combine well. Cook on Low 2–4 hours, or until potatoes are fully cooked.

Chicken and Ham Gumbo

Barbara Tenney Delta, PA

MAKES: **4 SERVINGS**
PREP. TIME: **20 MINUTES**
COOKING TIME: **6–8 HOURS**
IDEAL SLOW COOKER SIZE: **4-QUART**

1½ lbs. boneless, skinless chicken thighs, cubed

1 Tbsp. oil

10-oz. pkg. frozen okra

½ lb. smoked ham, cut into small chunks

1½ cups coarsely chopped onions

1½ cups coarsely chopped green peppers

2 or 3 10-oz. cans cannellini beans, drained

6 cups chicken broth

2 10-oz. cans diced tomatoes with green chilies

2 Tbsp. chopped fresh cilantro

1. Cook chicken pieces in oil in skillet until no longer pink.
2. Run hot water over okra until pieces separate easily.
3. Combine all ingredients but cilantro in slow cooker.
4. Cover. Cook on Low 6–8 hours. Stir in cilantro before serving.

Variations:

1. Stir in ½ cup long-grain dry rice with rest of ingredients.

2. Add ¾ tsp. salt and ¼ tsp. pepper with other ingredients.

Buffalo Chicken Wing Soup

Mary Lynn Miller Reinholds, PA • *Donna Neiter* Wausau, WI
Anna Stoltzfus Honey Brook, PA • *Joette Droz* Kalona, IA

MAKES: **8 SERVINGS**
PREP. TIME: **10 MINUTES**
COOKING TIME: **4–5 HOURS**
IDEAL SLOW COOKER SIZE: **3-QUART**

6 cups milk
3 10¾-oz. cans condensed cream of chicken soup,
 undiluted
3 cups (about 1 lb.) cooked chicken, shredded or cubed
1 cup (8 ozs.) sour cream
1–8 Tbsp. hot pepper sauce, according to your
 preference for heat! *

1. Combine milk and soups in slow cooker until smooth.
2. Stir in chicken.
3. Cover and cook on Low 3¾–4¾ hours.
4. Fifteen minutes before serving stir in sour cream and hot sauce.
5. Cover and continue cooking just until bubbly.

 * *Start with a small amount of hot sauce, and then add more to suit your—and your diners'—tastes!*

Keep cooked chicken in the freezer so it's ready when you need to quickly make a recipe.

Split Pea with Chicken Soup

Mary E. Wheatley Mashpee, MA

MAKES: **6–8 SERVINGS**
PREP. TIME: **20 MINUTES**
COOKING TIME: **4–10 HOURS**
IDEAL SLOW COOKER SIZE: **5-QUART**

16-oz. pkg. dried split peas
¾ cup finely diced carrots
3 cups cubed raw potatoes
8 cups chicken broth
1 cup cooked chicken, cubed

1. Combine peas, carrots, potatoes, and chicken broth in slow cooker.
2. Cook on High 4–5 hours, or on Low 8–10 hours, or until all vegetables are tender. Stir after the soup begins to slowly boil.
3. Ten minutes before serving, stir in cooked chicken.

Chicken Rice and Veggies Soup

Norma Grieser Clarksville, MI

MAKES: **8 SERVINGS**
PREP. TIME: **30 MINUTES**
COOKING TIME: **4–8 HOURS**
IDEAL SLOW COOKER SIZE: **4–6-QUART**

4 cups chicken broth
4 cups cooked chicken, cubed or shredded
1⅓ cups cut-up celery
1⅓ cups diced carrots
1 quart water
1 cup long-grain rice, uncooked

1. Put all ingredients in slow cooker.
2. Cover and cook on Low 4–8 hours, or until vegetables are cooked to your liking.

Tasty Chicken Soup

Rhonda Freed Lowville, NY

MAKES: **12 SERVINGS**
PREP. TIME: **10–15 MINUTES**
COOKING TIME: **6–7 HOURS**
IDEAL SLOW COOKER SIZE: **4-QUART**

12 cups chicken broth

2 cups cooked chicken, cubed

1 cup shredded carrots

3 whole cloves

small onion

16-oz. bag of dry noodles, cooked, *optional*

1. Place broth, chicken, and carrots in slow cooker.
2. Peel onion. Using a toothpick, poke 3 holes on the cut ends. Carefully press cloves into 3 of the holes until only their round part shows. Add to slow cooker.
3. Cover and cook on High 6–7 hours.
4. If you'd like a thicker soup, add a bag of cooked fine egg noodles before serving.

Variations: *You can make the broth and cook the chicken in your slow cooker, too. Just put 2–3 lbs. of cut-up chicken pieces into the slow cooker. Add 12 cups water. Cook on High 4–5 hours, or until chicken is tender and falling off the bone.*

Remove the chicken with a slotted spoon. Debone when cooled enough to handle.

Measure 2 cups of chicken meat and return to slow cooker. Completely cool the remaining chicken and freeze or refrigerate for future use.

Continue with the recipe above to make the soup.

Chinese Chicken Soup

Karen Waggoner Joplin, MO

MAKES: **6 SERVINGS**
PREP. TIME: **5 MINUTES**
COOKING TIME: **1–2 HOURS**
IDEAL SLOW COOKER SIZE: **4-QUART**

3 14½-oz. cans chicken broth

16-oz. pkg. frozen stir-fry vegetable blend

2 cups cooked chicken, cubed

1 tsp. minced fresh gingerroot

1 tsp. soy sauce

1. Mix all ingredients in slow cooker.
2. Cover and cook on High for 1–2 hours, depending upon how crunchy or soft you like your vegetables to be.

Chicken Noodle Soup

Jennifer J. Gehman Harrisburg, PA

MAKES: **6–8 SERVINGS**
PREP. TIME: **5–10 MINUTES**
COOKING TIME: **4–8 HOURS**
IDEAL SLOW COOKER SIZE: **5-QUART**

2 cups chicken, cubed

15¼-oz. can corn, *or* 2 cups frozen corn

1 cup frozen peas *or* green beans

10 cups water

10–12 chicken bouillon cubes

3 Tbsp. bacon drippings

½ pkg. dry kluski (or other very sturdy) noodles

1. Combine all ingredients except noodles in slow cooker.
2. Cover. Cook on High 4–6 hours, or on Low 6–8 hours. Add noodles during last 2 hours.
3. Serve with potato rolls and butter or grilled cheese sandwiches.

Chicken Vegetable Soup

Barbara Walker Sturgis, SD

Sheridy Steele Ardmore, OK

MAKES: **6 SERVINGS**
PREP. TIME: **10 MINUTES**
COOKING TIME: **6–8 HOURS**
IDEAL SLOW COOKER SIZE: **4-QUART**

28-oz. can low-sodium diced tomatoes, undrained

2 cups low-sodium, reduced-fat chicken broth

1 cup frozen corn

2 ribs celery, chopped

6-oz. can tomato paste

¼ cup dry lentils, rinsed

1 Tbsp. sugar

1 Tbsp. Worcestershire sauce

2 tsp. dried parsley flakes

1 tsp. dried marjoram

2 cups cooked chicken breast, cubed

1. Combine all ingredients in slow cooker except chicken.
2. Cover. Cook on Low 6–8 hours. Stir in chicken 1 hour before the end of the cooking time.

Per Serving: 190 calories (20 calories from fat), 2g total fat (0g saturated, 0g trans), 35mg cholesterol, 520mg sodium, 24g total carbohydrate (6g fiber, 7g sugar), 21g protein, 20%DV vitamin A, 20%DV vitamin C, 10%DV calcium, 20%DV iron.

You may want to revise herb amounts when using a slow cooker. Whole herbs and spices increase their flavoring power, while ground spices tend to lose some flavor. It's a good idea to season to taste before serving.

Chicken Stew

Carol Eberly Harrisonburg, VA

MAKES: **5 SERVINGS**
PREP. TIME: **15 MINUTES**
COOKING TIME: **8–10 HOURS**
IDEAL SLOW COOKER SIZE: **4 QUART**

1 lb. uncooked boneless, skinless chicken breasts, cubed

14½ oz.-can low-sodium Italian diced tomatoes, undrained

2 potatoes, peeled and cubed

5 carrots, chopped

3 celery ribs, chopped

1 onion, chopped

2 4-oz. cans mushroom stems and pieces, drained

3 chicken bouillon cubes

2 tsp. sugar

½ tsp. dried basil

½ tsp. dill weed

1 tsp. chili powder

¼ tsp. black pepper

1 Tbsp. cornstarch

1 cup water

1. Combine all ingredients except cornstarch and water in slow cooker.
2. Combine water and cornstarch. Stir into slow cooker.
3. Cover. Cook on Low 8–10 hours until vegetables are tender.

Per Serving: 300 calories (35 calories from fat), 4g total fat (1g saturated, 0g trans), 75mg cholesterol, 840mg sodium, 33g total carbohydrate (6g fiber, 10g sugar), 33g protein, 200%DV vitamin A, 30%DV vitamin C, 8%DV calcium, 15%DV iron.

Chicken Mushroom Stew

Bernice A. Esau North Newton, KS
Carol Sherwood Batavia, NY

MAKES: **6 SERVINGS**
PREP. TIME: **20 MINUTES**
COOKING TIME: **4 HOURS**
IDEAL SLOW COOKER SIZE: **3½–4-QUART**

6 boneless, skinless chicken breast halves (about 1½ lbs.),
    uncooked, cut in 1-inch cubes

2 Tbsp. cooking oil, *divided*

8 ozs. sliced fresh mushrooms

1 medium onion, diced

3 cups diced zucchini

1 cup diced green bell peppers

4 garlic cloves, diced

3 medium tomatoes, diced

6-oz. can tomato paste

¾ cup water

2 tsp. salt, *optional*

1 tsp. dried thyme

1 tsp. dried oregano

1 tsp. dried marjoram

1 tsp. dried basil

1. Brown chicken in 1 Tbsp. oil in a large skillet. Transfer to slow cooker, reserving drippings.
2. In same skillet, sauté mushrooms, onions, zucchini, green peppers, and garlic in drippings, and remaining 1 Tbsp. oil if needed, until crisp-tender. Place in slow cooker.
3. Add tomatoes, tomato paste, water, and seasonings.
4. Cover. Cook on Low 4 hours, or until vegetables are tender.

Per Serving: 260 calories (80 calories from fat), 8g total fat (1.5g saturated, 0g trans), 75mg cholesterol, 880mg sodium, 18g total carbohydrate (5g fiber, 5g sugar), 31g protein, 30%DV vitamin A, 40%DV vitamin C, 6%DV calcium, 20%DV iron.

Tip: *This is also good served over rice.*

All-Together Chicken Rice Soup

Michelle Steffen Harrisonburg, VA

MAKES: **14 SERVINGS**
PREP. TIME: **30 MINUTES**
COOKING TIME: **4–5 HOURS**
IDEAL SLOW COOKER SIZE: **6-QUART**

3 quarts hot water

1 medium onion, finely chopped

2–3 celery ribs, finely chopped

2 sprigs finely chopped fresh parsley

1 clove garlic, crushed

2 tsp. salt

½ cup thinly sliced carrots

4 large skinless chicken legs and thighs

½ cup chopped fresh parsley

3 cups hot cooked rice

1. Combine water, onion, celery, 2 sprigs parsley, garlic, salt, carrots, and chicken in slow cooker.
2. Cover. Cook on High 4–5 hours.
3. Remove chicken when tender and debone.
4. Stir cut-up chicken back into soup. Add ½ cup fresh chopped parsley
5. To serve, ladle soup into bowls. Add a rounded tablespoonful of hot cooked rice to each bowl.

Per Serving: 80 calories (5 calories from fat), 1g total fat (0g saturated, 0g trans), 15mg cholesterol, 530mg sodium, 11g total carbohydrate (0.5g fiber, 1g sugar), 7g protein, 20%DV vitamin A, 0%DV vitamin C, 2%DV calcium, 4%DV iron.

Variation: *If you want to eliminate washing another pan, add 1 cup raw long-grain rice to the slow cooker mixture after the chicken has cooked 3–4 hours. Cook on High another hour. When chicken and rice are tender, remove chicken and debone. Continue with Step 5.*

Barley and Chicken Soup

Millie Schellenburg Washington, NJ

MAKES: **5 SERVINGS**
PREP. TIME: **10 MINUTES**
COOKING TIME: **4–6 HOURS**
IDEAL SLOW COOKER SIZE: **5–6-QUART OVAL**

½ lb. dry barley

1 small soup chicken, cut up

fresh celery, as desired

parsley, as desired

basil, as desired

carrots, as desired

1. Combine all ingredients in slow cooker. Cover with water.
2. Cover. Cook on Low 4–6 hours.
3. Remove chicken from bones. Discard skin. Return chicken to soup. Continue cooking until barley is soft.

Per Serving: 310 calories (50 calories from fat), 6g total fat (1.5g saturated, 0g trans), 55mg cholesterol, 95mg sodium, 41g total carbohydrate (11g fiber, 4g sugar), 26g protein, 200%DV vitamin A, 10%DV vitamin C, 15%DV calcium, 30%DV iron.

Old-Fashioned Chicken and Dumplings

Colleen Heatwole Burton, MI

MAKES: **8 SERVINGS**
PREP. TIME: **30 MINUTES**
COOKING TIME: **4¼–6¼ HOURS**
IDEAL SLOW COOKER SIZE: **4-QUART**

Soup:

4 cups cooked chicken, cubed

6 cups fat-free, low-sodium chicken broth

1 Tbsp. fresh parsley, *or* 1½ tsp. dry parsley flakes

1 cup onions, chopped

1 cup celery, chopped

6 cups diced potatoes

1 cup green beans

1 cup carrots

1 cup peas, *optional*

Dumplings: (optional)

2 cups flour (half white and half whole wheat)

1 tsp. salt

4 tsp. baking powder

1 egg, beaten

2 Tbsp. olive oil

⅔ cup skim milk

1. Combine all soup ingredients, except peas.
2. Cover. Cook on Low 4–6 hours.
3. Transfer to large soup kettle with lid. Add peas, if desired. Bring to a boil. Reduce to simmer.
4. To make Dumplings, combine flour, salt, and baking powder in a large bowl.
5. In a separate bowl, combine egg, olive oil, and milk until smooth. Add to flour mixture.
6. Drop by large tablespoonsfuls on top of simmering broth until the dumplings cover the surface of the soup.
7. Cover. Simmer without lifting the lid for 18 minutes.

Per Serving: 400 calories (60 calories from fat), 7g total fat (1.5g saturated, 0g trans), 80mg cholesterol, 510mg sodium, 51g total carbohydrate (5g fiber, 5g sugar), 32g protein, 50%DV vitamin A, 20%DV vitamin C, 20%DV calcium, 30%DV iron.

Note: *I use this recipe a lot. I adapted it from a potpie recipe which needs to be baked in the oven. I like to make this because the soup can cook in the slow cooker while we're at church. When I get home, I transfer it to a soup kettle and make the dumplings while others set the table. The dish is good served with applesauce or fruit salad.*

Chicken Clam Chowder

Irene Klaeger Inverness, FL

MAKES: **10 SERVINGS**
PREP. TIME: **20 MINUTES**
COOKING TIME: **4–9 HOURS**
IDEAL SLOW COOKER SIZE: **4-QUART**

6 slices lean turkey bacon, diced

¼ lb. lean ham, cubed

2 cups chopped onions

2 cups diced celery

½ tsp. salt

¼ tsp. black pepper

2 cups diced potatoes

2 cups cooked, lean chicken, diced

4 cups fat-free, low-sodium clam juice, *or* 2 cans clams with juice

1-lb. can whole-kernel corn with liquid

¾ cup flour

4 cups fat-free milk

4 cups shredded fat-free cheddar *or* Monterey Jack cheese

½ cup fat-free evaporated milk

2 Tbsp. fresh parsley

1. Sauté bacon, ham, onions, and celery in nonstick skillet until bacon is crisp and onions and celery are limp. Add salt and pepper.
2. Combine all ingredients in slow cooker except flour, milk, cheese, evaporated milk, and parsley.
3. Cover. Cook on Low 6–8 hours, or on High 3-4 hours.
4. Whisk flour into milk. Stir into soup, along with cheese, evaporated milk, and parsley. Cook 1 more hour on High.

Per Serving: 250 calories (35 calories from fat), 3.5g total fat (1g saturated, 0g trans), 45mg cholesterol, 880mg sodium, 23g total carbohydrate (3g fiber, 9g sugar), 31g protein, 10%DV vitamin A, 10%DV vitamin C, 50%DV calcium, 10%DV iron.

Chicken Corn Soup

Eleanor Larson Glen Lyon, PA

MAKES: **4–6 SERVINGS**
PREP. TIME: **15 MINUTES**
COOKING TIME: **8–9 HOURS**
IDEAL SLOW COOKER SIZE: **4-QUART**

2 whole boneless, skinless chicken breasts, cubed

1 onion, chopped

1 garlic clove, minced

2 carrots, sliced

2 ribs celery, chopped

2 medium potatoes, cubed

1 tsp. mixed dried herbs

⅓ cup tomato sauce

12-oz. can cream-style corn

14-oz. can whole-kernel corn

3 cups chicken stock

¼ cup chopped Italian parsley

1 tsp. salt

¼ tsp. pepper

1. Combine all ingredients except parsley, salt, and pepper in slow cooker.
2. Cover. Cook on Low 8–9 hours, or until chicken is tender.
3. Add parsley and seasonings 30 minutes before serving.

Chili, Chicken, Corn Chowder

Jeanne Allen Rye, CO

MAKES: **6–8 SERVINGS**
PREP. TIME: **15 MINUTES**
COOKING TIME: **4 HOURS**
IDEAL SLOW COOKER SIZE: **4-QUART**

¼ cup oil

1 large onion, diced

1 garlic clove, minced

1 rib celery, finely chopped

2 cups frozen or canned corn

2 cups cooked chicken, deboned and cubed

4-oz. can diced green chilies

½ tsp. black pepper

2 cups chicken broth

salt to taste

1 cup half-and-half

1. In saucepan, sauté onion, garlic, and celery in oil until limp.
2. Stir in corn, chicken, and chilies. Sauté for 2–3 minutes.
3. Combine all ingredients except half-and-half in slow cooker.
4. Cover. Heat on Low 4 hours.
5. Stir in half-and-half before serving. Do not boil, but be sure cream is heated through.

Chicken Noodle Soup with Vegetables

Bernice A. Esau North Newton, KS

MAKES: **6 SERVINGS**
PREP. TIME: **15 MINUTES**
COOKING TIME: **5–7 HOURS**
IDEAL SLOW COOKER SIZE: **4–5-QUART**

2 onions, chopped

2 cups sliced carrots

2 cups sliced celery

10-oz. pkg. frozen peas, *optional*

2 tsp. salt, *optional*

¼ tsp. black pepper

½ tsp. dried basil

¼ tsp. dried thyme

3 Tbsp. dry parsley flakes

4 cups water

2½–3-lb. chicken, cut-up

1 cup thin noodles, uncooked

1. Place all ingredients in slow cooker, except chicken and noodles.
2. Remove skin and any fat from chicken pieces. Then place chicken in cooker, on top of the rest of the ingredients.
3. Cover. Cook on High 4–6 hours.
4. One hour before serving, remove chicken. Cool slightly. Cut meat from bones.
5. Return meat to cooker. Add noodles.
6. Cover. Cook on High 1 hour.

Per Serving: 440 calories (70 calories from fat), 8g total fat (2g saturated, 0g trans), 175mg cholesterol, 1030mg sodium, 25g total carbohydrate (6g fiber, 8g sugar), 64g protein, 200%DV vitamin A, 20%DV vitamin C, 8%DV calcium, 25%DV iron.

Variation:
1. Place chicken in cooker. Cover ⅔ of it with water and cook for 4 hours on High.
2. Remove chicken. Cool. Cut meat from bone.
3. Add some ice cubes to cooker broth. When cooled, remove fat.
4. Add all ingredients, except noodles.
5. Cover. Cook on High 2–3 hours.
6. Add noodles 1 hour before serving or place cooked noodles in individual bowls and serve chicken soup over noodles.

Chicken Stock for Soup (or other uses)

Stacy Schmucker Stoltzfus Enola, PA

MAKES: **3+ QUARTS**
PREP. TIME: **10 MINUTES**
COOKING TIME: **4–6 HOURS**
IDEAL SLOW COOKER SIZE: **6-QUART**

Light

3 lbs. chicken backs and necks, *or* whole chicken

3 quarts cold water

4 ribs celery, chopped coarsely

6 carrots, unpeeled, thickly sliced

2 onions, peeled and quartered

8 peppercorns

1. Rinse chicken. Place in slow cooker. Add water and vegetables.
2. Cover. Cook on High 4–6 hours.
3. Remove chicken and vegetables from broth.
4. When broth has cooled slightly, place in refrigerator to cool completely. Remove fat and any foam when chilled.
5. The stock is ready for soup. Freeze it in 1-cup containers.
6. Use the cooked chicken and vegetables for soup or stews.

Per Serving: 220 calories (45 calories from fat), 5g total fat (1g saturated, 0g trans), 110mg cholesterol, 170mg sodium, 8g total carbohydrate (2g fiber, 5g sugar), 36g protein, 200%DV vitamin A, 10%DV vitamin C, 6%DV calcium, 10%DV iron.

A note from the recipe's tester: *I made a chicken noodle soup with a portion of the stock just to see how it turned out. It was probably the best chicken noodle soup I've ever made! I did discover that the flavor of the stock was enhanced by adding salt.*

Cassoulet Chowder

Miriam Friesen Staunton, VA

MAKES: **8–10 SERVINGS**
PREP. TIME: **1¾ HOURS**
REFRIGERATION TIME: **4–8 HOURS**
COOKING TIME: **4–10 HOURS**
IDEAL SLOW COOKER SIZE: **5-QUART**

1¼ cups dry pinto beans

4 cups water

12-oz. pkg. brown-and-serve sausage links, cooked and drained

2 cups cooked chicken, cubed

2 cups cooked ham, cubed

1½ cups sliced carrots

8-oz. can tomato sauce

¾ cup dry red wine

½ cup chopped onions

½ tsp. garlic powder

1 bay leaf

1. Combine beans and water in large saucepan. Bring to boil. Reduce heat and simmer 1½ hours. Refrigerate beans and liquid 4–8 hours.
2. Combine all ingredients in slow cooker.
3. Cover. Cook on Low 8–10 hours, or on High 4 hours. If the chowder seems too thin, remove lid during last 30 minutes of cooking time to allow it to thicken.
4. Remove bay leaf before serving.

Slow cookers come in a variety of sizes, from 1–8-quarts. The best size for a family of four or five is a 5–6-quart size.

Soups, Stews, and Chilis

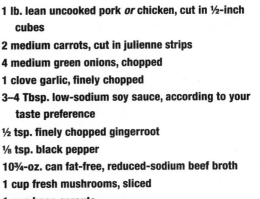

Elijah's Cucumber Soup

Shirley Unternahrer Hinh Wayland, IA

MAKES: **8 SERVINGS**
PREP. TIME: **30–40 MINUTES**
COOKING TIME: **1½–2 HOURS**
IDEAL SLOW COOKER SIZE: **4-QUART**

1 lb. ground pork
2 Tbsp. fish sauce
¼ tsp. black pepper
4 large cucumbers, peeled
2 quarts boiling water
2 green onions, chopped
⅛ tsp. black pepper
4 Tbsp. fish sauce
salt to taste

1. Combine pork, 2 Tbsp. fish sauce, and ¼ tsp. black pepper in mixing bowl.
2. Cut peeled cucumbers in half and scoop out seeds, creating a channel in each cuke. Stuff pork mixture into cucumbers.
3. Form remaining meat into 1-inch balls. Drop balls into stockpot with 2 quarts boiling water. Boil until a layer of foam develops on the water. Skim off foam and discard.
4. Drop stuffed cucumbers into boiling water. Simmer for 15 minutes. Transfer cucumbers and pork balls into slow cooker. Add hot liquid from stockpot.
5. Add green onions, ⅛ tsp. black pepper, and 4 Tbsp. fish sauce.
6. Cover. Cook on High 1½–2 hours.
7. Serve over rice in bowl, along with lemon juice and chili sauce.

Note: *This dish was brought into our family's recipe collection by my husband, Hai. Hai came to the United States, from Vietnam, 23 years ago. We eat this soup quite often at our house. Many of our friends and family have enjoyed it over the years and we've had many requests for it.*

Asian Pork Soup

Kristi See Weskan, KS

MAKES: **6 SERVINGS**
PREP. TIME: **20 MINUTES**
COOKING TIME: **3–9 HOURS**
IDEAL SLOW COOKER SIZE: **3–4-QUART**

1 lb. lean uncooked pork *or* chicken, cut in ½-inch cubes
2 medium carrots, cut in julienne strips
4 medium green onions, chopped
1 clove garlic, finely chopped
3–4 Tbsp. low-sodium soy sauce, according to your taste preference
½ tsp. finely chopped gingerroot
⅛ tsp. black pepper
10¾-oz. can fat-free, reduced-sodium beef broth
1 cup fresh mushrooms, sliced
1 cup bean sprouts

1. Cook meat in large nonstick skillet over medium heat for 8–10 minutes. Stir occasionally.
2. Mix meat and remaining ingredients except mushrooms and bean sprouts in slow cooker.
3. Cover. Cook on Low 7–9 hours, or on High 3–4 hours.
4. Stir in mushrooms and bean sprouts.
5. Cover. Cook on Low 1 hour.

Per Serving: 230 calories (70 calories from fat), 8g total fat (2.5g saturated, 0g trans), 70mg cholesterol, 430mg sodium, 12g total carbohydrate (3g fiber, 7g sugar), 28g protein, 80%DV vitamin A, 10%DV vitamin C, 4%DV calcium, 10%DV iron.

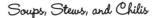

Creamy Pork Stew

Betty Moore Plano, IL

MAKES: 8 SERVINGS
PREP. TIME: 20 MINUTES
COOKING TIME: 8–10 HOURS
IDEAL SLOW COOKER SIZE: 5-QUART

Light

2 lbs. ground pork

2 10¾-oz. cans 98% fat-free cream of mushroom soup

2 14½-oz. cans green beans with liquid

4 potatoes, diced

4 carrots, chopped

2 small onions, diced

2 10¾-oz. cans condensed vegetarian vegetable soup

2 soup cans of water

3 ribs celery, chopped

½ tsp. salt

¼ tsp. black pepper

¼ tsp. garlic powder

½ tsp. dried marjoram

1. Brown ground pork in a nonstick skillet.
2. Combine all ingredients in slow cooker.
3. Cook on Low 8–10 hours.

Per Serving: 490 calories (170 calories from fat), 19g total fat (7g saturated, 1g trans), 80mg cholesterol, 1910mg sodium, 48g total carbohydrate (9g fiber, 12g sugar), 28g protein, 200%DV vitamin A, 20%DV vitamin C, 10%DV calcium, 25%DV iron.

Tips:

1. Add a can of diced tomatoes to Step 2 if you wish.

2. This recipe goes well with homemade bread.

Sauerkraut Potato Soup

Barbara Tenny Delta, PA

MAKES: 8 SERVINGS
PREP. TIME: 15 MINUTES
COOKING TIME: 2–8 HOURS
IDEAL SLOW COOKER SIZE: 5-QUART

1 lb. smoked Polish sausage, cut into ½-inch pieces

5 medium potatoes, cubed

2 large onions, chopped

2 large carrots, cut into ¼-inch slices

42–45-oz. can chicken broth

32-oz. can or bag sauerkraut, rinsed and drained

6-oz. can tomato paste

1. Combine all ingredients in large slow cooker. Stir to combine.
2. Cover. Cook on High 2 hours, and then on Low 6–8 hours.
3. Serve with rye bread.

Polish Sausage Bean Soup

Janie Steele   Moore, OK

MAKES: **10 SERVINGS**
PREP. TIME: **45 MINUTES**
SOAKING TIME: **8 HOURS**
COOKING TIME: **9½ HOURS**
IDEAL SLOW COOKER SIZE: **6-QUART**

1-lb. pkg. dried Great Northern beans

28-oz. can whole tomatoes

2 8-oz. cans tomato sauce

2 large onions, chopped

3 cloves garlic, minced

1 tsp. salt

¼–½ tsp. pepper, according to your taste preference

3 celery ribs, sliced

bell pepper, sliced

large ham bone or ham hock

1–2 lbs. smoked sausage links, sliced

1. Cover beans with water and soak for 8 hours. Rinse and drain.
2. Place beans in 6-qt. cooker and cover with water.
3. Combine all other ingredients, except sausage, in large bowl. Stir into beans in slow cooker.
4. Cover. Cook on High 1–1½ hours. Reduce to Low. Cook 7 hours.
5. Remove ham bone or hock and debone. Stir ham pieces back into soup.
6. Add sausage links.
7. Cover. Cook on Low 1 hour.

Note: *For enhanced flavor, brown sausage before adding to soup.*

Ruth's Split Pea Soup

Ruth Conrad Liechty   Goshen, IN

MAKES: **6–8 SERVINGS**
PREP. TIME: **15 MINUTES**
COOKING TIME: **12 HOURS**
IDEAL SLOW COOKER SIZE: **4-QUART**

1 lb. bulk sausage, browned and drained

6 cups water

1 bag (2¼ cups) dry split peas

2 medium potatoes, diced

1 onion, chopped

½ tsp. dried marjoram, *or* thyme

½ tsp. pepper

1. Wash and sort dried peas, removing any stones. Then combine all ingredients in slow cooker.
2. Cover. Cook on Low 12 hours.

Wrap cut-up onions or peppers in a paper towel before placing them in a Ziplock bag and refrigerating. The paper towel absorbs moisture and delays spoiling.

Karen's Split Pea Soup

Karen Stoltzfus Alto, MI

MAKES: **6 SERVINGS**
PREP. TIME: **15 MINUTES**
COOKING TIME: **7 HOURS**
IDEAL SLOW COOKER SIZE: **4–5-QUART**

2 carrots

2 ribs celery

1 onion

1 parsnip

1 leek (keep 3 inches of green)

1 ripe tomato

1 ham hock

1¾ cups (1 lb.) dried split peas, washed with stones removed

2 Tbsp. olive oil

1 bay leaf

1 tsp. dried thyme

4 cups chicken broth

4 cups water

1 tsp. salt

¼ tsp. pepper

2 tsp. chopped fresh parsley

1. Cut all vegetables into ¼-inch pieces and place in slow cooker. Add remaining ingredients except salt, pepper, and parsley.
2. Cover. Cook on High 7 hours.
3. Remove ham hock. Shred meat from bone and return meat to pot.
4. Season soup with salt and pepper. Stir in parsley. Serve immediately.

Split Pea Soup with Ham

Elena Yoder Carlsbad, NM

MAKES: **8 SERVINGS**
PREP. TIME: **15 MINUTES**
COOKING TIME: **4 HOURS**
IDEAL SLOW COOKER SIZE: **4-QUART**

2½ quarts water

1 ham hock *or* pieces of cut-up ham

2½ cups split peas, dried

1 medium onion, chopped

3 medium carrots, cut in small pieces

salt and pepper to taste

1. Bring water to a boil in a saucepan on your stovetop.
2. Place all other ingredients into slow cooker. Add water and stir together well.
3. Cover and cook on High for 4 hours, or until vegetables are tender.
4. If you've cooked a ham hock, remove it from the soup and debone the meat. Stir cut-up chunks of meat back into the soup before serving.

Mountain Bike Soup

Jonathan Gehman   Harrisonburg, VA

MAKES: **4 SERVINGS**
PREP. TIME: **10 MINUTES**
COOKING TIME: **2–6 HOURS**
IDEAL SLOW COOKER SIZE: **2–3-QUART**

12-oz. can chicken broth
12-oz. can V-8 juice, regular or spicy
⅓ cup barley, rice, *or* **broken spaghetti noodles, uncooked**
⅓ cup chopped pepperoni, ham, *or* **bacon**
15-oz. can cut green beans with liquid

1. Dump it all in. Put on the lid. Turn it on Low.
2. Go for a long ride on your bike, from 2–6 hours.

Tip: *This soup seems to accept whatever vegetables you throw in: a little corn, okra, diced potatoes, shredded zucchini, whatever … I often add more liquid before serving if it seems to be getting more like stew and less like soup.*

If you mistakenly add too much salt to a dish you're preparing, drop in a potato and continue cooking. The potato will help to absorb the extra salt.

Turkey Rosemary Veggie Soup

Willard E. Roth   Elkhart, IN

MAKES: **8 SERVINGS**
PREP. TIME: **15 MINUTES**
COOKING TIME: **8 HOURS**
IDEAL SLOW COOKER SIZE: **6-QUART**

1 lb. 99% fat-free ground turkey
3 parsley stalks with leaves, sliced
3 scallions, chopped
3 medium carrots, unpeeled, sliced
3 medium potatoes, unpeeled, sliced
3 celery ribs with leaves
3 small onions, sliced
1-lb. can whole-kernel corn with juice
1-lb. can green beans with juice
1-lb. can low-sodium diced Italian-style tomatoes
3 cans water
3 packets dry Herb-Ox vegetable broth
1 Tbsp. crushed rosemary, fresh or dry

1. Brown turkey with parsley and scallions in iron skillet. Drain. Pour into slow cooker sprayed with non-fat cooking spray.
2. Add vegetables, water, dry vegetable broth, and rosemary.
3. Cover. Cook on Low 8 hours.

Per Serving: 200 calories (15 calories from fat), 1.5g total fat (0g saturated, 0g trans), 25mg cholesterol, 510mg sodium, 31g total carbohydrate (6g fiber, 9g sugar), 18g protein, 100%DV vitamin A, 20%DV vitamin C, 6%DV calcium, 15%DV iron.

Tip: *This is tasty served topped with a dollop of non-fat yogurt and cornbread on the side.*

Meatball-Mushroom Soup

Nanci Keatley Salem, OR

MAKES: **8 SERVINGS**
PREP. TIME: **15 MINUTES**
COOKING TIME: **3–8 HOURS**
IDEAL SLOW COOKER SIZE: **3½-QUART**

½ lb. ground turkey

½ tsp. garlic powder

½ tsp. onion powder

¼ tsp. black pepper

1 large egg

1 Tbsp. olive oil

1 cup carrots, sliced

2 cloves garlic, crushed

2 cups sliced fresh mushrooms

10¾-oz. can low-fat or fat-free low-sodium beef broth

10¾-oz. can 98% fat-free cream of mushroom soup

2 Tbsp. tomato paste

Parmesan cheese for garnish

fresh parsley for garnish

1. In a small bowl mix together ground turkey and seasonings. Add egg, stirring until well blended. Form into small meatballs.
2. Heat olive oil in skillet. Brown meatballs. Drain well.
3. Transfer meatballs to slow cooker. Add remaining ingredients, except Parmesan cheese and parsley.
4. Cover. Cook on Low 6–8 hours, or on High 3–4 hours.

Per Serving: 100 calories (45 calories from fat), 5g total fat (1g saturated, 0g trans), 25mg cholesterol, 290mg sodium, 7g total carbohydrate (0.5g fiber, 2g sugar), 8g protein, 80%DV vitamin A, 4%DV vitamin C, 2%DV calcium, 4%DV iron.

Cheeseburger Soup

Nanci Keatley Salem, OR

MAKES: **6 SERVINGS**
PREP. TIME: **15 MINUTES**
COOKING TIME: **8–9 HOURS**
IDEAL SLOW COOKER SIZE: **4-QUART**

1 lb. ground turkey

1 cup chopped onions

½ cup chopped green bell peppers

2 ribs celery, chopped

20-oz. can beef broth

1 cup non-fat milk

2 cups water

2 Tbsp. flour

8 ozs. low-fat cheddar cheese, shredded

1. Brown turkey in nonstick skillet. Spoon into slow cooker.
2. Add vegetables to slow cooker.
3. Heat broth, milk, and water in skillet. Sprinkle flour over liquid. Stir until smooth and let boil for 3 minutes.
4. Pour into slow cooker.
5. Cover. Cook on Low 6 hours. Then add cheese and cook another 2–3 hours.

Per Serving: 240 calories (100 calories from fat), 11g total fat (3.5g saturated, 0g trans), 70mg cholesterol, 140mg sodium, 8g total carbohydrate (1g fiber, 5g sugar), 26g protein, 6%DV vitamin A, 10%DV vitamin C, 35%DV calcium, 8%DV iron.

Creamy Corn and Turkey Soup

Janessa Hochstedler   East Earl, PA

MAKES: **5–6 SERVINGS**
PREP. TIME: **15 MINUTES**
COOKING TIME: **3–8 HOURS**
IDEAL SLOW COOKER SIZE: **3-QUART**

2 cups cooked turkey, shredded

1 cup milk

2 cups chicken broth

15-oz. can Mexican-style corn

4 ozs. (half an 8-oz. pkg.) cream cheese, cubed

1 red bell pepper, chopped, *optional*

1. Place all ingredients in slow cooker.
2. Cover and cook on Low 7–8 hours, or on High 3 hours.

Leftover Turkey Soup

Janie Steele   Moore, OK

MAKES: **8–10 SERVINGS**
PREP. TIME: **10 MINUTES**
COOKING TIME: **2–3 HOURS**
IDEAL SLOW COOKER SIZE: **4-QUART**

1 small onion, chopped

1 cup chopped celery

1 Tbsp. oil

2–3 cups cooked turkey, diced

1 cup rice, cooked

leftover gravy *or* combination of leftover gravy and chicken broth

1. Sauté onion and celery in oil in saucepan until translucent.
2. Combine all ingredients in slow cooker, adding gravy and/or broth until of the consistency you want.
3. Cover. Cook on Low for at least 2–3 hours, or until heated through.

Cheesy Menudo

Eileen Eash   Carlsbad, NM

MAKES: **8 SERVINGS**
PREP. TIME: **10 MINUTES**
COOKING TIME: **4 HOURS**
IDEAL SLOW COOKER SIZE: **3½-QUART**

3 16-oz. cans white *or* yellow hominy, undrained

4-oz. can chopped green chilies

½ lb. Velveeta Light cheese, diced

1 tsp. garlic salt

½ tsp. black pepper

fresh cilantro *or* parsley, chopped

2 cups cooked chicken *or* lean beef, chopped

1. Combine all ingredients in slow cooker. Stir well.
2. Cover. Cook on Low 4 hours.

Per Serving: 240 calories (50 calories from fat), 6g total fat (2.5g saturated, 1g trans), 40mg cholesterol, 1000mg sodium, 28g total carbohydrate (5g fiber, 3g sugar), 18g protein, 6%DV vitamin A, 2%DV vitamin C, 20%DV calcium, 8%DV iron.

Wild Rice Soup

Joyce Shackelford Green Bay, WI

Light

MAKES: **8 SERVINGS**
PREP. TIME: **15 MINUTES**
COOKING TIME: **4–6 HOURS**
IDEAL SLOW COOKER SIZE: **4-QUART**

2 Tbsp. butter

½ cup dry wild rice

6 cups fat-free, low-sodium chicken stock

½ cup minced onions

½ cup minced celery

½ lb. winter squash, peeled, seeded, cut in ½-inch cubes

2 cups cooked chicken, chopped

½ cup browned, slivered almonds

1. Melt butter in small skillet. Add rice and sauté for 10 minutes over low heat. Transfer to slow cooker.
2. Add all remaining ingredients except chicken and almonds.
3. Cover. Cook on Low 4–6 hours. One hour before serving stir in chicken.
4. Top with browned slivered almonds just before serving.

Per Serving: 310 calories (70 calories from fat), 8g total fat (4g saturated, 0g trans), 70mg cholesterol, 320mg sodium, 25g total carbohydrate (3g fiber, 3g sugar), 33g protein, 2%DV vitamin A, 2%DV vitamin C, 8%DV calcium, 25%DV iron.

Don't be afraid to experiment and make changes in recipes. If a recipe calls for an ingredient you don't care for, either substitute something else, or leave it out.

Shrimp Chowder

Kristi See Weskan, KS • *Karen Waggoner* Joplin, MO

Light

MAKES: **8 SERVINGS**
PREP. TIME: **15 MINUTES**
COOKING TIME: **1–2 HOURS**
IDEAL SLOW COOKER SIZE: **5–6-QUART**

1 lb. red potatoes, cubed

2½ cups fat-free, reduced-sodium chicken broth

3 celery ribs, chopped

8 green onions, chopped

1½ lbs. medium-sized shrimp, uncooked, peeled, and deveined

½ cup sweet red bell peppers, chopped

1½ cups fat-free milk

¼ cup all-purpose flour

½ cup fat-free evaporated milk

2 Tbsp. minced fresh parsley

½ tsp. paprika

½ tsp. Worcestershire sauce

⅛ tsp. cayenne pepper

⅛ tsp. black pepper

1. Combine potatoes, broth, celery, onions, shrimp, and red bell peppers in slow cooker.
2. Cover. Cook on Low 2 hours, or until vegetables are done to your liking.
3. Stir in 1½ cups milk and gently mash vegetables with potato masher. Leave some small chunks of potato.
4. Combine flour and evaporated milk. Mix until smooth. Gradually stir into soup mixture.
5. Cook and stir uncovered on High until thickened.

Per Serving: 230 calories (15 calories from fat), 2g total fat (0g saturated, 0g trans), 130mg cholesterol, 240mg sodium, 28g total carbohydrate (4g fiber, 12g sugar), 25g protein, 15%DV vitamin A, 30%DV vitamin C, 20%DV calcium, 20%DV iron.

Tip: *This chowder is even better the next day after the flavors have melded overnight.*

Corn and Shrimp Chowder

Naomi E. Fast Hesston, KS

MAKES: **6 SERVINGS**
PREP. TIME: **20 MINUTES**
COOKING TIME: **3–4 HOURS**
IDEAL SLOW COOKER SIZE: **3½-QUART**

3 slices lean turkey bacon, diced
1 cup chopped onions
2 cups diced, unpeeled red potatoes
2 10-oz. pkgs. frozen corn
1 tsp. Worcestershire sauce
½ tsp. paprika
½ tsp. salt
⅛ tsp. black pepper
2 6-oz. cans shrimp, drained
2 cups water
2 Tbsp. butter
12-oz. can fat-free evaporated milk
chopped chives

1. Brown bacon in nonstick skillet until lightly crisp. Add onions to drippings and sauté until transparent. Using slotted spoon, transfer bacon and onions to slow cooker.
2. Add remaining ingredients to cooker except milk and chives.
3. Cover. Cook on Low 3–4 hours, adding milk and chives 30 minutes before end of cooking time.

Per Serving: 310 calories (70 calories from fat), 7g total fat (3g saturated, 0g trans), 115mg cholesterol, 480mg sodium, 41g total carbohydrate (4g fiber, 11g sugar), 23g protein, 10%DV vitamin A, 20%DV vitamin C, 25%DV calcium, 15%DV iron.

Note: *I learned to make this recipe in a 7th-grade home economics class. It made an impression on my father who liked seafood very much. The recipe calls only for canned shrimp, but I often increase its taste appeal with extra cooked shrimp.*

Hot & Sour Soup

Judy Govotsos Frederick, MD

MAKES: **4 SERVINGS**
PREP. TIME: **10 MINUTES**
COOKING TIME: **4–12 HOURS**
IDEAL SLOW COOKER SIZE: **3½-QUART**

4 cups fat-free, low-sodium chicken broth
8-oz. can sliced bamboo shoots, drained
1 carrot, julienned
8-oz. can water chestnuts, drained and sliced
3 Tbsp. quick-cooking tapioca
6-oz. can sliced mushrooms, drained
1 Tbsp. vinegar *or* rice wine vinegar
1 Tbsp. light soy sauce
1 tsp. sugar
¼ tsp. black pepper
¼–½ tsp. red pepper flakes, according to your taste preference
8-oz. pkg. frozen, peeled, and deveined shrimp, *optional*
4 ozs. firm tofu, drained and cubed
1 egg, beaten

1. Combine all ingredients, except shrimp, tofu, and egg in slow cooker.
2. Cover. Cook on Low 9–11 hours, or on High 3–4 hours.
3. Add shrimp and tofu.
4. Cover. Cook 45–60 minutes.
5. Pour egg into the soup in a thin stream. Stir the soup gently until the egg forms fine shreds instead of clumps.

Per Serving: 240 calories (45 calories from fat), 5g total fat (1g saturated, 0g trans), 135mg cholesterol, 600mg sodium, 24g total carbohydrate (4g fiber, 4g sugar), 26g protein, 80%DV vitamin A, 0%DV vitamin C, 25%DV calcium, 30%DV iron.

Variation: *You may want to stir in ½ tsp. garlic salt, if your diet permits, in Step 1.*

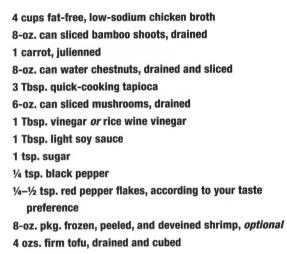

Soups, Stews, and Chilis

Southwestern Soup

Evelyn L. Ward Greeley, CO

MAKES: **4 SERVINGS**
PREP. TIME: **10–20 MINUTES**
COOKING TIME: **6–8 HOURS**
IDEAL SLOW COOKER SIZE: **4-QUART**

2 14-oz. cans beef broth
½ cup sliced carrots
½ cup diced onions
1 cup diced potatoes
1 garlic clove, minced
8-oz. can *or* 1 cup home-canned crushed tomatoes
1 Tbsp. Worcestershire sauce
salsa to taste

Garnishes:
shredded cheese
diced avocados
diced green peppers
diced cucumbers
2¼-oz. can sliced ripe olives
6-oz. fresh mushrooms, sliced and sautéed in butter
6-oz. can cooked and peeled tiny shrimp
1 cup cooked ham, diced
1 cup sliced green onion
3 hard-cooked eggs, chopped
1 cup diced tomatoes
sour cream

1. Combine broth, carrots, onions, potatoes, garlic, tomatoes, and Worcestershire sauce in slow cooker. Cook on Low 6–8 hours.
2. Before serving, stir in salsa, sampling as you go to get the right balance of flavors.
3. Serve the soup in bowls. Offer your choice of garnishes as toppings.

Crab Soup

Susan Alexander Baltimore, MD

MAKES: **10 SERVINGS**
PREP. TIME: **20 MINUTES**
COOKING TIME: **8–10 HOURS**
IDEAL SLOW COOKER SIZE: **5-QUART**

1 lb. carrots, sliced
½ bunch celery, sliced
1 large onion, diced
2 10-oz. bags frozen mixed vegetables, *or* your choice of frozen vegetables
12-oz. can tomato juice
1 lb. ham, cubed
1 lb. beef, cubed
6 slices bacon, chopped
1 tsp. salt
¼ tsp. pepper
1 Tbsp. Old Bay seasoning
1 lb. claw crabmeat

1. Combine all ingredients except seasonings and crab-meat in large slow cooker. Pour in water until cooker is half-full.
2. Add spices. Stir in thoroughly. Put crab on top.
3. Cover. Cook on Low 8–10 hours.
4. Stir well and serve.

Some new slow cookers cook hotter and faster than older models. So get to know your slow cooker. I suggest a range of cooking times for many of the recipes since cookers vary. When you've found the right length of time for a recipe done in your cooker, note that in your cookbook.

Creamy Salmon Chowder

Diane Shetler Hyde Park, MA

MAKES: **5 SERVINGS**
PREP. TIME: **10 MINUTES**
COOKING TIME: **3½–10 HOURS**
IDEAL SLOW COOKER SIZE: **3½-QUART**

2 cups fat-free chicken broth

2 cups water

10-oz. pkg. frozen corn

1 cup chopped celery

½ cup chopped onions

¾ cup wheat berries

8-oz. pkg. fat-free cream cheese, cut into cubes

16-oz. can salmon, drained, skin and bones removed, and coarsely flaked

1 Tbsp. dill weed

1. Combine chicken broth, water, corn, celery, onions, and wheat berries in slow cooker.
2. Cover. Cook on Low 8–10 hours, or on High 3½–4 hours.
3. Turn cooker to High. Add cheese, stirring until melted.
4. Stir in salmon and dill.
5. Cover. Cook 10 minutes longer.

Per Serving: 350 calories (60 calories from fat), 7g total fat (2g saturated, 0g trans), 40mg cholesterol, 790mg sodium, 42g total carbohydrate (6g fiber, 3g sugar), 34gprotein, 10%DV vitamin A, 10%DV vitamin C, 35%DV calcium, 15%DV iron.

Vegetable Salmon Chowder

Esther J. Yoder Hartville, OH

MAKES: **8 SERVINGS**
PREP. TIME: **15 MINUTES**
COOKING TIME: **3 HOURS**
IDEAL SLOW COOKER SIZE: **3½-QUART**

1½ cups cubed potatoes

1 cup diced celery

½ cup diced onions

2 Tbsp. fresh parsley, *or* 1 Tbsp. dried parsley

½ tsp. salt

¼ tsp. black pepper

water to cover

16-oz. can pink salmon

4 cups skim milk

2 tsp. lemon juice

2 Tbsp. finely cut red bell peppers

2 Tbsp. finely shredded carrots

½ cup instant potatoes

1. Combine cubed potatoes, celery, onions, parsley, salt, pepper, and water to cover in slow cooker.
2. Cook on High for 3 hours, or until soft. Add a bit more water if needed.
3. Add salmon, milk, lemon juice, red peppers, carrots, and instant potatoes.
4. Heat 1 hour more until very hot.

Per Serving: 140 calories (20 calories from fat), 2g total fat (0g saturated, 0g trans), 30mg cholesterol, 115mg sodium, 15g total carbohydrate (1g fiber, 7g sugar), 16g protein, 10%DV vitamin A, 10%DV vitamin C, 15%DV calcium, 4%DV iron.

Variations:

1. If you enjoy garlic, add a tablespoon or two of it, minced, to Step 1.

2. If you like a thicker chowder, and your diet allows, increase the instant potatoes in Step 3 to ¾–1 cup.

Wonderful Clam Chowder

Carlene Horne Bedford, NH

MAKES: **4–6 SERVINGS**
PREP. TIME: **10–15 MINUTES**
COOKING TIME: **6–7 HOURS**
IDEAL SLOW COOKER SIZE: **3½-QUART**

2 12-oz. cans evaporated milk

1 evaporated milk can of water

2 6-oz. cans whole clams, undrained

6-oz. can minced clams, undrained

1 small onion, chopped

2 small potatoes, diced

2 Tbsp. cornstarch

¼ cup water

1. Combine all ingredients except cornstarch and ¼ cup water in slow cooker.
2. Cover. Cook on Low 6–7 hours.
3. One hour before end of cooking time, mix cornstarch and ¼ cup water together. When smooth, stir into soup. Stir until soup thickens.

Tasty Clam Chowder

Jean H. Robinson Cinnaminson, NJ

MAKES: **8 SERVINGS**
PREP. TIME: **15 MINUTES**
COOKING TIME: **2½ HOURS**
IDEAL SLOW COOKER SIZE: **5-QUART**

2 1-lb. cans low-fat, low-sodium chicken broth

3 large potatoes, peeled and diced finely

2 large onions, chopped finely

1-lb. can creamed corn

1 carrot, chopped finely

1 dozen littleneck clams, *or* 3 6-oz. cans minced clams

2 cups low-fat milk

¼ tsp. black pepper

¼ tsp. salt

2 Tbsp. chopped fresh parsley

6 slices bacon, well cooked, drained and crumbled, *optional*

1. Pour broth into slow cooker.
2. Add potatoes, onions, creamed corn, and carrot.
3. Cover. Cook on High 1 hour. Stir. Cook on High another hour.
4. Using a potato masher, mash potatoes coarsely to thicken soup.
5. Add clams, milk, salt, black pepper, salt, and parsley.
6. Cover. Cook on High 20 minutes.
7. Garnish with crumbled bacon, if desired.

Per Serving: 210 calories (30 calories from fat), 3.5g total fat (1.5g saturated, 0g trans), 15mg cholesterol, 660mg sodium, 33g total carbohydrate (3g fiber, 8g sugar), 14g protein, 40%DV vitamin A, 20%DV vitamin C, 10%DV calcium, 15%DV iron.

Tip: *If your diet permits, you may want to increase the salt to ½ tsp.*

Manhattan Clam Chowder

Joyce Slaymaker Strasburg, PA
Louise Stackhouse Benton, PA

PICTURED
ON PAGE
100

MAKES: **8 SERVINGS**
PREP. TIME: **15 MINUTES**
COOKING TIME: **8–10 HOURS**
IDEAL SLOW COOKER SIZE: **3½-QUART**

¼ lb. lean turkey bacon, diced and browned

1 large onion, chopped

2 carrots, thinly sliced

3 ribs celery, sliced

1 Tbsp. dried parsley flakes

1-lb. 12-oz. can low-sodium tomatoes

½ tsp. salt

3 8-oz. cans clams with liquid

2 whole peppercorns

1 bay leaf

1½ tsp. dried crushed thyme

3 medium-sized potatoes, cubed

1. Combine all ingredients in slow cooker.
2. Cover. Cook on Low 8–10 hours, or until vegetables are done to your liking.

Per Serving: 260 calories (45 calories from fat), 5g total fat (1g saturated, 0g trans), 70mg cholesterol, 710mg sodium, 27g total carbohydrate (4g fiber, 5g sugar), 27g protein, 80%DV vitamin A, 40%DV vitamin C, 20%DV calcium, 100%DV iron.

Quick Clam and Corn Chowder

Carol L. Stroh Akron, NY

MAKES: **4–6 SERVINGS**
PREP. TIME: **5–10 MINUTES**
COOKING TIME: **3–4 HOURS**
IDEAL SLOW COOKER SIZE: **1½–2-QUART**

2 10½-oz. cans cream of potato soup

1 pint frozen corn

6½-oz. can minced clams, drained

2 soup cans milk

1. Place all ingredients in slow cooker. Stir to mix.
2. Cook on Low 3–4 hours, or until hot.

Clam Chowder

Marilyn Mowry Irving, TX

MAKES: **3 SERVINGS**
PREP. TIME: **10 MINUTES**
COOKING TIME: **2–3 HOURS**
IDEAL SLOW COOKER SIZE: **1–2-QUART**

15-oz. can New England-style clam chowder

1½ cups milk *or* half-and-half

6½-oz. can minced clams, undrained

half a stick (¼ cup) butter

¼ cup cooking sherry

1. Mix all ingredients together in slow cooker.
2. Heat on Low for 2–3 hours, or until good and hot.

Crabmeat Soup

Carol L. Stroh   Akron, NY

MAKES: **8 SERVINGS**
PREP. TIME: **5–10 MINUTES**
COOKING TIME: **5–6 HOURS**
IDEAL SLOW COOKER SIZE: **3½-QUART**

2 10¾-oz. cans cream of tomato soup

2 10½-oz. cans split pea soup

3 soup cans milk

1 cup heavy cream

1 or 2 6-oz. cans crabmeat, drained

¼ cup sherry, *optional*

1. Pour soups into slow cooker. Add milk and stir to mix.
2. Cover and cook on Low for 4 hours, or until hot.
3. Stir in cream and crabmeat. Continue to cook on Low for 1 hour, or until heated through.

Since I work full-time, I often put my dinner into the slow cooker to cook until I get home. My three teenagers and umpire/referee husband can all get a hot nutritious meal no matter what time they get home.

Shrimp Soup/Chowder

Joanne Good   Wheaton, IL

MAKES: **12 SERVINGS**
PREP. TIME: **25 MINUTES**
COOKING TIME: **7–8 HOURS**
IDEAL SLOW COOKER SIZE: **4-QUART**

1 medium onion, chopped

5 medium russet potatoes, peeled and cubed

1½ cups diced pre-cooked ham

4–6 cups water

salt and pepper to taste

2 lbs. shrimp, peeled, deveined, and cooked

Chowder option:

4 Tbsp. flour

1 cup heavy (whipping) cream

1. Place chopped onion in microwave-safe bowl and cook in microwave for 2 minutes on High.
2. Place onion, cubed potatoes, diced ham, and 4 cups water in slow cooker. (If you're making the Chowder option, whisk 4 Tbsp. flour into 4 cups water in bowl before adding to slow cooker.)
3. Cover and cook on Low for 7 hours, or until potatoes are softened. If soup base is thicker than you like, add up to 2 cups more water.
4. About 15–20 minutes before serving, turn heat to High and add shrimp. If making chowder, also add heavy cream. Cook until shrimp are hot, about 15 minutes.

Variation: *Add ½ tsp. thyme and 1 bay leaf in Step 2. Remove bay leaf before serving.*

Oyster Stew

Linda Overholt   Abbeville, SC

MAKES: **4 SERVINGS**
PREP. TIME: **15–20 MINUTES**
COOKING TIME: **2 HOURS**
IDEAL SLOW COOKER SIZE: **3½–4-QUART**

1 pint oysters with liquor
half a stick (¼ cup) butter
1 pint milk
1 pint half-and-half
salt and pepper to taste

1. In large nonstick skillet, heat oysters slowly in their own juice until edges begin to curl (do not boil).
2. Place oysters and their liquor in the slow cooker.
3. Add butter, milk, and half-and-half. Season with salt and pepper to taste.
4. Cook on Low for about 2 hours, or until heated through.

Variation: *Use 1 quart milk, instead of 1 pint milk and 1 pint half-and-half.*

Sara Kinsinger   Stuarts Draft, VA

Easy Southern Brunswick Stew

Barbara Sparks   Glen Burnie, MD

MAKES: **10–12 SERVINGS**
PREP. TIME: **10 MINUTES**
COOKING TIME: **6½–8½ HOURS**
IDEAL SLOW COOKER SIZE: **4-QUART**

2–3 lbs. pork butt
17-oz. can white corn
14-oz. bottle ketchup
2 cups diced potatoes, cooked
10-oz. pkg. frozen peas
2 10¾-oz. cans tomato soup
hot sauce to taste
salt to taste
pepper to taste

1. Place pork in slow cooker.
2. Cover. Cook on Low 6–8 hours. Remove meat from bone and shred.
3. Combine all ingredients in slow cooker.
4. Cover. Bring to boil on High. Reduce heat to Low and simmer 30 minutes.

Joy's Brunswick Stew

Joy Sutter Iowa City, IA

MAKES: **8 SERVINGS**
PREP. TIME: **10 MINUTES**
COOKING TIME: **4 HOURS**
IDEAL SLOW COOKER SIZE: **4-QUART**

1 lb. skinless, boneless chicken breasts, cubed
2 potatoes, thinly sliced
10¾-oz. can tomato soup
16-oz. can stewed tomatoes
10-oz. pkg. frozen corn
10-oz. pkg. frozen lima beans
3 Tbsp. onion flakes
¼ tsp. salt
⅛ tsp. pepper

1. Combine all ingredients in slow cooker.
2. Cover. Cook on High 2 hours. Reduce to Low and cook 2 hours.

Variation: *For more flavor, add 1 or 2 bay leaves during cooking.*

Brunswick Soup Mix

Joyce B. Suiter Garysburg, NC

MAKES: **14 SERVINGS**
PREP. TIME: **10–15 MINUTES**
COOKING TIME: **7 HOURS**
IDEAL SLOW COOKER SIZE: **5-QUART**

1 large onion, chopped
4 cups frozen, cubed, hash browns, thawed
4 cups chopped cooked chicken, *or* 2 20-oz. cans
    canned chicken
14½-oz. can diced tomatoes
15-oz. can tomato sauce
15¼-oz. can corn
15¼-oz. can lima beans, drained
2 cups chicken broth
½ tsp. salt
½ tsp. pepper
¼ tsp. Worcestershire sauce
¼ cup sugar

1. Combine all ingredients in large slow cooker.
2. Cover. Cook on High 7 hours.
3. Cool and freeze in 2-cup portions.
4. To use, empty 1 frozen portion into saucepan with small amount of liquid: tomato juice, V-8 juice, or broth. Cook slowly until soup mixture thaws. Stir frequently, adding more liquid until of desired consistency.

Soups, Stews, and Chilis

No-Fuss Potato Soup

Lucille Amos Greensboro, NC • *Betty Moore* Plano, IL
Lavina Hochstedler Grand Blanc, MI

MAKES: **8–10 SERVINGS**
PREP. TIME: **15 MINUTES**
COOKING TIME: **7–8 HOURS**
IDEAL SLOW COOKER SIZE: **5–6-QUART**

6 cups diced, peeled potatoes

5 cups water

2 cups diced onions

½ cup diced celery

½ cup chopped carrots

¼ cup butter

4 tsp. chicken bouillon granules

2 tsp. salt

¼ tsp. pepper

12-oz. can evaporated milk

3 Tbsp. chopped fresh parsley

8 oz. cheddar, *or* Colby, cheese, shredded

1. Combine all ingredients except milk, parsley, and cheese in slow cooker.
2. Cover. Cook on High 7–8 hours, or until vegetables are tender.
3. Stir in milk and parsley. Stir in cheese until it melts. Heat thoroughly.

Tip: *Top individual servings with chopped chives.*

Variation: *For added flavor, stir in 3 slices bacon, browned until crisp, and crumbled.*

"Baked" Potato Soup

Kristina Shuil Timberville, VA

MAKES: **6–8 SERVINGS**
PREP. TIME: **20 MINUTES**
WARMING TIME: **UNTIL THE COOKER IS EMPTY!**
IDEAL SLOW COOKER SIZE: **4-QUART**

4 large baked potatoes

⅔ cup butter

⅔ cup flour

6 cups milk, whole *or* 2%

¾ tsp. salt

½ tsp. pepper

4 green onions, chopped

12 slices bacon, fried and crumbled

2 cups shredded cheddar cheese

1 cup (8 oz.) sour cream

1. Cut potatoes in half. Scoop out pulp and put in small bowl.
2. Melt butter in large kettle. Add flour. Gradually stir in milk. Continue to stir until smooth, thickened, and bubbly.
3. Stir in potato pulp, salt, pepper, and three-quarters of the onions, bacon, and cheese. Cook until heated. Stir in sour cream.
4. Transfer to slow cooker set on Low to keep warm. Top with remaining onions, bacon, and cheese. Take to a potluck, or serve on a buffet table, straight from the cooker.

Variation: *Add several slices of Velveeta cheese to make soup extra cheesy and creamy.*

A baked potato will cook in about half the time if you boil it for 5 minutes before putting it in the oven to bake.

German Potato Soup

Lee Ann Hazlett   Freeport, IL

MAKES: **6–8 SERVINGS**
PREP. TIME: **15–20 MINUTES**
COOKING TIME: **4–10 HOURS**
IDEAL SLOW COOKER SIZE: **4-QUART**

1 onion, chopped

1 leek, trimmed and diced

2 carrots, diced

1 cup chopped cabbage

¼ cup chopped fresh parsley

4 cups beef broth

1 lb. potatoes, diced

1 bay leaf

1–2 tsp. black pepper

1 tsp. salt, *optional*

½ tsp. caraway seeds, *optional*

¼ tsp. nutmeg

1 lb. bacon, cooked and crumbled

½ cup sour cream

1. Combine all ingredients except bacon and sour cream.
2. Cover. Cook on Low 8-10 hours, or on High 4-5 hours.
3. Remove bay leaf. Use a slotted spoon to remove potatoes. Mash potatoes and mix with sour cream. Return to slow cooker. Stir in. Add bacon and mix together thoroughly.

Easy Potato Soup

Yvonne Kauffman Boettger   Harrisonburg, VA

MAKES: **8 SERVINGS**
PREP. TIME: **10 MINUTES**
COOKING TIME: **5 HOURS**
IDEAL SLOW COOKER SIZE: **4–6-QUART**

3 cups chicken broth

2-lb. bag frozen hash brown potatoes

1½ tsp. salt

¾ tsp. pepper

3 cups milk

3 cups shredded Monterey Jack *or* cheddar cheese

1. Place chicken broth, potatoes, salt, and pepper in slow cooker.
2. Cover and cook on High 4 hours, or until potatoes are soft.
3. Leaving the broth and potatoes in the slow cooker, mash the potatoes lightly, leaving some larger chunks.
4. Add milk and cheese. Blend in thoroughly.
5. Cover and cook on High until cheese melts and soup is hot.

Apple Butter — for Your Toast,
page 54

Nachos Dinner,
page 285

Asian-Style Tuna,
page 486

167

Boston Brown Bread,
page 78

168

Ham and Potato Chowder

Penny Blosser   Beavercreek, OH

MAKES: **5 SERVINGS**
PREP. TIME: **10 MINUTES**
COOKING TIME: **8 HOURS**
IDEAL SLOW COOKER SIZE: **4-QUART**

5-oz. pkg. scalloped potatoes

sauce mix from potato pkg.

1 cup cooked ham, cut into narrow strips

4 cups chicken broth

1 cup chopped celery

⅓ cup chopped onions

salt to taste

pepper to taste

2 cups half-and-half

⅓ cup flour

1. Combine potatoes, sauce mix, ham, broth, celery, onions, salt, and pepper in slow cooker.
2. Cover. Cook on Low 7 hours.
3. Combine half-and-half and flour. Gradually add to slow cooker, blending well.
4. Cover. Cook on Low up to 1 hour, stirring occasionally until thickened.

Ham 'n Cheese Soup

Janie Steele   Moore, OK

MAKES: **7 SERVINGS**
PREP. TIME: **15 MINUTES**
COOKING TIME: **6¼–8¼ HOURS**
IDEAL SLOW COOKER SIZE: **3½–4-QUART**

2 cups potatoes, cubed (you decide whether to peel or not)

1½ cups water

1½ cups cooked ham, cubed

1 large onion, chopped

3 Tbsp. butter *or* margarine

3 Tbsp. flour

¼ tsp. black pepper

3 cups fat-free milk

6 ozs. low-fat shredded cheese

1 cup frozen broccoli, thawed and chopped

1. Combine all ingredients except cheese and broccoli in slow cooker.
2. Cook on Low 6–8 hours.
3. Add cheese and broccoli. Stir well. Cook an additional 15 minutes, or until cheese is melted and broccoli is warm.

Per Serving: 250 calories (80 calories from fat), 9g total fat (5g saturated, 0g trans), 35mg cholesterol, 650mg sodium, 22g total carbohydrate (3g fiber, 7g sugar), 19g protein, 10%DV vitamin A, 20%DV vitamin C, 25%DV calcium, 8%DV iron.

Variations:

1. Wilt the onion in the microwave, or sauté it in a nonstick skillet, so that it is soft and its flavor well blended when the soup is served.

2. Cook the broccoli lightly in the microwave if you want to make sure it is softened when served.

Cream Cheese Potato Soup

Jean H. Robinson Cinnaminson, NJ

MAKES: **6 SERVINGS**
PREP. TIME: **15 MINUTES**
COOKING TIME: **4 HOURS**
IDEAL SLOW COOKER SIZE: **3½-QUART**

3 cups water

1 cup ham, diced

5 medium potatoes, diced finely

8-oz. pkg. fat-free cream cheese, cubed

half an onion, chopped

1 tsp. garlic salt

½ tsp. black pepper

½ tsp. dill weed

1. Combine all ingredients in slow cooker.
2. Cover. Cook on High 4 hours, stirring occasionally.
3. Turn to Low until ready to serve.

Per Serving: 220 calories (25 calories from fat), 3g total fat (1g saturated, 0g trans), 25mg cholesterol, 400mg sodium, 34g total carbohydrate (4g fiber, 2g sugar), 16g protein, 0%DV vitamin A, 30%DV vitamin C, 10%DV calcium, 10%DV iron.

Potato Chowder

Susan Wenger Lebanon, PA

MAKES: **12 SERVINGS**
PREP. TIME: **15 MINUTES**
COOKING TIME: **8½–10½ HOURS**
IDEAL SLOW COOKER SIZE: **5-QUART**

8 cups peeled, diced potatoes

3 14½-oz. cans chicken broth

10¾-oz. can cream of chicken soup

¼ tsp. pepper

8-oz. pkg. cream cheese, cubed

1. In slow cooker, combine potatoes, chicken broth, chicken soup, and pepper.
2. Cover and cook on Low 8–10 hours, or until potatoes are tender.
3. Add cream cheese, stirring until well blended.
4. Heat until cheese melts and soup is hot throughout.

Tip: *Garnish individual servings of the soup with ½ lb. cooked crumbled bacon and snipped chives, if you like.*

Variation: *Add ⅓ cup chopped onion to Step 1.*

If you wait until you have all your work done, you will never have company. Guests don't usually care about what's undone anyway.

Potato Soup with Possibilities

Janie Steele   Moore, OK

MAKES: **6 SERVINGS**
PREP. TIME: **20–30 MINUTES**
COOKING TIME: **5–6 HOURS**
IDEAL SLOW COOKER SIZE: **4–6-QUART**

5 cups homemade chicken broth, *or* 2 14-oz. cans chicken broth, plus ½ soup can water
1 large onion, chopped
3 celery stalks, chopped, including leaves, if you like
6 large white potatoes, peeled, chopped, cubed, or sliced
salt and pepper to taste

1. Place all ingredients in slow cooker.
2. Cover and cook on High 5 hours, or on Low 6 hours, or until vegetables are soft but not mushy.

   Variation: *Add shredded sharp cheddar cheese, 2–3 cups chopped clams, and a 10- or 16-oz. pkg. of frozen corn to the slow cooker.*

Potato Soup with Ground Beef

Sharon Timpe   Jackson, WI

MAKES: **6–8 SERVINGS**
PREP. TIME: **15–20 MINUTES**
COOKING TIME: **3½–4 HOURS**
IDEAL SLOW COOKER SIZE: **4–5-QUART**

1 lb. ground beef
4 cups potatoes, peeled and cut into ½-inch cubes
1 small onion, chopped
3 8-oz. cans tomato sauce
2 tsp. salt
½ tsp. pepper
4 cups water
½ tsp. hot pepper sauce, *optional*

1. Brown the ground beef in a nonstick skillet. Drain well. Place meat in slow cooker.
2. Add cubed potatoes, chopped onion, and tomato sauce.
3. Stir in salt, pepper, water, and hot pepper sauce, if you wish.
4. Cover and cook on High until mixture starts to simmer, about 1 hour.
5. Turn to Low and continue cooking until potatoes are tender, about 2½–3 hours.

   Tips:
   1. Garnish each bowl of soup with chopped parsley.
   2. I like to use red potatoes, because they stay more firm.

Spicy Potato Soup

Sharon Kauffman   Harrisonburg, VA

MAKES: **6–8 SERVINGS**
PREP. TIME: **15 MINUTES**
COOKING TIME: **5–10 HOURS**
IDEAL SLOW COOKER SIZE: **4-QUART**

1 lb. ground beef *or* **bulk sausage, browned**

4 cups cubed peeled potatoes

1 small onion, chopped

3 8-oz. cans tomato sauce

2 tsp. salt

1½ tsp. pepper

½–l tsp. hot pepper sauce

water

1. Combine all ingredients except water in slow cooker. Add enough water to cover ingredients.
2. Cover. Cook on Low 8–10 hours, or on High 5 hours, until potatoes are tender.

Hearty Potato-Sauerkraut Soup

Kathy Hertzler   Lancaster, PA

MAKES: **6–8 SERVINGS**
PREP. TIME: **15–20 MINUTES**
COOKING TIME: **10–12 HOURS**
IDEAL SLOW COOKER SIZE: **4-QUART**

4 cups chicken broth

10¾-oz. can cream of mushroom soup

16-oz. can sauerkraut, rinsed and drained

8 oz. fresh mushrooms, sliced

1 medium potato, cubed

2 medium carrots, peeled and sliced

2 ribs celery, chopped

2 lbs. Polish kielbasa (smoked), cubed

2½ cups cooked chicken, cubed

2 Tbsp. vinegar

2 tsp. dried dillweed

1½ tsp. pepper

1. Combine all ingredients in large slow cooker.
2. Cover. Cook on Low 10–12 hours.
3. If necessary, skim fat before serving.

Cabbage-Sausage Soup

Karen Waggoner   Joplin, MO

MAKES: **8 SERVINGS**
PREP. TIME: **15 MINUTES**
COOKING TIME: **6–7 HOURS**
IDEAL SLOW COOKER SIZE: **5-QUART**

4 cups low-fat, low-sodium chicken broth

1 medium head of cabbage, chopped

2 medium onions, chopped

½ lb. fully cooked smoked turkey sausage, halved lengthwise and sliced

½ cup all-purpose flour

¼ tsp. black pepper

1 cup skim milk

1. Combine chicken broth, cabbage, onions, and sausage in slow cooker.
2. Cover. Cook on High 5–6 hours, or until cabbage is tender.
3. Mix flour and black pepper in a bowl.
4. Gradually add milk, stirring until smooth.
5. Gradually stir into hot soup.
6. Cook, stirring occasionally for about 15 minutes, until soup is thickened. Serve.

Per Serving: 210 calories (100 calories from fat), 11g total fat (4g saturated, 0g trans), 20mg cholesterol, 790mg sodium, 17g total carbohydrate (3g fiber, 7g sugar), 11g protein, 4%DV vitamin A, 30%DV vitamin C, 10%DV calcium, 15%DV iron.

Sauerkraut Tomato Soup

Norma Grieser   Clarksville, MI

MAKES: **4 SERVINGS**
PREP. TIME: **10 MINUTES**
COOKING TIME: **4–6 HOURS**
IDEAL SLOW COOKER SIZE: **3–4-QUART**

2 14½-oz. cans stewed tomatoes

2 cups sauerkraut

1 cup diced potatoes

1 lb. fresh *or* smoked sausage, sliced

1. Combine all ingredients in slow cooker.
2. Cover and cook on Low 4–6 hours, or until the flavors have blended and the soup is thoroughly heated.

Variation: *Add to above ingredients 1 medium onion, chopped, and ⅓ cup brown sugar.*

Pork-Veggie Stew

Ruth E. Martin   Loysville, PA

MAKES: **8 SERVINGS**
PREP. TIME: **15 MINUTES**
COOKING TIME: **6 HOURS**
IDEAL SLOW COOKER SIZE: **4-QUART**

2 lbs. boneless pork loin, cut into 1-inch cubes

8 medium potatoes, peeled and cut into 2-inch pieces

6 large carrots, peeled and cut into 2-inch pieces

1 cup ketchup

2¼ cups water, *divided*

1. Brown pork cubes in a large nonstick skillet.
2. Lightly spray slow cooker with nonstick cooking spray.
3. Place all ingredients except ketchup and ¼ cup water in slow cooker.
4. Cover and cook on High 5 hours. One hour before serving, combine ketchup with

¼ cup water. Pour over stew. Cook one more hour.

Tip: *To prevent potatoes from turning black or discoloring, toss in water with a small amount of cream of tartar (6 cups water to 1 tsp. cream of tartar).*

Pork Potato Stew

Kristin Tice   Shipshewana, IN

MAKES: **4 SERVINGS**
PREP. TIME: **20 MINUTES**
COOKING TIME: **4 HOURS**
IDEAL SLOW COOKER SIZE: **3-QUART**

1 lb. ground pork

½ cup chopped onion

1 sweet potato, cubed and peeled, approximately 3 cups

2 beef bouillon cubes

½ tsp. dried rosemary

3 cups water

1. Place meat and onion in nonstick skillet. Brown on stovetop.
2. Place drained meat, along with onion, into slow cooker. Add remaining ingredients.
3. Cover and cook on Low for 4 hours.

Variation: *Add a bit of hot sauce to make the soup spicy, or serve on the side to accommodate those who don't like hot food.*

Invest in good quality knives. They make preparation much easier.

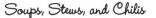

Curried Pork and Pea Soup

Kathy Hertzler Lancaster, PA

MAKES: **6–8 SERVINGS**
PREP. TIME: **15 MINUTES**
COOKING TIME: **4–12 HOURS**
IDEAL SLOW COOKER SIZE: **4-QUART**

1½-lb. boneless pork shoulder roast

1 cup yellow *or* green split peas, rinsed and drained

½ cup finely chopped carrots

½ cup finely chopped celery

½ cup finely chopped onions

49½-oz. can (approximately 6 cups) chicken broth

2 tsp. curry powder

½ tsp. paprika

¼ tsp. ground cumin

¼ tsp. pepper

2 cups torn fresh spinach

1. Trim fat from pork and cut pork into ½-inch pieces.
2. Combine split peas, carrots, celery, and onions in slow cooker.
3. Stir in broth, curry powder, paprika, cumin, and pepper. Stir in pork.
4. Cover. Cook on Low 10–12 hours, or on High 4 hours.
5. Stir in spinach. Serve immediately.

Navy Bean Vegetable Soup

Lavina Hochstedler Grand Blanc, MI

MAKES: **12 SERVINGS**
PREP. TIME: **10 MINUTES**
COOKING TIME: **9–10 HOURS**
IDEAL SLOW COOKER SIZE: **6-QUART**

4 medium carrots, thinly sliced

2 celery ribs, chopped

1 medium onion, chopped

2 cups fully cooked ham cubes, trimmed of fat

1½ cups dried navy beans

1.68-oz. pkg. dry vegetable soup mix

1 envelope dry onion soup mix

1 bay leaf

½ tsp. black pepper

8 cups water

1 tsp. salt, *optional*

1. Combine all ingredients in slow cooker.
2. Cover. Cook on Low 9–10 hours.
3. Discard bay leaf before serving.

Per Serving: 160 calories (20 calories from fat), 2.5g total fat (1g saturated, 0g trans), 20mg cholesterol, 520mg sodium, 22g total carbohydrate (8g fiber, 4g sugar), 14g protein, 100%DV vitamin A, 0%DV vitamin C, 6%DV calcium, 15%DV iron.

Variation: *If you like the taste, and your diet allows, you may want to substitute smoked turkey sausage or kielbasa in place of the ham.*

Vegetarian Soup

Jane Meiser   Harrisonburg, VA

MAKES: **6 SERVINGS**
PREP. TIME: **10 MINUTES**
COOKING TIME: **4–5 HOURS**
IDEAL SLOW COOKER SIZE: **3½-QUART**

16-oz. can low-sodium diced tomatoes

2 15-oz. cans kidney *or* pinto beans, drained, *divided*

1 cup chopped onions

1 clove garlic, minced

8¾-oz. can whole-kernel corn, drained

½ cup low-sodium picante sauce

½ cup water

½ tsp. salt

1 tsp. ground cumin

1 tsp. dried oregano

1 green bell pepper, diced

reduced-fat shredded cheddar cheese, *optional*

1. Drain tomatoes, reserving juice.
2. Combine juice and 1 can beans in food processor bowl. Process until fairly smooth.
3. Combine all ingredients except green peppers and cheese in slow cooker.
4. Cover. Cook on High 4–5 hours.
5. During last half hour add green peppers.
6. Ladle into bowls to serve. Top with cheese, if desired.

Per Serving: 180 calories (10 calories from fat), 1g total fat (0g saturated, 0g trans), 0mg cholesterol, 990mg sodium, 36g total carbohydrate (8g fiber, 9g sugar), 9g protein, 6%DV vitamin A, 30%DV vitamin C, 8%DV calcium, 15%DV iron.

Aunt Thelma's Homemade Soup

Janice Muller   Derwood, MD

MAKES: **10–12 SERVINGS**
PREP. TIME: **15 MINUTES**
COOKING TIME: **4½ HOURS**
IDEAL SLOW COOKER SIZE: **6-QUART**

7 cups water

4 chicken *or* vegetable bouillon cubes

1 cup thinly sliced carrots

1-lb. pkg. frozen peas

1-lb. pkg. frozen corn

1-lb. pkg. frozen lima beans

1 bay leaf

¼ tsp. dill seed

28-oz. can whole tomatoes

1 cup diced raw potatoes

1 cup chopped onions

2–3 tsp. salt

½ tsp. dried basil

¼ tsp. pepper

2 Tbsp. cornstarch

¼ cup cold water

1. Combine all ingredients except cornstarch and ¼ cup water in slow cooker.
2. Cover. Simmer on High 4 hours, or until vegetables are tender.
3. Thirty minutes before end of cooking time, mix cornstarch and cold water together until smooth. Remove 1 cup broth from cooker and mix with cornstarch-water. When smooth, stir into soup. Cover and continue cooking another half hour.
4. Serve with fresh Italian bread.

Note: *My aunt always makes this in the winter and freezes an extra batch for unexpected guests. I converted the recipe to crockpot-use a few years ago, but I think of her whenever I make it.*

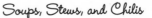

Minestrone

Bernita Boyts Shawnee Mission, KS

MAKES: **8–10 SERVINGS**
PREP. TIME: **20 MINUTES**
COOKING TIME: **4–9 HOURS**
IDEAL SLOW COOKER SIZE: **6-QUART**

1 large onion, chopped

4 carrots, sliced

3 ribs celery, sliced

2 garlic cloves, minced

1 Tbsp. olive oil

6-oz. can tomato paste

14½-oz. can chicken, beef, *or* vegetable broth

24-oz. can pinto beans, undrained

10-oz. pkg. frozen green beans

2–3 cups chopped cabbage

1 medium zucchini, sliced

8 cups water

2 Tbsp. parsley

2 Tbsp. Italian spice

1 tsp. salt, or more

½ tsp. pepper

¾ cup dry acini di pepe (small round pasta)

grated Parmesan *or* Asiago cheese

1. Sauté onion, carrots, celery, and garlic in oil until tender.
2. Combine all ingredients except pasta and cheese in slow cooker.
3. Cover. Cook 4–5 hours on High or 8–9 hours on Low, adding pasta 1 hour before cooking is complete.
4. Top individual servings with cheese.

The Soup

Joanne Kennedy Plattsburgh, NY

MAKES: **8 SERVINGS**
PREP. TIME: **20 MINUTES**
COOKING TIME: **9 HOURS**
IDEAL SLOW COOKER SIZE: **5–6-QUART**

2 14½-oz. cans vegetable broth

2 vegetable boullion cubes

4 cups water

1 quart canned tomatoes

3–4 garlic cloves, minced

1 large onion, chopped

1 cup chopped celery

2 cups chopped carrots

1 small zucchini, cubed

1 small yellow squash, cubed

2 tsp. fresh basil

1 tsp. fresh parsley

pepper to taste

3 dashes Tabasco sauce

1. Combine ingredients in slow cooker.
2. Cover. Cook on Low 9 hours.

Variation: *Add cooked pasta after soup is done.*

Soups, Stews, and Chilis

Soup to Get Thin On

Jean H. Robinson   Cinnaminson, NJ

MAKES: **20+ SERVINGS**
PREP. TIME: **15 MINUTES**
COOKING TIME: **6–8 HOURS**
IDEAL SLOW COOKER SIZE: **7-QUART, OR 2 4-QUART**

3 48-oz. cans low-fat, low-sodium chicken broth

2 medium onions, chopped

5 celery ribs, chopped

5 parsnips, chopped

1 head (8 cups) cabbage, shredded

4 bell peppers (red *or* green), chopped

8 ozs. mushrooms, chopped

10-oz. pkg. spinach, chopped

10-oz. pkg. frozen broccoli florets

10-oz. pkg. cauliflower

2–3 pieces chopped gingerroot

14½-oz. can crushed tomatoes

1 Tbsp. black pepper

1 Tbsp. salt

1. Combine all ingredients in slow cooker.
2. Cover. Cook on Low 6–8 hours.

Per Serving: 90 calories (0 calories from fat), 0g total fat (0g saturated, 0g trans), 0mg cholesterol, 660mg sodium, 16g total carbohydrate (15g fiber, 5g sugar), 7g protein, 20%DV vitamin A, 40%DV vitamin C, 8%DV calcium, 15%DV iron.

Cut up vegetables for your slow-cooker dish the night before and place them in Ziplock bags in the refrigerator. This cuts down on preparation time in the morning.

Low-Calorie Soup

Cindy Kiestynick   Glen Lyon, PA

MAKES: **14 SERVINGS**
PREP. TIME: **15 MINUTES**
COOKING TIME: **5 HOURS**
IDEAL SLOW COOKER SIZE: **4-5-QUART**

2 cups thinly sliced carrots

2 cups thinly sliced celery

2 cups chopped cabbage

8-oz. pkg. frozen green beans

1 onion, chopped

28-oz. can diced tomatoes

3 envelopes dry low-sodium beef-flavored soup mix

3 Tbsp. Worcestershire sauce

½ tsp. salt

¼ tsp. black pepper

water to cover

1. Combine all ingredients in slow cooker.
2. Cover. Cook on High 5 hours.

Per Serving: 80 calories (0 calories from fat), 0g total fat (0g saturated, 0g trans), 0mg cholesterol, 630mg sodium, 17g total carbohydrate (4g fiber, 5g sugar), 2g protein, 100%DV vitamin A, 10%DV vitamin C, 8%DV calcium, 6%DV iron.

Variation: *If you like, stir in a handful or two of baby spinach just before serving.*

 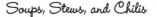

Barley-Cabbage Soup

Betty K. Drescher   Quakertown, PA

Light **MEATLESS**

MAKES: **8 SERVINGS**
PREP. TIME: **15 MINUTES**
COOKING TIME: **5–12 HOURS**
IDEAL SLOW COOKER SIZE: **3½–4-QUART**

¼ cup dry pearl barley
6 cups fat-free, low-sodium meat *or* vegetable broth
1 cup chopped onions
3–4 cups finely chopped green cabbage
¼ cup chopped fresh parsley
½ tsp. celery salt
½ tsp. salt
⅛ tsp. black pepper
1 Tbsp. minute tapioca

1. Combine all ingredients in slow cooker.
2. Cover. Cook on Low 10–12 hours, or on High 5–6 hours.

Per Serving: 60 calories (0 calories from fat), 0g total fat (0g saturated, 0g trans), 0mg cholesterol, 300mg sodium, 10g total carbohydrate (2g fiber, 2g sugar), 5g protein, 0%DV vitamin A, 10%DV vitamin C, 2%DV calcium, 4%DV iron.

Barley-Mushroom Soup

Janie Steele   Moore, OK

Light

MAKES: **8 SERVINGS**
PREP. TIME: **15 MINUTES**
COOKING TIME: **7–8 HOURS**
IDEAL SLOW COOKER SIZE: **5-QUART**

6 cups sliced fresh mushrooms
2 large onions, chopped
3 cloves garlic, minced
1 cup chopped celery
1 cup chopped carrots
5 cups water, *divided*
¼ cup dry quick-cooking pearl barley
4 cups low-sodium beef broth
4 tsp. Worcestershire sauce
1–1½ tsp. salt, *optional*
1½ tsp. dried basil
1½ tsp. dried parsley flakes
1 tsp. dill weed
1½ tsp. dried oregano
½ tsp. salt-free seasoning blend
½ tsp. dried thyme
½ tsp. garlic powder

1. Combine all ingredients in slow cooker.
2. Cook on Low 7–8 hours, or until vegetables are done to your liking.

Per Serving: 320 calories (10 calories from fat), 1g total fat (0g saturated, 0g trans), 0mg cholesterol, 310mg sodium, 69g total carbohydrate (14g fiber, 5g sugar), 12g protein, 30%DV vitamin A, 2%DV vitamin C, 6%DV calcium, 20%DV iron.

"Mom's Favorite" Vegetable Soup

Wendy McPhillips   Wichita, KS

MAKES: **5 SERVINGS**
PREP. TIME: **10 MINUTES**
COOKING TIME: **6–8 HOURS**
IDEAL SLOW COOKER SIZE: **4-QUART**

½ cup dry pearl barley

14½-oz. can low-sodium diced tomatoes

1 cup frozen corn

1 cup frozen peas

4 carrots, peeled and sliced

1 cup frozen green beans

water to cover

5 cubes low-sodium beef bouillon

5 cubes low-sodium chicken bouillon

½ tsp. salt

½ tsp. black pepper

½ tsp. dried basil

1 tsp. fresh thyme

½ tsp. fresh dill

1 tsp. fresh parsley

1. Combine all ingredients in slow cooker, except fresh herbs.
2. Cover. Cook on Low 6–8 hours.
3. Just before serving, stir in fresh thyme, dill, and parsley.

Per Serving: 190 calories (10 calories from fat), 1.5g total fat (0g saturated, 0g trans), 0mg cholesterol, 2340mg sodium, 40g total carbohydrate (9g fiber, 10g sugar), 7g protein, 200%DV vitamin A, 20%DV vitamin C, 10%DV calcium, 10%DV iron.

Tomato Green Bean Soup

Colleen Heatwole   Burton, MI

MAKES: **8 SERVINGS**
PREP. TIME: **10 MINUTES**
COOKING TIME: **6–8 HOURS**
IDEAL SLOW COOKER SIZE: **4-QUART**

1 cup chopped onions

1 cup chopped carrots

6 cups low-fat, reduced-sodium chicken broth

1 lb. fresh green beans, cut in 1-inch pieces

1 clove garlic, minced

3 cups fresh, diced tomatoes

1 tsp. dried basil

½ tsp. salt

¼ tsp. black pepper

1. Combine all ingredients in slow cooker.
2. Cover. Cook on Low 6–8 hours.

Per Serving: 70 calories (0 calories from fat), 0g total fat (0g saturated, 0g trans), 0mg cholesterol, 290mg sodium, 10g total carbohydrate (4g fiber, 6g sugar), 6g protein, 80%DV vitamin A, 10%DV vitamin C, 6%DV calcium, 10%DV iron.

Tip: *This recipe is best with fresh green beans and tomatoes, but if they are not in season you may use canned tomatoes and canned or frozen green beans—or corn. Remember, of course, that canned vegetables are likely to include salt.*

Fresh vegetables take longer to cook than meats, because, in a slow cooker, liquid simmers rather than boils. Remember this if you've adapted range-top recipes to slow cooking.

Quick-to-Mix Vegetable Soup

Cyndie Marrara   Port Matilda, PA

MAKES: **4 SERVINGS**
PREP. TIME: **5 MINUTES**
COOKING TIME: **5–7 HOURS**
IDEAL SLOW COOKER SIZE: **2-QUART**

2 cups frozen vegetables
¾ cup fat-free, low-sodium beef gravy
16-oz. can diced tomatoes
¼ cup dry red wine
½ cup diced onions
1 tsp. crushed garlic
¼ tsp. black pepper
½ cup water

1. Combine all ingredients in slow cooker.
2. Cover. Cook on High 5 hours or on Low 7 hours.

Per Serving: 130 calories (5 calories from fat), 0.5g total fat (0g saturated, 0g trans), 5mg cholesterol, 600mg sodium, 26g total carbohydrate (6g fiber, 4g sugar), 5g protein, 80%DV vitamin A, 10%DV vitamin C, 10%DV calcium, 8%DV iron.

Variation: *If your diet permits, you may want to add ¼–½ tsp. salt to Step 1.*

Dawn's Quick & Healthy Vegetable Soup

Dawn Day   Westminster, CA

MAKES: **8 SERVINGS**
PREP. TIME: **10 MINUTES**
COOKING TIME: **4½–8 HOURS**
IDEAL SLOW COOKER SIZE: **4-QUART**

4 cups vegetable *or* chicken broth
1 cup frozen corn
½ cup chopped carrots
½ cup green beans
1 cup cubed zucchini
12-oz. can chopped tomatoes
½ cup chopped onions
2 cloves garlic, minced
½ tsp. dried thyme
½ tsp. dried basil
¼ tsp. lemon pepper
1 cup chopped broccoli
½ cup frozen peas

1. Combine all ingredients except broccoli and peas in slow cooker.
2. Cover. Cook on Low 7 hours, or on High 3½ hours.
3. Stir in broccoli. Cook an additional 45 minutes on High.
4. Stir in peas. Cook an additional 15 minutes on High.

Per Serving: 70 calories (0 calories from fat), 0g total fat (0g saturated, 0g trans), 0mg cholesterol, 470mg sodium, 14g total carbohydrate (3g fiber, 6g sugar), 3g protein, 80%DV vitamin A, 20%DV vitamin C, 6%DV calcium, 6%DV iron.

Fresh Tomato Soup

Rebecca Leichty Harrisonburg, VA

MAKES: **6 SERVINGS**
PREP. TIME: **10 MINUTES**
COOKING TIME: **6–8 HOURS**
IDEAL SLOW COOKER SIZE: **3½–4-QUART**

5 cups ripe, diced tomatoes (your choice about whether or not to peel them)

1 Tbsp. tomato paste

4 cups salt-free chicken broth

1 carrot, grated

1 onion, minced

1 Tbsp. minced garlic

1 tsp. dried basil

pepper to taste

1 bay leaf

1. Combine all ingredients in a slow cooker.
2. Cook on Low for 6–8 hours. Stir once while cooking.
3. Remove bay leaf before serving.

Per Serving: 80 calories (5 calories from fat), 0.5g total fat (0g saturated, 0g trans), 0mg cholesterol, 135mg sodium, 14g total carbohydrate (3g fiber, 7g sugar), 6g protein, 40%DV vitamin A, 40%DV vitamin C, 4%DV calcium, 15%DV iron.

Variation: *To thicken the soup slightly, and if your diet allows, you may want to add a full 6-oz. can of tomato paste instead of just 1 Tbsp.*

Vegetarian Minestrone Soup

Connie Johnson Loudon, NH

MAKES: **6 SERVINGS**
PREP. TIME: **15 MINUTES**
COOKING TIME: **6–8 HOURS**
IDEAL SLOW COOKER SIZE: **4-QUART**

6 cups vegetable broth

2 carrots, chopped

2 large onions, chopped

3 ribs celery, chopped

2 garlic cloves, minced

1 small zucchini, cubed

1 handful fresh kale, chopped

½ cup dry barley

1 can chickpeas *or* white kidney beans, drained

1 Tbsp. parsley

½ tsp. dried thyme

1 tsp. dried oregano

28-oz. can crushed Italian tomatoes

1 tsp. salt

¼ tsp. pepper

shredded cheese

1. Combine all ingredients except cheese in slow cooker.
2. Cover. Cook on Low 6–8 hours, or until vegetables are tender.
3. Sprinkle individual servings with shredded cheese.

Have one or two "company specials" you can make when friends show up unexpectedly.

Joyce's Minestrone

Joyce Shackelford Green Bay, Wisconsin

MAKES: **6 SERVINGS**
PREP. TIME: **15 MINUTES**
COOKING TIME: **4–16 HOURS**
IDEAL SLOW COOKER SIZE: **4–5-QUART**

3½ cups beef broth

28-oz. can crushed tomatoes

2 medium carrots, thinly sliced

½ cup chopped onion

½ cup chopped celery

2 medium potatoes, thinly sliced

1–2 garlic cloves, minced

16-oz. can red kidney beans, drained

2 oz. thin spaghetti, broken into 2-inch pieces

2 Tbsp. parsley flakes

2–3 tsp. dried basil

1–2 tsp. dried oregano

1 bay leaf

1. Combine all ingredients in slow cooker.
2. Cover. Cook on Low 10–16 hours, or on High 4–6 hours.
3. Remove bay leaf. Serve.

Grace's Minestrone Soup

Grace Ketcham Marietta, GA

MAKES: **8 SERVINGS**
PREP. TIME: **15 MINUTES**
COOKING TIME: **8 HOURS**
IDEAL SLOW COOKER SIZE: **4–5-QUART**

¾ cup dry elbow macaroni

2 quarts chicken stock

2 large onions, diced

2 carrots, sliced

half a head of cabbage, shredded

½ cup diced celery

1-lb. can tomatoes

½ tsp. salt

½ tsp. dried oregano

1 Tbsp. minced parsley

¼ cup *each* frozen corn, peas, and lima beans

¼ tsp. pepper

grated Parmesan *or* Romano cheese

1. Cook macaroni according to package directions. Set aside.
2. Combine all ingredients except macaroni and cheese in large slow cooker.
3. Cover. Cook on Low 8 hours. Add macaroni during last 30 minutes of cooking time.
4. Garnish individual servings with cheese.

Tomato Vegetable Soup (Clean-the-Fridge-Monday-Night Soup)

Elaine Sue Good Tiskilwa, IL

MAKES: **8 SERVINGS**
PREP. TIME: **10 MINUTES**
COOKING TIME: **4–10 HOURS**
IDEAL SLOW COOKER SIZE: **3½-QUART**

2 cloves garlic, pressed and chopped

8- or 16-oz. pkg. frozen peppers and onions

3 Tbsp. Italian seasoning mix, *or* basil, oregano, etc.

32-oz. pkg. frozen mixed vegetables, *or* leftover vegetables from your refrigerator, chopped

46-oz. can vegetable *or* V-8 juice, *or* Bloody Mary mix, *or* beef broth

1. Place pressed garlic cloves into bottom of slow cooker. Add peppers and onions.
2. Sprinkle seasonings over top.
3. Add vegetables. Then pour juice over all ingredients.
4. Cover and cook on Low 8–10 hours, or on High 4 hours.

Note: *This recipe came about when our family was given 3 cases of Bloody Mary mix!*

Variations: *Being flexible is the key to this recipe. You can add:*
- *water if you like a thinner consistency.*
- *leftover meat—and/or cooked pasta or rice or barley—to bowls when serving.*
- *leftover or canned lentils or beans to each bowl before adding the soup.*

Veggie Stock

Char Hagner Montague, MI

MAKES: **6 CUPS**
PREP. TIME: **10 MINUTES**
COOKING TIME: **4–10 HOURS**
IDEAL SLOW COOKER SIZE: **4-QUART**

2 tomatoes, chopped

2 onions, cut up

4 carrots, cut up

1 stalk celery, cut up

1 potato, cut up

6 garlic cloves

dash of salt

½ tsp. dried thyme

1 bay leaf

6 cups water

1. Combine tomatoes, onions, carrots, celery, potato, garlic, salt, thyme, bay leaf, and water.
2. Cover. Cook on Low 8–10 hours, or on High 4–5 hours.
3. Strain stock through large sieve. Discard the solids.
4. Freeze until needed (up to 3 months). Use for soups or stews.

Per Serving: 70 calories (0 calories from fat), 0g total fat (0g saturated, 0g trans), 0mg cholesterol, 75mg sodium, 15g total carbohydrate (3g fiber, 5g sugar), 2g protein, 100%DV vitamin A, 10%DV vitamin C, 4%DV calcium, 6%DV iron.

Swiss Cheese and Veggie Soup

Sharon Miller   Holmesville, OH

MAKES: **4 SERVINGS**
PREP. TIME: **5 MINUTES**
COOKING TIME: **6–8 HOURS**
IDEAL SLOW COOKER SIZE: **3½-QUART**

2¼ cups frozen California-blend vegetables (broccoli, carrots, and cauliflower)

½ cup chopped onions

½ cup water

½ tsp. chicken bouillon granules

1 cup skim milk

3 ozs. shredded fat-free Swiss cheese

1. Combine vegetables, onions, water, and bouillon in slow cooker.
2. Cook on Low 6–8 hours, or until vegetables are tender.
3. Pour all ingredients into blender or food processor. Add milk. Process until smooth, or chunky smooth, whichever you prefer.
4. Serve, topped with shredded cheese.

Per Serving: 100 calories (0 calories from fat), 0g total fat (0g saturated, 0g trans), 5mg cholesterol, 290mg sodium, 11g total carbohydrate (3g fiber, 8g sugar), 11g protein, 40%DV vitamin A, 30%DV vitamin C, 40%DV calcium, 4%DV iron.

Variation: *If you want, and your diet permits, you may like to add ½ tsp. salt to Step 1.*

Vegetable Cheese Soup

Rosalie D. Miller   Mifflintown, PA

MAKES: **5 SERVINGS**
PREP. TIME: **15–20 MINUTES**
COOKING TIME: **4–10 HOURS**
IDEAL SLOW COOKER SIZE: **3-QUART**

2 cups cream-style corn

1 cup peeled and chopped potatoes

1 cup peeled and chopped carrots

2 14½-oz. cans vegetable *or* chicken broth

16-oz. jar processed cheese

1. Combine all ingredients except cheese in the slow cooker.
2. Cover and cook on Low 8–10 hours, or on High 4–5 hours.
3. Thirty to 60 minutes before serving, stir in the cheese. Then cook on High for 30–60 minutes to melt and blend the cheese.

Variation: *Add 1 tsp. celery seed, ½ tsp. black pepper, and ½ cup chopped onion to step one.*

Soups, Stews, and Chilis

Easy Cheese Soup

Nancy Wagner Graves　Manhattan, KS

MAKES: **4 SERVINGS**
PREP. TIME: **5–10 MINUTES**
COOKING TIME: **4–6 HOURS**
IDEAL SLOW COOKER SIZE: **3½-QUART**

2 10¾-oz. cans cream of mushroom *or* cream of
　chicken soup
1 cup beer *or* milk
1 lb. cheddar cheese, shredded
1 tsp. Worcestershire sauce
¼ tsp. paprika
croutons

1. Combine all ingredients except croutons in
   slow cooker.
2. Cover. Cook on Low 4–6 hours.
3. Stir thoroughly 1 hour before serving, to
   make sure cheese is well distributed and
   melted.
4. Serve topped with croutons or in bread bowls.

*Slow cookers fit any season. When it's
hot outside, they don't heat up your kitchen.
So turn on your cooker before heading to
the pool or the beach — or the garden. Or
put your dinner in the slow cooker, and then
go play or watch your favorite sport.*

Broccoli Soup

Betty B. Dennison　Grove City, PA

MAKES: **5 SERVINGS**
PREP. TIME: **10 MINUTES**
COOKING TIME: **1¼–2¼ HOURS**
IDEAL SLOW COOKER SIZE: **4-QUART**

2–3 lbs. fresh broccoli
1 Tbsp. margarine
water to cover
2 cups skim milk
½ cup Velveeta Light cheese, cut into small cubes

1. Chop broccoli. Remove any tough stalks and
   discard.
2. Place chopped broccoli, margarine, and
   water to cover in slow cooker.
3. Cover. Cook on High 1–2 hours.
4. Add skim milk. Cook for an additional 15
   minutes.
5. Stir in ½ cup Velveeta Light cheese and
   continue cooking until cheese is melted into
   soup.

Per Serving: 160 calories (35 calories from fat), 4g total fat (2g
saturated, 1g trans), 10mg cholesterol, 490mg sodium, 22g total
carbohydrate (8g fiber, 12g sugar), 16g protein, 100%DV vitamin A,
200%DV vitamin C, 40%DV calcium, 15%DV iron.

Cream of Broccoli and Mushroom Soup

Leona Miller Millersburg, OH

MAKES: **12 SERVINGS**
PREP. TIME: **10 MINUTES**
COOKING TIME: **3½–8 HOURS**
IDEAL SLOW COOKER SIZE: **5–6-QUART**

8 ozs. fresh mushrooms, sliced
2 lbs. fresh broccoli
3 10¾-oz. cans 98% fat-free cream of broccoli soup
½ tsp. dried thyme leaves, crushed, *optional*
3 bay leaves, optional
1 pint fat-free half-and-half
4 ozs. extra-lean smoked ham, chopped
¼ tsp. black pepper

1. Combine all ingredients in slow cooker.
2. Cook on Low 6–8 hours, or on High 3½–4 hours.
3. Remove bay leaves before serving.

Per Serving: 110 calories (25 calories from fat), 2.5g total fat (1g saturated, 0g trans), 10mg cholesterol, 580mg sodium, 16g total carbohydrate (3g fiber, 6g sugar), 7g protein, 30%DV vitamin A, 40%DV vitamin C, 10%DV calcium, 6%DV iron.

Broccoli, Potato, and Cheese Soup

Ruth Shank Gridley, IL

MAKES: **6 SERVINGS**
PREP. TIME: **20 MINUTES**
COOKING TIME: **4 HOURS**
IDEAL SLOW COOKER SIZE: **3-QUART**

2 cups cubed or diced potatoes
3 Tbsp. chopped onions
10-oz. pkg. frozen broccoli cuts, thawed
2 Tbsp. butter, melted
1 Tbsp. flour
1 cup cubed Velveeta Light cheese
½ tsp. salt
¼ tsp. black pepper
5½ cups fat-free milk

1. Cook potatoes and onions in boiling water in saucepan until potatoes are crisp-tender Drain. Place in slow cooker.
2. Add remaining ingredients. Stir together.
3. Cover. Cook on Low 4 hours.

Per Serving: 230 calories (70 calories from fat), 7g total fat (4.5g saturated, 1g trans), 25mg cholesterol, 780mg sodium, 27g total carbohydrate (3g fiber, 15g sugar), 16g protein, 10%DV vitamin A, 25%DV vitamin C, 40%DV calcium, 6%DV iron.

Variation: *If you prefer a thicker soup, and your diet allows, you may want to increase the flour to 3 Tbsp.*

Soups, Stews, and Chilis

Broccoli-Cheese Soup

Darla Sathre Baxter, MN

MAKES: **8 SERVINGS**
PREP. TIME: **10 MINUTES**
COOKING TIME: **8–10 HOURS**
IDEAL SLOW COOKER SIZE: **4-QUART**

MEATLESS

2 16-oz. pkgs. frozen chopped broccoli
2 10¾-oz. cans cheddar cheese soup
2 12-oz. cans evaporated milk
¼ cup finely chopped onions
½ tsp. seasoned salt
¼ tsp. pepper
sunflower seeds, *optional*
crumbled bacon, *optional*

1. Combine all ingredients except sunflower seeds and bacon in slow cooker.
2. Cover. Cook on Low 8–10 hours.
3. Garnish with sunflower seeds and bacon.

Broccoli-Cheese with Noodles Soup

Carol Sherwood Batavia, NY

MAKES: **8 SERVINGS**
PREP. TIME: **15 MINUTES**
COOKING TIME: **4 HOURS**
IDEAL SLOW COOKER SIZE: **4-QUART**

MEATLESS

2 cups noodles, cooked
10-oz. pkg. frozen chopped broccoli, thawed
3 Tbsp. chopped onions
2 Tbsp. butter
1 Tbsp. flour
2 cups cubed processed cheese
½ tsp. salt
5½ cups milk

1. Cook noodles just until soft in saucepan while combining rest of ingredients in slow cooker. Mix well.
2. Drain cooked noodles and stir into slow cooker.
3. Cover. Cook on Low 4 hours.

Double Cheese Cauliflower Soup

Zona Mae Bontrager Kokomo, IN

MAKES: **6 SERVINGS**
PREP. TIME: **15 MINUTES**
COOKING TIME: **2–3 HOURS**
IDEAL SLOW COOKER SIZE: **3–4-QUART**

4 cups (1 small head) cauliflower pieces
2 cups water
8-oz. pkg. cream cheese, cubed
5 oz. American cheese spread
¼ lb. dried beef, torn into strips or shredded
½ cup potato flakes or buds

1. Combine cauliflower and water in saucepan. Bring to boil. Set aside.
2. Heat slow cooker on Low. Add cream cheese and cheese spread. Pour in cauliflower and water. Stir to be sure the cheese is dissolved and mixed through the cauliflower.
3. Add dried beef and potato flakes. Mix well.
4. Cover. Cook on Low 2–3 hours.

Creamy Tomato Soup

Sara Kinsinger Stuarts Draft, VA

MEATLESS

MAKES: **6 SERVINGS**
PREP. TIME: **20 MINUTES**
COOKING TIME: **1½ HOURS**
IDEAL SLOW COOKER SIZE: **4-QUART**

26-oz. can condensed tomato soup, plus 6 ozs. water to
    equal 1 quart
½ tsp. salt, *optional*
half a stick (4 Tbsp.) butter
8 Tbsp. flour
1 quart milk (whole *or* reduced-fat)

1. Put tomato soup, salt if you wish, and butter
   in slow cooker. Blend well.
2. Cover and cook on High for 1 hour.
3. Meanwhile, place flour and 1 cup milk in
   2-quart microwave-safe container. Whisk
   together until big lumps disappear. Then
   whisk in remaining milk until only small
   lumps remain.
4. Place flour-milk mixture in microwave and
   cook on High for 3 minutes. Remove and
   stir until smooth. Return to microwave and
   cook on High for another 3 minutes.
5. Add thickened milk slowly to hot soup in
   slow cooker.
6. Heat thoroughly for 10 to 15 minutes.

Tip: *Serve with freshly ground pepper, dried
chives, or your choice of green herbs, and oyster
crackers or croutons.*

Corn Chowder

Charlotte Fry St. Charles, MO • *Jeanette Oberholtzer* Manheim, PA

MAKES: **4 SERVINGS**
PREP. TIME: **15 MINUTES**
COOKING TIME: **6–7 HOURS**
IDEAL SLOW COOKER SIZE: **3–4-QUART**

6 slices bacon, diced
½ cup chopped onions
2 cups diced peeled potatoes
2 10-oz. pkgs. frozen corn
16-oz. can cream-style corn
1 Tbsp. sugar
1 tsp. Worcestershire sauce
1 tsp. seasoned salt
¼ tsp. pepper
1 cup water

1. In skillet, brown bacon until crisp. Remove
   bacon, reserving drippings.
2. Add onions and potatoes to skillet and sauté
   for 5 minutes. Drain.
3. Combine all ingredients in slow cooker.
   Mix well.
4. Cover. Cook on Low 6–7 hours.

Variations:

*1. To make Clam Corn Chowder, drain and
add 2 cans minced clams during last hour of
cooking.*

*2. Substitute 1 quart home-frozen corn for the
store-bought frozen and canned corn.*

Cheese and Corn Chowder

Loretta Krahn Mt. Lake, MN

MAKES: **8 SERVINGS**
PREP. TIME: **10 MINUTES**
COOKING TIME: **5–7 HOURS**
IDEAL SLOW COOKER SIZE: **4-QUART**

¾ cup water

½ cup chopped onions

1½ cups sliced carrots

1½ cups chopped celery

1 tsp. salt

½ tsp. pepper

15¼-oz. can whole-kernel corn, drained

15-oz. can cream-style corn

3 cups milk

1½ cup shredded cheddar cheese

1. Combine water, onions, carrots, celery, salt, and pepper in slow cooker.
2. Cover. Cook on High 4–6 hours.
3. Add corn, milk, and cheese. Heat on High 1 hour, and then turn to Low until you are ready to eat.

Creamy Corn Chowder

Mary Rogers Waseca, MN

MAKES: **12 SERVINGS**
PREP. TIME: **30–40 MINUTES**
COOKING TIME: **2 HOURS**
IDEAL SLOW COOKER SIZE: **4-QUART**

½ lb. lean turkey bacon

4 cups diced potatoes

2 cups chopped onions

2 cups fat-free sour cream

1½ cups fat-free milk

2 10¾-oz. cans fat-free, low-sodium cream of chicken soup

2 15¼-oz. cans fat-free, low-sodium whole-kernel corn, undrained

1. Cut bacon into 1-inch pieces. Cook for 5 minutes in large nonstick skillet, doing it in two batches so all the pieces brown.
2. Add potatoes and onions and a bit of water. Cook 15–20 minutes, until vegetables are tender, stirring occasionally. Drain. Transfer to slow cooker.
3. Combine sour cream, milk, chicken soup, and corn. Place in slow cooker.
4. Cover. Cook on Low for 2 hours.

Per Serving: 260 calories (70 calories from fat), 8 total fat (2.5g saturated, 0g trans), 25mg cholesterol, 840mg sodium, 37g total carbohydrate (3g fiber, 10g sugar), 11g protein, 2%DV vitamin A, 20%DV vitamin C, 15%DV calcium, 10%DV iron.

Variation: *If you'll be gone for most of the day, you may want to use a different procedure from the one above. After Step 1, place bacon, potatoes, onions, 2 inches of water, the 2 cans of soup and the 2 cans of corn into the slow cooker. Cook on Low 8–10 hours, or until the vegetables are done to your liking. Thirty minutes before serving, stir in sour cream and milk and continue cooking on Low. Serve when soup is heated through and steaming.*

Double Corn and Cheddar Chowder

Maryann Markano Wilmington, DE

MAKES: **6 SERVINGS**
PREP. TIME: **10 MINUTES**
COOKING TIME: **4½ HOURS**
IDEAL SLOW COOKER SIZE: **4-QUART**

1 Tbsp. butter *or* margarine
1 cup onions, chopped
2 Tbsp. all-purpose flour
2½ cups fat-free, reduced-sodium chicken broth
16-oz. can creamed corn
1 cup frozen corn
½ cup finely chopped red bell peppers
½ tsp. hot pepper sauce
¾ cup shredded, reduced-fat, sharp cheddar cheese
freshly ground pepper to taste, *optional*

1. In saucepan on top of stove, melt butter or margarine. Stir in onions and sauté until wilted. Stir in flour. When well mixed, whisk in chicken broth. Stir frequently over medium heat until broth is thickened.
2. Pour into slow cooker. Mix in remaining ingredients except cheese.
3. Cook on Low 4½ hours. About an hour before the end of the cooking time, stir in cheese until melted and well blended.

Per Serving: 200 calories (60 calories from fat), 7g total fat (4g saturated, 0g trans), 20mg cholesterol, 530mg sodium, 25g total carbohydrate (2g fiber, 5g sugar), 12g protein, 20%DV vitamin A, 20%DV vitamin C, 20%DV calcium, 8%DV iron.

Variation: *You may also add a cup of cooked white or brown rice during the last hour if you like.*

Green Chili Corn Chowder

Kelly Evenson Pittsboro, NC

MAKES: **8 SERVINGS**
PREP. TIME: **15 MINUTES**
COOKING TIME: **7¼–8¼ HOURS**
IDEAL SLOW COOKER SIZE: **4-QUART**

16-oz. can cream-style corn
3 potatoes, peeled and diced
2 Tbsp. chopped fresh chives
4-oz. can diced green chilies, drained
2-oz. jar chopped pimentos, drained
½–¾ cup chopped cooked ham
2 10½-oz. cans chicken broth
salt to taste
pepper to taste
Tabasco sauce to taste
1 cup milk
shredded Monterey Jack cheese

1. Combine all ingredients except milk and cheese in slow cooker.
2. Cover. Cook on Low 7–8 hours or until potatoes are tender.
3. Stir in milk. Heat until hot.
4. Top individual servings with cheese. Serve with homemade bread.

Mexican Tomato-Corn Soup

Jeanne Heyerly   Chenoa, IL

MAKES: **8 SERVINGS**
PREP. TIME: **10 MINUTES**
COOKING TIME: **6–8 HOURS**
IDEAL SLOW COOKER SIZE: **4-QUART**

1 medium onion, diced

1 medium green bell pepper, diced

1 clove garlic, minced

1 cup diced carrots

14½-oz. can low-sodium diced Italian tomatoes

2½ cups low-sodium tomato juice

1 quart low-fat, low-sodium chicken broth

3 cups corn, frozen or canned

4-oz. can chopped chilies, undrained

1 tsp. chili powder

1½ tsp. ground cumin

dash cayenne powder

1. Combine all ingredients in slow cooker.
2. Cover. Cook on Low 6–8 hours.

Per Serving: 100 calories (10 calories from fat), 1g total fat (0g saturated, 0g trans), 0mg cholesterol, 115mg sodium, 20g total carbohydrate (4g fiber, 9g sugar), 6g protein, 50%DV vitamin A, 30%DV vitamin C, 4%DV calcium, 10%DV iron.

Tip: *Garnish individual servings with cilantro leaves, corn or tortilla chips, and/or low-fat shredded sharp cheddar cheese, if your diet permits.*

Southwest Corn Soup

Susan Tjon   Austin, TX

MAKES: **6 SERVINGS**
PREP. TIME: **10 MINUTES**
COOKING TIME: **4 HOURS**
IDEAL SLOW COOKER SIZE: **5-QUART**

2 4-oz. cans chopped green chilies, undrained

2 small zucchini, cut into bite-sized pieces

1 medium onion, thinly sliced

3 cloves garlic, minced

1 tsp. ground cumin

3 14½-oz. cans fat-free, sodium-reduced chicken broth

1½–2 cups cooked turkey, shredded

15-oz. can chickpeas *or* black beans, rinsed and drained

10-oz. pkg. frozen corn

1 tsp. dried oregano

½ cup chopped cilantro

1. Combine all ingredients in slow cooker.
2. Cook on Low 4 hours.

Per Serving: 240 calories (40 calories from fat), 4.5g total fat (1g saturated, 0g trans), 25mg cholesterol, 520mg sodium, 31g total carbohydrate (7g fiber, 5g sugar), 21g protein, 6%DV vitamin A, 20%DV vitamin C, 10%DV calcium, 20%DV iron.

Variation: *For a twist on the soup's flavor and consistency, substitute 1 14½-oz. can low-sodium diced tomatoes for one of the cans of chicken broth.*

Salsa Soup

Esther J. Yoder Hartville, OH

MAKES: **10 SERVINGS**
PREP. TIME: **10 MINUTES**
COOKING TIME: **4–10 HOURS**
IDEAL SLOW COOKER SIZE: **4-QUART**

1 lb. mild sausage, sliced

1 quart white navy beans, undrained

2 cups mild or medium salsa

4 cups fat-free chicken broth

1. Brown sausage in skillet and drain well.
2. Combine all ingredients in slow cooker.
3. Cook on Low 8-10 hours, or on High 4-6 hours.

Per Serving: 240 calories (80 calories from fat), 9g total fat (3g saturated, 0g trans), 15mg cholesterol, 480mg sodium, 27g total carbohydrate (6g fiber, 5g sugar), 14g protein, 6%DV vitamin A, 6%DV vitamin C, 10%DV calcium, 25%DV iron.

Variation: *If you like a thickened soup, mix ¼ cup cornstarch with ¼ cup water. Remove 1 cup hot soup broth from cooker about 15 minutes before end of cooking time. Whisk together with cornstarch mixture. When smooth, stir back into soup in cooker and stir until thickened. This can be served over rice, in addition to serving it as a soup.*

Green Bean and Ham Soup

Loretta Krahn Mountain Lake, MN

MAKES: **6 SERVINGS**
PREP. TIME: **15 MINUTES**
COOKING TIME: **4¼–6¼ HOURS**
IDEAL SLOW COOKER SIZE: **5-6-QUART**

1 meaty ham bone, *or* 2 cups cubed ham

1½ quarts water

1 large onion, chopped

2–3 cups cut-up green beans

3 large carrots, sliced

2 large potatoes, peeled and cubed

1 Tbsp. parsley

1 Tbsp. summer savory

½ tsp. salt

¼ tsp. pepper

1 cup cream *or* milk

1. Combine all ingredients except cream in slow cooker.
2. Cover. Cook on High 4-6 hours.
3. Remove ham bone. Cut off meat and return to slow cooker.
4. Turn to Low. Stir in cream or milk. Heat through and serve.

Green Bean and Sausage Soup

Bernita Boyts Shawnee Mission, KS

MAKES: **5-6 SERVINGS**
PREP. TIME: **20-25 MINUTES**
COOKING TIME: **7-10 HOURS**
IDEAL SLOW COOKER SIZE: **4-5-QUART**

1 medium onion, chopped

2 carrots, sliced

2 ribs celery, sliced

1 Tbsp. olive oil

5 medium potatoes, cubed

10-oz. pkg. frozen green beans

2 14½-oz. cans chicken broth

2 broth cans water

⅓ lb. link sausage, sliced, *or* bulk sausage, browned

2 Tbsp. chopped fresh parsley, or 2 tsp. dried

1–2 Tbsp. chopped fresh oregano, or 1–2 tsp. dried

1 tsp. Italian spice

salt to taste

pepper to taste

1. Sauté onion, carrots, and celery in oil in skillet until tender.
2. Combine all ingredients in slow cooker.
3. Cover. Cook on High 1–2 hours and then on Low 6–8 hours.
4. Serve with freshly baked bread or cornbread.

Variation: *If you like it hot, add ground red pepper or hot sauce just before serving.*

Curried Limas and Potato Soup

Barbara Gautcher   Harrisonburg, VA

MAKES: **6 SERVINGS**
PREP. TIME: **15 MINUTES**
COOKING TIME: **4–10 HOURS**
IDEAL SLOW COOKER SIZE: **3-QUART**

1½ cups dried large lima beans

4 cups water, *divided*

5–6 medium potatoes, finely chopped

½ head cauliflower, *optional*

2 cups (16 ozs.) sour cream

2 Tbsp. curry

1–2 tsp. salt and pepper, to taste

1. In a medium saucepan, bring dried limas to a boil in 2 cups water. Boil, uncovered, for 2 minutes. Cover, turn off heat, and wait 2 hours.
2. Drain water. Place beans in slow cooker.
3. Add 2 cups fresh water. Cover and cook 2 hours on High.
4. During the last hour of cooking, add diced potatoes and cauliflower florets. Cook longer if vegetables are not as tender as you like after 1 hour.
5. Ten minutes before serving, add sour cream, curry, and salt and pepper to taste.

Tip: *Sprinkle shredded cheese on top of each serving. And/or serve with chopped fresh fennel as a topping.*

Variation: *Soak limas in 2 cups water overnight. In the morning, drain water. Put limas in slow cooker and follow directions above, beginning with Step 3.*

Curried Carrot Soup

Ann Bender   Ft. Defiance, VA

MEATLESS

MAKES: **6–8 SERVINGS**
PREP. TIME: **20 MINUTES**
COOKING TIME: **2 HOURS**
IDEAL SLOW COOKER SIZE: **3-QUART**

1 garlic clove, minced

1 large onion, chopped

2 Tbsp. oil

1 Tbsp. butter

1 tsp. curry powder

1 Tbsp. flour

4 cups chicken *or* vegetable broth

6 large carrots, sliced

¼ tsp. salt

¼ tsp. ground red pepper, *optional*

1½ cups plain yogurt, *or* light sour cream

1. In skillet cook minced garlic and onion in oil and butter until limp but not brown.
2. Add curry and flour. Cook 30 seconds. Pour into slow cooker.
3. Add chicken broth and carrots.
4. Cover. Cook on High for about 2 hours, or until carrots are soft.
5. Puree mixture in blender. Season with salt and pepper. Return to slow cooker and keep warm until ready to serve.
6. Add a dollop of yogurt or sour cream to each serving.

Pumpkin Soup

Jane Meiser   Harrisonburg, VA

MAKES: **6 SERVINGS**
PREP. TIME: **5 MINUTES**
COOKING TIME: **5–6 HOURS**
IDEAL SLOW COOKER SIZE: **3½-QUART**

¼ cup chopped green bell pepper

1 small onion, finely chopped

2 cups low-sodium chicken stock *or* broth, fat removed

2 cups pumpkin puree

2 cups skim milk

⅛ tsp. dried thyme

¼ tsp. ground nutmeg

½ tsp. salt

2 Tbsp. cornstarch

¼ cup cold water

1 tsp. chopped fresh parsley

1. Combine all ingredients except cornstarch, cold water, and fresh parsley in slow cooker. Mix well.
2. Cover. Cook on Low 5–6 hours.
3. During the last hour add cornstarch mixed with water and stir until soup thickens.
4. Just before serving, stir in fresh parsley.

Per Serving: 70 calories (0 calories from fat), 0g total fat (0g saturated, 0g trans), 0mg cholesterol, 300mg sodium, 12g total carbohydrate (1g fiber, 8g sugar), 6g protein, 15%DV vitamin A, 10%DV vitamin C, 10%DV calcium, 6%DV iron.

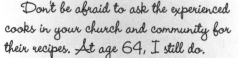

Don't be afraid to ask the experienced cooks in your church and community for their recipes. At age 64, I still do.

Onion Soup

Rosemarie Fitzgerald   Gibsonia, PA

MAKES: **8 SERVINGS**
PREP. TIME: **30 MINUTES**
COOKING TIME: **6–8 HOURS**
IDEAL SLOW COOKER SIZE: **3½-QUART**

3 medium onions, thinly sliced

2 Tbsp. butter

2 Tbsp. vegetable oil

1 tsp. salt

1 Tbsp. sugar

2 Tbsp. flour

1 quart fat-free, low-sodium vegetable broth

½ cup dry white wine

slices of French bread

½ cup grated fat-free Swiss *or* Parmesan cheese

1. Sauté onions in butter and oil in covered skillet until soft. Uncover. Add salt and sugar. Cook 15 minutes. Stir in flour. Cook 3 more minutes.
2. Combine onions, broth, and wine in slow cooker.
3. Cover. Cook on Low 6–8 hours.
4. Toast bread. Sprinkle with grated cheese and then broil.
5. Dish soup into individual bowls; then float a slice of broiled bread on top of each serving of soup.

Per Serving: 360 calories (50 calories from fat), 6g total fat (2.5g saturated, 0.5g trans), 10mg cholesterol, 1320mg sodium, 61g total carbohydrate (4g fiber, 7g sugar), 11g protein, 0%DV vitamin A, 0%DV vitamin C, 15%DV calcium, 15%DV iron.

Winter Squash and White Bean Stew

Mary E. Herr   Three Rivers, MI

MAKES: **6 SERVINGS**
PREP. TIME: **15 MINUTES**
COOKING TIME: **3–4 HOURS**
IDEAL SLOW COOKER SIZE: **4-QUART**

1 cup chopped onions

1 Tbsp. olive oil

½ tsp. ground cumin

¼ tsp. salt

¼ tsp. cinnamon

1 garlic clove, minced

3 cups peeled butternut squash, cut into ¾-inch cubes

1½ cups chicken broth

19-oz. can cannellini beans, drained

14½-oz. can diced tomatoes, undrained

1 Tbsp. chopped fresh cilantro

1. Combine all ingredients in slow cooker.
2. Cover. Cook on High 1 hour. Reduce heat to Low and heat 2–3 hours.

Variations:

1. Beans can be pureed in blender and added during the last hour.

2. Eight ounces dried beans can be soaked overnight, cooked until soft, and used in place of canned beans.

Butternut Squash Soup

Elaine Vigoda   Rochester, NY

MAKES: **4–6 SERVINGS**
PREP. TIME: **5 MINUTES**
COOKING TIME: **4–8 HOURS**
IDEAL SLOW COOKER SIZE: **4–5-QUART**

45-oz. can chicken broth

1 medium butternut squash, peeled and cubed

1 small onion, chopped

1 tsp. ground ginger

1 tsp. garlic, minced, *optional*

¼ tsp. nutmeg, *optional*

1. Place chicken broth and squash in slow cooker. Add remaining ingredients.
2. Cover and cook on High 4 hours, or on Low 6–8 hours, or until squash is tender.

Mjeddrah or Esau's Lentil Soup

MEATLESS

Dianna Milhizer   Springfield, VA

MAKES: **8 SERVINGS**
PREP. TIME: **15 MINUTES**
COOKING TIME: **6–8 HOURS**
IDEAL SLOW COOKER SIZE: **4-QUART**

1 cup chopped carrots

1 cup diced celery

2 cups chopped onions

1 Tbsp. olive oil *or* butter

2 cups brown rice

1 Tbsp. olive oil *or* butter

6 cups water

1 lb. lentils, washed and drained

garden salad

vinaigrette

1. Sauté carrots, celery, and onions in 1 Tbsp. oil in skillet. When soft and translucent place in slow cooker.
2. Brown rice in 1 Tbsp. oil until dry. Add to slow cooker.
3. Stir in water and lentils.
4. Cover. Cook on High 6–8 hours.
5. When thoroughly cooked, serve 1 cup each in individual soup bowls. Cover each with a serving of fresh garden salad (lettuce, spinach leaves, chopped tomatoes, minced onions, chopped bell peppers, sliced olives, sliced radishes). Pour favorite vinaigrette over all.

Russian Red-Lentil Soup

Naomi E. Fast   Hesston, KS

MAKES: **8 SERVINGS**
PREP. TIME: **15 MINUTES**
COOKING TIME: **3¾–4¾ HOURS**
IDEAL SLOW COOKER SIZE: **3½–4-QUART**

1 Tbsp. oil

1 large onion, chopped

3 cloves garlic, minced

½ cup diced, dried apricots

1½ cups dried red lentils

½ tsp. cumin

½ tsp. dried thyme

3 cups water

2 14½-oz. cans chicken *or* vegetable broth

14½-oz. can diced tomatoes

1 Tbsp. honey

¾ tsp. salt

½ tsp. coarsely ground black pepper

2 Tbsp. chopped fresh mint

1½ cups plain yogurt

1. Combine all ingredients except mint and yogurt in slow cooker.
2. Cover. Heat on High until soup starts to simmer, then turn to Low and cook 3–4 hours.
3. Add mint and dollop of yogurt to each bowl of soup.

Wild Rice and Lentil Soup

Maryann Markano   Wilmington, DE

MAKES: **8–10 SERVINGS**
PREP. TIME: **5 MINUTES**
SOAKING TIME: **6–8 HOURS, OR OVERNIGHT**
COOKING TIME: **5–8 HOURS**
IDEAL SLOW COOKER SIZE: **3½–4-QUART**

½ cup dried lentils, sorted, rinsed, and drained

3 cups water

6-oz. pkg. long-grain and wild rice blend, with spice packet

14-oz. can vegetable broth

10-oz. pkg. frozen mixed vegetables

1 cup skim milk

½ cup reduced-fat mild cheddar cheese, shredded

1. Cover lentils with water and soak overnight or for 6–8 hours. Drain and discard soaking water.
2. Put all ingredients into slow cooker, including the 3 cups fresh water. Mix well.
3. Cook on Low 5–8 hours, or until the vegetables are done to your liking.

Per Serving: 240 calories (25 calories from fat), 2.5g total fat (1.5g saturated, 0g trans), 5mg cholesterol, 280mg sodium, 42g total carbohydrate (7g fiber, 5g sugar), 13g protein, 30%DV vitamin A, 10%DV vitamin C, 15%DV calcium, 15%DV iron.

Tip: *It may be necessary to add more water if the soup seems too thick.*

Sweet Potato Lentil Stew

Mrs. Carolyn Baer Conrath, WI

MAKES: **6 SERVINGS**
PREP. TIME: **15 MINUTES**
COOKING TIME: **5–6 HOURS**
IDEAL SLOW COOKER SIZE: **4-QUART**

4 cups fat-free vegetable broth

3 cups (about 1¼ lbs.) sweet potatoes, peeled and cubed

1½ cups lentils, rinsed

3 medium carrots, cut into 1-inch pieces

1 medium onion, chopped

4 garlic cloves, minced

½ tsp. ground cumin

¼ tsp. ground ginger

¼ tsp. cayenne pepper

¼ cup minced fresh cilantro *or* parsley

¼ tsp. salt

1. Combine first nine ingredients in slow cooker.
2. Cook on Low 5–6 hours or just until vegetables are tender.
3. Stir in cilantro and salt just before serving.

Per Serving: 280 calories (5 calories from fat), 1g total fat (0g saturated, 0g trans), 0mg cholesterol, 580mg sodium, 54g total carbohydrate (19g fiber, 12g sugar), 16g protein, 300%DV vitamin A, 25%DV vitamin C, 8%DV calcium, 30%DV iron.

Variation: *For added flavor, you may want to increase the cumin to ¾–1 tsp. and the ginger to ½ tsp. And if your diet allows, you may also stir in ⅓ cup raisins, ¼ cup chopped nuts, and ¼ cup grated coconut just before serving.*

Crockpot Lentil Soup with Ham

Rhonda L. Burgoon Collingswood, NJ

MAKES: **8 SERVINGS**
PREP. TIME: **15 MINUTES**
COOKING TIME: **7–9 HOURS**
IDEAL SLOW COOKER SIZE: **4-QUART**

1 cup chopped onions

3 cloves garlic, minced

5 cups fat-free, low-sodium chicken broth

1 cup dried lentils

½ cup chopped carrots

2 bay leaves

3 cups chopped Swiss chard

1½ cups chopped potatoes

1 cup chopped ham

14½-oz. can low-sodium diced tomatoes

1 tsp. dried basil

½ tsp. dried thyme

½ tsp. black pepper

3 Tbsp. chopped fresh parsley

1. Combine all ingredients except fresh parsley in slow cooker.
2. Cover. Cook on Low 7–9 hours.
3. Stir in fresh parsley and serve.

Per Serving: 200 calories (30 calories from fat), 3.5g total fat (1g saturated, 0g trans), 15mg cholesterol, 290mg sodium, 25g total carbohydrate (10g fiber, 5g sugar),17g protein, 50%DV vitamin A, 20%DV vitamin C, 8%DV calcium, 25%DV iron.

Lentil-Tomato Stew

Marci Baum Annville, PA

Light
MEATLESS

MAKES: **8 SERVINGS**
PREP. TIME: **10 MINUTES**
COOKING TIME: **4–12 HOURS**
IDEAL SLOW COOKER SIZE: **6-QUART**

3 cups water

28-oz. can low-sodium peeled Italian tomatoes, undrained

6-oz. can low-sodium tomato paste

½ cup dry red wine

¾ tsp. dried basil

¾ tsp. dried thyme

½ tsp. crushed red pepper

1 lb. dried lentils, rinsed and drained with any stones removed

1 large onion, chopped

4 medium carrots, cut in ½-inch rounds

4 medium celery ribs, cut into ½-inch slices

3 garlic cloves, minced

1 tsp. salt

chopped fresh basil *or* parsley, for garnish

1. Combine water, tomatoes with juice, tomato paste, red wine, basil, thyme, and crushed red pepper in slow cooker.
2. Break up tomatoes with a wooden spoon and stir to blend them and the paste into the mixture.
3. Add lentils, onion, carrots, celery, and garlic.
4. Cover. Cook on Low 10–12 hours, or on High 4–5 hours.
5. Stir in the salt.
6. Serve in bowls, sprinkled with chopped basil or parsley.

Per Serving: 250 calories (10 calories from fat), 1g total fat (0g saturated, 0g trans), 0mg cholesterol, 530mg sodium, 44g total carbohydrate (16g fiber, 7g sugar), 17g protein, 20%DV vitamin A, 20%DV vitamin C, 8%DV calcium, 40%DV iron.

Lidia's Egg Drop Soup

Shirley Unternahrer Hinh Wayland, IA

Light

MAKES: **8 SERVINGS**
PREP. TIME: **10 MINUTES**
COOKING TIME: **1 HOUR**
IDEAL SLOW COOKER SIZE: **3½-QUART**

2 14½-oz. cans fat-free, low-sodium chicken broth

1 quart water

2 Tbsp. fish sauce

¼ tsp. salt

4 Tbsp. cornstarch

1 cup cold water

2 eggs, beaten

1 chopped green onion

¼ tsp. black pepper

1. Combine broth and water in large saucepan.
2. Add fish sauce and salt. Bring to boil.
3. Mix cornstarch into cold water until smooth. Add to soup. Bring to boil while stirring. Remove from heat.
4. Pour beaten eggs into thickened broth, but do not stir. Instead, pull fork through soup with 2 strokes.
5. Transfer to slow cooker. Add green onions and pepper.
6. Cover. Cook on Low 1 hour. Keep warm in cooker.
7. Eat plain or with rice.

Per Serving: 50 calories (10 calories from fat), 1g total fat (0g saturated, 0g trans), 45mg cholesterol, 510mg sodium, 5g total carbohydrate (0g fiber, 1g sugar), 4g protein, 0%DV vitamin A, 0%DV vitamin C, 0%DV calcium, 6%DV iron.

Note: *One day when the kids were sledding I surprised them with something other than hot cocoa when they came in. "Mmmmm," was all I heard, and, "This tastes great!" "You're the best, Mom!" They finished all the egg drop soup and wondered if I'd make more.*

Beef Main Dishes

So-Easy Roast Beef

Jean Binns Smith Bellefonte, PA • *Sarah Miller* Harrisonburg, VA
Heidi Hunsberger Harrisonburg, VA

MAKES: **6–8 SERVINGS**
PREP. TIME: **5 MINUTES**
COOKING TIME: **6–8 HOURS**
IDEAL SLOW COOKER SIZE: **4-QUART**

3–4-lb. beef roast
10¾-oz. can cream of mushroom soup
half or all of 1 envelope dry onion soup mix

1. Rinse beef, pat dry, and place in slow cooker.
2. Pour mushroom soup over top. Sprinkle with dry soup mix.
3. Cover and cook on Low 6–8 hours, or until meat is tender but not dry.

Variations:

1. You can add sliced carrots and halved potatoes after 4 hours of cooking.

2. For more sauce, mix mushroom soup with a soup-can of water before pouring into cooker.

Lena Hoover Ephrata, PA • *Michelle High* Fredericksburg, PA
Colleen Konetzni Rio Rancho, NM

3. For more sauce, mix mushroom soup with ½ cup white wine.

Karen Waggoner Joplin, MO

4. Brown the roast on all sides in 2 Tbsp. olive oil in a nonstick skillet. Place in the slow cooker. In a bowl, mix together mushroom soup, dry soup mix, ½ tsp. salt, ¼ tsp. pepper, and ½ cup water. Pour over meat. Proceed with Step 3 above.

Betty Moore Plano, IL

Zesty Italian Beef

Carol Eveleth   Wellman, IA

MAKES: **6 SERVINGS**
PREP. TIME: **5 MINUTES**
COOKING TIME: **4–10 HOURS**
IDEAL SLOW COOKER SIZE: **3½-QUART**

1 envelope dry onion soup mix
½ tsp. garlic powder
1 tsp. dried basil
½ tsp. dried oregano
¼ tsp. paprika, *optional*
½ tsp. red pepper, *optional*
2 cups water
2-lb. rump roast

1. Combine soup mix and seasonings with 2 cups water in slow cooker. Add roast.
2. Cook on High 4–6 hours, or on Low 8–10 hours, or until meat is tender but not dry.
3. Allow meat to rest for 10 minutes before slicing. Top slices with cooking juices.

Allow cooked meat to stand for 10–15 minutes before slicing it, so that it can re-gather its juices.

Beef Pot Roast

Nancy Wagner Graves   Manhattan, KS

MAKES: **6–8 SERVINGS**
PREP. TIME: **10 MINUTES**
COOKING TIME: **6–7 HOURS**
IDEAL SLOW COOKER SIZE: **4-QUART**

4–5-lb. beef chuck roast
1 garlic clove, cut in half
salt to taste
pepper to taste
1 carrot, chopped
1 rib celery, chopped
1 small onion, sliced
¾ cup sour cream
3 Tbsp. flour
½ cup dry white wine

1. Rub roast with garlic. Season with salt and pepper. Place in slow cooker.
2. Add carrots, celery, and onion.
3. Combine sour cream, flour, and wine. Pour into slow cooker.
4. Cover. Cook on Low 6-7 hours.

Beef Main Dishes

Pot Roast Complete

Naomi E. Fast Hesston, KS

MAKES: **6–8 SERVINGS**
PREP. TIME: **15 MINUTES**
COOKING TIME: **6½–7½ HOURS**
IDEAL SLOW COOKER SIZE: **4-QUART**

3–3½-lb. arm roast, boneless
2 large onions, sliced
½ cup brown sugar
⅓ cup soy sauce
⅓ cup cider vinegar
2 bay leaves
2–3 garlic cloves, minced
1 tsp. grated fresh ginger
1 cup julienned carrots, matchstick size
2 cups sliced button mushrooms
2–3 cups fresh spinach leaves, *or* 2 10-oz. pkgs. frozen
    spinach, drained
2 Tbsp. cornstarch

1. Place meat, topped with onions, in slow cooker.
2. Combine brown sugar, soy sauce, and vinegar. Pour over beef.
3. Add bay leaves, garlic, and ginger
4. Cover. Cook on High 6-7 hours.
5. Spread carrots, mushrooms, and spinach over beef.
6. Cover. Cook on High 20 minutes.
7. Mix cornstarch with ½ cup broth from slow cooker. Return to slow cooker.
8. Cover. Cook 10 minutes more.
9. Serve over rice.

Note: *I can't count how many times I have used this recipe over the last 15–20 years as a guest meal.*

Italian Beef au Jus

Carol Sherwood Batavia, NY

MAKES: **8 SERVINGS**
PREP. TIME: **10 MINUTES**
COOKING TIME: **8 HOURS**
IDEAL SLOW COOKER SIZE: **4-QUART**

3–5-lb. boneless beef roast
10-oz. pkg. dry au jus mix
1 pkg. dry Italian salad dressing mix
14½-oz. can beef broth
half a soup can water

1. Place beef in slow cooker.
2. Combine remaining ingredients. Pour over roast.
3. Cover. Cook on Low 8 hours.
4. Slice meat and spoon onto hard rolls with straining spoon to make sandwiches. Or shred with 2 forks and serve over noodles or rice in broth thickened with flour.

Variation: *To thicken broth, mix 3 Tbsp. cornstarch into ¼ cup cold water. Stir until smooth.*

Remove ½ cup beef broth from cooker and blend into cornstarch-water. Stir back into broth in cooker, stirring until smooth.

Cook 10–15 minutes on High until broth becomes of gravy consistency.

I-Forgot-to-Thaw-the-Roast Beef!

Thelma Good   Harrisonburg, VA

MAKES: **10 SERVINGS**
PREP. TIME: **20 MINUTES**
COOKING TIME: **7–9 HOURS**
IDEAL SLOW COOKER SIZE: **4–5-QUART**

3–4-lb. frozen beef roast
1½ tsp. salt
pepper to taste
1 large onion
¼ cup flour
¾ cup cold water

1. Place frozen roast in slow cooker. Sprinkle with 1½ tsp. salt and pepper to taste. Slice onion and lay over top.
2. Cover and cook on High 1 hour. Turn heat to Low and roast for 6–8 hours, or until meat is tender but not dry.
3. Spoon 1¼ cups broth from the slow cooker into a saucepan. Bring to a boil.
4. While broth is heating, whisk together flour and cold water in a small bowl until smooth.
5. When the broth boils, stir flour water into the broth, stirring continually until the broth is smooth and thickened.
6. Slice roast and return meat and onions to the slow cooker. Pour gravy over top. Turn on Low until ready to serve.

Tip: *This is a stress-free dish to serve to guests.*

Beef a la Mode

Gloria Julien   Gladstone, MI

MAKES: **6 SERVINGS**
PREP. TIME: **5–10 MINUTES**
COOKING TIME: **6–8 HOURS**
IDEAL SLOW COOKER SIZE: **4-QUART**

2-lb. boneless beef roast, cut into 6 serving-size pieces
½ lb. salt pork *or* bacon, cut up
3 onions, chopped
pepper to taste
water

1. Place beef and pork in slow cooker.
2. Sprinkle onions over top of meat.
3. Add pepper to taste.
4. Pour water in alongside meat, about 1-inch deep.
5. Cook on Low 6–8 hours.
6. Serve over mashed potatoes, cooked rice, or pasta.

Roast Venison with Gravy

Becky Gehman   Bergton, VA

MAKES: **4–6 SERVINGS**
PREP. TIME: **5 MINUTES**
COOKING TIME: **6–7 HOURS**
IDEAL SLOW COOKER SIZE: **3-QUART**

2–3-lb. venison roast
1–2 tsp. garlic powder *or* onion powder
10¾-oz. can golden mushroom soup
¾ soup can of water

1. Place roast in slow cooker. Sprinkle both sides with seasoning.
2. Cover and cook on Low 4–5 hours, turning the roast twice while cooking.
3. In a bowl, mix together soup and water. Add to meat after it's cooked for 4–5 hours.
4. Cover and cook on Low 2 more hours, turning roast once during this time.

Variations:

1. Instead of the garlic or onion powder, use 1 envelope dry beefy onion soup mix.

Krista Hershberger   Elverson, PA

Beef Main Dishes

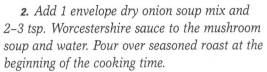

2. *Add 1 envelope dry onion soup mix and 2–3 tsp. Worcestershire sauce to the mushroom soup and water. Pour over seasoned roast at the beginning of the cooking time.*

Cover and cook on Low for 6 hours, or until meat is tender and not overcooked.

Anne Nolt Thompsontown, PA

Italian Pot Roast

Sandy Osborn Iowa City, IA

MAKES: **8 SERVINGS**
PREP. TIME: **5–10 MINUTES**
COOKING TIME: **5–8 HOURS**
IDEAL SLOW COOKER SIZE: **3½-QUART**

2½-lb. boneless beef round roast
1 medium onion, sliced
¼ tsp. salt
¼ tsp. pepper
2 8-oz. cans no-salt-added tomato sauce
1 envelope dry Italian salad dressing mix
½ cup flour *or* cornstarch
½ cup water

1. Slice roast in half for even cooking. Then place in your slow cooker.
2. Add onion and remaining ingredients in the order they are listed.
3. Cover and cook on High for 5 hours, or until the roast is tender but not dry. You can also cook it on High 1 hour, then reduce the heat to Low and cook for 7 hours.
4. When the meat is fully cooked, place it on a platter and cover it to keep it warm.
5. To turn cooking juices into gravy, turn the cooker to High to bring juices to a boil.
6. Mix ½ cup flour or cornstarch into ½ cup water. When smooth, pour in a thin stream into boiling juices, stirring continually. Continue to cook until juices thicken.
7. Slice meat. Serve gravy over meat, or place gravy in a separate bowl to serve.

Veal Hawaiian

Dorothy VanDeest Memphis, TN

MAKES: **4 SERVINGS**
PREP. TIME: **20 MINUTES**
COOKING TIME: **6 HOURS**
IDEAL SLOW COOKER SIZE: **4-QUART**

1½ lbs. boneless veal shoulder, trimmed of all fat and cut into 1-inch cubes
1 cup water
¼ cup sherry
2 Tbsp. low-sodium soy sauce
1 tsp. ground ginger
1 tsp. artificial sweetener

1. Lightly brown veal in a nonstick skillet.
2. Combine remaining ingredients in slow cooker. Stir in veal.
3. Cover. Cook on Low 6 hours.

Per Serving: 220 calories (60 calories from fat), 7g total fat (3g saturated, 0g trans), 130mg cholesterol, 470mg sodium, 1g total carbohydrate (0g fiber, 0g sugar), 32g protein, 0%DV vitamin A, 0%DV vitamin C, 4%DV calcium, 10%DV iron.

Variation:
You may substitute pork shoulder for the veal. This is tasty served over rice.

Don't be afraid to alter recipes to your liking.

Veal and Peppers

Irma H. Schoen   Windsor, CT

MAKES: **4 SERVINGS**
PREP. TIME: **10 MINUTES**
COOKING TIME: **4–7 MINUTES**
IDEAL SLOW COOKER SIZE: **4-QUART**

1½ lbs. boneless veal, cubed

3 green peppers, quartered

2 onions, thinly sliced

½ lb. fresh mushrooms, sliced

1 tsp. salt

½ tsp. dried basil

2 cloves garlic, minced

28-oz. can tomatoes

1. Combine all ingredients in slow cooker.
2. Cover. Cook on Low 7 hours, or on High 4 hours.
3. Serve over rice or noodles.

Variation: *Use boneless, skinless chicken breast, cut into chunks, instead of veal.*

Veggies and Beef Pot Roast

Alexa Slonin   Harrisonburg, VA

MAKES: **8–10 SERVINGS**
PREP. TIME: **15 MINUTES**
COOKING TIME: **10–12 HOURS**
IDEAL SLOW COOKER SIZE: **4–5 QUART**

12 oz. whole tiny new potatoes, *or* 2 medium potatoes, cubed, *or* 2 medium sweet potatoes, cubed

8 small carrots, cut in small chunks

2 small onions, cut in wedges

2 ribs celery, cut up

2½–3 lb. beef chuck *or* pot roast

2 Tbsp. cooking oil

¾ cup water, dry wine, *or* tomato juice

1 Tbsp. Worcestershire sauce

1 tsp. instant beef bouillon granules

1 tsp. dried basil

1. Place vegetables in bottom of slow cooker.
2. Brown roast in oil in skillet. Place on top of vegetables.
3. Combine water, Worcestershire sauce, bouillon, and basil. Pour over meat and vegetables.
4. Cover. Cook on Low 10–12 hours.

All-Day Pot Roast

Carol Shirk   Leola, PA

MAKES: **5 SERVINGS**
PREP. TIME: **15–20 MINUTES**
COOKING TIME: **5–12 HOURS**
IDEAL SLOW COOKER SIZE: **4-QUART**

1½-lb. boneless eye of beef round roast, round rump roast, *or* chuck roast

4 medium potatoes, quartered

16-oz. pkg. peeled baby carrots

10¾-oz. can golden mushroom soup

½ tsp. dried tarragon *or* basil, crushed

1. In a large nonstick skillet, brown meat on all sides.
2. Place potatoes and carrots in slow cooker. Place browned meat on top of vegetables.
3. In a small bowl, mix together soup and tarragon or basil. Pour over meat and vegetables.
4. Cover and cook on Low 10–12 hours, or on High 5–6 hours, until meat and vegetables are tender but not dry.

Beef Main Dishes

Italian Roast with Potatoes

Ruthie Schiefer   Vassar, MI

MAKES: **8 SERVINGS**
PREP. TIME: **30–35 MINUTES**
COOKING TIME: **6–7 HOURS**
IDEAL SLOW COOKER SIZE: **5-QUART**

6 medium potatoes, peeled if you wish, and quartered
1 large onion, sliced
3–4-lb. boneless beef roast
26-oz. jar tomato and basil pasta sauce, *divided*
½ cup water
3 beef bouillon cubes

1. Place potatoes and onion in bottom of slow cooker.
2. Meanwhile, brown roast on top and bottom in nonstick skillet.
3. Place roast on top of vegetables. Pour any drippings from the skillet over the beef.
4. Mix 1 cup pasta sauce and ½ cup water together in a small bowl. Stir in bouillon cubes. Spoon mixture over meat.
5. Cover and cook on Low 6–7 hours, or until meat is tender but not dry.
6. Transfer roast and vegetables to serving platter. Cover with foil.
7. Take 1 cup cooking juices from the slow cooker and place in medium-sized saucepan. Stir in remaining pasta sauce. Heat.
8. Slice or cube beef. Serve with heated sauce.

Browning the meat, onions, and vegetables before putting them in the cooker improves their flavor, but this extra step can be skipped in most recipes. The flavor will still be good.

Italian Beef Sandwiches

Carol Findling   Princeton, IL

MAKES: **6–8 SERVINGS**
PREP. TIME: **5–10 MINUTES**
COOKING TIME: **4–12 HOURS**
IDEAL SLOW COOKER SIZE: **4-QUART**

3–4-lb. lean rump roast
2 tsp. salt, *divided*
4 garlic cloves
2 tsp. Romano *or* **Parmesan cheese,** *divided*
12-oz. can beef broth
1 tsp. dried oregano

1. Place roast in slow cooker. Cut 4 slits in top of roast. Fill each slit with ½ tsp. salt, 1 garlic clove, and ½ tsp. cheese.
2. Pour broth over meat. Sprinkle with oregano.
3. Cover. Cook on Low 10–12 hours, or on High 4–6 hours.
4. Remove meat and slice or shred. Serve on buns with meat juices on the side.

Herbed Roast with Gravy

Sue Williams   Gulfport, MS

MAKES: **8–10 SERVINGS**
PREP. TIME: **5 MINUTES**
COOKING TIME: **4–10 HOURS**
IDEAL SLOW COOKER SIZE: **4-QUART**

4-lb. roast
2 tsp. salt
½ tsp. pepper
2 medium onions, sliced
half a can (10¾-oz.) condensed cheddar cheese soup
8-oz. can tomato sauce
4-oz. can mushroom pieces and stems, drained
¼ tsp. dried basil
¼ tsp. dried oregano

1. Season roast with salt and pepper. Place in slow cooker.
2. Combine remaining ingredients and pour over meat.
3. Cover. Cook on Low 8–10 hours, or on High 4–5 hours.
4. Serve with gravy.

Peppery Roast

Lovina Baer   Conrath, WI

MAKES: **8–10 SERVINGS**
PREP. TIME: **10 MINUTES**
COOKING TIME: **6–8 HOURS**
IDEAL SLOW COOKER SIZE: **4-QUART**

4-lb. beef *or* venison roast
1 tsp. garlic salt
1 tsp. onion salt
2 tsp. celery salt
1½ tsp. salt
2 tsp. Worcestershire sauce
2 tsp. pepper
½ cup ketchup
1 Tbsp. liquid smoke
3 Tbsp. brown sugar
1 Tbsp. dry mustard
dash of nutmeg
1 Tbsp. soy sauce
1 Tbsp. lemon juice
3 drops hot pepper sauce

1. Place roast in slow cooker.
2. Combine remaining ingredients and pour over roast.
3. Cover. Cook on High 6–8 hours.

Thirty minutes before making gravy, add flour to cold water in a jar with a screw-top lid. Close the lid tightly, shake the flour-water mixture vigorously, let it sit awhile, shake it again, let it sit awhile. Do this 3 or 4 times before you are ready to add it to the boiling broth. The lumps will disappear by the time you are ready to pour it into the hot broth to thicken it.

Beef Main Dishes

Savory Mexican Pot Roast

Bernice A. Esau   North Newton, KS

MAKES: **6–8 SERVINGS**
PREP. TIME: **15 MINUTES**
COOKING TIME: **10–12 HOURS**
IDEAL SLOW COOKER SIZE: **4-QUART**

3 lbs. beef brisket, cubed

2 Tbsp. oil

½ cup slivered almonds

2 cups mild picante sauce, or hot, if you prefer

2 Tbsp. vinegar

1 tsp. garlic powder

½ tsp. salt

¼ tsp. cinnamon

¼ tsp. dried thyme

¼ tsp. dried oregano

⅛ tsp. ground cloves

⅛ tsp. pepper

½–¾ cup water, as needed

1. Brown beef in oil in skillet. Place in slow cooker.
2. Combine remaining ingredients. Pour over meat.
3. Cover. Cook on Low 10–12 hours. Add water as needed.
4. Serve with potatoes, noodles, or rice.

Chuck Wagon Beef

Charlotte Bull   Cassville, MO

MAKES: **8 SERVINGS**
PREP. TIME: **20 MINUTES**
COOKING TIME: **8¼–10¼ HOURS**
IDEAL SLOW COOKER SIZE: **4-QUART**

4-lb. boneless chuck roast

1 tsp. garlic salt

¼ tsp. black pepper

2 Tbsp. oil

6–8 garlic cloves, minced

1 large onion, sliced

1 cup water

1 bouillon cube

2–3 tsp. instant coffee

1 bay leaf, *or* 1 Tbsp. mixed Italian herbs

3 Tbsp. cold water

2 Tbsp. cornstarch

1. Sprinkle roast with garlic salt and pepper. Brown on all sides in oil in saucepan. Place in slow cooker.
2. Sauté garlic and onion in meat drippings in saucepan. Add water, bouillon cube, and coffee. Cook over low heat for several minutes, stirring until drippings loosen. Pour over meat in cooker.
3. Add bay leaf or herbs.
4. Cover. Cook on Low 8–10 hours, or until very tender. Remove bay leaf and discard. Remove meat to serving platter and keep warm.
5. Mix water and cornstarch together until paste forms. Stir into hot liquid and onions in cooker. Cover. Cook 10 minutes on High, or until thickened.
6. Slice meat and serve with gravy over top or on the side.

CC Roast
(Company's Coming)

Anne Townsend Albuquerque, NM

MAKES: **8 SERVINGS**
PREP. TIME: **15 MINUTES**
COOKING TIME: **10–12 HOURS**
IDEAL SLOW COOKER SIZE: **4–5-QUART**

3-lb. boneless pot roast

2 Tbsp. flour

1 Tbsp. prepared mustard

1 Tbsp. chili sauce

1 Tbsp. Worcestershire sauce

1 tsp. red cider vinegar

1 tsp. sugar

4 potatoes, sliced

2 onions, sliced

1. Place pot roast in slow cooker.
2. Make a paste with the flour, mustard, chili sauce, Worcestershire sauce, vinegar, and sugar. Spread over the roast.
3. Top with potatoes and then the onions.
4. Cover. Cook on Low 10–12 hours.

Per Serving: 320 calories (70 calories from fat), 8g total fat (3g saturated, 0g trans), 100mg cholesterol, 160mg sodium, 24g total carbohydrate (3g fiber, 3g sugar), 36g protein, 0%DV vitamin A, 20%DV vitamin C, 2%DV calcium, 25%DV iron.

Never thaw meat at room temperature. Thaw meat safely in the microwave, as part of the cooking process, in a bowl of cold water, changing the water every 20 minutes, or in the refrigerator on the bottom shelf in a platter or deep dish.

Onion-Mushroom Pot Roast

Deb Herr Mountaintop, PA

MAKES: **6 SERVINGS**
PREP. TIME: **10 MINUTES**
COOKING TIME: **5–12 HOURS**
IDEAL SLOW COOKER SIZE: **6-QUART**

3–4-lb. pot roast *or* chuck roast

4-oz. can sliced mushrooms, drained

1 tsp. salt

¼ tsp. pepper

½ cup beef broth

1 envelope dry onion soup mix

1. Place pot roast in your slow cooker.
2. Add mushrooms, salt, and pepper.
3. In a small bowl, mix beef broth with the onion soup mix. Spoon over the roast.
4. Cover and cook on High 5–6 hours, or on Low 10–12 hours, or until meat is tender but not dry.

Variation: *To make gravy, prepare a smooth paste in a jar or small bowl, mixing ½ cup flour or cornstarch with ½ cup water.*

After the roast is fully cooked, remove the meat and keep it warm on a platter.

Turn cooker to High. When juices begin to boil, pour flour-water paste in a thin stream into the cooker, stirring continually.

Continue cooking and stirring until juices thicken. Serve over sliced roast, or in a bowl along with the meat.

Beef Main Dishes

Barbecued Roast Beef

Sherry H. Kauffman   Minot, ND

MAKES: **8 SERVINGS**
PREP. TIME: **15–20 MINUTES**
COOKING TIME: **6–7 HOURS**
IDEAL SLOW COOKER SIZE: **4-QUART**

4-lb. beef roast
1 cup ketchup
1 onion, chopped
¾ cup water
3 Tbsp. Worcestershire sauce
¾ cup brown sugar

1. Place roast in slow cooker.
2. In a small bowl, mix together all remaining ingredients except the brown sugar. Pour over roast.
3. Cover and cook on Low 6–7 hours. Approximately 1 hour before serving, sprinkle with ¾ cup brown sugar.

Barbecued Beef Brisket

Ruthie Schiefer   Vassar, MI

MAKES: **6–8 SERVINGS**
PREP. TIME: **10 MINUTES**
COOKING TIME: **6½–8½ HOURS**
IDEAL SLOW COOKER SIZE: **5-QUART**

2 cups Jack Daniel's Original No. 7 Barbecue Sauce,
  divided
1 medium onion, cut in wedges
3 beef bouillon cubes
3–4 lb. beef roast *or* brisket
3 bay leaves

1. In bottom of slow cooker, combine 1 cup barbecue sauce, onion, and bouillon cubes.
2. Place roast on top of sauce. Top with bay leaves.

3. Cover and cook on Low 6–8 hours or until beef is tender enough to shred easily.
4. Remove meat from slow cooker. Reserve cooking juices in slow cooker. Shred meat with two forks.
5. Return meat to slow cooker. Add remaining barbecue sauce. Mix well.
6. Cover and cook on High until heated through.
7. Serve on sandwich buns.

Savory Sweet Roast

Martha Ann Auker   Landisburg, PA

MAKES: **6–8 SERVINGS**
PREP. TIME: **10 MINUTES**
COOKING TIME: **12–16 HOURS**
IDEAL SLOW COOKER SIZE: **4-QUART**

3–4-lb. blade *or* chuck roast
oil
1 onion, chopped
10¾-oz. can cream of mushroom soup
½ cup water
¼ cup sugar
¼ cup vinegar
2 tsp. salt
1 tsp. prepared mustard
1 tsp. Worcestershire sauce

1. Brown meat in oil on both sides in saucepan. Put in slow cooker.
2. Blend together remaining ingredients. Pour over meat.
3. Cover. Cook on Low 12–16 hours.

Slow-Cooked Short Ribs

Jean A. Shaner York, PA • *Barbara L. McGinnis* Jupiter, FL

MAKES: **12 SERVINGS**
PREP. TIME: **35 MINUTES**
COOKING TIME: **9–10 HOURS**
IDEAL SLOW COOKER SIZE: **6-QUART**

⅔ cup flour

2 tsp. salt

½ tsp. pepper

4–4½ lbs. boneless beef short ribs, *or* 6–7 lbs. bone-in
   beef short ribs

oil *or* ⅓ cup butter

1 large onion, chopped

1½ cups beef broth

¾ cup wine *or* cider vinegar

½–¾ cup packed brown sugar, according to your taste
   preference

½ cup chili sauce

⅓ cup ketchup

⅓ cup Worcestershire sauce

5 garlic cloves, minced

1½ tsp. chili powder

1. Combine flour, salt, and pepper in plastic bag.
   Add ribs and shake to coat.
2. Brown meat in small amount of oil, or in
   butter, in batches in skillet. Transfer to slow
   cooker.
3. Combine remaining ingredients in saucepan.
   Cook, stirring up browned drippings, until
   mixture comes to boil. Pour over ribs.
4. Cover. Cook on Low 9–10 hours.
5. Debone and serve.

Tip: *It is ideal to cook these ribs one day in
advance of serving. Refrigerate for several hours
or overnight. Remove layer of congealed fat before
heating and serving over rice or noodles.*

Beef Ribs

Maryann Westerberg Rosamond, CA

MAKES: **8–10 SERVINGS**
PREP. TIME: **5 MINUTES**
COOKING TIME: **8½ HOURS**
IDEAL SLOW COOKER SIZE: **4-QUART**

3–4-lb. boneless beef *or* short ribs

1½ cups barbecue sauce, *divided*

½ cup apricot *or* pineapple jam

1 Tbsp. soy sauce

1. Place ribs in baking pan.
2. Combine ¾ cup barbecue sauce, jam, and
   soy sauce. Pour over ribs. Bake at 450° for
   30 minutes to brown.
3. Take out of oven. Layer beef and sauce used
   in oven in slow cooker.
4. Cover. Cook on Low 8 hours.
5. Mix remaining ¾ cup barbecue sauce with
   sauce from slow cooker. Pour over ribs and
   serve.

Tex-Mex Beef Ribs or Roast

Janie Steele Moore, OK

MAKES: **6 SERVINGS**
PREP. TIME: **5–10 MINUTES**
COOKING TIME: **4–10 HOURS**
IDEAL SLOW COOKER SIZE: **6-QUART**

3–4 lbs. beef short ribs *or* round steak, cut in serving-
   size pieces

1 cup sweet and tangy steak sauce

⅓ cup picante sauce

1 tsp. chili powder

½ tsp. dry mustard

1. Place ribs or steak in slow cooker.
2. Combine remaining ingredients in a bowl
   and pour over meat.

3. Cover and cook on Low 4–10 hours, or until meat is tender but not overcooked.

Beef Ribs with Sauerkraut

Rosaria Strachan Fairfield, CT

MAKES: **8–10 SERVINGS**
PREP. TIME: **10 MINUTES**
COOKING TIME: **3–8 HOURS**
IDEAL SLOW COOKER SIZE: **6-QUART**

3–4 lbs. beef short ribs
32-oz. bag or 27-oz. can sauerkraut, drained
2 Tbsp. caraway seeds
¼ cup water

1. Put ribs in 6-quart slow cooker.
2. Place sauerkraut and caraway seeds on top of ribs.
3. Pour in water.
4. Cover. Cook on High 3–4 hours, or on Low 7–8 hours.
5. Serve with mashed potatoes.

Variation: *If you really enjoy sauerkraut, double the amount of sauerkraut, and divide the recipe between 2 4–5-quart cookers.*

Ribs and Limas

Miriam Friesen Staunton, VA

MAKES: **6 SERVINGS**
PREP. TIME: **25 MINUTES**
COOKING TIME: **5½–12½ HOURS**
IDEAL SLOW COOKER SIZE: **6-QUART**

3 lbs. beef short ribs
2 Tbsp. oil
1 onion, chopped
4 carrots, sliced
¼ cup packed brown sugar
2 Tbsp. flour
2 tsp. dry mustard
1½ tsp. salt
¼ tsp. pepper
1¼ cups water
¼ cup cider vinegar
1 large bay leaf, broken in half
10-oz. pkg. frozen lima beans *or* peas, cooked

1. Cut ribs into serving-size pieces. Brown ribs in skillet in oil.
2. Place onions and carrots in slow cooker. Add ribs.
3. Combine brown sugar, flour, mustard, salt, and pepper. Stir in water and vinegar until smooth. Pour over ribs. Push bay leaves into liquid.
4. Cover. Cook on High 5–6 hours, or on Low 10–12 hours.
5. Stir in lima beans.
6. Cover. Cook on High 20–30 minutes.
7. Remove bay leaf before serving.
8. Serve with a citrus salad and crusty rolls.

Cabbage and Corned Beef

Elaine Vigoda   Rochester, NY

Light

MAKES: **12 SERVINGS**
PREP. TIME: **15 MINUTES**
COOKING TIME: **5–10 HOURS**
IDEAL SLOW COOKER SIZE: **5–6-QUART**

3 large carrots, cut into chunks

1 cup chopped celery

1 tsp. salt*

½ tsp. black pepper*

1 cup water

4-lb. corned beef

1 large onion, cut into pieces

4 potatoes, peeled and chunked

half a small head of cabbage, cut in wedges

1. Place carrots, celery, seasonings, and water in slow cooker.
2. Add beef. Cover with onions.
3. Cover. Cook on Low 8–10 hours, or on High 5–6 hours. (If your schedule allows, this dish has especially good taste and texture if you begin it on High for 1 hour, and then turn it to Low for 5–6 hours, before going on to Step 4.)
4. Lift corned beef out of cooker and add potatoes, pushing them to bottom of slow cooker. Return beef to cooker.
5. Cover. Cook on Low 1 hour.
6. Lift corned beef out of cooker and add cabbage, pushing the wedges down into the broth. Return beef to cooker.
7. Cover. Cook on Low 1 more hour.
8. Remove corned beef. Cool and slice on the diagonal. Serve surrounded by vegetables.

Per Serving: 340 calories (130 calories from fat), 15g total fat (5g saturated, 0.5g trans), 75mg cholesterol, 1110mg sodium, 35g total carbohydrate (7g fiber, 6g sugar), 19g protein, 80%DV vitamin A, 40%DV vitamin C, 8%DV calcium, 20%DV iron.

* *If the corned beef that you buy includes a spice packet, use either it or the salt and pepper called for in this recipe. Do not use both. (The nutritional analysis for this recipe was based on the 1 tsp. salt and ½ tsp. black pepper specified here, and not on a spice packet.)*

Tip: *Horseradish is a tasty condiment to serve alongside this dish.*

Fruity Corned Beef and Cabbage

Eleanor J. Ferreira   N. Chelmsford, MA

MAKES: **6 SERVINGS**
PREP. TIME: **10 MINUTES**
COOKING TIME: **5–12 HOURS**
IDEAL SLOW COOKER SIZE: **4-QUART**

2 medium onions, sliced

2½–3-lb. corned beef brisket

1 cup apple juice

¼ cup brown sugar, packed

2 tsp. finely shredded orange peel

6 whole cloves

2 tsp. prepared mustard

6 cabbage wedges

1. Place onions in slow cooker. Place beef on top of onions.
2. Combine apple juice, brown sugar, orange peel, cloves, and mustard. Pour over meat.
3. Place cabbage on top.
4. Cover. Cook on Low 10–12 hours, or on High 5–6 hours.

When cooking on High, stir occasionally for more even cooking and improved flavor.

Corned Beef Dinner

Shirley Sears Tiskilwa, IL

MAKES: **6 SERVINGS**
PREP. TIME: **10 MINUTES**
COOKING TIME: **10–11 HOURS**
IDEAL SLOW COOKER SIZE: **5-QUART**

2 onions, sliced

2 garlic cloves, minced

3 potatoes, pared and quartered

3 carrots, sliced

2 bay leaves

1 small head cabbage, cut into 4 wedges

3–4-lb. corned beef brisket

1 cup water

½ cup brown sugar

1 Tbsp. prepared mustard

dash of ground cloves

1. Layer onions, garlic, potatoes, carrots, bay leaves, and cabbage in slow cooker.
2. Place brisket on top.
3. Add water.
4. Cover. Cook on Low 10–11 hours.
5. During last hour of cooking, combine brown sugar, mustard, and cloves. Spread over beef.
6. Discard bay leaves. Slice meat and arrange on platter of vegetables.

Reuben Casserole

Melanie Thrower McPherson, KS

MAKES: **4 SERVINGS**
PREP. TIME: **10 MINUTES**
COOKING TIME: **2–4 HOURS**
IDEAL SLOW COOKER SIZE: **2-QUART**

2 cups deli-style corned beef, torn into bite-sized pieces, *divided*

15-oz. can sauerkraut, drained, *divided*

½ cup shredded *or* 8 slices Swiss cheese, *divided*

¼ cup Thousand Island salad dressing, *divided*

4 cups dry packaged stuffing mix, *divided*

1. Spray slow cooker with nonstick cooking spray.
2. Layer half of each ingredient in the order listed.
3. Repeat layers.
4. Cover and cook on Low 2–4 hours, until casserole is cooked through and cheese has melted.

Sauerkraut Chop Suey

Gloria Julien Gladstone, MI

MAKES: **10 SERVINGS**
PREP. TIME: **15 MINUTES**
COOKING TIME: **8–10 HOURS**
IDEAL SLOW COOKER SIZE: **6-QUART**

1 lb. beef stewing meat, trimmed of fat

1 lb. pork roast, cubed and trimmed of fat

2 10¾-oz. cans 98% fat-free cream of mushroom soup

1 envelope dry onion soup mix

27-oz. can sauerkraut

2 cups skim milk

12-oz. pkg. kluski (or extra-sturdy) noodles

1. Combine all ingredients except noodles in slow cooker.
2. Cook on Low 8–10 hours.
3. Add uncooked noodles 2 hours before serving, or cook noodles fully, drain, and stir into chop suey 15 minutes before serving.

Per Serving: 300 calories (60 calories from fat), 7g total fat (2.5g saturated, 0.5g trans), 95mg cholesterol, 780mg sodium, 33g total carbohydrate (2g fiber, 4g sugar), 25g protein, 2%DV vitamin A, 2%DV vitamin C, 8%DV calcium, 15%DV iron.

Roast Beef with Ginger Ale

Martha Bender   New Paris, IN

MAKES: **6–8 SERVINGS**
PREP. TIME: **15–20 MINUTES**
COOKING TIME: **8–10 HOURS**
IDEAL SLOW COOKER SIZE: **3½–4-QUART**

3-lb. beef roast

½ cup flour

1 envelope dry onion soup mix

1 envelope dry brown gravy mix

2 cups ginger ale

1. Coat the roast with flour. Reserve any flour that doesn't stick to the roast. Place roast in your slow cooker.
2. Combine the dry soup mix, gravy mix, remaining flour, and ginger ale in a bowl. Mix well.
3. Pour sauce over the roast.
4. Cover and cook on Low 8–10 hours or until the roast is tender.
5. Serve with mashed potatoes or rice.

8-Hour Tangy Beef

Mary Martins   Fairbank, IA

MAKES: **6–8 SERVINGS**
PREP. TIME: **5 MINUTES**
COOKING TIME: **8–9 HOURS**
IDEAL SLOW COOKER SIZE: **4-QUART**

3½–4-lb. beef roast

12-oz. can ginger ale

1½ cups ketchup

1. Put beef in slow cooker.
2. Pour ginger ale and ketchup over roast.
3. Cover. Cook on Low 8–9 hours.
4. Shred with 2 forks and serve on buns. Or break up into chunks and serve over rice, potatoes, or pasta.

Variations:

1. This recipe produces a lot of juice. You can add chopped onions, potatoes, and green beans in Step 2, if you want. Or stir in sliced mushrooms and/or peas 30 minutes before the end of the cooking time.

2. For a tangier finished dish, add chili powder or cumin, along with black pepper, in Step 2.

If you want to verify that meat in your cooker is fully cooked, use a meat thermometer to check that the internal temperature of poultry breasts has reached 160°F; thighs 175°F. Medium-done beef and pork should reach an internal temperature of 135°–140°F. Well-done beef and pork should reach an internal temperature of 155°–160°F.

Beef Main Dishes

Zippy Beef Roast

Colleen Heatwole   Burton, MI   •   *Joette Droz*   Kalona, IA
F. Elaine Asper   Norton, OH   •   *Ruth Ann Hoover*   New Holland, PA

MAKES: **6–8 SERVINGS**
PREP. TIME: **10–15 MINUTES**
COOKING TIME: **5–10 HOURS**
IDEAL SLOW COOKER SIZE: **4–5-QUART**

3–4 lb. beef roast
12-oz. can cola
10¾-oz. can cream of mushroom soup
1 envelope dry onion soup mix

1. Place beef in slow cooker.
2. In a small bowl, blend cola and mushroom soup together. Pour over roast.
3. Sprinkle with dry onion soup mix.
4. Cover and cook on Low for 10 hours, or on High for 5 hours, or until meat is tender but not dry.

Variations:

1. Add a 4-oz. can of mushroom stems and pieces, drained, to Step 2.

Ruth Liebelt   Rapid City, S.D.

2. Brown the roast on both sides in a nonstick skillet before placing in the slow cooker.

Shawn Eshleman   Ephrata, PA

3. Instead of the cola, use 1 cup cooking sherry. Instead of the can of mushroom soup, use 2 10¾-oz. cans of golden mushroom soup.

Janice Muller   Derwood, MD

Piquant Chuck Roast

Mary Jane Musser   Manheim, PA

MAKES: **6 SERVINGS**
PREP. TIME: **5 MINUTES**
COOKING TIME: **5–10 HOURS**
IDEAL SLOW COOKER SIZE: **3–4-QUART**

3-lb. chuck roast
½ cup orange juice
3 Tbsp. soy sauce
2 Tbsp. brown sugar
1 tsp. Worcestershire sauce

1. Place meat in slow cooker. In a mixing bowl, combine remaining ingredients and pour over meat.
2. Cover and cook on Low for 8–10 hours, or on High for 5 hours.

Tip: *Shred the meat with 2 forks. Mix well with sauce. Serve over cooked rice, noodles, or mashed potatoes.*

Beef Main Dishes

Sweet and Savory Brisket

Donna Neiter Wausau, WI • *Ellen Ranck* Gap, PA

MAKES: **8–10 SERVINGS**
PREP. TIME: **10–12 MINUTES**
COOKING TIME: **8–10 HOURS**
IDEAL SLOW COOKER SIZE: **5-QUART**

3–3½-lb. fresh beef brisket, cut in half, *divided*

1 cup ketchup

¼ cup grape jelly

1 envelope dry onion soup mix

½ tsp. pepper

1. Place half of the brisket in a slow cooker.
2. In a bowl, combine ketchup, jelly, dry soup mix, and pepper.
3. Spread half the mixture over half the meat. Top with the remaining meat and then the remaining ketchup mixture.
4. Cover and cook on Low 8–10 hours or until meat is tender but not dry.
5. Allow meat to rest for 10 minutes. Then slice and serve with cooking juices.

  * *Be sure to use fresh beef brisket, not corned beef.*

Barbecued Pot Roast

Leann Brown Ronks, PA

MAKES: **10 SERVINGS**
PREP. TIME: **5 MINUTES**
COOKING TIME: **5–6 HOURS**
IDEAL SLOW COOKER SIZE: **5–6-QUART**

5-lb. roast

16-oz. bottle honey barbecue sauce

1 small onion, chopped

1 clove garlic, minced

black pepper, *optional*

Montreal seasoning, *optional*

1. Place roast in slow cooker.
2. Pour barbecue sauce over top.
3. Sprinkle onion over roast, and garlic beside the roast.
4. If you wish, sprinkle with pepper and/or Montreal seasoning.
5. Cover and cook on Low 5–6 hours.
6. Remove roast from cooker and allow to rest for 10 minutes. Slice and serve with cooking juices.

Beef Roast with Tomatoes, Onions, and Peppers

Donna Treloar Hartford City, IN

MAKES: **10 SERVINGS**
PREP. TIME: **15 MINUTES**
COOKING TIME: **8–10 HOURS**
IDEAL SLOW COOKER SIZE: **4-QUART**

4–5-lb. beef roast

2 14½-oz. cans Mexican-style stewed tomatoes

16-oz. jar salsa, your choice of heat

2 or 3 medium onions, cut in chunks

1 or 2 green *or* red bell peppers, sliced

1. Brown the roast on top and bottom in a nonstick skillet and place in slow cooker.
2. In a bowl, combine stewed tomatoes and salsa. Spoon over meat.
3. Cover and cook on Low 8–10 hours, or until the meat is tender but not dry.
4. Add onions halfway through cooking time in order to keep fairly crisp. Push down into the sauce.
5. One hour before serving, add pepper slices. Push down into the sauce.
6. Remove meat from cooker and allow to rest 10 minutes before slicing. Place slices on serving platter and top with vegetables and sauce.

Beef Main Dishes

Tip: *Make beef burritos with the leftovers. Shred the beef and heat with remaining peppers, onions, and ½ cup of the broth. Add 1 Tbsp. chili powder, 2 tsp. cumin, and salt to taste. Heat thoroughly. Fill warm flour tortillas with mixture and serve with sour cream, salsa, and guacamole.*

Tomato-y Mexican Pot Roast

Susan Segraves Lansdale, PA

MAKES: **8 SERVINGS**
PREP. TIME: **5 MINUTES**
COOKING TIME: **8–10 HOURS**
IDEAL SLOW COOKER SIZE: **5-QUART**

1½ cups chunky salsa

6-oz. can tomato paste

1 envelope dry taco seasoning mix

1 cup water

3-lb. beef chuck roast

½ cup chopped cilantro

1. In a mixing bowl, combine first four ingredients.
2. Place roast in slow cooker and pour salsa mixture over top.
3. Cover and cook on Low 8–10 hours, or until beef is tender but not dry. Remove to a platter.
4. Stir cilantro into sauce before serving with beef.

To get the most flavor from herbs and spices when using them in a slow cooker, use whole fresh herbs rather than ground or crushed.

Machaca Beef

Jeanne Allen Rye, CO

MAKES: **12 SERVINGS**
PREP. TIME: **5–7 MINUTES**
COOKING TIME: **10–12 HOURS**
IDEAL SLOW COOKER SIZE: **4-QUART**

1½-lb. lean beef roast

1 large onion, sliced

4-oz. can chopped green chilies

2 low-sodium beef bouillon cubes

1½ tsp. dry mustard

½ tsp. garlic powder

¾ tsp. seasoned salt

½ tsp. black pepper

1 cup low-sodium salsa

1. Combine all ingredients except salsa in slow cooker. Add just enough water to cover.
2. Cover cooker and cook on Low 10–12 hours, or until beef is tender. Drain and reserve liquid.
3. Shred beef using two forks to pull it apart.
4. Combine beef, salsa, and enough of the reserved liquid to make a desired consistency.
5. Use this filling for burritos, chalupas, quesadillas, or tacos.

Per Serving: 80 calories (20 calories from fat), 2.5g total fat (1g saturated, 0g trans), 30mg cholesterol, 400mg sodium, 3g total carbohydrate (0g fiber, 1g sugar), 10g protein, 0%DV vitamin A, 0%DV vitamin C, 2%DV calcium, 8%DV iron.

Note: *After living in New Mexico for the past 30 years, I get homesick for New Mexican cuisine now that I live in Colorado. I keep memories of New Mexico alive by cooking foods that remind me of home.*

Salsa Beef

Sarah Niessen Akron, PA

MAKES: **5–6 SERVINGS**
PREP. TIME: **15 MINUTES**
COOKING TIME: **6–8 HOURS**
IDEAL SLOW COOKER SIZE: **5–6-QUART**

2–2½ lbs. beef, cut up in bite-sized cubes
1 Tbsp. oil
16-oz. jar salsa
8-oz. can tomato sauce
2 garlic cloves, minced
2 Tbsp. brown sugar
1 Tbsp. soy sauce
1 cup canned tomatoes

1. Brown beef in skillet in oil. Place in slow cooker.
2. Add remaining ingredients.
3. Cover. Cook on Low 6–8 hours.
4. Serve over rice.

Variation: *For added flavor, use Italian tomato sauce.*

Mexican Brisket

Veronica Sabo Shelton, CT

MAKES: **8 SERVINGS**
PREP. TIME: **20–30 MINUTES**
COOKING TIME: **2–10 HOURS**
IDEAL SLOW COOKER SIZE: **5-QUART**

1 lb. baking potatoes, peeled and cut into 1-inch cubes
1 lb. sweet potatoes, peeled and cut into 1-inch cubes
3–3½-lb. beef brisket, fat trimmed
1¼ cups salsa
2 Tbsp. flour, *or* quick-cooking tapioca

1. Place both kinds of potatoes in the slow cooker.
2. Top with the brisket.
3. Put salsa and flour in a small bowl and mix well. Pour evenly over the meat.
4. Cover and cook on Low 6½–10 hours, or on High 2–5½ hours, or until the meat is tender but not dry.
5. To serve, remove the meat from the cooker, keep warm, and allow to rest for 10 minutes. Then slice the meat across the grain. Place slices on a platter and top with the potatoes and sauce.

For a juicy beef roast to be ready by noon, put a roast in the slow cooker in the evening and let it on all night on Low.

Beef Main Dishes

Sour Beef

Rosanne Hankins Stevensville, MD

MAKES: **6–8 SERVINGS**
PREP. TIME: **5 MINUTES**
COOKING TIME: **8–10 HOURS**
IDEAL SLOW COOKER SIZE: **4-QUART**

3–4-lb. pot roast
⅓ cup cider vinegar
1 large onion, sliced
3 bay leaves
½ tsp. salt
¼ tsp. ground cloves
¼ tsp. garlic powder

1. Place roast in slow cooker. Add remaining ingredients.
2. Cover. Cook on Low 8–10 hours.

Old World Sauerbraten

C.J. Slagle Roann, IN • *Angeline Lang* Greeley, CO

MAKES: **8 SERVINGS**
PREP. TIME: **10 MINUTES**
MARINATING TIME: **24–36 HOURS**
COOKING TIME: **16–22 HOURS**
IDEAL SLOW COOKER SIZE: **4-QUART**

3½–4-lb. beef rump roast
1 cup water
1 cup vinegar
1 lemon, sliced but unpeeled
10 whole cloves
1 large onion, sliced
4 bay leaves
6 whole peppercorns
2 Tbsp. salt
2 Tbsp. sugar
12 gingersnaps, crumbled

1. Place meat in deep ceramic or glass bowl.
2. Combine water, vinegar, lemon, cloves, onion, bay leaves, peppercorns, salt, and sugar. Pour over meat. Cover and refrigerate 24–36 hours. Turn meat several times during marinating.
3. Place beef in slow cooker. Pour 1 cup marinade over meat.
4. Cover. Cook on Low 6–8 hours. Remove meat.
5. Strain meat juices and return to pot. Turn to High. Stir in gingersnaps. Cover and cook on High 10–14 minutes. Slice meat. Pour finished sauce over meat.

Italian Beef

Peggy Forsythe Bartlett, TN

MAKES: **6 SERVINGS**
PREP. TIME: **20 MINUTES**
COOKING TIME: **8 HOURS**
IDEAL SLOW COOKER SIZE: **4–6-QUART**

4–5-lb. beef roast, cut into 1–1½-inch cubes
2 or 3 beef bouillon cubes
1 tsp. garlic salt
2 Tbsp. Italian salad dressing

1. Place roast, bouillon cubes, garlic salt, and dressing in slow cooker. Stir.
2. Add 1–1½-inch water around the beef, being careful not to disturb the seasoning on the top of the meat.
3. Cover and cook on Low 8 hours, or until tender but not overcooked.
4. Remove beef from cooker and shred with 2 forks. Return shredded meat to cooker and stir into broth.
5. Serve over rice, or on rolls or garlic bread for a delicious open-face sandwich.

Beef and Gravy

Arlene Groff   Lewistown, PA

MAKES: **8 SERVINGS**
PREP. TIME: **25 MINUTES**
COOKING TIME: **6–8 HOURS**
IDEAL SLOW COOKER SIZE: **5-QUART**

1 onion, chopped

1 Tbsp. butter

3–4-lb. beef roast, cubed

1 tsp. salt

¼ tsp. pepper

2 cups water

3 beef bouillon cubes

½ cup flour

1. Sauté onion in skillet in butter until brown. Place onion in slow cooker, but reserve drippings.
2. Brown roast in skillet in drippings. Add meat to slow cooker, again reserving drippings.
3. Combine salt, pepper, water, bouillon, and flour. Add to meat drippings. Cook until thickened. Pour over meat.
4. Cover. Cook on Low 6–8 hours.
5. Serve over noodles.

Beef in Onion Gravy

Donna Neiter   Wausau, WI

MAKES: **3 SERVINGS**
PREP. TIME: **20 MINUTES**
COOKING TIME: **6–8 HOURS**
IDEAL SLOW COOKER SIZE: **3-QUART**

10¾-oz. can cream of mushroom soup

1 Tbsp. dry onion soup mix

2 Tbsp. beef bouillon granules

1 Tbsp. quick-cooking tapioca

1 lb. beef stew meat, cut into 1-inch cubes

1. Spray the interior of the cooker with cooking spray.
2. In the slow cooker, combine soup, soup mix, bouillon, and tapioca. Let stand 15 minutes.
3. Stir in beef.
4. Cover and cook on Low 6–8 hours, or until meat is tender but not dry.

Tip: *Serve over cooked noodles or mashed potatoes.*

Variation: *Add 2–3 Tbsp. chopped onions, ½ cup sliced fresh mushrooms, and/or ¼ tsp. pepper to the mixture in Step 2.*

Rosemarie Fitzgerald   Gibsonia, PA

Hungarian Beef

Audrey Romonosky   Austin, TX

MAKES: **5–6 SERVINGS**
PREP. TIME: **10 MINUTES**
COOKING TIME: **8¼ HOURS**
IDEAL SLOW COOKER SIZE: **4-QUART**

2 lbs. beef chuck, cubed

1 onion, sliced

½ tsp. garlic powder

½ cup ketchup

2 Tbsp. Worcestershire sauce

1 Tbsp. brown sugar

½ tsp. salt

2 tsp. paprika

½ tsp. dry mustard

1 cup cold water

¼ cup flour

½ cup water

1. Place meat in slow cooker. Add onion.
2. Combine garlic powder, ketchup, Worcestershire sauce, brown sugar, salt,

paprika, mustard, and 1 cup water. Pour over meat.

3. Cover. Cook on Low 8 hours.

4. Dissolve flour in ½ cup water. Stir into meat mixture. Cook on High until thickened, about 10 minutes.

5. Serve over noodles.

Horseradish Beef

Barbara Nolan   Pleasant Valley, NY

MAKES: **6–8 SERVINGS**
PREP. TIME: **10 MINUTES**
COOKING TIME: **8–10 HOURS**
IDEAL SLOW COOKER SIZE: **4-QUART**

3–4-lb. pot roast
2 Tbsp. oil
½ tsp. salt
½ tsp. pepper
1 onion, chopped
6-oz. can tomato paste
⅓ cup horseradish sauce

1. Brown roast on all sides in oil in skillet. Place in slow cooker. Add remaining ingredients.

2. Cover. Cook on Low 8–10 hours.

Don't salt meat or a roast as you're browning it. Instead, add it to taste at the end of the browning. The meat will stay more moist, since salt draws out moisture.

Chinese Pot Roast

Marsha Sabus   Fallbrook, CA

MAKES: **6 SERVINGS**
PREP. TIME: **10–15 MINUTES**
COOKING TIME: **8¼–10¼ HOURS**
IDEAL SLOW COOKER SIZE: **4-QUART**

3-lb. boneless beef pot roast
2 Tbsp. flour
1 Tbsp. oil
2 large onions, chopped
salt to taste
pepper to taste
½ cup soy sauce
1 cup water
½ tsp. ground ginger

1. Dip roast in flour and brown on both sides in oil in saucepan. Place in slow cooker.

2. Top with onions, salt, and pepper.

3. Combine soy sauce, water, and ginger. Pour over meat.

4. Cover. Cook on High 10 minutes. Reduce heat to Low and cook 8–10 hours.

5. Slice and serve with rice.

Dilled Pot Roast

Kathryn Yoder   Minot, ND

MAKES: **8 SERVINGS**
PREP. TIME: **5 MINUTES**
COOKING TIME: **7¼–9¼ HOURS**
IDEAL SLOW COOKER SIZE: **4–5-QUART**

2¾-lb. beef pot roast

1 tsp. salt

¼ tsp. black pepper

2 tsp. dried dill weed, *divided*

¼ cup water

2 Tbsp. wine vinegar

4 Tbsp. flour

½ cup water

2 cups fat-free sour cream

1. Sprinkle both sides of beef with salt, pepper, and 1 tsp. dill weed. Place in slow cooker.
2. Add ¼ cup water and vinegar.
3. Cover. Cook on Low 7–9 hours.
4. Remove meat from pot. Turn cooker to High.
5. Stir flour into ½ cup water. Stir into meat drippings.
6. Stir in additional 1 tsp. dill weed if you wish.
7. Cover. Cook on High 5 minutes.
8. Stir in sour cream.
9. Cover. Cook on High another 5 minutes.
10. Slice beef and serve with sour cream sauce.

Per Serving: 270 calories (80 calories from fat), 8g total fat (3g saturated, 0g trans), 100mg cholesterol, 390mg sodium, 13g total carbohydrate (0g fiber, 5g sugar), 34g protein, 0%DV vitamin A, 0%DV vitamin C, 6%DV calcium, 20%DV iron.

Apple and Onion Beef Pot Roast

Betty K. Drescher   Quakertown, PA

MAKES: **8–10 SERVINGS**
PREP. TIME: **20 MINUTES**
COOKING TIME: **5–6 HOURS**
IDEAL SLOW COOKER SIZE: **4-QUART**

3-lb. boneless beef roast, cut in half

oil

1 cup water

1 tsp. seasoned salt

½ tsp. soy sauce

½ tsp. Worcestershire sauce

¼ tsp. garlic powder

1 large tart apple, quartered

1 large onion, sliced

2 Tbsp. cornstarch

2 Tbsp. water

1. Brown roast on all sides in oil in skillet. Transfer to slow cooker.
2. Add water to skillet to loosen browned bits. Pour over roast.
3. Sprinkle with seasoned salt, soy sauce, Worcestershire sauce, and garlic powder.
4. Top with apple and onion.
5. Cover. Cook on Low 5–6 hours.
6. Remove roast and onion. Discard apple. Let stand 15 minutes.
7. To make gravy, pour juices from roast into saucepan and simmer until reduced to 2 cups. Combine cornstarch and water until smooth in small bowl. Stir into beef broth. Bring to boil. Cook and stir for 2 minutes until thickened.
8. Slice pot roast and serve with gravy.

Beef Main Dishes

Fruited Beef Tagine

Naomi E. Fast Hesston, KS

MAKES: **6–8 SERVINGS**
PREP. TIME: **20 MINUTES**
COOKING TIME: **5–6 HOURS**
IDEAL SLOW COOKER SIZE: **4-QUART**

1 Tbsp. oil

2 lbs. beef, cut into 2-inch cubes

4 cups sliced onions

2 tsp. ground coriander

1½ tsp. ground cinnamon

¾ tsp. ground ginger

14½-oz. can beef broth, plus enough water to equal 2 cups

16 ozs. pitted prunes

salt to taste

fresh ground pepper to taste

juice of one lemon

1. Brown beef cubes in oil in skillet. Place beef in slow cooker. Reserve drippings.
2. Sauté onions in drippings until lightly browned, adding more oil if needed. Add to slow cooker.
3. Add remaining ingredients, except lemon juice.
4. Simmer on Low 5–6 hours, adding lemon juice during the last 10 minutes.
5. This recipe, accompanied with a tossed green salad and rolls, makes a complete meal.

Variations:

1. Mix in a few very thin slices of lemon rind to add flavor and eye appeal.

2. You can substitute lamb cubes for the beef.

To get the most juice from a lime or lemon, heat it in the microwave for 10 seconds, then squeeze it.

Saucy Italian Roast

Sharon Miller Holmesville, OH

MAKES: **8–10 SERVINGS**
PREP. TIME: **5–10 MINUTES**
COOKING TIME: **8–9 HOURS**
IDEAL SLOW COOKER SIZE: **4-QUART**

3–3½-lb. boneless rump roast

½ tsp. salt

½ tsp. garlic powder

¼ tsp. pepper

4½-oz. jar mushroom pieces, drained

1 medium onion, diced

14-oz. jar spaghetti sauce

¼–½ cup beef broth

1. Cut roast in half.
2. Combine salt, garlic powder, and pepper. Rub over both halves of the roast. Place in slow cooker.
3. Top with mushrooms and onions.
4. Combine spaghetti sauce and broth. Pour over roast.
5. Cover. Cook on Low 8–9 hours.
6. Slice roast. Serve in sauce over pasta.

Simply Super Supper

Anne Townsend   Albuquerque, NM

MAKES: **4 SERVINGS**
PREP. TIME: **10 MINUTES**
COOKING TIME: **7–8 HOURS**
IDEAL SLOW COOKER SIZE: **3–4-QUART**

2 ribs celery, sliced

3 carrots, cut in strips

2 potatoes, cubed

2 onions, coarsely chopped

2-lb. beef roast

1 pkg. dry onion soup mix

1 Tbsp. liquid smoke

1½ cups water

1. Place vegetables in slow cooker.
2. Place roast on top of vegetables.
3. Sprinkle with dry soup mix.
4. Combine liquid smoke and water. Pour over roast.
5. Cover. Cook on Low 7–8 hours, or until vegetables are tender.
6. Slice meat and serve with cole slaw and French bread. Lemon pie makes a nice finish.

Note: *This is a welcoming dinner to come home to because the house smells so yummy as you walk in. And the wonderful aroma lingers.*

Meats usually cook faster than vegetables in slow cookers. If you want to know if your dish is fully cooked, check the vegetables to see if they're tender. If the recipe allows, place vegetables on the bottom and along the sides of your cooker as you're preparing it.

Tomato-y Beef Stew

Janie Steele   Moore, OK

MAKES: **6–8 SERVINGS**
PREP. TIME: **15 MINUTES**
COOKING TIME: **8 HOURS**
IDEAL SLOW COOKER SIZE: **5–6-QUART**

5 lbs. stewing meat, cubed

2 onions, chopped

14½-oz. can chopped tomatoes

10¾-oz. can tomato soup

5–6 carrots, sliced

5–6 potatoes, peeled and cubed

1 cup sliced celery

1 bell pepper, sliced

2 tsp. salt

½ tsp. pepper

2 cloves minced garlic

1. Combine all ingredients in slow cooker.
2. Cover. Cook on Low 8 hours.
3. Serve with warm bread or cornbread.

Note: *This recipe is very adaptable. You can reduce the amount of meat and increase the vegetables as you wish.*

Slow-Cooked Coffee Beef Roast

Mrs. Carolyn Baer   Conrath, WI

MAKES: **12 SERVINGS**
PREP. TIME: **20 MINUTES**
COOKING TIME: **8–10 HOURS**
IDEAL SLOW COOKER SIZE: **4–5-QUART**

1½ lbs. boneless beef sirloin tip roast, cut in half

2 tsp. canola oil

1½ cups sliced fresh mushrooms

½ cup sliced green onions

2 garlic cloves, minced

1½ cups brewed coffee

1 tsp. liquid smoke, *optional*

½ tsp. salt

½ tsp. chili powder

¼ tsp. black pepper

¼ cup cornstarch

½ cup cold water

1. In a large nonstick skillet, brown roast over medium-high heat on all sides in oil. Transfer roast to slow cooker.
2. In the same skillet, sauté mushrooms, onions, and garlic until tender.
3. Stir the coffee, liquid smoke if desired, salt, chili powder, and pepper into the vegetables. Pour over roast.
4. Cook on Low for 8–10 hours or until meat is tender.
5. Remove roast and keep warm.
6. Pour cooking juices into a 2-cup measuring cup; skim fat.
7. Combine cornstarch and water in a saucepan until smooth. Gradually stir in 2 cups of cooking juices.
8. Bring to a boil; cook and stir for 2 minutes or until thickened. Serve with sliced beef.

Per Serving: 100 calories (30 calories from fat), 3.5g total fat (1g saturated, 0g trans), 35mg cholesterol, 120mg sodium, 4g total carbohydrate (0.5g fiber, 1g sugar), 12g protein, 0%DV vitamin A, 2%DV vitamin C, 0%DV calcium, 8%DV iron.

Goodtime Beef Brisket

AmyMarlene Jensen   Fountain, CO

MAKES: **6–8 SERVINGS**
PREP. TIME: **10 MINUTES**
COOKING TIME: **8–10 HOURS**
IDEAL SLOW COOKER SIZE: **4–5 QUART**

3½–4-lb. beef brisket

1 can beer

2 cups tomato sauce

2 tsp. prepared mustard

2 Tbsp. balsamic vinegar

2 Tbsp. Worcestershire sauce

1 tsp. garlic powder

½ tsp. ground allspice

2 Tbsp. brown sugar

1 small green *or* red bell pepper, chopped

1 medium onion, chopped

1 tsp. salt

½ tsp. pepper

1. Place brisket in slow cooker.
2. Combine remaining ingredients. Pour over meat.
3. Cover. Cook on Low 8–10 hours.
4. Remove meat from sauce. Slice very thinly.
5. Serve on rolls or over couscous.

Slow-Cooked Round Steak

Kathy Lapp Halifax, PA

MAKES: **4–6 SERVINGS**
PREP. TIME: **15 MINUTES**
COOKING TIME: **4–5 HOURS**
IDEAL SLOW COOKER SIZE: **4-QUART**

1¾-lb. round steak

¼ cup flour

2 onions, sliced thickly

1 green pepper, sliced in strips

10¾-oz. can cream of mushroom soup

1. Cut steak into serving-size pieces. Dredge in flour. Brown in a nonstick skillet.
2. Place browned steak in slow cooker. Top with onion and pepper slices.
3. Pour soup over all, making sure steak pieces are covered.
4. Cover and cook on Low 4–5 hours.

Variations:

1. Add ½ tsp. salt and ¼ tsp. pepper to flour in Step 1.

2. If you like a lot of gravy, add a second can of soup to Step 3.

Steak in a Crock

Judith A. Govotsos Frederick, MD

MAKES: **4–5 SERVINGS**
PREP. TIME: **10–20 MINUTES**
COOKING TIME: **8–12 HOURS**
IDEAL SLOW COOKER SIZE: **4–5-QUART**

1 medium onion, sliced and separated into rings

4-oz. can of sliced mushrooms, liquid reserved

2½-lb. round steak, ¾-inch thick, cut into 4–5 pieces

10¾-oz. can cream of mushroom soup

2 Tbsp. dry sherry *or* water

1. Put onion rings and mushrooms in bottom of slow cooker.
2. Brown meat in nonstick skillet on all sides. Place in slow cooker over top vegetables.
3. In a bowl, mix reserved mushroom liquid, soup, and sherry together. Pour over all.
4. Cover and cook on Low 8–12 hours, or until meat is tender but not overcooked.

Slow Cooker Swiss Steak

Joyce Bowman Lady Lake, FL

MAKES: **4 SERVINGS**
PREP. TIME: **30 MINUTES**
COOKING TIME: **7 HOURS**
IDEAL SLOW COOKER SIZE: **3-QUART**

1-lb. round steak, ¾–1-inch thick, cubed

16-oz. can stewed tomatoes

3 carrots, halved lengthwise

2 potatoes, quartered

1 medium onion, quartered

garlic powder to taste, *optional*

1. Add all ingredients to your slow cooker in the order they are listed.
2. Cover and cook on Low for 7 hours, or until meat and vegetables are tender, but not overcooked or dry.

Beef Main Dishes

Italian Round Steak

Chris Peterson   Green Bay, WI   •   *Phyllis Wykes*   Plano, IL

MAKES: **5–6 SERVINGS**
PREP. TIME: **5–10 MINUTES**
COOKING TIME: **5–8 HOURS**
IDEAL SLOW COOKER SIZE: **4-QUART**

1½ lbs. round steak

1 tsp. salt

½ tsp. oregano

¼ tsp. pepper

medium or large onion, chopped coarsely

15½-oz. jar spaghetti sauce, your choice of flavors

1. Cut steak into 5–6 serving-size pieces.
2. In a bowl, mix together salt, oregano, and pepper. Sprinkle over both sides of pieces of meat. As you finish a piece, place the meat into the slow cooker.
3. Sprinkle with chopped onion.
4. Spoon spaghetti sauce over top, being careful not to disturb the seasoning and onions.
5. Cover and cook on Low 5–8 hours, or until the meat is tender but not overcooked.

Less tender, less expensive cuts of meat are better suited for slow cooking than expensive cuts of meat. If desired, you can brown meat on top of the stove first, for additional flavor.

Fajita Steak

Becky Harder   Monument, CO

MAKES: **6 SERVINGS**
PREP. TIME: **10 MINUTES**
COOKING TIME: **6–8 HOURS**
IDEAL SLOW COOKER SIZE: **4-QUART**

15-oz. can tomatoes with green chilies

¼ cup salsa, your choice of heat

8-oz. can tomato sauce

2 lbs. round steak, cut in 2-inch × 4-inch strips

1 envelope dry Fajita spice mix

1 cup water, *optional*

1. Combine all ingredients—except water—in your slow cooker.
2. Cover and cook on Low 6–8 hours, or until meat is tender but not overcooked.
3. Check meat occasionally to make sure it isn't cooking dry. If it begins to look dry, stir in water, up to 1 cup.

Tip: *Serve meat with fried onions and green peppers. Offer shredded cheese, avocado chunks, and sour cream as toppings. Let individual eaters wrap any or all of the ingredients in flour tortillas.*

Variation: *Instead of the salsa, add 1 small onion, chopped, and 1 red bell pepper, cut in 1-inch pieces to Step 1. Mix ¼ cup flour and ¼ cup water in a jar with a tight-fitting lid. Shake until smooth. Fifteen–20 minutes before the end of the cooking time, pour slowly into stew, stirring while you do so that it blends well. Cover and continue cooking until the stew thickens.*

Audrey L. Kneer   Williamsfield, IL

Mexicali Round Steak

Marcia S. Myer Manheim, PA

MAKES: **6 SERVINGS**
PREP. TIME: **10 MINUTES**
COOKING TIME: **8–9 HOURS**
IDEAL SLOW COOKER SIZE: **5-QUART**

1½ lbs. round steak, trimmed of fat

1 cup frozen corn, thawed

½–1 cup fresh cilantro, chopped, according to your
   taste preference

½ cup low-sodium, fat-free beef broth

3 ribs celery, sliced

1 large onion, sliced

20-oz. jar salsa

15-oz. can black beans *or* pinto beans, rinsed and
   drained

1 cup fat-free cheddar cheese

1. Cut beef into 6 pieces. Place in slow cooker.
2. Combine remaining ingredients, except cheese, and pour over beef.
3. Cover. Cook on Low 8–9 hours.
4. Sprinkle with cheese before serving.

Per Serving: 290 calories (60 calories from fat), 6g total fat (2g saturated, 0g trans), 70mg cholesterol, 900mg sodium, 26g total carbohydrate (7g fiber, 2g sugar), 35g protein, 20%DV vitamin A, 20%DV vitamin C, 25%DV calcium, 25%DV iron.

Roasting bags work well in the slow cooker. Simply fill with meat and vegetables and cook as directed in slow cooker recipes. Follow manufacturer's directions for filling and sealing bags.

Beef and Beans

Robin Schrock Millersburg, OH

MAKES: **8 SERVINGS**
PREP. TIME: **10 MINUTES**
COOKING TIME: **6½–8½ HOURS**
IDEAL SLOW COOKER SIZE: **4-QUART**

1 Tbsp. prepared mustard

1 Tbsp. chili powder

½ tsp. salt

¼ tsp. pepper

1½-lb. boneless round steak, cut into thin slices

2 14½-oz. cans diced tomatoes, undrained

1 medium onion, chopped

1 beef bouillon cube, crushed

16-oz. can kidney beans, rinsed and drained

1. Combine mustard, chili powder, salt, and pepper. Add beef slices and toss to coat. Place meat in slow cooker.
2. Add tomatoes, onion, and bouillon.
3. Cover. Cook on Low 6–8 hours.
4. Stir in beans. Cook 30 minutes longer.
5. Serve over rice.

Hearty Beef Stew

Lovina Baer Conrath, WI

MAKES: **4–6 SERVINGS**
PREP. TIME: **10 MINUTES**
COOKING TIME: **6–7 HOURS**
IDEAL SLOW COOKER SIZE: **4-QUART**

2-lb. round steak

4 large potatoes, cubed

2 large carrots, sliced

2 ribs celery, sliced

1 medium onion, chopped

1 quart tomato juice

1 Tbsp. Worcestershire sauce

2 tsp. salt

Beef Main Dishes

½ tsp. pepper

¼ cup sugar

1 Tbsp. clear jel

1. Combine meat, potatoes, carrots, celery, and onion in slow cooker.
2. Combine tomato juice, Worcestershire sauce, salt, and pepper. Pour into slow cooker.
3. Mix together sugar and clear jel. Add to remaining ingredients, stirring well.
4. Cover. Cook on High 6–7 hours.

Variation: *Instead of clear jel, use ¼ cup instant tapioca.*

New Mexico Steak

Mamie Christopherson   Rio Rancho, NM

MAKES: **4–6 SERVINGS**
PREP. TIME: **10 MINUTES**
COOKING TIME: **4 HOURS**
IDEAL SLOW COOKER SIZE: **3-QUART**

1 large onion, sliced

2-lb. round steak, cut into serving size pieces

salt and pepper to taste

2 7-oz. cans green chili salsa

1. Place onion slices in bottom of slow cooker.
2. Sprinkle steak with salt and pepper. Add steak pieces to cooker.
3. Spoon chili salsa over all, being careful not to wash off the seasonings.
4. Cover and cook on High 1 hour. Turn to Low and cook 3 hours, or until steak is tender but not overcooked.

Tips:

1. If the chili salsa is too hot, sprinkle a little white sugar over mixture before cooking. Or choose a milder salsa.

2. Add a little liquid (water or beer) if the dish seems too dry toward the end of the cooking time.

Pigs in Blankets

Linda Sluiter   Schererville, IN

MAKES: **4 SERVINGS**
PREP. TIME: **30 MINUTES**
COOKING TIME: **6–8 HOURS**
IDEAL SLOW COOKER SIZE: **4-QUART**

1–2-lb. round steak

1 lb. bacon

1 cup ketchup

¼ cup brown sugar

1 small onion

¼–½ cup water

1. Cut round steak into long strips. Roll up each meat strip, and then wrap with a slice of bacon. Secure with a toothpick to hold the roll shape.
2. Warm remaining ingredients in saucepan, bringing to a simmer to make a sauce.
3. Place meat rolls in slow cooker. Pour sauce over top.
4. Cover and cook on Low 6–8 hours, or until the meat is tender but not overcooked.

Beef Roulades

Karen Waggoner   Joplin, MO

MAKES: **12 SERVINGS**
PREP. TIME: **20 MINUTES**
COOKING TIME: **4–6 HOURS**
IDEAL SLOW COOKER SIZE: **5-QUART**

4 lbs. round steak

4 cups prepared packaged herb-seasoned stuffing mix

2 10¾-oz. cans cream of mushroom soup

1–2 cups water

1. Do it yourself—or ask your butcher—to cut steak into 12 long pieces. Pound each piece until thin and flattened.
2. Place ⅓ cup prepared stuffing on each slice of meat. Roll up and fasten with toothpick. Place in slow cooker.
3. In a bowl, mix soup and water together and then pour over steak.
4. Cover and cook on High 4–6 hours, or until meat is tender but not overcooked.

Buffet Beef

Kate Johnson   Rolfe, IA

MAKES: **8–10 SERVINGS**
PREP. TIME: **10 MINUTES**
COOKING TIME: **4–8 HOURS**
IDEAL SLOW COOKER SIZE: **4-QUART**

12-oz. can beer

1 envelope dry brown gravy mix

⅓ cup flour

2½–3-lb. round steak, cut into cubes

1. In the slow cooker mix beer and gravy mix together well.
2. In a plastic bag, shake flour and steak cubes together until meat is coated.

3. Empty entire contents of bag into slow cooker. Gently stir to coat meat with liquid.
4. Cover and cook on Low 6–8 hours, or on High 4 hours.

No-Peeking Beef Tips

Ruth C. Hancock   Earlsboro, OK

MAKES: **4 SERVINGS**
PREP. TIME: **15 MINUTES**
COOKING TIME: **4 HOURS**
IDEAL SLOW COOKER SIZE: **4-QUART**

2 lbs. stew meat

half or a whole envelope dry onion soup mix

12-oz. can lemon-lime soda

10¾-oz. can cream of mushroom soup *or* cream of chicken soup

1. Put meat in slow cooker. Sprinkle dry onion soup mix over meat.
2. Mix soda and cream of mushroom soup together in a bowl. Spoon over meat, being careful not to disturb the onion soup mix.
3. Cover and cook on High 4 hours. Do not stir or remove lid until the time is up.
4. Serve over cooked rice or noodles.

Variations:
1. Add a 4-oz. can of mushrooms, undrained, to Step 2.
Elaine Rineer   Lancaster, PA

2. Add a 4-oz. can of mushrooms, undrained, plus ½ cup red wine to Step 2.
Leona Yoder   Hartville, OH

3. Replace soda with 1 cup sour cream in original recipe. Add either a 4-oz. or an 8-oz. can of mushrooms, undrained, to Step 2.
Pauline Morrison   St. Marys, ON

Beef Main Dishes

Slow Cooker Pepper Steak

Esther Hartzler Carlsbad, NM

MAKES: **6–8 SERVINGS**
PREP. TIME: **15 MINUTES**
COOKING TIME: **6–7 HOURS**
IDEAL SLOW COOKER SIZE: **4-QUART**

1½–2 lbs. round beef steak

2 Tbsp. oil

¼ cup soy sauce

1 cup chopped onions

1 garlic clove, minced

1 tsp. sugar

½ tsp. salt

¼ tsp. pepper

¼ tsp. ground ginger

4 tomatoes, cut in eighths, *or* 16-oz. can tomatoes

2 large green peppers, cut in strips

½ cup cold water

1 Tbsp. cornstarch

1. Cut beef into 3-inch × 1-inch strips. Brown in oil in skillet. Drain. Transfer to slow cooker.
2. In separate bowl, combine soy sauce, onions, garlic, sugar, salt, pepper, and ginger. Pour over beef.
3. Cover. Cook on Low 5–6 hours.
4. Add tomatoes and green peppers. Cook 1 hour longer.
5. Combine cold water and cornstarch to make paste. Stir into slow cooker. Cook on High until thickened.
6. Serve over noodles or rice.

Always taste the food you've prepared before serving it, so you can correct the seasonings, if necessary.

Savory Pepper Steak

Grace W. Yoder Harrisonburg, VA

MAKES: **6 SERVINGS**
PREP. TIME: **15 MINUTES**
COOKING TIME: **8–10 HOURS**
IDEAL SLOW COOKER SIZE: **4-QUART**

1½-lb. beef round steak, cut ½-inch thick

¼ cup flour

½ tsp. salt

⅛ tsp. pepper

1 medium onion, chopped or sliced

1 garlic clove, minced

2 large green peppers, sliced in ½-inch strips, *divided*

29-oz. can whole tomatoes

1 Tbsp. beef flavor base, *or* 1 beef bouillon cube

1 Tbsp. soy sauce

2 tsp. Worcestershire sauce

3 Tbsp. flour

3 Tbsp. water

1. Cut beef into strips.
2. Combine ¼ cup flour, salt, and pepper. Toss with beef until well coated. Place in slow cooker.
3. Add onions, garlic, and half the green pepper slices. Mix well.
4. Combine tomatoes, beef base, soy sauce, and Worcestershire sauce. Pour into slow cooker.
5. Cover. Cook on Low 8–10 hours.
6. One hour before serving, turn to High and stir in remaining green pepper.
7. Combine 3 Tbsp. flour and water to make smooth paste. Stir into slow cooker. Cover. Cook until thickened.
8. Serve over rice.

Smothered Steak

Susan Yoder Graber Eureka, IL

MAKES: **6 SERVINGS**
PREP. TIME: **10 MINUTES**
COOKING TIME: **8 HOURS**
IDEAL SLOW COOKER SIZE: **4-QUART**

1½-lb. chuck *or* round steak, cut into strips
⅓ cup flour
½ tsp. salt
¼ tsp. pepper
1 large onion, sliced
1–2 green peppers, sliced
14½-oz. can stewed tomatoes
4-oz. can mushrooms, drained
2 Tbsp. soy sauce
10-oz. pkg. frozen French-style green beans

1. Layer steak in bottom of slow cooker. Sprinkle with flour, salt, and pepper. Stir well to coat steak.
2. Add remaining ingredients. Mix together gently.
3. Cover. Cook on Low 8 hours.
4. Serve over rice.

Variations:

1. Use 8-oz. can tomato sauce instead of stewed tomatoes.

2. Substitute 1 Tbsp. Worcestershire sauce in place of soy sauce.

Mary E. Martin Goshen, IN

A slow cooker set on Low does not burn food and will not spoil a meal if cooked somewhat beyond the designated time.

Spanish Round Steak

Shari Jensen Fountain, CO

MAKES: **4–6 SERVINGS**
PREP. TIME: **10 MINUTES**
COOKING TIME: **8 HOURS**
IDEAL SLOW COOKER SIZE: **4-QUART**

1 small onion, sliced, *divided*
1 rib celery, chopped, *divided*
1 green bell pepper, sliced in rings, *divided*
2 lbs. round steak
2 Tbsp. chopped fresh parsley, *or* 2 tsp. dried parsley
1 Tbsp. Worcestershire sauce
1 Tbsp. dry mustard
1 Tbsp. chili powder
2 cups canned tomatoes
2 tsp. dry minced garlic
½ tsp. salt
¼ tsp. pepper

1. Put half of onion, celery, and green pepper, in slow cooker.
2. Cut steak into serving-size pieces. Place steak pieces in slow cooker.
3. Put remaining onion, celery, and green pepper over steak.
4. Combine remaining ingredients. Pour over meat.
5. Cover. Cook on Low 8 hours.
6. Serve over noodles or rice.

Beef Main Dishes

Cherry Cobbler,
page 597

Mexican Goulash, page 286

Chicken Cordon Bleu Bundles, page 340

Red Beans and Pasta, page 508

Powerhouse Beef Roast with Tomatoes, Onions, and Peppers

Donna Treloar Gaston, IN

MAKES: **5–6 SERVINGS**
PREP. TIME: **PREP. TIME: 15 MINUTES**
COOKING TIME: **8–10 HOURS**
IDEAL SLOW COOKER SIZE: **4–5 QUART**

3-lb. boneless chuck roast

1 garlic clove, minced

1 Tbsp. oil

2–3 onions, sliced

2–3 sweet green and red peppers, sliced

16-oz. jar salsa

2 14½-oz. cans Mexican-style stewed tomatoes

1. Brown roast and garlic in oil in skillet. Place in slow cooker.
2. Add onions and peppers.
3. Combine salsa and tomatoes and pour over ingredients in slow cooker.
4. Cover. Cook on Low 8–10 hours.
5. Slice meat to serve.

Tip: *Make beef burritos with the leftovers. Shred the beef and heat with remaining peppers, onions, and ½ cup of the broth. Add 1 Tbsp. chili powder, 2 tsp. cumin, and salt to taste. Heat thoroughly. Fill warm flour tortillas with mixture and serve with sour cream, salsa, and guacamole.*

Steak Hi-Hat

Bonita Ensenberger Albuquerque, NM

MAKES: **8–10 SERVINGS**
PREP. TIME: **10 MINUTES**
COOKING TIME: **8–9 HOURS**
IDEAL SLOW COOKER SIZE: **4-QUART**

10¾-oz. can cream of chicken soup

10¾-oz. can cream of mushroom soup

1½ Tbsp. Worcestershire sauce

½ tsp. black pepper

1 tsp. paprika

2 cups chopped onion

1 garlic clove, minced

1 cup fresh, small button mushrooms, quartered

2 lbs. round steak, cubed

1 cup sour cream

cooked noodles with poppy seeds

crisp bacon bits, *optional*

1. Combine chicken soup, mushroom soup, Worcestershire sauce, pepper, paprika, onion, garlic, and mushrooms in slow cooker.
2. Stir in steak.
3. Cover. Cook on Low 8–9 hours.
4. Stir in sour cream during the last 20–30 minutes.
5. Serve on hot buttered noodles sprinkled with poppy seeds. Garnish with bacon bits.

Variation: *Add 1 tsp. salt with seasonings in Step 1.*

Fruited Flank Steak

Jean Butzer Batavia, NY

MAKES: **5 SERVINGS**
PREP. TIME: **5 MINUTES**
COOKING TIME: **7–9 HOURS**
IDEAL SLOW COOKER SIZE: **4–5-QUART**

1 lb. flank steak

¼ tsp. salt

dash of black pepper

30-oz. can fruit cocktail in light syrup

1 Tbsp. vegetable oil

1 Tbsp. lemon juice

¼ cup low-sodium teriyaki sauce

1 tsp. red wine vinegar

1 clove garlic, minced

1. Place flank steak in slow cooker. Sprinkle with salt and pepper.
2. Drain fruit cocktail, saving ¼ cup syrup.
3. Combine ¼ cup syrup with remaining ingredients, except fruit.
4. Pour syrup over steak.
5. Cover. Cook on Low 7–9 hours.
6. Add drained fruit during the last 10 minutes of cooking time.
7. Cut meat into thin slices across the grain to serve.

Per Serving: 250 calories (70 calories from fat), 7g total fat (2g saturated, 0g trans), 55mg cholesterol, 710mg sodium, 28g total carbohydrate (2g fiber, 25g sugar), 19g protein, 8%DV vitamin A, 2%DV vitamin C, 2%DV calcium, 15%DV iron.

Tender Texas-Style Steaks

Janice Muller Derwood, MD

MAKES: **4–6 SERVINGS**
PREP. TIME: **5 MINUTES**
COOKING TIME: **6 HOURS**
IDEAL SLOW COOKER SIZE: **3-QUART**

steaks *or* chops

1 cup brown sugar

1 cup ketchup

salt to taste

pepper to taste

few dashes of Worcestershire sauce

1. Lay steaks in bottom of slow cooker.
2. Combine sugar and ketchup. Pour over steaks.
3. Sprinkle with salt and pepper and a few dashes of Worcestershire sauce.
4. Cover. Cook on High 3 hours then on Low 3 hours.
5. Serve with wide egg noodles, green beans, and applesauce. Spoon some of the juice from the cooker over the noodles. Thicken the juice if you like with a little flour.

Beef Tongue

Lizzie Ann Yoder Hartville, OH

MAKES: **6 SERVINGS**
PREP. TIME: **15–20 MINUTES**
COOKING TIME: **7–8 HOURS**
IDEAL SLOW COOKER SIZE: **4–5-QUART**

1 beef tongue, fresh *or* smoked
2 scant Tbsp. salt
1½ cups water
1 bay leaf
2 lemons, squeezed, *or* 2 onions quartered
6 peppercorns

1. Place washed tongue in slow cooker.
2. In a bowl, mix all remaining ingredients together. Pour over tongue.
3. Cover and cook on Low 7–8 hours, or until the meat is tender. Cool until you're able to handle the meat, and then remove the outer skin by pulling on it gently.
4. Slice meat and serve hot.
5. Use chilled leftovers in sandwiches.

Burgundy Roast

Jane Hershberger Newton, KS

MAKES: **6–8 SERVINGS**
PREP. TIME: **10 MINUTES**
COOKING TIME: **5 HOURS**
IDEAL SLOW COOKER SIZE: **4-QUART**

4-lb. venison *or* beef roast
10¾-oz. can cream of mushroom soup
1 cup burgundy wine
1 large onion, finely chopped
2 Tbsp. chopped parsley

1. Place meat in slow cooker.
2. Blend soup and wine together in a mixing bowl. Pour over meat.
3. Top with onion and parsley.
4. Cover and cook on Low 5 hours, or until meat is tender but not dry.
5. Serve the sauce as a gravy over the sliced or cubed meat.

Variations:

1. Add 4 medium potatoes and 4 medium carrots, both quartered, and put them in the slow cooker first; then proceed with Step 1 above.

2. Replace the wine with 1 soup can of water.

Patricia Fleischer Carlisle, PA • *Ethel Mumaw* Millersburg, OH

Trim as much visible fat from meat as possible before placing it in the slow cooker in order to avoid greasy gravy.

Beef Stew Bourguignonne

Jo Haberkamp   Fairbank, IA

MAKES: **6 SERVINGS**
PREP. TIME: **15 MINUTES**
COOKING TIME: **10¼–12¼ HOURS**
IDEAL SLOW COOKER SIZE: **4-QUART**

2 lbs. stewing beef, cut in 1-inch cubes

2 Tbsp. cooking oil

10¾-oz. can condensed golden cream of mushroom soup

1 tsp. Worcestershire sauce

⅓ cup dry red wine

½ tsp. dried oregano

2 tsp. salt

½ tsp. pepper

½ cup chopped onions

½ cup chopped carrots

4-oz. can mushroom pieces, drained

½ cup cold water

¼ cup flour

noodles, cooked

1. Brown meat in oil in saucepan. Transfer to slow cooker.
2. Mix together soup, Worcestershire sauce, wine, oregano, salt and pepper, onions, carrots, and mushrooms. Pour over meat.
3. Cover. Cook on Low 10–12 hours.
4. Combine water and flour. Stir into beef mixture. Turn cooker to High.
5. Cook and stir until thickened and bubbly.
6. Serve over noodles.

For more flavorful gravy, first brown the meat in a skillet. Scrape all browned bits from the bottom of the skillet and add to the slow cooker along with the meat.

Burgundy Pot Roast

Rosemarie Fitzgerald   Gibsonia, PA

MAKES: **8–10 SERVINGS**
PREP. TIME: **15 MINUTES**
COOKING TIME: **9–11 HOURS**
IDEAL SLOW COOKER SIZE: **5-QUART**

2 beef bouillon cubes

¼ cup boiling water

14½-oz. can low-sodium diced or stewed tomatoes

1 cup dry red wine *or* burgundy

1.8-oz. box dry leek soup mix

1 Tbsp. Worcestershire sauce

4 cloves garlic, crushed or sliced

1 tsp. dried rosemary

1 tsp. dried thyme

1 tsp. dried marjoram

3 lbs. lean boneless beef pot roast, rolled and tied

2½ cups sliced carrots

½ cup parsnips, peeled, halved crosswise

4 Tbsp. flour

⅓ cup cold water

1. Dissolve bouillon cubes in boiling water. Pour into slow cooker.
2. Stir in tomatoes, wine, dry soup mix, Worcestershire sauce, garlic, and herbs.
3. Add meat. Roll in liquid to coat.
4. Put vegetables around meat.
5. Cover. Cook on Low 9–11 hours.
6. Remove meat to plate. Cover to keep warm. Turn slow cooker to High.
7. Whisk flour into ⅓ cup cold water. Stir into liquid and cook, covered, for 10 minutes.
8. Serve meat sliced with vegetables on the side and gravy.

Per Serving: 260 calories (70 calories from fat), 7g total fat (2.5g saturated, 0g trans), 80mg cholesterol, 740mg sodium, 16g total carbohydrate (3g fiber, 5g sugar), 29g protein, 100%DV vitamin A, 10%DV vitamin C, 6%DV calcium, 25%DV iron.

Beef Main Dishes

Variation: *You could add 5 red or white potatoes, quartered, to Step 4.*

Beef Burgundy

Joyce Kaut   Rochester, NY

MAKES: **8 SERVINGS**
PREP. TIME: **30 MINUTES**
COOKING TIME: **6¼–8¼ HOURS**
IDEAL SLOW COOKER SIZE: **4-QUART**

2 slices lean turkey bacon, cut in squares

2 lbs. lean sirloin tip *or* round steak, cubed

¼ cup flour

1 tsp. salt

½ tsp. seasoned salt

¼ tsp. dried marjoram

½ tsp. dried thyme

¼ tsp. black pepper

1 garlic clove, minced

1 low-sodium beef bouillon cube, crushed

1 cup burgundy wine

¼ lb. fresh mushrooms, sliced

2 Tbsp. cornstarch

2 Tbsp. cold water

1. Cook bacon in nonstick skillet until browned. Remove bacon, reserving drippings.
2. Coat beef with flour and brown on all sides in bacon drippings.
3. Combine steak, bacon drippings, bacon, seasonings, garlic, bouillon, and wine in slow cooker.
4. Cover. Cook on Low 6–8 hours.
5. Add mushrooms.
6. Dissolve cornstarch in water. Add to slow cooker.
7. Cover. Cook on High 15 minutes.
8. Serve over noodles.

Per Serving: 180 calories (45 calories from fat), 5g total fat (1.5g saturated, 0g trans), 55mg cholesterol, 630mg sodium, 7g total carbohydrate (0g fiber, 1g sugar), 18g protein, 0%DV vitamin A, 0%DV vitamin C, 2%DV calcium, 15%DV iron.

Variation: *If your diet allows, you may want to increase the salt to 1½ tsp. or the seasoned salt to 1 tsp.*

Creamy Hungarian Goulash

Kim Stoltzfus   New Holland, PA

MAKES: **8 SERVINGS**
PREP. TIME: **5 MINUTES**
COOKING TIME: **4–10 HOURS**
IDEAL SLOW COOKER SIZE: **4-QUART**

2-lb. round steak, cubed

½ tsp. onion powder

½ tsp. garlic powder

2 Tbsp. flour

½ tsp. salt

½ tsp. pepper

1½ tsp. paprika

10¾-oz. can tomato soup

½ soup can water

1 cup sour cream

1. Mix meat, onion powder, garlic powder, and flour together in slow cooker until meat is well coated.
2. Add remaining ingredients, except sour cream. Stir well.
3. Cover. Cook on Low 8–10 hours, or on High 4–5 hours.
4. Add sour cream 30 minutes before serving.
5. Serve over hot noodles.

Slow Cooker Beef

Sara Harter Fredette   Williamsburg, MA

MAKES: **4–6 SERVINGS**
PREP. TIME: **10 MINUTES**
COOKING TIME: **6–8 HOURS**
IDEAL SLOW COOKER SIZE: **4-QUART**

½ cup flour

2 tsp. salt

¼ tsp. pepper

2–3 lbs. stewing beef, cubed

2 Tbsp. oil

10¾-oz. can cream of mushroom soup

1 envelope dry onion soup mix

½ cup sour cream

1. Combine flour, salt, and pepper in plastic bag. Add beef in small batches. Shake to coat beef. Sauté beef in oil in saucepan. Place browned beef in slow cooker.
2. Stir in mushroom soup and onion soup mix.
3. Cover. Cook on Low 6–8 hours.
4. Stir in sour cream before serving. Heat for a few minutes.
5. Serve with noodles or mashed potatoes.

Keep a supply of cream of mushroom soup in your pantry. It is a quick and convenient staple for beef, veal, and pork roasts and casseroles. It makes a good sauce or gravy, with just a few additional seasonings or some sour cream.

Beef Cubes Stroganoff

Dale and Shari Mast   Harrisonburg, VA

MAKES: **4 SERVINGS**
PREP. TIME: **5 MINUTES**
COOKING TIME: **4–8 HOURS**
IDEAL SLOW COOKER SIZE: **4-QUART**

4 cups beef cubes

10¾-oz. can cream of mushroom soup

1 cup sour cream

1. Place beef in slow cooker. Cover with mushroom soup.
2. Cover. Cook on Low 8 hours, or on High 4–5 hours.
3. Before serving stir in sour cream.
4. Serve over cooked rice, pasta, or baked potatoes.

Easy Company Beef

Joyce B. Suiter   Garysburg, NC

MAKES: **8 SERVINGS**
PREP. TIME: **5 MINUTES**
COOKING TIME: **10 HOURS**
IDEAL SLOW COOKER SIZE: **4-QUART**

3 lbs. stewing beef, cubed

10¾-oz. can cream of mushroom soup

7-oz. jar mushrooms, undrained

½ cup red wine

1 envelope dry onion soup mix

1. Combine all ingredients in slow cooker.
2. Cover. Cook on Low 10 hours.
3. Serve over noodles, rice, or pasta.

Creamy Stroganoff

Evelyn Page Rapid City, SD

MAKES: **10 SERVINGS**
PREP. TIME: **10 MINUTES**
COOKING TIME: **6–7 HOURS**
IDEAL SLOW COOKER SIZE: **5–6-QUART**

1½-lb. round steak, trimmed of fat
¼ cup flour
½ tsp. black pepper
½ tsp. salt
1 tsp. garlic, minced
1 small onion, chopped
1 Tbsp. low-sodium soy sauce
1 beef bouillon cube
10¾-oz. can 98% fat-free cream of mushroom soup
1 cup water
8-oz. pkg. fat-free cream cheese, cubed

1. Cut steak into strips 1-inch long and ½-inch wide.
2. Mix with flour, pepper, salt, and garlic.
3. Combine with onion, soy sauce, bouillon, soup, and water in slow cooker.
4. Cook on Low 6–7 hours, stirring occasionally.
5. Add cream cheese cubes last 30 minutes of cooking.
6. Serve over cooked wide noodles.

Per Serving: 140 calories (40 calories from fat), 4.5g total fat (1.5g saturated, 0g trans), 45mg cholesterol, 760mg sodium, 8g total carbohydrate (0g fiber, 1g sugar), 18g protein, 4%DV vitamin A, 2%DV vitamin C, 6%DV calcium, 10%DV iron.

Beef-Lite

Rebecca Leichty Harrisonburg, VA

MAKES: **5 SERVINGS**
PREP. TIME: **5 MINUTES**
COOKING TIME: **6–8 HOURS**
IDEAL SLOW COOKER SIZE: **3-QUART**

1 lb. extra-lean ground beef
1 pkg. dry onion soup mix
10¾-oz. can 98% fat-free cream of celery soup
10¾-oz. can 98% fat-free cream of mushroom soup

1. Spray slow cooker with fat-free cooking spray.
2. Combine all ingredients in slow cooker.
3. Cook on Low for 6–8 hours.
4. Serve over hot rice.

Per Serving: 410 calories (110 calories from fat), 12 total fat (4.5g saturated, 1.5g trans), 40mg cholesterol, 1100mg sodium, 50g total carbohydrate (1g fiber, 2g sugar), 24g protein, 2%DV vitamin A, 0%DV vitamin C, 6%DV calcium, 20%DV iron.

Easy Stroganoff

Vicki Dinkel Sharon Springs, KS

MAKES: **6–8 SERVINGS**
PREP. TIME: **5 MINUTES**
COOKING TIME: **6¼–8¼ HOURS**
IDEAL SLOW COOKER SIZE: **3-QUART**

10¾-oz. can cream of mushroom soup

14½-oz. can beef broth

1 lb. beef stewing meat *or* round steak, cut in 1-inch
  pieces

1 cup sour cream

2 cups noodles, cooked

1. Combine soup and broth in slow cooker.
   Add meat.
2. Cover. Cook on High 3–4 hours. Reduce
   heat to Low and cook 3–4 hours.
3. Stir in sour cream.
4. Stir in noodles.
5. Cook on High 20 minutes.

Note: *Since I'm in school part-time and work
two part-time jobs, this nearly-complete meal is
great to come home to. It smells wonderful when
you open the door.*
  *A vegetable or salad and some crispy French
bread are good additions.*

Herby French Dip

Sara Wichert Hillsboro, KS

MAKES: **6–8 SANDWICHES**
PREP. TIME: **5 MINUTES**
COOKING TIME: **5–6 HOURS**
IDEAL SLOW COOKER SIZE: **4-QUART**

3-lb. chuck roast

2 cups water

½ cup soy sauce

1 tsp. garlic powder

1 bay leaf

3–4 whole peppercorns

1 tsp. dried rosemary, *optional*

1 tsp. dried thyme, *optional*

6–8 French rolls

1. Place roast in slow cooker.
2. Combine remaining ingredients in a mixing
   bowl. Pour over meat.
3. Cover and cook on High 5–6 hours, or until
   meat is tender but not dry.
4. Remove meat from broth and shred with
   fork. Stir back into sauce.
5. Remove meat from the cooker by large
   forkfuls and place on French rolls.

Zesty French Dip

Earnest Zimmerman Mechanicsburg, PA
Tracey Hanson Schramel Windom, MN

MAKES: **6–8 SANDWICHES**
PREP. TIME: **5 MINUTES**
COOKING TIME: **8 HOURS**
IDEAL SLOW COOKER SIZE: **4–6-QUART**

4-lb. beef roast

10½-oz. can beef broth

10½-oz. can condensed French onion soup

12-oz. bottle of beer

6–8 French rolls or baguettes

1. Pat roast dry and place in slow cooker.
2. In a mixing bowl, combine beef broth,
   onion soup, and beer. Pour over meat.
3. Cover and cook on Low 8 hours, or until
   meat is tender but not dry.
4. Split rolls or baguettes. Warm in the oven or
   microwave until heated through.
5. Remove meat from cooker and allow to rest
   for 10 minutes. Then shred with two forks,

or cut on the diagonal into thin slices, and place in rolls. Serve with dipping sauce on the side.

Beach Boy's Pot Roast

Jeanette Oberholtzer   Manheim, PA

MAKES: **6–8 SANDWICHES**
PREP. TIME: **10 MINUTES**
COOKING TIME: **8–12 HOURS**
IDEAL SLOW COOKER SIZE: **3–4-QUART**

3–4-lb. chuck *or* top round roast

8–12 slivers of garlic

32-oz. jar pepperoncini peppers, undrained

6–8 large hoagie rolls

12–16 slices of your favorite cheese

1. Cut slits into roast with a sharp knife and insert garlic slivers.
2. Place beef in slow cooker. Spoon peppers and all of their juice over top.
3. Cover and cook on Low 8–12 hours, or until meat is tender but not dry.
4. Remove meat from cooker and allow to cool. Then use 2 forks to shred the beef.
5. Spread on hoagie rolls and top with cheese.

Hot Beef Sandwiches

Evelyn L. Ward   Greeley, CO

MAKES: **10 SANDWICHES**
PREP. TIME: **5–10 MINUTES**
COOKING TIME: **8–10 HOURS**
IDEAL SLOW COOKER SIZE: **4-QUART**

3 lbs. beef chuck roast

1 large onion, chopped

¼ cup vinegar

1 clove garlic, minced

1–1½ tsp. salt

¼–½ tsp. pepper

1. Place meat in slow cooker. Top with onions.
2. Combine vinegar, garlic, salt, and pepper. Pour over meat.
3. Cover. Cook on Low 8–10 hours.
4. Drain broth but save for dipping.
5. Shred meat.
6. Serve on hamburger buns with broth on side.

Note: *I volunteer with Habitat for Humanity. I don't do construction, but I provide lunch sometimes for work crews. This sandwich is a favorite. I make the most colorful tossed salad that I can and serve fresh fruit that is in season and pie.*

Herby Beef Sandwiches

Jean A. Shaner   York, PA

MAKES: **10–12 SANDWICHES**
PREP. TIME: **5 MINUTES**
COOKING TIME: **7–8 HOURS**
IDEAL SLOW COOKER SIZE: **4-QUART**

3–4-lb. boneless beef chuck roast

3 Tbsp. fresh basil, *or* 1 Tbsp. dried basil

3 Tbsp. fresh oregano, *or* 1 Tbsp. dried oregano

1½ cups water

1 pkg. dry onion soup mix

10–12 Italian rolls

1. Place roast in slow cooker.
2. Combine basil, oregano, and water. Pour over roast.
3. Sprinkle with onion soup mix.
4. Cover. Cook on Low 7–8 hours. Shred meat with fork.
5. Serve on Italian rolls.

Middle-Eastern Sandwiches (for a crowd)

Esther Mast   East Petersburg, PA

MAKES: **10–16 SANDWICHES**
PREP. TIME: **50 MINUTES**
COOKING TIME: **6–8 HOURS**
IDEAL SLOW COOKER SIZE: **4-QUART**

4 lbs. boneless beef *or* venison, cut in ½-inch cubes

4 Tbsp. cooking oil

2 cups chopped onions

2 garlic cloves, minced

1 cup dry red wine

6-oz. can tomato paste

1 tsp. dried oregano

1 tsp. dried basil

½ tsp. dried rosemary

2 tsp. salt

dash of pepper

¼ cup cold water

¼ cup cornstarch

pita pocket breads

2 cups shredded lettuce

1 large tomato, seeded and diced

1 large cucumber, seeded and diced

8-ozs. plain yogurt

1. Brown meat, 1 lb. at a time, in skillet in 1 Tbsp. oil. Reserve drippings and transfer meat to slow cooker.
2. Sauté onion and garlic in drippings until tender. Add to meat.
3. Add wine, tomato paste, oregano, basil, rosemary, salt, and pepper.
4. Cover. Cook on Low 6–8 hours.
5. Turn cooker to High. Combine cornstarch and water in small bowl until smooth. Stir into meat mixture. Cook until bubbly and thickened, stirring occasionally.
6. Split pita breads to make pockets. Fill each with meat mixture, lettuce, tomato, cucumber, and yogurt.
7. Serve with jello salad or applesauce.

Beef Pitas

Dede Peterson   Rapid City, SD

MAKES: **2 SANDWICHES**
PREP. TIME: **15 MINUTES**
COOKING TIME: **3–4 HOURS**
IDEAL SLOW COOKER SIZE: **2-QUART**

½ lb. beef *or* pork, cut into small cubes

½ tsp. dried oregano

dash of black pepper

1 cup chopped fresh tomatoes

2 Tbsp. diced fresh green bell peppers

¼ cup nonfat sour cream

1 tsp. red wine vinegar

1 tsp. vegetable oil

2 large pita breads, heated and cut in half

1. Place meat in slow cooker. Sprinkle with oregano and black pepper.
2. Cook on Low 3–4 hours.
3. In a separate bowl, combine tomatoes, green peppers, sour cream, vinegar, and oil.
4. Fill pitas with meat. Top with vegetable and sour cream mixture.

Per Serving: 380 calories (80 calories from fat), 9g total fat (2.5g saturated, 0g trans), 75mg cholesterol, 410mg sodium, 44g total carbohydrate (3g fiber, 6g sugar), 30g protein, 20%DV vitamin A, 20%DV vitamin C, 10%DV calcium, 25%DV iron.

Beef Main Dishes

Tangy Barbecue Sandwiches

Lavina Hochstedler Grand Blanc, MI • *Lois M. Martin* Lititz, PA

MAKES: **14–18 SANDWICHES**
PREP. TIME: **20 MINUTES**
COOKING TIME: **7–9 HOURS**
IDEAL SLOW COOKER SIZE: **5-QUART**

3 cups chopped celery

1 cup chopped onions

1 cup ketchup

1 cup barbecue sauce

1 cup water

2 Tbsp. vinegar

2 Tbsp. Worcestershire sauce

2 Tbsp. brown sugar

1 tsp. chili powder

1 tsp. salt

½ tsp. pepper

½ tsp. garlic powder

3–4-lb. boneless chuck roast

14–18 hamburger buns

1. Combine all ingredients except roast and buns in slow cooker. When well mixed, add roast.
2. Cover. Cook on High 6–7 hours.
3. Remove roast. Cool and shred meat. Return to sauce. Heat well.
4. Serve on buns.

Easy Beef Stew

Judi Manos West Islip, NY

MAKES: **4–6 SERVINGS**
PREP. TIME: **20 MINUTES**
COOKING TIME: **7½–8½ HOURS**
IDEAL SLOW COOKER SIZE: **4-QUART**

4 medium red potatoes

1½ lbs. beef stew meat

⅓ cup flour

14-oz. can diced tomatoes, undrained

2 cups water

3 cups frozen stir-fry bell peppers and onions

1. Cut potatoes into quarters. Place on bottom of slow cooker.
2. In a mixing bowl, toss flour with beef to coat. Add to slow cooker.
3. Pour in undrained tomatoes and water.
4. Cover and cook on Low 7–8 hours, or until beef and potatoes are tender but not overcooked.
5. Gently fold stir-fry vegetables into stew. Cover and cook on Low 30–40 minutes, or until vegetables are hot and tender.

Variations:

1. Add 2–3 cups sliced carrots just after the potatoes in Step 1.

2. Add 2 tsp. salt and ¾ tsp. pepper to the flour in Step 2, before tossing with the beef.

When adapting range-top recipes to slow cooking, reduce the amount of onion you normally use because the onion flavor gets stronger during slow cooking.

Beef and Beans over Rice

Robin Schrock   Millersburg, OH

MAKES: **8 SERVINGS**
PREP. TIME: **15 MINUTES**
COOKING TIME: **5½–7½ HOURS**
IDEAL SLOW COOKER SIZE: **4-QUART**

1½ lbs. boneless round steak

1 Tbsp. prepared mustard

1 Tbsp. chili powder

½ tsp. salt, *optional*

¼ tsp. black pepper

1 garlic clove, minced

2 14½-oz. cans low-sodium diced tomatoes

1 medium onion, chopped

1 beef bouillon cube, crushed

16-oz. can kidney beans, rinsed and drained

1. Cut steak into thin strips.
2. Combine mustard, chili powder, salt (if desired), pepper, and garlic in a bowl.
3. Add steak. Toss to coat.
4. Transfer to slow cooker. Add tomatoes, onion, and bouillon.
5. Cover. Cook on Low 5–7 hours.
6. Stir in beans. Cook 30 minutes longer.
7. Serve over rice.

———————————

Per Serving: 190 calories (40 calories from fat), 4.5g total fat (1.5g saturated, 0g trans), 50mg cholesterol, 870mg sodium, 15g total carbohydrate (4g fiber, 4g sugar), 21g protein, 10%DV vitamin A, 8%DV vitamin C, 0%DV calcium, 15%DV iron.

Beef Barley Stew

Bonita Ensinberger   Albuquerque, NM

MAKES: **6 SERVINGS**
PREP. TIME: **15 MINUTES**
COOKING TIME: **9–10 HOURS**
IDEAL SLOW COOKER SIZE: **5-QUART**

½ lb. lean round steak, cut in ½-inch cubes

4 carrots, peeled and cut in ¼-inch slices

1 cup chopped yellow onions

½ cup coarsely chopped green bell peppers

1 clove garlic, pressed

½ lb. fresh button mushrooms, quartered

¾ cup dry pearl barley

½ tsp. salt

¼ tsp. ground black pepper

½ tsp. dried thyme

½ tsp. dried sweet basil

1 bay leaf

5 cups fat-free, low-sodium beef broth

1. Combine all ingredients in slow cooker.
2. Cover. Cook on Low 9–10 hours.

———————————

Per Serving: 220 calories (45 calories from fat), 5g total fat (1g saturated, 0g trans), 25mg cholesterol, 520mg sodium, 29g total carbohydrate (6g fiber, 5g sugar), 16g protein, 200%DV vitamin A, 20%DV vitamin C, 4%DV calcium, 15%DV iron.

Hungarian Barley Stew

Naomi E. Fast   Hesston, KS

MAKES: **8 SERVINGS**
PREP. TIME: **20 MINUTES**
COOKING TIME: **5 HOURS**
IDEAL SLOW COOKER SIZE: **5-QUART**

2 Tbsp. oil

1½ lbs. beef cubes

2 large onions, diced

1 medium green pepper, chopped

28-oz. can whole tomatoes

½ cup ketchup

⅔ cup dry small pearl barley

1 tsp. salt

½ tsp. pepper

1 Tbsp. paprika

10-oz. pkg. frozen baby lima beans

3 cups water

1 cup sour cream

1. Brown beef cubes in oil in skillet. Add onions and green peppers. Sauté. Pour into slow cooker.
2. Add remaining ingredients except sour cream.
3. Cover. Cook on High 5 hours.
4. Stir in sour cream before serving.
5. Serve with your favorite cabbage slaw.

I find that adding ¼–½ cup of a burgundy or Chablis wine to most soups and stew recipes brings out the flavor of the other seasonings.

Hungarian Beef Stew

Esther Becker   Gordonville, PA

MAKES: **6 SERVINGS**
PREP. TIME: **15 MINUTES**
COOKING TIME: **10–12 HOURS**
IDEAL SLOW COOKER SIZE: **4-QUART**

2 lbs. beef cubes

1 onion, chopped

2 medium potatoes, peeled and cubed

2 carrots, sliced

10-oz. pkg. frozen lima beans

2 tsp. parsley

½ cup beef broth

2 tsp. paprika

1 tsp. salt

16-oz. can diced tomatoes

1. Combine beef, onion, potatoes, carrots, lima beans, and parsley in slow cooker.
2. Combine remaining ingredients and pour into slow cooker.
3. Cover. Cook on Low 10–12 hours.
4. Serve with your favorite salad and whole wheat rolls.

Wash-Day Stew

Naomi E. Fast Hesston, KS

MAKES: **8–10 SANDWICHES**
PREP. TIME: **10 MINUTES**
COOKING TIME: **6–7 HOURS**
IDEAL SLOW COOKER SIZE: **5-QUART**

1½–2 lbs. lean lamb *or* beef, cubed

2 15-oz. cans garbanzo beans, drained

2 15-oz. cans white beans, drained

2 medium onions, peeled and quartered

1 quart water

1 tsp. salt

1 tomato, peeled and quartered

1 tsp. turmeric

3 Tbsp. fresh lemon juice

8–10 pita bread pockets

1. Combine ingredients in slow cooker.
2. Cover. Cook on High 6–7 hours.
3. Lift stew from cooker with a strainer spoon and stuff in pita bread pockets.

Note: *I learned to prepare this nutritious meal from a student from Iran, who was attending graduate school at the University of Nebraska. Fatimeh explained to me that her family prepared this dish every wash day.*

Very early in the morning, they made a fire in a large rock-lined pit outside. Then they placed a large covered kettle, filled with the above ingredients, over the coals to cook slowly all day. At the end of a day of doing laundry, the food was ready with a minimum of preparation. Of course, they started with dry beans and dry garbanzos, presoaked the night before. They served this Wash-Day Stew spooned into pita bread and ate it with their hands.

New Mexico Stew

Helen Kenagy Carlsbad, NM

MAKES: **8 SERVINGS**
PREP. TIME: **15 MINUTES**
COOKING TIME: **8½–10½ HOURS**
IDEAL SLOW COOKER SIZE: **5-QUART**

2 lbs. stewing meat *or* steak, cubed, *divided*

salt to taste

pepper to taste

1 Tbsp. oil

5–6 potatoes, cubed, *divided*

6–8 carrots, diced, *divided*

other vegetables, diced, *divided*

1–2 4¼-oz. cans chopped green chilies, *divided*

1½ lbs. raw pork sausage, crumbled, *divided*

1. Salt and pepper stewing meat. Brown in oil in skillet.
2. Place half the stewing meat in bottom of slow cooker.
3. Layer half the vegetables and chilies over the beef. Crumble half the sausage over top. Sprinkle each layer with salt and pepper.
4. Continue layering until all ingredients are used.
5. Cover. Cook on High until ingredients begin to boil. Then turn cooker to Low for 8–10 hours. Do not lift lid and do not stir during cooking.
6. Serve with a green salad and fresh bread.

Beef Main Dishes

Beef Stew with Shiitake Mushrooms

Kathy Hertzler Lancaster, PA

MAKES: **4–6 SERVINGS**
PREP. TIME: **10 MINUTES**
COOKING TIME: **8–9 HOURS**
IDEAL SLOW COOKER SIZE: **5-QUART**

12 new potatoes, cut into quarters

½ cup chopped onions

8-oz. pkg. baby carrots

3.4-oz. pkg. fresh shiitake mushrooms, sliced, *or* 2 cups regular white mushrooms, sliced

16-oz. can whole tomatoes

14½-oz. can beef broth

½ cup flour

1 Tbsp. Worcestershire sauce

1 tsp. salt.

1 tsp. sugar

1 tsp. dried marjoram leaves

¼ tsp. pepper

1 lb. beef stewing meat, cubed

1. Combine all ingredients except beef in slow cooker. Add beef.
2. Cover. Cook on Low 8–9 hours. Stir well before serving.

Many-Veggies Beef Stew

Janie Steele Moore, OK

MAKES: **14–18 SERVINGS**
PREP. TIME: **25 MINUTES**
COOKING TIME: **10–11 HOURS**
IDEAL SLOW COOKER SIZE: **2 4-QUART**

2–3 lbs. beef, cubed

16-oz. pkg. frozen green beans *or* mixed vegetables

16-oz. pkg. frozen corn

16-oz. pkg. frozen peas

2 lbs. carrots, chopped

1 large onion, chopped

4 medium potatoes, peeled and chopped

10¾-oz. can tomato soup

10¾-oz. can celery soup

10¾-oz. can mushroom soup

bell pepper, chopped, *optional*

1. Combine all ingredients in 2 4-quart slow cookers (this is a very large recipe).
2. Cover. Cook on Low 10–11 hours.

I often start the slow cooker on High until I'm ready for work, then switch it to Low as I go out the door. It may only be 45 minutes to 1 hour on High, but I feel it starts the cooking process faster, thus preserving flavor.

Bavarian Beef

Naomi E. Fast Hesston, KS

MAKES: **6 SERVINGS**
PREP. TIME: **15 MINUTES**
COOKING TIME: **6½–7½ HOURS**
IDEAL SLOW COOKER SIZE: **4-QUART**

3–3½-lb. boneless beef chuck roast

oil

3 cups sliced carrots

3 cups sliced onions

2 large kosher dill pickles, chopped

1 cup sliced celery

½ cup dry red wine *or* beef broth

⅓ cup German-style mustard

2 tsp. coarsely ground black pepper

2 bay leaves

¼ tsp. ground cloves

1 cup water

⅓ cup flour

1. Brown roast on both sides in oil in skillet. Transfer to slow cooker.
2. Add remaining ingredients.
3. Cover. Cook on Low 6–7 hours.
4. Remove meat and vegetables to large platter. Cover to keep warm.
5. Mix flour with 1 cup of broth until smooth. Return to cooker. Turn on High and stir, cooking until broth is smooth and thickened.
6. Serve over noodles or spaetzle.

Italian Beef Stew

Kathy Hertzler Lancaster, PA

MAKES: **4–6 SERVINGS**
PREP. TIME: **30 MINUTES**
COOKING TIME: **6 HOURS**
IDEAL SLOW COOKER SIZE: **4-QUART**

2 Tbsp. flour

2 tsp. chopped fresh thyme

1 tsp. salt

¼–½ tsp. freshly ground pepper

2¼ lbs. beef stewing meat, cubed

3 Tbsp. olive oil

1 onion, chopped

1 cup tomato sauce

1 cup beef stock

1 cup red wine

3 garlic cloves, minced

2 Tbsp. tomato paste

2 cups frozen peas, thawed but not cooked

1 tsp. sugar

1. Spoon flour into small dish. Season with thyme, salt, and pepper. Add beef cubes and coat evenly.
2. Heat oil in slow cooker on High. Add floured beef and brown on all sides.
3. Stir in remaining ingredients except peas and sugar.
4. Cover. Cook on Low 6 hours.
5. Add peas and sugar. Cook an additional 30 minutes, or until beef is tender and peas are warm.

Beef Main Dishes

Mushroom-Beef Stew

Dawn Day Westminster, CA

MAKES: **8–10 SERVINGS**
PREP. TIME: **20 MINUTES**
COOKING TIME: **6–7½ HOURS**
IDEAL SLOW COOKER SIZE: **3–4-QUART**

1 lb. sirloin, cubed

2 Tbsp. flour

oil

1 large onion, chopped

2 garlic cloves, minced

½ lb. button mushrooms, sliced

2 ribs celery, sliced

2 carrots, sliced

3–4 large potatoes, cubed

2 tsp. seasoned salt

14½-oz. can beef stock, *or* 2 bouillon cubes dissolved in
    1⅔ cups water

½–1 cup good red wine

1. Dredge sirloin in flour and brown in skillet. Reserve drippings. Place meat in slow cooker.
2. Sauté onion, garlic, and mushrooms in drippings just until soft. Add to meat.
3. Add all remaining ingredients.
4. Cover. Cook on Low 6 hours. Test to see if vegetables are tender. If not, continue cooking on Low for another 1–1½ hours.
5. Serve with crusty bread.

Try to have vegetable and meat pieces all cut about the same size and thickness. Pieces of uniform size tend to finish cooking at the same time.

Tempting Beef Stew

Patricia Howard Albuquerque, NM

MAKES: **10–12 SERVINGS**
PREP. TIME: **10 MINUTES**
COOKING TIME: **10–12 HOURS**
IDEAL SLOW COOKER SIZE: **5-QUART**

2–3 lbs. beef stewing meat

3 carrots, thinly sliced

1-lb. pkg. frozen green peas with onions

1-lb. pkg. frozen green beans

16-oz. can whole *or* stewed tomatoes

½ cup beef broth

½ cup white wine

½ cup brown sugar

4 Tbsp. tapioca

½ cup bread crumbs

2 tsp. salt

1 bay leaf

pepper to taste

1. Combine all ingredients in slow cooker.
2. Cover. Cook on Low 10–12 hours.
3. Serve over noodles, rice, couscous, or biscuits.

Variation: *In place of the tapioca, thicken stew with ¼ cup flour dissolved in ⅓–½ cup water. Mix in and turn cooker to High. Cover and cook for 15–20 minutes.*

Herbed Beef Stew

Carol Findling Princeton, IL

MAKES: **6–8 SERVINGS**
PREP. TIME: **15 MINUTES**
COOKING TIME: **4–12 HOURS**
IDEAL SLOW COOKER SIZE: **4-QUART**

1 lb. beef round, cubed
4 Tbsp. seasoned flour*
1½ cups beef broth
1 tsp. Worcestershire sauce
1 garlic clove
1 bay leaf
4 carrots, sliced
3 potatoes, cubed
2 onions, diced
1 rounded tsp. fresh thyme, *or* ½ tsp. dried thyme
1 rounded tsp. chopped fresh basil, *or* ½ tsp. dried basil
1 Tbsp. fresh parsley, *or* 1 tsp. dried parsley
1 rounded tsp. fresh marjoram, *or* 1 tsp. dried marjoram

1. Put meat in slow cooker. Add seasoned flour. Toss with meat. Stir in remaining ingredients. Mix well.
2. Cover. Cook on High 4–6 hours, or on Low 10–12 hours.

* Seasoned Flour
1 cup flour
1 tsp. salt
1 tsp. paprika
¼ tsp. pepper

I always keep 1-cup measuring cups in my sugar and flour canisters. That way I can reach in and measure what I need from that one cup.

Beef Stew Olé

Andrea O'Neil Fairfield, CT

MAKES: **6–8 SERVINGS**
PREP. TIME: **15 MINUTES**
COOKING TIME: **7–8 HOURS**
IDEAL SLOW COOKER SIZE: **4-QUART**

4 carrots, cubed
4 potatoes, peeled and cubed
1 onion, quartered
1½ lbs. beef stewing meat, cubed
8-oz. can tomato sauce
1 pkg. dry taco seasoning mix
2 cups water, *divided*
1½ Tbsp. cornstarch
2 tsp. salt
¼ tsp. pepper

1. Layer first four ingredients in slow cooker. Add tomato sauce.
2. Combine taco seasoning with 1½ cups water. Stir cornstarch into remaining ½ cup water until smooth. Stir into rest of water with taco seasoning. Pour over ingredients in slow cooker.
3. Sprinkle with salt and pepper.
4. Cover. Cook on Low 7–8 hours.
5. Serve over rice.

Tip: *If those eating at your table are cautious about spicy food, choose a "mild" taco seasoning mix and add 1 tsp. sugar to the seasonings.*

Lotsa-Tomatoes Beef Stew

Bernice A. Esau   North Newton, KS

MAKES: **6 SERVINGS**
PREP. TIME: **15 MINUTES**
COOKING TIME: **5½–6 HOURS**
IDEAL SLOW COOKER SIZE: **6–7-QUART**

2 lbs. extra-lean stewing beef cubes, trimmed of fat

5–6 carrots, cut in 1-inch pieces

1 large onion, cut in chunks

3 ribs celery, sliced

6 medium tomatoes, cut up and gently mashed

½ cup quick-cooking tapioca

1 whole clove, *or* ¼–½ tsp. ground cloves

1 tsp. dried basil

½ tsp. dried oregano

2 bay leaves

2 tsp. salt

½ tsp. black pepper

3–4 potatoes, cubed

1. Place all ingredients in slow cooker. Mix together well.
2. Cover. Cook on High 5½–6 hours.

Per Serving: 400 calories (70 calories from fat), 8g total fat (2.5g saturated, 0g trans), 90mg cholesterol, 110mg sodium, 48g total carbohydrate (7g fiber, 10g sugar), 34g protein, 200%DV vitamin A, 50%DV vitamin C, 60%DV calcium, 30%DV iron.

Tip: *Add 2–3 Tbsp. instant mashed potatoes during the last 30 minutes of cooking if the cooking juices are too thin.*

Santa Fe Stew

Jeanne Allen   Rye, CO

MAKES: **4–6 SERVINGS**
PREP. TIME: **20 MINUTES**
COOKING TIME: **4½–6½ HOURS**
IDEAL SLOW COOKER SIZE: **4-QUART**

2 lbs. sirloin *or* stewing meat, cubed

2 Tbsp. oil

1 large onion, diced

2 garlic cloves, minced

1½ cups water

1 Tbsp. dried parsley flakes

2 beef bouillon cubes

1 tsp. ground cumin

½ tsp. salt

3 carrots, sliced

14½-oz. can diced tomatoes

14½-oz. can green beans, drained, *or* 1 lb. frozen green beans

14½-oz. can corn, drained, *or* 1 lb. frozen corn

4-oz. can diced green chilies

3 zucchini squash, diced, *optional*

1. Brown meat, onion, and garlic in oil in saucepan until meat is no longer pink. Place in slow cooker.
2. Stir in remaining ingredients.
3. Cover. Cook on High 30 minutes. Reduce heat to Low and cook 4–6 hours.

Sweet-Sour Beef and Vegetables

Jo Haberkamp   Fairbank, IA

MAKES: **6 SERVINGS**
PREP. TIME: **10 MINUTES**
COOKING TIME: **4–6 HOURS**
IDEAL SLOW COOKER SIZE: **4-QUART**

2 lbs. round steak, cut in 1-inch cubes

2 Tbsp. oil

2 8-oz. cans tomato sauce

2 tsp. chili powder

2 cups sliced carrots

2 cups small white onions

1 tsp. paprika

¼ cup sugar

1 tsp. salt

⅓ cup vinegar

½ cup light molasses

1 large green pepper, cut in 1-inch pieces

1. Brown steak in oil in saucepan.
2. Combine all ingredients in slow cooker.
3. Cover. Cook on High 4–6 hours.

Best Everyday Stew

Elizabeth L. Richards   Rapid City SD

MAKES: **8 SERVINGS**
PREP. TIME: **20 MINUTES**
COOKING TIME: **10 HOURS**
IDEAL SLOW COOKER SIZE: **6-QUART**

2¼ lbs. flank steak, 1½-inch thick

8 red potatoes, small to medium in size

10 baby carrots

1 large clove garlic, diced

1 medium to large onion, chopped

1 cup baby peas

3 ribs celery, cut in 1-inch pieces

3 cups cabbage, in chunks

2 8-oz. cans low-sodium tomato sauce

1 Tbsp. Worcestershire sauce

2 bay leaves

¼–½ tsp. dried thyme, according to your taste preference

¼–½ tsp. dried basil, according to your taste preference

¼–½ tsp. dried marjoram, according to your taste preference

1 Tbsp. parsley

2 cups water or more, if desired

4 cubes beef *or* vegetable bouillon

1. Trim flank steak of fat. Cut in 1½-inch cubes. Brown slowly in nonstick skillet.
2. Quarter potatoes.
3. Combine all ingredients in large slow cooker.
4. Cover. Cook on High 1 hour. Turn to Low and cook 9 additional hours.

Per Serving: 260 calories (60 calories from fat), 7g total fat (2g saturated, 0g trans), 75mg cholesterol, 1330mg sodium, 22g total carbohydrate (4g fiber, 6g sugar), 29g protein, 40%DV vitamin A, 20%DV vitamin C, 6%DV calcium, 25%DV iron.

Tip: *Let all soups and stews sit overnight in refrigerator and skim off any fat in the morning.*

Beef Main Dishes

Gone-All-Day Dinner

Susan Scheel   West Fargo, ND

MAKES: **8 SERVINGS**
PREP. TIME: **15 MINUTES**
COOKING TIME: **6–8 HOURS**
IDEAL SLOW COOKER SIZE: **5-QUART**

1 cup uncooked wild rice, rinsed and drained

1 cup chopped celery

1 cup chopped carrots

2 4-oz. cans mushrooms, drained

1 large onion, chopped

½ cup slivered almonds

3 beef bouillon cubes

2½ tsp. seasoned salt

2 lbs. boneless round steak, cut in bite-sized pieces

3 cups water

1. Layer ingredients in slow cooker in order listed. Do not stir.
2. Cover. Cook on Low 6–8 hours.
3. Stir before serving.

Per Serving: 300 calories (90 calories from fat), 10g total fat (2g saturated, 0g trans), 70mg cholesterol, 1110mg sodium, 24g total carbohydrate (4g fiber, 3g sugar), 28g protein, 80%DV vitamin A, 2%DV vitamin C, 4%DV calcium, 20%DV iron.

Lazy Day Stew

Ruth Ann Gingrich   New Holland, PA

MAKES: **8 SERVINGS**
PREP. TIME: **15 MINUTES**
COOKING TIME: **8 HOURS**
IDEAL SLOW COOKER SIZE: **4-QUART**

2 lbs. stewing beef, cubed

2 cups diced carrots

2 cups diced potatoes

2 medium onions, chopped

1 cup chopped celery

10-oz. pkg. lima beans

2 tsp. quick-cooking tapioca

1 tsp. salt

½ tsp. pepper

8-oz. can tomato sauce

1 cup water

1 Tbsp. brown sugar

1. Place beef in bottom of slow cooker. Add vegetables.
2. Sprinkle tapioca, salt, and pepper over ingredients.
3. Mix together tomato sauce and water. Pour over top.
4. Sprinkle brown sugar over all.
5. Cover. Cook on Low 8 hours.

Variation: *Instead of lima beans, use 1½ cups green beans.*

Rose M. Hoffman   Schuylkill Haven, PA

If your recipe calls for 3 Tablespoons of fresh basil, and you have only dried basil, use 1 Tablespoon of dried basil. In other words, 1 portion of dried herbs can be substituted for 3 portions of fresh herbs. And vice versa.

Veggie Surprise Beef Stew

Irene Hull   Anderson, IN

MAKES: **5 SERVINGS**
PREP. TIME: **20 MINUTES**
COOKING TIME: **5½–6½ HOURS**
IDEAL SLOW COOKER SIZE: **3–4-QUART**

¾ lb. lean stewing meat, trimmed of fat and cut into
   ½-inch cubes

2 tsp. canola oil

14½-oz. can low-sodium, low-fat beef broth

14½-oz. can low-sodium stewed tomatoes

1½ cups butternut squash, peeled and cubed

1 cup frozen corn

½ cup chopped carrots

dash of salt

dash of black pepper

dash of dried oregano

2 Tbsp. cornstarch

¼ cup water

1. In a skillet, brown stewing meat in canola oil over medium heat. Transfer to slow cooker.
2. Add beef broth, vegetables, salt, pepper, and oregano.
3. Cover. Cook on High 5–6 hours.
4. Combine cornstarch and water until smooth. Stir into stew.
5. Cover. Cook on High 30 minutes.

Per Serving: 200 calories (50 calories from fat), 5g total fat (1.5g saturated, 0g trans), 40mg cholesterol, 180mg sodium, 22g total carbohydrate (4g fiber, 6g sugar), 17g protein, 150%DV vitamin A, 20%DV vitamin C, 6%DV calcium, 15%DV iron.

Fruity Vegetable Beef Stew

Esther S. Martin   Ephrata, PA

Mrs. Carolyn Baer   Conrath, WI

MAKES: **4 SERVINGS**
PREP. TIME: **25 MINUTES**
COOKING TIME: **5½–6½ HOURS**
IDEAL SLOW COOKER SIZE: **4-QUART**

¾ lb. lean beef stewing meat, cut into ½-inch cubes

2 tsp. canola oil

14½-oz. can fat-free beef broth

14½-oz. can stewed tomatoes, cut up

1½ cups peeled and cubed butternut squash

1 cup thawed, frozen corn

6 dried apricot *or* peach halves, quartered

½ cup chopped carrots

1 tsp. dried oregano

¼ tsp. salt

¼ tsp. black pepper

2 Tbsp. cornstarch

¼ cup water

2 Tbsp. minced fresh parsley

1. Brown meat in oil in a nonstick skillet over medium heat.
2. Combine meat, broth, tomatoes, squash, corn, apricots, carrots, oregano, salt, and pepper in slow cooker.
3. Cook on High 5–6 hours, or until vegetables and meat are tender.
4. Combine cornstarch and water until smooth. Stir into stew.
5. Cook on High 30 minutes, or until stew is thickened.
6. Add parsley just before serving.

Per Serving: 280 calories (60 calories from fat), 7g total fat (1.5g saturated, 0g trans), 50mg cholesterol, 510mg sodium, 35g total carbohydrate (5g fiber, 13g sugar), 23g protein, 150%DV vitamin A, 20%DV vitamin C, 8%DV calcium, 20%DV iron.

Beef Main Dishes

Note: *With the sweet flavor from apricots and squash, we think this dish has a South American or Cuban flair. The addition of corn makes it even more hearty.*

Hamburger Potatoes

Juanita Marner   Shipshewana, IN

MAKES: **3–4 SERVINGS**
PREP. TIME: **15 MINUTES**
COOKING TIME: **6–8 HOURS**
IDEAL SLOW COOKER SIZE: **4-QUART**

3 medium potatoes, sliced

3 carrots, sliced

1 small onion, sliced

2 Tbsp. dry rice

1 tsp. salt

½ tsp. pepper

1 lb. ground beef, browned and drained

1½–2 cups tomato juice, as needed to keep dish from getting too dry

1. Combine all ingredients in slow cooker.
2. Cover. Cook on Low 6–8 hours.

10-Layer Slow Cooker Dish

Norma Saltzman   Shickley, NE

MAKES: **8 SERVINGS**
PREP. TIME: **20 MINUTES**
COOKING TIME: **4 HOURS**
IDEAL SLOW COOKER SIZE: **5-QUART**

1½ lbs. lean ground chuck

6 medium potatoes, thinly sliced, *divided*

1 medium onion, thinly sliced, *divided*

½ tsp. salt, *divided*

½ tsp. black pepper, *divided*

15-oz. can corn, undrained, *divided*

15-oz. can peas, undrained, *divided*

¼ cup water

10¾-oz. can fat-free, low-sodium cream of mushroom soup

1. Brown ground chuck in nonstick skillet. Then create the following layers in the slow cooker.
2. Layer 1: one-fourth of the potatoes, mixed with one-half the onions, salt, and pepper.
3. Layer 2: half-can of corn.
4. Layer 3: one-fourth of the potatoes.
5. Layer 4: half-can of peas.
6. Layer 5: one-fourth of the potatoes, mixed with one-half the onions, salt, and pepper.
7. Layer 6: remaining corn.
8. Layer 7: remaining potatoes.
9. Layer 8: remaining peas and water.
10. Layer 9: ground chuck.
11. Layer 10: soup.
12. Cover. Cook on High 4 hours.

Per Serving: 370 calories (90 calories from fat), 9g total fat (3.5g saturated, 0.5g trans), 30mg cholesterol, 720mg sodium, 49g total carbohydrate (7g fiber, 6g sugar), 25g protein, 0%DV vitamin A, 30%DV vitamin C, 4%DV calcium, 25%DV iron.

1-2-3-4 Casserole

Betty K. Drescher Quakertown, PA

MAKES: **8 SERVINGS**
PREP. TIME: **35 MINUTES**
COOKING TIME: **7–9 HOURS**
IDEAL SLOW COOKER SIZE: **4-QUART**

1 lb. ground beef

2 onions, sliced

3 carrots, thinly sliced

4 potatoes, thinly sliced

½ tsp. salt

⅛ tsp. pepper

1 cup cold water

½ tsp. cream of tartar

10¾-oz. can cream of mushroom soup

¼ cup milk

½ tsp. salt

⅛ tsp. pepper

1. Layer in greased slow cooker: ground beef, onions, carrots, ½ tsp. salt, and ⅛ tsp. pepper.
2. Dissolve cream of tartar in water in bowl. Toss sliced potatoes with water. Drain.
3. Combine soup and milk. Toss with potatoes. Add remaining salt and pepper. Arrange potatoes in slow cooker.
4. Cover. Cook on Low 7–9 hours.

Variations:

1. Substitute sour cream for the milk.

2. Top potatoes with ½ cup shredded cheese.

Taters 'n Beef

Maryland Massey Millington, MD

MAKES: **6–8 SERVINGS**
PREP. TIME: **20 MINUTES**
COOKING TIME: **4¼–6¼ HOURS**
IDEAL SLOW COOKER SIZE: **4-QUART**

2 lbs. ground beef, browned

1 tsp. salt

½ tsp. pepper

¼ cup chopped onions

1 cup canned tomato soup

6 potatoes, sliced

1 cup milk

1. Combined beef, salt, pepper, onions, and soup.
2. Place a layer of potatoes in bottom of slow cooker. Cover with a portion of the meat mixture. Repeat layers until ingredients are used.
3. Cover. Cook on Low 4–6 hours. Add milk and cook on High 15–20 minutes.

Variations:

1. Use home-canned spaghetti sauce instead of tomato soup.

2. Add a layer of chopped raw cabbage after each layer of sliced potatoes to add to the flavor, texture, and nutritional value of the meal.

Hamburger Vegetable Stew

Jeanne Heyerly Chenoa, IL

MAKES: **8 SERVINGS**
PREP. TIME: **20 MINUTES**
COOKING TIME: **8–10 HOURS**
IDEAL SLOW COOKER SIZE: **2–3 QUART**

2 lbs. ground beef

1 medium onion, chopped

1 garlic clove, minced

2 cups tomato juice

2–3 carrots, sliced

2–3 ribs celery, sliced

half a green pepper, chopped

2 cups green beans

2 medium potatoes, cubed

2 cups water

1 Tbsp. Worcestershire sauce

¼ tsp. dried oregano

¼ tsp. dried basil

¼ tsp. dried thyme

dash of hot pepper sauce

2 Tbsp. dry onion soup mix, *or* 1 beef bouillon cube

1 tsp. salt

¼ tsp. pepper

1. Brown meat and onion in saucepan. Drain. Stir in garlic and tomato juice. Heat to boiling.
2. Combine all ingredients in slow cooker.
3. Cover. Cook on Low 8–10 hours.

Variation: *Use 1 cup barley in place of potatoes.*

Place cooked hamburger in a strainer and rinse it under hot water to eliminate extra fat.

Supper-in-a-Dish

Martha Hershey Ronks, PA

MAKES: **8 SERVINGS**
PREP. TIME: **20 MINUTES**
COOKING TIME: **4 HOURS**
IDEAL SLOW COOKER SIZE: **4-QUART**

1 lb. ground beef, browned and drained

1½ cups sliced raw potatoes

1 cup sliced carrots

1 cup peas

½ cup chopped onions

½ cup chopped celery

¼ cup chopped green peppers

1 tsp. salt

¼ tsp. pepper

10¾-oz. can cream of chicken, *or* mushroom, soup

¼ cup milk

⅔ cup shredded sharp cheese

1. Layer ground beef, potatoes, carrots, peas, onions, celery, green peppers, salt, and pepper in slow cooker.
2. Combine soup and milk. Pour over layered ingredients. Sprinkle with cheese.
3. Cover. Cook on High 4 hours.

New Mexico Cheeseburgers

Colleen Konetzni Rio Rancho, NM

MAKES: **8 SERVINGS**
PREP. TIME: **30 MINUTES**
COOKING TIME: **7–9 HOURS**
IDEAL SLOW COOKER SIZE: **4-QUART**

1 lb. ground beef, browned

6 potatoes, peeled and sliced

½ cup chopped green chilies

1 onion, chopped

10¾-oz. can cream of mushroom soup

2 cups cubed Velveeta cheese

1. Layer beef, potatoes, green chilies, and onions in slow cooker.
2. Spread soup over top.
3. Top with cheese.
4. Cover. Cook on High 1 hour. Reduce heat to Low and cook 6–8 hours.

Halloween Hash

Sharon Miller Holmesville, OH

MAKES: **4 SERVINGS**
PREP. TIME: **20–25 MINUTES**
COOKING TIME: **2–4 HOURS**
IDEAL SLOW COOKER SIZE: **2-QUART**

1 lb. lean ground beef

½ cup chopped onion

16-oz. can whole-kernel corn, drained

16-oz. can kidney beans, drained

16-oz. can diced tomatoes

½ cup shredded cheddar cheese, *optional*

1. Brown beef and onion in a nonstick skillet until no longer pink. Drain. Place mixture in your slow cooker.
2. Layer in all remaining ingredients except the cheese.

3. Cover and cook on Low 2–4 hours, or until thoroughly hot.
4. Serve as is, or over a bed of rice or noodles. Sprinkle each serving with cheese, if you wish.

A Hearty Western Casserole

Karen Ashworth Duenweg, MO

MAKES: **5 SERVINGS**
PREP. TIME: **10 MINUTES**
COOKING TIME: **1 HOUR**
IDEAL SLOW COOKER SIZE: **4-QUART**

1 lb. ground beef, browned

16-oz. can whole corn, drained

16-oz. can red kidney beans, drained

10¾-oz. can condensed tomato soup

1 cup (4 oz.) Colby cheese

¼ cup milk

1 tsp. minced dry onion flakes

½ tsp. chili powder

1. Combine beef, corn, beans, soup, cheese, milk, onion, and chili powder in slow cooker.
2. Cover. Cook on Low 1 hour.

Variation:

1 pkg. (of 10) refrigerator biscuits

2 Tbsp. margarine

¼ cup yellow cornmeal

Dip biscuits in margarine and then in cornmeal. Bake 20 minutes or until brown. Top beef mixture with biscuits before serving.

Beef Main Dishes

Green Chili Stew

Jeanne Allen Rye, CO

MAKES: **6–8 SERVINGS**
PREP. TIME: **20 MINUTES**
COOKING TIME: **4–6 HOURS**
IDEAL SLOW COOKER SIZE: **4-QUART**

3 Tbsp. oil
2 garlic cloves, minced
1 large onion, diced
1 lb. ground sirloin
½ lb. ground pork
3 cups chicken broth
2 cups water
2 4-oz. cans diced green chilies
4 large potatoes, diced
10-oz. pkg. frozen corn
1 tsp. black pepper
1 tsp. crushed dried oregano
½ tsp. ground cumin
1 tsp. salt

1. Brown onion, garlic, sirloin, and pork in oil in skillet. Cook until meat is no longer pink.
2. Combine all ingredients in slow cooker.
3. Cover. Cook on Low 4–6 hours, or until potatoes are soft.

Tip: *Excellent served with warm tortillas or cornbread.*

Shipwreck

Betty Lahman Elkton, VA

MAKES: **8 SERVINGS**
PREP. TIME: **15 MINUTES**
COOKING TIME: **6–8 HOURS**
IDEAL SLOW COOKER SIZE: **4-QUART**

1 lb. ground beef, browned
4–5 potatoes, cut in French-fry-like strips
1–2 onions, chopped
16-oz. can light red kidney beans, drained
¼-lb. Velveeta cheese, cubed
10¾-oz. can tomato soup
1½ tsp. salt
¼ tsp. pepper
butter

1. Layer in slow cooker in this order: ground beef, potatoes, onions, kidney beans, and cheese. Pour soup over top. Season with salt and pepper. Dot with butter.
2. Cover. Cook on Low 6–8 hours.

Tip: *This is particularly good served with Parmesan cheese sprinkled on top at the table.*

Beef and Lentils

Esther Porter   Minneapolis, MN

MAKES: **12 SERVINGS**
PREP. TIME: **35 MINUTES**
COOKING TIME: **6–8 HOURS**
IDEAL SLOW COOKER SIZE: **4–5 QUART**

1 medium onion

3 whole cloves

5 cups water

1 lb. lentils

1 tsp. salt

1 bay leaf

1 lb. (or less) ground beef, browned and drained

½ cup ketchup

¼ cup molasses

2 Tbsp. brown sugar

1 tsp. dry mustard

¼ tsp. Worcestershire sauce

1 onion, finely chopped

1. Stick cloves into whole onion. Set aside.
2. In large saucepan, combine water, lentils, salt, bay leaf, and whole onion with cloves. Simmer 30 minutes.
3. Meanwhile, combine all remaining ingredients in slow cooker. Stir in simmered ingredients from saucepan. Add additional water if mixture seems dry.
4. Cover. Cook on Low 6–8 hours (check to see if lentils are tender).

Tips:
1. This freezes well.
2. Top with sour cream and/or salsa when serving.

Zucchini Hot Dish

Sharon Wantland   Menomonee Falls, WI

MAKES: **4 SERVINGS**
PREP. TIME: **15–20 MINUTES**
COOKING TIME: **2–3 HOURS**
IDEAL SLOW COOKER SIZE: **1½-QUART**

1 lb. ground beef

1 small onion, chopped, *optional*

salt and pepper to taste

4–5 6-inch-long zucchini, sliced

10¾-oz. can cream of mushroom soup

1–2 cups shredded cheddar cheese

1. Brown ground beef with onions, if you wish, along with salt and pepper in a nonstick skillet until crumbly. Drain.
2. Layer zucchini and beef mixture alternately in slow cooker.
3. Top with soup. Sprinkle with cheese.
4. Cover and cook on Low 2–3 hours, or until the zucchini is done to your liking.

Ground Beef 'n Biscuits

Karen Waggoner   Joplin, MO

MAKES: **8 SERVINGS**
PREP. TIME: **20 MINUTES**
COOKING TIME: **1–1½ HOURS**
IDEAL SLOW COOKER SIZE: **6-QUART OVAL**

1½ lbs. extra-lean ground beef

½ cup chopped celery

½ cup chopped onions

2 Tbsp. flour

1 tsp. salt

¼ tsp. black pepper

½ tsp. dried oregano

2 8-oz. cans tomato sauce

10-oz. pkg. frozen peas, thawed

2 7½-oz. cans refrigerated buttermilk biscuits

2 cups fat-free shredded cheddar cheese

1. Brown ground beef, celery, and onions in nonstick skillet.
2. Stir in flour, salt, pepper, and oregano.
3. Add tomato sauce and peas.
4. Pour into slow cooker. (A large oval cooker allows the biscuits to be arranged over top. You can also divide the mixture between two round slow cookers and accommodate the biscuits in that way.)
5. Arrange biscuits over top and sprinkle with cheese.
6. Cook uncovered on High for 1–1½ hours.

Per Serving: 370 calories (80 calories from fat), 9g total fat (3.5g saturated, 0g trans), 35mg cholesterol, 1470mg sodium, 38g total carbohydrate (3g fiber, 5g sugar), 34g protein, 20%DV vitamin A, 10%DV vitamin C, 30%DV calcium, 25%DV iron.

German Dinner

Sharon Miller Holmesville, OH

MAKES: **6 SERVINGS**
PREP. TIME: **10 MINUTES**
COOKING TIME: **9–11 HOURS**
IDEAL SLOW COOKER SIZE: **4–5-QUART**

32-oz. bag sauerkraut, drained
1 lb. extra-lean ground beef
1 small green bell pepper, grated
2 11½-oz. cans V-8 juice
½ cup chopped celery, *optional*

1. Combine all ingredients in slow cooker.
2. Cook for 1 hour on High, and then on Low 8–10 hours.

Per Serving: 170 calories (60 calories from fat), 7g total fat (3g saturated, 0g trans), 30mg cholesterol, 1160mg sodium, 10g total carbohydrate (4g fiber, 3g sugar), 17g protein, 10%DV vitamin A, 40%DV vitamin C, 6%DV calcium, 25%DV iron.

Beef-Vegetable Casserole

Edwina Stoltzfus Narvon, PA

MAKES: **8 SERVINGS**
PREP. TIME: **20 MINUTES**
COOKING TIME: **4–5 HOURS**
IDEAL SLOW COOKER SIZE: **5-QUART**

1 lb. extra-lean ground beef *or* **turkey**
1 medium onion, chopped
½ cup chopped celery
4 cups chopped cabbage
2½ cups canned stewed tomatoes, slightly mashed
1 Tbsp. flour
1 tsp. salt
1 Tbsp. sugar
¼–½ tsp. black pepper, according to your taste preference

1. Sauté meat, onion, and celery in nonstick skillet until meat is browned.
2. Pour into slow cooker.
3. Top with layers of cabbage, tomatoes, flour, salt, sugar, and pepper.
4. Cover. Cook on High 4–5 hours.

Per Serving: 140 calories (50 calories from fat), 5g total fat (2g saturated, 0g trans), 20mg cholesterol, 710mg sodium, 10g total carbohydrate (2g fiber, 6g sugar), 13g protein, 8%DV vitamin A, 20%DV vitamin C, 8%DV calcium, 10%DV iron.

Assemble all of your measured ingredients first. Then add as the recipe calls for them.

Stuffed Cabbage

Miriam Nolt New Holland, PA

MAKES: **8 SERVINGS**
PREP. TIME: **25 MINUTES**
COOKING TIME: **8–10 HOURS**
IDEAL SLOW COOKER SIZE: **5-QUART**

4 cups water

12 large cabbage leaves, cut from head at base and washed

1 lb. lean ground beef *or* lamb

½ cup rice, cooked

½ tsp. salt

¼ tsp. black pepper

¼ tsp. dried thyme

¼ tsp. nutmeg

¼ tsp. cinnamon

6-oz. can tomato paste

¾ cup water

1. Boil 4 cups water in saucepan. Turn off heat. Soak cabbage leaves in water for 5 minutes. Remove. Drain. Cool.
2. Combine ground beef, rice, salt, pepper, thyme, nutmeg, and cinnamon.
3. Place 2 Tbsp. of mixture on each cabbage leaf. Roll firmly. Stack in slow cooker.
4. Combine tomato paste and ¾ cup water. Pour over stuffed cabbage.
5. Cover. Cook on Low 8–10 hours.

Per Serving: 140 calories (50 calories from fat), 5g total fat (2g saturated, 0g trans), 20mg cholesterol, 220mg sodium, 10g total carbohydrate (2g fiber, 2g sugar), 13g protein, 10%DV vitamin A, 20%DV vitamin C, 4%DV calcium, 10%DV iron.

Stuffed Ground Beef

Mary B. Sensenig New Holland, PA

MAKES: **4 SERVINGS**
PREP. TIME: **10 MINUTES**
COOKING TIME: **4–6 HOURS**
IDEAL SLOW COOKER SIZE: **4-QUART**

2 cups ground beef

2 cups shredded cabbage

salt and pepper to taste

2 cups bread filling

2 cups tomato juice

1. Brown ground beef in a nonstick skillet. Drain.
2. Spray the inside of the cooker with nonstick cooking spray. Layer ingredients in slow cooker in this order: ground beef, cabbage, salt and pepper, bread filling.
3. Pour tomato juice over top.
4. Cook on Low 4–6 hours, or until cabbage is just tender.

Beef Main Dishes

Cedric's Casserole

Kathy Purcell Dublin, OH

MAKES: **4–6 SERVINGS**
PREP. TIME: **30 MINUTES**
COOKING TIME: **3–4 HOURS**
IDEAL SLOW COOKER SIZE: **3-QUART**

1 medium onion, chopped

3 Tbsp. butter *or* margarine

1 lb. ground beef

½–¾ tsp. salt

¼ tsp. pepper

3 cups shredded cabbage

10¾-oz. can tomato soup

1. Sauté onion in skillet in butter.
2. Add ground beef and brown. Season with salt and pepper.
3. Layer half of cabbage in slow cooker, followed by half of meat mixture. Repeat layers.
4. Pour soup over top.
5. Cover. Cook on Low 3–4 hours.
6. Serve with garlic bread and canned fruit.

Note: *I grew up with this recipe and remember my mother serving it often. It makes a wonderful potluck take-along.*

Grate ends of cheese blocks (cheddar, Swiss, Monterey Jack, etc.) together into a Ziploc bag and keep the grated cheese on hand for sprinkling over salads, casseroles, and toasted cheese bread.

Meal-in-One

Melanie L. Thrower McPherson, KS

MAKES: **6–8 SERVINGS**
PREP. TIME: **25 MINUTES**
COOKING TIME: **4 HOURS**
IDEAL SLOW COOKER SIZE: **4–5-QUART**

2 lbs. ground beef

1 onion, diced

1 green bell pepper, diced

1 tsp. salt

¼ tsp. pepper

1 large bag frozen hash brown potatoes

16-oz. container sour cream

24-oz. container cottage cheese

1 cup Monterey Jack cheese, shredded

1. Brown ground beef, onion, and green pepper in skillet. Drain. Season with salt and pepper.
2. In slow cooker, layer one-third of the potatoes, meat, sour cream, and cottage cheese. Repeat twice.
3. Cover. Cook on Low 4 hours, sprinkling Monterey Jack cheese over top during last hour.
4. Serve with red or green salsa.

Variation: *For a cheesier dish, prepare another cup of shredded cheese and sprinkle ½ cup over the first layer of potatoes, meat, sour cream, and cottage cheese, and another ½ cup over the second layer of those ingredients.*

Bean Tator Tot Casserole

Marjora Miller Archbold, OH

MAKES: **6 SERVINGS**
PREP. TIME: **5–10 MINUTES**
COOKING TIME: **4 HOURS**
IDEAL SLOW COOKER SIZE: **4-QUART**

1 lb. ground beef
½ tsp. salt
¼ tsp. pepper
1 onion, chopped
1-lb. bag frozen string beans
10¾-oz. can cream of mushroom soup
1 cup shredded cheese
21-oz. bag. frozen tator tots

1. Crumble raw ground beef in bottom of slow cooker. Sprinkle with salt and pepper.
2. Layer remaining ingredients on beef in order listed.
3. Cover. Cook on High 1 hour. Reduce heat to Low and cook 3 hours.

Variation: *In order to reduce the calorie content of this dish, use raw shredded potatoes instead of tater tots.*

Meal-in-One-Casserole

Elizabeth Yoder Millersburg, OH • *Marcella Stalter* Flanagan, IL

MAKES: **4–6 SERVINGS**
PREP. TIME: **20 MINUTES**
COOKING TIME: **4 HOURS**
IDEAL SLOW COOKER SIZE: **4-QUART**

1 lb. ground beef
1 medium onion, chopped
1 medium green pepper, chopped
15¼-oz. can whole-kernel corn, drained
4-oz. can mushrooms, drained
1 tsp. salt
¼ tsp. pepper
11-oz. jar salsa
5 cups medium egg noodles, uncooked
28-oz. can diced tomatoes, undrained
1 cup shredded cheddar cheese

1. Cook beef and onion in saucepan over medium heat until meat is no longer pink. Drain. Transfer to slow cooker.
2. Top with green pepper, corn, and mushrooms. Sprinkle with salt and pepper. Pour salsa over mushrooms. Cover and cook on Low 3 hours.
3. Cook noodles according to package in separate pan. Drain and add to slow cooker after mixture in cooker has cooked for 3 hours. Top with tomatoes. Sprinkle with cheese.
4. Cover. Cook on Low 1 more hour.

Variation: *Add uncooked noodles after salsa. Pour tomatoes and 1 cup water over all. Sprinkle with cheese. Cover and cook on Low 4 hours, or until noodles are tender.*

Nadine Martinitz Salina, KS

Beef Main Dishes

Chinese Hamburger

Esther J. Yoder Hartville, OH

MAKES: **8 SERVINGS**
PREP. TIME: **15 MINUTES**
COOKING TIME: **3–4 HOURS**
IDEAL SLOW COOKER SIZE: **4-QUART**

1 lb. ground beef, browned and drained

1 onion, diced

2 ribs celery, diced

10¾-oz. can chicken noodle soup

10¾-oz. can cream of mushroom soup

12-oz. can Chinese vegetables

salt to taste, about ¼–½ tsp.

pepper to taste, about ¼ tsp.

1 green pepper, diced

1 tsp. soy sauce

1. Combine all ingredients in slow cooker.
2. Cover. Cook on High 3–4 hours.
3. Serve over rice.

Stuffed Green Peppers with Corn

Jean Butzer Batavia, NY

MAKES: **6 SERVINGS**
PREP. TIME: **20 MINTUES**
COOKING TIME: **5–6 HOURS**
IDEAL SLOW COOKER SIZE: **5-QUART**

6 green bell peppers

½ lb. extra-lean ground beef

¼ cup finely chopped onions

1 Tbsp. chopped pimento

¾ tsp. salt

¼ tsp. black pepper

12-oz. can low-sodium whole-kernel corn, drained

1 Tbsp. Worcestershire sauce

1 tsp. prepared mustard

10¾-oz. can condensed low-sodium cream of tomato soup

1. Cut a slice off the top of each pepper. Remove core, seeds, and white membrane.
2. In a small bowl, combine beef, onions, pimento, salt, black pepper, and corn.
3. Spoon into peppers. Stand peppers up in slow cooker.
4. Combine Worcestershire sauce, mustard, and tomato soup. Pour over peppers.
5. Cover. Cook on Low 5–6 hours.

Per Serving: 170 calories (40 calories from fat), 4.5g total fat (2g saturated, 0g trans), 15mg cholesterol, 650mg sodium, 24g total carbohydrate (4g fiber, 8g sugar), 11g protein, 25%DV vitamin A, 120%DV vitamin C, 2%DV calcium, 15%DV iron.

Stuffed Green Peppers with Rice

Patricia Howard   Albuquerque, NM

MAKES: **6 SERVINGS**
PREP. TIME: **40 MINUTES**
COOKING TIME: **5–7 HOURS**
IDEAL SLOW COOKER SIZE: **5–6-QUART**

6 green peppers

1 lb. ground beef

¼ cup chopped onions

1 tsp. salt

¼ tsp. pepper

1¼ cups rice, cooked

1 Tbsp. Worcestershire sauce

8-oz. can tomato sauce

¼ cup beef broth

1. Cut stem ends from peppers. Carefully remove seeds and membrane without breaking pepper apart. Parboil in water for 5 minutes. Drain. Set aside.
2. Brown ground beef and onions in skillet. Drain off drippings. Place meat and onions in mixing bowl.
3. Add seasonings, rice, and Worcestershire sauce to meat and combine well. Stuff green peppers with mixture. Stand stuffed peppers upright in large slow cooker.
4. Mix together tomato sauce and beef broth. Pour over peppers.
5. Cover. Cook on Low 5–7 hours.

Surprise Stuffed Peppers

Dorothy VanDeest   Memphis, TN

MAKES: **4 SERVINGS**
PREP. TIME: **15 MINUTES**
COOKING TIME: **8–9 HOURS**
IDEAL SLOW COOKER SIZE: **5-QUART, OR LARGE ENOUGH THAT EACH PEPPER CAN SIT ON THE BOTTOM OF THE COOKER**

2 cups low-sodium tomato juice

6-oz. can tomato paste

2 7-oz. cans chunk-style tuna, drained and rinsed

2 Tbsp. dried onion flakes

2 Tbsp. dried veggie flakes

¼ tsp. garlic powder

4 medium green bell peppers, tops removed and seeded

1. Mix tomato juice and tomato paste, reserving 1 cup.
2. Mix remaining tomato-juice mixture with tuna, onion flakes, veggie flakes, and garlic powder.
3. Fill peppers equally with mixture. Place upright in slow cooker.
4. Pour the reserved 1 cup tomato-juice mixture over peppers.
5. Cover. Cook on Low 8–9 hours, or until peppers are done to your liking.

Per Serving: 220 calories (5 calories from fat), 0.5g total fat (0g saturated, 0g trans), 60mg cholesterol, 460mg sodium, 23g total carbohydrate (5g fiber, 9g sugar), 30g protein, 20%DV vitamin A, 200%DV vitamin C, 4%DV calcium, 10%DV iron.

Don't give up if a particular dish doesn't turn out well. Practice makes perfect. Brainstorm with experienced cooks who may be able to help solve your problem.

Pizza Rice Casserole

Jennie Martin   Richfield, PA

MAKES: **6–8 SERVINGS**
PREP. TIME: **20 MINUTES**
COOKING TIME: **6 HOURS**
IDEAL SLOW COOKER SIZE: **5-QUART**

1 lb. ground beef

1 medium onion, chopped

3 cups long-grain rice, uncooked

1 quart pizza sauce

3 cups shredded cheese, your choice of flavor

1 cup cottage cheese, *optional*

4 cups water

1. Place ground beef and chopped onion in a nonstick skillet. Brown and then drain.
2. Mix all ingredients in slow cooker.
3. Cover and cook on High for 6 hours, or until the rice is tender.

Spanish Rice

Loretta Krahn   Mt. Lake, MN

MAKES: **8 SERVINGS**
PREP. TIME: **15 MINUTES**
COOKING TIME: **6–10 HOURS**
IDEAL SLOW COOKER SIZE: **4–5 QUART**

2 lbs. ground beef, browned

2 medium onions, chopped

2 green peppers, chopped

28-oz. can tomatoes

8-oz. can tomato sauce

1½ cups water

2½ tsp. chili powder

2 tsp. salt

2 tsp. Worcestershire sauce

1½ cups rice, uncooked

1. Combine all ingredients in slow cooker.
2. Cover. Cook on Low 8–10 hours, or on High 6 hours.

Hamburger Rice Casserole

Shari Mast   Harrisonburg, VA

MAKES: **6–8 SERVINGS**
PREP. TIME: **25 MINUTES**
COOKING TIME: **4 HOURS**
IDEAL SLOW COOKER SIZE: **4-QUART**

½ lb. ground beef

1 onion, chopped

1 cup diced celery

1 tsp. dried basil

1 tsp. dried oregano

10¾-oz. can cream of mushroom soup

1 soup can water

4 cups rice, cooked

4-oz. can mushroom pieces, drained

Velveeta cheese slices

1. Brown ground beef, onion, and celery in skillet. Season with basil and oregano.
2. Combine soup and water in bowl.
3. In well greased slow cooker, layer half of rice, half of mushrooms, half of ground-beef mixture, and half of soup. Repeat layers.
4. Cover. Cook on High 4 hours.
5. Top with cheese 30 minutes before serving.
6. This casserole, served with cornbread and applesauce, makes a well-rounded meal that is quick and easy to prepare and well-received by children and adults.

Beef and Pepper Rice

Liz Ann Yoder Hartville, OH

MAKES: **4–6 SERVINGS**
PREP. TIME: **20 MINUTES**
COOKING TIME: **3–6 HOURS**
IDEAL SLOW COOKER SIZE: **3-QUART**

1 lb. ground beef
2 green peppers, *or* 1 green and 1 red pepper, coarsely chopped
1 cup chopped onions
1 cup brown rice, uncooked
2 beef bouillon cubes, crushed
3 cups water
1 Tbsp. soy sauce

1. Brown beef in skillet. Drain.
2. Combine all ingredients in slow cooker. Mix well.
3. Cover. Cook on Low 5-6 hours or on High 3 hours, or until liquid is absorbed.

Hearty Rice Casserole

Dale Peterson Rapid City, SD

MAKES: **12–16 SERVINGS**
PREP. TIME: **25 MINUTES**
COOKING TIME: **6–7 HOURS**
IDEAL SLOW COOKER SIZE: **4-QUART**

10¾-oz. can cream of mushroom soup
10¾-oz. can creamy onion soup
10¾-oz. can cream of chicken soup
1 cup water
1 lb. ground beef, browned
1 lb. pork sausage, browned
1 large onion, chopped
1 large green pepper, chopped
1½ cups long-grain rice
shredded cheese, *optional*

1. Combine all ingredients except cheese in slow cooker. Mix well.
2. Cover. Cook on Low 6-7 hours, sprinkling with cheese during last hour, if you wish.

Chili and Cheese on Rice

Dale and Shari Mast Harrisonburg, VA

MAKES: **6 SERVINGS**
PREP. TIME: **15 MINUTES**
COOKING TIME: **4 HOURS**
IDEAL SLOW COOKER SIZE: **4-QUART**

1 lb. ground beef
1 onion, diced
1 tsp. dried basil
1 tsp. dried oregano
16-oz. can light red kidney beans
15½-oz. can chili beans
1 pint stewed tomatoes, drained
rice, cooked
shredded cheddar cheese

1. Brown ground beef and onion in skillet. Season with basil and oregano.
2. Combine all ingredients except rice and cheese in slow cooker.
3. Cover. Cook on Low 4 hours.
4. Serve over cooked rice. Top with cheese.

Chili Haystacks

Judy Buller   Bluffton, OH

MAKES: **10–12 SERVINGS**
PREP. TIME: **20 MINUTES**
COOKING TIME: **1–3 HOURS**
IDEAL SLOW COOKER SIZE: **5-QUART**

2 lbs. ground beef, browned

1 small onion, chopped

2 8-oz. cans tomato sauce

2 15-oz. cans chili beans with chili gravy, *or* **red beans**

2 10-oz. cans mild enchilada sauce, *or* **mild salsa**

½ tsp. chili powder

1 tsp. garlic salt

pepper to taste

raisins

chopped apples

shredded lettuce

chopped tomatoes

shredded cheese

corn chips

rice *or* **baked potatoes**

1. Combine beef, onion, tomato sauce, chili beans, enchilada sauce, chili powder, garlic salt, and pepper. Pour into slow cooker.
2. Cover. Cook on Low 2–3 hours, or on High 1 hour.
3. Serve over baked potatoes or rice and add your choice of remaining ingredients on top.

Note: *Because this recipe offers such a wide choice of toppings, all diners are sure to find something they like. Haystacks are easy to serve buffet-style. The wide array of condiments sparks conversation—and becomes an adventure in eating. Members of my family like a little of each topping over the chili.*

Guests are often surprised to see how large their haystacks are when they're finished serving themselves. They frequently fill their entire

plates! The atmosphere can be comfortable when everything is prepared ahead. And with this recipe, the serving time can vary. Do the rice or baked potatoes in a second slow cooker.

China Dish

Lois Stoltzfus   Honey Brook, PA

MAKES: **6 SERVINGS**
PREP. TIME: **20 MINUTES**
COOKING TIME: **6–8 HOURS**
IDEAL SLOW COOKER SIZE: **4-QUART**

1½ lbs. extra-lean ground beef

10¾-oz. can cream of chicken soup

10¾-oz. can 98% fat-free cream of mushroom soup

3½ cups water

2 cups chopped celery

1 cup chopped onions

1 cup brown rice, uncooked

3 Tbsp. Worcestershire sauce

1. Brown ground beef in a nonstick skillet.
2. Combine all ingredients in slow cooker.
3. Cover. Cook on Low 6–8 hours.

Per Serving: 400 calories (140 calories from fat), 15g total fat (6g saturated, 1g trans), 45mg cholesterol, 950mg sodium, 36g total carbohydrate (2g fiber, 3g sugar), 28g protein, 6%DV vitamin A, 8%DV vitamin C, 8%DV calcium, 20%DV iron.

African Beef Curry

Rebecca Leichty   Harrisonburg, VA

MAKES: **6 SMALL SERVINGS**
PREP. TIME: **20 MINUTES**
COOKING TIME: **6–8 HOURS**
IDEAL SLOW COOKER SIZE: **3-QUART**

1 lb. extra-lean ground beef, browned

1 large onion, thinly sliced

1 green bell pepper, diced

1 tomato, peeled and diced

1 apple, peeled, cored, and diced

1–2 tsp. curry (or more to taste)

4 cups prepared rice

1. Spray slow cooker with fat-free cooking spray.
2. Add all ingredients except rice in slow cooker and mix well.
3. Cover and cook on High 6–8 hours.
4. Serve over hot rice.

Per Serving: 340 calories (70 calories from fat), 7g total fat (3g saturated, 0g trans), 30mg cholesterol, 50mg sodium, 47g total carbohydrate (2g fiber, 6g sugar), 20g protein, 6%DV vitamin A, 20%DV vitamin C, 4%DV calcium, 20%DV iron.

Tip: *This is interesting served with a spoonful of low-fat or non-fat "lemon-enhanced" vanilla yogurt on top of each individual dish.*

Variation: *You can thicken this by stirring in 6-oz. can of tomato paste in Step 2, if you wish.*

Beef and Noodle Casserole

Delores Scheel   West Fargo, N

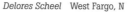

MAKES: **10 SERVINGS**
PREP. TIME: **20 MINUTES**
COOKING TIME: **4 HOURS**
IDEAL SLOW COOKER SIZE: **4-QUART**

1 lb. extra-lean ground beef

1 medium onion, chopped

1 medium green bell pepper, chopped

17-oz. can whole-kernel corn, drained

4-oz. can mushroom stems and pieces, drained

1 tsp. salt

¼ tsp. black pepper

11-oz. jar salsa

5 cups dry medium egg noodles, cooked

28-oz. can low-sodium diced tomatoes, undrained

1 cup low-fat shredded cheddar cheese

1. Brown ground beef and onion in nonstick skillet over medium heat. Transfer to slow cooker.
2. Top with remaining ingredients in order listed.
3. Cover. Cook on Low 4 hours.

Per Serving: 460 calories (100 calories from fat), 11g total fat (4g saturated, 0g trans), 75mg cholesterol, 1300mg sodium, 61g total carbohydrate (7g fiber, 9g sugar), 31g protein, 15%DV vitamin A, 30%DV vitamin C, 25%DV calcium, 30%DV iron.

Noodle Hamburger Dish

Esther J. Yoder Hartville, OH

MAKES: **10 SERVINGS**
PREP. TIME: **20 MINUTES**
COOKING TIME: **3–4 HOURS**
IDEAL SLOW COOKER SIZE: **4–5-QUART**

1½ lbs. ground beef, browned and drained

1 green pepper, diced

1 quart whole tomatoes

10¾-oz. can cream of mushroom soup

1 large onion, diced

1½ Tbsp. Worcestershire sauce

8-oz. pkg. noodles, uncooked

1 tsp. salt

¼ tsp. pepper

1 cup shredded cheese

1. Combine all ingredients except cheese in slow cooker.
2. Cover. Cook on High 3–4 hours.
3. Sprinkle with cheese before serving.

Yum-e-setti

Elsie Schlabach Millersburg, OH

MAKES: **6–8 SERVINGS**
PREP. TIME: **20 MINUTES**
COOKING TIME: **2–3 HOURS**
IDEAL SLOW COOKER SIZE: **4–5-QUART**

1½ lbs. ground beef, browned and drained

10¾-oz. can tomato soup

8-oz. pkg. wide noodles, cooked

10¾-oz. can cream of chicken soup

1 cup chopped celery, cooked tender

2 tsp. salt

1 lb. frozen mixed vegetables

½ lb. Velveeta cheese, cubed

1. Combine ground beef and tomato soup.
2. Combine chicken soup, noodles, and celery.
3. Layer beef mixture, chicken mixture, and vegetables. Sprinkle with salt. Lay cheese over top.
4. Cover. Cook on Low 2–3 hours.

Variation: *For more "bite," use shredded cheddar cheese instead of cubed Velveeta.*

Brown large quantities (10 lbs.) of ground beef, seasoned with onion, basil, and oregano to taste. Drain and cool. Freeze in pint freezer containers. The meat is readily available with no prep time or cleanup needed when preparing a slow cooker recipe or casserole that calls for browned ground beef.

Shell Casserole

Jean Butzer   Batavia, NY

MAKES: **4–5 SERVINGS**
PREP. TIME: **20 MINUTES**
COOKING TIME: **2¼–3¼ HOURS**
IDEAL SLOW COOKER SIZE: **4-QUART**

1 lb. ground beef

1 small onion, chopped

¾ tsp. salt

¼ tsp. garlic powder

1 tsp. Worcestershire sauce

¼ cup flour

1¼ cups hot water

2 tsp. beef bouillon granules

2 Tbsp. red wine

6 oz. medium-sized shell pasta, uncooked

4-oz. can sliced mushrooms, drained

1 cup sour cream

1. Brown ground beef and onion in saucepan. Drain. Place in slow cooker.
2. Stir in salt, garlic powder, Worcestershire sauce, and flour.
3. Add water, bouillon, and wine. Mix well.
4. Cover. Cook on Low 2–3 hours.
5. Cook pasta in separate pan according to package directions. Stir cooked pasta, mushrooms, and sour cream into slow cooker. Cover. Cook on High 10–15 minutes.

Add 3 Tbsp. oil to water before cooking pasta. It keeps it from sticking together.

Beef and Macaroni

Esther J. Yoder   Hartville, OH

MAKES: **4–5 SERVINGS**
PREP. TIME: **20 MINUTES**
COOKING TIME: **2–2½ HOURS**
IDEAL SLOW COOKER SIZE: **3-QUART**

1 lb. ground beef

1 small onion, chopped

half a green pepper, chopped

1 cup macaroni, cooked

½ tsp. dried basil

½ tsp. dried thyme

1 tsp. Worcestershire sauce

1 tsp. salt

10¾-oz. can cheddar cheese soup

1. Brown beef, onions, and green pepper in skillet. Pour off drippings and place meat and vegetables in slow cooker.
2. Combine all ingredients in cooker.
3. Cover. Cook on High 2–2½ hours, stirring once or twice.
4. Serve with broccoli and applesauce.

Plenty More in the Kitchen

Jean Robinson   Cinnaminson, NJ

MAKES: **12–16 SERVINGS**
PREP. TIME: **30 MINUTES**
COOKING TIME: **5 HOURS**
IDEAL SLOW COOKER SIZE: **6-QUART**

3 lbs. ground beef

1 cup chopped onions

1 Tbsp. oil

26-oz. jar tomato sauce *or* spaghetti sauce

1 tsp. salt

2 tsp. chili powder

1 tsp. pepper

2 Tbsp. dark brown sugar

16-oz. can whole-kernel corn

2 14½-oz. cans beef broth

8-oz. pkg. dry elbow macaroni

1 cup shredded sharp cheese

1. Brown beef and onion in oil.
2. Combine all ingredients except cheese. Pour into slow cooker.
3. Cover. Cook on High 1 hour. Turn to Low and cook 4 more hours.
4. Sprinkle with cheese and cook 10 minutes more.

Note: *This is a tried and true recipe adapted from an old 1984 Pennsylvania Grange Cookbook. An easy meal to carry outside to the picnic table or a Little League game.*

Variation: *You can change the balance of ingredients by using only 1–1½ lbs. ground beef and adding another ½–1 cup dry macaroni.*

Chili Spaghetti

Clara Newswanger   Gordonville, PA

MAKES: **8–10 SERVINGS**
PREP. TIME: **25 MINUTES**
COOKING TIME: **4 HOURS**
IDEAL SLOW COOKER SIZE: **4-QUART**

½ cup diced onions

2 cups tomato juice

2 tsp. chili powder

1 tsp. salt

¾ cup shredded mild cheese

1½ lbs. ground beef, browned

12-oz. dry spaghetti, cooked

1. Combine all ingredients in slow cooker.
2. Cover. Cook on Low 4 hours. Check mixture about halfway through the cooking time. If it's becoming dry, stir in an additional cup of tomato juice.

Variations:
1. Add 8-oz. can sliced mushrooms to Step 1.
2. Use 2 Tbsp. chili powder instead of 2 tsp. chili powder for added flavor.

Granny's Delight

Anna B. Stoltzfus Honey Brook, PA

MAKES: **5 SERVINGS**
PREP. TIME: **20 MINUTES**
COOKING TIME: **1½ HOURS**
IDEAL SLOW COOKER SIZE: **6-QUART**

1 lb. ground beef

1 small onion, chopped

3 cups dry macaroni

1 cup shredded cheddar cheese

4 cups spaghetti sauce, your favorite packaged or homemade

½ cup water

1. Brown beef with chopped onion in a nonstick skillet. Drain.
2. Spray interior of slow cooker with nonstick cooking spray. Place all ingredients into slow cooker and fold together gently.
3. Cover and cook on High for 1½ hours, or until macaroni is tender but not mushy.

Variation: *Add ½ tsp. salt, ¼–½ tsp. pepper, according to your taste preference, and 2 cloves minced garlic.*

Karen Waggoner Joplin, MO

Creamy Hamburger Topping

Andrea Cunningham Arlington, KS

MAKES: **8 SERVINGS**
PREP. TIME: **15 MINUTES**
COOKING TIME: **3–5 HOURS**
IDEAL SLOW COOKER SIZE: **4–6-QUART**

1 lb. ground beef

8 ozs. shredded cheese, your choice of flavors

1 onion, diced

10¾-oz. can cream of mushroom soup

12-oz. can diced tomatoes, undrained

1. Brown ground beef in a nonstick skillet. Drain.
2. Combine all ingredients in your slow cooker.
3. Cook on Low 3-5 hours, or until heated through.
4. Serve over cooked pasta.

Ground Beef Goulash

Pat Bertsche Flanagan, IL

MAKES: **10 SERVINGS**
PREP. TIME: **10 MINUTES**
COOKING TIME: **5–6 HOURS**
IDEAL SLOW COOKER SIZE: **4-QUART**

1 lb. extra-lean ground beef

1 large onion, sliced

1 clove garlic, minced

½ cup ketchup

2 Tbsp. Worcestershire sauce

1 Tbsp. brown sugar

1–1½ tsp. salt

2 tsp. paprika

½ tsp. dry mustard

1 cup water

¼ cup flour

¼ cup cold water

1. Place meat in slow cooker. Cover with onions.
2. Combine garlic, ketchup, Worcestershire sauce, sugar, salt, paprika, mustard, and 1 cup water. Pour over meat.
3. Cook on Low 5–6 hours.
4. Dissolve flour in ¼ cup cold water. Stir into meat mixture.
5. Cook on High 10–15 minutes, or until slightly thickened.
6. Serve over noodles or rice.

———————————

Per Serving: 90 calories (20 calories from fat), 2.5g total fat (1g saturated, 0g trans), 25mg cholesterol, 660mg sodium, 9g total carbohydrate (0.5g fiber, 3g sugar), 10g protein, 8%DV vitamin A, 2%DV vitamin C, 2%DV calcium, 8%DV iron.

Variation: *To brighten the flavor, you may add ¼ cup pickle cubes or 2 Tbsp. lemon zest when stirring in thickening in Step 4.*

Cheese and Pasta in a Pot

Cathy Boshart Lebanon, PA

MAKES: **8 SERVINGS**
PREP. TIME: **35–40 MINUTES**
COOKING TIME: **2–3 HOURS**
IDEAL SLOW COOKER SIZE: **5-QUART**

2 lbs. ground beef

1 Tbsp. oil

2 medium onions, chopped

1 garlic clove, minced

14-oz. jar spaghetti sauce

16-oz. can stewed tomatoes

4-oz. can sliced mushrooms, undrained

8 ozs. dry shell macaroni, cooked al dente

1½ pints sour cream

½ lb. provolone cheese, sliced

½ lb. mozzarella cheese, thinly sliced or shredded

1. Brown ground beef in oil in skillet. Drain off all but 2 Tbsp. drippings.
2. Add onions, garlic, spaghetti sauce, stewed tomatoes, and undrained mushrooms to drippings. Mix well. Simmer 20 minutes, or until onions are soft.
3. Pour half of macaroni into slow cooker. Cover with half the tomato/meat sauce. Spread half the sour cream over sauce. Top with provolone cheese. Repeat, ending with mozzarella cheese.
4. Cover. Cook on High 2 hours, or on Low 3 hours.

Cheeseburger Casserole

Erma Kauffman   Cochranville, PA

MAKES: **6 SERVINGS**
PREP. TIME: **20 MINUTES**
COOKING TIME: **3 HOURS**
IDEAL SLOW COOKER SIZE: **3-QUART**

1 lb. ground beef
1 small onion, chopped
1 tsp. salt
dash of pepper
½ cup bread crumbs
1 egg
tomato juice to moisten
4½ cups mashed potatoes (leftover mashed potatoes work well)
9 slices American cheese

1. Combine beef, onions, salt, pepper, bread crumbs, egg, and tomato juice. Place one-third of mixture in slow cooker.
2. Spread with one-third of mashed potatoes and 3 slices cheese. Repeat 2 times.
3. Cover. Cook on Low 3 hours.

Stuffed "Baked" Topping

Fannie Miller   Hutchinson, KS

MAKES: **12 SERVINGS**
PREP. TIME: **35 MINUTES**
COOKING TIME: **1 HOUR**
IDEAL SLOW COOKER SIZE: **5-QUART**

3 lbs. ground beef
1 cup chopped green peppers
½ cup chopped onions
6 Tbsp. butter
¼ cup flour
3 cups milk
½ cup pimento *or* chopped sweet red peppers
¾ lb. cheddar cheese

¾ lb. your favorite mild cheese
½ tsp. hot pepper sauce
¼ tsp. dry mustard
salt to taste
12 baked potatoes

1. Brown ground beef, green peppers, and onions in butter. Transfer mixture to slow cooker, reserving drippings.
2. Stir flour into drippings. Slowly add milk. Cook until thickened.
3. Add pimento, cheeses, and seasonings. Pour over ingredients in slow cooker.
4. Cover. Heat on Low.
5. Serve over baked potatoes, each one split open on an individual dinner plate.

Tastes-Like-Turkey

Lizzie Weaver   Ephrata, PA

MAKES: **6 SERVINGS**
PREP. TIME: **10–15 MINUTES**
COOKING TIME: **3–8 HOURS**
IDEAL SLOW COOKER SIZE: **4–5 QUART**

2 lbs. hamburger, browned
1 tsp. salt
½ tsp. pepper
2 10¾-oz. cans cream of chicken soup
10¾-oz. can cream of celery soup
4 scant cups milk
1 large pkg. bread stuffing *or* large loaf of bread, torn in pieces

1. Combine all ingredients in large buttered slow cooker.
2. Cover. Cook on High 3 hours, or on Low 6–8 hours.

Dried Beef and Noodles Casserole

Mary B. Sensenig New Holland, PA

MAKES: **4 SERVINGS**
PREP. TIME: **5 MINUTES**
COOKING TIME: **3–3½ HOURS**
IDEAL SLOW COOKER SIZE: **4-QUART**

8-oz. pkg. dry noodles

10¾-oz. can cream of mushroom soup

1 cup milk

¼ lb. dried beef, shredded

1 cup shredded cheese, *optional*

1. Cook noodles as directed on package. Drain and rinse with cold water.
2. In a mixing bowl, blend soup and milk together.
3. Spray the interior of the cooker. Layer ingredients in cooker in this order: cooked noodles, soup-milk mixture, dried beef.
4. Cover and cook on Low for 2½–3 hours. Sprinkle cheese over top, if you wish. Cover and continue cooking another half hour.

Shredded Beef for Tacos

Dawn Day Westminster, CA

MAKES: **6–8 SERVINGS**
PREP. TIME: **15 MINUTES**
COOKING TIME: **6–8 HOURS**
IDEAL SLOW COOKER SIZE: **4-QUART**

2–3-lb. round roast, cut into large chunks

1 large onion, chopped

3 Tbsp. oil

2 serrano chilies, chopped

3 garlic cloves, minced

1 tsp. salt

1 cup water

1. Brown meat and onion in oil. Transfer to slow cooker.
2. Add chilies, garlic, salt, and water.
3. Cover. Cook on High 6–8 hours.
4. Pull meat apart with two forks until shredded.
5. Serve with fresh tortillas, lettuce, tomatoes, cheese, and guacamole.

Southwestern Flair

Phyllis Attig Reynolds, IL

MAKES: **8–12 SERVINGS**
PREP. TIME: **5 MINUTES**
COOKING TIME: **9 HOURS**
IDEAL SLOW COOKER SIZE: **4-QUART**

3–4-lb. chuck roast *or* flank steak

1 envelope dry taco seasoning

1 cup chopped onions

1 Tbsp. white vinegar

1¼ cup green chilies

flour tortillas

shredded cheese

refried beans

shredded lettuce

chopped tomatoes

salsa

sour cream

guacamole

1. Combine meat, taco seasoning, onions, vinegar, and chilies in slow cooker.
2. Cover. Cook on Low 9 hours.
3. Shred meat with fork.
4. Serve with tortillas and your choice of the remaining ingredients.

Beef Enchiladas

Jane Talso   Albuquerque, NM

MAKES: **12–16 SERVINGS**
PREP. TIME: **15 MINUTES**
COOKING TIME: **4–5 HOURS**
IDEAL SLOW COOKER SIZE: **5–6-QUART**

4-lb. boneless chuck roast

2 Tbsp. oil

4 cups sliced onions

2 tsp. salt

2 tsp. black pepper

2 tsp. cumin seeds

2 4½-oz. cans peeled, diced green chilies

14½-oz. can peeled, diced tomatoes

8 large tortillas (10–12 inch size)

1 lb. cheddar cheese, shredded

4 cups green *or* red enchilada sauce

1. Brown roast on all sides in oil in saucepan. Place roast in slow cooker.
2. Add remaining ingredients except tortillas, cheese, and sauce.
3. Cover. Cook on High 4–5 hours.
4. Shred meat with fork and return to slow cooker.
5. Warm tortillas in oven. Heat enchilada sauce. Fill each tortilla with ¾ cup beef mixture and ½ cup cheese. Roll up and serve with sauce.

Variation: *Use 2 lbs. ground beef instead of chuck roast. Brown without oil in saucepan, along with chopped onions.*

Slow-Cooked Steak Fajitas

Virginia Graybill   Hershey, PA

MAKES: **12 SERVINGS**
PREP. TIME: **25 MINUTES**
COOKING TIME: **8½–9½ HOURS**
IDEAL SLOW COOKER SIZE: **4-QUART**

1½ lbs. beef flank steak

15-oz. can low-sodium diced tomatoes with garlic and onion, undrained

1 jalapeño pepper, seeded and chopped*

2 garlic cloves, minced

1 tsp. ground coriander

1 tsp. ground cumin

1 tsp. chili powder

½ tsp. salt

2 medium onions, sliced

2 medium green bell peppers, julienned

2 medium sweet red bell peppers, julienned

1 Tbsp. minced fresh parsley

2 tsp. cornstarch

1 Tbsp. water

12 6-inch flour tortillas, warmed

¾ cup fat-free sour cream

¾ cup low-sodium salsa

1. Slice steak thinly into strips across grain. Place in slow cooker.
2. Add tomatoes, jalapeño, garlic, coriander, cumin, chili powder, and salt.
3. Cover. Cook on Low 7 hours.
4. Add onions, peppers, and parsley.
5. Cover. Cook 1–2 hours longer, or until meat is tender.
6. Combine cornstarch and water until smooth. Gradually stir into slow cooker.
7. Cover. Cook on High 30 minutes, or until slightly thickened.
8. Using a slotted spoon, spoon about ½ cup of meat mixture down the center of each tortilla.

9. Add 1 Tbsp. sour cream and 1 Tbsp. salsa to each.
10. Fold bottom of tortilla over filling and roll up.

———————————

Per Serving: 250 calories (60 calories from fat), 7g total fat (2g saturated, 0g trans), 35mg cholesterol, 570mg sodium, 31g total carbohydrate (2g fiber, 4g sugar), 16g protein, 30%DV vitamin A, 60%DV vitamin C, 10%DV calcium, 20%DV iron.

* *When cutting jalapeño peppers, use rubber or plastic gloves to protect your hands. Avoid touching your face.*

Slow Cooker Fajita Stew

Sara Puskar Abingdon, MD
Nancy Wagner Graves Manhattan, KS

MAKES: **8 SERVINGS**
PREP. TIME: **15 MINTUES**
COOKING TIME: **6½–8½ HOURS**
IDEAL SLOW COOKER SIZE: **3–4-QUART**

2½ lbs. boneless beef top round steak
1 onion, chopped
1-oz. envelope dry fajita seasoning mix (about 2 Tbsp.)
14-oz. can diced tomatoes, undrained
1 red bell pepper, cut into 1-inch pieces
¼ cup flour
¼ cup water

1. Trim excess fat from beef and cut into 2-inch pieces. Combine with onion in slow cooker.
2. Mix together fajita seasoning and undrained tomatoes. Pour over beef.
3. Place cut-up peppers on top.
4. Cover. Cook on Low 6–8 hours, or until beef is tender.
5. Combine flour and water in a small bowl. Stir well to mix.
6. Gradually add to slow cooker.

7. Cover. Cook on High 15–20 minutes until thickened, stirring occasionally.

———————————

Per Serving: 320 calories (60 calories from fat), 7g total fat (2.5g saturated, 0g trans), 85mg cholesterol, 330mg sodium, 31g total carbohydrate (2g fiber, 3g sugar), 31g protein, 20%DV vitamin A, 20%DV vitamin C, 4%DV calcium, 25%DV iron.

Tip: *This is delicious served over hot rice.*

Mexican Cornbread

Jeanne Heyerly Chenoa, IL

MAKES: **6 SERVINGS**
PREP. TIME: **20 MINUTES**
COOKING TIME: **4½–6 HOURS**
IDEAL SLOW COOKER SIZE: **4-QUART**

16-oz. can cream-style corn
1 cup cornmeal
½ tsp. baking soda
1 tsp. salt
¼ cup oil
1 cup milk
2 eggs, beaten
½ cup taco sauce
2 cups shredded cheddar cheese
1 medium onion, chopped
1 garlic clove, minced
4-oz. can diced green chilies
1 lb. ground beef, lightly cooked and drained

1. Combine corn, cornmeal, baking soda, salt, oil, milk, eggs, and taco sauce. Pour half of mixture into slow cooker.
2. Layer cheese, onion, garlic, green chilies, and ground beef on top of cornmeal mixture. Cover with remaining cornmeal mixture.
3. Cover. Cook on High 1 hour and on Low 3½–4 hours, or only on Low 6 hours.

Tamale Pie

Jeannine Janzen   Elbing, KS

MAKES: **8 SERVINGS**
PREP. TIME: **10 MINUTES**
COOKING TIME: **4 HOURS**
IDEAL SLOW COOKER SIZE: **4-QUART**

¾ cup cornmeal

1½ cups milk

1 egg, beaten

1 lb. ground beef, browned and drained

1 envelope dry chili seasoning mix

16-oz. can diced tomatoes

16-oz. can corn, drained

1 cup shredded cheddar cheese

1. Combine cornmeal, milk, and egg.
2. Stir in meat, chili seasoning mix, tomatoes, and corn until well blended. Pour into slow cooker.
3. Cover. Cook on High 1 hour, then on Low 3 hours.
4. Sprinkle with cheese. Cook another 5 minutes until cheese is melted.

Tostadas

Elizabeth L. Richards   Rapid City, SD

MAKES: **6–10 SERVINGS**
PREP. TIME: **15 MINUTES**
COOKING TIME: **6 HOURS**
IDEAL SLOW COOKER SIZE: **3–4-QUART**

1 lb. ground beef, browned

2 cans refried beans

1 envelope dry taco seasoning mix

8-oz. can tomato sauce

½ cup water

10 tostada shells

1½ cups shredded lettuce

2 tomatoes, diced

½ lb. shredded cheddar cheese

1 can sliced black olives

1 pint sour cream

guacamole

salsa

1. Combine ground beef, refried beans, taco seasoning mix, tomato sauce, and water in slow cooker.
2. Cover. Cook on Low 6 hours.
3. Crisp tostada shells.
4. Spread hot mixture on tostada shells. Top with remaining ingredients.

Pecos River Red-Frito Pie

Donna Barnitz   Jenks, OK

MAKES: **6 SERVINGS**
PREP. TIME: **10 MINUTES**
COOKING TIME: **8–10 HOURS**
IDEAL SLOW COOKER SIZE: **4-QUART**

1 large onion, chopped coarsely

3 lbs. coarsely ground hamburger

2 garlic cloves, minced

3 Tbsp. ground hot red chili peppers

2 Tbsp. ground mild red chili peppers

1½ cups water

corn chips

shredded Monterey Jack cheese

shredded cheddar cheese

1. Combine onion, hamburger, garlic, chilies, and water in slow cooker.
2. Cover. Cook on Low 8–10 hours. Drain.
3. Serve over corn chips. Top with mixture of Monterey Jack and cheddar cheeses.

Nachos Dinner

Arlene Miller Hutchinson, KS

PICTURED
ON PAGE
166

MAKES: **8 SERVINGS**
PREP. TIME: **15 MINUTES**
COOKING TIME: **1 HOUR**
IDEAL SLOW COOKER SIZE: **4-QUART**

1 lb. ground beef

¼ cup diced onions

¼ cup diced green peppers

1 pint taco sauce

1 can refried beans

10¾-oz. can cream of mushroom soup

1 envelope dry taco seasoning

salt to taste

2 cups Velveeta *or* cheddar cheese

tortilla chips

lettuce

chopped tomatoes

sour cream

1. Brown ground beef, onions, and green peppers in saucepan. Drain.
2. Combine all ingredients except tortilla chips, lettuce, tomatoes, and sour cream in slow cooker.
3. Cover. Cook on High 1 hour, stirring occasionally until cheese is fully melted.
4. Pour into serving bowl and serve immediately with chips, lettuce, tomatoes, and sour cream, or turn to Low to keep warm and serve from cooker.

Keep a clean work area — as clean as possible. Clutter can cause confusion which can lead to mistakes.

Slow Cooker Enchiladas

Robin Schrock Millersburg, OH

MAKES: **6 SERVINGS**
PREP. TIME: **30 MINTUES**
COOKING TIME: **5–7 HOURS**
IDEAL SLOW COOKER SIZE: **4-QUART**

1 lb. lean ground beef

1 cup onions, chopped

½ cup green bell pepper, chopped

16-oz. can pinto *or* kidney beans, rinsed and drained

10-oz. can diced tomatoes and green chilies

1 cup water

1 tsp. chili powder

16-oz. can black beans, rinsed and drained

½ tsp. ground cumin

½ tsp. salt

¼ tsp. black pepper

dash of dried red pepper flakes and/or several drops Tabasco sauce, if you like

1 cup shredded low-fat sharp cheddar cheese

1 cup shredded low-fat Monterey Jack cheese

6 flour tortillas (6 or 7 inches)

1. In a nonstick skillet, brown beef, onions, and green pepper.
2. Add remaining ingredients, except cheeses and tortillas. Bring to a boil.
3. Reduce heat. Cover and simmer for 10 minutes.
4. Combine cheeses in a bowl.
5. In slow cooker, layer about ¾ cup beef mixture, one tortilla, and about ¼ cup cheese. Repeat layers until all ingredients are used.
6. Cover. Cook on Low 5–7 hours.

Per Serving: 490 calories (110 calories from fat), 12g total fat (4.5g saturated, 0g trans), 35mg cholesterol, 1480mg sodium, 51g total carbohydrate (8g fiber, 6g sugar), 43g protein, 10%DV vitamin A, 20%DV vitamin C, 80%DV calcium, 30%DV iron.

Mexican Goulash

Sheila Plock Boalsburg, PA

PICTURED
ON PAGE
234

MAKES: **8–10 SERVINGS**
PREP. TIME: **45 MINUTES**
COOKING TIME: **3–4 HOURS**
IDEAL SLOW COOKER SIZE: **5-QUART**

1½–2 lbs. ground beef
2 onions, chopped
1 green pepper, chopped
½ cup celery, chopped
1 garlic clove, minced
28-oz. can whole tomatoes, cut up
6-oz. can tomato paste
4¼-oz. can sliced black olives, drained
14½-oz. can green beans, drained
15¼-oz. can Mexicorn, drained
15-oz. can dark red kidney beans
diced jalapeño peppers to taste
1 tsp. salt
¼ tsp. pepper
1 Tbsp. chili powder
3 dashes Tabasco sauce
shredded cheddar cheese

1. Brown ground beef. Reserve drippings and transfer beef to slow cooker.
2. Sauté onions, pepper, celery, and garlic in drippings in skillet. Transfer to slow cooker.
3. Add remaining ingredients. Mix well.
4. Cover. Cook on High 3–4 hours.
5. Sprinkle individual servings with shredded cheese. Serve with tortilla chips.

Tortilla Bake

Kelly Evenson Pittsboro, NC

MAKES: **6–8 SERVINGS**
PREP. TIME: **20 MINUTES**
COOKING TIME: **6–8 HOURS**
IDEAL SLOW COOKER SIZE: **3-QUART**

10¾-oz. can cheddar cheese soup
1½-oz. pkg. dry taco seasoning mix
8 corn tortillas
1½ lbs. ground beef, browned and drained
3 medium tomatoes, coarsely chopped
sour cream
shredded cheese
green onions, thinly sliced
bell peppers, cut-up
diced avocado
shredded lettuce

1. Combine soup and taco seasoning.
2. Cut each tortilla into 6 wedges. Spoon one-quarter of ground beef into slow cooker. Top with one-quarter of all tortilla wedges. Spoon one-quarter of soup mixture on tortillas. Top with one-quarter of tomatoes. Repeat layers 3 times.
3. Cover. Cook on Low 6–8 hours.
4. To serve, spoon onto plates and offer remaining ingredients as toppings.

When testing new recipes have your family rate them. Write comments, along with the date that you made the recipe, in the page margins next to the recipe.

Three-Bean Burrito Bake

Darla Sathre   Baxter, MN

MAKES: **6 SERVINGS**
PREP. TIME: **30 MINUTES**
COOKING TIME: **8–10 HOURS**
IDEAL SLOW COOKER SIZE: **4-QUART**

1 Tbsp. oil

1 onion, chopped

1 green bell pepper, chopped

2 garlic cloves, minced

16-oz. can pinto beans, drained

16-oz. can kidney beans, drained

15-oz. can black beans, drained

4-oz. can sliced black olives, drained

4-oz. can green chilies

2 15-oz. cans diced tomatoes

1 tsp. chili powder

1 tsp. ground cumin

6–8 6-inch flour tortillas

2 cups shredded Co-Jack cheese

sour cream

1. Sauté onions, green peppers, and garlic in large skillet in oil.
2. Add beans, olives, chilies, tomatoes, chili powder, and cumin.
3. In greased slow cooker, layer ¾ cup vegetables, a tortilla, ⅓ cup cheese. Repeat layers until all those ingredients are used, ending with sauce.
4. Cover. Cook on Low 8–10 hours.
5. Serve with dollops of sour cream on individual servings.

Taco Casserole

Marcia S. Myer   Manheim, PA

MAKES: **6 SERVINGS**
PREP. TIME: **25 MINUTES**
COOKING TIME: **7–8 HOURS**
IDEAL SLOW COOKER SIZE: **3-QUART**

1½ lbs. ground beef, browned

14½-oz. can diced tomatoes with chilies

10¾-oz. can cream of onion soup

1 pkg. dry taco seasoning mix

¼ cup water

6 corn tortillas cut in ½-inch strips

½ cup sour cream

1 cup shredded cheddar cheese

2 green onions, sliced, *optional*

1. Combine beef, tomatoes, soup, seasoning mix, and water in slow cooker.
2. Stir in tortilla strips.
3. Cover. Cook on Low 7–8 hours.
4. Spread sour cream over casserole. Sprinkle with cheese.
5. Cover. Let stand 5 minutes until cheese melts.
6. Remove cover. Garnish with green onions. Allow to stand for 15 more minutes before serving.

Casserole Verde

Julia Fisher New Carlisle, OH

MAKES: **6 SERVINGS**
PREP. TIME: **35 MINUTES**
COOKING TIME: **4 HOURS**
IDEAL SLOW COOKER SIZE: **4-QUART**

1 lb. ground beef
1 small onion, chopped
⅛ tsp. garlic powder
8-oz. can tomato sauce
⅓ cup chopped black olives
4-oz. can sliced mushrooms
8-oz. container sour cream
8-oz. container cottage cheese
4¼-oz. can chopped green chilies
12-oz. pkg. tortilla chips
8 ozs. Monterey Jack cheese, shredded

1. Brown ground beef, onions, and garlic in skillet. Drain. Add tomato sauce, olives, and mushrooms.
2. In a separate bowl, combine sour cream, cottage cheese, and green chilies.
3. In slow cooker, layer a third of the chips, and half the ground beef mixture, half the sour cream mixture, and half the shredded cheese. Repeat all layers, except reserve last third of the chips to add just before serving.
4. Cover. Cook on Low 4 hours.
5. Ten minutes before serving time, scatter reserved chips over top and continue cooking, uncovered.

Tiajuana Tacos

Helen Kenagy Carlsbad, NM

MAKES: **6 SERVINGS**
PREP. TIME: **20 MINUTES**
COOKING TIME: **2 HOURS**
IDEAL SLOW COOKER SIZE: **3½-QUART**

3 cups cooked chopped beef
1-lb. can refried beans
½ cup chopped onions
½ cup chopped green peppers
½ cup chopped ripe olives
8-oz. can tomato sauce
3 tsp. chili powder
1 Tbsp. Worcestershire sauce
½ tsp. garlic powder
¼ tsp. pepper
¼ tsp. paprika
⅛ tsp. celery salt
⅛ tsp. ground nutmeg
¾ cup water
1 tsp. salt
1 cup crushed corn chips
6 taco shells
shredded lettuce
chopped tomatoes
shredded cheddar cheese

1. Combine first 15 ingredients in slow cooker.
2. Cover. Cook on High 2 hours.
3. Just before serving, fold in corn chips.
4. Spoon mixture into taco shells. Top with lettuce, tomatoes, and cheese.

Easy Crock Taco Filling

Joanne Good   Wheaton, IL

MAKES: **4–6 SERVINGS**
PREP. TIME: **20 MINUTES**
COOKING TIME: **6–8 HOURS**
IDEAL SLOW COOKER SIZE: **4-QUART**

1 large onion, chopped

1 lb. ground beef

2 15-oz. cans chili beans

15-oz. can Santa Fe, *or* Mexican, *or* Fiesta corn

¾ cup water

¼ tsp. cayenne pepper, *optional*

½ tsp. garlic powder, *optional*

1. Brown ground beef and chopped onion in a nonstick skillet. Drain.
2. Mix all ingredients together in the slow cooker, blending well.
3. Cover and cook on Low for 6–8 hours.

Tips:

1. You may want to add more or less than ¾ cup water to this recipe, depending upon how hot and fast your slow cooker cooks and how tight-fitting its lid is.

2. Serve in warmed, soft corn tortillas or hard taco shells. Or serve as a taco dip with plain corn tortilla chips.

3. Good garnishes for this taco filling include sour cream, guacamole, shredded cheese, diced tomatoes, shredded lettuce, and salsa.

Easy Beef Tortillas

Karen Waggoner   Joplin, MO

MAKES: **6 SERVINGS**
PREP. TIME: **20 MINUTES**
COOKING TIME: **1½–3 HOURS**
IDEAL SLOW COOKER SIZE: **4-QUART**

1½ lbs. ground beef

10¾-oz. can cream of chicken soup

2½ cups crushed tortilla chips, *divided*

16-oz. jar salsa

1½ cups (6 ozs.) shredded cheddar cheese

1. Brown ground beef in a nonstick skillet. Drain. Stir in soup.
2. Spray inside of cooker with nonstick cooking spray. Sprinkle 1½ cups tortilla chips in slow cooker. Top with beef mixture, then salsa, and then cheese.
3. Cover and cook on High for 1½ hours, or on Low for 3 hours.
4. Sprinkle with remaining chips just before serving.

Beef Main Dishes

Tortilla Casserole

Christie Detamore-Hunsberger   Harrisonburg, VA

MAKES: **4 SERVINGS**
PREP. TIME: **20 MINUTES**
COOKING TIME: **3¼–4¼ HOURS**
IDEAL SLOW COOKER SIZE: **3-QUART**

4–6 white *or* whole wheat tortillas, *divided*

1 lb. ground beef

1 envelope dry taco seasoning

16-oz. can fat-free refried beans

1½ cups (6 ozs.) shredded low-fat cheese of your
   choice, *divided*

3–4 Tbsp. sour cream, *optional*

1. Spray the inside of the cooker with nonstick cooking spray. Tear about ¾ of the tortillas into pieces and line the sides and bottom of the slow cooker.
2. Brown the ground beef in a nonstick skillet. Drain. Return to skillet and mix in taco seasoning.
3. Layer refried beans, browned and seasoned meat, 1 cup cheese, and sour cream if you wish, over tortilla pieces.
4. Place remaining tortilla pieces on top. Sprinkle with remaining cheese.
5. Cover and cook on Low 3-4 hours.

If cooked rice is called for, stir in raw rice with the other ingredients. Add 1 cup extra liquid per cup of raw rice. Use long grain converted rice for best results in all-day cooking.

Tamale Casserole

Mamie Christopherson   Rio Rancho, NM

MAKES: **6–8 SERVINGS**
PREP. TIME: **10 MINUTES**
COOKING TIME: **5–7 HOURS**
IDEAL SLOW COOKER SIZE: **4-QUART**

2 lbs. frozen meatballs

28-oz. can chopped tomatoes

1 cup yellow cornmeal

14- to 16-oz. can cream-style corn

1 cup chopped stuffed green olives

½ tsp. chili powder, *optional*

1. Microwave frozen meatballs for 4 minutes on Power 3, or until thawed. Place in slow cooker.
2. Combine remaining ingredients in a mixing bowl. Pour over meatballs and mix well.
3. Cover and cook on High 1 hour. Turn to Low and cook 4–6 hours. Check after 4 hours of cooking. The casserole is finished when it reaches a "loaf" consistency.

Meatballs with Veggies Sauce

Barbara Katrine Rose Woodbridge, VA

MAKES: **4–6 SERVINGS**
PREP. TIME: **30 MINUTES**
COOKING TIME: **3½–4½ HOURS**
IDEAL SLOW COOKER SIZE: **4-QUART**

Meatballs:

1 lb. ground beef

½–¾ cup tomato juice

2 slices crumbled whole wheat bread

2 tsp. instant minced onion

2 tsp. Worcestershire sauce

¼ tsp. garlic powder

¼ tsp. dry mustard

¼ tsp. pepper

1. Combine all meatball ingredients. Shape into meatballs, using 1 heaping tablespoon mixture for each. Place on rack in baking pan.
2. Bake in oven at 350° for 30 minutes, or until done.

Sauce:

4 tsp. Worcestershire sauce

2 tsp. vinegar

1 tsp. dried Italian seasoning

¼ tsp. garlic powder

¼ tsp. cinnamon

¼ tsp. pepper

2 4-oz. cans sliced mushrooms, undrained

2 cups sliced carrots

3 cups tomato juice

4 tsp. instant minced onion

4 Tbsp. minced green peppers

1. Combine meatballs and sauce ingredients in slow cooker.
2. Cover. Cook on High 3-4 hours.
3. Serve over rice.

BBQ Meatballs

Kathryn Yoder Minot, ND

MAKES: **12–15 MAIN-DISH SERVINGS, OR 20–25 APPETIZER**
PREP. TIME: **20 MINUTES**
COOKING TIME: **7–10 HOURS**
IDEAL SLOW COOKER SIZE: **4-QUART**

Meatballs:

3 lbs. ground beef

5-oz. can evaporated milk

1 cup dry oatmeal (rolled *or* instant)

1 cup cracker crumbs

2 eggs

½ cup chopped onions

½ tsp. garlic powder

2 tsp. salt

½ tsp. pepper

2 tsp. chili powder

Sauce:

2 cups ketchup

1 cup brown sugar

1½ tsp. liquid smoke

½ tsp. garlic powder

¼ cup chopped onions

1. Combine all meatball ingredients. Shape into walnut-sized balls. Place on waxed paper-lined cookie sheets. Freeze. When fully frozen, place in plastic bag and store in freezer until needed.
2. When ready to use, place frozen meatballs in slow cooker. Cover. Cook on High as you mix up sauce.
3. Pour combined sauce ingredients over meatballs. Stir.
4. Cover. Continue cooking on High 1 hour. Stir. Turn to Low and cook 6–9 hours.

Variation: *Instead of using barbecue sauce, cook meatballs with spaghetti sauce or cream of mushroom soup.*

Saucy Barbecued Meatballs

Mary Ellen Wilcox Scatia, NY

MAKES: **ABOUT 60 APPETIZERS**
PREP. TIME: **30 MINUTES**
COOKING TIME: **5 HOURS**
IDEAL SLOW COOKER SIZE: **4-QUART**

Meatballs:

¾ lb. ground beef
¾ cup bread crumbs
1½ Tbsp. minced onion
½ tsp. horseradish
3 drops Tabasco sauce
2 eggs, beaten
¾ tsp. salt
½ tsp. pepper
butter

Sauce:

¾ cup ketchup
½ cup water
¼ cup cider vinegar
2 Tbsp. brown sugar
1 Tbsp. minced onion
2 tsp. horseradish
1 tsp. salt
1 tsp. dry mustard
3 drops Tabasco
dash pepper

1. Combine all meatball ingredients except butter. Shape into ¾-inch balls. Brown in butter in skillet. Place in slow cooker.
2. Combine all sauce ingredients. Pour over meatballs.
3. Cover. Cook on Low 5 hours.

Festive Cocktail Meatballs

Irene Klaeger Inverness, FL

MAKES: **6 MAIN-DISH SERVINGS, OR 12 APPETIZERS**
PREP. TIME: **35 MINUTES**
COOKING TIME: **4 HOURS**
IDEAL SLOW COOKER SIZE: **4-QUART**

2 lbs. ground beef
⅓ cup ketchup
3 tsp. dry bread crumbs
1 egg, beaten
2 tsp. onion flakes
¾ tsp. garlic salt
½ tsp. pepper
1 cup ketchup
1 cup packed brown sugar
6-oz. can tomato paste
¼ cup soy sauce
¼ cup cider vinegar
1–1½ tsp. hot pepper sauce

1. Combine ground beef, ⅓ cup ketchup, bread crumbs, egg, onion flakes, garlic salt, and pepper. Mix well. Shape into 1-inch meatballs. Place on jelly roll pan. Bake at 350° for 18 minutes, or until brown. Place in slow cooker.
2. Combine 1 cup ketchup, brown sugar, tomato paste, soy sauce, vinegar, and hot pepper sauce. Pour over meatballs.
3. Cover. Cook on Low 4 hours.

I use bread that is older or stale to make bread crumbs. I try to always have some in the freezer.

Sweet and Sour Tomato-y Meatballs

Elaine Unruh   Minneapolis, MN

MAKES: **6–8 MAIN-DISH SERVINGS, OR 20–30 APPETIZERS**
PREP. TIME: **40–45 MINUTES**
COOKING TIME: **6 HOURS**
IDEAL SLOW COOKER SIZE: **4-QUART**

Meatballs:

2 lbs. ground beef

1¼ cups bread crumbs

1½ tsp. salt

1 tsp. pepper

2–3 Tbsp. Worcestershire sauce

1 egg

½ tsp. garlic salt

¼ cup finely chopped onions

Sauce:

1 can pineapple chunks, juice reserved

3 Tbsp. cornstarch

¼ cup cold water

1–1¼ cups ketchup

¼ cup Worcestershire sauce

¼ tsp. salt

¼ tsp. pepper

¼ tsp. garlic salt

½ cup chopped green peppers

1. Combine all meatball ingredients. Shape into 15–20 meatballs. Brown in skillet, rolling so all sides are browned. Place meatballs in slow cooker.
2. Pour juice from pineapples into skillet. Stir into drippings.
3. Combine cornstarch and cold water. Add to skillet and stir until thickened.
4. Stir in ketchup and Worcestershire sauce. Season with salt, pepper, and garlic salt. Add green peppers and pineapples. Pour over meatballs.
5. Cover. Cook on Low 6 hours.

Flavorful Meatballs

Alice Miller   Stuarts Draft, VA

MAKES: **4 MAIN-DISH SERVINGS**
PREP. TIME: **30 MINUTES**
COOKING TIME: **3–4 HOURS**
IDEAL SLOW COOKER SIZE: **4-QUART**

1 lb. extra-lean ground chuck

½ cup dry bread crumbs

¼ cup fat-free milk

¾ tsp. salt

¼ tsp. black pepper

1 egg, beaten

2 Tbsp. finely chopped onions

½ tsp. Worcestershire sauce

Sauce:

⅓ cup packed brown sugar

2 Tbsp. cornstarch

13½-oz. can unsweetened pineapple chunks, undrained

⅓ cup vinegar

1 Tbsp. soy sauce

1 green bell pepper, chopped

⅓ cup water

1. Combine meatball ingredients. Shape into ¾–1-inch balls. Brown in nonstick skillet. Drain. Place in slow cooker.
2. Add brown sugar and cornstarch to skillet. Stir in remaining ingredients. Heat to boiling, stirring constantly. Pour over meatballs.
3. Cover. Cook on Low 3–4 hours.

Per Serving: 380 calories (110 calories from fat), 12g total fat (4.5g saturated, 0g trans), 90mg cholesterol, 850mg sodium, 40g total carbohydrate (2g fiber, 28g sugar), 28g protein, 0%DV vitamin A, 20%DV vitamin C, 10%DV calcium, 20%DV iron.

Variation: *If you like pineapples, use a 20-oz. can of chunks, instead of the 13½-oz. can.*

Give-Me-More Meatballs

Esther Becker Gordonville, PA • *Ruth Shank* Gridley, IL

MAKES: **30 APPETIZERS**
PREP. TIME: **25–30 MINUTES**
COOKING TIME: **6–10 HOURS**
IDEAL SLOW COOKER SIZE: **4-QUART**

1½ cups chili sauce

1 cup grape *or* apple jelly

3 tsp. brown spicy mustard

1 lb. ground beef

1 egg

3 Tbsp. dry bread crumbs

½ tsp. salt

1. Combine chili sauce, jelly, and mustard in slow cooker. Mix well.
2. Cover. Cook on High while preparing meatballs.
3. Mix together remaining ingredients. Shape into 30 balls. Place in baking pan and bake at 400° for 15–20 minutes. Drain well. Spoon into slow cooker. Stir gently to coat well.
4. Cover. Cook on Low 6–10 hours.

Variations:

1. To increase flavor, add ¼ tsp. pepper, ¼ tsp. Italian spice, and a dash of garlic powder to the meatball mixture.

Sandra Thom Jenks, OK

2. Use Italian or seasoned bread crumbs in meatball mixture. Add 1 tsp. Worcestershire sauce and 1½ Tbsp. fresh parsley to meatball mixture.

Barbara Sparks Glen Burnie, MD

3. Make meatballs larger and serve with rice or noodles.

Holiday Meatballs

Jean Robinson Cinnaminson, NJ

MAKES: **20 APPETIZERS**
PREP. TIME: **10 MINUTES**
COOKING TIME: **3–6 HOURS**
IDEAL SLOW COOKER SIZE: **5-QUART**

2 15-oz. bottles hot ketchup

2 cups blackberry wine

2 12-oz. jars apple jelly

2 lbs. frozen, precooked meatballs, or your own favorite meatballs, cooked

1. Heat ketchup, wine, and jelly in slow cooker on High.
2. Add frozen meatballs.
3. Cover. Cook on High 4–6 hours. (If the meatballs are not frozen, cook on High 3–4 hours.)

Tip: *For those who like it hotter and spicier, put a bottle of XXXtra hot sauce on the table for them to add to their individual servings.*

Variation: *If you prefer a less wine-y flavor, use 1 cup water and only 1 cup wine.*

Beef Main Dishes

Piquant Meatballs

Arlene Leaman Kliewer Lakewood, Co

MAKES: **8–10 MAIN-DISH SERVINGS, OR 30 APPETIZERS**
PREP. TIME: **1 HOUR**
COOKING TIME: **LOW HEAT UNTIL READY TO SERVE**
IDEAL SLOW COOKER SIZE: **4-QUART**

2 lbs. ground beef

2 eggs, slightly beaten

1 cup bread crumbs

2 tsp. salt

¼ tsp. pepper

Sauce:

12-oz. bottle chili sauce

10-oz. jar grape jelly

½ cup ketchup

1 tsp. Worcestershire sauce

1. Combine ground beef, eggs, bread crumbs, salt, and pepper. Form into 30 small balls. Place on baking sheet.
2. Bake at 400° for 15–17 minutes. Place in slow cooker.
3. Combine sauce ingredients in saucepan. Heat. Pour over meatballs.
4. Heat on Low until ready to serve.

Note: *We often make this recipe for our family's Christmas evening snack.*

Variations:

1. Liven up the meatballs by adding ⅔ cup chopped onions, 2 Tbsp. snipped fresh parsley, and 1 tsp. Worcestershire sauce in Step 1.

Joan Rosenberger Stephens City, VA

2. Add juice of half a lemon to the Sauce in Step 3.

Linda Sluiter Schererville, IN

3. Use ½ cup crushed cornflakes in place of the 1 cup bread crumbs in the meatball mixture. Add 1 Tbsp. bottled lemon juice to the Sauce in Step 3.

Alice Miller Stuarts Draft, VA

Tangy Cranberry Meatballs

Char Hagner Montague, MI

MAKES: **4 MAIN-DISH SERVINGS**
PREP. TIME: **10 MINUTES**
COOKING TIME: **3–4 HOURS**
IDEAL SLOW COOKER SIZE: **3-QUART**

1 lb. frozen prepared meatballs

12-oz. bottle chili sauce

16-oz. can jellied cranberry sauce

½ cup brown sugar

1. Place meatballs in slow cooker.
2. In a mixing bowl, combine chili sauce, cranberry sauce, and brown sugar, breaking up the cranberry sauce as well as you can. Pour over the meatballs.
3. Cover and cook on Low 3-4 hours.

Tip: *You can serve this as an appetizer (with toothpicks) or as a main dish over rice, pasta, or mashed potatoes.*

Variation: *Add 1 Tbsp. lemon juice to Step 2.*

Lena Mae Janes Lane, KS

Citrus-Cranberry Meatballs

Mary Ann Wasick   West Allis, WI

MAKES: **5–6 MAIN-DISH SERVINGS**
PREP. TIME: **5–10 MINUTES**
COOKING TIME: **2–4 HOURS**
IDEAL SLOW COOKER SIZE: **4-QUART**

1 medium onion, finely chopped
2 Tbsp. butter
16-oz. can jellied cranberry sauce
16-oz. pkg. prepared frozen beef *or* turkey meatballs
(approx. 32)
1 tsp. dried orange peel

1. In small saucepan, sauté onion in butter.
2. Stir cranberry sauce into saucepan. Heat on low until melted.
3. Combine all ingredients in slow cooker.
4. Cover and cook on Low 2–4 hours.

Creamy Cranberry Meatballs

F. Elaine Asper   Norton, OH

MAKES: **6 MAIN-DISH SERVINGS, OR 18–20 APPETIZERS**
PREP. TIME: **15 MINUTES**
COOKING TIME: **2–6 HOURS**
IDEAL SLOW COOKER SIZE: **4-QUART**

50 meatballs, about 1½ lbs.
1 cup brown gravy, from a jar, or made from a mix
1 cup whole-berry cranberry sauce
2 Tbsp. heavy cream
2 tsp. Dijon mustard

1. Put meatballs in slow cooker.
2. Mix remaining ingredients in a bowl. Pour over meatballs.
3. Cover and cook on High 2–3 hours or on Low 5–6 hours.

May-I-Have-More Party Meatballs

Marie Miller   Scotia, NY

MAKES: **8–10 MAIN-DISH SERVINGS**
PREP. TIME: **10 MINUTES**
COOKING TIME: **2–4 HOURS**
IDEAL SLOW COOKER SIZE: **4-QUART**

16-oz. jar salsa
16-oz. can jellied cranberry sauce
2 lbs. frozen meatballs (see recipe for making BBQ Meatballs on page 291)

1. Melt cranberry sauce in saucepan. Stir in salsa and meatballs. Bring to boil. Stir. Pour into slow cooker.
2. Cover. Cook on Low 2–4 hours.

Tangy Swedish Meatballs

Lucy O'Connell   Goshen, MA

MAKES: **12 MAIN-DISH SERVINGS**
PREP. TIME: **10 MINUTES**
COOKING TIME: **6–8 HOURS**
IDEAL SLOW COOKER SIZE: **5–6-QUART**

3 lbs. Swedish-style meatballs (frozen is fine)
16-oz. can whole berry cranberry sauce
18-oz. bottle barbecue sauce
½ cup spicy prepared mustard

1. Place meatballs in slow cooker.
2. Combine remaining ingredients in a bowl; then pour over meatballs.
3. Cover and cook on Low 6–8 hours.

Tip: *You can serve this as an appetizer, or as a main dish served over rice.*

Quick-and-Easy Sweet and Sour Meatballs

Charlotte Shaffer East Earl, PA • *Michele Ruvola* Selden, NY
Velma Sauder Leola, PA

MAKES: **8–10 MAIN-DISH SERVINGS**
PREP. TIME: **15 MINUTES**
COOKING TIME: **2 HOURS**
IDEAL SLOW COOKER SIZE: **3–4-QUART**

2 lbs. precooked meatballs

1 cup grape jelly

2 cups cocktail sauce

1. Place precooked meatballs in your slow cooker.
2. In a medium-sized bowl, mix jelly and cocktail sauce together with a whisk (it will be a little lumpy).
3. Pour jelly and cocktail sauce over meatballs. Stir well.
4. Cook on High 1–2 hours, or until the sauce is heated through.
5. Turn heat to Low until you're ready to serve.

Fruity Meatballs

Donna Lantgen Chadron, NE

MAKES: **8–10 MAIN-DISH SERVINGS**
PREPARATION TIME: **5–10 MINUTES**
COOKING TIME: **4–5 HOURS**
IDEAL SLOW COOKER SIZE: **4-QUART**

2 lbs. frozen meatballs

1 cup brown sugar

16-oz. can crushed pineapple with juice

1. Combine ingredients in slow cooker.
2. Cover and cook on Low 4–5 hours. If you're home and able, stir every 2 hours.

Creamy Easy Meatballs

Carlene Horne Bedford, NH

MAKES: **10–12 MAIN-DISH SERVINGS**
PREP. TIME: **7 MINUTES**
COOKING TIME: **4–5 HOURS**
IDEAL SLOW COOKER SIZE: **5-QUART**

2 10¾-oz. cans cream of mushroom soup

2 8-oz. pkgs. cream cheese, softened

4-oz. can sliced mushrooms, undrained

1 cup milk

2–3 lbs. frozen meatballs

1. Combine soup, cream cheese, mushrooms, and milk in slow cooker.
2. Add meatballs. Stir.
3. Cover. Cook on Low 4–5 hours.
4. Serve over noodles.

Meatballs with Chili

Colleen Konetzni Rio Rancho, NM

MAKES: **8 MAIN-DISH SERVINGS**
PREP. TIME: **10 MINUTES**
COOKING TIME: **8 HOURS**
IDEAL SLOW COOKER SIZE: **5-QUART**

2 lbs. frozen beef meatballs

16-oz. jar 505 green chili sauce, or any other good green chili sauce

chili-sauce jar of water

1. Place frozen meatballs in slow cooker.
2. In a mixing bowl, combine green chili sauce and water.
3. Pour sauce and water over meatballs.
4. Cover and cook on Low 8 hours.

Tip: *This is good as a main dish served with flour tortillas. Or put out toothpicks and serve the meatballs as party food.*

My Norwegian Meatballs

Mamie Christopherson Rio Rancho, NM

MAKES: **10–12 MAIN-DISH SERVINGS**
PREP. TIME: **5 MINUTES**
COOKING TIME: **45 MINUTES**
IDEAL SLOW COOKER SIZE: **3-QUART**

2–2½-lb. pkg. frozen meatballs

2 or 3 10¾-oz. cans cream of mushroom soup, depending
  upon how saucy you'd like the finished dish to be

12-oz. can evaporated milk

1½ cups sour cream

1 cup beef broth

1 tsp. dill weed, *optional*

1. Lay frozen meatballs in a long, microwave-safe dish and microwave on High for 4 minutes.
2. Meanwhile, in a large mixing bowl, combine all other ingredients.
3. Place meatballs in slow cooker. Cover with soup mixture.
4. Cover and cook on High 45 minutes (sauce should not boil).
5. Turn to Low. Keep warm until serving time.

Tips:
1. Serve these as an appetizer (with toothpicks), or as a main dish with mashed potatoes or noodles.
2. Substitute other herbs for the dill weed.

Beef and Ham Meatballs

Jean Butzer Batavia, NY

MAKES: **5–7 MAIN-DISH SERVINGS**
PREP. TIME: **20 MINUTES**
COOKING TIME: **2¾–3¾ HOURS**
IDEAL SLOW COOKER SIZE: **4-QUART**

1½ lbs. ground beef

4½-oz. can deviled ham

⅔ cup evaporated milk

2 eggs, beaten slightly

1 Tbsp. grated onion

2 cups soft bread crumbs

1 tsp. salt

¼ tsp. allspice

¼ tsp. pepper

¼ cup flour

¼ cup water

1 Tbsp. ketchup

2 tsp. dill weed

1 cup sour cream

1. Combine beef, ham, milk, eggs, onion, bread crumbs, salt, allspice, and pepper. Shape into 2-inch meatballs. Arrange in slow cooker.
2. Cover. Cook on Low 2½–3½ hours. Turn control to High.
3. Dissolve flour in water until smooth. Stir in ketchup and dill weed. Add to meatballs, stirring gently.
4. Cook on High 15–20 minutes, or until slightly thickened.
5. Turn off heat. Stir in sour cream.
6. Serve over rice or pasta.

Mushrooms and Cheese Meatballs

Betty Richards Rapid City, SD

MAKES: **12-15 MAIN-DISH SERVINGS, OR 20–25 APPETIZERS**
PREP. TIME: **10 MINUTES**
COOKING TIME: **6–8 HOURS**
IDEAL SLOW COOKER SIZE: **4-QUART**

3–4-lb. bag prepared meatballs (or make your own,
  using recipe for meatballs with BBQ Meatballs,
  page 291)

3 10¾-oz. cans cream of mushroom *or* cream of celery,
  soup

4-oz. can button mushrooms

16-oz. jar Cheese Whiz

1 medium onion, diced

1. Combine all ingredients in slow cooker.
2. Cover. Cook on Low 6–8 hours.
3. Use as an appetizer, or as a main dish
   served over noodles or rice.

Chinese Meatballs

Evelyn L. Ward Greeley, CO

MAKES: **6 MAIN-DISH SERVINGS**
PREP. TIME: **40 MINUTES**
COOKING TIME: **3 HOURS**
IDEAL SLOW COOKER SIZE: **3-QUART**

1 lb. ground beef

1 egg

5 Tbsp. cornstarch, *divided*

½ tsp. salt

2 Tbsp. minced onions

2 cups pineapple juice

2 Tbsp. soy sauce

½ cup wine vinegar

¾ cup water

½ cup sugar

1 green pepper, cut in strips

1 can water chestnuts, drained

canned chow mein noodles

6 slices pineapple, cut into halves

1. Combine beef, egg, 1 Tbsp. cornstarch,
   salt, and onions. Mix well. Shape into
   1-inch meatballs. Brown on all sides under
   broiler.
2. Mix remaining cornstarch with pineapple
   juice. When smooth, mix in soy sauce,
   vinegar, water, and sugar. Bring to boil.
   Simmer, stirring until thickened.
3. Combine meatballs and sauce in slow
   cooker.
4. Cover. Cook on Low 2 hours.
5. Add green peppers and water chestnuts.
6. Cover. Cook 1 hour.
7. Serve over chow mein noodles and garnish
   with pineapple slices.

Applesauce Meatballs

Mary E. Wheatley Mashpee, MA

MAKES: **6 MAIN-DISH SERVINGS**
PREP. TIME: **40 MINUTES**
COOKING TIME: **4–6 HOURS**
IDEAL SLOW COOKER SIZE: **3-QUART**

¾ lb. ground beef

¼ lb. ground pork

1 egg

¾ cup soft bread crumbs

½ cup unsweetened applesauce

¾ tsp. salt

¼ tsp. pepper

oil

¼ cup ketchup

¼ cup water

1. Combine beef, pork, egg, bread crumbs, applesauce, salt, and pepper. Form into 1½-inch balls.
2. Brown in oil in batches in skillet. Transfer meat to slow cooker, reserving drippings.
3. Combine ketchup and water and pour into skillet. Stir up browned drippings and mix well. Spoon over meatballs.
4. Cover. Cook on Low 4–6 hours.
5. Serve with steamed rice and green salad.

Meatball Sauce

Norma Grieser Clarksville, MI

MAKES: **10 SERVINGS**
PREP. TIME: **10 MINUTES**
COOKING TIME: **3–8 HOURS**
IDEAL SLOW COOKER SIZE: **6-QUART**

32-oz. bottle of ketchup

16 ozs. ginger ale

3 Tbsp. brown sugar

3 Tbsp. vinegar

3 Tbsp. Worcestershire sauce, *optional*

3 lbs. fully cooked meatballs

1. Combine sauce ingredients in slow cooker. Cover, turn to High, and bring to a simmer.
2. Gently spoon in meatballs, being careful not to splash yourself with the hot sauce.
3. Cover and simmer 3–4 hours on Low if the meatballs are thawed; 6–8 hours if they're frozen when you put them in.

Variations: *You can use little smokies instead of meatballs. In fact, this sauce is good on most meats you grill or barbecue. To serve as a sauce for grilled meat, follow Step 1; then brush on grilled meat.*

To make your own bread crumbs, drop dried bread into a sturdy plastic bag. Close it, lay it out flat on the counter top, and crush with a rolling pin. That will contain the crumbs and you can store any leftover crumbs in the bag.

Give-Me-More Barbecued Ribs, page 442

301

Snack Mix, page 61

Barbecued Beef Sandwiches,
page 326

Sesame Chicken Wings, page 395

Porcupine Tomato Meatballs

Esther J. Yoder Hartville, OH • *Jean Binns Smith* Bellefonte, PA

MAKES: **6 MAIN-DISH SERVINGS**
PREP. TIME: **30 MINUTES**
COOKING TIME: **2–4 HOURS**
IDEAL SLOW COOKER SIZE: **4-QUART**

1 lb. ground beef

¼ cup long-grain rice, uncooked

¼–½ tsp. salt, *optional*

10½-oz. can tomato soup, *divided*

2 Tbsp. shortening *or* butter

1 cup water

1. In a medium-sized bowl, mix ground beef, rice, salt, and ¼ cup of tomato soup. Shape into 1½-inch balls.
2. Brown the balls in 2 Tbsp. shortening or butter in a large nonstick skillet, being careful not to crowd them. (If your skillet is small, brown them in two batches.)
3. Place the browned meatballs in your slow cooker.
4. In the bowl, mix together 1 cup of water and the remaining tomato soup. Pour over meatballs.
5. Cover and cook on High 2–4 hours, or until the rice is fully cooked.

Creamy Porcupine Meatballs

Jennifer Dzialonski Brishton, MI

MAKES: **5 MAIN-DISH SERVINGS**
PREP. TIME: **20 MINUTES**
COOKING TIME: **5 HOURS**
IDEAL SLOW COOKER SIZE: **3½-QUART**

¾ lb. extra-lean ground beef *or* ground turkey

1 cup skim milk

½ cup long-grain rice, uncooked

1 medium onion, chopped

1 cup dry bread crumbs

½ tsp. salt

dash of black pepper

10¾-oz. can low-fat, low-sodium cream of mushroom soup

½ cup skim milk

1. Combine meat, 1 cup skim milk, rice, onion, bread crumbs, salt, and pepper in a bowl.
2. Shape with an ice cream scoop. Place in slow cooker.
3. Mix together soup and ½ cup milk. Pour over meatballs.
4. Cover. Cook on Low 5 hours.
5. Serve with mushroom-soup gravy.

Per Serving: 140 calories (80 calories from fat), 9g total fat (3.5g saturated, 1g trans), 30mg cholesterol, 920mg sodium, 40g total carbohydrate (1g fiber, 6g sugar), 21g protein, 0%DV vitamin A, 0%DV vitamin C, 15%DV calcium, 20%DV iron.

We eat with our "eyes" as well as our mouths. Vary the colors and textures of food you serve at a meal.

Sour Cream Meatballs

Zona Mae Bontrager Kokomo, IN

MAKES: **6–8 MAIN-DISH SERVINGS**
PREP. TIME: **35 MINUTES**
COOKING TIME: **4¼–5¼ HOURS**
IDEAL SLOW COOKER SIZE: **4–5-QUART**

1 lb. ground beef
½ lb. ground pork
½ cup minced onions
¾ cup fine dry bread crumbs
1 Tbsp. minced parsley
1 tsp. salt
⅛ tsp. pepper
½ tsp. garlic powder
1 Tbsp. Worcestershire sauce
1 egg
½ cup milk
¼ cup oil

Gravy:

¼ cup flour
¼ tsp. salt
¼ tsp. garlic powder
⅛ tsp. pepper
1 tsp. paprika
2 cups boiling water
¾ cup sour cream

1. Combine meats, onions, bread crumbs, parsley, salt, pepper, garlic powder, Worcestershire sauce, egg, and milk.
2. Shape into balls the size of a walnut. Brown in oil in skillet. Reserve drippings, and place meatballs in slow cooker.
3. Cover. Cook on High 10–15 minutes.
4. Stir flour, salt, garlic powder, pepper, and paprika into hot drippings in skillet. Stir in water and sour cream. Pour over meatballs.
5. Cover. Reduce heat to Low. Cook 4–5 hours.
6. Serve over rice or noodles.

Party Meatballs to Please

Kathy Purcell Dublin, OH

MAKES: **10–12 MAIN-DISH SERVINGS**
PREP. TIME: **50 MINUTES**
COOKING TIME: **3–4 HOURS**
IDEAL SLOW COOKER SIZE: **5–6-QUART**

3 lbs. ground beef
1 pkg. dry onion soup mix
14-oz. can sweetened condensed milk

Sauce:

18-oz. bottle ketchup
½ cup brown sugar
¼ cup Worcestershire sauce

1. Combine beef, soup mix, and condensed milk. Form into about 3 dozen meatballs, each about 1½-inches around.
2. Place meatballs on baking sheet. Brown in 350° oven for 30 minutes. Remove from oven and drain. Place meatballs in slow cooker.
3. Combine sauce ingredients. Pour over meatballs.
4. Cover. Cook on Low 3–4 hours.

Note: *I have made these meatballs for many different parties and events and they are always a big hit. Everyone asks for the recipe.*

Beef Main Dishes

Easy Meatballs for a Group

Penny Blosser Beavercreek, OH

MAKES: **10–12 MAIN-DISH SERVINGS**
PREP. TIME: **5 MINUTES**
COOKING TIME: **4 HOURS**
IDEAL SLOW COOKER SIZE: **5–6-QUART**

80–100 frozen small meatballs
16-oz. jar barbecue sauce
16-oz. jar apricot jam

1. Fill slow cooker with meatballs.
2. Combine sauce and jam. Pour over meatballs.
3. Cover. Cook on Low 4 hours, stirring occasionally.
4. This works well as an appetizer, or as a main dish over rice.

Sweet 'n Tangy Meatballs

Donna Lantgen Rapid City, SD

MAKES: **8 MAIN-DISH SERVINGS**
PREP. TIME: **45 MINUTES**
COOKING TIME: **5 HOURS**
IDEAL SLOW COOKER SIZE: **4-QUART**

1½ lbs. ground beef
¼ cup plain dry bread crumbs
3 Tbsp. prepared mustard
1 tsp. Italian seasoning
¾ cup water
¼ cup ketchup
2 Tbsp. honey
1 Tbsp. red-hot cayenne pepper sauce
¾-oz. pkg. brown gravy mix

1. Combine ground beef, bread crumbs, mustard, and Italian seasoning. Shape into 1-inch balls. Bake or microwave until cooked. Drain. Place meatballs in slow cooker.
2. Cover. Cook on Low 3 hours.
3. Combine remaining ingredients in saucepan. Cook for 5 minutes. Pour over meatballs.
4. Cover. Cook on Low 2 hours.

Variation: *For a fuller flavor, use orange juice instead of water in sauce.*

Always use big bowls and big utensils when cooking. You have to wash them anyway. Bowls and pans that are too small make for frustration.

Meatballs and Spaghetti Sauce

Carol Sommers Millersburg, OH

MAKES: **6–8 SERVINGS**
PREP. TIME: **35 MINUTES**
COOKING TIME: **6–8 HOURS**
IDEAL SLOW COOKER SIZE: **4-QUART**

PICTURED
ON PAGE
32

Meatballs:

1½ lbs. ground beef

2 eggs

1 cup bread crumbs

oil

Sauce:

28-oz. can tomato puree

6-oz. can tomato paste

10¾-oz. can tomato soup

¼–½ cup grated Romano *or* Parmesan cheese

1 tsp. oil

1 garlic clove, minced

sliced mushrooms (either canned or fresh), *optional*

1. Combine ground beef, eggs, and bread crumbs. Form into 16 meatballs. Brown in oil in skillet.
2. Combine sauce ingredients in slow cooker. Add meatballs. Stir together gently.
3. Cover. Cook on Low 6–8 hours. Add mushrooms 1–2 hours before sauce is finished.
4. Serve over cooked spaghetti.

Mexican Meatballs

Anna Kenagy Carlsbad, NM

MAKES: **4–5 MAIN-DISH SERVINGS**
PREP. TIME: **35 MINUTES**
COOKING TIME: **3–8 HOURS**
IDEAL SLOW COOKER SIZE: **3–4-QUART**

1 lb. ground beef

4 slices bread, torn into small pieces

1 onion, chopped

⅓ cup milk

1 egg yolk, beaten (reserve white)

1 tsp. salt

dash of pepper

1 egg white, beaten

1 cup cornflakes, crushed

oil

10¾-oz. can tomato soup

1 small green bell pepper, chopped

½ cup water

1. Combine ground beef, bread, onion, milk, egg yolk, salt, and pepper. Form into balls.
2. Roll balls in egg white and then in crumbs. Brown in hot oil in skillet and then place in slow cooker.
3. Combine soup, pepper, and water. Pour over meatballs.
4. Cover. Cook on Low 8 hours, or on High 3–4 hours.

Italian Meatball Subs

Bonnie Miller Louisville, OH

MAKES: **6–7 SUBS**
PREP. TIME: **45 MINUTES**
COOKING TIME: **4–6 HOURS**
IDEAL SLOW COOKER SIZE: **4–5-QUART**

2 eggs, beaten

¼ cup milk

½ cup dry bread crumbs

2 Tbsp. grated Parmesan cheese

1 tsp. salt

¼ tsp. pepper

⅛ tsp. garlic powder

1 lb. ground beef

½ lb. bulk pork sausage

Sauce:

15-oz. can tomato sauce

6-oz. can tomato paste

1 small onion, chopped

½ cup chopped green bell pepper

½ cup red wine *or* beef broth

⅓ cup water

2 garlic cloves, minced

1 tsp. dried oregano

1 tsp. salt

½ tsp. pepper

½ tsp. sugar

1. Make meatballs by combining eggs and milk. Add bread crumbs, cheese and seasonings. Add meats. Mix well. Shape into 1-inch balls. Broil or sauté until brown. Put in slow cooker.
2. Combine sauce ingredients. Pour over meatballs.
3. Cover. Cook on Low 4–6 hours.
4. Serve on rolls with creamy red potatoes, salad, and dessert.

Just-One-More Meatball

Arlene Groff Lewistown, PA

MAKES: **8 SERVINGS**
PREP. TIME: **35 MINUTES**
COOKING TIME: **4 HOURS**
IDEAL SLOW COOKER SIZE: **5-QUART**

2 lbs. ground beef

2 eggs

1 small onion, chopped

¼ cup milk

1½ cup crushed crackers (equal to one packaged column of saltines)

1 tsp. prepared mustard

1 tsp. salt

½ tsp. pepper

oil

1½ cups tomato juice

⅓ cup vinegar

1 Tbsp. soy sauce

1 Tbsp. Worcestershire sauce

¾ cup brown sugar

2 Tbsp. cornstarch

1 tsp. prepared mustard

1. Combine beef, eggs, onion, milk, crackers, 1 tsp. mustard, salt, and pepper. Form into small balls. Brown in oil in skillet. Place in slow cooker.
2. Combine remaining ingredients. Pour over meatballs.
3. Cover. Cook on High 2 hours. Stir well. Cook an additional 2 hours.

To easily and cleanly crush crackers, put them in a plastic bag. Then crush them with a rolling pin.

Snappy Meatballs

Clara Newswanger Gordonville, PA

MAKES: **6–8 MAIN-DISH SERVINGS, OR 25 APPETIZER SERVINGS**
PREP. TIME: **35 MINUTES**
COOKING TIME: **4 HOURS**
IDEAL SLOW COOKER SIZE: **4-QUART**

Meatballs:

2 lbs. ground beef
½ cup chopped onions
1 cup bread crumbs
2 eggs
1 tsp. salt

Sauce:

3½ cups tomato juice
1 cup brown sugar
¼ cup vinegar
1 tsp. grated onion
12 gingersnap cookies, crushed

1. Combine meatball ingredients. Shape into balls. Brown in skillet. Drain well. Spoon into slow cooker.
2. Combine sauce ingredients in slow cooker. Pour over meatballs. Mix gently.
3. Cover. Cook on Low 4 hours.

Note: *Our son married a woman from the West Coast. He brought his new bride "home" on their honeymoon. We held an informal reception for friends who could not attend their wedding. Served with a light lunch, this recipe brought raves! Now we think of our children 3,000 miles away whenever we make these meatballs.*

Flavor-Filled Meatballs

Alice Miller Stuarts Draft, VA

MAKES: **4 MAIN-DISH SERVINGS**
PREP. TIME: **35 MINUTES**
COOKING TIME: **3–4 HOURS**
IDEAL SLOW COOKER SIZE: **4-QUART**

1 lb. ground beef
½ cup dry bread crumbs
¼ cup milk
1 tsp. salt
1 egg, beaten
2 Tbsp. finely chopped onions
½ tsp. Worcestershire sauce

Sauce:

½ cup packed brown sugar
2 Tbsp. cornstarch
13¼-oz. can pineapple chunks, undrained
⅓ cup vinegar
1 Tbsp. soy sauce
1 green pepper, chopped

1. Combine meatball ingredients. Shape into 1½-inch balls. Brown in skillet. Drain. Place in slow cooker.
2. Add brown sugar and cornstarch to skillet. Stir in remaining ingredients. Heat to boiling, stirring constantly. Pour over meatballs.
3. Cover. Cook on Low 3–4 hours.

Variation: *If you like pineapples, use a 20-oz. can of chunks, instead of the 13¼-oz. can.*

Beef Main Dishes

Amazing Meat Loaf

Sara Kinsinger Stuarts Draft, VA • *Miriam Nolt* New Holland, PA
Ruth Zendt Mifflintown, PA • *Karen Ceneviva* New Haven, CT

MAKES: **8 SERVINGS**
PREP. TIME: **15 MINUTES**
COOKING TIME: **2–8 HOURS**
IDEAL SLOW COOKER SIZE: **4-QUART**

½ cup ketchup, *divided*
2 lbs. ground beef
2 eggs
⅔ cup dry quick oats
1 envelope dry onion soup mix

1. Reserve 2 Tbsp. ketchup. Combine ground beef, eggs, dry oats, soup mix, and remaining ketchup. Shape into loaf. Place in slow cooker.
2. Top with remaining ketchup.
3. Cover and cook on Low for 6–8 hours, or on High for 2–4 hours.

Tip: *Chill leftovers, and then slice for sandwiches.*

Easy Meat Loaf

Karen Waggoner Joplin, MO

MAKES: **5–6 SERVINGS**
PREP. TIME: **5 MINUTES**
COOKING TIME: **2 HOURS**
IDEAL SLOW COOKER SIZE: **3–4-QUART**

2 lbs. ground beef *or* turkey
6¼-oz. pkg. stuffing mix for beef, plus seasoning
2 eggs, beaten
½ cup ketchup, *divided*

1. Mix beef or turkey, dry stuffing, eggs, and ¼ cup ketchup. Shape into an oval loaf.
2. Place in slow cooker. Pour remaining ketchup over top.
3. Cover and cook on High for 2 hours.

Cheese Meat Loaf

Mary Sommerfeld Lancaster, PA

MAKES: **8 SERVINGS**
PREP. TIME: **15 MINUTES**
COOKING TIME: **6–8 HOURS**
IDEAL SLOW COOKER SIZE: **4-QUART**

2 lbs. ground chuck *or* ground beef
2 cups shredded sharp cheddar *or* American cheese
1 tsp. salt
1 tsp. dry mustard
¼ tsp. pepper
½ cup chili sauce
2 cups crushed cornflakes
2 eggs
½ cup milk

1. Combine all ingredients. Shape into loaf. Place in greased slow cooker.
2. Cover. Cook on Low 6–8 hours.
3. Slice and serve with your favorite tomato sauce or ketchup.

Variation: *Before baking, surround meat loaf with quartered potatoes, tossed lightly in oil.*

When camping, always prepare extra food. You'll likely need six servings to feed four ravenous campers!

Savory Meat Loaf

Betty B. Dennison   Grove City, PA

MAKES: **6–8 SERVINGS**
PREP. TIME: **20 MINUTES**
COOKING TIME: **7 HOURS**
IDEAL SLOW COOKER SIZE: **4-QUART**

2 lbs. ground beef *or* **turkey**

1 cup dry rolled oats

tomato juice (just enough to moisten meat if needed)

2 eggs

1 onion, diced

1 Tbsp. prepared mustard

1 tsp. garlic salt

2 Tbsp. ketchup

1 Tbsp. Worcestershire sauce

1 tsp. salt

Sauce:

26-oz. can *or* **2 10¾-oz. cans mushroom soup**

6–10 fresh mushrooms, diced

1 Tbsp. onion flakes

half soup can water

¼ tsp. salt

⅛ tsp. pepper

1. Combine all meat loaf ingredients. Shape into either a round or an oval loaf, to fit the shape of your slow cooker, and place in greased cooker.
2. Cover. Cook on High 1 hour.
3. Combine sauce ingredients. Pour over meat loaf.
4. Cover. Cook on Low 6 hours.

Tip: *Be careful when you remove the lid, not to let the moisture that has gathered on the lid drop back into the sauce, thereby thinning it.*

A-Touch-of-Italy Meat Loaf

Tracey Yohn   Harrisburg, PA

MAKES: **8 SERVINGS**
PREP. TIME: **10 MINUTES**
COOKING TIME: **2½–6 HOURS**
IDEAL SLOW COOKER SIZE: **4–5-QUART**

2 lbs. ground beef

2 cups soft bread crumbs

½ cup spaghetti sauce

1 large egg

2 Tbsp. dried onion

¼ tsp. pepper

1¼ tsp. salt

1 tsp. garlic salt

½ tsp. dried Italian herbs

¼ tsp. garlic powder

2 Tbsp. spaghetti sauce

1. Fold a 30-inch-long piece of foil in half lengthwise. Place in bottom of slow cooker with both ends hanging over the edge of cooker. Grease foil.
2. Combine beef, bread crumbs, ½ cup spaghetti sauce, egg, onion, and seasonings. Shape into loaf. Place on top of foil in slow cooker. Spread 2 Tbsp. spaghetti sauce over top.
3. Cover. Cook on High 2½–3 hours, or on Low 5–6 hours.

Beef Main Dishes

Meat Loaf Sensation

Andrea O'Neil Fairfield, CT

MAKES: **8 SERVINGS**
PREP. TIME: **5–10 MINUTES**
COOKING TIME: **8–10 HOURS**
IDEAL SLOW COOKER SIZE: **4–5-QUART**

2½ lbs. ground beef
half of an 8-oz. jar salsa
1 pkg. dry taco seasoning, *divided*
1 egg, slightly beaten
1 cup bread crumbs
12-oz. pkg. shredded Mexican-mix cheese
2 tsp. salt
½ tsp. pepper

1. Combine all ingredients, except half of taco seasoning. Mix well. Shape into loaf and place in slow cooker. Sprinkle with remaining taco seasoning.
2. Cover. Cook on Low 8–10 hours.

Nutritious Meat Loaf

Elsie Russett Fairbank, IA

MAKES: **6 SERVINGS**
PREP. TIME: **10 MINUTES**
COOKING TIME: **3–4 HOURS**
IDEAL SLOW COOKER SIZE: **4-QUART**

1 lb. ground beef
2 cups finely shredded cabbage
1 medium green pepper, diced
1 Tbsp. dried onion flakes
½ tsp. caraway seeds
1 tsp. salt

1. Combine all ingredients. Shape into loaf and place on rack in slow cooker.
2. Cover. Cook on High 3–4 hours.

Meat Loaf and Mexico

Karen Waggoner Joplin, MO

MAKES: **6 SERVINGS**
PREP. TIME: **15 MINUTES**
COOKING TIME: **4–4½ HOURS**
IDEAL SLOW COOKER SIZE: **4-QUART**

1¼ lbs. extra-lean ground beef
4 cups hash browns, thawed
1 egg, lightly beaten, *or* egg substitute
2 Tbsp. dry vegetable soup mix
2 Tbsp. low-sodium taco seasoning
2 cups fat-free shredded cheddar cheese, *divided*

1. Mix together ground beef, hash browns, egg, soup mix, taco seasoning, and 1 cup of cheese. Shape into loaf.
2. Line slow cooker with tin foil, allowing ends of foil to extend out over edges of cooker, enough to grab hold of and to lift the loaf out when it's finished cooking. Spray the foil with nonfat cooking spray.
3. Place loaf in cooker. Cover. Cook on Low 4 hours.
4. Sprinkle with remaining cheese and cover until melted.
5. Gently lift loaf out, using foil handles. Allow to rest 10 minutes, then slice and serve.

Per Serving: 350 calories (80 calories from fat), 9g total fat (3.5g saturated, 0g trans), 70mg cholesterol, 1040mg sodium, 32g total carbohydrate (4g fiber, 1g sugar), 34g protein, 15%DV vitamin A, 10%DV vitamin C, 35%DV calcium, 15%DV iron.

Meat Loaf Dinner

Esther Lehman Croghan, NY

MAKES: **4 SERVINGS**
PREP. TIME: **15 MINUTES**
COOKING TIME: **9–10 HOURS**
IDEAL SLOW COOKER SIZE: **4–5-QUART**

6 potatoes, cubed
4 carrots, thinly sliced
¼ tsp. salt
1 egg, slightly beaten
1 large shredded wheat biscuit, crushed
¼ cup chili sauce
¼ cup finely chopped onion
½ tsp. salt
¼ tsp. dried marjoram
tsp. pepper
1 lb. ground beef

1. Place potatoes and carrots in slow cooker. Season with salt.
2. Combine egg, shredded wheat, chili sauce, onion, salt, marjoram, and pepper. Add ground beef. Mix well. Shape into loaf, slightly smaller in diameter than the cooker. Place on top of vegetables, not touching sides of cooker.
3. Cover. Cook on Low 9–10 hours.

Variation: *Substitute ½ cup bread crumbs or dry oatmeal for crushed shredded wheat biscuit.*

Magic Meat Loaf

Carolyn Baer Conrath, WI

MAKES: **6 SERVINGS**
PREP. TIME: **20 MINUTES**
COOKING TIME: **9–11 HOURS**
IDEAL SLOW COOKER SIZE: **4-QUART**

1 egg, beaten
¼ cup milk
1½ tsp. salt
2 slices bread, crumbled
1½ lbs. ground beef
half a small onion, chopped
2 Tbsp. chopped green peppers
2 Tbsp. chopped celery
ketchup
green pepper rings
4–6 potatoes, cubed
3 Tbsp. butter, melted

1. Combine egg, milk, salt, and bread crumbs in large bowl. Allow bread crumbs to soften.
2. Add meat, onions, green peppers, and celery. Shape into loaf and place off to the side in slow cooker.
3. Top with ketchup and green pepper rings.
4. Toss potatoes with melted butter. Spoon into cooker alongside meat loaf.
5. Cover. Cook on High 1 hour, then on Low 8–10 hours.

Most slow cookers perform best when more than half full.

Beef Main Dishes

Gourmet Meat Loaf

Anne Townsend Albuquerque, NM

MAKES: **8 SERVINGS**
PREP. TIME: **25 MINUTES**
COOKING TIME: **8–12 HOURS**
IDEAL SLOW COOKER SIZE: **4-QUART**

2 medium potatoes, cut in strips

Meat loaf:
2 lbs. ground beef
½ lb. bulk sausage
1 onion, finely chopped
**2–3 cloves garlic, minced, according to your taste
    preference**
½ cup ketchup
¾ cup crushed saltines
2 eggs
2 tsp. Worcestershire sauce
2 tsp. seasoned salt
¼ tsp. pepper

Sauce:
½ cup ketchup
¼ cup brown sugar
1½ tsp. dry mustard
½ tsp. ground nutmeg

1. Place potatoes in bottom of slow cooker.
2. Combine meat loaf ingredients. Form into loaf and place on top of potatoes.
3. Combine sauce ingredients. Spoon over meat loaf.
4. Cover. Cook on Low 8–12 hours.

Tip: *The potatoes take longer to cook than the meat so make sure you allow enough time.*

Note: *My husband has this at the top of his list of favorite meat loaf recipes.*

Turkey-Beef Loaf

Jody Moore Pendleton, IN

MAKES: **8 SERVINGS**
PREP. TIME: **10 MINUTES**
COOKING TIME: **4–10 HOURS**
IDEAL SLOW COOKER SIZE: **3–4-QUART**

½ lb. extra-lean ground beef
1 lb. lean ground turkey
1 medium onion, chopped
2 eggs
⅔ cup dry quick oats
1 envelope dry onion soup mix
½–1 tsp. liquid smoke
1 tsp. dry mustard
1 cup ketchup, *divided*

1. Mix beef, turkey, and chopped onion thoroughly.
2. Combine with eggs, oats, dry soup mix, liquid smoke, mustard, and all but 2 Tbsp. of ketchup.
3. Shape into loaf and place in slow cooker sprayed with non-fat cooking spray. Top with remaining ketchup.
4. Cover. Cook on Low 8–10 hours, or on High 4–6 hours.

Per Serving: 210 calories (45 calories from fat), 5g total fat (1.5g saturated, 0g trans), 80mg cholesterol, 1040mg sodium, 18g total carbohydrate (2g fiber, 5g sugar), 23g protein, 8%DV vitamin A, 6%DV vitamin C, 4%DV calcium, 10%DV iron.

Meat Loaf and Mushrooms

Rebecca Meyerkorth Wamego, KS

MAKES: **6 SERVINGS**
PREP. TIME: **20 MINUTES**
COOKING TIME: **5 HOURS**
IDEAL SLOW COOKER SIZE: **3½–4-QUART**

2 1-oz. slices whole wheat bread

½ lb. extra-lean ground beef

¾ lb. fat-free ground turkey

1½ cups mushrooms, sliced

½ cup minced onions

1 tsp. Italian seasoning

¾ tsp. salt

2 eggs

1 clove garlic, minced

3 Tbsp. ketchup

1½ tsp. Dijon mustard

⅛ tsp. ground red pepper

1. Fold two strips of tin foil, each long enough to fit from the top of the cooker, down inside and up the other side, plus a 2-inch overhang on each side of the cooker—to function as handles for lifting the finished loaf out of the cooker.
2. Process bread slices in food processor until crumbs measure 1⅓ cups.
3. Combine bread crumbs, beef, turkey, mushrooms, onions, Italian seasoning, salt, eggs, and garlic in bowl. Shape into loaf to fit in slow cooker.
4. Mix together ketchup, mustard, and pepper. Spread over top of loaf.
5. Cover. Cook on Low 5 hours.
6. When finished, pull loaf up gently with foil handles. Place loaf on warm platter. Pull foil handles away. Allow loaf to rest for 10 minutes before slicing.

Per Serving: 230 calories (60 calories from fat), 7g total fat (2g saturated, 0g trans), 100mg cholesterol, 1190mg sodium, 15g total carbohydrate (2g fiber, 4g sugar), 27g protein, 4%DV vitamin A, 0%DV vitamin C, 4%DV calcium, 15%DV iron.

Party Meatball Subs

Tamara McCarthy Pennsburg, PA

MAKES: **30 SERVINGS**
PREP. TIME: **15 MINUTES**
COOKING TIME: **8–10 HOURS**
IDEAL SLOW COOKER SIZE: **8–10-QUART**

10-lb. bag prepared meatballs

1 large onion, sliced

10 good-sized fresh mushrooms, sliced

2 26-oz. jars spaghetti sauce, your choice of flavors

2 cloves garlic, minced

1 lb. mozzarella cheese, shredded, *optional*

1. Combine all ingredients except the cheese in your slow cooker. Stir well to coat the meatballs with sauce.
2. Cover and cook on Low 8–10 hours, stirring occasionally throughout cooking time to mix juices.
3. Serve in hoagie rolls and sprinkle mozzarella cheese over top, if you wish.

Tip: *This makes a lot of meatball subs! The recipe also works if you reduce the ingredients by half, or even make only a quarter of the amounts that are called for.*

Meatball Stew

Nanci Keatley Salem, OR • *Ada Miller* Sugarcreek, OH

MAKES: **8 SERVINGS**
PREP. TIME: **20–25 MINUTES**
COOKING TIME: **4–5 HOURS**
IDEAL SLOW COOKER SIZE: **4-QUART**

2 lbs. ground beef

½ tsp. salt

½ tsp. pepper

6 medium potatoes, cubed

1 large onion, sliced

6 medium carrots, sliced

1 cup ketchup

1 cup water

1½ tsp. balsamic vinegar

1 tsp. dried basil

1 tsp. dried oregano

½ tsp. salt

½ tsp. pepper

1. Combine beef, ½ tsp. salt, and ½ tsp. pepper. Mix well. Shape into 1-inch balls. Brown meatballs in saucepan over medium heat. Drain.
2. Place potatoes, onion, and carrots in slow cooker. Top with meatballs.
3. Combine ketchup, water, vinegar, basil, oregano, ½ tsp. salt, and ½ tsp. pepper. Pour over meatballs.
4. Cover. Cook on High 4–5 hours, or until vegetables are tender.

Meatball-Barley Casserole

Marjorie Y. Guengerich Harrisonburg, VA

MAKES: **6 SERVINGS**
PREP. TIME: **40 MINUTES**
COOKING TIME: **4–8 HOURS**
IDEAL SLOW COOKER SIZE: **4-QUART**

⅔ cup pearl barley

1 lb. ground beef

½ cup soft bread crumbs

1 small onion, chopped

¼ cup milk

¼ tsp. pepper

1 tsp. salt

oil

½ cup thinly sliced celery

½ cup finely chopped sweet peppers

10¾-oz. can cream of celery soup

⅓ cup water

paprika

1. Cook barley as directed on package. Set aside.
2. Combine beef, bread crumbs, onion, milk, pepper, and salt. Shape into 20 balls. Brown on all sides in oil in skillet. Drain and place in slow cooker.
3. Add barley, celery, and peppers.
4. Combine soup and water. Pour into slow cooker. Mix all together gently.
5. Sprinkle with paprika.
6. Cover. Cook on Low 6–8 hours, or on High 4 hours.

Pork and Beef Barbecue

Susan Scheel   West Fargo, ND

MAKES: **14 SERVINGS**
PREP. TIME: **15 MINUTES**
COOKING TIME: **6–8 HOURS**
IDEAL SLOW COOKER SIZE: **5–6-QUART**

8-oz. can tomato sauce

½ cup brown sugar, packed

¼ cup chili powder, or less

¼ cup cider vinegar

2 tsp. Worcestershire sauce

1 tsp. salt

1 lb. lean beef stewing meat, cut into ¾-inch cubes

1 lb. lean pork tenderloin,
cut into ¾-inch cubes

3 green bell peppers, chopped

3 large onions, chopped

1. Combine tomato sauce, brown sugar, chili powder, cider vinegar, Worcestershire sauce, and salt in slow cooker.
2. Stir in meats, green peppers, and onions.
3. Cover. Cook on High 6–8 hours.
4. Shred meat with two forks. Stir all ingredients together well.
5. Serve on buns.

Per Serving: 270 calories (50 calories from fat), 6g total fat (1.5g saturated, 0.5g trans), 40mg cholesterol, 480mg sodium, 38g total carbohydrate (3g fiber, 14g sugar), 18g protein, 20%DV vitamin A, 20%DV vitamin C, 8%DV calcium, 20%DV iron.

Mile-High Shredded Beef Sandwiches

Miriam Christophel   Battle Creek, MI   •   *Mary Seielstad*   Sparks, NV

MAKES: **8 SANDWICHES**
PREP. TIME: **20 MINUTES**
COOKING TIME: **7–9 HOURS**
IDEAL SLOW COOKER SIZE: **4-QUART**

3-lb. chuck roast *or* round steak

2 Tbsp. oil

1 cup chopped onions

½ cup sliced celery

2 cups beef broth, *or* 4 bouillon dissolved in 2 cups water

1 garlic clove

1 tsp. salt

¾ cup ketchup

4 Tbsp. brown sugar

2 Tbsp. vinegar

1 tsp. dry mustard

½ tsp. chili powder

3 drops Tabasco sauce

1 bay leaf

¼ tsp. paprika

¼ tsp. garlic powder

1 tsp. Worcestershire sauce

1. In skillet brown both sides of meat in oil. Add onions and celery and sauté briefly. Transfer to slow cooker. Add broth or bouillon.
2. Cover. Cook on Low 6–8 hours, or until tender. Remove meat from cooker and cool. Shred beef.
3. Remove vegetables from cooler and drain, reserving 1½ cups broth. Combine vegetables and meat.
4. Return shredded meat and vegetables to cooker. Add broth and remaining ingredients and combine well.
5. Cover. Cook on High 1 hour. Remove bay leaf.
6. Pile into 8 sandwich rolls and serve.

Beef Main Dishes

Slow Cooker Beef Sandwiches

Elaine Unruh Minneapolis, MN • *Winifred Ewy* Newton, KS

MAKES: **8–10 SANDWICHES**
PREP. TIME: **5 MINUTES**
COOKING TIME: **8–10 HOURS**
IDEAL SLOW COOKER SIZE: **4-QUART**

2–3-lb. chuck roast, cubed
1 pkg. dry onion soup mix
12-oz. can cola

1. Place meat in slow cooker.
2. Sprinkle soup mix over meat. Pour cola over all.
3. Cover. Cook on Low 8–10 hours.
4. Serve as roast or shred the beef, mix with sauce, and serve on buns.

Variation: *Layer 4 medium potatoes, sliced, and 4 carrots, sliced, in bottom of pot. Place meat and rest of ingredients on top, and follow recipe for cooking.*

Barbecue Beef on Rolls

Elizabeth Yoder Millersburg, OH

MAKES: **12 SERVINGS**
PREP. TIME: **10 MINUTES**
COOKING TIME: **6½–8½ HOURS**
IDEAL SLOW COOKER SIZE: **4-QUART**

3-lb. boneless chuck roast
1 cup barbecue sauce
½ cup apricot preserves
⅓ cup chopped green peppers
1 small onion, chopped
1 Tbsp. Dijon mustard
2 tsp. brown sugar

1. Cut roast into quarters. Place in greased slow cooker.
2. Combine barbecue sauce, preserves, green peppers, onion, mustard, and brown sugar. Pour over roast.
3. Cover. Cook on Low 6–8 hours. Remove roast and slice thinly. Return to slow cooker. Stir gently.
4. Cover. Cook 20–30 minutes.
5. Serve beef and sauce on rolls.

A sharp knife is a safe knife. Keep your knives sharp!

Ranch Hand Beef

Sharon Timpe   Mequon, WI

MAKES: **10–12 SERVINGS**
PREP. TIME: **10 MINUTES**
COOKING TIME: **4–9 HOURS**
IDEAL SLOW COOKER SIZE: **4-QUART**

3–3½-lb. boneless beef chuck roast

1 cup thinly sliced onions

10¾-oz. can cream of celery soup

4-oz. can sliced mushrooms

12-oz. can beer

½ cup ketchup

1 large bay leaf

½ tsp. salt

¼ tsp. lemon pepper

2 Tbsp. chopped fresh parsley, *or* 1½ tsp. dried parsley

1. Place roast in slow cooker.
2. Combine remaining ingredients. Pour over roast.
3. Cover. Cook on Low 7–9 hours or on Medium setting 4–6 hours, until meat is tender.
4. Remove bay leaf.
5. Shred roast with two forks. Mix meat through sauce.
6. Serve on buns for sandwiches or over cooked noodles as a main dish.

Variations:

1. If you prefer a thicker sauce, stir 2 Tbsp. cornstarch into ¼ cup water. When smooth, stir into hot sauce, 15 minutes before serving.

2. To give this dish a Mexican theme, serve the beef over tortilla chips or fritos and have bowls of shredded lettuce, diced avocado, sliced green onions, sliced ripe olives, sour cream, diced tomatoes, and shredded cheese for garnishing the meat.

Easy Roast Beef Barbecue

Rose Hankins   Stevensville, MD

MAKES: **12–16 SANDWICHES**
PREP. TIME: **10 MINUTES**
COOKING TIME: **12 HOURS**
IDEAL SLOW COOKER SIZE: **4-QUART**

3–4-lb. beef roast

12-oz. bottle barbecue sauce

½ cup water

½ cup ketchup

½ cup chopped onions

½ cup chopped green pepper

1. Combine ingredients in slow cooker.
2. Cover. Cook on Low 12 hours.
3. Shred meat using 2 forks. Mix thoroughly through sauce.
4. Serve on rolls with cole slaw.

Barbecued Beef Sauce

Eleanor Larson   Glen Lyon, PA

MAKES: **18–20 SANDWICHES**
PREP. TIME: **10 MINUTES**
COOKING TIME: **10–12 HOURS**
IDEAL SLOW COOKER SIZE: **4–5 QUART**

3½–4-lb. beef round steak, cubed

1 cup finely chopped onions

½ cup firmly packed brown sugar

1 Tbsp. chili powder

½ cup ketchup

⅓ cup cider vinegar

12-oz. can beer

6-oz. can tomato paste

buns

1. Combine all ingredients except buns in slow cooker.
2. Cover. Cook on Low 10–12 hours.

3. Remove beef from sauce with slotted spoon. Place in large bowl. Shred with 2 forks.
4. Add 2 cups sauce from slow cooker to shredded beef. Mix well.
5. Pile into buns and serve immediately.
6. Reserve any remaining sauce for serving over pasta, rice, or potatoes.

Hearty Italian Sandwiches

Rhonda Lee Schmidt Scranton, PA • *Robin Schrock* Millersburg, OH

MAKES: **8 SANDWICHES**
PREP. TIME: **15 MINUTES**
COOKING TIME: **6 HOURS**
IDEAL SLOW COOKER SIZE: **4-QUART**

1½ lbs. ground beef
1½ lbs. bulk Italian sausage
2 large onions, chopped
2 large green peppers, chopped
2 large sweet red peppers, chopped
1 tsp. salt
1 tsp. pepper
shredded Monterey Jack cheese

1. In skillet brown beef and sausage. Drain.
2. Place one-third onions and peppers in slow cooker. Top with half of meat mixture. Repeat layers. Sprinkle with salt and pepper.
3. Cover. Cook on Low 6 hours, or until vegetables are tender.
4. With a slotted spoon, serve about 1 cup mixture on each roll. Top with cheese.

   Tip: *For some extra flavor, add a spoonful of salsa to each roll before topping with cheese.*

Barbecued Spoonburgers

Mrs. Paul Gray Beatrice, NE

MAKES: **6–8 SANDWICHES**
PREP. TIME: **15 MINUTES**
COOKING TIME: **3–8 HOURS**
IDEAL SLOW COOKER SIZE: **4-QUART**

2 Tbsp. oil
1½ lbs. ground beef
½ cup chopped onions
½ cup diced celery
half a green pepper, chopped
1 Tbsp. Worcestershire sauce
½ cup ketchup
1 garlic clove, minced
1 tsp. salt
¾ cup water
⅛ tsp. pepper
½ tsp. paprika
6-oz. can tomato paste
2 Tbsp. vinegar
2 tsp. brown sugar
1 tsp. dry mustard

1. Brown beef in oil in saucepan. Drain.
2. Combine all ingredients in slow cooker.
3. Cover. Cook on Low 6–8 hours, or on High 3–4 hours.
4. Serve on buns or over mashed potatoes, pasta, or rice.

"High" on most slow cookers is approximately 300°F. "Low" is approximately 200°F.

Low-Fat Slow Cooker Barbecue

Martha Hershey   Ronks, PA

MAKES: **12 SANDWICHES**
PREP. TIME: **20 MINUTES**
COOKING TIME: **4 HOURS**
IDEAL SLOW COOKER SIZE: **3-QUART**

1 lb. extra-lean ground beef

2 cups celery, chopped fine

1 cup onions, chopped

1 Tbsp. whipped butter

2 Tbsp. red wine vinegar

1 Tbsp. brown sugar

3 Tbsp. Worcestershire sauce

1 tsp. salt

1 tsp. yellow prepared mustard

1 cup ketchup

2 cups water

1. Brown ground beef, celery, and onions in a nonstick skillet.
2. Combine all ingredients in slow cooker.
3. Cover and cook on High for 4 hours.
4. Serve in sandwich rolls.

Per Serving: 110 calories (45 calories from fat), 5g total fat (2g saturated, 0g trans), 15mg cholesterol, 540mg sodium, 8g total carbohydrate (0.5g fiber, 3g sugar), 8g protein, 6%DV vitamin A, 6%DV vitamin C, 2%DV calcium, 8%DV iron.

Tangy Sloppy Joes

Jean Shaner   York, PA   •   *Tammy Smoker*   Cochranville, PA

MAKES: **12 SANDWICHES**
PREP. TIME: **15 MINUTES**
COOKING TIME: **3–10 HOURS**
IDEAL SLOW COOKER SIZE: **4-QUART**

3 lbs. ground beef, browned and drained

1 onion, finely chopped

1 green pepper, chopped

2 8-oz. cans tomato sauce

¾ cup ketchup

1 Tbsp. Worcestershire sauce

1 tsp. chili powder

¼ tsp. pepper

¼ tsp. garlic powder

1. Combine all ingredients except rolls in slow cooker.
2. Cover. Cook on Low 8–10 hours, or on High 3–4 hours.
3. Serve in sandwich rolls.

Creamy Sloppy Joes

Penny Blosser   Beavercreek, OH

MAKES: **6 SANDWICHES**
PREP. TIME: **10 MINUTES**
COOKING TIME: **1–2 HOURS**
IDEAL SLOW COOKER SIZE: **4-QUART**

1 lb. ground beef, browned and drained

10¾-oz. can cream of mushroom soup

¼ cup ketchup

1 small onion, diced

1. Combine all ingredients in slow cooker.
2. Cover. Cook on Low 1–2 hours.
3. Serve on rolls or over baked potatoes.

Beef Main Dishes

Unforgettable Sloppy Joes

Nan Decker Albuquerque, NM

MAKES: **4–6 SANDWICHES**
PREP. TIME: **10 MINUTES**
COOKING TIME: **4–5 HOURS**
IDEAL SLOW COOKER SIZE: **4-QUART**

1 lb. ground beef

1 onion, chopped

¾ cup ketchup

2 Tbsp. chili sauce

1 Tbsp. Worcestershire sauce

1 Tbsp. prepared mustard

1 Tbsp. vinegar

1 Tbsp. sugar

1. Brown beef and onion in saucepan. Drain.
2. Combine all ingredients in slow cooker.
3. Cover. Cook on Low 4–5 hours.
4. Serve on buns.

Barbecued Hamburgers

Martha Hershey Ronks, PA

MAKES: **4 SANDWICHES**
PREP. TIME: **20 MINUTES**
COOKING TIME: **3–6 HOURS**
IDEAL SLOW COOKER SIZE: **3-QUART**

1 lb. ground beef

¼ cup chopped onions

3 Tbsp. ketchup

1 tsp. salt

1 egg, beaten

¼ cup seasoned bread crumbs

18-oz. bottle of your favorite barbecue sauce

1. Combine beef, onions, ketchup, salt, egg, and bread crumbs. Form into 4 patties. Brown both sides lightly in skillet. Place in slow cooker.
2. Cover with barbecue sauce.
3. Cover. Bake on High 3 hours, or on Low 6 hours.

Note: *We first had Barbecued Hamburgers at a 4-H picnic, and they have been a family favorite ever since.*

Tip: *Mix the hamburger patties, brown them, and freeze them in advance, and you'll have little to do at the last minute.*

Keep hot dishwater in the sink so you can clean up the kitchen as you go and while the food is baking or cooking.

Barbecue Sauce and Hamburgers

Dolores Kratz Souderton, PA

MAKES: **6 SANDWICHES**
PREP. TIME: **25 MINUTES**
COOKING TIME: **5–6 HOURS**
IDEAL SLOW COOKER SIZE: **4-QUART**

14¾-oz. can beef gravy

½ cup ketchup

½ cup chili sauce

1 Tbsp. Worcestershire sauce

1 Tbsp. prepared mustard

6 grilled hamburger patties

6 slices cheese, *optional*

1. Combine all ingredients except hamburger patties and cheese slices in slow cooker.
2. Add hamburger patties.
3. Cover. Cook on Low 5-6 hours.
4. Serve in buns, each topped with a slice of cheese if you like.

Tips:

1. Freeze leftover sauce for future use.

2. This is both a practical and a tasty recipe for serving a crowd (picnics, potlucks, etc). You can grill the patties early in the day, rather than at the last minute when your guests are arriving.

Date all containers that you put in the freezer so you're sure to use the oldest food first.

Italian Barbecue Sandwiches

Mary B. Sensenig New Holland, PA

MAKES: **4 SANDWICHES**
PREP. TIME: **10 MINUTES**
COOKING TIME: **2–6 HOURS**
IDEAL SLOW COOKER SIZE: **3-QUART**

1 lb. ground beef

1 cup tomato sauce

half an envelope dry spaghetti sauce mix

salt and pepper to taste

8 ozs. Velveeta *or* American cheese, cubed

1. In a nonstick skillet, brown ground beef. Drain.
2. Place meat in slow cooker. Stir in sauce and seasonings.
3. Cover and cook on Low 2-6 hours.
4. One hour before serving, stir in cheese.
5. Stir before serving over long rolls.

Savory Sloppy Joes

Clara Yoder Byler Hartville, OH

MAKES: **8–10 SANDWICHES**
PREP. TIME: **30 MINUTES**
COOKING TIME: **2–3 HOURS**
IDEAL SLOW COOKER SIZE: **4-QUART**

2 lbs. ground beef

1 onion, finely chopped

½ cup ketchup

1 tsp. Worcestershire sauce

10¾-oz. can cream of mushroom soup

1 tsp. salt, *optional*

1. Brown ground beef and onion together in nonstick skillet. Drain.
2. Place in slow cooker. Stir in remaining ingredients.
3. Cook on High for 2-3 hours, or until heated through.
4. Serve in rolls.

Pizzaburgers

Deborah Swartz Grottoes, VA

MAKES: **4–6 SANDWICHES**
PREP. TIME: **20 MINUTES**
COOKING TIME: **1–2 HOURS**
IDEAL SLOW COOKER SIZE: **4-QUART**

1 lb. ground beef
½ cup chopped onions
¼ tsp. salt
⅛ tsp. pepper
8 ozs. pizza sauce
10¾-oz. can cream of mushroom soup
2 cups shredded cheddar cheese

1. Brown ground beef and onion in skillet. Drain.
2. Add remaining ingredients. Mix well. Pour into slow cooker.
3. Cover. Cook on Low 1–2 hours.
4. Serve on hamburger buns.

Yum-Yums

Evelyn L. Ward Greeley, CO

MAKES: **12 SANDWICHES**
PREP. TIME: **35 MINUTES**
COOKING TIME: **4–6 HOURS**
IDEAL SLOW COOKER SIZE: **4-QUART**

3 lbs. ground beef
2 onions, chopped
10¾-oz. can cream of chicken soup
1½ cups tomato juice
1 tsp. prepared mustard
1 tsp. Worcestershire sauce
1 tsp. salt
¼ tsp. pepper

1. Brown beef and onions in skillet. Drain.
2. Add remaining ingredients. Pour into slow cooker.
3. Cover. Cook on Low 4–6 hours.
4. Serve on hamburger buns.

Note: *This is a great recipe for serving a crowd. A club I am a part of serves it when we do fund raisers. Our menu is Yum-yums, marinated bean salad, and strawberry short cake. We make the food in our homes and carry it to the meeting site.*

Pulled Beef or Pork

Pat Bechtel Dillsburg, PA

MAKES: **16–18 SERVINGS**
PREP. TIME: **5–10 MINUTES**
COOKING TIME: **8–10 HOURS**
IDEAL SLOW COOKER SIZE: **3½-QUART**

4-lb. beef *or* pork roast
2 envelopes dry ranch dressing mix
2 envelopes dry Italian dressing mix

1. Cook roast in slow cooker on Low for 8–10 hours, or until tender but not overcooked. Do not add water or seasonings! By the end of the cooking time there will be broth from cooking—do not discard it!
2. Just before serving remove meat from slow cooker. Using 2 forks, pull meat apart.
3. Add dry dressing mixes to broth and stir thoroughly. Stir pulled meat back into broth in the cooker. Serve immediately in rolls, or over cooked rice or pasta, or over mashed potatoes.

Barbecued Beef Sandwiches

Arianne Hochstetler Goshen, IN

MAKES: **24 SANDWICHES**
PREP. TIME: **15 MINUTES**
COOKING TIME: **5½–6½ HOURS**
IDEAL SLOW COOKER SIZE: **4-QUART**

PICTURED
ON PAGE
303

4-lb. round steak, ¾-inch thick, cut into 3-inch cubes
2 cups ketchup
1 cup cola
½ cup chopped onion
2 garlic cloves, minced

1. Spray slow cooker with nonstick cooking spray.
2. Place beef pieces in cooker.

3. Mix remaining ingredients in a large bowl and pour over meat.
4. Cover and cook on High 5–6 hours.
5. About 30 minutes before serving, remove beef from slow cooker and shred with 2 forks. Return beef to slow cooker and mix well with sauce.
6. Cover and cook on High an additional 20 minutes.
7. Spoon about ⅓ cup beef mixture into individual sandwich buns.

Super Beef Barbecue

Linda E. Wilcox Blythewood, SC

MAKES: **10–12 SANDWICHES**
PREP. TIME: **15 MINUTES**
COOKING TIME: **9–10 HOURS**
IDEAL SLOW COOKER SIZE: **6-QUART**

3–4-lb. rump roast
1 clove garlic, minced, *or* ¼ cup finely chopped onion
18-oz. bottle barbecue sauce
1 cup ketchup
16-oz. jar whole dill pickles, undrained

1. Cut roast into quarters and place in slow cooker.
2. In a bowl, stir together garlic, barbecue sauce, and ketchup. When well blended, fold in pickles and their juice. Pour over meat.
3. Cover and cook on Low 8–9 hours, or until meat begins to fall apart.
4. Remove the pickles and discard them.
5. Lift the meat out onto a platter and shred by pulling it apart with 2 forks.
6. Return meat to sauce and heat thoroughly on Low, about 1 hour.
7. Serve in sandwich rolls.

Beef Main Dishes

Junior Beef

Barbara Jean Fabel Wausau, WI

MAKES: **15–20 SANDWICHES**
PREP. TIME: **10 MINUTES**
COOKING TIME: **5–6 HOURS**
IDEAL SLOW COOKER SIZE: **4-QUART**

3½–5 lb. beef roast

½ tsp. salt

½ tsp. cayenne pepper

½ tsp. black pepper

1 tsp. seasoned salt

1 medium onion, chopped

1 quart dill pickle juice

4 dill pickles, chopped

½ lb. fresh mushrooms, sliced and sautéed

2 cups shredded cheddar *or* Swiss cheese

1. Combine all ingredients except rolls, mushrooms, and cheese in slow cooker.
2. Cover. Cook on High 4–5 hours.
3. Shred meat using two forks. Reduce heat to Low and cook 1 hour, or until meat is very tender.
4. Serve on hamburger buns with sautéed, sliced, fresh mushrooms, and shredded cheddar or Swiss cheese.

Beef Roast Barbecue Sandwiches

Melba Eshleman Manheim, PA

MAKES: **10–12 SANDWICHES**
PREP. TIME: **10 MINUTES**
REFRIGERATION TIME: **8–10 HOURS**
COOKING TIME: **10–12 HOURS**
IDEAL SLOW COOKER SIZE: **4-QUART**

3–4 lb. beef roast (bottom round *or* rump is best)

½ cup water

½ cup ketchup

1 tsp. chili powder

1½ Tbsp. Worcestershire sauce

2 Tbsp. vinegar

1 tsp. salt

1 Tbsp. sugar

1 tsp. dry mustard

1 medium onion, finely chopped

½ cup water

1. The night before serving, place roast in slow cooker with ½ cup water.
2. Cover. Cook on Low 10–12 hours.
3. Also the night before serving, combine remaining ingredients and refrigerate 8–10 hours.
4. In the morning, shred roast with fork and return to cooker. Pour remaining ingredients over top. Mix together.
5. Heat on Low until mealtime.
6. Serve on kaiser rolls.

Keep peeled onions covered in a jar when refrigerated.

Potluck Beef Barbecue Sandwiches

Carol Sommers   Millersburg, OH

MAKES: **16 SANDWICHES**
PREP. TIME: **5–10 MINUTES**
COOKING TIME: **6½–8¾ HOURS**
IDEAL SLOW COOKER SIZE: **5-QUART**

4-lb. beef chuck roast

1 cup brewed coffee *or* water

1 Tbsp. cider *or* red-wine vinegar

1 tsp. salt

½ tsp. pepper

14-oz. bottle ketchup

15-oz. can tomato sauce

1 cup sweet pickle relish

2 Tbsp. Worcestershire sauce

¼ cup brown sugar

1. Place roast, coffee, vinegar, salt, and pepper in slow cooker.
2. Cover. Cook on High 6–8 hours, or until meat is very tender.
3. Pour off cooking liquid. Shred meat with two forks.
4. Add remaining ingredients. Stir well.
5. Cover. Cook on High 30–45 minutes. Reduce heat to Low for serving.

No-More-Bottled Barbecue Sauce

Lauren Eberhard   Seneca, IL

MAKES: **2–2½ CUPS SAUCE**
PREP. TIME: **10 MINUTES**
COOKING TIME: **3 HOURS**
IDEAL SLOW COOKER SIZE: **1½-QUART**

1 cup finely chopped onions

¼ cup oil

6-oz. can tomato paste

½ cup water

¼ cup brown sugar

¼ cup lemon juice (freshly squeezed juice is best)

3 Tbsp. Worcestershire sauce

2 Tbsp. prepared mustard

2 tsp. salt

¼ tsp. pepper

1. Combine ingredients in slow cooker.
2. Cover. Cook on Low 3 hours.
3. Use on hamburgers, sausage, pork chops, ribs, steaks, chicken, turkey, or fish.

Tip: *Sauce will keep in refrigerator for up to 2 weeks.*

Beef Main Dishes

Chicken and Turkey Main Dishes

Sunday Roast Chicken

Ruth A. Feister   Narvon, PA

MAKES: **4–5 SERVINGS**
PREP. TIME: **30–35 MINUTES**
COOKING TIME: **6 HOURS**
IDEAL SLOW COOKER SIZE: **6-QUART**

Seasoning Mix:

1 Tbsp. salt
2 tsp. paprika
1½ tsp. onion powder
1½ tsp. garlic powder
1½ tsp. dried basil
1 tsp. dry mustard
1 tsp. cumin
2 tsp. pepper
½ tsp. dried thyme
½ tsp. savory

2 Tbsp. butter
2 cups chopped onions
1 cup chopped green pepper
1 roasting chicken

¼ cup flour
1–2 cups chicken stock

1. Combine seasoning mix ingredients in small bowl.
2. Melt butter over high heat in skillet. When butter starts to sizzle, add chopped onions and peppers, and 3 Tbsp. seasoning mix. Cook until onions are golden brown. Cool.
3. Stuff cavity of chicken with cooled vegetables.
4. Sprinkle outside of chicken with 1 Tbsp. seasoning mix. Rub in well.
5. Place chicken in large slow cooker.
6. Cover. Cook on Low 6 hours.
7. Empty vegetable stuffing and juices into saucepan. Whisk in flour and 1 cup stock. Cook over high heat until thickened. Add more stock if you prefer a thinner gravy.

Note: *The first time I served this dish was when we had family visiting us from Mississippi. We had a wonderful time sitting around a large table sharing many laughs and catching up on the years since our last visit.*

Chicken in a Pot

Carolyn Baer Conrath, WI • *Evie Hershey* Atglen, PA
Judy Koczo Plano, IL • *Mary Puskar* Forest Hill, MD
Mary Wheatley Mashpee, MA

MAKES: **6 SERVINGS**
PREP. TIME: **10 MINUTES**
COOKING TIME: **3½–10 HOURS**
IDEAL SLOW COOKER SIZE: **5-QUART**

2 carrots, sliced

2 onions, sliced

2 celery ribs, cut in 1-inch pieces

3 lb. chicken, whole or cut up

2 tsp. salt

½ tsp. dried coarse black pepper

1 tsp. dried basil

½ cup water, chicken broth, *or* white cooking wine

1. Place vegetables in bottom of slow cooker. Place chicken on top of vegetables. Add seasonings and water.
2. Cover. Cook on Low 8–10 hours, or on High 3½–5 hours (use 1 cup liquid if cooking on High).
3. This is a great foundation for soups—chicken vegetable, chicken noodle…

Variation: *To make this a full meal, add 2 medium-sized potatoes, quartered, to vegetables before cooking.*

Healthy Chicken

Carla Koslowskay Hillsboro, KS

MAKES: **8 SERVINGS**
PREP. TIME: **10 MINUTES**
COOKING TIME: **3½–4 HOURS**
IDEAL SLOW COOKER SIZE: **6-QUART**

3½ lbs. chicken pieces *or* whole chicken, cut up

2 cups skim milk

5 cups rice *or* corn cereal, finely crushed

1 tsp. salt

½ tsp. black pepper

1. Remove skin from chicken. Dip in milk.
2. Put crumbs in a plastic bag. Drop chicken pieces into bag to coat with cereal. Shake well.
3. Place chicken pieces in slow cooker. Sprinkle with salt and pepper.
4. Cover. Cook on High 3½–4 hours.

Per Serving: 480 calories (120 calories from fat), 14g total fat (4g saturated, 0g trans), 165mg cholesterol, 480mg sodium, 26g total carbohydrate (0.5g fiber, 5g sugar), 59g protein, 4%DV vitamin A, 0%DV vitamin C, 15%DV calcium, 15%DV iron.

Always defrost meat or poultry before putting it into the slow cooker, or cook recipes containing frozen meats an additional 4–6 hours on Low, or 2 hours on High.

Chicken and Turkey Main Dishes

Slow-Cooked Chicken & Mushroom Stew

Joette Proz Kalona, IA

MAKES: **4 SERVINGS**
PREP. TIME: **15 MINUTES**
COOKING TIME: **6–8 HOURS**
IDEAL SLOW COOKER SIZE: **4–5-QUART**

10¾-oz. can 98% fat-free cream of mushroom soup

half a soup can water

4 boneless, skinless chicken breast halves

½ tsp. salt

¼ tsp. black pepper

½ lb. fresh medium-sized white mushrooms, *or a
   variety of mushrooms, including portabella, cut-up*

1 cup baby carrots

2 ribs celery, cut into small pieces

½ tsp. garlic powder

1. Combine soup and water in slow cooker.
2. Cut chicken into 2-inch chunks. Sprinkle with salt and pepper. Place in slow cooker.
3. Add mushrooms, carrots, celery, and garlic powder. Stir gently to mix.
4. Cover. Cook on Low 6–8 hours or until chicken is done and internal temperature reaches 170°.
5. Serve with rice.

Per Serving: 230 calories (50 calories from fat), 5g total fat (1.5g saturated, 0.5g trans), 75mg cholesterol, 900mg sodium, 14g total carbohydrate (2g fiber, 4g sugar), 30g protein, 150%DV vitamin A, 8%DV vitamin C, 6%DV calcium, 10%DV iron.

Tip: *If you're a mushroom lover, double the amount of mushrooms! You may want to increase the salt, pepper, and garlic powder if you add mushrooms.*

Easy Mushroom Chicken

Trish Dick Ladysmith, WI • *Janice Burkholder* Richfield, PA
Carol Shirk Leola, PA • *Clara Newswanger,* Gordonville, PA
Sara Kinsinger Stuarts Draft, VA • *Carrie Darby* Wayland, IA

MAKES: **4–6 SERVINGS**
PREP. TIME: **5–10 MINUTES**
COOKING TIME: **3–8 HOURS**
IDEAL SLOW COOKER SIZE: **4-QUART**

4–6 chicken legs and thighs (joined), skinned

salt and pepper to taste

½ cup chicken broth *or* dry white wine

10¾-oz. can cream of mushroom *or* celery soup

4-oz. can sliced mushrooms, drained

1. Sprinkle salt and pepper on each piece of chicken. Place chicken in slow cooker.
2. In a small bowl, mix broth and soup together. Pour over chicken.
3. Spoon mushrooms over top.
4. Cover and cook on Low 6-8 hours, or on High 3-4 hours, or until chicken is tender but not dry.

Variation: *Add 1 clove garlic, minced, in Step 2, and scant ¼ tsp. rosemary leaves, fresh or dried, in Step 2.*

Carolyn Spohn Shawnee, KS

Chicken in Mushroom Sauce

Carol Eberly Harrisonburg, VA • *Ruthie Schiefer* Vassar, MI

MAKES: **4 SERVINGS**
PREP. TIME: **10–15 MINUTES**
COOKING TIME: **4–5 HOURS**
IDEAL SLOW COOKER SIZE: **4–5-QUART**

4 boneless, skinless chicken breast halves

10¾-oz. can cream of mushroom soup

1 cup sour cream

7-oz. can mushroom stems and pieces, drained, *optional*

4 bacon strips, cooked and crumbled, *or* ¼ cup pre-cooked bacon crumbles

1. Place chicken in slow cooker.
2. In a mixing bowl, combine soup and sour cream, and mushroom pieces if you wish. Pour over chicken.
3. Cover and cook on Low 4–5 hours, or until chicken is tender, but not dry.
4. Sprinkle with bacon before serving.
5. Serve over cooked rice or pasta.

Variations: *If you like, add 2 cloves crushed garlic to Step 2. And lay 2 sprigs of fresh rosemary over the chicken and sauce in Step 2. Add a sprinkling of paprika and freshly snipped parsley to the bacon topping, just before serving.*

Stanley Kropf Elkhart, IN

Creamy Nutmeg Chicken

Amber Swarey Donalds, SC

MAKES: **6 SERVINGS**
PREP. TIME: **25 MINUTES**
COOKING TIME: **3 HOURS**
IDEAL SLOW COOKER SIZE: **4-QUART**

6 boneless chicken breast halves

oil

¼ cup chopped onions

¼ cup minced parsley

2 10¾-oz. cans cream of mushroom soup

½ cup sour cream

½ cup milk

1 Tbsp. ground nutmeg

¼ tsp. sage

¼ tsp. dried thyme

¼ tsp. crushed rosemary

1. Brown chicken in skillet in oil. Reserve drippings and place chicken in slow cooker.
2. Sauté onions and parsley in drippings until onions are tender.
3. Stir in remaining ingredients. Mix well. Pour over chicken.
4. Cover. Cook on Low 3 hours, or until juices run clear.
5. Serve over mashed or fried potatoes, or rice.

Herbed Chicken

LaVerne A. Olson   Lititz, PA

MAKES: **8 SERVING**
PREP. TIME: **10 MINUTES**
COOKING TIME: **2¼–2¾ HOURS**
IDEAL SLOW COOKER SIZE: **5-QUART**

4 whole chicken breasts, halved

10¾-oz. can cream of mushroom *or* chicken soup

¼ cup soy sauce

¼ cup oil

¼ cup wine vinegar

¾ cup water

½ tsp. minced garlic

1 tsp. ground ginger

½ tsp. dried oregano

1 Tbsp. brown sugar

1. Place chicken in slow cooker.
2. Combine remaining ingredients. Pour over chicken.
3. Cover. Cook on Low 2–2½ hours. Uncover and cook 15 minutes more. Serve with rice.

Note: *A favorite with the whole family, even the grandchildren. The gravy is delicious.*

Delicious Chicken

Nadine L. Martinitz   Salina, KS

MAKES: **6 SERVINGS**
PREP. TIME: **10 MINUTES**
COOKING TIME: **8–10 HOURS**
IDEAL SLOW COOKER SIZE: **4–5-QUART**

3 whole chicken breasts, skin removed and halved

10¾-oz. can low-sodium condensed cream of chicken soup

½ cup cooking sherry

4-oz. can sliced mushrooms, drained

1 tsp. Worcestershire sauce

1 tsp. dried tarragon leaves *or* dried rosemary

¼ tsp. garlic powder

1. Rinse chicken breasts and pat dry. Place in slow cooker.
2. Combine remaining ingredients and pour over chicken breasts, making sure that all pieces are glazed with the sauce.
3. Cover and cook on Low 8–10 hours, or on High 4–5 hours.
4. Serve over mashed potatoes or noodles.

Per Serving: 340 calories (70 calories from fat), 7 total fat (2.5g saturated, 0g trans), 150mg cholesterol, 750mg sodium, 11g total carbohydrate (0g fiber, 4g sugar), 55g protein, 4%DV vitamin A, 0%DV vitamin C, 8%DV calcium, 10%DV iron.

Chicken in Wine

Mary Seielstad   Sparks, NV

MAKES: **4–6 SERVINGS**
PREP. TIME: **5 MINUTES**
COOKING TIME: **6–8 HOURS**
IDEAL SLOW COOKER SIZE: **4-QUART**

2–3 lbs. chicken breasts or pieces

10¾-oz. can cream of mushroom soup

10¾-oz. can French onion soup

1 cup dry white wine *or* chicken broth

1. Put chicken in slow cooker.
2. Combine soups and wine. Pour over chicken.
3. Cover. Cook on Low 6–8 hours.
4. Serve over rice, pasta, or potatoes.

Golden Chicken and Noodles

Sue Pennington   Bridgewater, VA

MAKES: **6 SERVINGS**
PREP. TIME: **5–7 MINUTES**
COOKING TIME: **6–7 HOURS**
IDEAL SLOW COOKER SIZE: **4-QUART**

6 boneless, skinless chicken breast halves

2 10¾-oz. cans broccoli cheese soup

2 cups milk

1 small onion, chopped

½–1 tsp. salt

½–1 tsp. dried basil

⅛ tsp. pepper

1. Place chicken pieces in slow cooker.
2. Combine remaining ingredients. Pour over chicken.
3. Cover. Cook on High 1 hour. Reduce heat to Low. Cook 5–6 hours.
4. Serve over noodles.

Honey-"Baked" Chicken

Mary Kennell   Roanoke, IL

MAKES: **4 SERVINGS**
PREP. TIME: **15 MINUTES**
COOKING TIME: **3–6 HOURS**
IDEAL SLOW COOKER SIZE: **5-QUART**

4 skinless, bone-in chicken breast halves

2 Tbsp. butter, melted

2 Tbsp. honey

2 tsp. prepared mustard

2 tsp. curry powder

salt and pepper, *optional*

1. Spray slow cooker with nonstick cooking spray and add chicken
2. Mix butter, honey, mustard, and curry powder together in a small bowl. Pour sauce over chicken.
3. Cover and cook on High 3 hours, or on Low 5–6 hours.

Variations:

1. Use chicken thighs instead of breasts. Drop the curry powder if you wish.

Cathy Boshart   Lebanon, PA

2. Use a small fryer chicken, quartered, instead of breasts or thighs.

Frances Kruba   Dundalk, MD

3. Instead of curry powder, use ½ tsp. paprika.

Jena Hammond   Traverse City, MI

Picnic Chicken

Anne Townsend Albuquerque, NM

MAKES: **4 SERVINGS**
PREP. TIME: **5 MINUTES**
COOKING TIME: **6–7 HOURS**
IDEAL SLOW COOKER SIZE: **3-QUART**

2 lbs. *or* **4 large chicken thighs**

¼ cup dill pickle relish

¼ cup Dijon mustard

¼ cup mayonnaise

½ cup chicken broth

1. Rinse chicken well. Pat dry. Place in slow cooker with the skin side up.
2. In a mixing bowl, stir together the relish, mustard, and mayonnaise. When well blended, stir in chicken broth. Mix well.
3. Pour sauce over chicken.
4. Cover cooker and cook on Low 6–7 hours, or until chicken is tender but not dry or mushy.

Orange-Garlic Chicken

Susan Kasting Jenks, OK

MAKES: **6 SERVINGS**
PREP. TIME: **15 MINUTES**
COOKING TIME: **2½–6 HOURS**
IDEAL SLOW COOKER SIZE: **4-QUART**

6 skinless, bone-in chicken breast halves

1½ tsp. dry thyme

6 cloves garlic, minced

1 cup orange juice concentrate

2 Tbsp. balsamic vinegar

1. Rub thyme and garlic over chicken. (Reserve any leftover thyme and garlic.) Place chicken in slow cooker.
2. Mix orange juice concentrate and vinegar together in a small bowl. Stir in reserved thyme and garlic. Spoon over chicken.
3. Cover and cook on Low 5-6 hours, or on High 2½–3 hours, or until chicken is tender but not dry.

Tip: *Remove chicken from slow cooker and keep warm on a platter. Skim fat from sauce. Bring remaining sauce to boil in a saucepan to reduce. Serve sauce over chicken and cooked rice.*

Be careful about adding liquids to food in a slow cooker. Foods have natural juices in them, and unlike oven cooking which is dry, food juices remain in the slow cooker as the food cooks.

Oregano Chicken

Tina Goss   Duenweg, MO

MAKES: **6 SERVINGS**
PREP. TIME: **5 MINUTES**
COOKING TIME: **4–6 HOURS**
IDEAL SLOW COOKER SIZE: **4–5-QUART**

3½–4 lbs. chicken, cut-up
half a stick (¼ cup) butter, melted
1 envelope dry Italian salad dressing mix
2 Tbsp. lemon juice
1–2 Tbsp. dried oregano

1. Place chicken in bottom of slow cooker. Mix butter, dressing mix, and lemon juice together and pour over top.
2. Cover and cook on High for 4–6 hours, or until chicken is tender but not dry.
3. Baste occasionally with sauce mixture and sprinkle with oregano 1 hour, or just before, serving.

Greek Chicken Pita Filling

Judi Manos   Wist Islip, NY • *Jeanette Oberholtzer*   Manheim, PA

MAKES: **4 SERVINGS**
PREP. TIME: **10 MINUTES**
COOKING TIME: **6–8 HOURS**
IDEAL SLOW COOKER SIZE: **2–3-QUART**

1 onion, chopped
1 lb. boneless, skinless chicken thighs
1 tsp. lemon pepper
½ tsp. dried oregano
½ cup plain yogurt

1. Combine first 3 ingredients in slow cooker. Cover and cook on Low 6–8 hours, or until chicken is tender.
2. Just before serving, remove chicken and shred with two forks.
3. Add shredded chicken back into slow cooker and stir in oregano and yogurt.
4. Serve as a filling for pita bread.

Bacon-Feta Stuffed Chicken

Tina Goss   Duenweg, MO

MAKES: **4 SERVINGS**
PREP. TIME: **10 MINUTES**
COOKING TIME: **1½–3 HOURS**
IDEAL SLOW COOKER SIZE: **3-QUART**

¼ cup crumbled cooked bacon
¼ cup crumbled feta cheese
4 boneless, skinless chicken breast halves
2 14½-oz. cans diced tomatoes
1 Tbsp. dried basil

1. In a small bowl, mix bacon and cheese together lightly.
2. Cut a pocket in the thicker side of each chicken breast. Fill each with ¼ of the bacon and cheese. Pinch shut and secure with toothpicks.
3. Place chicken in slow cooker. Top with tomatoes and sprinkle with basil.
4. Cover and cook on High 1½–3 hours, or until chicken is tender, but not dry or mushy.

Savory Chicken, Meal #1

Shari Mast   Harrisonburg, VA

MAKES: **8 SERVINGS**
PREP. TIME: **15 MINUTES**
COOKING TIME: **4–5 HOURS**
IDEAL SLOW COOKER SIZE: **5-QUART**

4 boneless, skinless chicken breast halves

4 skinless chicken quarters

10¾-oz. can cream of chicken soup

1 Tbsp. water

¼ cup chopped sweet red peppers

1 Tbsp. chopped fresh parsley, *or* **1 tsp. dried parsley,**
    optional

1 Tbsp. lemon juice

½ tsp. paprika, *optional*

1. Layer chicken in slow cooker.
2. Combine remaining ingredients and pour over chicken. Make sure all pieces are covered with sauce.
3. Cover. Cook on High 4–5 hours.

Savory Chicken, Meal #2

Shari Mast   Harrisonburg, VA

MAKES: **3–4 SERVINGS**
PREP. TIME: **20 MINUTES**
COOKING TIME: **3¼–4¼ HOURS**
IDEAL SLOW COOKER SIZE: **3-QUART**

leftover chicken and broth from Savory Chicken Meal #1

2 carrots

1 rib celery

2 medium onions

2 Tbsp. flour *or* cornstarch

¼ cup cold water

1. For a second Savory Chicken Meal, pick leftover chicken off bone. Set aside.
2. Return remaining broth to slow cooker and stir in thinly sliced carrots and celery, and onions cut up in chunks. Cook 3–4 hours on High.
3. In separate bowl, mix flour or cornstarch with cold water. When smooth, stir into hot broth.
4. Stir in cut-up chicken. Heat 15–20 minutes, or until broth thickens and chicken is hot.
5. Serve over rice or pasta.

Don't peek. It takes 15–20 minutes for the cooker to regain lost steam and return to the right temperature.

Company Chicken

Jeanne Allen   Rye, CO

MAKES: **6 SERVINGS**
PREP. TIME: **10 MINUTES**
COOKING TIME: **3–8 HOURS**
IDEAL SLOW COOKER SIZE: **6-QUART**

1 envelope liquid Butter Bud mix

6 boneless, skinless chicken breast halves

6 fat-free mozzarella cheese slices

10¾-oz. can cream of mushroom soup

¼ cup water

6-oz. package stuffing mix

1. Prepare liquid Butter Bud mix according to package directions.
2. Place chicken breasts in slow cooker sprayed with non-fat cooking spray.
3. Top each breast with a slice of cheese.
4. Combine soup and water. Pour over chicken.
5. Toss the stuffing mix, its seasoning packet, and prepared Butter Buds together. Sprinkle over chicken breasts.
6. Cover. Cook on Low 6–8 hours, or on High 3–4 hours.

Per Serving: 350 calories (60 calories from fat), 7g total fat (2g saturated, 0g trans), 80mg cholesterol, 1310mg sodium, 30g total carbohydrate (1g fiber, 3g sugar), 39g protein, 0%DV vitamin A, 0%DV vitamin C, 45%DV calcium, 10%DV iron.

Variation: *For additional seasoning, add 1 tsp. dried sage to Step 5.*

Put stuffing mix in a one-gallon sized Ziplock bag. Crush with a rolling pin. Good for crushing crackers, too.

Chicken, Corn, and Stuffing

Karen Waggoner   Joplin, MO

MAKES: **4 SERVINGS**
PREP. TIME: **5 MINUTES**
COOKING TIME: **2–2½ HOURS**
IDEAL SLOW COOKER SIZE: **4-QUART**

4 boneless, skinless chicken breast halves

6-oz. box stuffing mix for chicken

16-oz. pkg. frozen whole-kernel corn

half a stick (4 Tbsp.) butter, melted

2 cups water

1. Place chicken in bottom of slow cooker.
2. Mix remaining ingredients together in a mixing bowl. Spoon over chicken.
3. Cover and cook on High 2–2½ hours, or until chicken is tender and the stuffing is dry.

Scalloped Chicken with Stuffing

Brenda Joy Sonnie   Newton, PA

MAKES: **4–6 SERVINGS**
PREP. TIME: **10 MINUTES**
COOKING TIME: **2–3 HOURS**
IDEAL SLOW COOKER SIZE: **3-QUART**

4 cups cooked chicken

1 box stuffing mix for chicken

2 eggs

1 cup water

1½ cups milk

1 cup frozen peas

1. Combine chicken and dry stuffing mix. Place in slow cooker.
2. Beat eggs, water, and milk together in a bowl. Pour over chicken and stuffing.
3. Cover. Cook on High 2–3 hours.
4. Add frozen peas during last hour of cooking.

Variation: *For more flavor, use chicken broth instead of water.*

Apricot Stuffing and Chicken

Elizabeth Colucci Lancaster, PA

MAKES: **5 SERVINGS**
PREP. TIME: **10 MINUTES**
COOKING TIME: **2–3½ HOURS**
IDEAL SLOW COOKER SIZE: **5-QUART**

1 stick (8 Tbsp.) butter, *divided*

1 box cornbread stuffing mix

4 boneless, skinless chicken breast halves

6–8-oz. jar apricot preserves

1. In a mixing bowl, make stuffing, using ½ stick (4 Tbsp.) butter and amount of water called for in instructions on box. Set aside.
2. Cut up chicken into 1-inch pieces. Place on bottom of slow cooker. Spoon stuffing over top.
3. In microwave, or on stovetop, melt remaining ½ stick (4 Tbsp.) butter with preserves. Pour over stuffing.
4. Cover and cook on High for 2 hours, or on Low for 3½ hours, or until chicken is tender but not dry.

One-Dish Chicken Supper

Louise Stackhouse Benton, PA

MAKES: **4 SERVINGS**
PREP. TIME: **5 MINUTES**
COOKING TIME: **6–8 HOURS**
IDEAL SLOW COOKER SIZE: **4-QUART**

4 boneless, skinless chicken breast halves

10¾-oz. can cream of chicken *or* celery *or* mushroom soup

⅓ cup milk

1 pkg. Stove Top stuffing mix and seasoning packet

1⅔ cups water

1. Place chicken in slow cooker.
2. Combine soup and milk. Pour over chicken.
3. Combine stuffing mix, seasoning packet, and water. Spoon over chicken.
4. Cover. Cook on Low 6–8 hours.

Herby Chicken and Stuffing

Janice Yoskovich Carmichaels, PA • *Jo Ellen Moore* Pendleton, IN

MAKES: **14–16 SERVINGS**
PREP. TIME: **20 MINUTES**
COOKING TIME: **4½–5 HOURS**
IDEAL SLOW COOKER SIZE: **6-QUART**

2½ cups chicken broth

1 cup butter, melted

½ cup chopped onions

½ cup chopped celery

4-oz. can mushrooms, stems and pieces, drained

¼ cup dried parsley flakes

1½ tsp. rubbed sage

1 tsp. poultry seasoning

1 tsp. salt

½ tsp. pepper

12 cups day-old bread cubes (½-inch pieces)

2 eggs

10¾-oz. can cream of chicken soup

5–6 cups cubed cooked chicken

1. Combine all ingredients except bread, eggs, soup, and chicken in saucepan. Simmer for 10 minutes.
2. Place bread cubes in large bowl.
3. Combine eggs and soup. Stir into broth mixture until smooth. Pour over bread and toss well.
4. Layer half of stuffing and then half of chicken into very large slow cooker (or two medium-sized cookers). Repeat layers.
5. Cover. Cook on Low 4½–5 hours.

Layered Chicken Cordon Bleu

Beth Peachey   Belleville, PA

MAKES: **4 SERVINGS**
PREP. TIME: **10 MINUTES**
COOKING TIME: **6–8 HOURS**
IDEAL SLOW COOKER SIZE: **4–5-QUART**

4 boneless, skinless chicken breast halves
½ lb. deli-sliced cooked ham
½ lb. baby Swiss cheese, sliced
10¾-oz. can cream of chicken soup
1 box dry stuffing mix, prepared according to box
directions

1. Layer all ingredients in the order they are listed into your slow cooker.
2. Cover and cook on Low 6-8 hours, or until chicken is tender but not dry.

Chicken Cordon Bleu Bundles

Melanie Thrower   McPherson, KS

MAKES: **6 SERVINGS**
PREP. TIME: **15 MINUTES**
COOKING TIME: **4–5 HOURS**
IDEAL SLOW COOKER SIZE: **4-QUART**

PICTURED
ON PAGE
235

3 whole chicken breasts, split and deboned
6 pieces thinly sliced ham
6 slices Swiss cheese
salt to taste
pepper to taste
6 slices bacon
¼ cup water
1 tsp. chicken bouillon granules
½ cup white cooking wine
1 tsp. cornstarch
¼ cup cold water

1. Flatten chicken to ⅛–¼-inch thickness. Place a slice of ham and a slice of cheese on top of each flattened breast. Sprinkle with salt and pepper. Roll up and wrap with strip of bacon. Secure with toothpick. Place in slow cooker.
2. Combine ¼ cup water, granules, and wine. Pour into slow cooker.
3. Cover. Cook on High 4 hours.
4. Combine cornstarch and ¼ cup cold water. Add to slow cooker. Cook until sauce thickens.

Chicken with Dried Beef and Bacon

Rhonda Freed Lowville, NY • *Darlene G. Martin* Richfield, PA
Sharon Miller Holmesville, OH • *Jena Hammond* Traverse City, MI

MAKES: **4–6 SERVINGS**
PREP. TIME: **15 MINUTES**
COOKING TIME: **3–8 HOURS**
IDEAL SLOW COOKER SIZE: **4-QUART**

4–6 slices bacon
8–12 slices low-sodium dried beef, *divided*
4–6 boneless, skinless chicken breasts, *divided*
10¾-oz. can low-fat, low-sodium cream of mushroom
  soup
1 cup sour cream

1. Place a paper towel on a paper plate. Top with 4-6 slices of bacon. Cover with another paper towel. Microwave on High for 2 minutes, until bacon is partially cooked. Lift bacon onto fresh paper towel and allow towel to absorb fat.
2. Line slow cooker with half the slices of dried beef.
3. Wrap a slice of bacon around each chicken breast and place the first layer of chicken into the slow cooker. Cover first layer of chicken breasts with the remaining slices of dried beef. Add second layer of chicken.
4. In a mixing bowl, combine soup and sour cream. Pour over the chicken and dried beef.
5. Cover and cook on Low 7-8 hours, or on High 3-4 hours.
6. Serve over cooked noodles or rice.

Variation: *Peel and cube 6 large potatoes. Add half the cubed potatoes after placing the first layer of chicken into the slow cooker (Step 3). Add the other half of the potatoes after the second layer of chicken (Step 3.) Add another can of mushroom soup to Step 4.*

Janie Steele Moore, OK

Scalloped Potatoes and Chicken

Carol Sommers Millersburg, OH

MAKES: **6–8 SERVINGS**
PREP. TIME: **15 MINUTES**
COOKING TIME: **4½–5½ HOURS**
IDEAL SLOW COOKER SIZE: **4-QUART**

¼ cup chopped green peppers
½ cup chopped onions
1½ cups diced Velveeta cheese
7–8 medium potatoes, sliced
salt to taste
10¾-oz. can cream of celery soup
1 soup can milk
3–4 whole boneless, skinless chicken breasts
salt to taste

1. Place layers of green peppers, onions, cheese, and potatoes and a sprinkling of salt in slow cooker.
2. Sprinkle salt over chicken breasts and lay on top of potatoes.
3. Combine soup and milk and pour into slow cooker, pushing meat down into liquid.
4. Cover. Cook on High 1½ hours. Reduce temperature to Low and cook 3-4 hours. Test that potatoes are soft. If not, continue cooking on Low another hour and test again, continuing to cook until potatoes are finished.

Scalloped Chicken with Potatoes

Carolyn W. Carmichael Berkeley Heights, NJ

MAKES: **4 SERVINGS**
PREP. TIME: **5 MINUTES**
COOKING TIME: **4–10 HOURS**
IDEAL SLOW COOKER SIZE: **4-QUART**

5-oz. pkg. scalloped potatoes
scalloped potatoes dry seasoning pack
4 chicken breast halves *or* 8 legs
10-oz. pkg. frozen peas
2 cups water

1. Put potatoes, seasoning pack, chicken, and peas in slow cooker. Pour water over all.
2. Cover. Cook on Low 8–10 hours, or on High 4 hours.

One-Pot Easy Chicken

Jean Robinson Cinnaminson, NJ

MAKES: **6 SERVINGS**
PREP. TIME: **25–30 MINUTES**
COOKING TIME: **6 HOURS**
IDEAL SLOW COOKER SIZE: **6-QUART**

6–8 potatoes, quartered
1–2 large onions, sliced
3–5 carrots, cubed
5-lbs. chicken, skin removed (quarters or legs and thighs work well)
1 small onion, chopped
1 tsp. black pepper
1 Tbsp. whole cloves
1 Tbsp. garlic salt
1 Tbsp. chopped fresh oregano
1 tsp. dried rosemary
½ cup lemon juice *or* chicken broth

1. Layer potatoes, sliced onions, and carrots in bottom of slow cooker.

2. Rinse and pat chicken dry. In bowl mix together chopped onions, pepper, cloves, and garlic salt. Dredge chicken in seasonings. Place in cooker over vegetables. Spoon any remaining seasonings over chicken.
3. Sprinkle with oregano and rosemary. Pour lemon juice over chicken.
4. Cover. Cook on Low 6 hours.

Note: *This is a lifesaver when the grandchildren come for a weekend. I get to play with them, and dinner is timed and ready when we are.*

Chicken and Rice

Batty Chalker Dalhart, TX

MAKES: **6 SERVINGS**
PREP. TIME: **10 MINUTES**
COOKING TIME: **5–6 HOURS**
IDEAL SLOW COOKER SIZE: **4-QUART**

10¾-oz. can cream of chicken soup
1 pkg. dry onion soup mix
2½ cups water
1 cup long-grain rice, uncooked
6 ozs. boneless, skinless chicken breast tenders
¼ tsp. black pepper

1. Combine all ingredients in slow cooker.
2. Cook on Low 5–6 hours.
3. Stir occasionally.

Per Serving: 140 calories (35 calories from fat), 4g total fat (1g saturated, 0g trans), 20mg cholesterol, 520mg sodium, 16g total carbohydrate (0.5g fiber, 1g sugar), 8g protein, 4%DV vitamin A, 0%DV vitamin C, 2%DV calcium, 4%DV iron.

Chicken and Turkey Main Dishes

Spicy Chicken with Rice

Dawn Hahn   Lititz, PA

MAKES: **4 SERVINGS**
PREP. TIME: **10 MINUTES**
COOKING TIME: **4–6 HOURS**
IDEAL SLOW COOKER SIZE: **4–5-QUART**

1 cup long-grain rice, uncooked

1¼ cups chicken broth

1 cup salsa, your choice of heat

4 boneless, skinless chicken breast halves

¾ cup shredded cheddar cheese

1. Spray interior of slow cooker with nonstick cooking spray.
2. Pour rice into bottom of slow cooker.
3. Add chicken broth and salsa. Stir together well.
4. Place chicken breasts on top.
5. Cover and cook for 4–6 hours on Low, or until chicken and rice are tender but not dry.
6. Garnish with cheese just before serving.

Fiesta Chicken

Stacie Skelly   Millersville, PA

MAKES: **8 SERVINGS**
PREP. TIME: **5 MINUTES**
COOKING TIME: **6½ HOURS**
IDEAL SLOW COOKER SIZE: **4–5-QUART**

8 boneless, skinless chicken breast halves

16-oz. jar salsa

2 cups instant rice

1. Place chicken in slow cooker. Pour salsa over chicken.
2. Cover and cook on Low 6 hours, or until chicken is tender but not dry.
3. Remove chicken to a serving platter and keep warm.

4. Add rice to hot salsa in slow cooker and cook on High 30 minutes. Serve chicken and rice together on a large platter.

Spicy Chicken Curry

Joan Miller   Wayland, IA

MAKES: **10 SERVINGS**
PREP. TIME: **15–20 MINUTES**
COOKING TIME: **3–4½ HOURS**
IDEAL SLOW COOKER SIZE: **4–5-QUART**

10 skinless, bone-in chicken breast halves, *divided*

16-oz. jar salsa, your choice of heat

1 medium onion, chopped

2 Tbsp. curry powder

1 cup sour cream

1. Place half the chicken in the slow cooker.
2. Combine salsa, onion, and curry powder in a medium-sized bowl. Pour half the sauce over the meat in the cooker.
3. Repeat Steps 1 and 2.
4. Cover and cook on High for 3 hours. Or cook on High for 1½ hours, and then turn cooker to Low and cook 3 more hours.
5. Remove chicken to serving platter and cover to keep warm.
6. Add sour cream to slow cooker and stir into salsa until well blended. Serve over the chicken.

One hour on High equals about 2 to 2½ hours on Low.

Chicken, Broccoli, and Rice Casserole

Wanda Roth Napoleon, OH

MAKES: **8 SERVINGS**
PREP. TIME: **10 MINUTES**
COOKING TIME: **3–7 HOURS**
IDEAL SLOW COOKER SIZE: **6-QUART**

1 cup long-grain rice, uncooked

3 cups water

2 tsp. low-sodium chicken bouillon granules

10¾-oz. can fat-free, low-sodium cream of chicken soup

2 cups chopped, cooked chicken breast

¼ tsp. garlic powder

1 tsp. onion salt

1 cup shredded, fat-free cheddar cheese

16-oz. bag frozen broccoli, thawed

1. Combine all ingredients except broccoli in slow cooker.
2. One hour before end of cooking time, stir in broccoli.
3. Cook on High for a total of 3–4 hours, or on Low for a total of 6–7 hours.

Per Serving: 200 calories (20 calories from fat), 2.5g total fat (0.5g saturated, 0g trans), 30mg cholesterol, 960mg sodium, 25g total carbohydrate (2g fiber, 1g sugar), 18g protein, 15%DV vitamin A, 20%DV vitamin C, 20%DV calcium, 10%DV iron.

Tip: *If casserole is too runny as the end of the cooking time nears, remove lid from slow cooker for 15 minutes while continuing to cook on High.*

Chicken with Broccoli Rice

Maryann Markano Wilmington, DE

MAKES: **6 SERVINGS**
PREP. TIME: **20 MINUTES**
COOKING TIME: **6–8 HOURS**
IDEAL SLOW COOKER SIZE: **5-QUART**

1¼ cups long-grain rice, uncooked

pepper to taste

2 lbs. boneless, skinless chicken breasts, cut into strips

1 pkg. Knorr's cream of broccoli dry soup mix

2½ cups chicken broth

1. Spray slow cooker with nonstick cooking spray. Place rice in cooker. Sprinkle with pepper.
2. Top with chicken pieces.
3. In a mixing bowl, combine soup mix and broth. Pour over chicken and rice.
4. Cover and cook on Low 6–8 hours, or until rice and chicken are tender but not dry.

Wild Rice Hot Dish

Barbara Tenney Delta, PA

MAKES: **8–10 SERVINGS**
PREP. TIME: **15 MINUTES**
COOKING TIME: **4–6 HOURS**
IDEAL SLOW COOKER SIZE: **4-QUART**

2 cups wild rice, uncooked

½ cup slivered almonds

½ cup chopped onions

½ cup chopped celery

8–12-oz. can mushrooms, drained

2 cups cooked, cut-up chicken

6 cups chicken broth

¼-½ tsp. salt

¼ tsp. pepper

¼ tsp. garlic powder

1 Tbsp. chopped parsley

1. Wash and drain rice.
2. Combine all ingredients in slow cooker. Mix well.
3. Cover. Cook on Low 4–6 hours, or until rice is finished. Do not remove lid before rice has cooked 4 hours.

Company Casserole

Vera Schmucker   Goshen, IN

MAKES: **4–6 SERVINGS**
PREP. TIME: **15–20 MINUTES**
COOKING TIME: **3–8 HOURS**
IDEAL SLOW COOKER SIZE: **5-QUART**

1¼ cups rice, uncooked

½ cup (1 stick) butter, melted

3 cups chicken broth

3–4 cups cut-up cooked chicken breast

2 4-oz. cans sliced mushrooms, drained

⅓ cup soy sauce

12-oz. pkg. shelled frozen shrimp

8 green onions, chopped, 2 Tbsp. reserved

⅔ cup slivered almonds

1. Combine rice and butter in slow cooker. Stir to coat rice well.
2. Add remaining ingredients except almonds and 2 Tbsp. green onions.
3. Cover. Cook on Low 6–8 hours, or on High 3–4 hours, until rice is tender.
4. Sprinkle almonds and green onions over top before serving.
5. Serve with green beans, tossed salad, and fruit salad.

Chicken-Vegetable Dish

Cheri Jantzen   Houston, TX

MAKES: **4 SERVINGS**
PREP. TIME: **10 MINUTES**
COOKING TIME: **2–5 HOURS**
IDEAL SLOW COOKER SIZE: **4–5-QUART**

4 skinless bone-in chicken breast halves

15-oz. can crushed tomatoes

10-oz. pkg. frozen green beans

2 cups water *or* chicken broth

1 cup brown rice, uncooked

1 cup sliced mushrooms

2 carrots, chopped

1 onion, chopped

½ tsp. minced garlic

½ tsp. herb-blend seasoning

¼ tsp. dried tarragon

1. Combine all ingredients in slow cooker.
2. Cover. Cook on High 2 hours, and then on Low 3–5 hours.

Cape Breton Chicken

Joanne Kennedy Plattsburgh, NY

MAKES: **5 SERVINGS**
PREP. TIME: **15 MINUTES**
COOKING TIME: **7 HOURS**
IDEAL SLOW COOKER SIZE: **4-QUART**

4 boneless, skinless chicken breast halves, uncooked, cubed
1 medium onion, chopped
1 medium green bell pepper, chopped
1 cup chopped celery
1 quart low-sodium stewed *or* crushed tomatoes
1 cup water
½ cup tomato paste
2 Tbsp. Worcestershire sauce
2 Tbsp. brown sugar
1 tsp. black pepper

1. Combine all ingredients in slow cooker.
2. Cover. Cook on Low 7 hours.
3. Serve over rice.

Per Serving: 240 calories (25 calories from fat), 2.5g total fat (0.5g saturated, 0g trans), 60mg cholesterol, 190mg sodium, 27g total carbohydrate (6g fiber, 16g sugar), 25g protein, 30%DV vitamin A, 40%DV vitamin C, 10%DV calcium, 25%DV iron.

Chicken and Bean Torta

Vicki Dinkel Sharon Springs, KS

MAKES: **6 SERVINGS**
PREP. TIME: **20 MINUTES**
COOKING TIME: **4–5 HOURS**
IDEAL SLOW COOKER SIZE: **4–5-QUART**

1 lb. uncooked boneless, skinless chicken breasts
1 medium onion
½ tsp. garlic salt
¼ tsp. black pepper
15-oz. can ranch-style black beans
15-oz. can low-sodium diced tomatoes with green chilies
4 tortillas
1½ cups shredded low-fat cheddar cheese
salsa
fat-free sour cream
lettuce
tomatoes

1. Cut chicken in small pieces. Brown with onion in nonstick skillet. Drain well.
2. Season with garlic salt and pepper. Stir in beans and tomatoes.
3. Place strips of foil on bottom and up sides of slow cooker, forming an X. Spray foil and cooker lightly with non-fat cooking spray.
4. Place 1 tortilla on bottom of cooker. Spoon on one-third of chicken mixture and one-quarter of the cheese.
5. Repeat layers, ending with a tortilla sprinkled with cheese on top.
6. Cover. Cook on Low 4–5 hours.
7. Remove to platter using foil strips as handles. Gently pull out foil and discard.
8. Serve with salsa, sour cream, lettuce, and tomatoes.

Per Serving: 510 calories (90 calories from fat), 10g total fat (3.5g saturated, 0.5g trans), 75mg cholesterol, 1250mg sodium, 60g total carbohydrate (9g fiber, 11g sugar), 45g protein, 20%DV vitamin A, 30%DV vitamin C, 45%DV calcium, 25%DV iron.

Variation: *If your diet allows, use mild Rotel tomatoes in place of the tomatoes with green chilies.*

Italian Chicken Stew

Mary Longenecker Bethel, PA

MAKES: **4 SERVINGS**
PREP. TIME: **20 MINUTES**
COOKING TIME: **3–6 HOURS**
IDEAL SLOW COOKER SIZE: **5–6-QUART**

2 boneless, skinless chicken breast halves, uncooked, cut in 1½-inch pieces

19-oz. can cannellini beans, drained and rinsed

15½-oz. can kidney beans, drained and rinsed

14½-oz. can low-sodium diced tomatoes, undrained

1 cup chopped celery

1 cup sliced carrots

2 small garlic cloves, coarsely chopped

1 cup water

½ cup dry red wine *or* low-fat chicken broth

3 Tbsp. tomato paste

1 Tbsp. sugar

1½ tsp. dried Italian seasoning

1. Combine chicken, cannellini beans, kidney beans, tomatoes, celery, carrots, and garlic in slow cooker. Mix well.
2. In medium bowl, combine all remaining ingredients. Mix well. Pour over chicken and vegetables. Mix well.
3. Cover. Cook on Low 5-6 hours, or on High 3 hours.

Per Serving: 340 calories (25 calories from fat), 2.5g total fat (0.5g saturated, 0g trans), 35mg cholesterol, 1460mg sodium, 53g total carbohydrate (14g fiber, 12g sugar), 29g protein, 100%DV vitamin A, 20%DV vitamin C, 20%DV calcium, 25%DV iron.

Chicken Tortilla Casserole

Jeanne Allen Rye, CO

MAKES: **8–10 SERVINGS**
PREP. TIME: **25 MINUTES**
COOKING TIME: **3–6 HOURS**
IDEAL SLOW COOKER SIZE: **5–6-QUART**

4 whole boneless, skinless chicken breasts, cooked and cut in 1-inch pieces (reserve ¼ cup broth chicken was cooked in)

10 6-inch flour tortillas, cut in strips about ½-inch wide × 2-inches long

2 medium onions, chopped

1 tsp. canola oil

10¾-oz. can fat-free chicken broth

10¾-oz. can 98% fat-free cream of mushroom soup

2 4-oz. cans mild green chilies, chopped

1 egg

1 cup shredded low-fat cheddar cheese

1. Pour reserved chicken broth in slow cooker sprayed with non-fat cooking spray.
2. Scatter half the tortilla strips in bottom of slow cooker.
3. Mix remaining ingredients together, except the second half of the tortilla strips and the cheese.
4. Layer half the chicken mixture into the cooker, followed by the other half of the tortillas, followed by the rest of the chicken mix.
5. Cover. Cook on Low 4-6 hours, or on High 3-5 hours.
6. Add the cheese to the top of the dish during the last 20-30 minutes of cooking.
7. Uncover and allow casserole to rest 15 minutes before serving.

Per Serving: 280 calories (70 calories from fat), 7g total fat (2.5g saturated, 1g trans), 65mg cholesterol, 570mg sodium, 28g total carbohydrate (2g fiber, 3g sugar), 23g protein, 2%DV vitamin A, 2%DV vitamin C, 20%DV calcium, 15%DV iron.

Chicken Soft Tacos

Kristen Allen   Houston, TX

MAKES: **6 SERVINGS**
PREP. TIME: **5 MINUTES**
COOKING TIME: **6–8 HOURS**
IDEAL SLOW COOKER SIZE: **5–6-QUART**

1–1½ lbs. frozen, boneless, skinless chicken breasts

14½-oz. can low-sodium diced tomatoes with green chilies

1 envelope low-sodium taco seasoning

1. Place chicken breasts in slow cooker.
2. Mix tomatoes and taco seasoning. Pour over chicken.
3. Cover. Cook on Low 6–8 hours.
4. Serve in soft tortillas. Top with salsa, low-fat shredded cheddar cheese, guacamole if your diet allows, and fresh tomatoes.

Per Serving: 100 calories (20 calories from fat), 2.5g total fat (0.5g saturated, 0g trans), 50mg cholesterol, 300mg sodium, 2g total carbohydrate (0.5g fiber, 1g sugar), 18g protein, 0%DV vitamin A, 0%DV vitamin C, 2%DV calcium, 4%DV iron.

Another Chicken in a Pot

Jennifer J. Gehman   Harrisburg, PA

MAKES: **4–6 SERVINGS**
PREP. TIME: **10 MINUTES**
COOKING TIME: **3½–10 HOURS**
IDEAL SLOW COOKER SIZE: **4–5-QUART**

1-lb. bag baby carrots

1 small onion, diced

14½-oz. can green beans

3-lb. whole chicken, cut into serving-size pieces

2 tsp. salt

½ tsp. black pepper

½ cup chicken broth

¼ cup white wine

½–1 tsp. dried basil

1. Put carrots, onion, and beans on bottom of slow cooker. Add chicken. Top with salt, pepper, broth, and wine. Sprinkle with basil.
2. Cover. Cook on Low 8–10 hours, or on High 3½–5 hours.

Savory Slow Cooker Chicken

Sara Harter Fredette   Williamsburg, MA

MAKES: **4 SERVINGS**
PREP. TIME: **10–15 MINUTES**
COOKING TIME: **8–10 HOURS**
IDEAL SLOW COOKER SIZE: **4–5-QUART**

2½ lbs. chicken pieces, skinned

1 lb. fresh tomatoes, chopped, *or* **15-oz. can stewed tomatoes**

2 Tbsp. white wine

1 bay leaf

¼ tsp. pepper

2 garlic cloves, minced

1 onion, chopped

½ cup chicken broth

1 tsp. dried thyme

1½ tsp. salt

2 cups broccoli, cut into bite-sized pieces

1. Combine all ingredients except broccoli in slow cooker.
2. Cover. Cook on Low 8–10 hours.
3. Add broccoli 30 minutes before serving.

Convenient Chicken and Dumplings

Annabelle Unternahrer   Shipshewana, IN

MAKES: **5–6 SERVINGS**
PREP. TIME: **10 MINUTES**
COOKING TIME: **2½ HOURS**
IDEAL SLOW COOKER SIZE: **3–4-QUART**

1 lb. boneless, skinless chicken breasts, uncooked and cut in 1-inch cubes
1 lb. frozen vegetables of your choice
1 medium onion, diced
2 12-oz. jars fat-free low-sodium chicken broth, *divided*
1½ cups low-fat buttermilk biscuit mix

1. Combine chicken, vegetables, onion, and chicken broth (reserve ½ cup, plus 1 Tbsp., broth) in slow cooker.
2. Cover. Cook on High 2 hours.
3. Mix biscuit mix with reserved broth until moistened. Drop by tablespoonfuls over hot chicken and vegetables.
4. Cover. Cook on High 10 minutes.
5. Uncover. Cook on High 20 minutes more.

Per Serving: 330 calories (70 calories from fat), 8g total fat (2g saturated, 0g trans), 65mg cholesterol, 600mg sodium, 31g total carbohydrate (5g fiber, 7g sugar), 33g protein, 6%DV vitamin A, 10%DV vitamin C, 10%DV calcium, 20%DV iron.

Tip: *For a less brothy stew, add another ½ pound vegetables.*

Asian Chicken Ginger

Dianna R. Milhizer   Brighton, MI

MAKES: **6 SERVINGS**
PREP. TIME: **15 MINUTES**
COOKING TIME: **4–6 HOURS**
IDEAL SLOW COOKER SIZE: **6-QUART**

6 chicken breast halves, uncooked, cut-up
1 cup diced carrots
½ cup minced onion
½ cup low-sodium soy sauce
¼ cup rice vinegar
¼ cup sesame seeds
1 Tbsp. ground ginger, *or* ¼ cup grated gingerroot
¾ tsp. salt
1 tsp. sesame oil
2 cups broccoli florets
1 cup cauliflower florets

1. Combine all ingredients except broccoli and cauliflower in slow cooker.
2. Cover. Cook on Low 3–5 hours. Stir in broccoli and cauliflower and cook an additional hour.
3. Serve over brown rice.

Per Serving: 230 calories (60 calories from fat), 7g total fat (1.5g saturated, 0g trans), 75mg cholesterol, 1090mg sodium, 12g total carbohydrate (4g fiber, 4g sugar), 31g protein, 100%DV vitamin A, 30%DV vitamin C, 10%DV calcium, 15%DV iron.

Variation: *You can use a variety of vegetables that are in season for this recipe—zucchini, celery, Chinese peas, and turnips. Chop or slice them and add during the last hour of cooking.*

Do not put your good knife in the dishwasher.

Szechwan-Style Chicken and Broccoli

Jane Meiser   Harrisonburg, VA

MAKES: **4 SERVINGS**
PREP. TIME: **20 MINUTES**
COOKING TIME: **1–3 HOURS**
IDEAL SLOW COOKER SIZE: **4-QUART**

2 whole boneless, skinless chicken *or* turkey breasts

oil

½ cup picante sauce

2 Tbsp. soy sauce

½ tsp. sugar

½ Tbsp. quick-cooking tapioca

1 medium onion, chopped

2 garlic cloves, minced

½ tsp. ground ginger

2 cups broccoli florets

1 medium red pepper, cut into pieces

1. Cut chicken into 1-inch cubes and brown lightly in oil in skillet. Place in slow cooker.
2. Stir in remaining ingredients.
3. Cover. Cook on High 1–1½ hours, or on Low 2–3 hours.

If a recipe calls for cooked noodles, macaroni, etc., cook them before adding to the cooker. Don't overcook; instead, cook just till slightly tender.

Mix-It-and-Run Chicken

Shelia Heil   Lancaster, PA

MAKES: **4 SERVINGS**
PREP. TIME: **10 MINUTES**
COOKING TIME: **8–10 HOURS**
IDEAL SLOW COOKER SIZE: **4–5-QUART**

2 15-oz. cans cut green beans, undrained

2 10¾-oz. cans cream of mushroom soup

4–6 boneless, skinless chicken breast halves

½ tsp. salt

1. Drain beans, reserving juice in a medium-sized mixing bowl.
2. Stir soups into bean juice, blending thoroughly. Set aside.
3. Place beans in slow cooker. Sprinkle with salt.
4. Place chicken in cooker. Sprinkle with salt.
5. Top with soup.
6. Cover and cook on Low 8–10 hours, or until chicken is tender, but not dry or mushy.

Creamy Chicken and Noodles

Rhonda Burgoon Collingswood, NJ

MAKES: **4–6 SERVINGS**
PREP. TIME: **25 MINUTES**
COOKING TIME: **4¼–9¼ HOURS**
IDEAL SLOW COOKER SIZE: **4-QUART**

2 cups sliced carrots

1½ cups chopped onions

1 cup sliced celery

2 Tbsp. snipped fresh parsley

bay leaf

3 medium chicken legs and thighs (about 2 lbs.)

2 10¾-oz. cans cream of chicken soup

½ cup water

1 tsp. dried thyme

1 tsp. salt

¼ tsp. pepper

1 cup peas

10 ozs. wide noodles, cooked

1. Place carrots, onions, celery, parsley, and bay leaf in bottom of slow cooker.
2. Place chicken on top of vegetables.
3. Combine soup, water, thyme, salt, and pepper. Pour over chicken and vegetables.
4. Cover. Cook on Low 8–9 hours, or on High 4–4½ hours.
5. Remove chicken from slow cooker. Cool slightly. Remove from bones, cut into bite-sized pieces and return to slow cooker.
6. Remove and discard bay leaf.
7. Stir peas into mixture in slow cooker. Allow to cook for 5–10 more minutes.
8. Pour over cooked noodles. Toss gently to combine.
9. Serve with crusty bread and a salad.

Creamy Chicken a la King

Lafaye M. Musser Denver, PA

MAKES: **4 SERVINGS**
PREP. TIME: **20 MINUTES**
COOKING TIME: **7½–8½ HOURS**
IDEAL SLOW COOKER SIZE: **4-QUART**

10¾-oz. can cream of chicken soup

3 Tbsp. flour

½ tsp. salt

¼ tsp. pepper

dash cayenne pepper

1 lb. boneless chicken, uncooked and cut in pieces

1 rib celery, chopped

½ cup chopped green pepper

¼ cup chopped onions

9-oz. bag frozen peas, thawed

1. Combine soup, flour, salt, pepper, and cayenne pepper in slow cooker.
2. Stir in chicken, celery, green pepper, and onion.
3. Cover. Cook on Low 7–8 hours.
4. Stir in peas.
5. Cover. Cook 30 minutes longer.
6. Serve in pastry cups or over rice, waffles, or toast.

Chicken Pot Roast

Carol Eberly Harrisonburg, VA • *Sarah Miller* Harrisonburg, VA

MAKES: **4 SERVINGS**
PREP. TIME: **10–15 MINUTES**
COOKING TIME: **3–4 HOURS**
IDEAL SLOW COOKER SIZE: **4–5-QUART**

4 boneless, skinless chicken breast halves

salt and pepper to taste

4–6 medium carrots, peeled and sliced

2 cups lima beans, fresh *or* frozen

1 cup water

1. Salt and pepper chicken breasts. Use garlic salt if you wish. Place chicken in slow cooker and start cooking on High.
2. Prepare carrots and place on top of chicken. Add limas on top. Pour water over all.
3. Cover and cook on Low 3–4 hours, or until chicken and vegetables are tender but not dry or mushy.
4. This is good served over rice.

One-Pot Chicken Dinner

Arianne Hochstetler Goshen, IN

MAKES: **6 SERVINGS**
PREP. TIME: **15 MINUTES**
COOKING TIME: **3–6 HOURS**
IDEAL SLOW COOKER SIZE: **4–5-QUART**

12 chicken drumsticks or thighs, skin removed

3 medium sweet potatoes, cut into 2-inch pieces

12-oz. jar chicken gravy, *or* 10¾-oz. can cream of chicken soup

2 Tbsp. unbleached flour, if using chicken gravy

1 tsp. dried parsley flakes, *optional*

½ tsp. dried rosemary, *optional*

salt and pepper to taste, *optional*

10-oz. pkg. frozen cut green beans

1. Place chicken in slow cooker. Top with sweet potatoes chunks.
2. In small bowl, combine remaining ingredients, except beans, and mix until smooth. Pour over chicken.
3. Cover and cook on High 1½ hours, or on Low 3½ hours.
4. One and one-half hours before serving, stir green beans into chicken mixture. Cover and cook on Low 1–2 hours, or until chicken, sweet potatoes, and green beans are tender, but not dry or mushy.

Variation: *Instead of adding the green beans into the slow cooker, stir-fry 1 lb. French-cut green beans with 1 chopped onion. Serve alongside chicken and sweet potatoes.*

Chicken Vegetable Gala

Janie Steele Moore, OK

MAKES: **4 SERVINGS**
PREP. TIME: **10–15 MINUTES**
COOKING TIME: **6–8 HOURS**
IDEAL SLOW COOKER SIZE: **6-QUART**

4 bone-in chicken breast halves

1 small head of cabbage, quartered

1-lb. pkg. baby carrots

2 14½-oz. cans Mexican-flavored stewed tomatoes

1. Place all ingredients in slow cooker in order listed.
2. Cover and cook on Low 6–8 hours, or until chicken and vegetables are tender.

Reuben Chicken Casserole

Maryann Markano   Wilmington, DE

MAKES: **6 SERVINGS**
PREP. TIME: **25–30 MINUTES**
COOKING TIME: **4 HOURS**
IDEAL SLOW COOKER SIZE: **5-QUART**

2 16-oz. cans sauerkraut, rinsed and drained, *divided*
1 cup Light Russian salad dressing, *divided*
6 boneless, skinless chicken breast halves, *divided*
1 Tbsp. prepared mustard, *divided*
6 slices Swiss cheese
fresh parsley for garnish, *optional*

1. Place half the sauerkraut in the slow cooker. Drizzle with ⅓ cup dressing.
2. Top with 3 chicken breast halves. Spread half the mustard on top of the chicken.
3. Top with remaining sauerkraut and chicken breasts. Drizzle with another ⅓ cup dressing. (Save the remaining dressing until serving time.)
4. Cover and cook on Low for 4 hours, or until the chicken is tender, but not dry or mushy.
5. To serve, place a breast half on each of 6 plates. Divide the sauerkraut over the chicken. Top each with a slice of cheese and a drizzle of the remaining dressing. Garnish with parsley if you wish, just before serving.

Be sure to read a recipe the whole way through before beginning to cook, so you are certain you have all the ingredients you need.

Tomato Chicken Curry

Dawn Ranck   Harrisonburg, VA

MAKES: **6–8 SERVINGS**
PREP. TIME: **25–30 MINUTES**
COOKING TIME: **2–6 HOURS**
IDEAL SLOW COOKER SIZE: **6-QUART**

28-oz. can tomatoes
4 whole chicken breasts, cut in half
1 onion, chopped
half a green pepper, chopped
2 carrots, chopped
2 ribs celery, chopped
1–2 Tbsp. curry
1 tsp. turmeric
½ tsp. salt
¼ tsp. pepper
1 Tbsp. sugar
1 chicken bouillon cube dissolved in ¼ cup hot water

1. Combine all ingredients in slow cooker.
2. Cover. Cook on High 2–3 hours, or on Low 5–6 hours.

Dad's Spicy Chicken Curry

Tom & Sue Ruth   Lancaster, PA

MAKES: **8 SERVINGS**
PREP. TIME: **25 MINUTES**
COOKING TIME: **6–8 HOURS**
IDEAL SLOW COOKER SIZE: **6-QUART**

4 lbs. chicken pieces, with bones

water

2 onions, diced

10-oz. pkg. frozen chopped spinach, thawed and
   squeezed dry

1 cup plain yogurt

2–3 diced red potatoes

3 tsp. salt

1 tsp. garlic powder

1 tsp. ground ginger

1 tsp. ground cumin

1 tsp. ground coriander

1 tsp. pepper

1 tsp. ground cloves

1 tsp. ground cardamom

1 tsp. ground cinnamon

½ tsp. chili powder

1 tsp. red pepper flakes

3 tsp. turmeric

1. Place chicken in large slow cooker. Cover
   with water.
2. Cover. Cook on High 2 hours, or until tender.
3. Drain chicken. Remove from slow cooker.
   Cool briefly and cut/shred into small pieces.
   Return to slow cooker.
4. Add remaining ingredients.
5. Cover. Cook on Low 4–6 hours, or until
   potatoes are tender.
6. Serve on rice. Accompany with fresh mango
   slices or mango chutney.

Variation: *Substitute 5 tsp. curry powder for
the garlic, ginger, cumin, coriander, and pepper.*

Sweet Potatoes and Chicken Curry

Maricarol Magill   Freehold, NJ

MAKES: **4 SERVINGS**
PREP. TIME: **10 MINUTES**
COOKING TIME: **5¼–6¼ HOURS**
IDEAL SLOW COOKER SIZE: **4-QUART**

4 boneless, skinless chicken breast halves

1 small onion, chopped

2 sweet potatoes (about 1½ lbs.), cubed

⅔ cup orange juice

1 garlic clove, minced

1 tsp. chicken bouillon granules

1 tsp. salt

¼ tsp. pepper

4 tsp. curry powder

2 Tbsp. cornstarch

2 Tbsp. cold water

sliced green onions

shredded coconut

peanuts

raisins

1. Place chicken in slow cooker. Cover with
   onions and sweet potatoes.
2. Combine orange juice, garlic, chicken
   bouillon granules, salt, pepper, and curry
   powder. Pour over vegetables.
3. Cover. Cook on Low 5–6 hours.
4. Remove chicken and vegetables and keep
   warm.
5. Turn slow cooker to High. Dissolve
   cornstarch in cold water. Stir into sauce in
   slow cooker. Cover. Cook on High 15–20
   minutes.
6. Serve chicken and sauce over rice. Top with
   your choice of remaining ingredients.

Creamy Chicken Curry

Gloria Frey Lebanon, PA

MAKES: **4–6 SERVINGS**
PREP. TIME: **20 MINUTES**
COOKING TIME: **2–4 HOURS**
IDEAL SLOW COOKER SIZE: **3–4-QUART**

2 10¾-oz. cans cream of mushroom soup

1 soup can water

2 tsp. curry powder

⅓–½ cup chopped almonds, toasted

4 skinless chicken breast halves, cooked and cubed

1. Combine ingredients in slow cooker.
2. Cover and cook on Low 2–4 hours. Stir occasionally.
3. Serve over cooked rice.

A vegetable peeler works nicely to peel the brown skin from a coconut after you remove the hard shell.

Fruity Curried Chicken

Marlene Bogard Newton, KS

MAKES: **5 SERVINGS**
PREP. TIME: **20 MINUTES**
COOKING TIME: **4¼–6¼ HOURS**
IDEAL SLOW COOKER SIZE: **5-QUART**

2½–3½-lb. fryer chicken, cut up

salt to taste

pepper to taste

1 Tbsp. curry powder

1 garlic clove, crushed or minced

1 Tbsp. butter, melted

½ cup chicken broth, *or* 1 chicken bouillon cube
    dissolved in ½ cup water

2 Tbsp. finely chopped onion

29-oz. can cling peaches

½ cup pitted prunes

3 Tbsp. cornstarch

3 Tbsp. cold water

peanuts

shredded coconut

fresh pineapple chunks

1. Sprinkle chicken with salt and pepper. Place in slow cooker.
2. Combine curry, garlic, butter, broth, and onions in bowl.
3. Drain peaches, reserving syrup. Add ½ cup syrup to curry mixture. Pour over chicken.
4. Cover. Cook on Low 4–6 hours. Remove chicken from pot. Turn on High.
5. Stir in prunes.
6. Dissolve cornstarch in cold water. Stir into pot.
7. Cover. Cook on High 10 minutes, or until thickened. Add peaches. Add cooked chicken.
8. Serve over rice. Offer remaining ingredients as condiments.

Curried Chicken with Apples

Sharon Miller   Holmesville, OH

MAKES: **7 SERVINGS**
PREP. TIME: **15 MINUTES**
COOKING TIME: **6–7 HOURS**
IDEAL SLOW COOKER SIZE: **4-QUART**

1½ lbs. uncooked boneless skinless chicken breasts, cubed

2½ cups finely chopped apples

10¾-oz. can 98% fat-free cream of mushroom soup, undiluted

4-oz. can mushroom pieces

1 medium onion, chopped

½ cup skim milk

2–3 tsp. curry powder, according to your taste preference

¼ tsp. paprika

1 cup peas, thawed

1. Combine all ingredients except peas in greased slow cooker.
2. Cook on Low 5-6 hours.
3. Add peas.
4. Cook an additional hour.
5. Serve over noodles or rice if desired.

Per Serving: 200 calories (35 calories from fat), 4g total fat (1g saturated, 0g trans), 55mg cholesterol, 490mg sodium, 20g total carbohydrate (4g fiber, 11g sugar), 22g protein, 6%DV vitamin A, 4%DV vitamin C, 6%DV calcium, 8%DV iron.

Aloha Chicken Cosmopolitan

Dianna Milhizer   Brighton, MI

MAKES: **12 SERVINGS**
PREP. TIME: **10–15 MINUTES**
REFRIGERATION TIME: **30 MINUTES**
COOKING TIME: **6 HOURS**
IDEAL SLOW COOKER SIZE: **5-QUART**

5 lbs. boneless, skinless chicken breasts, cut into strips or cubed

dash of salt

1 cup frozen orange juice

1 cup coconut milk

1 cup soy sauce

¼ cup sesame oil

1. Lightly salt chicken and then refrigerate for 30 minutes.
2. Drain chicken of any juices that have gathered and combine with other ingredients in large slow cooker.
3. Cover. Cook on Low 6 hours.
4. Serve with white rice.

Sweet Aromatic Chicken

Anne Townsend   Albuquerque, NM

MAKES: **6–8 SERVINGS**
PREP. TIME: **5 MINUTES**
COOKING TIME: **5–6 HOURS**
IDEAL SLOW COOKER SIZE: **4-QUART**

½ cup coconut milk

½ cup water

8 chicken thighs, skinned

½ cup brown sugar

2 Tbsp. soy sauce

⅛ tsp. ground cloves

2 garlic cloves, minced

1. Combine coconut milk and water. Pour into greased slow cooker.
2. Add remaining ingredients in order listed.
3. Cover. Cook on Low 5–6 hours.

Tips: *What to do with leftover coconut milk?*
1. Two or three spoonfuls over vanilla ice cream, topped with a cherry, makes a flavorful, quick dessert.
2. Family Pina Coladas are good. Pour the coconut milk into a pitcher and add one large can pineapple juice, along with some ice cubes. Decorate with pineapple chunks and cherries.

Curried Chicken Dinner

Janessa Hochstedler   East Earl, PA

MAKES: **6 SERVINGS**
PREP. TIME: **20 MINUTES**
COOKING TIME: **5–10 HOURS**
IDEAL SLOW COOKER SIZE: **3-QUART**

1½ lbs. boneless, skinless chicken thighs, quartered
3 potatoes, peeled and cut into chunks, about 2 cups
1 apple, chopped
2 Tbsp. curry powder
14½-oz. can chicken broth
1 medium onion, chopped, *optional*

1. Place all ingredients in slow cooker. Mix together gently.
2. Cover and cook on Low 8–10 hours, or on High 5 hours, or until chicken is tender but not dry.
3. Serve over cooked rice.

Chicken Divan

Kristin Tice   Shipshewana, IN

MAKES: **4 SERVINGS**
PREP. TIME: **15 MINUTES**
COOKING TIME: **3–4 HOURS**
IDEAL SLOW COOKER SIZE: **3-QUART**

4 boneless, skinless chicken breast halves
4 cups chopped broccoli, fresh *or* frozen
2 10¾-oz. cans cream of chicken soup
1 cup mayonnaise
½–1 tsp. curry powder, depending upon your taste preference

1. Place chicken breasts in slow cooker.
2. Top with broccoli.
3. In a small mixing bowl, blend soup, mayonnaise, and curry powder together. Pour over top of chicken and broccoli.
4. Cover and cook on High 3–4 hours, or until chicken and broccoli are tender but not mushy or dry. Serve with rice.

A slow cooker is great for taking food to a potluck supper, even if you didn't prepare it in the cooker.

Chicken Sweet and Sour

Willard E. Roth   Elkhart, IN

MAKES: **8 SERVINGS**
PREP. TIME: **10 MINUTES**
COOKING TIME: **6½ HOURS**
IDEAL SLOW COOKER SIZE: **4–5-QUART**

4 medium potatoes, sliced

8 boneless, skinless chicken breast halves

2 Tbsp. cider vinegar

¼ tsp. ground nutmeg

1 tsp. dry basil, *or* **1 Tbsp. chopped fresh basil**

2 Tbsp. brown sugar

1 cup orange juice

dried parsley flakes

17-oz. can waterpack sliced peaches, drained

fresh parsley

fresh orange slices

1. Place potatoes in greased slow cooker. Arrange chicken on top.
2. In separate bowl, combine vinegar, nutmeg, basil, brown sugar, and orange juice. Pour over chicken. Sprinkle with parsley.
3. Cover. Cook on Low 6 hours.
4. Remove chicken and potatoes from sauce and arrange on warm platter.
5. Turn cooker to High. Add peaches. When warm, spoon peaches and sauce over chicken and potatoes. Garnish with fresh parsley and orange slices.

Don't be afraid to experiment. Not everything will be successful, but sometimes there will be a fantastic discovery.

Chicken with Tropical Barbecue Sauce

Lois Stoltzfus   Honey Brook, PA

MAKES: **6 SERVINGS**
PREP. TIME: **5 MINUTES**
COOKING TIME: **3–9 HOURS**
IDEAL SLOW COOKER SIZE: **4-QUART**

¼ cup molasses

2 Tbsp. cider vinegar

2 Tbsp. Worcestershire sauce

2 tsp. prepared mustard

⅛–¼ tsp. hot pepper sauce

2 Tbsp. orange juice

3 whole chicken breasts, halved

1. Combine molasses, vinegar, Worcestershire sauce, mustard, hot pepper sauce, and orange juice. Brush over chicken.
2. Place chicken in slow cooker.
3. Cover. Cook on Low 7–9 hours, or on High 3–4 hours.

Fruited Barbecue Chicken

Barbara Katrine Rose   Woodbridge, VA

MAKES: **6–8 SERVINGS**
PREP. TIME: **5 MINUTES**
COOKING TIME: **4 HOURS**
IDEAL SLOW COOKER SIZE: **4-QUART**

29-oz. can tomato sauce

20-oz. can unsweetened crushed pineapple, undrained

2 Tbsp. brown sugar

3 Tbsp. vinegar

1 Tbsp. instant minced onion

1 tsp. paprika

2 tsp. Worcestershire sauce

¼ tsp. garlic powder

⅛ tsp. pepper

3 lbs. chicken, skinned and cubed

11-oz. can mandarin oranges, drained

1. Combine all ingredients except chicken and oranges. Add chicken pieces.
2. Cover. Cook on High 4 hours.
3. Just before serving, stir in oranges. Serve over hot rice.

Orange Chicken Leg Quarters

Kimberly Jensen Bailey, CO

MAKES: **8 SERVINGS**
PREP. TIME: **25 MINUTES**
COOKING TIME: **5–6 HOURS**
IDEAL SLOW COOKER SIZE: **5–6-QUART**

4 chicken drumsticks, skin removed

4 chicken thighs, skin removed

1 cup strips of green and red bell peppers

½ cup fat-free, low-sodium chicken broth

½ cup prepared orange juice

½ cup ketchup

2 Tbsp. soy sauce

1 Tbsp. light molasses

1 Tbsp. prepared mustard

½ tsp. garlic salt

11-oz. can mandarin oranges

2 tsp. cornstarch

1 cup frozen peas

2 green onions, sliced

1. Place chicken in slow cooker. Top with pepper strips.
2. Combine broth, juice, ketchup, soy sauce, molasses, mustard, and garlic salt. Pour over chicken.
3. Cover. Cook on Low 5–6 hours.
4. Remove chicken and vegetables from slow cooker. Keep warm.
5. Measure out 1 cup of cooking sauce. Put in saucepan and bring to boil.
6. Drain oranges, reserving 1 Tbsp. juice. Stir cornstarch into reserved juice. Add to boiling sauce in pan.
7. Add peas to sauce and cook, stirring 2–3 minutes until sauce thickens and peas are warm. Stir in oranges.
8. Arrange chicken pieces on platter of cooked white rice, fried cellophane noodles, or lo mein noodles. Pour orange sauce over chicken and rice or noodles. Top with sliced green onions.

Per Serving: 170 calories (40 calories from fat), 4g total fat (1g saturated, 0g trans), 45mg cholesterol, 520mg sodium, 18g total carbohydrate (2g fiber, 11g sugar), 16g protein, 10%DV vitamin A, 30%DV vitamin C, 4%DV calcium, 10%DV iron.

Chicken and Turkey Main Dishes

Chicken in Piquant Sauce

Beth Shank Wellman, IA • *Karen Waggoner* Joplin, MO
Carol Armstrong Winston, OR • *Lois Niebauer* Pedricktown, NJ
Jean Butzer Batavia, NY • *Veronica Sabo* Shelton, CT
Charlotte Shaffer East Earl, PA

MAKES: **4–6 SERVINGS**
PREP. TIME: **10–15 MINUTES**
COOKING TIME: **3–4 HOURS**
IDEAL SLOW COOKER SIZE: **3–4-QUART**

16-oz. jar Russian *or* Creamy French salad dressing
12-oz. jar apricot preserves
1 envelope dry onion soup mix
4–6 boneless, skinless chicken breast halves

1. In a bowl, mix together the dressing, preserves, and dry onion soup mix.
2. Place the chicken breasts in your slow cooker.
3. Pour the sauce over top of the chicken.
4. Cover and cook on High 3 hours, or on Low 4 hours, or until chicken is tender but not dry.

Variations:

1. Serve over cooked brown rice. Top individual servings with broken cashews.

Crystal Brunk Singers Glen, VA

2. Substitute K.C. Masterpiece BBQ Sauce with Hickory Brown Sugar for the salad dressing. Add 1 cup pineapple chunks and/or 1 cup mandarin oranges, with or without juice, to Step 1.

Jane Hershberger Newton, KS

3. Drop the salad dressing and use 2 12-oz. jars apricot preserves. And substitute ham or turkey for the chicken breasts.

Shirley Sears Sarasota, FL • *Jennifer Eberly* Harrisonburg, VA
Marcia S. Myer Manheim, PA

Chicken, Sweet Chicken

Anne Townsend Albuquerque, NM

MAKES: **6–8 SERVINGS**
PREP. TIME: **15 MINUTES**
COOKING TIME: **5–6 HOURS**
IDEAL SLOW COOKER SIZE: **3-QUART**

2 medium raw sweet potatoes, peeled and cut into ¼-inch thick slices
8 boneless, skinless chicken thighs
8-oz. jar orange marmalade
¼ cup water
¼–½ tsp. salt
½ tsp. pepper

1. Place sweet potato slices in slow cooker.
2. Rinse and dry chicken pieces. Arrange on top of the potatoes.
3. Spoon marmalade over the chicken and potatoes.
4. Pour water over all. Season with salt and pepper.
5. Cover and cook on High 1 hour, and then turn to Low and cook 4–5 hours, or until potatoes and chicken are both tender.

Orange Chicken and Sweet Potatoes

Kimberlee Greenawalt Harrisonburg, VA

MAKES: **6 SERVINGS**
PREP. TIME: **10 MINUTES**
COOKING TIME: **3–10 HOURS**
IDEAL SLOW COOKER SIZE: **4-QUART**

2–3 sweet potatoes, peeled and sliced

3 whole chicken breasts, halved

⅔ cup flour

1 tsp. salt

1 tsp. nutmeg

½ tsp. cinnamon

dash pepper

dash garlic powder

10¾-oz. can cream of celery *or* cream of chicken soup

4-oz. can sliced mushrooms, drained

½ cup orange juice

½ tsp. grated orange rind

2 tsp. brown sugar

3 Tbsp. flour

1. Place sweet potatoes in bottom of slow cooker.
2. Rinse chicken breasts and pat dry. Combine flour, salt, nutmeg, cinnamon, pepper, and garlic powder. Thoroughly coat chicken in flour mixture. Place on top of sweet potatoes.
3. Combine soup with remaining ingredients. Stir well. Pour over chicken breasts.
4. Cover. Cook on Low 8–10 hours, or on High 3–4 hours.
5. Serve over rice.

Orange-Glazed Chicken Breasts

Leona Miller Millersburg, OH

MAKES: **6 SERVINGS**
PREP. TIME: **5 MINUTES**
COOKING TIME: **7¼–9¼ HOURS**
IDEAL SLOW COOKER SIZE: **4-QUART**

6-oz. can frozen orange juice concentrate, thawed

½ tsp. dried marjoram

6 boneless, skinless chicken breast halves

¼ cup cold water

2 Tbsp. cornstarch

1. Combine orange juice and marjoram in shallow dish. Dip each breast in orange-juice mixture and place in slow cooker. Pour remaining sauce over breasts.
2. Cover. Cook on Low 7–9 hours, or on High 3½–4 hours.
3. Remove chicken from slow cooker. Turn cooker to High and cover.
4. Combine water and cornstarch. Stir into liquid in slow cooker. Place cover slightly ajar on slow cooker. Cook until sauce is thick and bubbly, about 15–20 minutes. Serve over chicken.

Variation: *To increase "spice" in dish, add ½–1 tsp. Worcestershire sauce to orange juice-marjoram glaze.*

Mandarin Orange Chicken

Ann VanDoren Lady Lake, FL

MAKES: **4 SERVINGS**
PREP. TIME: **20 MINUTES**
COOKING TIME: **4½–5½ HOURS**
IDEAL SLOW COOKER SIZE: **3–4-QUART**

4 boneless, skinless chicken breast halves

1 medium onion, thinly sliced

¼ cup orange juice concentrate

1 tsp. poultry seasoning

½ tsp. salt

11-oz. can mandarin oranges, drained, with 3 Tbsp. juice reserved

2 Tbsp. flour

1. Place chicken in slow cooker.
2. Combine onion, orange juice concentrate, poultry seasoning, and salt. Pour over chicken.
3. Cover. Cook on Low 4–5 hours.
4. Remove chicken and keep warm. Reserve cooking juices.
5. In a saucepan, combine 3 Tbsp. reserved mandarin orange juice and flour. Stir until smooth.
6. Stir in chicken cooking juices. Bring to a boil. Stir and cook for 2 minutes to thicken.
7. Stir in mandarin oranges. Pour over chicken.
8. Serve with rice or pasta.

Per Serving: 240 calories (30 calories from fat), 3.5g total fat (1g saturated, 0g trans), 75mg cholesterol, 360mg sodium, 25g total carbohydrate (1g fiber, 20g sugar), 28g protein, 10%DV vitamin A, 30%DV vitamin C, 4%DV calcium, 10%DV iron.

Apricot Mustard Chicken

Lee Ann Hazlett Delavan, WI

MAKES: **6 SERVINGS**
PREP. TIME: **10 MINUTES**
COOKING TIME: **2½–6 HOURS**
IDEAL SLOW COOKER SIZE: **5–6-QUART**

11½-oz. can apricot nectar

2 Tbsp. Dijon mustard

1 clove garlic, minced

¼ tsp. fresh grated ginger

¼ tsp. cayenne pepper

¼ tsp. ground allspice

¼ tsp. turmeric

¼ tsp. ground cardamom

6 boneless, skinless chicken breast halves

4 cups prepared couscous *or* wild rice (blended is good, too)

1. Combine all ingredients except chicken and couscous in slow cooker.
2. Add chicken, turning it to make sure all sides are covered in sauce.
3. Cover. Cook on Low 5–6 hours, or on High 2½–3 hours.
4. Remove chicken and arrange over warm couscous or rice. Pour the sauce over the chicken and serve.

Per Serving: 300 calories (35 calories from fat), 4g total fat (1g saturated, 0g trans), 75mg cholesterol, 200mg sodium, 33g total carbohydrate (2g fiber, 8g sugar), 31g protein, 15%DV vitamin A, 2%DV vitamin C, 4%DV calcium, 10%DV iron.

Maui Chicken

John D. Allen   Rye, CO

MAKES: **6 SERVINGS**
PREP. TIME: **20 MINUTES**
COOKING TIME: **4–6 HOURS**
IDEAL SLOW COOKER SIZE: **4–5-QUART**

6 boneless chicken breast halves

2 Tbsp. oil

14½-oz. can chicken broth

20-oz. can pineapple chunks

¼ cup vinegar

2 Tbsp. brown sugar

2 tsp. soy sauce

1 garlic clove, minced

1 medium green bell pepper, chopped

3 Tbsp. cornstarch

¼ cup water

1. Brown chicken in oil. Transfer chicken to slow cooker.
2. Combine remaining ingredients. Pour over chicken.
3. Cover. Cook on High 4–6 hours.
4. Serve over rice.

Chicken a la Fruit

Teresa Kennedy   Mt. Pleasant, IA

MAKES: **5–6 SERVINGS**
PREP. TIME: **20 MINUTES**
COOKING TIME: **6–8 HOURS**
IDEAL SLOW COOKER SIZE: **6-QUART**

½ cup crushed pineapple, drained

3 whole peaches, mashed

2 Tbsp. lemon juice

2 Tbsp. soy sauce

½–¾ tsp. salt

¼ tsp. pepper

1 chicken, cut up

1. Spray slow cooker with nonstick cooking spray.
2. Mix pineapple, peaches, lemon juice, soy sauce, and salt and pepper in a large bowl.
3. Dip chicken pieces in sauce and then place in slow cooker. Pour remaining sauce over all.
4. Cover and cook on Low 6–8 hours, or until chicken is tender but not dry.

Easy Teriyaki Chicken

Barbara Shie   Colorado Springs, CO

MAKES: **5–6 SERVINGS**
PREP. TIME: **5 MINUTES**
COOKING TIME: **4–8 HOURS**
IDEAL SLOW COOKER SIZE: **4-QUART**

2–3 lbs. skinless chicken pieces

20-oz. can pineapple chunks

dash of ground ginger

1 cup teriyaki sauce

1. Place chicken in slow cooker. Pour remaining ingredients over chicken.
2. Cover. Cook on Low 6–8 hours, or on High 4–6 hours.

Never thaw meat at room temperature. Thaw meat safely in the microwave, as part of the cooking process, in a bowl of cold water, changing the water every 20 minutes, or in the refrigerator on the bottom shelf in a platter or deep dish.

Garlic-Lime Chicken

Loretta Krahn   Mountain Lake, MN

MAKES: **5 SERVINGS**
PREP. TIME: **10 MINUTES**
COOKING TIME: **4–8 HOURS**
IDEAL SLOW COOKER SIZE: **4-QUART**

5 chicken breast halves

½ cup soy sauce

¼–⅓ cup lime juice, according to your taste preference

1 Tbsp. Worcestershire sauce

2 garlic cloves, minced, *or* 1 tsp. garlic powder

½ tsp. dry mustard

½ tsp. ground pepper

1. Place chicken in slow cooker.
2. Combine remaining ingredients and pour over chicken.
3. Cover. Cook on High 4–6 hours, or on Low 6–8 hours.

Lemon-Honey Chicken

Carolyn W. Carmichael   Berkeley Heights, NJ

MAKES: **4–6 SERVINGS**
PREP. TIME: **5 MINUTES**
COOKING TIME: **8 HOURS**
IDEAL SLOW COOKER SIZE: **4-QUART**

1 lemon

1 whole roasting chicken, rinsed

½ cup orange juice

½ cup honey

1. Pierce lemon with fork. Place in chicken cavity. Place chicken in slow cooker.
2. Combine orange juice and honey. Pour over chicken.
3. Cover. Cook on Low 8 hours. Remove lemon and squeeze over chicken.
4. Carve chicken and serve.

Stewed Asian Chicken

Stanley Kropf   Elkhart, IN

MAKES: **4–6 SERVINGS**
PREP. TIME: **15–20 MINUTES**
COOKING TIME: **4 HOURS**
IDEAL SLOW COOKER SIZE: **4–5-QUART**

1 whole chicken, cut up

3 Tbsp. hot sweet mustard, *or* 2 Tbsp. hot mustard and
   1 Tbsp. honey

2 Tbsp. soy sauce

1 tsp. ground ginger

1 tsp. cumin

1. Wash chicken and place in slow cooker. Pat dry.
2. Mix the remaining ingredients in a bowl. Taste and adjust seasonings if you want. Pour over chicken.
3. Cover and cook on High for at least 4 hours, or until tender.

Tips:

1. This is a folk recipe so the cook should experiment to taste. I often use a variety of optional ingredients, depending on how I'm feeling. These include teriyaki sauce, oyster sauce, cardamom, sesame and olive oil, dry vermouth, and garlic, in whatever amount and combination seems right.

2. If you cook the dish longer than 4 hours, the chicken tends to fall apart. In any event, serve it in a bowl large enough to hold the chicken and broth.

3. I like to serve this with cooked plain or saffron rice.

Slice chicken when it is partly frozen. It is much easier to slice cleanly.

Asian-Style Sesame Chicken

Anne Townsend   Albuquerque, NM

MAKES: **4 SERVINGS**
PREP. TIME: **5 MINUTES**
COOKING TIME: **4–8 HOURS**
IDEAL SLOW COOKER SIZE: **3-QUART**

1 Tbsp. hot chili sesame oil

4 large chicken thighs

3 cloves garlic, sliced

½ cup brown sugar

3 Tbsp. soy sauce

1. Spread oil around the bottom of your slow cooker.
2. Rinse chicken well and remove excess fat. Pat dry. Place in your slow cooker.
3. Sprinkle garlic slices over top of the chicken. Crumble brown sugar over top. Drizzle with soy sauce.
4. Cover and cook on Low 4–8 hours, or until thighs are tender, but not dry.
5. Serve over rice, prepared with the juice from the cooked chicken instead of water.

Pacific Chicken

Colleen Konetzni Rio Rancho, NM

MAKES: **6 SERVINGS**
PREP. TIME: **10 MINUTES**
COOKING TIME: **7–8 HOURS**
IDEAL SLOW COOKER SIZE: **3–4-QUART**

6–8 skinless chicken thighs

½ cup soy sauce

2 Tbsp. brown sugar

2 Tbsp. grated fresh ginger

2 garlic cloves, minced

1. Wash and dry chicken. Place in slow cooker.
2. Combine remaining ingredients. Pour over chicken.
3. Cover. Cook on High 1 hour. Reduce heat to Low and cook 6-7 hours.
4. Serve over rice with a fresh salad.

Asian Chicken Cashew Dish

Dorothy Horst Tiskilwa, IL

MAKES: **6 SERVINGS**
PREP. TIME: **15 MINUTES**
COOKING TIME: **2-9 HOURS**
IDEAL SLOW COOKER SIZE: **3-QUART**

14-oz. can bean sprouts, drained

3 Tbsp. butter, melted

4 green onions, chopped

4-oz. can mushroom pieces

10¾-oz. can cream of mushroom soup

1 cup sliced celery

12½-oz. can chunk chicken breast, *or* **1 cup cooked chicken, cubed**

1 Tbsp. soy sauce

1 cup cashew nuts

1. Combine all ingredients except nuts in slow cooker.
2. Cover. Cook on Low 4–9 hours, or on High 2-3 hours.
3. Stir in cashew nuts before serving.
4. Serve over rice.

Note: *I teach English as a Second Language to Vietnamese women. Occasionally they invite us to join them for dinner on Vietnamese New Year. We enjoy the fellowship and Vietnamese traditions immensely. They always have a "Lucky Tree," a tree with yellow flowers which blooms in Vietnam on New Year's. They decorate the tree by hanging red envelopes in it. Each contains a money gift; one is given to each unmarried person present, including the babies.*

Thai Chicken

Joanne Good   Wheaton, IL

MAKES: **6 SERVINGS**
PREP. TIME: **5 MINUTES**
COOKING TIME: **8–9 HOURS**
IDEAL SLOW COOKER SIZE: **4-QUART**

6 skinless chicken thighs

¾ cup salsa, your choice of heat

¼ cup chunky peanut butter

1 Tbsp. low-sodium soy sauce

2 Tbsp. lime juice

1 tsp. grated gingerroot, *optional*

2 Tbsp. chopped cilantro, *optional*

1 Tbsp. chopped dry-roasted peanuts, *optional*

1. Put chicken in slow cooker.
2. In a bowl, mix remaining ingredients together, except cilantro and chopped peanuts.
3. Cover and cook on Low 8–9 hours, or until chicken is cooked through but not dry.
4. Skim off any fat. Remove chicken to a platter and serve topped with sauce. Sprinkle with peanuts and cilantro, if you wish.
5. Serve over cooked rice.

Variation: *Vegetarians can substitute 2 15-oz. cans of white beans, and perhaps some tempeh, for the chicken.*

Raspberried Chicken Drumsticks

Pat Bechtel   Dillsburg, PA

MAKES: **3 SERVINGS**
PREP. TIME: **10 MINUTES**
COOKING TIME: **5¼–6¼ HOURS**
IDEAL SLOW COOKER SIZE: **3½-QUART**

3 Tbsp. soy sauce

⅓ cup red raspberry fruit spread *or* **jam**

5 chicken drumsticks *or* **chicken thighs**

2 Tbsp. cornstarch

2 Tbsp. cold water

1. Mix soy sauce and raspberry spread or jam together in a small bowl until well blended.
2. Brush chicken with the sauce and place in slow cooker. Spoon remainder of the sauce over top.
3. Cook on Low 5–6 hours, or until chicken is tender but not dry.
4. Mix together cornstarch and cold water in a small bowl until smooth. Then remove chicken to a serving platter and keep warm. Turn slow cooker to High and stir in cornstarch and water to thicken. When thickened and bubbly, after about 10–15 minutes, spoon sauce over chicken before serving.

Don't be afraid to try new or unusual ingredients.

Chicken and Apples

Jean Butzer Batavia, NY

MAKES: **6 SERVINGS**
PREP. TIME: **20 MINUTES**
COOKING TIME: **7–8 HOURS**
IDEAL SLOW COOKER SIZE: **5–6-QUART**

6-oz. can frozen orange concentrate, thawed

½ tsp dried marjoram leaves

dash ground nutmeg

dash garlic powder

1 onion, chopped

6 skinless, boneless chicken breast halves

3 Granny Smith apples, cored and sliced

¼ cup water

2 Tbsp. cornstarch

1. In a small bowl, combine orange juice concentrate, marjoram, nutmeg, and garlic powder.
2. Place onions in bottom of slow cooker.
3. Dip each chicken breast into the orange mixture to coat. Then place in slow cooker over onions.
4. Pour any remaining orange juice concentrate mixture over the chicken.
5. Cover. Cook on Low 6–7 hours.
6. Add apples and cook on Low 1 hour longer.
7. Remove chicken, apples, and onions to a serving platter.
8. Pour the sauce that remains into a medium saucepan.
9. Mix together water and cornstarch. Stir into the juices.
10. Cook over medium heat, stirring constantly until the sauce is thick and bubbly.
11. Serve the sauce over the chicken.

Per Serving: 240 calories (30 calories from fat), 3g total fat (1g saturated, 0g trans), 75mg cholesterol, 65mg sodium, 24g total carbohydrate (2g fiber, 19g sugar), 28g protein, 2%DV vitamin A, 20%DV vitamin C, 4%DV calcium, 6%DV iron.

Variation: *You can also thicken the sauce by adding cornstarch and water mixture to sauce in the slow cooker. Cook on High 10–15 minutes until thickened.*

Cran-Apple Chicken

Joyce Shackellord Green Bay, WI

MAKES: **6 SERVINGS**
PREP. TIME: **10 MINUTES**
COOKING TIME: **6–8 HOURS**
IDEAL SLOW COOKER SIZE: **5–6-QUART**

6 boneless, skinless chicken breast halves

1 cup fresh *or* frozen cranberries

1 green apple, peeled, cored, and sliced

1 Tbsp. brown sugar

1 cup unsweetened apple juice *or* cider

1. Place chicken in slow cooker.
2. Sprinkle with cranberries and apples.
3. Mix brown sugar and apple juice. Pour over chicken and fruit.
4. Cover. Cook on Low 6–8 hours.

Per Serving: 190 calories (30 calories from fat), 3g total fat (1g saturated, 0g trans), 75mg cholesterol, 65mg sodium, 13g total carbohydrate (2g fiber, 11g sugar), 27g protein, 0%DV vitamin A, 20%DV vitamin C, 2%DV calcium, 6%DV iron.

Cranberry Chicken

Janie Steele   Moore, OK   •   *Sheila Soldner*   Lititz, PA

MAKES: **6 SERVINGS**
PREP. TIME: **10 MINUTES**
COOKING TIME: **6–8 HOURS**
IDEAL SLOW COOKER SIZE: **4–5-QUART**

6 chicken breast halves, *divided*

8-oz. bottle Catalina *or* Creamy French salad dressing

1 envelope dry onion soup mix

16-oz. can whole cranberry sauce

1. Place 3 chicken breasts in slow cooker.
2. Mix other ingredients together in a mixing bowl. Pour half the sauce over chicken in the cooker.
3. Repeat Steps 1 and 2.
4. Cover and cook on Low 6–8 hours, or until chicken is tender but not dry.

Teriyaki Chicken with Snow Peas

Elaine Vigoda   Rochester, NY

MAKES: **6 SERVINGS**
PREP. TIME: **15 MINUTES**
COOKING TIME: **5–6 HOURS**
IDEAL SLOW COOKER SIZE: **5-QUART**

1 lb. boneless, skinless chicken thighs, cut into chunks

1 lb. boneless, skinless chicken breasts, cut into large chunks

10-oz. bottle teriyaki sauce

½ lb. snow peas, *optional*

8-oz. can water chestnuts, drained, *optional*

1. Place chicken in slow cooker. Cover with sauce. Stir until sauce is well distributed.
2. Cover and cook on Low 4–5 hours, or until chicken is tender. Add snow peas and water chestnuts, if you wish.
3. Cover and cook another hour on Low.
4. Serve over cooked white rice or Chinese rice noodles.

Buy sturdy kitchen tools. Buy ones that fit well into your hands. Take care of them and they will last a very long time.

Spicy Italian Chicken

Ilene Bontrager Arlington, KS

MAKES: **6 SERVINGS**
PREP. TIME: **15 MINUTES**
COOKING TIME: **4–5 HOURS**
IDEAL SLOW COOKER SIZE: **5-QUART**

1 medium onion, chopped
½ cup fat-free Italian dressing
½ cup water
¼ tsp. salt
½ tsp. garlic powder
1 tsp. chili powder
½ tsp. paprika
¼ tsp. black pepper
6 boneless, skinless chicken breast halves
2 Tbsp. cornstarch
2 Tbsp. cold water

1. Spray the inside of the slow cooker with nonfat cooking spray. Combine all ingredients except chicken, cornstarch, and water in slow cooker.
2. Add chicken. Turn to coat.
3. Cover. Cook on Low 4–5 hours.
4. Remove chicken and keep warm.
5. In a saucepan, combine cornstarch and cold water.
6. Add cooking juices gradually. Stir and bring to a boil until thickened.
7. Pour sauce over chicken and then serve over noodles or rice.

Per Serving: 180 calories (30 calories from fat), 3.5g total fat (1g saturated, 0g trans), 75mg cholesterol, 550mg sodium, 7g total carbohydrate (0.5g fiber, 3g sugar), 27g protein, 2%DV vitamin A, 0%DV vitamin C, 2%DV calcium, 6%DV iron.

Tip: *The flavor of the chicken improves if you marinate it in the Italian dressing for a few hours before cooking.*

Chicken and Veggie Bake

Sara Puskar Abingdon, MD

MAKES: **8 SERVINGS**
PREP. TIME: **10 MINUTES**
COOKING TIME: **4–8 HOURS**
IDEAL SLOW COOKER SIZE: **4-QUART**

8 boneless, skinless chicken breast halves
black pepper to taste
1 tsp. garlic powder
16-oz. bottle fat-free Italian salad dressing, *divided*
2 15-oz. cans whole potatoes, drained
1 lb. frozen Italian veggies *or* green beans
8-oz. can water chestnuts, *optional*

1. Sprinkle chicken with pepper and garlic powder.
2. Put chicken in bottom of slow cooker. Pour half of salad dressing over meat, making sure that all pieces are glazed.
3. Add potatoes, vegetables, and water chestnuts. Pour remaining salad dressing over, again making sure that the vegetables are all lightly coated.
4. Cover. Cook on High 4 hours, or on Low 7–8 hours.

Per Serving: 200 calories (35 calories from fat), 3.5g total fat (1g saturated, 0g trans), 75mg cholesterol, 480mg sodium, 12g total carbohydrate (3g fiber, 2g sugar), 29g protein, 50%DV vitamin A, 4%DV vitamin C, 4%DV calcium, 10%DV iron.

Zesty Italian Chicken

Yvonne Kauffman Boettger   Harrisonburg, VA

MAKES: **4–6 SERVINGS**
PREP. TIME: **5 MINUTES**
COOKING TIME: **4–8 HOURS**
IDEAL SLOW COOKER SIZE: **4-QUART**

**2–3 lbs. boneless, skinless chicken breasts, cut into
chunks**
16-oz. bottle Italian dressing
¼ cup Parmesan cheese

1. Place chicken in bottom of slow cooker and pour dressing over chicken. Stir together gently.
2. Sprinkle cheese on top.
3. Cover and cook on High 4 hours, or on Low 8 hours, or until chicken is tender but not dry.
4. Serve over cooked rice, along with extra sauce from the chicken.

Creamy Italian Chicken

Kathy Esh   New Holland, PA   •   *Mary Ann Bowman*   East Earl, PA

MAKES: **4 SERVINGS**
PREP. TIME: **5–10 MINUTES**
COOKING TIME: **4 HOURS**
IDEAL SLOW COOKER SIZE: **5-QUART**

4 boneless, skinless chicken breast halves
1 envelope dry Italian salad dressing mix
¼ cup water
8-oz. pkg. cream cheese, softened
10¾-oz. can cream of chicken *or* celery soup
4-oz. can mushroom stems and pieces, drained, *optional*

1. Place chicken in slow cooker. Combine salad dressing and water. Pour over chicken.
2. Cover and cook on Low 3 hours.
3. In a small bowl, beat cream cheese and soup until blended. Stir in mushrooms if you wish. Pour over chicken.
4. Cover and cook on Low 1 hour, or until chicken is tender but not dry.

Tips:

1. Remove chicken from sauce and serve on a platter. Serve the sauce over cooked noodles.

2. Shred chicken after cooking, and then stir into the sauce. Serve over cooked noodles.

Liquids don't boil down in a slow cooker. At the end of the cooking time, remove the cover, set dial on High and allow the liquid to evaporate, if the dish is soup-ier than you want.

Chicken Cacciatore with Spaghetti

Phyllis Pellman Good Lancaster, PA

MAKES: **4–5 SERVINGS**
PREP. TIME: **15 MINUTES**
COOKING TIME: **6–6½ HOURS**
IDEAL SLOW COOKER SIZE: **4-QUART**

2 onions, sliced

2½–3 lbs. chicken legs

2 garlic cloves, minced

16-oz. can stewed tomatoes

8-oz. can tomato sauce

1 tsp. salt

¼ tsp. pepper

1–2 tsp. dried oregano

½ tsp. dried basil

1 bay leaf

¼ cup white wine

1. Place onions in bottom of slow cooker.
2. Lay chicken legs over onions.
3. Combine remaining ingredients. Pour over chicken.
4. Cover. Cook on Low 6–6½ hours.
5. Remove bay leaf. Serve over hot buttered spaghetti, linguini, or fettucini.

Low-Fat Chicken Cacciatore

Dawn Day Westminster, CA

MAKES: **10 SERVINGS**
PREP. TIME: **15 MINUTES**
COOKING TIME: **8 HOURS**
IDEAL SLOW COOKER SIZE: **3-QUART**

2 lbs. uncooked boneless, skinless chicken breasts, cubed

½ lb. fresh mushrooms

1 bell pepper, chopped

1 medium-sized onion, chopped

12-oz. can low-sodium chopped tomatoes

6-oz. can low-sodium tomato paste

12-oz. can low-sodium tomato sauce

½ tsp. dried oregano

½ tsp. dried basil

½ tsp. garlic powder

½ tsp. salt

½ tsp. black pepper

1. Combine all ingredients in slow cooker.
2. Cover. Cook on Low 8 hours.
3. Serve over rice or whole wheat, or semolina, pasta.

Per Serving: 200 calories (30 calories from fat), 3.5g total fat (1g saturated, 0g trans), 75mg cholesterol, 500mg sodium, 10g total carbohydrate (2g fiber, 4g sugar), 30g protein, 10%DV vitamin A, 20%DV vitamin C, 6%DV calcium, 10%DV iron.

Variations:

1. You can substitute 2 cups fresh diced tomatoes for 12-oz. can tomatoes.

2. If you are not concerned about increasing your sodium intake, you may want to use 1 tsp. salt instead of ½ tsp.

Con Pollo

Dorothy Van Deest Memphis, TN

MAKES: **4–6 SERVINGS**
PREP. TIME: **10 MINUTES**
COOKING TIME: **3–10 HOURS**
IDEAL SLOW COOKER SIZE: **5-QUART**

3–4-lb. whole chicken

salt to taste

pepper to taste

paprika to taste

garlic salt to taste

6-oz. can tomato paste

½ cup beer

3-oz. jar stuffed olives with liquid

1. Wash chicken. Sprinkle all over with salt, pepper, paprika, and garlic salt. Place in slow cooker.
2. Combine tomato paste and beer. Pour over chicken. Add olives.
3. Cover. Cook on Low 8–10 hours, or on High 3-4 hours.
4. Serve over rice or noodles, along with salad and cornbread, and sherbet for dessert.

Note: *This is chicken with a Spanish flair. This easy supper is quick, too, by slow cooker standards, if you use the high temperature. Let your slow cooker be the chef.*

Chicken and Sausage Cacciatore

Joyce Kaut Rochester, NY

MAKES: **4–6 SERVINGS**
PREP. TIME: **25–35 MINUTES**
COOKING TIME: **8 HOURS**
IDEAL SLOW COOKER SIZE: **5-QUART**

1 large green pepper, sliced in 1-inch strips

1 cup sliced mushrooms

1 medium onion, sliced in rings

1 lb. skinless, boneless chicken breasts, browned

1 lb. Italian sausage, browned

½ tsp. dried oregano

½ tsp. dried basil

1½ cups Italian-style tomato sauce

1. Layer vegetables in slow cooker.
2. Top with meat.
3. Sprinkle with oregano and basil.
4. Top with tomato sauce.
5. Cover. Cook on Low 8 hours.
6. Remove cover during last 30 minutes of cooking time to allow sauce to cook off and thicken.
7. Serve over cooked spiral pasta.

Use your slow cooker to cook a hen, turkey, or roast beef for use in salads or casseroles. The meat can even be frozen when you put it in the slow cooker. Set the cooker on Low, and let the meat cook all night while you sleep.

Chicken Jambalaya

Martha Ann Auker Landisburg, PA

MAKES: **6 SERVINGS**
PREP. TIME: **20 MINUTES**
COOKING TIME: **6 HOURS**
IDEAL SLOW COOKER SIZE: **5-QUART**

1 lb. uncooked boneless, skinless chicken breast, cubed

3 cups fat-free chicken broth

¾ cup water

1½ cups brown rice, uncooked

4 ozs. reduced-fat, smoked turkey sausage, diced

½ cup thinly sliced celery with leaves

½ cup chopped onion

½ cup chopped green bell pepper

2 tsp. Cajun seasoning

2 garlic cloves, minced

⅛ tsp. hot pepper sauce, *optional*

1 bay leaf

14½-oz. can no-salt diced tomatoes, undrained

1. In a large nonstick skillet, sauté chicken 2–3 minutes.
2. Stir together remaining ingredients in slow cooker.
3. Add sautéed chicken.
4. Cover. Cook on High 6 hours.

_____

Per Serving: 370 calories (60 calories from fat), 7g total fat (1.5g saturated, 0g trans), 75mg cholesterol, 620mg sodium, 42g total carbohydrate (4g fiber, 4g sugar), 34g protein, 4%DV vitamin A, 10%DV vitamin C, 10%DV calcium, 15%DV iron.

Variation: *You can substitute 1 cup low-sodium tomato juice for ¾ cup water.*

Zesty Chicken Breasts

Barb Yoder Angola, IN

MAKES: **6 SERVINGS**
PREP. TIME: **15 MINUTES**
COOKING TIME: **3–8 HOURS**
IDEAL SLOW COOKER SIZE: **4-QUART**

6 bone-in chicken breast halves

2 14½-oz. cans diced tomatoes, undrained

1 small can jalapeños, sliced and drained, *optional*

¼ cup reduced-fat, creamy peanut butter

2 Tbsp. fresh cilantro, chopped, *optional*

1. Remove skin from chicken, but leave bone in.
2. Mix all ingredients, except chicken, in medium-sized bowl.
3. Pour one-third of sauce in bottom of slow cooker sprayed with non-fat cooking spray. Place chicken on top.
4. Pour remaining sauce over chicken.
5. Cover. Cook on High 3–4 hours, or on Low 6–8 hours.
6. Remove from slow cooker gently. Chicken will be very tender and will fall off the bones.

_____

Per Serving: 230 calories (60 calories from fat), 7g total fat (1.5g saturated, 0g trans), 75mg cholesterol, 650mg sodium, 11g total carbohydrate (4g fiber, 5g sugar), 31g protein, 8%DV vitamin A, 10%DV vitamin C, 10%DV calcium, 8%DV iron.

If you have them available, use whole or leaf herbs and spices rather than crushed or ground ones.

Parmesan Chicken

Karen Waggoner   Joplin, MO

MAKES: **8 SERVINGS**
PREP. TIME: **10 MINUTES**
COOKING TIME: **4–4½ HOURS**
IDEAL SLOW COOKER SIZE: **4–5-QUART**

8 boneless, skinless chicken breast halves (about 2 lbs.)
½ cup water
1 cup fat-free mayonnaise
½ cup grated fat-free Parmesan cheese
2 tsp. dried oregano
¼ tsp. black pepper
¼ tsp. paprika

1. Place chicken and water in slow cooker.
2. Cover. Cook on High 2 hours.
3. Mix remaining ingredients. Spread over chicken.
4. Cover. Cook on High 2–2½ hours.

Per Serving: 180 calories (35 calories from fat), 4g total fat (1g saturated, 0g trans), 75mg cholesterol, 400mg sodium, 4g total carbohydrate (0.5g fiber, 2g sugar), 28g protein, 2%DV vitamin A, 0%DV vitamin C, 8%DV calcium, 6%DV iron.

Chicken Parmigiana

Brenda Pope   Dundee, OH

MAKES: **6 SERVINGS**
PREP. TIME: **10–15 MINUTES**
COOKING TIME: **6–8 HOURS**
IDEAL SLOW COOKER SIZE: **4-QUART**

1 egg
1 tsp. salt
¼ tsp. pepper
6 boneless, skinless chicken breast halves
1 cup Italian bread crumbs
2–4 Tbsp. butter
14-oz. jar pizza sauce

6 slices mozzarella cheese
grated Parmesan cheese

1. Beat egg, salt, and pepper together. Dip chicken into egg and coat with bread crumbs. Sauté chicken in butter in skillet. Arrange chicken in slow cooker.
2. Pour pizza sauce over chicken.
3. Cover. Cook on Low 6–8 hours.
4. Layer mozzarella cheese over top and sprinkle with Parmesan cheese. Cook an additional 15 minutes.

Can-You-Believe-It's-So-Simple Salsa Chicken

Leesa DeMartyn   Enola, PA

MAKES: **4–6 SERVINGS**
PREP. TIME: **5 MINUTES**
COOKING TIME: **5–8 HOURS**
IDEAL SLOW COOKER SIZE: **3-QUART**

4–6 boneless, skinless chicken breast halves
16-oz. jar chunky-style salsa, your choice of heat
2 cups shredded cheese, your choice of flavor

1. Place chicken in slow cooker. Pour salsa over chicken.
2. Cover and cook on Low 5–8 hours, or until chicken is tender but not dry.
3. Top individual servings with shredded cheese.
4. Serve this over cooked rice, or in a whole wheat or cheddar cheese wrap.

Cheesy Chicken Chili

Jennifer Kuh   Bay Village, OH

MAKES: **4 SERVINGS**
PREP. TIME: **5–7 MINUTES**
COOKING TIME: **6–8 HOURS**
IDEAL SLOW COOKER SIZE: **3–4-QUART**

4 boneless, skinless chicken breast halves
16-oz. jar salsa, your choice of heat
2 16-oz. cans Great Northern beans, drained
8 ozs. shredded Colby Jack, *or* Pepper Jack, cheese

1. Place chicken in the bottom of your slow cooker.
2. Cover with salsa.
3. Cover and cook on Low 5½–7½ hours, or until chicken is tender but not dry.
4. Shred or cube chicken in the sauce.
5. Stir in beans and cheese.
6. Cover and cook another 30 minutes on Low.
7. Serve over cooked rice or noodles.

Chicken Enchiladas

Jennifer Yoder Sommers   Harrisonburg, VA

MAKES: **4 SERVINGS**
PREP. TIME: **20 MINUTES**
COOKING TIME: **4 HOURS**
IDEAL SLOW COOKER SIZE: **3-QUART**

2 10¾-oz. cans cream of chicken *or* mushroom soup
4½-oz. can diced green chilies
2–3 boneless, skinless whole chicken breasts, cut into pieces
2 cups shredded cheddar cheese
5 6-inch flour tortillas

1. In a mixing bowl, combine soups, chilies, and chicken.
2. Spray the interior of the cooker with nonstick cooking spray. Put foil handles in place (see Step 1 of Meat Loaf and Mushrooms, page 316).
3. Spoon in ⅕ of the sauce on the bottom. Top with ⅕ of the cheese and then 1 tortilla. Continue layering in that order, and with those amounts, 4 more times, ending with cheese on top.
4. Cover cooker and cook on Low 4 hours.

Chicken Olé

Barb Yoder   Angola, IN

MAKES: **8 SERVINGS**
PREP. TIME: **10 MINUTES**
COOKING TIME: **4½–5½ HOURS**
IDEAL SLOW COOKER SIZE: **4-QUART**

10¾-oz. can cream of mushroom soup
10¾-oz. can cream of chicken soup
1 cup sour cream
2 Tbsp. grated onion
1½ cups shredded cheddar cheese
12 flour tortillas, each torn into 6–8 pieces
3–4 cups cubed, cooked chicken
7-oz. jar salsa
½ cup shredded cheddar cheese

1. In separate bowl, combine soups, sour cream, onion, and 1½ cups cheese.
2. Place one-third of each of the following in layers in slow cooker: torn tortillas, soup mixture, chicken, and salsa. Repeat layers 2 more times.
3. Cover. Cook on Low 4–5 hours. (This recipe does not respond well to cooking on High.)
4. Gently stir. Sprinkle with remaining ½ cup cheese. Cover. Cook on Low another 15–30 minutes.
5. Serve with tortilla chips and lettuce.

Chicken Enchilada Casserole

Marsha Sabus   Fallbrook, CA

MAKES: **4–6 SERVINGS**
PREP. TIME: **30 MINUTES**
COOKING TIME: **6–8 HOURS**
IDEAL SLOW COOKER SIZE: **4-QUART**

1 onion, chopped

1 garlic clove, minced

1 Tbsp. oil

10-oz. can enchilada sauce

8-oz. can tomato sauce

salt to taste

pepper to taste

8 corn tortillas

3 boneless chicken breast halves, cooked and cubed

15-oz. can ranch-style beans, drained

11-oz. can Mexicorn, drained

¾-lb. cheddar cheese, shredded

2¼-oz. can sliced black olives, drained

1. Sauté onion and garlic in oil in saucepan. Stir in enchilada sauce and tomato sauce. Season with salt and pepper.
2. Place two tortillas in bottom of slow cooker. Layer one-third chicken on top. Top with one-third sauce mixture, one-third beans, one-third corn, one-third cheese, and one-third black olives. Repeat layers 2 more times. Top with 2 tortillas.
3. Cover. Cook on Low 6–8 hours.

Variation: *Substitute 1 lb. cooked and drained hamburger for the chicken.*

Chicken Creole Cosmo

Cathy Boshart   Lebanon, PA

MAKES: **6 SERVINGS**
PREP. TIME: **15 MINUTES**
COOKING TIME: **2–3 HOURS**
IDEAL SLOW COOKER SIZE: **4-QUART**

2 Tbsp. butter

half a medium green pepper, chopped

2 medium onions, chopped

½ cup chopped celery

1 lb. 4 oz.-can tomatoes

½ tsp. pepper *or* your choice of dried herbs

1½ tsp. salt *or* your choice of dried herbs

⅛ tsp. red pepper

1 cup water

2 Tbsp. cornstarch

1 tsp. sugar

1½ Tbsp. cold water

2 cups cooked and cubed chicken

6 green *or* black olives, sliced

½ cup sliced mushrooms

1. Melt butter in slow cooker. Add green pepper, onions, and celery. Heat.
2. Add tomatoes, pepper, salt, and 1 cup water.
3. Cover. Cook on High while preparing remaining ingredients.
4. Combine cornstarch and sugar. Add 1½ Tbsp. cold water and make a smooth paste. Stir into mixture in slow cooker. Add chicken, olives, and mushrooms.
5. Cover. Cook on Low 2–3 hours.

Chicken and Vegetables

Barbara McGinnis Jupiter, FL

MAKES: **4 SERVINGS**
PREP. TIME: **15 MINUTES**
COOKING TIME: **6 HOURS**
IDEAL SLOW COOKER SIZE: **4-QUART**

2 (.9-oz.) pkgs. dry bearnaise sauce mix

½ cup dry white wine

1 lb. boneless, skinless chicken breasts, cut into bite-sized cubes

9-oz. pkg. frozen mixed vegetables

1 lb. cooked ham, cubed

1 lb. red potatoes, cubed

1 red bell pepper, chopped

1 green bell pepper, chopped

3 shallots, minced

½ tsp. garlic powder

½ tsp. turmeric powder

½ tsp. dried tarragon

1. Combine all ingredients in slow cooker.
2. Cover. Cook on Low 6 hours.

Chicken Azteca

Katrine Rose Woodbridge, VA

MAKES: **10–12 SERVINGS**
PREP. TIME: **15–20 MINUTES**
COOKING TIME: **2½–6½ HOURS**
IDEAL SLOW COOKER SIZE: **7-QUART**

2 15-oz. cans black beans, drained

4 cups frozen corn kernels

2 garlic cloves, minced

¾ tsp. ground cumin

2 cups chunky salsa, *divided*

10 skinless, boneless chicken breast halves

2 8-oz. pkgs. cream cheese, cubed

rice, cooked

shredded cheddar cheese

1. Combine beans, corn, garlic, cumin, and half of salsa in slow cooker.
2. Arrange chicken breasts over top. Pour remaining salsa over top.
3. Cover. Cook on High 2–3 hours, or on Low 4–6 hours.
4. Remove chicken and cut into bite-sized pieces. Return to cooker.
5. Stir in cream cheese. Cook on High until cream cheese melts.
6. Spoon chicken and sauce over cooked rice. Top with shredded cheese.

Don't lift the lid on the rice pan before it's time.

Chicken and Turkey Main Dishes

Tamale Chicken

Jeanne Allen Rye, CO

MAKES: **6 SERVINGS**
PREP. TIME: **30 MINUTES**
COOKING TIME: **3–4 HOURS**
IDEAL SLOW COOKER SIZE: **4-QUART**

1 medium onion, chopped

4-oz. can chopped green chilies

2 Tbsp. oil

10¾-oz. can cream of chicken soup

2 cups sour cream

1 cup sliced ripe olives

1 cup chopped stewed tomatoes

2 cups shredded cheddar cheese

8 chicken breast halves, cooked and chopped

16-oz. can beef tamales, chopped

1 tsp. chili powder

1 tsp. garlic powder

1 tsp. pepper

½ cup shredded cheddar cheese

fresh tomatoes

shredded lettuce

sour cream

salsa

guacamole

1. Sauté onion and chilies in oil in skillet.
2. Combine all ingredients except ½ cup shredded cheese. Pour into slow cooker.
3. Top with remaining cheese.
4. Cover. Cook on High 3-4 hours.
5. Serve with your choice of remaining ingredients as toppings.

Easy Chicken a la King

Jenny R. Unternahrer Wayland, IA

MAKES: **6 SERVINGS**
PREP. TIME: **5 MINUTES**
COOKING TIME: **3–6 HOURS**
IDEAL SLOW COOKER SIZE: **4-QUART**

1½ lbs. uncooked boneless, skinless chicken breast

10¾-oz. can fat-free, low-sodium cream of chicken soup

3 Tbsp. flour

¼ tsp. black pepper

9-oz. pkg. frozen peas and onions, thawed and drained

2 Tbsp. chopped pimentos

½ tsp. paprika

1. Cut chicken into bite-sized pieces and place in slow cooker.
2. Combine soup, flour, and pepper. Pour over chicken. Do not stir.
3. Cover. Cook on High 2½ hours, or on Low 5-5½ hours.
4. Stir in peas and onions, pimentos, and paprika.
5. Cover. Cook on High 20-30 minutes.

Per Serving: 280 calories (70 calories from fat), 7g total fat (2g saturated, 0g trans), 100mg cholesterol, 510mg sodium, 13g total carbohydrate (2g fiber, 0g sugar), 39g protein, 10%DV vitamin A, 10%DV vitamin C, 4%DV calcium, 15%DV iron.

Variations:

1. Add ¼–½ cup chopped green peppers to Step 2.

Sharon Brubaker Myerstown, PA

2. If your diet allows, you may want to add ½ tsp. salt to the mixture in Step 2.

Chickenetti

Miriam Nolt   New Holland, PA

Ruth Hershey   Paradise, PA

MAKES: **10 SERVINGS**
PREP. TIME: **25 MINUTES**
COOKING TIME: **2–3 HOURS**
IDEAL SLOW COOKER SIZE: **6–7-QUART**

1 cup fat-free, low-sodium chicken broth

16-oz. pkg. spaghetti, cooked

4–6 cups cubed and cooked chicken *or* turkey breast

10¾-oz. can fat-free, low-sodium cream of mushroom *or* celery soup

1 cup water

¼ cup chopped green bell peppers

½ cup diced celery

½ tsp. black pepper

1 medium onion, grated

½ lb. fat-free white *or* yellow American cheese, cubed

1. Put chicken broth into very large slow cooker. Add spaghetti and chicken.
2. In large bowl, combine soup and water until smooth. Stir in remaining ingredients; then pour into slow cooker.
3. Cover. Cook on Low 2–3 hours.

Per Serving: 210 calories (25 calories from fat), 3g total fat (1g saturated, 0g trans), 50mg cholesterol, 630mg sodium, 20g total carbohydrate (1g fiber, 4g sugar), 24g protein, 0%DV vitamin A, 0%DV vitamin C, 20%DV calcium, 6%DV iron.

Variation: *If your diet allows, you may want to add ½ tsp. salt to Step 2, when stirring together the diluted soup and chopped vegetables.*

Chicken Tetrazzini

Joyce Slaymaker   Strasburg, PA

MAKES: **4 SERVINGS**
PREP. TIME: **10 MINUTES**
COOKING TIME: **6–8 HOURS**
IDEAL SLOW COOKER SIZE: **3–4-QUART**

2–3 cups diced cooked chicken

2 cups chicken broth

1 small onion, chopped

¼ cup sauterne, white wine, *or* milk

½ cup slivered almonds

2 4-oz. cans sliced mushrooms, drained

10¾-oz. can cream of mushroom soup

1 lb. spaghetti, cooked

grated Parmesan cheese

1. Combine all ingredients except spaghetti and cheese in slow cooker.
2. Cover. Cook on Low 6–8 hours.
3. Serve over buttered spaghetti. Sprinkle with Parmesan cheese.

Variations:

1. Place spaghetti in large baking dish. Pour sauce in center. Sprinkle with Parmesan cheese. Broil until lightly browned.

2. Add 10-oz. pkg. frozen peas to Step 1.

Darlene Raber   Wellman, IA

I keep cooked, deboned chicken in the freezer for times when recipes call for prepped chicken. It cuts down on meal prepping time.

Chicken at a Whim

Colleen Heatwole Burton, MI

MAKES: **6–8 SERVINGS**
PREP. TIME: **10 MINUTES**
COOKING TIME: **4½ HOURS**
IDEAL SLOW COOKER SIZE: **4-QUART**

6 medium, boneless, skinless chicken breast halves

1 small onion, sliced

1 cup dry white wine, chicken broth, *or* water

15-oz. can chicken broth

2 cups water

6-oz. can sliced black olives, with juice

1 small can artichoke hearts, with juice

5 garlic cloves, minced

1 cup dry elbow macaroni *or* small shells

1 envelope dry savory garlic soup

1. Place chicken in slow cooker. Spread onion over chicken.
2. Combine remaining ingredients, except dry soup mix, and pour over chicken. Sprinkle with dry soup.
3. Cover. Cook on Low 4½ hours.

Coq au Vin

Nancy Savage Factoryville, PA

MAKES: **6 SERVINGS**
PREP. TIME: **25 MINUTES**
COOKING TIME: **5–6 HOURS**
IDEAL SLOW COOKER SIZE: **4–5-QUART**

4 slices turkey bacon

1½ cups frozen pearl onions

1 cup fresh, sliced, button mushrooms

1 clove garlic, minced

1 tsp. dried thyme leaves

¼ tsp. coarse ground black pepper

6 boneless, skinless chicken breast halves

½ cup dry red wine

¾ cup fat-free, low-sodium chicken broth

¼ cup tomato paste

3 Tbsp. flour

1. Cook bacon in medium skillet over medium heat. Drain and crumble.
2. Layer ingredients in slow cooker in the following order: onions, crumbled bacon, mushrooms, garlic, thyme, pepper, chicken, wine, and broth.
3. Cover. Cook on Low 5–6 hours.
4. Remove chicken and vegetables. Cover. Keep warm.
5. Ladle ½ cup cooking liquid into small bowl. Allow to cool slightly.
6. Turn slow cooker to High. Cover.
7. Mix removed liquid, tomato paste, and flour until smooth.
8. Return tomato mixture to slow cooker.
9. Cover. Cook 15 minutes or until thickened.
10. Serve over egg noodles, if desired.

Per Serving: 230 calories (45 calories from fat), 5g total fat (1.5g saturated, 0g trans), 80mg cholesterol, 230mg sodium, 11g total carbohydrate (2g fiber, 4g sugar), 31g protein, 6%DV vitamin A, 6%DV vitamin C, 4%DV calcium, 15%DV iron.

Chicken Alfredo

Dawn M. Propst   Levittown, PA

MAKES: **4–6 SERVINGS**
PREP. TIME: **20 MINUTES**
COOKING TIME: **8 HOURS**
IDEAL SLOW COOKER SIZE: **4-QUART**

16-oz. jar Alfredo sauce

4–6 boneless, skinless chicken breast halves

8 ozs. dry noodles, cooked

4-oz. can mushroom pieces and stems, drained

**1 cup shredded mozzarella cheese, *or* ½ cup grated
   Parmesan cheese**

1. Pour about one-third of Alfredo sauce in bottom of slow cooker.
2. Add chicken and cover with remaining sauce.
3. Cover. Cook on Low 8 hours.
4. Fifteen minutes before serving, add noodles and mushrooms, mixing well. Sprinkle top with cheese. Dish is ready to serve when cheese is melted.
5. Serve with green salad and Italian bread.

Chicken in a Hurry

Yvonne Boettger   Harrisonburg, VA

MAKES: **4–5 SERVINGS**
PREP. TIME: **10 MINUTES**
COOKING TIME: **4–8 HOURS**
IDEAL SLOW COOKER SIZE: **4–5-QUART**

2½–3 lbs. skinless chicken drumsticks

½ cup ketchup

¼ cup water

¼ cup brown sugar

1 pkg. dry onion soup mix

1. Arrange chicken in slow cooker.
2. Combine remaining ingredients. Pour over chicken.
3. Cover. Cook on High 4–5 hours, or on Low 7–8 hours.

Tender Barbecued Chicken

Betty Stoltzfus   Honeybrook, PA

MAKES: **4–6 SERVINGS**
PREP. TIME: **10 MINUTES**
COOKING TIME: **8–10 HOURS**
IDEAL SLOW COOKER SIZE: **6-QUART**

3–4 lb. broiler chicken

1 medium onion, thinly sliced

1 medium lemon, thinly sliced

18-oz. bottle barbecue sauce

¾ cup cola-flavored soda

1. Place chicken in slow cooker.
2. Top with onion and lemon.
3. Combine barbecue sauce and cola. Pour into slow cooker.
4. Cover. Cook on Low 8–10 hours, or until chicken juices run clear.
5. Cut into serving-sized pieces and serve with barbecue sauce. Slice any leftovers and use in sandwiches.

Onions, Peppers, and Celery Barbecued Chicken

Dawn M. Propst Levittown, PA

MAKES: **6 SERVINGS**
PREP. TIME: **15 MINUTES**
COOKING TIME: **8 HOURS**
IDEAL SLOW COOKER SIZE: **4-QUART**

3 whole boneless, skinless chicken breasts, cut in half

¼ cup flour

¼ cup oil

1 medium onion, sliced

1 green *or* yellow pepper, sliced

½ cup chopped celery

2 Tbsp. Worcestershire sauce

1 cup ketchup

2 cups water

¼ tsp. salt

¼ tsp. paprika

1. Roll chicken breasts in flour. Brown in oil in skillet. Transfer chicken to slow cooker.
2. Sauté onion, peppers, and celery in skillet, also, cooking until tender. Add remaining ingredients and bring to boil. Pour over chicken.
3. Cover. Cook on Low 8 hours.
4. Serve over noodles or rice.

Herby Barbecued Chicken

Lauren M. Eberhard Seneca, IL

MAKES: **4–6 SERVINGS**
PREP. TIME: **10 MINUTES**
COOKING TIME: **6–8 HOURS**
IDEAL SLOW COOKER SIZE: **4–5-QUART**

1 whole chicken, cut up, *or* 8 of your favorite pieces

1 onion, thinly sliced

1 bottle Sweet Baby Ray's Barbecue Sauce

1 tsp. dried oregano

1 tsp. dried basil

1. Place chicken in slow cooker.
2. Mix onion slices, sauce, oregano, and basil together in a bowl. Pour over chicken, covering as well as possible.
3. Cover and cook on Low 6–8 hours, or until chicken is tender but not dry.

Come-Back-for-More Barbecued Chicken

Leesa DeMartyn Enola, PA

MAKES: **6–8 SERVINGS**
PREP. TIME: **10 MINUTES**
COOKING TIME: **6–8 HOURS**
IDEAL SLOW COOKER SIZE: **5-QUART**

6–8 chicken breast halves

1 cup ketchup

⅓ cup Worcestershire sauce

½ cup brown sugar

1 tsp. chili powder

½ cup water

1. Place chicken in slow cooker.
2. Whisk remaining ingredients in a large bowl. Pour sauce mixture over chicken.
3. Cover and cook on Low 6–8 hours, or until chicken is tender but not overcooked.

Tip: *If the sauce begins to dry out as the dish cooks, stir in another ½ cup water.*

Easy Chicken

Ruth Liebelt   Rapid City, SD

MAKES: **6–8 SERVINGS**
PREP. TIME: **10 MINUTES**
COOKING TIME: **8 HOURS**
IDEAL SLOW COOKER SIZE: **5–6-QUART**

8–10 chicken wings *or* legs and thighs

½ cup soy sauce

½ cup sugar

½ tsp. Tabasco sauce

pinch of ground ginger

1. Place chicken in greased slow cooker.
2. Combine remaining ingredients and pour over chicken.
3. Cover. Cook on Low 8 hours.
4. Serve with cooked rice, rolls, and salad.

Cranberry Barbecued Chicken

Teena Wagner   Waterloo, ON

MAKES: **6–8 SERVINGS**
PREP. TIME: **5–10 MINUTES**
COOKING TIME: **4–8 HOURS**
IDEAL SLOW COOKER SIZE: **4-QUART**

3–4-lb. chicken pieces

½ tsp. salt

¼ tsp. pepper

½ cup diced celery

½ cup diced onions

16-oz. can whole berry cranberry sauce

1 cup barbecue sauce

1. Combine all ingredients in slow cooker.
2. Cover. Bake on High for 4 hours, or on Low 6–8 hours.

Barbecued Chicken Breasts

Jeanne Allen   Rye, CO

MAKES: **8 SERVINGS**
PREP. TIME: **10 MINUTES**
COOKING TIME: **3–8 HOURS**
IDEAL SLOW COOKER SIZE: **3–4-QUART**

8 boneless, skinless chicken breast halves

8-oz. can low-sodium tomato sauce

8-oz. can water

2 Tbsp. brown sugar

2 Tbsp. prepared mustard

2 Tbsp. Worcestershire sauce

¼ cup cider vinegar

½ tsp. salt

¼ tsp. black pepper

dash of garlic powder

dash of dried oregano

3 Tbsp. onion, chopped

1. Place chicken in slow cooker sprayed with non-fat cooking spray. Overlap chicken as little as possible.
2. Combine remaining ingredients. Pour over chicken.
3. Cover. Cook on Low 6–8 hours, or on High 3–4 hours.
4. To thicken the sauce a bit, remove the lid during the last hour of cooking.

Per Serving: 170 calories (30 calories from fat), 3g total fat (1g saturated, 0g trans), 75mg cholesterol, 470mg sodium, 7g total carbohydrate (0.5g fiber, 5g sugar), 27g protein, 2%DV vitamin A, 4%DV vitamin C, 2%DV calcium, 8%DV iron.

Chicken and Potatoes Barbecue

Betty B. Dennison   Grove City, PA

MAKES: **8 SERVINGS**
PREP. TIME: **5–10 MINUTES**
COOKING TIME: **4–9 HOURS**
IDEAL SLOW COOKER SIZE: **4–5-QUART**

8 boneless, skinless chicken breast halves, *divided*

8 small or medium potatoes, quartered, *divided*

1 cup honey barbecue sauce

16-oz. can jellied cranberry sauce

1. Spray slow cooker with nonstick cooking spray. Place 4 chicken breasts in slow cooker.
2. Top with 4 cut-up potatoes.
3. Mix barbecue sauce and cranberry sauce together in a bowl. Spoon half the sauce over the chicken and potatoes in the cooker.
4. Place remaining breasts in cooker, followed by the remaining potato chunks. Pour rest of sauce over all.
5. Cover and cook on Low 8–9 hours, or on High 4 hours, or until chicken and potatoes are tender but not dry.

Tip: *You may peel the potatoes or leave the skins on. Red potatoes are especially appealing with their skins on.*

California Chicken

Shirley Sears   Tiskilwa, IL

MAKES: **4–6 SERVINGS**
PREP. TIME: **10 MINUTES**
COOKING TIME: **8½–9½ HOURS**
IDEAL SLOW COOKER SIZE: **4-QUART**

3-lb. chicken, quartered

1 cup orange juice

⅓ cup chili sauce

2 Tbsp. soy sauce

1 Tbsp. molasses

1 tsp. dry mustard

1 tsp. garlic salt

2 Tbsp. chopped green peppers

3 medium oranges, peeled and separated into slices, *or* 13½-oz. can mandarin oranges

1. Arrange chicken in slow cooker.
2. In separate bowl, combine juice, chili sauce, soy sauce, molasses, dry mustard, and garlic salt. Pour over chicken.
3. Cover. Cook on Low 8–9 hours.
4. Stir in green peppers and oranges. Heat 30 minutes longer.

Variation: *Stir 1 tsp. curry powder in with sauces and seasonings. Stir 1 small can pineapple chunks and juice in with green peppers and oranges.*

When you find a recipe that you love, make a notation in the cookbook that it is a great recipe.

Chicken with Applesauce

Kelly Evenson   Pittsboro, NC

MAKES: **4 SERVINGS**
PREP. TIME: **20 MINUTES**
COOKING TIME: **2–3 HOURS**
IDEAL SLOW COOKER SIZE: **4-QUART**

4 boneless, skinless chicken breast halves

salt to taste

pepper to taste

4–5 Tbsp. oil

2 cups applesauce

¼ cup barbecue sauce

½ tsp. poultry seasoning

2 tsp. honey

½ tsp. lemon juice

1. Season chicken with salt and pepper. Brown in oil for 5 minutes per side.
2. Cut up chicken into 1-inch chunks and transfer to slow cooker.
3. Combine remaining ingredients. Pour over chicken and mix together well.
4. Cover. Cook on High 2–3 hours, or until chicken is tender.
5. Serve over rice or noodles.

Chicken Breasts with Rosemary

Marla Folkerts   Holland, OH

MAKES: **4 SERVINGS**
PREP. TIME: **10 MINUTES**
COOKING TIME: **3–6 HOURS**
IDEAL SLOW COOKER SIZE: **3–4-QUART**

4 boneless, skinless chicken breast halves (4 ozs. each)

1½ tsp. balsamic vinegar

1 tsp. minced garlic

1 Tbsp. grated lemon rind

¼ tsp. salt

⅛ tsp. black pepper

½ cup dry white wine *or* reduced-sodium chicken broth

1 tsp. finely chopped fresh rosemary, *or* ½ tsp. dried

½ cup fresh diced tomato

1. Place chicken breasts in slow cooker.
2. Mix vinegar, garlic, lemon rind, salt, pepper, and wine. Pour over chicken.
3. Cover. Cook on Low 6 hours, or on High 3 hours.
4. One-half hour before the end of the cooking time, stir in rosemary and fresh tomato.

Per Serving: 170 calories (30 calories from fat), 3 total fat (1g saturated, 0g trans), 75mg cholesterol, 210mg sodium, 3g total carbohydrate (0.5g fiber, 1g sugar), 27g protein, 4%DV vitamin A, 8%DV vitamin C, 2%DV calcium, 6%DV iron.

Chicken and Turkey Main Dishes

Southwestern Chicken

Joyce Shackelford   Green Bay, WI

MAKES: **6 SERVINGS**
PREP. TIME: **5 MINUTES**
COOKING TIME: **3–8 HOURS**
IDEAL SLOW COOKER SIZE: **6-QUART**

2 15¼-oz. cans corn, drained

15-oz. can black beans, rinsed and drained

16-oz. jar chunky salsa, *divided*

6 boneless, skinless chicken breast halves

1 cup low-fat shredded cheddar cheese

1. Combine corn, black beans, and ½ cup salsa in slow cooker.
2. Top with chicken. Pour remaining salsa over chicken.
3. Cover. Cook on High 3–4 hours, or on Low 7–8 hours.
4. Sprinkle with cheese. Cover 5 minutes for cheese to melt.

Per Serving: 370 calories (50 calories from fat), 6g total fat (2g saturated, 0g trans), 75mg cholesterol, 1210mg sodium, 43g total carbohydrate (7g fiber, 7g sugar), 39g protein, 6%DV vitamin A, 10%DV vitamin C, 15%DV calcium, 20%DV iron.

Tip: *This dish goes well with rice.*

Tex-Mex Chicken and Rice

Kelly Evenson   Pittsboro, NC

MAKES: **8 SERVINGS**
PREP. TIME: **25 MINUTES**
COOKING TIME: **4–4½ HOURS**
IDEAL SLOW COOKER SIZE: **4-QUART**

1 cup converted white rice, uncooked

28-oz. can diced peeled tomatoes

6-oz. can tomato paste

3 cups hot water

1 pkg. dry taco seasoning mix

4 whole boneless, skinless chicken breasts, uncooked and cut into ½-inch cubes

2 medium onions, chopped

1 green pepper, chopped

4-oz. can diced green chilies

1 tsp. garlic powder

½ tsp. pepper

1. Combine all ingredients except chilies and seasonings in large slow cooker.
2. Cover. Cook on Low 4–4½ hours, or until rice is tender and chicken is cooked.
3. Stir in green chilies and seasonings and serve.
4. Serve with mixed green leafy salad and refried beans.

When I use mushrooms or green peppers in the slow cooker, I usually stir them in during the last hour so they don't get too mushy.

Red Pepper Chicken

Sue Graber   Eureka, IL

MAKES: **4 SERVINGS**
PREP. TIME: **10 MINUTES**
COOKING TIME: **4–6 HOURS**
IDEAL SLOW COOKER SIZE: **4-QUART**

4 boneless, skinless chicken breast halves

15-oz. can black beans, drained

12-oz. jar roasted red peppers, undrained

14½-oz. can Mexican stewed tomatoes, undrained

1 large onion, chopped

½ tsp. salt

pepper to taste

1. Place chicken in slow cooker.
2. Combine beans, red peppers, stewed tomatoes, onion, salt, and pepper. Pour over chicken.
3. Cover. Cook on Low 4–6 hours, or until chicken is no longer pink.
4. Serve over rice.

Chicken Gumbo

Virginia Bender   Dover, DE

MAKES: **6–8 SERVINGS**
PREP. TIME: **25 MINUTES**
COOKING TIME: **3–10 HOURS**
IDEAL SLOW COOKER SIZE: **4-QUART**

1 large onion, chopped

3–4 garlic cloves, minced

1 green pepper, diced

2 cups okra, sliced

2 cups tomatoes, chopped

4 cups chicken broth

1 lb. chicken breast, cut into 1-inch pieces

2 tsp. Old Bay Seasoning

1. Combine all ingredients in slow cooker.
2. Cover. Cook on Low 8–10 hours, or on High 3–4 hours.
3. Serve over rice.

Greek Chicken

Judy Govotsus   Monrovia, MD

MAKES: **8 SERVINGS**
PREP. TIME: **10 MINUTES**
COOKING TIME: **5–10 HOURS**
IDEAL SLOW COOKER SIZE: **6-QUART**

6 medium potatoes, quartered

3 lbs. chicken pieces, skin removed

2 large onions, quartered

1 whole bulb garlic, minced

½ cup water

3 tsp. dried oregano

1 tsp. salt

½ tsp. black pepper

1 Tbsp. olive oil

1. Place potatoes in bottom of slow cooker. Add chicken, onions, and garlic.

2. In small bowl mix water with oregano, salt, and pepper.
3. Pour over chicken and potatoes. Top with oil.
4. Cover. Cook on High 5–6 hours, or on Low 9–10 hours.

Per Serving: 430 calories (70 calories from fat), 8g total fat (2g saturated, 0g trans), 145mg cholesterol, 430mg sodium, 31g total carbohydrate (4g fiber, 3g sugar), 56g protein, 0%DV vitamin A, 30%DV vitamin C, 6%DV calcium, 20%DV iron.

Twenty-Clove Chicken

Nancy Savage   Factoryville, PA

MAKES: **6 SERVINGS**
PREP. TIME: **10 MINUTES**
COOKING TIME: **5–6 HOURS**
IDEAL SLOW COOKER SIZE: **4-QUART**

PICTURED
ON PAGE
404

¼ cup dry white wine
2 Tbsp. chopped dried parsley
2 tsp. dried basil leaves
1 tsp. dried oregano
pinch of crushed red pepper flakes
20 cloves of garlic (about 1 head)
4 celery ribs, chopped
6 boneless, skinless chicken breast halves
1 lemon, juice and zest
fresh herbs, *optional*

1. Combine wine, dried parsley, dried basil, dried oregano, and dried red peppers in large bowl.
2. Add garlic cloves and celery. Coat well.
3. Transfer garlic and celery to slow cooker with slotted spoon.
4. Add chicken to herb mixture. Coat well. Place chicken on top of vegetables in slow cooker.

5. Sprinkle lemon juice and zest in slow cooker. Add any remaining herb mixture.
6. Cover. Cook on Low for 5–6 hours, or until chicken is no longer pink in center.
7. Garnish with fresh herbs if desired.

Per Serving: 170 calories (30 calories from fat), 3.5g total fat (1g saturated, 0g trans), 75mg cholesterol, 90mg sodium, 7g total carbohydrate (2g fiber, 1g sugar), 28g protein, 4%DV vitamin A, 10%DV vitamin C, 6%DV calcium, 10%DV iron.

Variation: *For browned chicken, sauté uncooked breasts in large skillet in 1 Tbsp. olive oil over medium heat. Cook for 5 minutes on each side, or until golden brown. Then proceed with steps above.*

To preserve garlic longer, separate garlic cloves from the bud. Place in plastic containers and freeze. Take out what you need when you need it.

Lemon Chicken

Judi Manos West Islip, NY • *Joette Droz* Kalona, IA
Cindy Krestynick Glen Lyon, PA

MAKES: **6 SERVINGS**
PREP. TIME: **20 MINUTES**
COOKING TIME: **3½–4½ HOURS**
IDEAL SLOW COOKER SIZE: **5-QUART**

6 boneless, skinless chicken breast halves

1 tsp. dried oregano

½ tsp. seasoned salt

¼ tsp. black pepper

¼ cup water

3 Tbsp. lemon juice

2 garlic cloves, minced

2 tsp. chicken bouillon granules

2 tsp. fresh parsley, minced

1. Pat chicken dry with paper towels.
2. Combine oregano, seasoned salt, and pepper. Rub over chicken.
3. Brown chicken in a nonstick skillet over medium heat.
4. Place chicken in slow cooker.
5. Combine water, lemon juice, garlic, and bouillon in skillet. Bring to a boil, stirring to loosen browned bits. Pour over chicken.
6. Cover. Cook on Low 3–4 hours.
7. Baste chicken. Add parsley.
8. Remove lid and cook 15–30 minutes longer, allowing juices to thicken slightly.
9. Serve chicken and juices over rice.

Per Serving: 150 calories (30 calories from fat), 3g total fat (1g saturated, 0g trans), 75mg cholesterol, 320mg sodium, 1g total carbohydrate (0g fiber, 0g sugar), 27g protein, 2%DV vitamin A, 4%DV vitamin C, 2%DV calcium, 6%DV iron.

Tip: *If you want to make sure the chicken absorbs the flavors of the sauce as fully as possible, cut it into 1-inch cubes just before placing in slow cooker.*

Dill-Lemon Chicken

Vera Schmucker Goshen, IN

MAKES: **4 SERVINGS**
PREP. TIME: **10 MINUTES**
COOKING TIME: **3–4 HOURS**
IDEAL SLOW COOKER SIZE: **4-QUART**

1 cup fat-free sour cream

1 Tbsp. fresh dill, minced

1 tsp. lemon pepper seasoning

1 tsp. lemon zest

4 boneless, skinless chicken breast halves

1. Combine sour cream, dill, lemon pepper, and lemon zest in a small bowl. Spoon one-fourth of the sour cream-lemon-dill mixture into bottom of slow cooker.
2. Arrange chicken breasts on top in a single layer.
3. Pour remaining sauce over chicken. Spread evenly.
4. Cover. Cook on Low 3–4 hours, or until juices run clear.

Per Serving: 200 calories (35 calories from fat), 4g total fat (1.5g saturated, 0g trans), 80mg cholesterol, 230mg sodium, 10g total carbohydrate (0g fiber, 5g sugar), 30g protein, 8%DV vitamin A, 0%DV vitamin C, 10%DV calcium, 6%DV iron.

Mediterranean Chicken

Barbara Jean Fabel   Wausau, WI

MAKES: **4 SERVINGS**
PREP. TIME: **5 MINUTES**
COOKING TIME: **4–6 HOURS**
IDEAL SLOW COOKER SIZE: **3-QUART**

1 yellow onion, thinly sliced

14-oz. jar marinated artichoke hearts, drained

14-oz. can low-sodium peeled tomatoes

6 Tbsp. red wine vinegar

1 tsp. minced garlic

½ tsp. salt

½ tsp. black pepper

4 boneless, skinless chicken breast halves

1. Combine all ingredients except chicken in slow cooker.
2. Place chicken in cooker, pushing down into vegetables and sauce until it's as covered as possible.
3. Cover. Cook on Low 4–6 hours.
4. Serve over rice.

Per Serving: 270 calories (80 calories from fat), 8g total fat (1g saturated, 0g trans), 75mg cholesterol, 900mg sodium, 18g total carbohydrate (4g fiber, 4g sugar), 31g protein, 4%DV vitamin A, 30%DV vitamin C, 6%DV calcium, 6%DV iron.

Chicken and Sun-Dried Tomatoes

Joyce Shackelford   Green Bay, WI

MAKES: **8 SERVINGS**
PREP. TIME: **20 MINUTES**
COOKING TIME: **4–6 HOURS**
IDEAL SLOW COOKER SIZE: **6-QUART**

1 Tbsp. olive oil

3 lbs. boneless, skinless chicken breasts, cut in 8 serving pieces

2 garlic cloves, minced

½ cup white wine

1½ cups fat-free, low-sodium chicken stock

1 tsp. dried basil

½ cup chopped, sun-dried tomatoes, cut into slivers

1. Heat oil in skillet. Add several pieces of chicken at a time, but make sure not to crowd the skillet so the chicken can brown evenly.
2. Transfer chicken to slow cooker as it finishes browning.
3. Add garlic, wine, chicken stock, and basil to skillet. Bring to a boil. Scrape up any bits from the bottom of the pan.
4. Pour over chicken. Scatter tomatoes over the top.
5. Cover. Cook on Low 4–6 hours.

Per Serving: 320 calories (70 calories from fat), 8g total fat (2g saturated, 0g trans), 145mg cholesterol, 230mg sodium, 2g total carbohydrate (0.5g fiber, 1g sugar), 54g protein, 0%DV vitamin A, 0%DV vitamin C, 4%DV calcium, 15%DV iron.

Chicken Casablanca

Joyce Kaut   Rochester, NY

MAKES: **6–8 SERVINGS**
PREP. TIME: **30 MINUTES**
COOKING TIME: **4½–6½ HOURS**
IDEAL SLOW COOKER SIZE: **4–5-QUART**

2 Tbsp. oil
2 large onions, sliced
1 tsp. ground ginger
3 garlic cloves, minced
3 large carrots, diced
2 large potatoes, diced
3 lbs. skinless chicken pieces
½ tsp. ground cumin
½ tsp. salt
½ tsp. pepper
¼ tsp. cinnamon
2 Tbsp. raisins
14½-oz. can chopped tomatoes
3 small zucchini, sliced
15-oz. can garbanzo beans, drained
2 Tbsp. chopped parsley

1. Sauté onions, ginger, and garlic in oil in skillet. (Reserve oil.) Transfer to slow cooker. Add carrots and potatoes.
2. Brown chicken over medium heat in reserved oil. Transfer to slow cooker. Mix gently with vegetables.
3. Combine seasonings in separate bowl. Sprinkle over chicken and vegetables. Add raisins and tomatoes.
4. Cover. Cook on High 4–6 hours.
5. Add sliced zucchini, beans, and parsley 30 minutes before serving.
6. Serve over cooked rice or couscous.

Variation: *Add ½ tsp. turmeric and ¼ tsp. cayenne pepper to Step 3.*

Michelle Mann   Mt. Joy, PA

Groundnut Stew

Cathy Boshart   Lebanon, PA

MAKES: **8 SERVINGS**
PREP. TIME: **10 MINUTES**
COOKING TIME: **3½ HOURS**
IDEAL SLOW COOKER SIZE: **4-QUART**

2 green peppers, cut into rings
1 medium onion, cut into rings
2 Tbsp. shortening
6-oz. can tomato paste
¾ cup peanut butter
3 cups chicken broth
1½ tsp. salt
1 tsp. chili powder
1 tsp. sugar
½ tsp. ground nutmeg
4 cups cubed, cooked chicken
coconut
peanuts
raisins
chopped hard-boiled eggs
chopped bananas
cut up oranges
chopped eggplant
chopped apples
chopped tomatoes
shredded carrots
chopped green pepper
chopped onion
chopped pineapple

1. Cook and stir green pepper and onion rings in shortening in hot slow cooker.
2. Combine tomato paste and peanut butter. Stir into slow cooker.
3. Add broth and seasonings. Stir in chicken.
4. Cover. Cook on Low 3 hours.
5. Serve over hot rice and top with your choice of remaining ingredients.

African Chicken Treat

Anne Townsend Albuquerque, NM

MAKES: **4 SERVINGS**
PREP. TIME: **10 MINUTES**
COOKING TIME: **5–6 HOURS**
IDEAL SLOW COOKER SIZE: **4-QUART**

1½ cups water

2 tsp. chicken bouillon granules

2 ribs celery, thinly sliced

2 onions, thinly sliced

1 red bell pepper, sliced

1 green bell pepper, sliced

8 chicken thighs, skinned

½ cup extra crunchy peanut butter

crushed chili pepper of your choice

1. Combine water, chicken bouillon granules, celery, onions, and peppers in slow cooker.
2. Spread peanut butter over both sides of chicken pieces. Sprinkle with chili pepper. Place on top of ingredients in slow cooker.
3. Cover. Cook on Low 5–6 hours.

To save peeling time when using fresh tomatoes, dip the tomatoes into boiling water until their skins begin to crack. Then the skins will peel off easily.

Mulligan Stew

Carol Ambrose Ripon, CA

MAKES: **8–10 SERVINGS**
PREP. TIME: **15 MINUTES**
COOKING TIME: **7 HOURS**
IDEAL SLOW COOKER SIZE: **4–5-QUART**

3-lb. stewing hen, cut up, *or* 4 lbs. chicken legs and thighs

1½ tsp. salt

¼-lb. salt pork *or* bacon, cut in 1-inch squares

4 cups tomatoes, peeled and sliced

2 cups fresh corn, *or* 1-lb. pkg. frozen corn

1 cup coarsely chopped potatoes

10-oz. pkg. lima beans, frozen

½ cup chopped onions

1 tsp. salt

¼ tsp. pepper

dash of cayenne pepper

1. Place chicken in very large slow cooker. Add water to cover. Add 1½ tsp. salt.
2. Cover. Cook on Low 2 hours. Add more water if needed.
3. Add remaining ingredients. (If you don't have a large cooker, divide the stew between 2 average-sized ones.) Simmer on Low 5 hours longer.

Tip: *Flavor improves if stew is refrigerated and reheated the next day. May also be made in advance and frozen.*

Variation: *You can debone the chicken after the first cooking for 2 hours. Stir chicken pieces back into cooker with other ingredients and continue with directions above.*

Gran's Big Potluck

Carol Ambrose Ripon, CA

MAKES: **10–15 SERVINGS**
PREP. TIME: **20 MINUTES**
COOKING TIME: **10–12 HOURS**
IDEAL SLOW COOKER SIZE: **5–6-QUART**

2½–3 lb. stewing hen, cut into pieces

½ lb. stewing beef, cubed

½-lb. veal shoulder *or* roast, cubed

1½ quarts water

½ lb. small red potatoes, cubed

½ lb. small onions, cut in half

1 cup sliced carrots

1 cup chopped celery

1 green pepper, chopped

1-lb. pkg. frozen lima beans

1 cup okra, whole or diced, fresh *or* frozen

1 cup whole-kernel corn

8-oz. can whole tomatoes with juice

15-oz. can tomato puree

1 tsp. salt

¼-½ tsp. pepper

1 tsp. dry mustard

½ tsp. chili powder

¼ cup chopped fresh parsley

1. Combine all ingredients except last 5 seasonings in one very large slow cooker, or divide between two medium-sized ones.
2. Cover. Cook on Low 10–12 hours. Add seasonings during last hour of cooking.

Tip: *You may want to debone the chicken and mix it back into the cooker before serving the meal.*

Chicken and Seafood Gumbo

Dianna Milhizer Brighton, MI

MAKES: **12 SERVINGS**
PREP. TIME: **40–45 MINUTES**
COOKING TIME: **10–12 HOURS**
IDEAL SLOW COOKER SIZE: **6-QUART**

1 cup chopped celery

1 cup chopped onions

½ cup chopped green peppers

¼ cup olive oil

¼ cup, plus 1 Tbsp., flour

6 cups chicken stock

2 lbs. chicken, cut up

3 bay leaves

1½ cups sliced okra

12-oz. can diced tomatoes

1 tsp. Tabasco sauce

salt to taste

pepper to taste

1 lb. ready-to-eat shrimp

½ cup snipped fresh parsley

1. Sauté celery, onions, and peppers in oil. Blend in flour and chicken stock until smooth. Cook 5 minutes. Pour into slow cooker.
2. Add remaining ingredients except seafood and parsley.
3. Cover. Cook on Low 10–12 hours.
4. One hour before serving add shrimp and parsley.
5. Remove bay leaves before serving.
6. Serve with white rice.

Use a kitchen shears to cut up chicken. It is fast, safe, and easy.

Sesame Chicken Wings

Shirley Unternahrer Hinh   Wayland, IA

MAKES: **6–8 MAIN-DISH SERVINGS,
OR 16 APPETIZERS**
PREP. TIME: **35–40 MINUTES**
COOKING TIME: **2½–5 HOURS**
IDEAL SLOW COOKER SIZE: **4-QUART**

PICTURED
ON PAGE
304

3 lbs. chicken wings

salt to taste

pepper to taste

1¾ cups honey

1 cup soy sauce

½ cup ketchup

2 Tbsp. canola oil

2 Tbsp. sesame oil

2 garlic cloves, minced

toasted sesame seeds

1. Rinse wings. Cut at joint. Sprinkle with salt and pepper. Place on broiler pan.
2. Broil 5 inches from top, 10 minutes on each side. Place chicken in slow cooker.
3. Add remaining ingredients except sesame seeds. Pour over chicken.
4. Cover. Cook on Low 5 hours, or on High 2½ hours.
5. Sprinkle sesame seeds over top just before serving.
6. Serve as appetizer, or with white or brown rice and shredded lettuce to turn this appetizer into a meal.

Note: *My husband and his co-workers have a "pot-luck-lunch" at work. I think this is a nice way to break the monotony of the week or month. And it gives them a chance to share. What better way to keep food ready than with a slow cooker!*

Kickin' Chicken Wings

Tracy Supcoe   Barclay, MD

MAKES: **8 MAIN-DISH SERVINGS**
PREP. TIME: **20 MINUTES**
COOKING TIME: **5–6 HOURS**
IDEAL SLOW COOKER SIZE: **4-QUART**

4-lb. chicken wings

2 large onions, chopped

2 6-oz. cans tomato paste

2 large garlic cloves, minced

¼ cup Worcestershire sauce

¼ cup cider vinegar

½ cup brown sugar

½ cup sweet pickle relish

½ cup red *or* white wine

2 tsp. salt

2 tsp. dry mustard

1. Cut off wing tips. Cut wings at joint. Place in slow cooker.
2. Combine remaining ingredients. Add to slow cooker. Stir.
3. Cover. Cook on Low 5–6 hours.

Chili Barbecued Chicken Wings

Rosemarie Fitzgerald   Gibsonia, PA

MAKES: **10 MAIN-DISH SERVINGS**
PREP. TIME: **5 MINUTES**
COOKING TIME: **2–8 HOURS**
IDEAL SLOW COOKER SIZE: **5-QUART**

5 lbs. chicken wings, tips cut off

12-oz. bottle chili sauce

⅓ cup lemon juice

1 Tbsp. Worcestershire sauce

2 Tbsp. molasses

1 tsp. salt

2 tsp. chili powder

¼ tsp. hot pepper sauce

dash garlic powder

1. Place wings in cooker.
2. Combine remaining ingredients and pour over chicken.
3. Cover. Cook on Low 6–8 hours, or on High 2–3 hours.

Note: *These wings are also a great appetizer, yielding about 15 appetizer-size servings. Take any leftover chicken off the bone and combine with leftover sauce. Serve over cooked pasta for a second meal.*

Five-Spice Chicken Wings

Marcia Parker   Lansdale, PA

MAKES: **6–8 SERVINGS**
PREP. TIME: **30 MINUTES**
COOKING TIME: **2½–5½ HOURS**
IDEAL SLOW COOKER SIZE: **3½–4-QUART**

3 lbs. (about 16) chicken wings

1 cup bottled plum sauce (check an Asian grocery, or the Asian food aisle in a general grocery store)

2 Tbsp. butter, melted

1 tsp. five-spice powder (check an Asian grocery, or the Asian food aisle in a general grocery store)

thinly sliced orange wedges, *optional*

pineapple slices, *optional*

1. In a foil-lined baking pan arrange the wings in a single layer. Bake at 375° for 20 minutes. Drain well.
2. Meanwhile, combine the plum sauce, melted butter, and five-spice powder in your slow cooker. Add wings. Then stir to coat the wings with sauce.
3. Cover and cook on Low 4–5 hours, or on High 2–2½ hours.
4. Serve immediately, or keep them warm in your slow cooker on Low for up to 2 hours.
5. Garnish with orange wedges and pineapple slices to serve, if you wish.

Variation: *For Kentucky Chicken Wings, create a different sauce in Step 2. Use ½ cup maple syrup, ½ cup whiskey, and 2 Tbsp. melted butter. Then stir in the wings. Continue with Step 3.*

A slow cooker set on Low does not burn food and will not spoil a meal if cooked somewhat beyond the designated time.

Marinated Chinese Chicken Salad

Lee Ann Hazlett   Delavan, WI

PICTURED ON PAGE 502

MAKES: **8 SERVINGS**
PREP. TIME: **25 MINUTES**
COOKING TIME: **3–8 HOURS**
IDEAL SLOW COOKER SIZE: **5–6-QUART**

Marinade:

3 cloves minced garlic

1 Tbsp. fresh ginger, grated

1 tsp. dried red pepper flakes

2 Tbsp. honey

3 Tbsp. low-sodium soy sauce

6 boneless, skinless chicken breast halves

Dressing:

½ cup rice wine vinegar

1 clove garlic, minced

1 tsp. fresh grated ginger

1 Tbsp. honey

Salad:

1 large head iceberg lettuce, shredded

2 carrots, julienned

½ cup chopped roasted peanuts

¼ cup chopped cilantro

½ package maifun noodles, fried in hot oil

1. Mix marinade ingredients in a small bowl.
2. Place chicken in slow cooker and pour marinade over chicken, coating each piece well.
3. Cover. Cook on Low 6–8 hours, or on High 3–4 hours.
4. Remove chicken from slow cooker and cool. Reserve juices. Shred chicken into bite-sized pieces.
5. In a small bowl, combine the dressing ingredients with ½ cup of the juice from the slow cooker.
6. In a large serving bowl toss together the shredded chicken, lettuce, carrots, peanuts, cilantro, and noodles.
7. Just before serving, drizzle with the salad dressing. Toss well and serve.

Per Serving: 130 calories (20 calories from fat), 2.5g total fat (0.5g saturated, 0g trans), 55mg cholesterol, 250mg sodium, 6g total carbohydrate (0g fiber, 4g sugar), 21g protein, 8%DV vitamin A, 2%DV vitamin C, 2%DV calcium, 6%DV iron.

Variation: *You may substitute chow mein noodles for the maifun noodles.*

Loretta's Hot Chicken Sandwiches

Loretta Krahn   Mt. Lake, MN

MAKES: **12 SERVINGS**
PREP. TIME: **15 MINUTES**
COOKING TIME: **2 HOURS**
IDEAL SLOW COOKER SIZE: **4-QUART**

8 cups cubed cooked chicken *or* turkey

1 medium onion, chopped

1 cup chopped celery

2 cups mayonnaise

1 cup cubed American cheese

1. Combine all ingredients except buns in slow cooker.
2. Cover. Cook on High 2 hours.
3. Serve on buns.

Barbecue Chicken for Buns

Linda Sluiter   Schererville, IN

MAKES: **16–20 SERVINGS**
PREP. TIME: **15 MINUTES**
COOKING TIME: **8 HOURS**
IDEAL SLOW COOKER SIZE: **4-QUART**

6 cups diced cooked chicken

2 cups chopped celery

1 cup chopped onions

1 cup chopped green peppers

4 Tbsp. butter

2 cups ketchup

2 cups water

2 Tbsp. brown sugar

4 Tbsp. vinegar

2 tsp. dry mustard

1 tsp. pepper

1 tsp. salt

1. Combine all ingredients in slow cooker.
2. Cover. Cook on Low 8 hours.
3. Stir chicken until it shreds.
4. Pile into steak rolls and serve.

Tender Turkey Breast

Becky Gehman   Bergton, VA

MAKES: **10 SERVINGS**
PREP. TIME: **5 MINUTES**
COOKING TIME: **2–9 HOURS**
IDEAL SLOW COOKER SIZE: **6-QUART**

6-lb. turkey breast, boneless *or* bone-in

2–3 Tbsp. water

1. Place the turkey breast in the slow cooker. Add water.
2. Cover and cook on High 2–4 hours, or on Low 4–9 hours, or until tender but not dry and mushy.
3. Turn over once during cooking time.
4. If you'd like to brown the turkey, place it in your oven and bake it uncovered at 325° for 15–20 minutes after it's finished cooking in the slow cooker.

Tips:

1. Save the drippings in the bottom of the slow cooker when you remove the meat. Transfer them to a nonstick skillet. Add ½ cup water to ½ cup drippings. Heat until simmering. In a small jar, blend 2 Tbsp. flour into 1 cup water. When smooth, stir into simmering broth, continuing to heat and stir until smooth and thickened. Use as gravy over sliced hot turkey.

2. Slice cooked turkey and serve hot. Or allow to cool and then either shred, slice, or cut into chunks for making salads or sandwiches. Freeze any leftovers.

Chicken and Turkey Main Dishes

Slow Cooker Turkey Breast

Liz Ann Yoder   Hartville, OH

MAKES: **8–10 SERVINGS**
PREP. TIME: **10 MINUTES**
COOKING TIME: **9–10 HOURS**
IDEAL SLOW COOKER SIZE: **6–7-QUART**

6-lb. turkey breast

2 tsp. oil

salt to taste

pepper to taste

1 medium onion, quartered

4 garlic cloves, peeled

½ cup water

1. Rinse turkey and pat dry with paper towels.
2. Rub oil over turkey. Sprinkle with salt and pepper. Place, meaty side up, in large slow cooker.
3. Place onion and garlic around sides of cooker.
4. Cover. Cook on Low 9–10 hours, or until meat thermometer stuck in meaty part of breast registers 180°.
5. Remove from slow cooker and let stand 10 minutes before slicing.
6. Serve with mashed potatoes, cranberry salad, and corn or green beans.

Tips:

1. Reserve broth for soups, or thicken with flour-water paste and serve as gravy over sliced turkey.

2. Freeze broth in pint-sized containers for future use.

3. Debone turkey and freeze in pint-sized containers for future use. Or freeze any leftover turkey after serving the meal described above.

Variation: *Add carrot chunks and chopped celery to Step 3 to add more flavor to the turkey broth.*

Turkey in the Slow Cooker

Earnest Zimmerman   Mechanicsburg, PA

MAKES: **6–8 SERVINGS**
PREP. TIME: **5 MINUTES**
COOKING TIME: **1–5 HOURS**
IDEAL SLOW COOKER SIZE: **6-QUART**

3–5-lb. bone-in turkey breast

salt and pepper to taste

2 carrots, cut in chunks

1 onion, cut in eighths

2 ribs celery, cut in chunks

1. Rinse turkey breast and pat dry. Season well inside with salt.
2. Place vegetables in bottom of slow cooker. Sprinkle with pepper. Place turkey breast on top of vegetables.
3. Cover and cook on High 1–3 hours, on Low 4–5 hours, or until tender but not dry or mushy.

Tips:

1. Strain broth and reserve it. Discard vegetables. The broth makes excellent gravy or base for soups. You can freeze whatever you don't need immediately.

2. Debone the turkey. Slice and serve hot, or chill and use for turkey salad or sandwiches.

Easy Turkey Breast

Susan Stephani Smith Monument, CO

MAKES: **12 SERVINGS**
PREP. TIME: **5 MINUTES**
COOKING TIME: **6–7 HOURS**
IDEAL SLOW COOKER SIZE: **5–6-QUART**

**1 Jenny O'Turkey Breast—with bone in and with gravy
    packet**

salt

1. Wash frozen breast and sprinkle with salt.
2. Place turkey, gravy packet up, in slow
   cooker that's large enough to be covered
   when the turkey breast is in it.
3. Cover. Cook turkey on Low 6–7 hours, or
   until tender, removing gravy packet when
   the turkey is partially thawed. (Keep packet
   in refrigerator.)
4. Make gravy according to directions on
   packet. Warm before serving.

Turkey Breast with Orange Sauce

Jean Butzer Batavia, NY

MAKES: **4–6 SERVINGS**
PREP. TIME: **15–20 MINUTES**
COOKING TIME: **7–8 HOURS**
IDEAL SLOW COOKER SIZE: **5–6-QUART**

1 large onion, chopped

3 garlic cloves, minced

1 tsp. dried rosemary

½ tsp. pepper

2–3-lb. boneless, skinless turkey breast

1½ cups orange juice

1. Place onions in slow cooker.
2. Combine garlic, rosemary, and pepper.

3. Make gashes in turkey, about ¾ of the way
   through at 2-inch intervals. Stuff with herb
   mixture. Place turkey in slow cooker.
4. Pour juice over turkey.
5. Cover. Cook on Low 7–8 hours, or until
   turkey is no longer pink in center.

Note: *This very easy, impressive-looking
and -tasting recipe is perfect for company.*

Onion Turkey Breast

Mary Ann Wasick West Allis, WI

MAKES: **6–8 SERVINGS**
PREP. TIME: **5 MINUTES**
COOKING TIME: **8–10 HOURS**
IDEAL SLOW COOKER SIZE: **4–5-QUART**

4–6-lb. boneless, skinless turkey breast

1 tsp. garlic powder

1 envelope dry onion soup mix

1. Place turkey in slow cooker. Sprinkle garlic
   powder and onion soup mix over breast.
2. Cover. Cook on Low 8–10 hours.

Tip: *Use au jus over rice or pasta.*

Saucy Turkey Breast, page 406

Cottage Cheese Bread,
page 79

Welsh Rarebit, page 66

Twenty-Clove Chicken, page 389

Lemony Turkey Breast

Joyce Shackelford   Green Bay, WI
Mrs. Carolyn Baer   Conrath, WI

MAKES: **12 SERVINGS**
PREP. TIME: **10 MINUTES**
COOKING TIME: **5–7 HOURS**
IDEAL SLOW COOKER SIZE: **6-QUART**

1 5-lb. bone-in turkey breast, cut in half and skin
   removed, partially frozen in center
1 medium lemon, halved
1 tsp. lemon-pepper seasoning
1 tsp. garlic salt
4 tsp. cornstarch
½ cup fat-free, reduced-sodium chicken broth

1. Place turkey, meaty side up, in slow cooker
   sprayed with non-fat cooking spray.
2. Squeeze half of lemon over turkey. Sprinkle
   with lemon pepper and garlic salt.
3. Place lemon halves under turkey.
4. Cover. Cook on Low 5–7 hours.
5. Remove turkey. Discard lemons.
6. Allow turkey to rest 15 minutes before
   slicing.

Per Serving: 190 calories (10 calories from fat), 1g total fat (0g
saturated, 0g trans), 110mg cholesterol, 260mg sodium, 1g total
carbohydrate (0g fiber, 0g sugar), 40g protein, 0%DV vitamin A, 0%DV
vitamin C, 2%DV calcium, 10%DV iron.

Tip: *To make gravy, pour cooking liquid
into a cup. Skim the fat. In saucepan, combine
cornstarch and broth until smooth. Gradually stir
in cooking liquid. Bring to a boil. Cook and stir
for 2 minutes. Serve over turkey slices.*

Cranberry-Orange Turkey Breast

Lee Ann Hazlett   Delavan, WI

MAKES: **9 SERVINGS**
PREP. TIME: **10 MINUTES**
COOKING TIME: **3½–8 HOURS**
IDEAL SLOW COOKER SIZE: **6-QUART**

½ cup orange marmalade
16-oz. can whole cranberries in sauce
2 tsp. orange zest, grated
3-lb. turkey breast

1. Combine marmalade, cranberries, and zest in
   a bowl.
2. Place the turkey breast in the slow cooker
   and pour half the orange-cranberry mixture
   over the turkey.
3. Cover. Cook on Low 7–8 hours, or on High
   3½–4 hours, until turkey juices run clear.
4. Add remaining half of orange-cranberry
   mixture for the last half hour of cooking.
5. Remove turkey to warm platter and allow to
   rest for 15 minutes before slicing.
6. Serve with orange-cranberry sauce.

Per Serving: 270 calories (10 calories from fat), 1g total fat (0g
saturated, 0g trans), 125mg cholesterol, 90mg sodium, 18g total
carbohydrate (2g fiber, 16 sugar), 46g protein, 0%DV vitamin A, 4%DV
vitamin C, 2%DV calcium, 15%DV iron.

*Food is always more tasty when served
attractively. Add a garnish and a special
touch whenever possible.*

Saucy Turkey Breast

Kelly Bailey Mechanicsburg, PA • *Michele Ruvola* Selden, NY
Ruth Fisher Leicester, NY

MAKES: **6–8 SERVINGS**
PREP. TIME: **5 MINUTES**
COOKING TIME: **1–5 HOURS**
IDEAL SLOW COOKER SIZE: **4–6-QUART**

PICTURED
ON PAGE
401

3–5-lb. turkey breast, bone-in *or* boneless

1 envelope dry onion soup mix

salt and pepper to taste

16-oz. can cranberry sauce, jellied *or* whole-berry

2 Tbsp. cornstarch

2 Tbsp. cold water

1. Sprinkle salt and pepper and soup mix on the top and bottom of turkey breast. Place turkey in slow cooker.
2. Add cranberry sauce to top of turkey breast.
3. Cover and cook on Low 4–5 hours, or on High 1–3 hours, or until tender but not dry and mushy. (A meat thermometer should read 180°.)
4. Remove turkey from cooker and allow to rest for 10 minutes. (Keep sauce in cooker.)
5. Meanwhile, cover cooker and turn to High. In a small bowl, mix together cornstarch and cold water until smooth. When sauce is boiling, stir in cornstarch paste. Continue to simmer until sauce thickens.
6. Slice turkey and serve topped with sauce from cooker.

Try out a recipe you've never had before. It is fun to see the family react to it.

Turkey with Mushroom Sauce

Judi Manos West Islip, NY

MAKES: **12 SERVINGS**
PREP. TIME: **15 MINUTES**
COOKING TIME: **7–8 HOURS**
IDEAL SLOW COOKER SIZE: **6-QUART**

1 large boneless, skinless turkey breast, halved

2 Tbsp. butter, melted

2 Tbsp. dried parsley

½ tsp. dried oregano

½ tsp. salt

¼ tsp. black pepper

½ cup white wine

1 cup sliced fresh mushrooms

2 Tbsp. cornstarch

¼ cup cold water

1. Place turkey in slow cooker. Brush with butter.
2. Mix together parsley, oregano, salt, pepper, and wine. Pour over turkey.
3. Top with mushrooms.
4. Cover. Cook on Low 7–8 hours.
5. Remove turkey and keep warm.
6. Skim any fat from cooking juices.
7. In a saucepan, combine cornstarch and water until smooth. Gradually add cooking juices. Bring to a boil. Cook and stir 2 minutes until thickened.
8. Slice turkey and serve with sauce.

Per Serving: 100 calories (20 calories from fat), 2.5g total fat (1.5g saturated, 0g trans), 45mg cholesterol, 140mg sodium, 2g total carbohydrate (0g fiber, 0g sugar), 16g protein, 2%DV vitamin A, 0%DV vitamin C, 0%DV calcium, 6%DV iron.

Chicken and Turkey Main Dishes

Stuffed Turkey Breast

Jean Butzer Batavia, NY

MAKES: **8 SERVINGS**
PREP. TIME: **25 MINUTES**
COOKING TIME: **7–9 HOURS**
IDEAL SLOW COOKER SIZE: **6-QUART**

¼ cup butter, melted

1 small onion, finely chopped

½ cup finely chopped celery

2½-oz. pkg. croutons with real bacon bits

1 cup chicken broth

2 Tbsp. fresh minced parsley

½ tsp. poultry seasoning

1 whole turkey breast, uncooked, *or* **2 halves (about 5 lbs.)**

salt to taste

pepper to taste

24-inch × 26-inch piece of cheesecloth for each breast half

dry white wine

1. Combine butter, onion, celery, croutons, broth, parsley, and poultry seasoning.
2. Cut turkey breast in thick slices from breastbone to rib cage, leaving slices attached to bone (crosswise across breast).
3. Sprinkle turkey with salt and pepper.
4. Soak cheesecloth in wine. Place turkey on cheesecloth. Stuff bread mixture into slits between turkey slices. Fold one end of cheesecloth over the other to cover meat. Place on metal rack or trivet in 5–6-quart slow cooker.
5. Cover. Cook on Low 7–9 hours, or until tender. Pour additional wine over turkey during cooking.
6. Remove from pot and remove cheesecloth immediately. If browner breast is preferred, remove from pot and brown in 400° oven for 15–20 minutes. Let stand 10 minutes before slicing through and serving.
7. Thicken the drippings, if you wish, for gravy. Mix together 3 Tbsp. cornstarch and ¼ cup cold water. When smooth, stir into broth (with turkey removed from cooker). Turn cooker to High and stir until cornstarch paste is dissolved. Allow to cook for about 10 minutes, until broth is thickened and smooth.

Slow Cooker Turkey and Dressing

Carol Sherwood Batavia, NY

MAKES: **4–6 SERVINGS**
PREP. TIME: **10–15 MINUTES**
COOKING TIME: **5–6 HOURS**
IDEAL SLOW COOKER SIZE: **5–6-QUART**

8-oz. pkg., or 2 6-oz. pkgs., stuffing mix

½ cup hot water

2 Tbsp. butter, softened

1 onion, chopped

½ cup chopped celery

¼ cup sweetened, dried cranberries

3-lb. boneless turkey breast

¼ tsp. dried basil

½ tsp. salt

½ tsp. pepper

1. Spread dry stuffing mix in greased slow cooker.
2. Add water, butter, onion, celery, and cranberries. Mix well.
3. Sprinkle turkey breast with basil, salt, and pepper. Place over stuffing mixture.
4. Cover. Cook on Low 5–6 hours, or until turkey is done but not dry.
5. Remove turkey. Slice and set aside.
6. Gently stir stuffing and allow to sit for 5 minutes before serving.
7. Place stuffing on platter, topped with sliced turkey.

Chicken and Turkey Main Dishes

Slow-Cooked Turkey Dinner

Miriam Nolt New Holland, PA

MAKES: **4–6 SERVINGS**
PREP. TIME: **15 MINUTES**
COOKING TIME: **7½ HOURS**
IDEAL SLOW COOKER SIZE: **4-QUART**

1 onion, diced

6 small red potatoes, quartered

2 cups sliced carrots

1½–2 lbs. boneless, skinless turkey thighs

¼ cup flour

2 Tbsp. dry onion soup mix

10¾-oz. can cream of mushroom soup

⅔ cup chicken broth *or* water

1. Place vegetables in bottom of slow cooker.
2. Place turkey thighs over vegetables.
3. Combine remaining ingredients. Pour over turkey.
4. Cover. Cook on High 30 minutes. Reduce heat to Low and cook 7 hours.

Barbecued Turkey Legs

Barbara Walker Sturgis, SC

MAKES: **4–6 SERVINGS**
PREP. TIME: **10 MINUTES**
COOKING TIME: **5–7 HOURS**
IDEAL SLOW COOKER SIZE: **4–5-QUART**

4 turkey drumsticks

1–2 tsp. salt

¼–½ tsp. pepper

⅓ cup molasses

¼ cup vinegar

½ cup ketchup

3 Tbsp. Worcestershire sauce

¾ tsp. hickory smoke

2 Tbsp. instant minced onion

1. Sprinkle turkey with salt and pepper. Place in slow cooker.
2. Combine remaining ingredients. Pour over turkey.
3. Cover. Cook on Low 5–7 hours.

Barbecued Turkey Cutlets

Maricarol Magill Freehold, NJ

MAKES: **6–8 SERVINGS**
PREP. TIME: **10 MINUTES**
COOKING TIME: **4 HOURS**
IDEAL SLOW COOKER SIZE: **4–5-QUART**

6–8 (1½–2 lbs.) turkey cutlets

¼ cup molasses

¼ cup cider vinegar

¼ cup ketchup

3 Tbsp. Worcestershire sauce

1 tsp. garlic salt

3 Tbsp. chopped onion

2 Tbsp. brown sugar

¼ tsp. pepper

1. Place turkey cutlets in slow cooker.
2. Combine remaining ingredients. Pour over turkey.
3. Cover. Cook on Low 4 hours.
4. Serve over white or brown rice.

Turkey and Sweet Potato Casserole

Michele Ruvola Selden, NY

MAKES: **4 SERVINGS**
PREP. TIME: **15 MINUTES**
COOKING TIME: **8–10 HOURS**
IDEAL SLOW COOKER SIZE: **4-QUART**

3 medium sweet potatoes, peeled and cut into 2-inch pieces

10-oz. pkg. frozen cut green beans

2 lbs. turkey cutlets

12-oz. jar home-style turkey gravy

2 Tbsp. flour

1 tsp. parsley flakes

¼–½ tsp. dried rosemary

⅛ tsp. pepper

1. Layer sweet potatoes, green beans, and turkey in slow cooker.
2. Combine remaining ingredients until smooth. Pour over mixture in slow cooker.
3. Cover. Cook on Low 8–10 hours.
4. Remove turkey and vegetables and keep warm. Stir sauce. Serve with sauce over meat and vegetables, or with sauce in a gravy boat.
5. Serve with biscuits and cranberry sauce.

Indonesian Turkey

Elaine Sue Good Tiskilwa, IL

MAKES: **4 SERVINGS**
PREP. TIME: **10 MINUTES**
COOKING TIME: **6–8 HOURS**
IDEAL SLOW COOKER SIZE: **2–3½-QUART**

3 turkey breast tenderloins (about 1½–2 lbs.)

6 cloves garlic, pressed and chopped

1½ Tbsp. grated fresh ginger

1 Tbsp. sesame oil

3 Tbsp. soy sauce, *optional*

½ tsp. cayenne pepper, *optional*

⅓ cup peanut butter, your choice of chunky or smooth

1. Place the turkey on the bottom of your slow cooker.
2. Sprinkle with garlic, ginger, and sesame oil.
3. Cover and cook on Low 8 hours, or until meat thermometer registers 180°.
4. With a slotted spoon, remove turkey pieces from slow cooker. Stir peanut butter into remaining juices. If the sauce is thicker than you like, stir in ¼–⅓ cup water.
5. Spoon peanut butter sauce over turkey to serve.

Tips:

1. If you like spicier foods, be sure to include the cayenne pepper and add it as part of Step 2. And, if your diet allows, add the soy sauce during Step 2 also.

2. The more meat you have the more evenly it will cook, especially if your slow cooker cooks hot.

Variation: *You may substitute 4 whole boneless, skinless chicken breasts or 12 boneless, skinless chicken thighs for the 3 turkey breast tenderloins. I have used both and was pleased with the results.*

Maple-Glazed Turkey Breast with Rice

Jeanette Oberholtzer Manheim, PA

MAKES: **4 SERVINGS**
PREP. TIME: **10–15 MINUTES**
COOKING TIME: **4–6 HOURS**
IDEAL SLOW COOKER SIZE: **3–4-QUART**

6-oz. pkg. long-grain wild rice mix

1½ cups water

2-lb. boneless turkey breast, cut into 1½–2-inch chunks

¼ cup maple syrup

1 onion, chopped

¼ tsp. ground cinnamon

½ tsp. salt, *optional*

1. Combine all ingredients in the slow cooker.
2. Cook on Low 4–6 hours, or until turkey and rice are both tender, but not dry or mushy.

Broccoli-Turkey Supreme

Karen Waggoner Joplin, MO

MAKES: **8 SERVINGS**
PREP. TIME: **10 MINUTES**
COOKING TIME: **2–2½ HOURS**
IDEAL SLOW COOKER SIZE: **5–6-QUART**

4 cups cooked turkey breast, cubed

10¾-oz. can condensed cream of chicken soup

10-oz. pkg. frozen broccoli florets, thawed and drained

6.9-oz. pkg. low-sodium plain rice mix

1½ cups fat-free milk

1 cup fat-free chicken broth

1 cup chopped celery

8-oz. can sliced water chestnuts, drained

¾ cup low-fat mayonnaise

½ cup chopped onions

1. Combine all ingredients in slow cooker.
2. Cook uncovered on High for 2–2½ hours, or until rice is tender.

Per Serving: 380 calories (100 calories from fat),11g total fat (2.5g saturated, 0g trans), 70mg cholesterol, 630mg sodium, 37g total carbohydrate (3g fiber, 9g sugar), 32g protein, 10%DV vitamin A, 20%DV vitamin C, 10%DV calcium, 10%DV iron.

Turkey Meat Loaf

PICTURED ON PAGE 98

Martha Ann Auker Landisburg, PA

MAKES: **8 SERVINGS**
PREP. TIME: **15 MINUTES**
COOKING TIME: **6–8 HOURS**
IDEAL SLOW COOKER SIZE: **4-QUART**

1½ lbs. lean ground turkey

2 egg whites

⅓ cup ketchup

1 Tbsp. Worcestershire sauce

1 tsp. dried basil

½ tsp. salt

½ tsp. black pepper

2 small onions, chopped

2 potatoes, finely shredded

2 small red bell peppers, finely chopped

1. Combine all ingredients in a large bowl.
2. Shape into a loaf to fit in your slow cooker. Place in slow cooker.
3. Cover. Cook on Low 6–8 hours.

Per Serving: 200 calories (60 calories from fat), 7g total fat (2g saturated, 0g trans), 65mg cholesterol, 380mg sodium, 16g total carbohydrate (2g fiber, 4g sugar), 17g protein, 20%DV vitamin A, 40%DV vitamin C, 4%DV calcium, 10%DV iron.

Turkey Roast

Donna Lantgen   Rapid City, SD

MAKES: **10 SERVINGS**
PREP. TIME: **10 MINUTES**
COOKING TIME: **6–7 HOURS**
IDEAL SLOW COOKER SIZE: **4–5-QUART**

2 lbs. fat-free ground turkey

2 Tbsp. poultry seasoning

2 slices bread, cubed

1 egg

1. Combine all ingredients. Form into a round or oval loaf (according to the shape of your slow cooker) and place in the cooker.
2. Cook 6–7 hours on Low. Remove from cooker and allow to sit for 15 minutes before slicing and serving.

Per Serving: 120 calories (15 calories from fat), 2g total fat (0g saturated, 0g trans), 55mg cholesterol, 85mg sodium, 3g total carbohydrate (0g fiber, 0g sugar), 23g protein, 2%DV vitamin A, 0%DV vitamin C, 2%DV calcium, 10%DV iron.

Variation: *Mix in any of the following when combining ingredients to add flavor to the Roast:*

1 medium onion, finely chopped

1 green *or* red bell pepper, finely chopped

6 ozs. fresh mushrooms, sliced

½ cup low-fat, low-sodium barbecue sauce

½ cup ketchup

1 tsp. salt

½ tsp. black pepper

1 can 98% fat-free, low-sodium condensed cream of mushroom soup

Savory Turkey Meatballs in Italian Sauce

Marla Folkerts   Holland, OH

MAKES: **8 SERVINGS**
PREP. TIME: **30 MINUTES**
COOKING TIME: **6–8 HOURS**
IDEAL SLOW COOKER SIZE: **4-QUART**

28-oz. can crushed tomatoes

1 Tbsp. red wine vinegar

1 medium onion, finely chopped

2 garlic cloves, minced

¼ tsp. Italian herb seasoning

1 tsp. dried basil

1 lb. ground turkey

⅛ tsp. garlic powder

⅛ tsp. black pepper

⅓ cup dried parsley

2 egg whites

¼ tsp. dried minced onion

⅓ cup quick oats

¼ cup grated Parmesan cheese

¼ cup flour

oil

1. Combine tomatoes, vinegar, onions, garlic, Italian seasonings, and basil in slow cooker. Turn to Low.
2. Combine remaining ingredients, except flour and oil. Form into 1-inch balls. Dredge each ball in flour. Brown in oil in skillet over medium heat. Transfer to slow cooker. Stir into sauce.
3. Cover. Cook on Low 6–8 hours.
4. Serve over pasta or rice.

Tip: *The meatballs and sauce freeze well.*

Saucy Turkey Meatballs

Michelle Steffen Harrisonburg, VA

MAKES: **6 SERVINGS**
PREP. TIME: **20 MINUTES**
COOKING TIME: **6–8 HOURS**
IDEAL SLOW COOKER SIZE: **3-QUART**

½ lb. lean ground turkey

1 cup oat bran

1 clove garlic, crushed

2 Tbsp. water

1 Tbsp. low-sodium soy sauce

3 egg whites

½ cup onions, diced

½ cup low-sodium chili sauce

½ cup grape jelly

¼ cup Dijon mustard

1. Combine turkey, oat bran, garlic, water, soy sauce, egg whites, and onions. Shape into 24 balls (1 Tbsp. per ball).
2. Place meatballs on baking sheet and bake at 350° for 15–20 minutes until browned. (They can be made ahead and frozen.)
3. Mix together chili sauce, grape jelly, and Dijon mustard.
4. Combine meatballs and sauce in slow cooker.
5. Cover. Cook on Low 6–8 hours.

Per Serving: 210 calories (45 calories from fat), 5g total fat (1g saturated, 0g trans), 30mg cholesterol, 650mg sodium, 36g total carbohydrate (3g fiber, 22g sugar), 12g protein, 0%DV vitamin A, 0%DV vitamin C, 4%DV calcium, 10%DV iron.

Turkey Meatballs and Gravy

Betty Sue Good Broadway, VA

MAKES: **8 SERVINGS**
PREP. TIME: **30 MINUTES**
COOKING TIME: **3–8 HOURS**
IDEAL SLOW COOKER SIZE: **4-QUART**

2 eggs, beaten

¾ cup bread crumbs

½ cup finely chopped onions

½ cup finely chopped celery

2 Tbsp. chopped fresh parsley

¼ tsp. pepper

⅛ tsp. garlic powder

1 tsp. salt

2 lbs. ground turkey

1½ Tbsp. cooking oil

10¾-oz. can cream of mushroom soup

1 cup water

⅞-oz. pkg. turkey gravy mix

½ tsp. dried thyme

2 bay leaves

1. Combine eggs, bread crumbs, onions, celery, parsley, pepper, garlic powder, salt, and meat. Shape into 1½-inch balls.
2. Brown meat balls in oil in skillet. Drain meatballs and transfer to slow cooker.
3. Combine soup, water, dry gravy mix, thyme, and bay leaves. Pour over meatballs.
4. Cover. Cook on Low 6–8 hours, or on High 3–4 hours. Discard bay leaves before serving.
5. Serve over mashed potatoes or buttered noodles.

Chicken and Turkey Main Dishes

Southern Barbecue Spaghetti Sauce

Mrs. Carolyn Baer   Conrath, WI

Lavina Hochstedler   Grand Blanc, MI

MAKES: **12 SERVINGS**
PREP. TIME: **20 MINUTES**
COOKING TIME: **4–5 HOURS**
IDEAL SLOW COOKER SIZE: **4–5-QUART**

1 lb. lean ground turkey

2 medium onions, chopped

1½ cups sliced fresh mushrooms

1 medium green bell pepper, chopped

2 garlic cloves, minced

14½-oz. can diced tomatoes, undrained

12-oz. can tomato paste

8-oz. can tomato sauce

1 cup ketchup

½ cup fat-free beef broth

2 Tbsp. Worcestershire sauce

2 Tbsp. brown sugar

1 Tbsp. ground cumin

2 tsp. chili powder

12 cups spaghetti, cooked

1. In a large nonstick skillet, cook the turkey, onions, mushrooms, green pepper, and garlic over medium heat until meat is no longer pink. Drain.
2. Transfer to slow cooker. Stir in tomatoes, tomato paste, tomato sauce, ketchup, broth, Worcestershire sauce, brown sugar, cumin, and chili powder. Mix well.
3. Cook on Low 4–5 hours. Serve over spaghetti.

Per Serving: 330 calories (20 calories from fat), 2g total fat (0g saturated, 0g trans), 15mg cholesterol, 530mg sodium, 60g total carbohydrate (6g fiber, 10g sugar), 20g protein, 30%DV vitamin A, 20%DV vitamin C, 6%DV calcium, 20%DV iron.

Noodleless Lasagna

Nanci Keatley   Salem, OR

MAKES: **4 SERVINGS**
PREP. TIME: **20 MINUTES**
COOKING TIME: **4–4½ HOURS**
IDEAL SLOW COOKER SIZE: **4–5-QUART**

1½ lbs. fat-free ground turkey

1½ cups meat-free, low-sodium spaghetti sauce

8 ozs. sliced mushrooms

1½ cups fat-free ricotta cheese

1 egg, beaten

1 cup shredded mozzarella cheese (part skim), *divided*

1½ tsp. Italian seasoning

10 slices turkey pepperoni

1. Brown ground turkey in a nonstick skillet.
2. Add spaghetti sauce and mushrooms and mix with meat.
3. Pour half of turkey mixture into slow cooker sprayed with nonfat cooking spray.
4. In a small bowl, mix together the ricotta cheese, egg, ¼ cup of mozzarella, and the Italian seasoning. Beat well with a fork.
5. Lay half of pepperoni slices on top of turkey mixture.
6. Spread half of cheese mixture over pepperoni.
7. Repeat layers, finishing by sprinkling the remaining mozzarella on top.
8. Cover. Cook on Low 4–4½ hours.

Per Serving: 480 calories (130 calories from fat), 15g total fat (5g saturated, 0g trans), 190mg cholesterol, 2070mg sodium, 19g total carbohydrate (2g fiber, 8g sugar), 67g protein, 10%DV vitamin A, 6%DV vitamin C, 30%DV calcium, 25%DV iron.

Variation: *If you are not concerned about increasing your sodium intake, you could add ½ tsp. salt and an additional cup of spaghetti sauce to Step 2.*

Sloppy Joes Italia

Nanci Keatley   Salem, OR

MAKES: **12 SANDWICHES**
PREP. TIME: **15 MINUTES**
COOKING TIME: **3–4 HOURS**
IDEAL SLOW COOKER SIZE: **4–5-QUART**

1½ lbs. ground turkey, browned in nonstick skillet

1 cup chopped onions

2 cups low-sodium tomato sauce

1 cup fresh mushrooms, sliced

2 Tbsp. Splenda

1–2 Tbsp. Italian seasoning, according to your taste
   preference

12 reduced-calorie hamburger buns

12 slices low-fat mozzarella cheese, *optional*

1. Place ground turkey, onions, tomato sauce,
   and mushrooms in slow cooker.
2. Stir in Splenda and Italian seasoning.
3. Cover. Cook on Low 3–4 hours.
4. Serve ¼ cup of Sloppy Joe mixture on each
   bun, topped with cheese, if desired.

———————————

Per Serving: 200 calories (50 calories from fat), 6g total fat (1.5g
saturated, 0g trans), 45mg cholesterol, 680mg sodium, 25g total
carbohydrate (4g fiber, 6g sugar), 15g protein, 8%DV vitamin A, 4%DV
vitamin C, 4%DV calcium, 15%DV iron.

Ground Turkey
Potato Dinner

Marjorie Yoder Guengerich   Harrisonburg, VA

MAKES: **6 SERVINGS**
PREP. TIME: **15 MINUTES**
COOKING TIME: **4–8 HOURS**
IDEAL SLOW COOKER SIZE: **4–5-QUART**

1 lb. ground turkey

5 cups raw sliced potatoes

1 onion, sliced

½ tsp. salt

dash of black pepper

14½-oz. can cut green beans, undrained

4-oz. can mushroom pieces, undrained, *optional*

10¾-oz. can cream of chicken soup

1. Crumble uncooked ground turkey in slow
   cooker.
2. Add potatoes, onions, salt, and pepper.
3. Add beans and mushrooms. Pour soup over
   top.
4. Cover. Cook on High 4 hours, or on Low
   6–8 hours.

———————————

Per Serving: 250 calories (40 calories from fat), 4g total fat (1g
saturated, 0g trans), 35mg cholesterol, 900mg sodium, 31g total
carbohydrate (5g fiber, 3g sugar), 24g protein, 2%DV vitamin A,
20%DV vitamin C, 6%DV calcium, 15%DV iron.

*Always have ingredients for simple recipes
on hand.*

Cabbage Joe

Sue Hamilton   Minooka, IL

MAKES: **6 SERVINGS**
PREP. TIME: **10 MINUTES**
COOKING TIME: **6–9 HOURS**
IDEAL SLOW COOKER SIZE: **5-QUART**

1 lb. lean ground turkey

3 cups shredded cabbage

2 cups barbecue sauce

1. Brown turkey in a nonstick skillet over medium heat.
2. Combine cabbage, turkey, and sauce in slow cooker.
3. Cover. Cook on Low 6–8 hours.

Per Serving: 230 calories (60 calories from fat), 7g total fat (1.5g saturated, 0g trans), 60mg cholesterol, 1210mg sodium, 26g total carbohydrate (2g fiber, 21g sugar), 14g protein, 8%DV vitamin A, 10%DV vitamin C, 4%DV calcium, 10%DV iron.

Tip: *Use as sandwich filling, if you wish, in rolls.*

Savory Stuffed Green Peppers

Jean Moore   Pendleton, IN

MAKES: **8 SERVINGS**
PREP. TIME: **20 MINUTES**
COOKING TIME: **3–9 HOURS**
IDEAL SLOW COOKER SIZE: **4–6-QUART OVAL, SO THAT THE PEPPERS CAN ALL SIT ON THE BOTTOM OF THE COOKER**

8 small green peppers, tops removed and seeded

10-oz. pkg. frozen corn

¾ lb. 99% fat-free ground turkey

¾ lb. extra-lean ground beef

8-oz. can low-sodium tomato sauce

½ tsp. garlic powder

¼ tsp. black pepper

1 cup shredded low-fat American cheese

½ tsp. Worcestershire sauce

¼ cup chopped onions

3 Tbsp. water

2 Tbsp. ketchup

1. Wash peppers and drain well. Combine all ingredients except water and ketchup in mixing bowl. Stir well.
2. Stuff peppers ⅔ full.
3. Pour water in slow cooker. Arrange peppers on top.
4. Pour ketchup over peppers.
5. Cover. Cook on High 3–4 hours, or on Low 7–9 hours.

Per Serving: 200 calories (35 calories from fat), 4g total fat (1.5g saturated, 0g trans), 30mg cholesterol, 530mg sodium, 21g total carbohydrate (4g fiber, 7g sugar), 23g protein, 20%DV vitamin A, 100%DV vitamin C, 20%DV calcium, 10%DV iron.

Variation: *For a zestier flavor, use 99% fat-free Italian turkey sausage instead of the ground turkey, and use 1 cup salsa instead of the tomato sauce.*

Turkey Macaroni

Jean Moore Pendleton, IN • *Jeanne Allen* Rye, CO

MAKES: **6 SERVINGS**
PREP. TIME: **20 MINUTES**
COOKING TIME: **3–6 HOURS**
IDEAL SLOW COOKER SIZE: **5-QUART**

1 tsp. vegetable oil

1½ lbs. 99% fat-free ground turkey

2 10¾-oz. cans condensed low-sodium tomato soup,
  undiluted

16-oz. can corn, drained

½ cup onions, chopped

4-oz. can sliced mushrooms, drained

2 Tbsp. ketchup

1 Tbsp. prepared mustard

¼ tsp. black pepper

¼ tsp. garlic powder

2 cups dry macaroni, cooked and drained

1. Heat oil in medium skillet. Brown turkey. Drain.
2. Combine all ingredients except macaroni in slow cooker. Stir to blend. Cover.
3. Cook on High 3–4 hours, or on Low 4–6 hours. Stir in cooked and drained macaroni 15 minutes before serving.

Per Serving: 300 calories (40 calories from fat), 4.5g total fat (0g saturated, 0g trans), 45mg cholesterol, 420mg sodium, 38g total carbohydrate (3g fiber, 4g sugar), 34g protein, 8%DV vitamin A, 30%DV vitamin C, 2%DV calcium, 20%DV iron.

Sausage Pasta

Rose Hankins Stevensville, MD

MAKES: **6 SERVINGS**
PREP. TIME: **20 MINUTES**
COOKING TIME: **8–10 HOURS**
IDEAL SLOW COOKER SIZE: **5-QUART**

1 lb. turkey sausage, cut in 1-inch chunks

1 cup chopped green and/or red bell peppers

1 cup chopped celery

1 cup chopped red onions

1 cup chopped green zucchini

8-oz. can tomato paste

2 cups water

14-oz. can tomatoes, chopped

¼ cup cooking wine

1 Tbsp. Italian seasoning

1 lb. pasta, cooked

1. Combine all ingredients except pasta in slow cooker.
2. Cover. Cook on Low 8–10 hours.
3. Add pasta 10 minutes before serving.

Per Serving: 220 calories (60 calories from fat), 7g total fat (2g saturated, 0g trans), 55mg cholesterol, 730mg sodium, 27g total carbohydrate (4g fiber, 5g sugar), 14g protein, 15%DV vitamin A, 20%DV vitamin C, 6%DV calcium, 15%DV iron.

Tip: *If diets allow, enjoy this served with a thick slice of Italian bread for each person. Sprinkle with olive oil and garlic. Broil 1–2 minutes.*

Sauerkraut and Turkey Sausage

Vera F. Schmucker   Goshen, IN

MAKES: **8 SERVINGS**
PREP. TIME: **5 MINUTES**
COOKING TIME: **4–6 HOURS**
IDEAL SLOW COOKER SIZE: **3-QUART**

1 large can sauerkraut

¼–½ cup brown sugar, according to your taste
   preference

8-inch link spicy *or* smoked turkey sausage

1. Pour sauerkraut into slow cooker.
2. Sprinkle with brown sugar.
3. Cut turkey sausage into ¼-inch slices and arrange over sauerkraut.
4. Cook on Low 4–6 hours.

Italian Turkey Sandwiches

Light

Joette Droz   Kalona, IA   •   *Barbara Walker*   Sturgis, SD

MAKES: **10 SANDWICHES**
PREP. TIME: **20 MINUTES**
COOKING TIME: **5–6 HOURS**
IDEAL SLOW COOKER SIZE: **6-QUART**

1 bone-in turkey breast (5½ lbs.), skin removed

½ cup chopped green bell pepper

1 medium onion, chopped

¼ cup chili sauce

3 Tbsp. white vinegar

2 Tbsp. dried oregano *or* Italian seasoning

4 tsp. beef bouillon granules

1. Place turkey breast, green pepper, and onion in slow cooker.
2. Combine chili sauce, vinegar, oregano, and bouillon. Pour over turkey and vegetables.
3. Cover. Cook on Low 5–6 hours, or until meat juices run clear and vegetables are tender.
4. Remove turkey, reserving cooking liquid. Shred the turkey with 2 forks.
5. Return to cooking juices.
6. For each serving, spoon approximately ½ cup onto a kaiser or hard sandwich roll.

Per Serving: 270 calories (30 calories from fat), 3g total fat (0.5g saturated, 0g trans), 50mg cholesterol, 760mg sodium, 35g total carbohydrate (2g fiber, 5g sugar), 24g protein, 4%DV vitamin A, 10%DV vitamin C, 8%DV calcium, 20%DV iron.

Slow cookers fit any season. When it's hot outside, they don't heat up your kitchen. So turn on your cooker before heading to the pool or the beach — or the garden.

Turkey Sloppy Joes

Marla Folkerts   Holland, OH

MAKES: **6 SANDWICHES**
PREP. TIME: **20 MINUTES**
COOKING TIME: **4½–6 HOURS**
IDEAL SLOW COOKER SIZE: **4-QUART**

1 red onion, chopped

1 sweet pepper, chopped

1½ lbs. boneless turkey, finely chopped

1 cup chili sauce *or* **ketchup**

¼ tsp. salt

1 garlic clove, minced

1 tsp. Dijon-style mustard

⅛ tsp. pepper

1. Place onion, sweet pepper, and turkey in slow cooker.
2. Combine chili sauce, salt, garlic, mustard, and pepper. Pour over turkey mixture. Mix well.
3. Cover. Cook on Low 4½–6 hours.
4. Serve on homemade bread or sandwich rolls.

Hot Turkey Sandwiches

Tracey Hanson Schramel   Windom, MN

MAKES: **8 SANDWICHES**
PREP. TIME: **20–30 MINUTES**
COOKING TIME: **4–5 HOURS**
IDEAL SLOW COOKER SIZE: **3-QUART**

6 cups cooked turkey, cut into bite-sized chunks

1½ cups mayonnaise *or* **salad dressing**

1 lb. Velveeta cheese, cubed

1½ cups chopped celery

1 small onion, minced

¼ tsp. salt

⅛ tsp. pepper

1. Combine all ingredients and place in slow cooker.
2. Cover and cook on Low 4–5 hours.
3. Serve in rolls.

I like to slow-cook a turkey in advance of needing it. I slice the cooked breast meat into serving pieces and freeze it. And I chop all the rest of the meat and freeze it in 3-cup batches. The chopped turkey is ready for any recipe calling for cooked turkey or chicken, such as turkey or chicken salad, turkey pot pie, and so on.

Pork Main Dishes

Tender Pork Roast

Renee Baum Chambersburg, PA • *Mary Lynn Miller* Reinholds, PA

MAKES: **8 SERVINGS**
PREP. TIME: **10 MINUTES**
COOKING TIME: **3–8 HOURS**
IDEAL SLOW COOKER SIZE: **5-QUART**

3-lb. boneless pork roast, cut in half

8-oz. can tomato sauce

¾ cup soy sauce

½ cup sugar

2 tsp. dry mustard

1. Place roast in slow cooker.
2. Combine remaining ingredients in a bowl. Pour over roast.
3. Cover and cook on Low 6–8 hours, or on High 3–4 hours, or until meat is tender but not dry.
4. Remove roast from slow cooker to a serving platter. Discard juices or thicken for gravy.

Tip: *To thicken the juices, mix 2 Tbsp. cornstarch with 2 Tbsp. water in a small bowl. After removing meat from the cooker, turn it to High. When juices are simmering, stir in cornstarch-water mixture. Continue stirring until it is absorbed. Simmer until juices thicken, about 10 minutes, stirring occasionally. Serve over or alongside sliced pork.*

Flavorful Pork Roast

Betty A. Holt   St. Charles, MO

MAKES: **8–10 SERVINGS**
PREP. TIME: **5 MINUTES**
COOKING TIME: **7 HOURS**
IDEAL SLOW COOKER SIZE: **4-QUART**

4–5-lb. pork loin roast

large onion, sliced

1 bay leaf

2 Tbsp. soy sauce

1 Tbsp. garlic powder

1. Place roast and onion in slow cooker. Add bay leaf, soy sauce, and garlic powder.
2. Cover. Cook on High 1 hour and then on Low 6 hours.
3. Slice and serve.

Apricot-Glazed Pork Roast

Jean Butzer   Batavia, NY • *Virginia Blish*   Akron, NY

MAKES: **10–12 SERVINGS**
PREP. TIME: **10 MINUTES**
COOKING TIME: **3–6 HOURS**
IDEAL SLOW COOKER SIZE: **5–6-QUART**

10½-oz. can condensed chicken broth

18-oz. jar apricot preserves

1 large onion, chopped

2 Tbsp. Dijon mustard

3½–4-lb. boneless pork loin

1. Mix broth, preserves, onion, and mustard in a bowl.
2. Cut roast to fit, if necessary, and place in cooker. Pour glaze over meat.
3. Cover and cook on Low 4–6 hours, or on High 3 hours, or until tender.
4. Remove pork loin from slow cooker to a serving platter. Discard juices or thicken for gravy.

Tip: *To thicken the juices, mix 2 Tbsp. cornstarch with 2 Tbsp. water in a small bowl. After removing meat from the cooker, turn it to High. When juices are simmering, stir in cornstarch-water mixture. Continue stirring until it is absorbed. Simmer until juices thicken, about 10 minutes, stirring occasionally. Serve over or alongside sliced pork.*

Pork Main Dishes

Autumn Harvest Pork Loin

Stacy Schmucker Stoltzfus Enola, PA

MAKES: **4–6 SERVINGS**
PREP. TIME: **30 MINUTES**
COOKING TIME: **5–6 HOURS**
IDEAL SLOW COOKER SIZE: **5-QUART**

1 cup cider *or* apple juice

1½–2-lb. pork loin

salt

pepper

2 large Granny Smith apples, peeled and sliced

1½ whole butternut squashes, peeled and cubed

½ cup brown sugar

¼ tsp. cinnamon

¼ tsp. dried thyme

¼ tsp. dried sage

1. Heat cider in hot skillet. Sear pork loin on all sides in cider.
2. Sprinkle meat with salt and pepper on all sides. Place in slow cooker, along with juices.
3. Combine apples and squash. Sprinkle with sugar and herbs. Stir. Place around pork loin.
4. Cover. Cook on Low 5–6 hours.
5. Remove pork from cooker. Let stand 10–15 minutes. Slice into ½-inch-thick slices.
6. Serve topped with apples and squash.

When using fresh herbs you may want to experiment with the amounts to use, because their strength is enhanced in the slow cooker, rather than becoming weaker.

Apple-Cranberry Pork Roast

Dawn Day Westminster, CA

MAKES: **8 SERVINGS**
PREP. TIME: **20 MINUTES**
COOKING TIME: **6–8 HOURS**
IDEAL SLOW COOKER SIZE: **4-QUART**

2 lbs. pork tenderloin, fat trimmed

2 Tbsp. canola oil

3 cups apple juice

3 Granny Smith apples

1 cup fresh cranberries

¾ tsp. salt

½ tsp. black pepper

1. Brown roast on all sides in skillet in canola oil. Place in slow cooker.
2. Add remaining ingredients.
3. Cover. Cook on Low 6–8 hours.

Per Serving: 290 calories (80 calories from fat), 9g total fat (2g saturated, 0g trans), 90mg cholesterol, 290mg sodium, 19g total carbohydrate (2g fiber, 16g sugar), 32g protein, 0%DV vitamin A, 0%DV vitamin C, 0%DV calcium, 8%DV iron.

Cranberry-Mustard Pork Tenderloin

Valerie Drobel   Carlisle, PA

MAKES: **6 SERVINGS**
PREP. TIME: **15 MINUTES**
COOKING TIME: **6–8 HOURS**
IDEAL SLOW COOKER SIZE: **5-QUART**

16-oz. can whole cranberry sauce

3 Tbsp. lemon juice

4 Tbsp. Dijon mustard

3 Tbsp. brown sugar

2 pork tenderloins, about 2 lbs. total

1. In a small bowl, combine first four ingredients. Place about ⅓ of mixture in bottom of slow cooker.
2. Place tenderloins on top of sauce. Pour remaining sauce over tenderloins.
3. Cover and cook on Low 6–8 hours, or until meat is tender.
4. Allow meat to stand for 10 minutes before slicing.

Tip: *To thicken the juices, mix 2 Tbsp. cornstarch with 2 Tbsp. water in a small bowl. After removing meat from the cooker, turn it to High. When juices are simmering, stir in cornstarch-water mixture. Continue stirring until it is absorbed. Simmer until juices thicken, about 10 minutes, stirring occasionally. Serve over or alongside sliced pork.*

Cranberry Orange Pork Roast

Barbara Aston   Ashdown, AR

MAKES: **6–8 SERVINGS**
PREP. TIME: **10 MINUTES**
COOKING TIME: **8–10 HOURS**
IDEAL SLOW COOKER SIZE: **4-QUART**

3–4-lb. pork roast

salt to taste

pepper to taste

1 cup ground or finely chopped cranberries

¼ cup honey

1 tsp. grated orange peel

⅛ tsp. ground cloves

⅛ tsp. ground nutmeg

1. Sprinkle roast with salt and pepper. Place in slow cooker.
2. Combine remaining ingredients. Pour over roast.
3. Cover. Cook on Low 8–10 hours.

Fruited Pork

Jeanette Oberholtzer   Manheim, PA

MAKES: **6 SERVINGS**
PREP. TIME: **10 MINUTES**
COOKING TIME: **4–6 HOURS**
IDEAL SLOW COOKER SIZE: **3-4-QUART**

2-lb. boneless pork loin roast

½ tsp. salt

¼ tsp. pepper

1½ cups mixed dried fruit

½ cup apple juice

1. Place pork in slow cooker. Sprinkle with salt and pepper.
2. Top with fruit. Pour apple juice over top.
3. Cover and cook on Low 4–6 hours, or until pork is tender.

Savory Tenderloins

Barbara Jean Fabel   Wausau, WI

MAKES: **6–8 SERVINGS**
PREP. TIME: **25 MINUTES**
COOKING TIME: **3–5 HOURS**
IDEAL SLOW COOKER SIZE: **4–5-QUART**

½ cup sliced celery

¼ lb. fresh mushrooms, quartered

1 medium onion, sliced

¼ cup butter, melted

2 1¼-lb. pork tenderloins

1 Tbsp. butter

2 tsp. salt

¼ tsp. pepper

1 Tbsp. butter

½ cup beef broth

1 Tbsp. flour

1. Placed celery, mushrooms, onion, and ¼ cup melted butter in slow cooker.
2. Brown tenderloins in skillet in 1 Tbsp. butter. Layer over vegetables in slow cooker.
3. Sprinkle with salt and pepper.
4. Combine bouillon and flour until smooth. Pour over tenderloins.
5. Cover. Cook on High 3 hours, or on Low 4–5 hours.

Pork Roast with Potatoes and Onions

Trudy Kutter   Corfu, NY

MAKES: **6–8 SERVINGS**
PREP. TIME: **15 MINUTES**
COOKING TIME: **8½ HOURS**
IDEAL SLOW COOKER SIZE: **4-QUART**

2½–3-lb. boneless pork loin roast

1 large garlic clove, slivered

5–6 potatoes, cubed

1 large onion, sliced

¾ cup broth, tomato juice, *or* water

1½ Tbsp. soy sauce

1 Tbsp. cornstarch

1 Tbsp. cold water

1. Make slits in roast and insert slivers of garlic. Put under broiler to brown.
2. Put potatoes in slow cooker. Add half of onions. Place roast on onions and potatoes. Cover with remaining onions.
3. Combine broth and soy sauce. Pour over roast.
4. Cover. Cook on Low 8 hours. Remove roast and vegetables from liquid.
5. Combine cornstarch and water. Add to liquid in slow cooker. Turn to High until thickened. Serve over sliced meat and vegetables.

Variation: *Use sweet potatoes instead of white potatoes.*

To remove onion odor from your fingers, rub a metal spoon between your finger and thumb under running water.

Slow-Cooked Pork Stew

Virginia Graybill Hershey, PA

MAKES: **8 SERVINGS**
PREP. TIME: **20 MINUTES**
COOKING TIME: **4–6 HOURS**
IDEAL SLOW COOKER SIZE: **5-QUART**

2 lbs. lean pork loin, cut into 1-inch cubes
½ lb. baby carrots
3 large potatoes, cut into 1-inch cubes
2 parsnips, cut into 1-inch cubes
2 onions, cut into wedges, slices, or chopped coarsely
3 garlic cloves, minced
1–2 tsp. ground black pepper, depending on your taste preferences
1 tsp. dried thyme
1 tsp. salt
2½ cups low-sodium canned vegetable juice
2 Tbsp. brown sugar
1 Tbsp. prepared mustard
4 tsp. tapioca

1. Place pork in slow cooker.
2. Add carrots, potatoes, parsnips, onions, garlic, pepper, thyme, and salt. Mix together well.
3. In a medium bowl, combine vegetable juice, brown sugar, mustard, and tapioca. Pour over meat and vegetables.
4. Cover. Cook on Low 6 hours, or on High 4 hours.

Per Serving: 300 calories (60 calories from fat), 7g total fat (2.5g saturated, 0g trans), 65mg cholesterol, 490mg sodium, 34g total carbohydrate (5g fiber, 11g sugar), 26g protein, 60%DV vitamin A, 30%DV vitamin C, 8%DV calcium, 15%DV iron.

German Pot Roast

Eleanor Larson Glen Lyon, PA

MAKES: **12 SERVINGS**
PREP. TIME: **15 MINUTES**
COOKING TIME: **4–8 HOURS**
IDEAL SLOW COOKER SIZE: **5-QUART**

2 lbs. boneless, lean pork roast
1 tsp. garlic salt
½ tsp. black pepper
4 large sweet potatoes, peeled and diced
2 medium onions, sliced
½ tsp. dried oregano
14½-oz. can low-sodium tomatoes

1. Place pork roast in slow cooker.
2. Sprinkle with garlic salt and pepper.
3. Add remaining ingredients.
4. Cover. Cook on Low 7–8 hours, or on High 4–5 hours.

Per Serving: 170 calories (45 calories from fat), 5g total fat (2g saturated, 0g trans), 45mg cholesterol, 290mg sodium, 14g total carbohydrate (2g fiber, 4g sugar), 16g protein, 100%DV vitamin A, 4%DV vitamin C, 4%DV calcium, 4%DV iron.

Carolina Pot Roast

Jonathan Gehman Harrisonburg, VA

MAKES: **3–4 SERVINGS**
PREP. TIME: **20 MINUTES**
COOKING TIME: **3 HOURS**
IDEAL SLOW COOKER SIZE: **3-QUART**

3 medium-large sweet potatoes, peeled and cut into 1-inch chunks
½ cup brown sugar
1-lb. pork roast
scant ¼ tsp. cumin
salt to taste
water

1. Place sweet potatoes in bottom of slow cooker. Sprinkle brown sugar over potatoes.
2. Heat nonstick skillet over medium-high heat. Add roast and brown on all sides. Sprinkle meat with cumin and salt while browning. Place pork on top of potatoes.
3. Add an inch of water to the cooker, being careful not to wash the seasoning off the meat.
4. Cover and cook on Low 3 hours, or until meat and potatoes are tender but not dry or mushy.

Vegetable Pork Dish

Cyndie Marrara   Port Matilda, PA

MAKES: **6 SERVINGS**
PREP. TIME: **15 MINUTES**
COOKING TIME: **7 HOURS**
IDEAL SLOW COOKER SIZE: **4-QUART**

2 sweet potatoes *or* yams, peeled and cut in small pieces
10-oz. pkg. frozen corn
10-oz. pkg. frozen Italian beans
1 medium onion, chopped
1½ lbs. lean pork, cut in small pieces
14½-oz. can low-sodium diced tomatoes, undrained
¾ cup water
1 tsp. garlic, chopped
¼ tsp. salt
⅛ tsp. black pepper

1. Combine potatoes, corn, beans, and onion in slow cooker.
2. Place pork on top.
3. Stir together tomatoes, water, garlic, salt, and pepper. Pour over pork.
4. Cover. Cook on Low 7 hours.

Per Serving: 340 calories (100 calories from fat), 11g total fat (4g saturated, 0g trans), 105mg cholesterol, 370mg sodium, 22g total carbohydrate (4g fiber, 10g sugar), 36g protein, 100%DV vitamin A, 20%DV vitamin C, 0%DV calcium, 15%DV iron.

Chalupa

Jeannine Janzen   Elbing, KS

MAKES: **12–16 SERVINGS**
PREP. TIME: **5–10 MINUTES**
SOAKING TIME: **8 HOURS, OR OVERNIGHT**
COOKING TIME: **8 HOURS**
IDEAL SLOW COOKER SIZE: **5-QUART**

3-lb. pork roast
1 lb. dry pinto beans
2 garlic cloves, minced
1 Tbsp. ground cumin
1 Tbsp. dried oregano
2 Tbsp. chili powder
1 Tbsp. salt
4-oz. can chopped green chilies
water
lettuce
shredded cheese
chopped onions
chopped tomatoes

1. Cover beans with water and soak overnight in slow cooker.
2. In the morning, remove beans (reserve soaking water), and put roast in bottom of cooker. Add remaining ingredients (including the beans and their soaking water) and more water if needed to cover all the ingredients.
3. Cook on High 1 hour, and then on Low 6 hours. Remove meat and shred with two forks. Return meat to slow cooker.
4. Cook on High 1 more hour.
5. Serve over a bed of lettuce. Top with shredded cheese and chopped onions and tomatoes.

Nutritious Pork with Veggies Dinner

Judy Miles   Centreville, MD

MAKES: **6 SERVINGS**
PREP. TIME: **20 MINUTES**
COOKING TIME: **6–8 HOURS**
IDEAL SLOW COOKER SIZE: **3½-QUART**

1 lb. pork roast, cut into strips ½-inch thick

1 large onion, chopped

1 small green bell pepper, sliced

8 ozs. fresh mushrooms, sliced

8-oz. can low-sodium tomato sauce

4 carrots, sliced

1½ Tbsp. vinegar

1 tsp. salt

2 tsp. Worcestershire sauce

1. Brown pork in a skillet over medium heat in a nonstick skillet.
2. Combine all ingredients in slow cooker.
3. Cover. Cook on Low 6–8 hours.
4. Serve over hot rice.

Per Serving: 210 calories (70 calories from fat), 7g total fat (2.5g saturated, 0g trans), 70mg cholesterol, 700mg sodium, 12g total carbohydrate (3g fiber, 6g sugar), 25g protein, 200%DV vitamin A, 20%DV vitamin C, 4%DV calcium, 10%DV iron.

When browning meats, don't crowd the skillet or cooking pan. If the pieces are too close to each other, they'll steam in each other's juices rather than browning.

Spicy Pork Olé

Mary Kennell   Roanoke, IL

MAKES: **5 SERVINGS**
PREP. TIME: **10–15 MINUTES**
COOKING TIME: **3½–4 HOURS**
IDEAL SLOW COOKER SIZE: **4-QUART**

1½ lbs. pork loin, cut into bite-sized pieces

2 Tbsp. taco seasoning

2 cups mild salsa

⅓ cup peach jam

2 Tbsp. cornstarch

¼ cup water

1. Spray slow cooker with nonstick cooking spray.
2. Place pork in slow cooker. Sprinkle with taco seasoning and stir to coat.
3. Add salsa and jam. Stir.
4. Cook on High 3–3½ hours, or until meat is tender. Remove meat to serving dish and keep warm.
5. In a bowl, blend cornstarch and water. Turn cooker to High. When sauce simmers, stir in cornstarch-water mixture. Continue stirring until fully absorbed. Continue cooking, stirring occasionally, until sauce thickens. Serve over or alongside pork.

As-Basic-As-It-Gets Pork and Sauerkraut

Earnest Zimmerman   Mechanicsburg, PA

MAKES: **8–12 SERVINGS**
PREP. TIME: **5 MINUTES**
COOKING TIME: **3–8 HOURS**
IDEAL SLOW COOKER SIZE: **6–8-QUART**

3–4 lb. pork roast

32-oz. bag *or* 2 14½-oz. cans sauerkraut, *divided*

salt and/or pepper, *optional*

1. Rinse pork roast; pat dry.
2. Place half the sauerkraut in bottom of slow cooker. Place roast on top.
3. Cover roast with remaining sauerkraut. Season with salt and/or pepper, if you wish.
4. Cover and cook on Low 6–8 hours, or on High 3–4 hours.

Variation: *For added flavor, choose a crisp apple, core it, peel it or not, and slice it. Lay over seasoned sauerkraut at the end of Step 3. Crumble 1–2 Tbsp. brown sugar over top.*

Ethel Mumaw Millersburg, OH

No-Fuss Sauerkraut

Vera M. Kuhns Harrisonburg, VA

MAKES: **12 SERVINGS**
PREP. TIME: **7 MINUTES**
COOKING TIME: **4–5 HOURS**
IDEAL SLOW COOKER SIZE: **7–8-QUART**

3-lb. pork roast
3 2-lb. pkgs. sauerkraut (drain and discard juice from 1 pkg.)
2 apples, peeled and sliced
½ cup brown sugar
1 cup apple juice

1. Place meat in large slow cooker.
2. Place sauerkraut on top of meat.
3. Add apples and brown sugar. Add apple juice.
4. Cover. Cook on High 4–5 hours.
5. Serve with mashed potatoes.

Tip: *If your slow cooker isn't large enough to hold all the ingredients, cook one package of sauerkraut and half the apples, brown sugar, and apple juice in another cooker. Mix the ingredients of both cookers together before serving.*

Savory Pork Roast with Sauerkraut

Eleya Raim Oxford, IA

MAKES: **6 SERVINGS**
PREP. TIME: **10 MINUTES**
COOKING TIME: **3–6 HOURS**
IDEAL SLOW COOKER SIZE: **4-QUART OVAL**

2-lb. pork roast
1 clove garlic, minced
1 medium onion, sliced
1 pint sauerkraut, or more if you wish
1 tsp. caraway seed

1. If you have time, heat a nonstick skillet over medium-high heat. Place the roast in the hot pan and brown on all sides.
2. Place the roast, browned or not, in the slow cooker.
3. Add remaining ingredients in the order listed.
4. Cover and cook on High 3 hours, or on Low 4–6 hours, or until meat is tender but not dry.

Variation: *Salt and pepper the roast before you place it in the cooker.*

Flavor-Filled Pork and Sauerkraut

Sheila Soldner Lititz, PA

MAKES: **10–15 SERVINGS**
PREP. TIME: **30 MINUTES**
COOKING TIME: **10–11 HOURS**
IDEAL SLOW COOKER SIZE: **6–7-QUART**

4–5-lb. lean pork loin roast

1–2-lb. bag sauerkraut, *divided*

half a small head of cabbage, thinly sliced, *divided*

1 large onion, thinly sliced, *divided*

1 apple, quartered, cored, and sliced, but not peeled,
    divided

1 tsp. dill weed, *optional*

½ cup brown sugar, *optional*

1 cup water

1. Brown roast for 10 minutes in a heavy nonstick skillet. Place roast in slow cooker.
2. Cover with a layer of half the sauerkraut, then a layer of half the cabbage, a layer of half the onion, and a layer of half the apple.
3. Repeat the layers.
4. If you wish to use the dill weed and brown sugar, mix them and the water together in a bowl. Pour over layers. Or simply pour water over top.
5. Cover and cook on High 1 hour. Turn to Low and cook until meat is tender, about 9–10 hours.

Pork and Sauerdogs

Leesa DeMartyn Enola, PA

MAKES: **12–15 SERVINGS**
PREP. TIME: **5 MINUTES**
COOKING TIME: **4–11 HOURS**
IDEAL SLOW COOKER SIZE: **5–6-QUART**

5-lb. pork roast

32-oz. can sauerkraut, undrained

1 pkg. of 8 hot dogs

1. Place pork in slow cooker. Spoon sauerkraut over pork.
2. Cover and cook on Low 9–11 hours, or on High 4–5 hours, or until meat is tender but not dry.
3. Lift roast onto a platter and, using a fork, separate the meat into small pieces.
4. Return pork to cooker and stir into sauerkraut.
5. Cut hot dogs into ½-inch slices and stir into pork and sauerkraut.
6. Cover and cook for an additional 30 minutes. Serve over a bed of mashed potatoes.

Shredded Pork

Cindy Krestynick Glen Lyon, PA

MAKES: **8–12 SERVINGS**
PREP. TIME: **10 MINUTES**
COOKING TIME: **4–10 HOURS**
IDEAL SLOW COOKER SIZE: **4–5-QUART**

3–4-lb. pork butt roast

1½ envelopes taco seasoning

3–5 cloves garlic, sliced, according to your taste
    preference

1 large onion, quartered

4-oz. can whole green chilies, drained

1 cup water

1. Place roast in slow cooker.
2. In a bowl, mix all remaining ingredients together. Spoon over meat in cooker.
3. Cover and cook on Low 8–10 hours, or on High 4–6 hours, or until meat is tender but not dry.
4. Place pork on a platter and shred with 2 forks. Stir shredded meat back into sauce.
5. Serve in tortillas, topped with shredded lettuce, tomato, and sour cream, or over steamed rice.

North Carolina Barbecue

J. B. Miller   Indianapolis, IN

MAKES: **8–12 SERVINGS**
PREP. TIME: **15 MINUTES**
COOKING TIME: **5–8 HOURS**
IDEAL SLOW COOKER SIZE: **4–5-QUART**

3–4-lb. pork loin, roast *or* shoulder
1 cup apple cider vinegar
¼ cup, plus 1 Tbsp., prepared mustard
¼ cup, plus 1 Tbsp., Worcestershire sauce
2 tsp. red pepper flakes

1. Trim fat from pork. Place in slow cooker.
2. In a bowl, mix remaining ingredients together. Spoon over meat.
3. Cover and cook on High 5 hours, or on Low 8 hours, or until meat is tender but not dry.
4. Slice, or break meat apart, and serve drizzled with the cooking juices. If you use the meat for sandwiches, you'll have enough for 8–12 sandwiches.

Barbecued Pork

Grace Ketcham   Marietta, GA   •   *Mary Seielstad*   Sparks, NV

MAKES: **8 SERVINGS**
PREP. TIME: **15 MINUTES**
COOKING TIME: **8 HOURS**
IDEAL SLOW COOKER SIZE: **4-QUART**

3 lbs. pork, cubed
2 cups chopped onions
3 green peppers, chopped
½ cup brown sugar
¼ cup vinegar
6-oz. can tomato paste
1½ Tbsp. chili powder
1 tsp. dry mustard
2 tsp. Worcestershire sauce
2 tsp. salt

1. Combine all ingredients in slow cooker.
2. Cover. Cook on High 8 hours.
3. Shred meat with fork. Mix into sauce and heat through.
4. Serve on hamburger buns with shredded cheese and cole slaw on top.

Variation: *Substitute cubed chuck roast or stewing beef for the pork, or use half beef, half pork.*

A slow cooker is perfect for less tender meats such as a round steak. Because the meat is cooked in liquid for hours, it turns out tender and juicy.

Pork Barbecue

Mary Sommerfeld Lancaster, PA

MAKES: **10–12 SANDWICHES**
PREP. TIME: **10 MINUTES**
COOKING TIME: **12–20 HOURS**
IDEAL SLOW COOKER SIZE: **4–5 QUART**

2 onions, sliced

4–5-lb. pork roast *or* fresh picnic ham

5–6 whole cloves

2 cups water

1 large onion, chopped

16-oz. bottle barbecue sauce

1. Put half of sliced onions in bottom of slow cooker. Add meat, cloves, and water. Cover with remaining sliced onions.
2. Cover. Cook on Low 8–12 hours.
3. Remove bone from meat. Cut up meat. Drain liquid.
4. Return meat to slow cooker. Add chopped onion and barbecue sauce.
5. Cover. Cook on High 1–3 hours, or on Low 4–8 hours, stirring two or three times.
6. Serve on buns.

Tip: *This freezes well.*

Poppin' Pork Barbecue

Barbara L. McGinnis Jupiter, FL

MAKES: **8–12 SANDWICHES**
PREP. TIME: **5–10 MINUTES**
COOKING TIME: **8 HOURS**
IDEAL SLOW COOKER SIZE: **5-QUART**

3–4-lb. pork loin

salt to taste

pepper to taste

2 cups cider vinegar

2 tsp. sugar

½ cup ketchup

crushed red pepper to taste

Tabasco sauce to taste

1. Sprinkle pork with salt and pepper. Place in slow cooker.
2. Pour vinegar over meat. Sprinkle sugar on top.
3. Cover. Cook on Low 8 hours.
4. Remove pork from cooker and shred meat.
5. In bowl mix together ketchup, red pepper, Tabasco sauce, and ½ cup vinegar-sugar drippings. Stir in shredded meat.
6. Serve on sandwich rolls with cole slaw.

Variation: *To increase the tang, add 1 tsp. dry mustard in Step 5. Use ¼ cup ketchup and ¼ cup orange juice, instead of ½ cup ketchup.*

Slow cookers come in a variety of sizes, from 1–8-quarts. The best size for a family of four or five is a 5–6-quart size.

Pork 'n Beef Barbecue Sandwiches

Sherry L. Lapp   Lancaster, PA

MAKES: **6–8 SANDWICHES**
PREP. TIME: **15 MINUTES**
COOKING TIME: **8 HOURS**
IDEAL SLOW COOKER SIZE: **4-QUART**

1½ lbs. cubed pork

1 lb. stewing beef, cubed

6-oz. can tomato paste

¼ cup vinegar

½ cup brown sugar

1 tsp. salt

1 Tbsp. chili powder

1 large onion, chopped

1 green pepper, chopped

1. Combine ingredients in slow cooker.
2. Cover. Cook on Low 8 hours.
3. Shred meat with fork before serving on rolls.
4. Bring to the table with creamy cole slaw.

Honey Barbecue Pork Chops

Tamara McCarthy   Pennsburg, PA

MAKES: **8 SERVINGS**
PREP. TIME: **15 MINUTES**
COOKING TIME: **6–8 HOURS**
IDEAL SLOW COOKER SIZE: **4-QUART**

8 pork chops, *divided*

1 large onion, sliced, *divided*

1 cup barbecue sauce

⅓ cup honey

1. Place one layer of pork chops in your slow cooker.
2. Arrange a proportionate amount of sliced onions over top.

3. Mix barbecue sauce and honey together in a small bowl. Spoon a proportionate amount of sauce over the chops.
4. Repeat the layers.
5. Cover and cook on Low 3–4 hours.
6. If the sauce barely covers the chops, flip them over at this point. If they're well covered, simply allow them to cook another 3–4 hours on Low, or until they're tender but the meat is not dry.

Pork Chops with Tomato Sauce

Margaret H. Moffitt   Bartlett, TN

MAKES: **4–6 SERVINGS**
PREP. TIME: **25 MINUTES**
COOKING TIME: **3–7 HOURS**
IDEAL SLOW COOKER SIZE: **3-QUART**

4 thickly-cut pork chops

1 medium onion, sliced or chopped

½ cup ketchup

¼ cup brown sugar

½ tsp. chili powder

½ cup water

1. Place pork chops in bottom of slow cooker. Top with onions.
2. In a bowl, mix ketchup, brown sugar, chili powder and water together. Spoon sauce over all. (If the chops need to be stacked in order to fit into your cooker, make sure to top each one with sauce.)
3. Cover and cook on High 3–4 hours, or on Low for up to 6–7 hours, or until meat is tender but not dry.

Saucy Pork Chops

Mary Puskar   Forest Hill, MD

MAKES: **5 SERVINGS**
PREP. TIME: **15 MINUTES**
COOKING TIME: **6–8 HOURS**
IDEAL SLOW COOKER SIZE: **4-QUART**

5–6 center-cut loin pork chops
3 Tbsp. oil
1 onion, sliced
1 green pepper, cut in strips
8-oz. can tomato sauce
3–4 Tbsp. brown sugar
1 Tbsp. vinegar
1½ tsp. salt
1–2 tsp. Worcestershire sauce

1. Brown chops in oil in skillet. Transfer to slow cooker.
2. Add remaining ingredients to cooker.
3. Cover. Cook on Low 6–8 hours.
4. Serve over rice.

Tangy Pork Chops

Tracy Clark   Mt. Crawford, VA   •   *Lois M. Martin*   Lititz, PA
Becky Oswald   Broadway, PA

MAKES: **4 SERVINGS**
PREP. TIME: **15 MINUTES**
COOKING TIME: **5½–6½ HOURS**
IDEAL SLOW COOKER SIZE: **4-QUART**

4 ½-inch thick pork chops
½ tsp. salt
⅛ tsp. pepper
2 medium onions, chopped
2 celery ribs, chopped
1 large green pepper, sliced
14½-oz. can stewed tomatoes
½ cup ketchup
2 Tbsp. cider vinegar

2 Tbsp. brown sugar
2 Tbsp. Worcestershire sauce
1 Tbsp. lemon juice
1 beef bouillon cube
2 Tbsp. cornstarch
2 Tbsp. water

1. Place chops in slow cooker. Sprinkle with salt and pepper.
2. Add onions, celery, pepper, and tomatoes.
3. Combine ketchup, vinegar, brown sugar, Worcestershire sauce, lemon juice, and bouillon. Pour over vegetables.
4. Cover. Cook on Low 5–6 hours.
5. Combine cornstarch and water until smooth. Stir into slow cooker.
6. Cover. Cook on High 30 minutes, or until thickened.
7. Serve over rice.

Variation: *Use chunks of beef or chicken legs and thighs instead of pork.*

Chops and Beans

Shirley Sears   Tiskilwa, IL

MAKES: **6 SERVINGS**
PREP. TIME: **15–20 MINUTES**
COOKING TIME: **7–8 HOURS**
IDEAL SLOW COOKER SIZE: **4-QUART**

6 pork chops
⅓ cup chopped onions
½ tsp. salt
⅓ tsp. garlic salt
⅛ tsp. pepper
28-oz. can vegetarian *or* baked beans
¼ tsp. hot pepper sauce
13½-oz. can crushed pineapple, undrained
⅓ cup chili sauce

Pork Main Dishes

1. Brown pork chops in skillet five minutes per side. Place in slow cooker.
2. Sauté onion in skillet in meat juices. Spread over pork chops.
3. Sprinkle with salt, garlic salt, and pepper.
4. Combine beans and hot sauce. Pour over chops.
5. Combine pineapple and chili sauce. Spread evenly over beans.
6. Cover. Cook on Low 7–8 hours.

Hearty Baked Beans and Chops

John D. Allen   Rye, CO

MAKES: **6 SERVINGS**
PREP. TIME: **10 MINUTES**
COOKING TIME: **4–6 HOURS**
IDEAL SLOW COOKER SIZE: **5-QUART**

2 16½-oz. cans baked beans
6 rib pork chops, ½-inch thick
1½ tsp. prepared mustard
1½ Tbsp. brown sugar
1½ Tbsp. ketchup
6 onion slices, ¼-inch thick

1. Pour baked beans into bottom of greased slow cooker.
2. Layer pork chops over beans.
3. Spread mustard over pork chops. Sprinkle with brown sugar and drizzle with ketchup.
4. Top with onion slices.
5. Cover. Cook on High 4–6 hours.

Oxford Canal Chops Deluxe

Willard E. Roth   Elkhart, IN

MAKES: **6 SERVINGS**
PREP. TIME: **25 MINUTES**
COOKING TIME: **4–6 HOURS**
IDEAL SLOW COOKER SIZE: **5-QUART**

6 6-oz. boneless pork chops
¼ cup flour
1 tsp. powdered garlic
1 tsp. sea salt
1 tsp. black pepper
1 tsp. dried basil and/or dried oregano
2 Tbsp. oil
2 medium onions, sliced
1 cup burgundy wine
14½-oz. can beef broth
1 soup can water
6-oz. can tomato sauce
8 ozs. dried apricots
½ lb. fresh mushroom caps

1. Shake chops in bag with flour and seasonings.
2. Glaze onions in oil in medium hot skillet. Add chops and brown.
3. Pour extra flour over chops in skillet. In large bowl mix together wine, broth, water, and tomato sauce, then pour over meat. Bring to boil.
4. Remove chops from skillet and place in cooker. Layer in apricots and mushrooms. Pour broth over top.
5. Cover. Cook on High 4 hours, or on Low 6 hours.
6. Serve with the Celtic speciality Bubble and Squeak—Irish potatoes mashed with green cabbage or brussels sprouts.

Note: *This was a hit when prepared in the tiny kitchen of a houseboat on the Oxford Canal and then shared by six friends.*

Easy Sweet and Sour Pork Chops

Jeanne Hertzog   Bethlehem, PA

MAKES: **6 SERVINGS**
PREP. TIME: **5 MINUTES**
COOKING TIME: **5–8 HOURS**
IDEAL SLOW COOKER SIZE: **4-QUART**

16-oz. bag frozen Asian vegetables
6 pork chops
12-oz. bottle sweet and sour sauce
½ cup water
1 cup frozen pea pods

1. Place partially thawed Asian vegetables in slow cooker. Arrange chops on top.
2. Combine sauce and water. Pour over chops.
3. Cover. Cook on Low 7–8 hours.
4. Turn to High and add pea pods.
5. Cover. Cook on High 5 minutes.

Golden Glow Pork Chops

Pam Hochstedler   Kalona, IA

MAKES: **5–6 SERVINGS**
PREP. TIME: **5 MINUTES**
COOKING TIME: **3–4 HOURS**
IDEAL SLOW COOKER SIZE: **4-QUART**

5–6 pork chops
salt to taste
pepper to taste
29-oz. can cling peach halves, drained (reserve juice)
¼ cup brown sugar
½ tsp. ground cinnamon
¼ tsp. ground cloves
8-oz. can tomato sauce
¼ cup vinegar

1. Lightly brown pork chops on both sides in saucepan. Drain. Arrange in slow cooker. Sprinkle with salt and pepper.
2. Place drained peach halves on top of pork chops.
3. Combine brown sugar, cinnamon, cloves, tomato sauce, ¼ cup peach syrup, and vinegar. Pour over peaches and pork chops.
4. Cover. Cook on Low 3–4 hours.

Perfect Pork Chops

Brenda Pope   Dundee, OH

MAKES: **2 SERVINGS**
PREP. TIME: **15 MINUTES**
COOKING TIME: **3–4 HOURS**
IDEAL SLOW COOKER SIZE: **3-QUART**

2 small onions
2 ¾-inch thick, boneless, center loin pork chops, frozen
fresh ground pepper to taste
1 chicken bouillon cube
¼ cup hot water
2 Tbsp. prepared mustard with white wine
fresh parsley sprigs *or* lemon slices *optional*

1. Cut off ends of onions and peel. Cut onions in half crosswise to make 4 thick "wheels." Place in bottom of slow cooker.
2. Sear both sides of frozen chops in heavy skillet. Place in cooker on top of onions. Sprinkle with pepper.
3. Dissolve bouillon cube in hot water. Stir in mustard. Pour into slow cooker.
4. Cover. Cook on High 3–4 hours.
5. Serve topped with fresh parsley sprigs or lemon slices, if desired.

Keep peeled onions covered in a jar when refrigerated.

Creamy Pork Chops

Judi Manos West Islip, NY

MAKES: **6 SERVINGS**
PREP. TIME: **5–7 MINUTES**
COOKING TIME: **4–5 HOURS**
IDEAL SLOW COOKER SIZE: **3-QUART**

10¾-oz. can 98% fat-free cream of chicken soup

1 onion, chopped

3 Tbsp. ketchup

2 tsp. Worcestershire sauce

6 whole pork chops, boneless *or* bone-in, *divided*

1. Mix soup and chopped onions together in a bowl. Stir in ketchup and Worcestershire sauce. Pour half of mixture into slow cooker.
2. Place pork chops in slow cooker. If you have to stack them, spoon a proportionate amount of the remaining sauce over the first layer of meat.
3. Add the rest of the chops. Cover with the remaining sauce.
4. Cover and cook on Low 4–5 hours, or until meat is tender but not dry.

Pork Chops with Mushroom Sauce

Jennifer J. Gehman Harrisburg, PA

MAKES: **4–6 SERVINGS**
PREP. TIME: **5–10 MINUTES**
COOKING TIME: **4½–10 HOURS**
IDEAL SLOW COOKER SIZE: **4-QUART**

4–6 boneless thin *or* thick pork chops

10¾-oz. can cream of mushroom soup

¾ cup white wine

4-oz. can sliced mushrooms

2 Tbsp. quick cooking tapioca

2 tsp. Worcestershire sauce

1 tsp. beef bouillon granules, *or* 1 beef bouillon cube

¼ tsp. minced garlic

¾ tsp. dried thyme, *optional*

1. Place pork chops in slow cooker.
2. Combine remaining ingredients and pour over pork chops.
3. Cook on Low 8–10 hours, or on High 4½–5 hours.
4. Serve over rice.

Spicy Pork Chops

Cynthia Morris Grottoes, VA

MAKES: **4 SERVINGS**
PREP. TIME: **5 MINUTES**
COOKING TIME: **6–8 HOURS**
IDEAL SLOW COOKER SIZE: **4-QUART**

4 frozen pork chops

1 cup Italian salad dressing

½ cup brown sugar

⅓ cup prepared spicy mustard

1. Place pork chops in slow cooker.
2. Mix remaining 3 ingredients together in a bowl. Pour over chops.
3. Cover and cook on Low 6–8 hours, or until meat is tender but not dry.

Tip: *Check the meat after cooking for 4 hours to make sure the meat is not getting dry or overcooking.*

Variation: *You can substitute chicken breasts for pork chops.*

Pork Chops and Apple Slices

Dorothy VanDeest Memphis, TN • *Dale Peterson* Rapid City, SD

MAKES: **4 SERVINGS**
PREP. TIME: **15 MINUTES**
COOKING TIME: **6–8 HOURS**
IDEAL SLOW COOKER SIZE: **3–4-QUART**

4 pork loin chops, about 1-inch thick, well trimmed
2 medium apples, peeled, cored, and sliced
1 tsp. butter
¼ tsp. nutmeg, optional
salt and pepper to taste

1. Heat a nonstick skillet until hot. Add chops and brown quickly. Turn and brown on the other side.
2. While chops are browning, place half the sliced apples in the slow cooker. Top with 2 chops. Repeat the layers.
3. Dot with butter and sprinkle with nutmeg. Sprinkle generously with salt and pepper.
4. Cover and cook on Low 6-8 hours, or until meat is tender but not dry.

Variation: *Finely chop one small onion. Sprinkle half the onion pieces over the first layer of chops, and the rest of it over the second layer of chops.*

Kate Johnson Rolfe, IA

Pork Chops in Orange Sauce

Kelly Evenson Pittsboro, NC

MAKES: **4 SERVINGS**
PREP. TIME: **25 MINUTES**
COOKING TIME: **5¼–6¼ HOURS**
IDEAL SLOW COOKER SIZE: **5-QUART**

4 thick, center-cut pork chops
salt to taste
pepper to taste
1 Tbsp. oil
1 orange
¼ cup ketchup
¾ cup orange juice
1 Tbsp. orange marmalade
1 Tbsp. cornstarch
¼ cup water

1. Season pork chops on both sides with salt and pepper.
2. Brown chops lightly on both sides in skillet in oil. Transfer to slow cooker. Reserve 2 Tbsp. drippings and discard the rest.
3. Grate ½ tsp. orange zest from top or bottom of orange. Combine zest with ketchup, orange juice, and marmalade. Pour into skillet. Simmer 1 minute, stirring constantly. Pour over chops.
4. Cover. Cook on Low 5-6 hours. Remove chops and keep warm.
5. Dissolve cornstarch in water. Stir into slow cooker until smooth. Cook on High 15 minutes, or until thickened.
6. Serve with orange sauce on top, along with slices of fresh orange.
7. Serve over noodles or rice with a green salad.

When you're browning meat, use tongs or a metal spatula to flip it over or remove it from the pan. Resist using a fork; tasty juices escape if you jag the meat.

Fruited Pork Chops

Mrs. Carolyn Baer   Conrath, WI

MAKES: **6 SERVINGS**
PREP. TIME: **20 MINUTES**
COOKING TIME: **3½–4 HOURS**
IDEAL SLOW COOKER SIZE: **5–6-QUART**

3 Tbsp. all-purpose flour

1½ tsp. dried oregano

¾ tsp. salt

¼ tsp. garlic powder

¼ tsp. black pepper

6 lean boneless pork loin chops (about 5 ozs. each)

1 Tbsp. olive *or* canola oil

20-oz. can unsweetened pineapple chunks

1 cup water

2 Tbsp. brown sugar

2 Tbsp. dried minced onion

2 Tbsp. tomato paste

¼ cup raisins

1. In a large resealable plastic bag, combine flour, oregano, salt, garlic powder, and pepper.
2. Add pork chops one at a time and shake to coat.
3. Brown pork chops on both sides in a nonstick skillet using canola oil. Transfer browned chops to slow cooker.
4. Drain pineapple, reserving juice. Set pineapple aside.
5. In a mixing bowl, combine ¾ cup reserved pineapple juice, water, brown sugar, dried onion, and tomato paste. Pour over chops.
6. Sprinkle raisins over top.
7. Cook on High 3–3½ hours, or until meat is tender and a meat thermometer reads 160°. Stir in reserved pineapple chunks. Cook 10 minutes longer or until heated through.

Per Serving: 280 calories (80 calories from fat), 9g total fat (2.5g saturated, 0g trans), 65mg cholesterol, 350mg sodium, 28g total carbohydrate (2g fiber, 22g sugar), 24g protein, 4%DV vitamin A, 20%DV vitamin C, 6%DV calcium, 10%DV iron.

Tip: *This is good served over brown rice.*

Variation: *If your diet allows, you may want to place 1 tsp. salt (instead of the ¾ tsp.) in coating mixture in Step 1.*

Pork and Cabbage Dinner

Mrs. Paul Gray   Beatrice, NE

MAKES: **8 SERVINGS**
PREP. TIME: **10 MINUTES**
COOKING TIME: **5–6 HOURS**
IDEAL SLOW COOKER SIZE: **4–5-QUART**

2 lbs. pork steaks, *or* chops, *or* shoulder

¾ cup chopped onions

¼ cup chopped fresh parsley, *or* 2 Tbsp. dried parsley

4 cups shredded cabbage

1 tsp. salt

⅛ tsp. pepper

½ tsp. caraway seeds

⅛ tsp. allspice

½ cup beef broth

2 cooking apples, cored and sliced ¼-inch thick

1. Place pork in slow cooker. Layer onions, parsley, and cabbage over pork.
2. Combine salt, pepper, caraway seeds, and allspice. Sprinkle over cabbage. Pour broth over cabbage.
3. Cover. Cook on Low 5–6 hours.
4. Add apple slices 30 minutes before serving.

Slow-Cooked Pork Chops with Green Beans

Vonnie Oyer   Hubbard, OR

MAKES: **3–4 SERVINGS**
PREP. TIME: **10 MINUTES**
COOKING TIME: **4–8 HOURS**
IDEAL SLOW COOKER SIZE: **3-QUART**

3–4 boneless pork chops

salt and pepper to taste

2 cups green beans, frozen *or* fresh

2 slices bacon, cut up

½ cup water

1 Tbsp. lemon juice

1. Place pork chops in bottom of slow cooker. Salt and pepper to taste.
2. Top with remaining ingredients in the order listed.
3. Cover and cook on Low 4–8 hours, or until meat and green beans are tender but not dry or overcooked.

Pork and Sweet Potatoes

Vera F. Schmucker   Goshen, IN

MAKES: **4 SERVINGS**
PREP. TIME: **15 MINUTES**
COOKING TIME: **4–4½ HOURS**
IDEAL SLOW COOKER SIZE: **4-QUART**

4 pork loin chops

salt and pepper to taste

4 sweet potatoes, cut in large chunks

2 onions cut in quarters

½ cup apple cider

1. Place meat in bottom of slow cooker. Salt and pepper to taste.
2. Arrange sweet potatoes and onions over top of the pork.
3. Pour apple cider over all.
4. Cook on High 30 minutes, and then on Low 3½–4 hours, or until meat and vegetables are tender but not dry.

Pork Chops and Yams

Tamara McCarthy Pennsburg, PA

MAKES: **4 SERVINGS**
PREP. TIME: **15 MINUTES**
COOKING TIME: **6–7 HOURS**
IDEAL SLOW COOKER SIZE: **4-QUART**

4–6 pork chops

**16-oz. can yams, drained, *or* 3 medium raw yams,
    peeled and sliced**

10¾-oz. can cream of mushroom soup

½ cup sour cream

¼ cup water

1. In a nonstick skillet, brown pork chops over medium heat. Transfer to slow cooker.
2. Place yams over pork chops.
3. In a mixing bowl, combine condensed soup, sour cream, and water. Stir until well blended.
4. Pour sauce over yams and pork chops.
5. Cover and cook on Low 6–7 hours, or until meat and yams are tender but not dry.

Sturdy Pork Chop Casserole

Nancy Wagner Graves Manhattan, KS

MAKES: **4–6 SERVINGS**
PREP. TIME: **25 MINUTES**
COOKING TIME: **3–10 HOURS**
IDEAL SLOW COOKER SIZE: **5-QUART**

6–8 pork chops

salt to taste

pepper to taste

oil

2 medium potatoes, peeled and sliced

1 large onion, sliced

1 large green pepper, sliced

½ tsp. dried oregano

16-oz. can tomatoes

1. Season pork chops with salt and pepper. Brown in oil in skillet. Transfer to slow cooker.
2. Add remaining ingredients in order listed.
3. Cover. Cook on Low 8–10 hours, or on High 3–4 hours.

Three-Ingredient Sauerkraut Meal

Esther J. Yoder Hartville, OH

MAKES: **8 SERVINGS**
PREP. TIME: **5 MINUTES**
COOKING TIME: **8–10 HOURS**
IDEAL SLOW COOKER SIZE: **5-QUART**

2 cups low-sodium barbecue sauce

1 cup water

2 lbs. thinly sliced lean pork chops, trimmed of fat

2 lbs. sauerkraut, rinsed

1. Mix together barbecue sauce and water.
2. Combine barbecue sauce, pork chops, and sauerkraut in slow cooker.
3. Cover. Cook on Low 8–10 hours

Per Serving: 300 calories (90 calories from fat), 11g total fat (3.5g saturated, 0g trans), 90mg cholesterol, 1450mg sodium, 18g total carbohydrate (3g fiber, 12g sugar), 32g protein, 4%DV vitamin A, 10%DV vitamin C, 6%DV calcium, 20%DV iron.

Yams and sweet potatoes are not the same. Yams are much drier. Learn to recognize the difference. Likewise, there are many varieties of apples, from very tart to very sweet, firm texture to soft. Experiment with different kinds to discover your favorite for a recipe.

Apples, Sauerkraut, and Chops

Carol Sherwood Batavia, NY

MAKES: **4 SERVINGS**
PREP. TIME: **25 MINUTES**
COOKING TIME: **4–8 HOURS**
IDEAL SLOW COOKER SIZE: **5-QUART**

4 pork chops, ½-inch thick, browned
1 onion, sliced and separated into rings
⅛ tsp. garlic flakes or powder
3 cups sauerkraut, drained
1 cup unpeeled apple slices
1½ tsp. caraway seeds
¼ tsp. salt
¼ tsp. dried thyme
¼ tsp. pepper
¾ cup apple juice

1. Place half of onions, garlic flakes, sauerkraut, apple slices, and caraway seeds in slow cooker. Season with half the salt, thyme, and pepper.
2. Add pork chops.
3. Layer remaining ingredients in order given.
4. Pour apple juice over all.
5. Cover. Cook on Low 6–8 hours, or on High 4 hours.

Pork Chops on Rice

Hannah D. Burkholder Bridgewater, VA

MAKES: **4 SERVINGS**
PREP. TIME: **30 MINUTES**
COOKING TIME: **4–9 HOURS**
IDEAL SLOW COOKER SIZE: **5-QUART**

½ cup brown rice
⅔ cup converted white rice
¼ cup butter
½ cup chopped onions
4-oz. can sliced mushrooms, drained
½ tsp. dried thyme
½ tsp. sage
½ tsp. salt
¼ tsp. black pepper
4 boneless pork chops, ¾–1-inch thick
10½-oz. can beef consomme
2 Tbsp. Worcestershire sauce
½ tsp. dried thyme
½ tsp. paprika
¼ tsp. ground nutmeg

1. Sauté white and brown rice in butter in skillet until rice is golden brown.
2. Remove from heat and stir in onions, mushrooms, thyme, sage, salt, and pepper. Pour into greased slow cooker.
3. Arrange chops over rice.
4. Combine consomme and Worcestershire sauce. Pour over chops.
5. Combine thyme, paprika, and nutmeg. Sprinkle over chops.
6. Cover. Cook on Low 7–9 hours, or on High 4–5 hours.

Pork Main Dishes

Pork Chops with Stuffing

Erma Kauffman Cochranville, PA

MAKES: **2 SERVINGS**
PREP. TIME: **15 MINUTES**
COOKING TIME: **4–5 HOURS**
IDEAL SLOW COOKER SIZE: **1½-QUART**

4 slices bread, cubed

1 egg

¼ cup grated or finely chopped celery

¼–½ tsp. salt

⅛ tsp. pepper

2 thickly cut pork chops

1 cup water

1. Combine bread cubes, eggs, celery, salt, and pepper.
2. Cut pork chops part way through, creating a pocket. Fill with stuffing.
3. Pour water into slow cooker. Add chops.
4. Cover. Cook on Low 4–5 hours.

Pork Chops and Stuffing with Curry

Mary Martins Fairbank, IA

MAKES: **3–4 SERVINGS**
PREP. TIME: **10 MINUTES**
COOKING TIME: **6–7 HOURS**
IDEAL SLOW COOKER SIZE: **4-QUART**

1 box stuffing mix

1 cup water

10¾-oz. can cream of mushroom soup

1 tsp., or more, curry powder, according to your taste preference

3–4 pork chops

1. Combine stuffing mix and water. Place half in bottom of slow cooker.

2. Combine soup and curry powder. Pour half over stuffing. Place pork chops on top.
3. Spread remaining stuffing over pork chops. Pour rest of soup on top.
4. Cover. Cook on Low 6–7 hours.
5. Serve with a tossed salad and a cooked vegetable.

Barbecued Spareribs

Mrs. Paul Gray Beatrice, NE

MAKES: **4 SERVINGS**
PREP. TIME: **5 MINUTES**
COOKING TIME: **6–8 HOURS**
IDEAL SLOW COOKER SIZE: **4-QUART**

4-lb. country-style spareribs, cut into serving-size pieces

10¾-oz. can tomato soup

½ cup cider vinegar

½ cup brown sugar

1 Tbsp. soy sauce

1 tsp. celery seed

1 tsp. salt

1 tsp. chili powder

dash cayenne pepper

1. Place ribs in slow cooker.
2. Combine remaining ingredients and pour over ribs.
3. Cover. Cook on Low 6–8 hours.
4. Skim fat from juices before serving.

Put your cooker meal together the night before you want to cook it. The following morning put the mixture in the slow cooker, cover, and turn it on.

Sesame Pork Ribs

Joette Droz   Kalona, IA

MAKES: **6 SERVINGS**
PREP. TIME: **10 MINUTES**
COOKING TIME: **5–6 HOURS**
IDEAL SLOW COOKER SIZE: **5-QUART**

1 medium onion, sliced

¾ cup packed brown sugar

¼ cup soy sauce

½ cup ketchup

¼ cup honey

2 Tbsp. cider *or* white vinegar

3 garlic cloves, minced

1 tsp. ground ginger

¼–½ tsp. crushed red pepper flakes

5 lbs. country-style pork ribs

2 Tbsp. sesame seeds, toasted

2 Tbsp. chopped green onions

1. Place onions in bottom of slow cooker.
2. Combine brown sugar, soy sauce, ketchup, honey, vinegar, garlic, ginger, and red pepper flakes in large bowl. Add ribs and turn to coat. Place on top of onions in slow cooker. Pour sauce over meat.
3. Cover. Cook on Low 5–6 hours.
4. Place ribs on serving platter. Sprinkle with sesame seeds and green onions. Serve sauce on the side.

Just Peachy Ribs

Amymarlene Jensen   Fountain, CO

MAKES: **4–6 SERVINGS**
PREP. TIME: **10 MINUTES**
COOKING TIME: **8–10 HOURS**
IDEAL SLOW COOKER SIZE: **4-QUART**

4-lb. boneless pork spareribs

½ cup brown sugar

¼ cup ketchup

¼ cup white vinegar

1 garlic clove, minced

1 tsp. salt

1 tsp. pepper

2 Tbsp. soy sauce

15-oz. can spiced cling peaches, cubed, with juice

1. Cut ribs in serving-size pieces and brown in broiler or in saucepan in oil. Drain. Place in slow cooker.
2. Combine remaining ingredients. Pour over ribs.
3. Cover. Cook on Low 8–10 hours.

Give-Me-More Barbecued Ribs

Virginia Bender   Dover, DE

MAKES: **6 SERVINGS**
PREP. TIME: **10 MINUTES**
COOKING TIME: **8–10 HOURS**
IDEAL SLOW COOKER SIZE: **6-QUART**

PICTURED
ON PAGE
301

4 lbs. pork ribs

½ cup brown sugar

12-oz. jar chili sauce

¼ cup balsamic vinegar

2 Tbsp. Worcestershire sauce

2 Tbsp. Dijon mustard

1 tsp. hot sauce

1. Place ribs in slow cooker.
2. Combine remaining ingredients. Pour half of sauce over ribs.
3. Cover. Cook on Low 8–10 hours.
4. Serve with remaining sauce.

Sweet and Sour Ribs

Cassandra Ly   Carlisle, PA

MAKES: **8–10 SERVINGS**
PREP. TIME: **15 MINUTES**
COOKING TIME: **8–10 HOURS**
IDEAL SLOW COOKER SIZE: **6-QUART**

3–4 lbs. boneless country-style pork ribs

20-oz. can pineapple tidbits

2 8-oz. cans tomato sauce

½ cup thinly sliced onions

½ cup thinly sliced green peppers

½ cup packed brown sugar

¼ cup cider vinegar

¼ cup tomato paste

2 Tbsp. Worcestershire sauce

1 garlic clove, minced

1 tsp. salt

½ tsp. pepper

1. Place ribs in slow cooker.
2. Combine remaining ingredients. Pour over ribs.
3. Cook on Low 8–10 hours.
4. Serve over rice.

Pineapple Pork

Anne Townsend   Albuquerque, NM

MAKES: **4 SERVINGS**
PREP. TIME: **10 MINUTES**
COOKING TIME: **6–8 HOURS**
IDEAL SLOW COOKER SIZE: **4-QUART**

8 country-style pork ribs

black pepper to taste

¼ tsp. paprika

20-oz. can unsweetened pineapple tidbits

2 Tbsp. Dijon mustard

2 Tbsp. fast-cooking tapioca, *optional*

1. Slice ribs into 8 sections. Place in slow cooker sprayed with nonfat cooking spray.
2. Combine remaining ingredients. Pour over ribs.
3. Cover. Cook on Low 6–8 hours.
4. If you wish, 30 minutes before the end of the cooking time, stir in tapioca in order to thicken the cooking juices.

Per Serving: 130 calories (45 calories from fat), 5g total fat (1.5g saturated, 0g trans), 25mg cholesterol, 210mg sodium, 13g total carbohydrate (1g fiber, 11g sugar), 9g protein, 0%DV vitamin A, 10%DV vitamin C, 4%DV calcium, 8%DV iron.

Tip: *These ribs are great the next day. Refrigerate them after cooking, and then remove the fat before reheating to serve.*

Don't have enough time? A lot of dishes can be made in less time by increasing the temperature to High and cooking the dish for about half the time as is necessary on Low.

Seasoned Pork Ribs

Melanie Thrower McPherson, KS

MAKES: **2–3 SERVINGS**
PREP. TIME: **5–10 MINUTES**
COOKING TIME: **4 HOURS**
IDEAL SLOW COOKER SIZE: **4–5-QUART**

3 lbs. pork shoulder ribs, cut in serving-size pieces
2 tsp. chipotle seasoning spice
1 tsp. coarse black pepper, *optional*
1 Tbsp. prepared horseradish
¼ cup ketchup
¼ cup apricot jelly

1. Heat a nonstick skillet over medium-high heat.
2. Season pork with chipotle seasonings and then place in hot skillet, browning each piece on top and bottom. Do in batches so all the pieces brown well.
3. As you finish browning ribs, place them in the slow cooker.
4. Cover and cook on High for 3 hours.
5. Meanwhile, mix together pepper if you wish, horseradish, ketchup, and apricot jelly in a bowl. Spread over cooked pork.
6. Cover and cook on High 1 hour, or until the meat is tender.

When buying kitchen tools, spend the extra money for good quality.

A-Touch-of-Asia Ribs

Sharon Shank Bridgewater, VA

MAKES: **8–10 SERVINGS**
PREP. TIME: **5–10 MINUTES**
COOKING TIME: **4–8 HOURS**
IDEAL SLOW COOKER SIZE: **5–6-QUART**

6 lbs. country-style pork ribs, cut into serving-size pieces
¼ cup teriyaki sauce
¼ cup cornstarch
27-oz. jar duck sauce
2 Tbsp. minced garlic, *optional*

1. Place ribs in the bottom of your slow cooker.
2. In a large bowl, stir together teriyaki sauce and cornstarch. Blend in duck sauce and garlic if you wish.
3. Pour the sauce over the ribs, making sure that each layer is well covered.
4. Cover and cook on Low 8 hours, or on High 4–5 hours.

Italian Country-Style Pork Ribs

Kay Kassinger Port Angeles, WA

MAKES: **8–10 SERVINGS**
PREP. TIME: **20 MINUTES**
COOKING TIME: **7–8 HOURS**
IDEAL SLOW COOKER SIZE: **5-QUART**

3–3½ lbs. country-style pork ribs, cut into serving-size pieces
2 14½-oz. cans Italian-seasoned diced tomatoes
1 cup frozen pearl onions
1½ tsp. Italian seasoning
1 tsp. salt
water as needed

1. Brown ribs on top and bottom in nonstick skillet. Do in batches to assure that each piece browns well.

Pork Main Dishes

2. Spray cooker with nonstick cooking spray. Transfer browned meat to slow cooker.
3. Drain tomatoes into hot skillet. Deglaze skillet with tomato juice by stirring up the drippings with a wooden spoon.
4. Layer tomatoes, onions, and seasonings over top of ribs. Pour deglazed pan drippings into slow cooker. Add about 2-inch of water.
5. Cover and cook on Low 7–8 hours, or until meat is tender but not overcooked.

Country-Style Ribs and Sauerkraut

Rhonda Burgoon   Collingswood, NJ

MAKES: **4–6 SERVINGS**
PREP. TIME: **15 MINUTES**
COOKING TIME: **8–10 HOURS**
IDEAL SLOW COOKER SIZE: **5-QUART**

16-oz. bag sauerkraut, rinsed and drained

1 onion, diced

1 red-skinned apple, chopped

2–3 lbs. country-style pork ribs

1 cup beer

1. Combine sauerkraut, onion, and apple in bottom of slow cooker.
2. Layer ribs over sauerkraut.
3. Pour beer over ribs just before turning on cooker.
4. Cover. Cook on Low 8–10 hours.
5. Serve with homemade cornbread and mashed potatoes, or serve deboned on a kaiser roll as a sandwich.

Barbecued Ribs & Sauce

Mary Longenecker   Bethel, PA

MAKES: **10 SERVINGS**
PREP. TIME: **5 MINUTES**
COOKING TIME: **8–10 HOURS**
IDEAL SLOW COOKER SIZE: **4-QUART**

3 lbs. lean country-style pork ribs

2½ lbs. sauerkraut, rinsed

2 cups low-sodium barbecue sauce

1 cup water

1. Place ribs on bottom of cooker.
2. Layer sauerkraut over ribs.
3. Mix barbecue sauce and water together. Pour over meat and kraut.
4. Cover. Cook on Low 8–10 hours.

Per Serving: 230 calories (80 calories from fat), 9g total fat (3g saturated, 0g trans), 50mg cholesterol, 1470mg sodium, 19g total carbohydrate (3g fiber, 13g sugar), 17g protein, 4%DV vitamin A, 20%DV vitamin C, 6%DV calcium, 15%DV iron.

Country Pork and Squash

Jean Halloran   Green Bay, WI

MAKES: **6 SERVINGS**
PREP. TIME: **15 MINUTES**
COOKING TIME: **6–8 HOURS**
IDEAL SLOW COOKER SIZE: **5-QUART**

6 boneless country-style pork ribs, trimmed of fat

2 medium acorn squash

¾ cup brown sugar

2 Tbsp. orange juice

¾ tsp. Kitchen Bouquet browning and seasoning sauce

1. Place ribs on bottom of slow cooker.
2. Cut each squash in half. Remove seeds. Cut each half into 3 slices.
3. Place the squash slices over top of the ribs.
4. Combine remaining ingredients in a small bowl. Pour sauce over the ribs and squash.
5. Cover and cook on Low 6-8 hours, or until the meat is tender.
6. Serve 2 rings of squash with each pork rib.

Variation: *Add ¾ tsp. salt to Step 4.*

Ham in Foil

Jeanette Oberholtzer   Manheim, PA   •   *Janet Roggie*   Lowville, NY

Vicki Dinkel   Sharon Springs, KS

MAKES: **8 SERVINGS**
PREP. TIME: **5 MINUTES**
COOKING TIME: **7 HOURS**
IDEAL SLOW COOKER SIZE: **5-QUART**

½ cup water

3–4-lb. precooked ham

liquid smoke

1. Pour water into slow cooker.
2. Sprinkle ham with liquid smoke. Wrap in foil. Place in slow cooker.
3. Cover. Cook on High 1 hour, then on Low 6 hours.
4. Cut into thick chunks or ½-inch slices and serve.

Ham 'n Cola

Carol Peachey   Lancaster, PA

MAKES: **8–10 SERVINGS**
PREP. TIME: **5 MINUTES**
COOKING TIME: **2–10 HOURS**
IDEAL SLOW COOKER SIZE: **4–5-QUART**

½ cup brown sugar

1 tsp. dry mustard

1 tsp. prepared horseradish

¼ cup cola-flavored soda

3–4-lb. precooked ham

1. Combine brown sugar, mustard, and horse-radish. Moisten with just enough cola to make a smooth paste. Reserve remaining cola.
2. Rub entire ham with mixture. Place ham in slow cooker and add remaining cola.
3. Cover. Cook on Low 6-10 hours, or on High 2-3 hours.

Country Ham

Esther Burkholder   Millerstown, PA

MAKES: **12 SERVINGS**
PREP. TIME: **10 MINUTES**
COOKING TIME: **6 HOURS**
IDEAL SLOW COOKER SIZE: **4-QUART**

3-lb. boneless, fully cooked ham
½–¾ cup brown sugar, according to your taste
    preferences
2 Tbsp. prepared mustard
¼ cup peach preserves

1. Place ham in slow cooker.
2. Combine remaining ingredients in a small bowl. Spread over ham.
3. Cover and cook on Low 6 hours, or until heated through.

Variation: *Use apricot preserves instead of peach.*

Edwina Stoltzfus   Narvon, PA

Glazed Ham in a Bag

Eleanor J. Ferreira   North Chelmsford, MA

MAKES: **12 SERVINGS**
PREP. TIME: **7 MINUTES**
COOKING TIME: **6–8 HOURS**
IDEAL SLOW COOKER SIZE: **6–7-QUART**

5-lb. cooked ham
3 Tbsp. orange juice
1 Tbsp. Dijon mustard

1. Rinse meat. Place in cooking bag.
2. Combine orange juice and mustard. Spread over ham.
3. Seal bag with twist tie. Poke 4 holes in top of bag. Place in slow cooker.
4. Cover. Cook on Low 6–8 hours.

5. To serve, remove ham from bag, reserving juices. Slice ham; spoon over juices.

Tip: *Serve additional juice alongside in small bowl.*

Apricot-Glazed Ham

Dede Peterson   Rapid City, SD

MAKES: **4 SERVINGS**
PREP. TIME: **20 MINUTES**
COOKING TIME: **4–6 HOURS**
IDEAL SLOW COOKER SIZE: **6-QUART**

4 ham steaks
⅓ cup apricot jam
¾–1 cup honey, depending upon how much sweetness
    you like
⅓ cup soy sauce
¼ tsp. nutmeg

1. Place ham in slow cooker.
2. In a bowl, mix all other ingredients together. Pour over ham.
3. Cook on Low 4–6 hours, or until meat is heated through but not dry.

Some really good dishes can be very easy to make. Learn to enjoy the pleasure of simple foods.

Cranberry Ham

Janie Steele   Moore, OK

MAKES: **4 SERVINGS**
PREP. TIME: **5–10 MINUTES**
COOKING TIME: **4½ HOURS**
IDEAL SLOW COOKER SIZE: **3-QUART**

1–2-lb. fully cooked ham, or 2-inch-thick slice of fully cooked ham

1 cup whole cranberry sauce

2 Tbsp. brown sugar

1. Place ham in slow cooker. Cover with cranberry sauce. Sprinkle brown sugar over top.
2. Cook on Low 4½ hours, or until meat is heated through but not drying out.

Apple-Raisin Ham

Betty B. Dennison   Grove City, PA

MAKES: **6 SERVINGS**
PREP. TIME: **10–15 MINUTES**
COOKING TIME: **4–5 HOURS**
IDEAL SLOW COOKER SIZE: **4-QUART**

1½ lbs. fully cooked ham

21-oz. can apple pie filling

⅓ cup golden raisins

⅓ cup orange juice

¼ tsp. ground cinnamon

2 Tbsp. water

1. Cut ham slices into six equal pieces.
2. In a mixing bowl, combine pie filling, raisins, orange juice, cinnamon, and water.
3. Place 1 slice of ham in your slow cooker. Spread ⅙ of the apple mixture over top.
4. Repeat layers until you have used all the ham and apple mixture.
5. Cover and cook on Low 4–5 hours.

Tips:

1. This is a great way to use leftovers.

2. And you can use any leftovers from this to make wonderful sandwiches.

Scalloped Potatoes and Ham

Carol Sherwood Batavia, NY • *Sharon Anders* Alburtis, PA
Mary Stauffer Ephrata, PA • *Esther Hartzler* Carlsbad, NM
Dawn Hahn Lititz, PA • *Diann J. Dunham* State College, PA

MAKES: **4–6 SERVINGS**
PREP. TIME: **20 MINUTES**
COOKING TIME: **6–8 HOURS**
IDEAL SLOW COOKER SIZE: **5-QUART**

2–3 lbs. potatoes, peeled, sliced, *divided*

12-oz. pkg., or 1 lb., cooked ham, cubed, *divided*

1 small onion, chopped, *divided*

2 cups shredded cheddar cheese, *divided*

10¾-oz. can cream of celery *or* mushroom soup

1. Spray the interior of the cooker with nonstick cooking spray.
2. Layer ⅓ each of the potatoes, ham, onion, and cheese into the cooker.
3. Repeat twice.
4. Spread soup on top.
5. Cover and cook on Low 6–8 hours, or until potatoes are tender.

Variation: *For a creamier sauce, combine can of creamed soup with ½ cup water in a bowl before pouring over contents of cooker in Step 4.*

Jeannine Janzen Elbing, KS

Pork Main Dishes

Creamy Scalloped Potatoes and Ham

Rhonda Freed Lowville, NY

MAKES: **6 SERVINGS**
PREP. TIME: **20 MINUTES**
COOKING TIME: **4–5 HOURS**
IDEAL SLOW COOKER SIZE: **4-QUART**

6 cups sliced, raw potatoes

salt and pepper to taste

10¾-oz. can cream of mushroom *or* celery soup

1½ cups milk

1 lb. cooked ham, cubed

1. Place potatoes in slow cooker. Salt and pepper each layer.
2. In a bowl, mix soup, milk, and ham together. Pour over potatoes.
3. Cover and cook on High for 3½ hours. Continue cooking ½–1½ hours more if needed, or until potatoes are tender.

Variation: *Substitute 12-oz. can evaporated milk for the 1½ cups milk.*

Mary Kay Nolt Newmanstown, PA

Ham and Chunky Potatoes

Ruth Shank Gridley, IL

MAKES: **6–8 SERVINGS**
PREP. TIME: **5 MINUTES**
COOKING TIME: **10 HOURS**
IDEAL SLOW COOKER SIZE: **4–5-QUART**

6–8 medium red *or* russet potatoes, cut into chunks

2–3-lb. boneless ham

½ cup brown sugar

1 tsp. dry mustard

1. Prick potato pieces with fork. Place in slow cooker.
2. Place ham on top of potatoes. Crumble brown sugar over ham. Sprinkle with dry mustard.
3. Cover. Cook on Low 10 or more hours, until potatoes are tender.
4. Pour juices over ham and potatoes to serve.

Potatoes and Green Beans with Ham

Mary B. Sensenig New Holland, PA

MAKES: **4 SERVINGS**
PREP. TIME: **5 MINUTES**
COOKING TIME: **6–8 HOURS**
IDEAL SLOW COOKER SIZE: **3-QUART**

1-lb. ham slice, cut in chunks

2 cups green beans, frozen *or* fresh

2 cups red-skinned potatoes, quartered, but not peeled

½ cup water

½ cup chopped onion

4 slices American cheese

1. Place all ingredients, except cheese, in slow cooker. Gently mix together.
2. Cover and cook on Low 6–8 hours, or until vegetables are tender.
3. One hour before the end of the cooking time, lay cheese slices over top.

Cut up vegetables for your slow-cooker dish the night before and place them in Ziplock bags in the refrigerator. This cuts down on preparation time in the morning.

Green Bean Supper for a Crowd

Beverly Flatt-Getz Warriors Mark, PA

MAKES: **24–28 SERVINGS**
PREP. TIME: **10 MINUTES**
COOKING TIME: **6–8 HOURS**
IDEAL SLOW COOKER SIZE: **6–7-QUART**

2 lbs. new potatoes, *or* 5 white potatoes halved and
  scrubbed
6 lb. 5-oz. can green beans, drained
15-oz. can whole corn, drained
1 large onion (or 2 medium), diced
5-oz. can lean chunk ham in water
10¾-oz. can fat-free, low-sodium chicken broth
½ tsp. garlic powder
½ tsp. onion powder
1 chicken bouillon cube

1. Place potatoes in slow cooker.
2. Add remainder of ingredients.
3. Fill pot half full of water.
4. Cook on Low 6–8 hours, or until the
   vegetables are done to your liking.

Per Serving: 70 calories (0 calories from fat), 0g total fat (0g
saturated, 0g trans), 0mg cholesterol, 510mg sodium, 14g total
carbohydrate (3g fiber, 3g sugar), 3g protein, 6%DV vitamin A, 10%DV
vitamin C, 2%DV calcium, 6%DV iron.

Variation: *You can use fresh green beans in
place of the canned ones.*

Ham and Cabbage

Tim Smith Rutledge, PA

MAKES: **4 SERVINGS**
PREP. TIME: **30 MINUTES**
COOKING TIME: **6–7 HOURS**
IDEAL SLOW COOKER SIZE: **6–7-QUART**

2 lbs. uncooked ham
12 whole cloves
8 medium red potatoes
1 medium head green cabbage
water

1. Rinse ham, then stick cloves evenly into
   ham. Place in center of slow cooker.
2. Cut potatoes in half. Add to slow cooker
   around the ham.
3. Quarter cabbage and remove center stem.
   Add to cooker, again surrounding the ham.
4. Fill with water to cover.
5. Cover and cook on High 6–7 hours, or until
   vegetables and meat are tender, but not dry
   or mushy.
6. Serve with mustard for the ham, and butter
   for the potatoes.

Ham-Broccoli Casserole

Rebecca Meyerkorth Wamego, KS

MAKES: **4 SERVINGS**
PREP. TIME: **20 MINUTES**
COOKING TIME: **4–5 HOURS**
IDEAL SLOW COOKER SIZE: **4–5-QUART**

16-oz. pkg. frozen broccoli cuts, thawed and drained

2–3 cups cubed, cooked ham

10¾-oz. can cream of mushroom soup

4 ozs. of your favorite mild cheese, cubed

1 cup milk

1 cup instant rice, uncooked

1 rib celery, chopped

1 small onion, chopped

1. Combine broccoli and ham in slow cooker.
2. Combine soup, cheese, milk, rice, celery, and onion. Stir into broccoli.
3. Cover. Cook on Low 4–5 hours.

Ham & Yam Dish

Leona Miller Millersburg, OH

MAKES: **8 SERVINGS**
PREP. TIME: **10 MINUTES**
COOKING TIME: **1½–6 HOURS**
IDEAL SLOW COOKER SIZE: **4–5-QUART**

40-oz. can yams in water, drained

1½ lbs. extra-lean smoked ham, cut into bite-sized cubes

20-oz. can unsweetened pineapple chunks *or* crushed pineapple in light juice, drained

¼ cup dark brown sugar

1. Spray slow cooker with nonfat cooking spray.
2. Stir all ingredients together gently in the slow cooker.
3. Cook on High 1½–2 hours, or on Low 4–6 hours.

Per Serving: 320 calories (45 calories from fat), 5g total fat (1.5g saturated, 0g trans), 45mg cholesterol, 930mg sodium, 47g total carbohydrate (3g fiber, 36g sugar), 21g protein, 300%DV vitamin A, 10%DV vitamin C, 6%DV calcium, 20%DV iron.

Ham-Yam-Apple

Joan Rosenberger Stephens City, VA

MAKES: **4 SERVINGS**
PREP. TIME: **10 MINUTES**
COOKING TIME: **4–5 HOURS**
IDEAL SLOW COOKER SIZE: **5-QUART**

1 slice fully cooked ham (about 1 lb.)

29-oz. can sweet potatoes *or* yams, drained

2 apples, thinly sliced

¼ cup light brown sugar

2 Tbsp. orange juice

1. Cube ham.
2. Combine all ingredients in slow cooker.
3. Cook on Low 4–5 hours, or until apples are tender.

Per Serving: 460 calories (60 calories from fat), 7g total fat (2g saturated, 0g trans), 60mg cholesterol, 1520mg sodium, 73g total carbohydrate (5g fiber, 57g sugar), 28g protein, 200%DV vitamin A, 20%DV vitamin C, 8%DV calcium, 25%DV iron.

When cooking meats and vegetables together, especially when cooking on Low, place the vegetables on the bottom where they will be kept moist.

Ham and Lima Beans

Charlotte Shaffer   East Earl, PA

MAKES: **6 SERVINGS**
PREP. TIME: **15 MINUTES**
SOAKING TIME: **8 HOURS, OR OVERNIGHT**
COOKING TIME: **4–7 HOURS**
IDEAL SLOW COOKER SIZE: **4-QUART**

1 lb. dry lima beans

1 onion, chopped

1 bell pepper, chopped

1 tsp. dry mustard

1 tsp. salt

1 tsp. pepper

½ lb. ham, finely cubed

1 cup water

10¾-oz. can tomato soup

1. Cover beans with water. Soak 8 hours. Drain.
2. Combine ingredients in slow cooker.
3. Cover. Cook on Low 7 hours, or on High 4 hours.
4. If mixture begins to dry out, add ½ cup water or more and stir well.
5. This is delicious served with hot cornbread.

Ham and Mushrooms Hash Browns

Evelyn Page   Riverton, WY   •   *Anna Stoltzfus*   Honey Brook, PA

MAKES: **6–8 SERVINGS**
PREP. TIME: **15 MINUTES**
COOKING TIME: **6–8 HOURS**
IDEAL SLOW COOKER SIZE: **5-QUART**

28-oz. pkg. frozen hash brown potatoes

2½ cups cubed cooked ham

2-oz. jar pimentos, drained and chopped

4-oz. can mushrooms, *or* ¼-lb. sliced fresh mushrooms

10¾-oz. can cheddar cheese soup

¾ cup half-and-half

dash of pepper

salt to taste

1. Combine potatoes, ham, pimentos, and mushrooms in slow cooker.
2. Combine soup, half-and-half, and seasonings. Pour over potatoes.
3. Cover. Cook on Low 6–8 hours. (If you turn the cooker on when you go to bed, you'll have a wonderfully tasty breakfast in the morning.)

Variation: *Add a 4-oz. can of mushrooms, drained, or ¼ lb. sliced fresh mushrooms, to Step 1.*

Don't be afraid to experiment and make changes in recipes. If a recipe calls for an ingredient you don't care for, either substitute something else, or leave it out.

Black Beans with Ham

Colleen Heatwole   Burton, MI

MAKES: **8–10 SERVINGS**
PREP. TIME: **20 MINUTES**
SOAKING TIME: **8 HOURS OR OVERNIGHT**
COOKING TIME: **10–12 HOURS**
IDEAL SLOW COOKER SIZE: **5-QUART**

4 cups dry black beans

1–2 cups diced ham

1 tsp. salt, *optional*

1 tsp. cumin

½–1 cup minced onion

2 garlic cloves, minced

3 bay leaves

1 quart diced tomatoes

1 Tbsp. brown sugar

1. Cover black beans with water and soak for 8 hours, or over night. Drain and pour beans into slow cooker.
2. Add all remaining ingredients and stir well. Cover with water.
3. Cover cooker. Cook on Low 10–12 hours.
4. Serve over rice.

   Note: *This is our favorite black bean recipe. We make it frequently in the winter.*

Smothered Lentils

Tracey B. Stenger   Gretna, LA

MAKES: **6 SERVINGS**
PREP. TIME: **10 MINUTES**
COOKING TIME: **8 HOURS**
IDEAL SLOW COOKER SIZE: **4-QUART**

2 cups dry lentils, rinsed and sorted

1 medium onion, chopped

½ cup chopped celery

2 garlic cloves, minced

1 cup ham, cooked and chopped

½ cup chopped carrots

1 cup diced tomatoes

1 tsp. dried marjoram

1 tsp. ground coriander

salt to taste

pepper to taste

3 cups water

1. Combine all ingredients in slow cooker.
2. Cover. Cook on Low 8 hours. (Check lentils after 5 hours of cooking. If they've absorbed all the water, stir in 1 more cup water.)

Ham with Sweet Potatoes and Oranges

Esther Becker   Gordonville, PA

MAKES: **4 SERVINGS**
PREP. TIME: **15 MINUTES**
COOKING TIME: **7–8 HOURS**
IDEAL SLOW COOKER SIZE: **3-QUART**

2–3 sweet potatoes, peeled and sliced ¼-inch thick

1 large ham slice

3 seedless oranges, peeled and sliced

3 Tbsp. orange juice concentrate

3 Tbsp. honey

½ cup brown sugar

2 Tbsp. cornstarch

1. Place sweet potatoes in slow cooker.
2. Arrange ham and orange slices on top.
3. Combine remaining ingredients. Drizzle over ham and oranges.
4. Cover. Cook on Low 7–8 hours.
5. Delicious served with lime jello salad.

Southwest Hominy and Hot Dogs

MAKES: **12–14 SERVINGS**
PREP. TIME: **15 MINUTES**
COOKING TIME: **2–4 HOURS**
IDEAL SLOW COOKER SIZE: **6-QUART**

3 29-oz. cans hominy, drained

10¾-oz. can cream of mushroom soup

10¾-oz. can cream of chicken soup

1 cup diced green chilies

½ lb. Velveeta cheese, cubed

1 lb. hot dogs, diced

1. Combine all ingredients in slow cooker.
2. Cover. Cook on Low 2–4 hours. Stir before serving.

Underground Ham and Cheese

Carol Sommers   Millersburg, OH

MAKES: **12–16 SERVINGS**
PREP. TIME: **30–40 MINUTES**
COOKING TIME: **3–4 HOURS**
IDEAL SLOW COOKER SIZE: **2 4–5-QUART**

4 cups cooked ham, cut into chunks

4 Tbsp. butter

½ cup chopped onions

1 Tbsp. Worcestershire sauce

2 10¾-oz. cans cream of mushroom soup

1 cup milk

2 cups Velveeta cheese, cubed

4 quarts mashed potatoes

1 pint sour cream

browned and crumbled bacon

1. Combine ham, butter, onions, and Worcestershire sauce in saucepan. Cook until onions are tender. Place in large slow cooker, or divide between 2 4–5-quart cookers.

2. In saucepan, heat together soup, milk, and cheese until cheese melts. Pour into cooker(s).
3. Combine potatoes and sour cream. Spread over mixture in slow cooker(s).
4. Sprinkle with bacon.
5. Cover. Cook on Low 3–4 hours, or until cheese mixture comes to top when done (hence, the name "underground").

Ham and Cheese Casserole

Kendra Dreps   Liberty, PA

MAKES: **8–10 SERVINGS**
PREP. TIME: **15–30 MINUTES**
COOKING TIME: **2–4 HOURS**
IDEAL SLOW COOKER SIZE: **3½-QUART**

12- *or* 16-oz. pkg. medium egg noodles, *divided*

10¾-oz. can condensed cream of celery soup

1 pint sour cream

2 cups fully cooked ham, cubed, *divided*

2 cups shredded cheese, your choice, *divided*

1. Prepare noodles according to package instructions. Drain.
2. In a small bowl combine soup and sour cream until smooth. Set aside.
3. In a greased slow cooker, layer one-third of the cooked noodles, one-third of the ham, and one-third of the cheese.
4. Top with one-fourth of soup mixture.
5. Repeat steps 3 and 4 twice until all ingredients are used. The final layer should be the soup-sour cream mixture.
6. Cook 2–4 hours on Low, or until heated through.

Pork Main Dishes

Ham and Hash Browns

Joette Droz Kalona, IA • *Jonice Crist* Quinter, KS

MAKES: **4 SERVINGS**
PREP. TIME: **10 MINUTES**
COOKING TIME: **4–6 HOURS**
IDEAL SLOW COOKER SIZE: **4-QUART**

26-oz. pkg. frozen hash browns

2 cups fully cooked ham, cubed

2-oz. jar diced pimentos, drained

10¾-oz. can cheddar cheese soup

¾ cup milk

¼ tsp. pepper, *optional*

1. In a slow cooker combine potatoes, ham, and pimentos.
2. Combine soup, milk, and pepper if you wish in a bowl until smooth. Mix well and pour over potato mixture. Stir.
3. Cover and cook on Low 4–6 hours, or until potatoes are tender.

Barbecued Ham Sandwiches

Jane Steiner Orrville, OH

MAKES: **4–6 SANDWICHES**
PREP. TIME: **5–7 MINUTES**
COOKING TIME: **5 HOURS**
IDEAL SLOW COOKER SIZE: **3-QUART**

1 lb. chipped turkey ham *or* chipped honey-glazed ham

1 small onion, finely diced

½ cup ketchup

1 Tbsp. vinegar

3 Tbsp. brown sugar

buns

1. Place half of meat in greased slow cooker.
2. Combine other ingredients. Pour half of mixture over meat. Repeat layers.
3. Cover. Cook on Low 5 hours.
4. Fill buns and serve.

Ham Barbecue

Janet V. Yocum Elizabethtown, PA

MAKES: **6–8 SANDWICHES**
PREP. TIME: **5 MINUTES**
COOKING TIME: **8 HOURS**
IDEAL SLOW COOKER SIZE: **3-QUART**

1 lb. boiled ham, cut into cubes

1 cup cola-flavored soda

1 cup ketchup

1. Place ham in slow cooker. Pour cola and ketchup over ham.
2. Cover. Cook on Low 8 hours.
3. Serve in hamburger rolls.

Verenike Casserole

Jennifer Yoder Sommers Harrisonburg, VA

MAKES: **8–10 SERVINGS**
PREP. TIME: **10–15 MINUTES**
COOKING TIME: **5–6 HOURS**
IDEAL SLOW COOKER SIZE: **5-QUART**

24 ozs. cottage cheese

3 eggs

1 tsp. salt

½ tsp. pepper

1 cup sour cream

2 cups evaporated milk

2 cups cubed cooked ham

7–9 dry lasagna noodles

1. Combine all ingredients except noodles.
2. Place half of creamy ham mixture in bottom of cooker. Add uncooked noodles. Cover with remaining half of creamy ham sauce. Be sure noodles are fully submerged in sauce.
3. Cover. Cook on Low 5–6 hours.
4. Serve with green salad, peas, and zwieback or bread.

Note: *This is an easy way to make the traditional Russian Mennonite dish—verenike, or cheese pockets. Its great taste makes up for its appearance!*

I bake a casserole on Saturday. Then on Sunday morning I put it into a slow cooker, turn it on High for 30 minutes, then on Low while I'm at church.

Shepherd's Pie

Melanie Thrower McPherson, KS

MAKES: **3–4 SERVINGS**
PREP. TIME: **30–40 MINUTES**
COOKING TIME: **3 HOURS**
IDEAL SLOW COOKER SIZE: **4-QUART**

1 lb. ground pork

1 Tbsp. vinegar

1 tsp. salt

¼ tsp. hot pepper

1 tsp. paprika

¼ tsp. dried oregano

¼ tsp. black pepper

1 tsp. chili powder

1 small onion, chopped

15-oz. can corn, drained

3 large potatoes

¼ cup milk

1 tsp. butter

¼ tsp. salt

dash of pepper

shredded cheese

1. Combine pork, vinegar, and spices. Cook in skillet until brown. Add onion and cook until onions begin to glaze. Spread in bottom of slow cooker.
2. Spread corn over meat.
3. Boil potatoes until soft. Mash with milk, butter, ¼ tsp. salt, and dash of pepper. Spread over meat and corn.
4. Cover. Cook on Low 3 hours. Sprinkle top with cheese a few minutes before serving.

Note: *This is my 9-year-old son's favorite dish.*

Variation: *You can substitute ground beef for the pork.*

Pork Main Dishes

Ham Loaf or Balls

Michelle Strite   Goshen, IN

MAKES: **8–10 SERVINGS**
PREP. TIME: **30 MINUTES**
COOKING TIME: **4–6 HOURS**
IDEAL SLOW COOKER SIZE: **4–5-QUART**

Ham Loaf or Balls:

1 lb. ground ham

1 lb. ground pork *or* ground beef

1 cup soft bread crumbs

2 eggs, slightly beaten

1 cup milk

2 Tbsp. minced onions

1¼ tsp. salt

⅛ tsp. pepper

Glaze:

¾ cup brown sugar

1 tsp. dry mustard

1 Tbsp. cornstarch

¼ cup vinegar

½ cup water

1. Combine ham loaf or balls ingredients. Form into loaf or balls and place in slow cooker.
2. Combine dry ingredients for glaze in bowl. Mix in vinegar and water until smooth. Pour into saucepan. Cook until slightly thickened. Pour over meat.
3. Cover. Cook on High 4–6 hours.

   Variations:
   1. For a firmer loaf, or balls, use dry bread crumbs instead of soft. Use only ¾ cup milk instead of 1 cup.

   2. Form meat mixture into 1-inch balls. Brown lightly by baking on cookie sheet in 400° oven for 5–10 minutes. Place balls in slow cooker. Pour cooked glaze over balls, cover, and cook on High 2–4 hours.

Julia A. Fisher   New Carlisle, OH

Pork and Beef Spaghetti Sauce

Doris Perkins   Mashpee, MA

MAKES: **18–24 SERVINGS**
PREP. TIME: **30 MINUTES**
COOKING TIME: **4–5 HOURS**
IDEAL SLOW COOKER SIZE: **4–5-QUART**

¼-lb. bacon, diced

1¼-lb. ground beef

½ lb. ground pork

1 cup chopped onions

½ cup chopped green peppers

3 garlic cloves, minced

2 2-lb., 3-oz. cans Italian tomatoes

2 6-oz. cans tomao paste

1 cup dry red wine *or* water

2½ tsp. dried oregano

2½ tsp. dried basil

1 bay leaf, crumbled

¾ cup water

¼ cup chopped fresh parsley

1 tsp. dried thyme

1 Tbsp. salt

¼ tsp. pepper

¼ cup dry red wine *or* water

1. Brown bacon in skillet until crisp. Remove. Add ground beef and pork. Crumble and cook until brown. Stir in onions, green peppers, and garlic. Cook 10 minutes.
2. Pour tomatoes into slow cooker and crush with back of spoon.
3. Add all other ingredients, except ¼ cup wine, in slow cooker.
4. Cover. Bring to boil on High. Reduce heat to Low for 3–4 hours.
5. During last 30 minutes, stir in ¼ cup red wine or water.

Pork Main Dishes   457

Harvest Kielbasa

Christ Kaczynski Schenectady, NY

MAKES: **6 SERVINGS**
PREP. TIME: **20 MINUTES**
COOKING TIME: **4–8 HOURS**
IDEAL SLOW COOKER SIZE: **4-QUART**

2 lbs. smoked kielbasa

3 cups unsweetened applesauce

½ cup brown sugar

3 medium onions, sliced

1. Slice kielbasa into ¼-inch slices. Brown in skillet. Drain.
2. Combine applesauce and brown sugar.
3. Layer kielbasa, onions, and applesauce mixture in slow cooker.
4. Cover. Cook on Low 4–8 hours.

Tip: *The longer it cooks, the better the flavor.*

Sweet and Spicy Kielbasa

Michele Ruvola Selden, NY

MAKES: **6–8 SERVINGS**
PREP. TIME: **5 MINUTES**
COOKING TIME: **2½–3 HOURS**
IDEAL SLOW COOKER SIZE: **3-QUART**

1 cup brown sugar

1 Tbsp. spicy mustard

2 lbs. smoked fully cooked kielbasa, cut into 1-inch pieces

1. Combine brown sugar and mustard in slow cooker.
2. Add kielbasa; stir to coat evenly.
3. Cover and cook on Low 2½–3 hours, stirring occasionally.

Sausage and Apples

Linda Sluiter Schererville, IN

MAKES: **4 SERVINGS**
PREP. TIME: **10 MINUTES**
COOKING TIME: **1–3 HOURS**
IDEAL SLOW COOKER SIZE: **3-QUART**

1 lb. smoked sausage

2 large apples, cored and sliced

¼ cup brown sugar

½ cup apple juice

1. Cut meat into 2-inch pieces.
2. Place all ingredients in slow cooker and mix together well.
3. Cover and cook on Low 1–3 hours, or until heated through and until apples are as tender as you like them.

To chop onions painlessly, place your cutting board on a front unheated burner. Turn on the rear burner and chop the onions. The heat from the back burner will pull the "teary" oils away from you.

Pork Main Dishes

Sweet and Sour Sausage Dish

Jena Hammond   Traverse City, MI

MAKES: **8–10 SERVINGS**
PREP. TIME: **15 MINUTES**
COOKING TIME: **3–6 HOURS**
IDEAL SLOW COOKER SIZE: **4-QUART**

2 20-oz. cans pineapple chunks, drained

2 large green peppers, sliced into bite-sized strips

3 16-oz. pkgs. smoked sausage, cut into 1-inch chunks

18-oz. bottle honey barbecue sauce

1. Combine pineapples, peppers, and sausage chunks in slow cooker.
2. Pour barbecue sauce over mixture and stir.
3. Cover and cook on High 3 hours, or on Low 6 hours, or until dish is heated through.

Sausage and Sweet Potatoes

Ruth Hershey   Paradise, PA

MAKES: **4–6 SERVINGS**
PREP. TIME: **15–20 MINUTES**
COOKING TIME: **4–10 HOURS**
IDEAL SLOW COOKER SIZE: **3-QUART**

1 lb. bulk sausage

2 sweet potatoes, peeled and sliced

3 apples, peeled and sliced

2 Tbsp. brown sugar

1 Tbsp. flour

¼ cup water

1. Brown loose sausage in skillet, breaking up chunks of meat with a wooden spoon. Drain.
2. Layer sausage, sweet potatoes, and apples in slow cooker.
3. Combine remaining ingredients and pour over ingredients in slow cooker.
4. Cover. Cook on Low 8–10 hours, or on High 4 hours.

Green Beans with Sausage

Mary B. Sensenig   New Holland, PA

MAKES: **4–5 SERVINGS**
PREP. TIME: **5 MINUTES**
COOKING TIME: **4–5 HOURS**
IDEAL SLOW COOKER SIZE: **4-QUART**

16-oz.-pkg. miniature smoked sausage links

1 quart green beans, with most of the juice drained

1 small onion, chopped

½ cup brown sugar

¼ cup ketchup

1. Place sausage in slow cooker. Top with beans and then onion.
2. In a bowl, stir together sugar and ketchup. Spoon over top.
3. Cover and cook on Low 4–5 hours.

Sausage and Scalloped Potatoes

Melissa Warner Broad Top, PA • *Carolyn Baer* Conrath, WI

MAKES: **8 SERVINGS**
PREP. TIME: **20 MINUTES**
COOKING TIME: **4–10 HOURS**
IDEAL SLOW COOKER SIZE: **3½–4-QUART**

2 lbs. potatoes, sliced ¼-inch thick, *divided*

1 lb. fully cooked smoked sausage link, sliced ½-inch thick, *divided*

2 medium-sized onions, chopped, *divided*

10¾-oz. can condensed cheddar cheese soup, *divided*

10¾-oz. can condensed cream of celery soup

10-oz. pkg. frozen peas, thawed, *optional*

1. Spray interior of cooker with nonstick cooking spray.
2. Layer into the cooker one-third of the potatoes, one-third of the sausage, one-third of the onion, and one-third of the cheddar cheese soup.
3. Repeat layers two more times.
4. Top with cream of celery soup.
5. Cover and cook on Low 8–10 hours, or on High 4–5 hours, or until vegetables are tender.
6. If you wish, stir in peas. Cover and let stand 5 minutes. (If you forgot to thaw the peas, stir them in but let stand 10 minutes.)

Golden Autumn Stew

Naomi E. Fast Hesston, KS

MAKES: **8–10 SERVINGS**
PREP. TIME: **30–40 MINUTES**
COOKING TIME: **2–4 HOURS**
IDEAL SLOW COOKER SIZE: **5-QUART**

2 cups cubed Yukon gold potatoes

2 cups cubed, peeled sweet potatoes

2 cups cubed, peeled butternut squash

1 cup cubed, peeled rutabaga

1 cup diced carrots

1 cup sliced celery

1 lb. smoked sausage

2 cups apple juice *or* cider

1 tart apple, thinly sliced

salt to taste

pepper to taste

1 Tbsp. sugar *or* honey

1. Combine vegetables in slow cooker.
2. Place ring of sausage on top.
3. Add apple juice and apple slices.
4. Cover. Cook on High 2 hours and on Low 4 hours, or until vegetables are tender. Do not stir.
5. To serve, remove sausage ring. Season with salt, pepper, and sugar as desired. Place vegetables in bowl. Slice meat into rings and place on top.
6. Serve with hot baking-powder biscuits and honey, and a green salad or cole slaw.

Tip: *Don't omit the rutabaga! Get acquainted with its rich uniqueness. It will surprise and please your taste buds.*

Pork Main Dishes

Creamy Sausage and Potatoes

Janet Oberholtzer Ephrata, PA

MAKES: **6 SERVINGS**
PREP. TIME: **15 MINUTES**
COOKING TIME: **6–8 HOURS**
IDEAL SLOW COOKER SIZE: **3½-QUART**

3 lbs. small potatoes, peeled and quartered

1 lb. smoked sausage, cut into ¼-inch slices

8-oz. pkg. cream cheese, softened

10¾-oz. can cream of celery soup

1 envelope dry ranch salad dressing mix

1. Place potatoes in slow cooker. Add sausage.
2. In a bowl, beat together cream cheese, soup, and salad dressing mix until smooth. Pour over potatoes and sausage.
3. Cover and cook on Low 6–8 hours, or until the potatoes are tender, stirring half-way through cooking time if you're home. Stir again before serving.

Tip: *Small red potatoes are great in this dish. If you use them, don't peel them!*

Variation: *You may substitute smoked turkey sausage for the smoked pork sausage.*

When testing new recipes have your family rate them. Write comments, along with the date that you made the recipe, in the page margins next to the recipe.

Italian Sausage Dinner

Janessa Hochstedler East Earl, PA

MAKES: **6 SERVINGS**
PREP. TIME: **10 MINUTES**
COOKING TIME: **5–10 HOURS**
IDEAL SLOW COOKER SIZE: **4-QUART**

1½ lbs. Italian sausage, cut in ¾-inch slices

2 Tbsp. A-1 steak sauce

28-oz. can diced Italian-style tomatoes, with juice

2 chopped green peppers

½ tsp. red pepper flakes, *optional*

2 cups minute rice, uncooked

1. Place all ingredients, except rice, in slow cooker.
2. Cover and cook on Low 7½–9½ hours, or on High 4½ hours.
3. Stir in uncooked rice. Cover and cook an additional 20 minutes on High or Low.

Sausage and a Rainbow of Peppers

Dawn Day Westminster, CA

MAKES: **8–10 SERVINGS**
PREP. TIME: **25–30 MINUTES**
COOKING TIME: **6 HOURS**
IDEAL SLOW COOKER SIZE: **5-QUART**

3 medium onions, sliced

1 sweet red pepper, sliced

1 sweet green pepper, sliced

1 sweet yellow pepper, sliced

4 garlic cloves, minced

1 Tbsp. oil

28 oz.-can chopped tomatoes

1 tsp. salt

½ tsp. red crushed pepper

2–3 lbs. sweet Italian sausage, cut into 3-inch pieces

1. Sauté onions, peppers, and garlic in oil in skillet. When just softened, place in slow cooker.
2. Add tomatoes, salt, and crushed red pepper. Mix well.
3. Add sausage links.
4. Cover. Cook on Low 6 hours.
5. Serve on rolls, or over pasta or baked potatoes.

Variation: *For a thicker sauce, stir in 3 Tbsp. ClearJell during the last 15 minutes of the cooking time.*

Sausage in Spaghetti Sauce

Mary Ann Bowman East Earl, PA

MAKES: **10–12 SERVINGS**
PREP. TIME: **15 MINUTES**
COOKING TIME: **3–6 HOURS**
IDEAL SLOW COOKER SIZE: **5-QUART**

4 lbs. sausage of your choice

1 red bell pepper

1 green bell pepper

1 large onion

26-oz. jar spaghetti sauce

1. Heat nonstick skillet over medium-high heat. Brown sausage in nonstick skillet in batches. As a batch is finished browning on all sides, cut into 1½-inch chunks. Then place in slow cooker.
2. Slice or chop peppers and onion and put on top of sausage.
3. Add spaghetti sauce over all.
4. Cover and cook on Low 6 hours, or on High 3 hours.

When I use mushrooms or green peppers in the slow cooker, I usually stir them in during the last hour so they don't get too mushy.

Pork Main Dishes

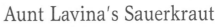

Italian Spaghetti Sauce

Michele Ruvola   Selden, NY

MAKES: **8–10 SERVINGS**
PREP. TIME: **20 MINUTES**
COOKING TIME: **8–9 HOURS**
IDEAL SLOW COOKER SIZE: **5–6-QUART**

2 lbs. sausage *or* ground beef

3 medium onions, chopped (about 2¼ cups)

2 cups sliced mushrooms

6 garlic cloves, minced

2 14½-oz. cans diced tomatoes, undrained

29-oz. can tomato sauce

12-oz. can tomato paste

2 Tbsp. dried basil

1 Tbsp. dried oregano

1 Tbsp. sugar

1 tsp. salt

½ tsp. crushed red pepper flakes

1. Cook sausage, onions, mushrooms, and garlic in skillet over medium heat for 10 minutes. Drain. Transfer to slow cooker.
2. Stir in remaining ingredients.
3. Cover. Cook on Low 8–9 hours.

Tip: *This is also a good sauce to use in lasagna.*

Aunt Lavina's Sauerkraut

Pat Unternahrer   Wayland, IA

MAKES: **8–12 SERVINGS**
PREP. TIME: **10 MINUTES**
COOKING TIME: **3–6 HOURS**
IDEAL SLOW COOKER SIZE: **4-QUART**

2–3 lbs. smoked sausage, cut into 1-inch pieces

2 Tbsp. water *or* oil

2 bell peppers, chopped

2 onions, sliced

½ lb. fresh mushrooms, sliced

1 quart sauerkraut, drained

2 14½-oz. cans diced tomatoes with green peppers

1 tsp. salt

½ tsp. pepper

2 Tbsp. brown sugar

1. Place sausage in slow cooker. Heat on Low while you prepare other ingredients.
2. Sauté peppers, onions, and mushrooms in small amount of water or oil in saucepan.
3. Combine all ingredients in slow cooker.
4. Cover. Cook on Low 5–6 hours, or on High 3–4 hours.
5. Serve with mashed potatoes.

Polish Sausage Stew

Jeanne Heyerly Chenoa, IL • *Joyce Kaut* Rochester, NY
Joyce B. Suiter Garysburg, NC

MAKES: **6–8 SERVINGS**
PREP. TIME: **15 MINUTES**
COOKING TIME: **4–8 HOURS**
IDEAL SLOW COOKER SIZE: **4–5-QUART**

10¾-oz. can cream of celery soup
⅓ cup packed brown sugar
27-oz. can sauerkraut, drained
1½ lbs. Polish sausage, cut into 2-inch pieces and browned
4 medium potatoes, cubed
1 cup chopped onions
1 cup (4 oz.) shredded Monterey Jack cheese

1. Combine soup, sugar, and sauerkraut. Stir in sausage, potatoes, and onions.
2. Cover. Cook on Low 8 hours, or on High 4 hours.
3. Stir in cheese and serve.

Sausage-Sauerkraut Supper

Ruth Ann Hoover New Holland, PA • *Robin Schrock* Millersburg, OH

MAKES: **10–12 SERVINGS**
PREP. TIME: **20 MINUTES**
COOKING TIME: **8–9 HOURS**
IDEAL SLOW COOKER SIZE: **4–5-QUART**

4 cups cubed carrots
4 cups cubed red potatoes
2 14-oz. cans sauerkraut, rinsed and drained
2½ lbs. fresh Polish sausage, cut into 3-inch pieces
1 medium onion, thinly sliced
3 garlic cloves, minced
1½ cups dry white wine *or* chicken broth
½ tsp. pepper
1 tsp. caraway seeds

1. Layer carrots, potatoes, and sauerkraut in slow cooker.
2. Brown sausage in skillet. Transfer to slow cooker. Reserve 1 Tbsp. drippings in skillet.
3. Sauté onion and garlic in drippings until tender. Stir in wine. Bring to boil. Stir to loosen brown bits. Stir in pepper and caraway seeds. Pour over sausage.
4. Cover. Cook on Low 8–9 hours.

Pork Main Dishes

Kielbasa and Cabbage

Barbara McGinnis Jupiter, FL

MAKES: **6 SERVINGS**
PREP. TIME: **15 MINUTES**
COOKING TIME: **7–8 HOURS**
IDEAL SLOW COOKER SIZE: **4–5-QUART**

1½ lb.-head green cabbage, shredded

2 medium onions, chopped

3 medium red potatoes, peeled and cubed

1 red bell pepper, chopped

2 garlic cloves, minced

⅔ cup dry white wine

1½ lbs. Polish kielbasa, cut into 3-inch long links

28-oz. can cut-up tomatoes with juice

1 Tbsp. Dijon mustard

¾ tsp. caraway seeds

½ tsp. pepper

¾ tsp. salt

1. Combine all ingredients in slow cooker.
2. Cover. Cook on Low 7–8 hours, or until cabbage is tender.

When choosing cabbage, select a bright green head that is firm and solid.

Kielbasa Stew

Fannie Miller Hutchinson, KS

MAKES: **6–8 SERVINGS**
PREP. TIME: **40–45 MINUTES**
COOKING TIME: **8–10 HOURS**
IDEAL SLOW COOKER SIZE: **5-QUART**

6 strips of bacon

1 onion, chopped

1–1½ lbs. smoked, fully cooked kielbasa, thinly sliced

2 15½-oz. cans Great Northern beans

2 8-oz. cans tomato sauce

4-oz. can chopped green chilies

2 medium carrots, thinly sliced

1 medium green pepper, chopped

½ tsp. Italian seasoning

½ tsp. dried thyme

½ tsp. black pepper

1. Fry bacon in skillet until crisp. Crumble bacon and place in large slow cooker. Add onions and kielbasa to drippings in skillet. Cook until onions are soft.
2. Transfer onions and kielbasa to slow cooker.
3. Add all remaining ingredients to cooker and stir together well.
4. Cover. Cook on Low 8–10 hours, or until vegetables are tender.

Rice and Beans—and Sausage

Marcia S. Myer   Manheim, PA

MAKES: **8 SERVINGS**
PREP. TIME: **25 MINUTES**
COOKING TIME: **4–6 HOURS**
IDEAL SLOW COOKER SIZE: **5-QUART**

3 celery ribs, chopped

1 onion, chopped

2 garlic cloves, minced

1¾ cups tomato juice

2 16-oz. cans kidney beans, drained

¾ tsp. dried oregano

¾ tsp. dried thyme

¼ tsp. red pepper flakes

¼ tsp. pepper

½ lb. (or more) fully cooked smoked turkey sausage *or* kielbasa, cut into ¼-inch slices

4 cups rice, cooked

shredded cheese, *optional*

1. Combine all ingredients except rice and shredded cheese in slow cooker.
2. Cover. Cook on Low 4–6 hours.
3. Serve over rice. Garnish with shredded cheese, if you wish.

Economy One-Dish Supper

Betty Drescher   Quakertown, PA

MAKES: **6 SERVINGS**
PREP. TIME: **15 MINUTES**
COOKING TIME: **4–10 HOURS**
IDEAL SLOW COOKER SIZE: **5-QUART**

½ lb. lean sausage

1½ cups potatoes, grated or cubed

1 cup water

½ tsp. cream of tartar

1 cup raw carrots, grated or thinly sliced

¼ cup rice, uncooked

1 onion, minced

¼ tsp. salt

¼ tsp. black pepper

¼ tsp. curry powder

3 cups low-sodium tomato juice

1. Brown sausage in nonstick skillet. Cut into ¼-inch-thick slices.
2. Mix water and cream of tartar. Toss with potatoes. Drain.
3. Layer sausage, potatoes, carrots, rice, and onion in slow cooker.
4. Combine salt, pepper, curry powder, and tomato juice. Pour over all.
5. Cover. Cook on Low 8–10 hours, or on High 4–5 hours.

Per Serving: 150 calories (60 calories from fat), 7g total fat (2.5g saturated, 0g trans), 15mg cholesterol, 280mg sodium, 18g total carbohydrate (3g fiber, 7g sugar), 5g protein, 100%DV vitamin A, 20%DV vitamin C, 2%DV calcium, 8%DV iron.

Sausage-Vegetable Stew

Rosann Zeiset   Stevens, PA

MAKES: **10 SERVINGS**
PREP. TIME: **30 MINUTES**
COOKING TIME: **3–10 HOURS**
IDEAL SLOW COOKER SIZE: **5–6-QUART**

1 lb. sausage (regular, turkey, *or* smoked)

4 cups potatoes, cooked and cubed

4 cups carrots, cooked and sliced

4 cups green beans, cooked

28-oz. can tomato sauce

1 tsp. onion powder

¼ or ½ tsp. black pepper, according to your taste

1. Slice sausage into 1½-inch pieces. Place in slow cooker.
2. Add cooked vegetables. Pour tomato sauce over top.
3. Sprinkle with onion powder and pepper. Stir.
4. Cook on High 3–4 hours, or on Low 8–10 hours.

Per Serving: 230 calories (80 calories from fat), 9g total fat (3g saturated, 0g trans), 15mg cholesterol, 930mg sodium, 32g total carbohydrate (6g fiber, 9g sugar), 8g protein, 200%DV vitamin A, 30%DV vitamin C, 6%DV calcium, 15%DV iron.

Variation: *If your diet allows, you may want to add ½ tsp. salt to Step 3.*

It's quite convenient to use a slow cooker to cook potatoes for salads or for fried potatoes or as "baked" potatoes. Just fill the slow cooker with cleaned potatoes and cook all day until done.

Bratwursts

Dede Peterson   Rapid City, SD

MAKES: **8 SERVINGS**
PREP. TIME: **15 MINUTES**
COOKING TIME: **4–5 HOURS**
IDEAL SLOW COOKER SIZE: **4-QUART**

8 bratwursts

1 large onion, sliced

12-oz. can of beer

1 cup chili sauce

1 Tbsp. Worcestershire sauce

1 cup ketchup

2 Tbsp. vinegar

½ tsp. salt

2 Tbsp. brown sugar

1 Tbsp. paprika

1. Boil bratwursts in water in skillet for 10 minutes to remove fat.
2. Drain bratwursts and place in slow cooker.
3. Mix together remaining ingredients in bowl and then pour over meat.
4. Cook on Low 4–5 hours.

Per Serving: 160 calories (45 calories from fat), 5g total fat (1.5g saturated, 0g trans), 10mg cholesterol, 1000mg sodium, 24g total carbohydrate (0.5g fiber, 17g sugar), 3g protein, 20%DV vitamin A, 10%DV vitamin C, 2%DV calcium, 4%DV iron.

Bratwurst Stew

Lauren M. Eberhard   Senecca, IL

MAKES: **8 SERVINGS**
PREP. TIME: **15 MINUTES**
COOKING TIME: **3–4 HOURS**
IDEAL SLOW COOKER SIZE: **5-QUART**

2 10¾-oz. cans fat-free chicken broth

4 medium carrots, sliced

2 ribs of celery, cut in chunks

1 medium onion, chopped

1 tsp. dried basil

½ tsp. garlic powder

3 cups chopped cabbage

2 1-lb. cans Great Northern beans, drained

5 fully cooked bratwurst links, cut into ½-inch slices

1. Combine all ingredients in slow cooker.
2. Cook on High 3–4 hours, or until veggies are tender.

Per Serving: 120 calories (30 calories from fat), 3.5g total fat (1g saturated, 0g trans), 5mg cholesterol, 320mg sodium, 15g total carbohydrate (5g fiber, 4g sugar), 7g protein, 150%DV vitamin A, 10%DV vitamin C, 6%DV calcium, 10%DV iron.

Note: *You can eat this as a stew, or over hot cornbread or rice.*

Election Lunch

Alix Nancy Botsford   Seminole, OK

MAKES: **6–12 SERVINGS**
PREP. TIME: **30 MINUTES**
COOKING TIME: **2–4 HOURS**
IDEAL SLOW COOKER SIZE: **6-QUART**

2–3 Tbsp. olive oil

1 large onion, chopped

1 lb. sausage, cut into thin slices, or casings removed and crumbled

1 rib celery, sliced

1 Tbsp. Worcestershire sauce

1½ tsp. dry mustard

¼ cup honey

10-oz. can tomatoes with green chili peppers

1-lb. can lima *or* butter beans, drained, with liquid reserved

1-lb. can red kidney beans, drained, with liquid reserved

1-lb. can garbanzo beans, drained, with liquid reserved

1. Brown onion and sausage in oil.
2. Combine ingredients in 6-quart slow cooker, or divide between 2 4-quart cookers and stir to combine. Add reserved juice from lima, kidney, and garbanzo beans if there's enough room in the cookers.
3. Cover. Cook on Low 2–4 hours.

Note: *I mixed up this hearty stew the night before Election Day and took it to the voting site the next morning. I plugged it in, and all day long we could smell the stew cooking. I work at a very sparsely populated, country polling place and ended up giving out the recipe and little water-cup samples to many voters!*

I have four different sizes of slow cookers. One is very tiny, with only an on and off switch, for keeping cheese sauce hot. One I use for heating gravy. Another I often use to keep mashed potatoes warm.

Pork Main Dishes

Chili Casserole

Sharon Miller   Holmesville, OH

MAKES: **6 SERVINGS**
PREP. TIME: **20–25 MINUTES**
COOKING TIME: **7 HOURS**
IDEAL SLOW COOKER SIZE: **5-QUART**

1 lb. bulk pork sausage, browned

2 cups water

15½-oz. can chili beans

14½-oz. can diced tomatoes

¾ cup brown rice

¼ cup chopped onions

1 Tbsp. chili powder

1 tsp. Worcestershire sauce

1 tsp. prepared mustard

¾ tsp. salt

⅛ tsp. garlic powder

1 cup shredded cheddar cheese

1. Combine all ingredients except cheese in slow cooker.
2. Cover. Cook on Low 7 hours.
3. Stir in cheese during last 10 minutes of cooking time.

Sausage-Pasta Stew

Betty K. Drescher   Quakertown, PA

MAKES: **8 SERVINGS**
PREP. TIME: **30–35 MINUTES**
COOKING TIME: **7¼–9¼ HOURS**
IDEAL SLOW COOKER SIZE: **6-QUART**

1 lb. Italian sausage, casings removed

4 cups water

26-oz. jar meatless spaghetti sauce

16-oz. can kidney beans, rinsed and drained

1 medium yellow summer squash, cut in 1-inch pieces

2 medium carrots, cut in ¼-inch slices

1 medium red *or* green sweet pepper, diced

⅓ cup chopped onions

1½ cups spiral pasta, uncooked

1 cup frozen peas

1 tsp. sugar

½ tsp. salt

¼ tsp. pepper

1. Sauté sausage in skillet until no longer pink. Drain and place in slow cooker.
2. Add water, spaghetti sauce, kidney beans, squash, carrots, pepper, and onions. Mix well.
3. Cover. Cook on Low 7–9 hours, or until vegetables are tender.
4. Add remaining ingredients. Mix well.
5. Cover. Cook on High 15–20 minutes until pasta is tender.

Tip: *Add 1 Tbsp. tapioca in Step 5 if you like a thicker stew.*

Pizza Rigatoni

Tina Snyder   Manheim, PA

MAKES: **6–8 SERVINGS**
PREP. TIME: **25 MINUTES**
COOKING TIME: **4 HOURS**
IDEAL SLOW COOKER SIZE: **5-QUART**

1½ lbs. bulk sausage

3 cups rigatoni, lightly cooked

4 cups shredded mozzarella cheese

10¾-oz. can cream of mushroom soup

1 small onion, sliced

15-oz. can pizza sauce

8-oz. can pizza sauce

3½-oz. pkg. sliced pepperoni

6-oz. can sliced ripe olives

1. Cook and drain sausage. Place half in 4-quart, or larger, slow cooker.
2. Layer half of pasta, cheese, soup, onion, pizza sauce, pepperoni, and olives over sausage. Repeat layers.
3. Cover. Cook on Low 4 hours.

Variation: *If your store doesn't carry 8-oz. cans pizza sauce, substitute an 8-oz. can tomato sauce with basil, garlic, and oregano.*

Crockpot Pizza

Sharon Miller   Holmesville, OH

MAKES: **6 SERVINGS**
PREP. TIME: **25 MINUTES**
COOKING TIME: **6–8 HOURS**
IDEAL SLOW COOKER SIZE: **5-QUART**

1½ lbs. bulk sausage

1 small onion, chopped

1-lb. pkg. pasta *or* noodles, uncooked

28-oz. jar spaghetti sauce

16-oz. can tomato sauce

¾ cup water

4-oz. can mushrooms, drained

16-oz. pkg. shredded mozzarella cheese

8-oz. pkg. pepperoni, chopped

1. Brown sausage and onion in skillet. Drain. Place one-third of mixture in cooker.
2. Layer in one-third of uncooked pasta.
3. Combine spaghetti sauce, tomato sauce, water, and mushrooms in bowl. Ladle one-third of that mixture over noodles.
4. Repeat the above layers 2 more times.
5. Top with pepperoni. Top that with shredded cheese.
6. Cover. Cook on Low 6–8 hours.

Leave the lid on while the slow cooker cooks. The steam that condenses on the lid helps cook the food from the top. Every time you take the lid off, the cooker loses steam. After you put the lid back on, it takes up to 20 minutes to regain the lost steam and temperature. That means it takes longer for the food to cook.

Pork Main Dishes

Melt-in-Your-Mouth Sausages

Ruth Ann Gingrich New Holland, PA • *Ruth Hershey* Paradise, PA
Carol Sherwood Batavia, NY • *Nancy Zimmerman* Loysville, PA

MAKES: **6–8 SERVINGS**
PREP. TIME: **5 MINUTES**
COOKING TIME: **6–8 HOURS**
IDEAL SLOW COOKER SIZE: **4-QUART**

2 lbs. sweet Italian sausage, cut into 5-inch lengths

48-oz. jar spaghetti sauce

6-oz. can tomato paste

1 large green pepper, thinly sliced

1 large onion, thinly sliced

1 Tbsp. grated Parmesan cheese

1 tsp. dried parsley, *or* 1 Tbsp. chopped fresh parsley

1 cup water

1. Place sausage in skillet. Cover with water. Simmer 10 minutes. Drain.
2. Combine remaining ingredients in slow cooker. Add sausage.
3. Cover. Cook on Low 6 hours.
4. Serve in buns, or cut sausage into bite-sized pieces and serve over cooked spaghetti.

Tip: *Sprinkle with more Parmesan cheese.*

Sauerkraut & Trail Bologna

Carol Sommers Millersburg, OH

MAKES: **10 SERVINGS**
PREP. TIME: **5 MINUTES**
COOKING TIME: **6–8 HOURS**
IDEAL SLOW COOKER SIZE: **4-QUART**

32-oz. bag sauerkraut, rinsed

¼–½ cup brown sugar

1 ring Trail Bologna

1. Combine sauerkraut and brown sugar in slow cooker.
2. Remove casing from bologna and cut into ¼-inch slices. Add to sauerkraut. Stir.
3. Cover. Cook on Low 6–8 hours.

Variation: *If you don't have access to Holmes County, Ohio's specialty Trail Bologna, use 1 large ring bologna.*

Spiced Hot Dogs

Tracey Yohn   Harrisburg, PA

MAKES: **3–4 SERVINGS**
PREP. TIME: **5 MINUTES**
COOKING TIME: **2 HOURS**
IDEAL SLOW COOKER SIZE: **3-QUART**

1 lb. hot dogs, cut in pieces
2 Tbsp. brown sugar
3 Tbsp. vinegar
½ cup ketchup
2 tsp. prepared mustard
½ cup water
½ cup chopped onions

1. Place hot dogs in slow cooker.
2. Combine all ingredients except hot dogs in saucepan. Simmer. Pour over hot dogs.
3. Cover. Cook on Low 2 hours.

Barbecued Hot Dogs

Jeanette Oberholtzer   Manheim, PA

MAKES: **8 SERVINGS**
PREP. TIME: **5 MINUTES**
COOKING TIME: **4½ HOURS**
IDEAL SLOW COOKER SIZE: **4-QUART**

1 cup apricot preserves
4 oz. tomato sauce
⅓ cup vinegar
2 Tbsp. soy sauce
2 Tbsp. honey
1 Tbsp. oil
1 tsp. salt
¼ tsp. ground ginger
2 lbs. hot dogs, cut into 1-inch pieces

1. Combine all ingredients except hot dogs in slow cooker.

2. Cover. Cook on High 30 minutes. Add hot dog pieces. Cook on Low 4 hours.
3. Serve over rice as a main dish, or as an appetizer.

Bits and Bites

Betty Richards   Rapid City, SD

MAKES: **12 SERVINGS**
PREP. TIME: **5 MINUTES**
COOKING TIME: **3–4 HOURS**
IDEAL SLOW COOKER SIZE: **4-QUART**

12-oz. can beer
1 cup ketchup
1 cup light brown sugar
½–1 cup barbecue sauce
1 lb. all-beef hot dogs, sliced 1½-inches thick
2 lbs. cocktail sausages

1. Combine beer, ketchup, brown sugar, and barbecue sauce. Pour into slow cooker.
2. Add hot dogs and sausages. Mix well.
3. Cover. Cook on Low 3–4 hours.

Keep it simple! Use prepared foods if you need to. Grandma had more time at home to cook even though she was busy with other housework.

Bandito Chili Dogs

Sue Graber Eureka, IL

MAKES: **10 SERVINGS**
PREP. TIME: **10 MINUTES**
COOKING TIME: **3–3½ HOURS**
IDEAL SLOW COOKER SIZE: **4-QUART**

1 lb. hot dogs

2 15-oz. cans chili, with *or* without beans

10¾-oz. can condensed cheddar cheese soup

4-oz. can chopped green chilies

10 hot dog buns

1 medium onion, chopped

1–2 cups corn chips, coarsely crushed

1 cup shredded cheddar cheese

1. Place hot dogs in slow cooker.
2. Combine chili, soup, and green chilies. Pour over hot dogs.
3. Cover. Cook on Low 3–3½ hours.
4. Serve hot dogs in buns. Top with chili mixture, onion, corn chips, and cheese.

Note: *This is a fun recipe for after a football game or outside activity. The main part of your meal is ready when you get home.*

Sloppy Jane Sandwiches

Kathleen Rogge Alexandria, IN

MAKES: **4–5 SERVINGS**
PREP. TIME: **5–10 MINUTES**
COOKING TIME: **2–3 HOURS**
IDEAL SLOW COOKER SIZE: **2-QUART**

1 pkg. hot dogs, cut into ¾-inch slices

28-oz. can baked beans

1 tsp. prepared mustard

1 tsp. instant minced onion

⅓ cup chili sauce

1. In slow cooker, combine all ingredients.
2. Cover and cook on Low 2–3 hours.
3. Spoon into toasted hot dog buns.

Tip: *This recipe doubles easily.*

Frankwiches

Esther Mast   East Petersburg, PA

MAKES: **16–18 SERVINGS**
PREP. TIME: **15 MINUTES**
COOKING TIME: **4¼ HOURS**
IDEAL SLOW COOKER SIZE: **4-QUART**

2 10¾-oz. cans cheddar cheese soup

½ cup finely chopped onions

½ cup sweet pickle relish

4 tsp. prepared mustard

2 lbs. hot dogs, thinly sliced

8-oz. container sour cream

1. Combine soup, onions, relish, and mustard. Stir in sliced hot dogs.
2. Cover. Cook on Low 4 hours.
3. Stir in sour cream.
4. Cover. Cook on High 10–15 minutes, stirring occasionally.
5. Serve over toasted English muffin halves or squares of hot cornbread.

Notes: *Instead of using this as sandwich filling you can serve it over rice as a main dish. Add a green vegetable and a jello salad and you have an easy, refreshing, quick meal!*

This will also bring smiles to the faces of your grandchildren! Add a relish tray and some chips, and you have a quick summer meal on the patio. Top it off with frozen popsicles.

Most slow cookers perform best when more than half full.

Saucy Hot Dogs

Donna Conto   Saylorsburg, PA

MAKES: **8 SERVINGS**
PREP. TIME: **15 MINUTES**
COOKING TIME: **2 HOURS**
IDEAL SLOW COOKER SIZE: **5-QUART**

1 lb. all-beef hot dogs

10-oz. jar grape jelly

⅓ cup prepared mustard

¼ cup red wine

¼ tsp. dry mustard

1. Cut hot dogs into ½-inch slices. Place in slow cooker.
2. Mix remaining ingredients together with the hot dogs in the cooker.
3. Cover and cook on Low for 2 hours.
4. Serve in rolls or over cooked pasta.

Tip: *This is also a great buffet dish. Serve it from the warm slow cooker with toothpicks.*

Cranberry Franks

Loretta Krahn   Mountain Lake, MN

MAKES: **15–20 SERVINGS**
PREP. TIME: **10 MINUTES**
COOKING TIME: **1–2 HOURS**
IDEAL SLOW COOKER SIZE: **3-QUART**

2 pkgs. cocktail wieners *or* little smoked sausages

16-oz. can jellied cranberry sauce

1 cup ketchup

3 Tbsp. brown sugar

1 Tbsp. lemon juice

1. Combine all ingredients in slow cooker.
2. Cover. Cook on High 1–2 hours.

Tip: *Great picnic, potluck, or buffet food.*

Zesty Wieners

Sherril Bieberly   Salina, KS

MAKES: **10–12 SERVINGS**
PREP. TIME: **5 MINUTES**
COOKING TIME: **1–2 HOURS**
IDEAL SLOW COOKER SIZE: **2–3-QUART**

12-oz. bottle chili sauce

12-oz. jar hot pepper jelly

1½ lbs. little smokie wieners

1. Combine chili sauce and jelly in slow cooker. Add wieners.
2. Simmer on High until sauce thickens, about 1–2 hours.
3. Serve in buns, or over cooked rice or pasta. Or serve on a buffet from the warm cooker, along with toothpicks to spear the wieners.

Hot Dogs and Noodles

Dolores Kratz   Souderton, PA

MAKES: **6 SERVINGS**
PREP. TIME: **25 MINUTES**
COOKING TIME: **5–6 HOURS**
IDEAL SLOW COOKER SIZE: **5-QUART**

8-oz. pkg. medium egg noodles, cooked and drained

1¼ cups grated Parmesan cheese

1 cup milk

¼ cup butter *or* margarine, melted

1 Tbsp. flour

¼ tsp. salt

1-lb. pkg. hot dogs, sliced

¼ cup packed brown sugar

¼ cup mayonnaise

2 Tbsp. prepared mustard

1. Place noodles, cheese, milk, butter, flour, and salt in slow cooker. Mix well.
2. Combine hot dogs with remaining ingredients. Spoon evenly over noodles.
3. Cover. Cook on Low 5–6 hours.

Pot-Luck Wiener Bake

Ruth Ann Penner   Hillsboro, KS

MAKES: **6 SERVINGS**
PREP. TIME: **8 MINUTES**
COOKING TIME: **3 HOURS**
IDEAL SLOW COOKER SIZE: **3-QUART**

4 cups cooked potatoes, peeled and diced

10¾-oz. can cream of mushroom soup

1 cup mayonnaise

1 cup sauerkraut, drained

1 lb. wieners, sliced

1. Mix all ingredients in slow cooker.
2. Cover and cook on Low 3 hours.

Frankfurter Succotash

June S. Groff   Denver, PA

MAKES: **4–6 SERVINGS**
PREP. TIME: **10 MINUTES**
COOKING TIME: **4–6 HOURS**
IDEAL SLOW COOKER SIZE: **2-QUART**

1 lb. hot dogs, cut into ½-inch slices

2 10-oz. pkgs. frozen succotash, thawed and drained

10¾-oz. can cheddar cheese soup

1. Stir all ingredients together in slow cooker.
2. Cover and cook on Low 4–6 hours, or until vegetables are tender.

Variation: *Substitute cooked ham chunks for the hot dogs.*

Pizza Rice

Sue Hamilton   Minooka, IL

MAKES: **6 SERVINGS**
PREP. TIME: **5 MINUTES**
COOKING TIME: **6–10 HOURS**
IDEAL SLOW COOKER SIZE: **4-QUART**

2 cups rice, uncooked

3 cups chunky pizza sauce

2½ cups water

7-oz. can mushrooms, undrained

4 oz. pepperoni, sliced

1 cup shredded cheese

1. Combine rice, sauce, water, mushrooms, and pepperoni. Stir.
2. Cover. Cook on Low 10 hours, or on High 6 hours. Sprinkle with cheese before serving.

Seafood Main Dishes

Tex-Mex Luau

Dorothy VanDeest   Memphis, TN

MAKES: **6 SERVINGS**
PREP. TIME: **10 MINUTES**
COOKING TIME: **3–4 HOURS**
IDEAL SLOW COOKER SIZE: **3–4-QUART**

1½ lbs. frozen firm-textured fish fillets, thawed

2 onions, thinly sliced

2 lemons, *divided*

2 Tbsp. butter, melted

2 tsp. salt

1 bay leaf

4 whole peppercorns

1 cup water

1. Cut fillets into serving portions.
2. Combine onion slices and 1 sliced lemon in butter, along with salt, bay leaf, and peppercorns. Pour into slow cooker.
3. Place fillets on top of onion and lemon slices. Add water.
4. Cover. Cook on High 3–4 hours.
5. Before serving, carefully remove fish fillets with slotted spoon. Place on heatproof plate.
6. Sprinkle with juice of half of the second lemon. Garnish with remaining lemon slices.
7. Serve hot with Avocado Sauce (see below), if desired. Or chill and serve cold, also with Avocado Sauce, if you wish.

Per Serving: 160 calories (50 calories from fat), 5g total fat (2.5g saturated, 0g trans), 65mg cholesterol, 870mg sodium, 7g total carbohydrate (2g fiber, 3g sugar), 22g protein, 4%DV vitamin A, 20%DV vitamin C, 6%DV calcium, 4%DV iron.

Avocado Sauce

7½ ozs. frozen low-fat avocado dip, thawed

½ cup fat-free sour cream

2 Tbsp. lemon juice

half a small onion, finely chopped

Combine all ingredients. Mix well.

Lemon-Dijon Fish

June S. Groff   Denver, PA

MAKES: **4 SERVINGS**
PREP. TIME: **10 MINUTES**
COOKING TIME: **3 HOURS**
IDEAL SLOW COOKER SIZE: **2-QUART**

1½ lbs. orange roughy fillets
2 Tbsp. Dijon mustard
3 Tbsp. butter, melted
1 tsp. Worcestershire sauce
1 Tbsp. lemon juice

1. Cut fillets to fit in slow cooker.
2. In a bowl, mix remaining ingredients together. Pour sauce over fish. (If you have to stack the fish, spoon a portion of the sauce over the first layer of fish before adding the second layer.)
3. Cover and cook on Low 3 hours, or until fish flakes easily but is not dry or overcooked.

Herb Potato-Fish Bake

Barbara Sparks   Glen Burnie, MD

MAKES: **4 SERVINGS**
PREP. TIME: **20 MINUTES**
COOKING TIME: **1–2 HOURS**
IDEAL SLOW COOKER SIZE: **4-QUART**

10¾-oz. can cream of celery soup
½ cup water
1-lb. perch fillet, fresh *or* thawed
2 cups cooked, diced potatoes, drained
¼ cup grated Parmesan cheese
1 Tbsp. chopped parsley
½ tsp. salt
½ tsp. dried basil
¼ tsp. dried oregano

1. Combine soup and water. Pour half in slow cooker. Spread fillet on top. Place potatoes on fillet. Pour remaining soup mix over top.
2. Combine cheese and herbs. Sprinkle over ingredients in slow cooker.
3. Cover. Cook on High 1–2 hours, being careful not to overcook fish.

Buy dried herbs and spices in small amounts because they lose their flavor over time.

Herbed Flounder

Dorothy VanDeest Memphis, TX

MAKES: **6 SERVINGS**
PREP. TIME: **5 MINUTES**
COOKING TIME: **3–4 HOURS**
IDEAL SLOW COOKER SIZE: **6-QUART OVAL**

2 lbs. flounder fillets, fresh *or* frozen

½ tsp. salt

¾ cup chicken broth

2 Tbsp. lemon juice

2 Tbsp. dried chives

2 Tbsp. dried minced onion

½–1 tsp. leaf marjoram

4 Tbsp. chopped fresh parsley

1. Wipe fish as dry as possible. Cut fish into portions to fit slow cooker.
2. Sprinkle with salt.
3. Combine broth and lemon juice. Stir in remaining ingredients.
4. Place a meat rack in the slow cooker. Lay fish on rack. Pour liquid mixture over each portion.
5. Cover. Cook on High 3–4 hours.

Per Serving: 160 calories (20 calories from fat), 2.5g total fat (0.5 saturated, 0g trans), 75mg cholesterol, 2590mg sodium, 5g total carbohydrate (0.5g fiber, 2g sugar), 29g protein, 8%DV vitamin A, 10%DV vitamin C, 6%DV calcium, 4%DV iron.

Fish Feast

Anne Townsend Albuquerque, NM

MAKES: **8 SERVINGS**
PREP. TIME: **10 MINUTES**
COOKING TIME: **2–3 HOURS**
IDEAL SLOW COOKER SIZE: **6-QUART OVAL**

3 lbs. red snapper fillets

1 Tbsp. garlic, minced

1 large onion, sliced

1 green bell pepper, cut in 1-inch pieces

2 unpeeled zucchini, sliced

14-oz. can low-sodium diced tomatoes

½ tsp. dried basil

½ tsp. dried oregano

¼ tsp. salt

¼ tsp. black pepper

¼ cup dry white wine *or* white grape juice

1. Rinse snapper and pat dry. Place in slow cooker sprayed with non-fat cooking spray.
2. Mix remaining ingredients together and pour over fish.
3. Cover. Cook on High 2–3 hours, being careful not to overcook the fish.

Per Serving: 200 calories (25 calories from fat), 2.5g total fat (0.5g saturated, 0g trans), 65mg cholesterol, 260mg sodium, 7g total carbohydrate (2g fiber, 3g sugar), 36g protein, 4%DV vitamin A, 20%DV vitamin C, 8%DV calcium, 6%DV iron.

Tips:

1. Red snapper can be pricey. You may substitute a sturdy white fish.

2. Serve in a bowl; the Feast is juicy. Or serve as a topping for rice.

Company Seafood Pasta

Jennifer Yoder Sommers   Harrisonburg, VA

MAKES: **4–6 SERVINGS**
PREP. TIME: **15 MINUTES**
COOKING TIME: **1–2 HOURS**
IDEAL SLOW COOKER SIZE: **4-QUART**

2 cups sour cream

3 cups shredded Monterey Jack cheese

2 Tbsp. butter, melted

½ lb. crabmeat *or* imitation flaked crabmeat

⅛ tsp. pepper

½ lb. bay scallops, lightly cooked

1 lb. medium shrimp, cooked and peeled

1. Combine sour cream, cheese, and butter in slow cooker.
2. Stir in remaining ingredients.
3. Cover. Cook on Low 1–2 hours.
4. Serve immediately over linguine. Garnish with fresh parsley.

Spaghetti Sauce with Crab

Dawn Day   Westminster, CA

MAKES: **4–6 SERVINGS**
PREP. TIME: **15 MINUTES**
COOKING TIME: **4–6 HOURS**
IDEAL SLOW COOKER SIZE: **2–3-QUART**

1 medium onion, chopped

½ lb. fresh mushrooms, sliced

2 12-oz. cans low-sodium tomato sauce, *or* 1 12-oz. can low-sodium tomato sauce and 1 12-oz. can low-sodium chopped tomatoes

6-oz. can tomato paste

½ tsp. garlic powder

½ tsp. dried basil

½ tsp. dried oregano

½ tsp. salt

1 lb. crabmeat

16 ozs. angel-hair pasta, cooked

1. Sauté onions and mushrooms in nonstick skillet over low heat. When wilted, place in slow cooker.
2. Add tomato sauce, tomato paste, and seasonings. Stir in crab.
3. Cover. Cook on Low 4–6 hours.
4. Serve over angel-hair pasta.

Per Serving: 550 calories (45 calories from fat), 5g total fat (0g saturated, 0g trans), 80mg cholesterol, 1710mg sodium, 88g total carbohydrate (9g fiber, 12g sugar), 42g protein, 20%DV vitamin A, 30%DV vitamin C, 15%DV calcium, 35%DV iron.

Date all containers that you put in the freezer so you're sure to use the oldest food first.

Crockpot Shrimp Marinara

Judy Miles Centreville, MD

MAKES: **6 SERVINGS**
PREP. TIME: **15 MINUTES**
COOKING TIME: **6¾–7¾ HOURS**
IDEAL SLOW COOKER SIZE: **3½-QUART**

16-oz. can low-sodium tomatoes, cut up

2 Tbsp. minced parsley

1 clove garlic, minced

½ tsp. dried basil

½ tsp. salt

¼ tsp. black pepper

1 tsp. dried oregano

6-oz. can tomato paste

½ tsp. seasoned salt

1 lb. shrimp, cooked and shelled

3 cups spaghetti

grated Parmesan cheese

1. Combine tomatoes, parsley, garlic, basil, salt, pepper, oregano, tomato paste, and seasoned salt in slow cooker.
2. Cover. Cook on Low 6–7 hours.
3. Stir shrimp into sauce.
4. Cover. Cook on High 10–15 minutes.
5. Serve over cooked spaghetti. Top with Parmesan cheese.

Per Serving: 210 calories (15 calories from fat), 1.5g total fat (0g saturated, 0g trans), 145mg cholesterol, 720mg sodium, 29g total carbohydrate (4g fiber, 4g sugar), 21g protein, 10%DV vitamin A, 10%DV vitamin C, 10%DV calcium, 25%DV iron.

Chicken and Shrimp Casserole

Vera Schmucker Goshen, IN

MAKES: **6 SERVINGS**
PREP. TIME: **15–20 MINUTES**
COOKING TIME: **3–8 HOURS**
IDEAL SLOW COOKER SIZE: **5-QUART**

1¼ cups rice, uncooked

2 Tbsp. butter, melted

3 cups fat-free, low-sodium chicken broth

1 cup water

3 cups cut-up, cooked skinless chicken breast

2 4-oz. cans sliced mushrooms, drained

⅓ cup light soy sauce

12-oz. pkg. shelled frozen shrimp

8 green onions, chopped, 2 Tbsp. reserved

⅔ cup slivered almonds

1. Combine rice and butter in slow cooker. Stir to coat rice well.
2. Add remaining ingredients except almonds and 2 Tbsp. green onions.
3. Cover. Cook on Low 6–8 hours, or on High 3–4 hours, until rice is tender.
4. Sprinkle almonds and green onions over top before serving.

Per Serving: 410 calories (130 calories from fat), 15g total fat (3.5g saturated, 0g trans), 150mg cholesterol, 850mg sodium, 26g total carbohydrate (5g fiber, 10g sugar), 42g protein, 0%DV vitamin A, 10%DV vitamin C, 15%DV calcium, 25%DV iron.

Variation: *If your diet allows, add ½ tsp. salt to Step 2.*

Shrimp Jambalaya

Karen Ashworth   Duenweg, MO

MAKES: **8 SERVINGS**
PREP. TIME: **15 MINUTES**
COOKING TIME: **2¼ HOURS**
IDEAL SLOW COOKER SIZE: **5-QUART**

2 Tbsp. margarine

2 medium onions, chopped

2 green bell peppers, chopped

3 ribs celery, chopped

1 cup chopped, cooked lean ham

2 garlic cloves, chopped

1½ cups minute rice, uncooked

1½ cups fat-free low sodium beef broth

28-oz. can low-sodium chopped tomatoes

2 Tbsp. chopped parsley, fresh *or* dried

1 tsp. dried basil

½ tsp. dried thyme

¼ tsp. black pepper

⅛ tsp. cayenne pepper

1 lb. shelled, deveined, medium-sized shrimp

1 Tbsp. chopped parsley for garnish

1. One-half hour before assembling recipe, melt margarine in slow cooker set on High. Add onions, peppers, celery, ham, and garlic. Cook 30 minutes.
2. Add rice. Cover and cook 15 minutes.
3. Add broth, tomatoes, 2 Tbsp. parsley, and remaining seasonings. Cover and cook on High 1 hour.
4. Add shrimp. Cook on High 30 minutes, or until liquid is absorbed.
5. Garnish with 1 Tbsp. parsley.

Per Serving: 160 calories (35 calories from fat), 4g total fat (1g saturated, 0g trans), 15mg cholesterol, 350mg sodium, 23g total carbohydrate (3g fiber, 5g sugar), 9g protein, 10%DV vitamin A, 30%DV vitamin C, 8%DV calcium, 6%DV iron.

Variation: *If you wish, and your diet allows, you may add ½ tsp. salt to Step 3.*

Chicken and Shrimp Jambalaya

Doris M. Coyle-Zipp   South Ozone Park, NY

MAKES: **5–6 SERVINGS**
PREP. TIME: **15 MINUTES**
COOKING TIME: **2¼–3¾ HOURS**
IDEAL SLOW COOKER SIZE: **4-QUART**

3½–4-lb. roasting chicken, cut up

3 onions, diced

1 carrot, sliced

3–4 garlic cloves, minced

1 tsp. dried oregano

1 tsp. dried basil

1 tsp. salt

⅛ tsp. white pepper

14-oz. can crushed tomatoes

1 lb. shelled raw shrimp

2 cups rice, cooked

1. Combine all ingredients except shrimp and rice in slow cooker.
2. Cover. Cook on Low 2–3½ hours, or until chicken is tender.
3. Add shrimp and rice.
4. Cover. Cook on High 15–20 minutes, or until shrimp are done.

Seafood Main Dishes

Shrimp Creole

Carol Findling   Princeton, IL

MAKES: **8–10 SERVINGS**
PREP TIME: **30 MINUTES**
COOKING TIME: **6–8 HOURS**
IDEAL SLOW COOKER SIZE: **4–5-QUART**

½ cup butter

⅓ cup flour

1¾ cups sliced onions

1 cup diced green peppers

1 cup diced celery

1½ large carrots, shredded

2¾-lb. can tomatoes

¾ cup water

½ tsp. dried thyme

1 garlic clove, minced

pinch of rosemary

1 Tbsp. sugar

3 bay leaves

1 Tbsp. Worcestershire sauce

1 Tbsp. salt

⅛ tsp. dried oregano

2 lbs. shelled shrimp, deveined

1. Melt butter in skillet. Add flour and brown, stirring constantly. Add onions, green peppers, celery, and carrots. Cook 5–10 minutes. Transfer to slow cooker.
2. Add remaining ingredients, except shrimp, and stir well.
3. Cover. Cook on Low 6–8 hours.
4. Add shrimp during last hour.
5. Serve over rice.

Seafood Gumbo

Barbara Katrine Rose   Woodbridge, VA

MAKES: **10 SERVINGS**
PREP. TIME: **45 MINUTES**
COOKING TIME: **3–4 HOURS**
IDEAL SLOW COOKER SIZE: **4–5-QUART**

1 lb. okra, sliced

2 Tbsp. butter, melted

¼ cup butter, melted

¼ cup flour

1 bunch green onions, sliced

½ cup chopped celery

2 garlic cloves, minced

16-oz. can tomatoes and juice

1 bay leaf

1 Tbsp. chopped fresh parsley

1 fresh thyme sprig

1½ tsp. salt

½–1 tsp. red pepper

3–5 cups water, depending upon the consistency you like

1 lb. peeled and deveined fresh shrimp

½ lb. fresh crabmeat

1. Sauté okra in 2 Tbsp. butter until okra is lightly browned. Transfer to slow cooker.
2. Combine remaining butter and flour in skillet. Cook over medium heat, stirring constantly until roux is the color of chocolate, 20–25 minutes. Stir in green onions, celery, and garlic. Cook until vegetables are tender. Add to slow cooker. Gently stir in remaining ingredients.
3. Cover. Cook on High 3–4 hours.
4. Serve over rice.

Seafood Medley

Susan Alexander   Baltimore, MD

MAKES: **10–12 SERVINGS**
PREP. TIME: **20 MINUTES**
COOKING TIME: **3–4 HOURS**
IDEAL SLOW COOKER SIZE: **4-QUART**

1 lb. shrimp, peeled and deveined

1 lb. crabmeat

1 lb. bay scallops

2 10¾-oz. cans cream of celery soup

2 soup cans milk

2 Tbsp. butter, melted

1 tsp. Old Bay seasoning

¼–½ tsp. salt

¼ tsp. pepper

1. Layer shrimp, crab, and scallops in slow cooker.
2. Combine soup and milk. Pour over seafood.
3. Mix together butter and spices and pour over top.
4. Cover. Cook on Low 3–4 hours.
5. Serve over rice or noodles.

Be careful about adding liquids to food in a slow cooker. Foods have natural juices in them, and unlike oven cooking which is dry, food juices remain in the slow cooker as the food cooks.

Curried Shrimp

Charlotte Shaffer   East Earl, PA

MAKES: **4–5 SERVINGS**
PREP. TIME: **5–10 MINUTES**
COOKING TIME: **4–6 HOURS**
IDEAL SLOW COOKER SIZE: **3-QUART**

1 small onion, chopped

2 cups cooked shrimp

1 tsp. curry powder

10¾-oz. can cream of mushroom soup

1 cup sour cream

1. Combine all ingredients except sour cream in slow cooker.
2. Cover. Cook on Low 2–3 hours.
3. Ten minutes before serving, stir in sour cream.
4. Serve over rice or puff pastry.

Variation: *Add another ½ tsp. curry for some added flavor.*

Asian Shrimp Casserole

Sharon Wantland   Menomonee Falls, WI

MAKES: **10 SERVINGS**
PREP. TIME: **10–15 MINUTES**
COOKING TIME: **45 MINUTES**
IDEAL SLOW COOKER SIZE: **5-QUART**

4 cups rice, cooked

2 cups cooked *or* canned shrimp

1 cup cooked *or* canned chicken

1-lb. can (2 cups) Chinese vegetables

10¾-oz. can cream of celery soup

½ cup milk

½ cup chopped green peppers

1 Tbsp. soy sauce

can of Chinese noodles

1. Combine all ingredients except noodles in slow cooker.
2. Cover. Cook on Low 45 minutes.
3. Top with noodles just before serving.

Salmon Cheese Casserole

Light

Wanda S. Curtin Bradenton, FL

MAKES: **6 SERVINGS**
PREP. TIME: **10 MINUTES**
COOKING TIME: **2½–3½ HOURS**
IDEAL SLOW COOKER SIZE: **2-QUART**

14¾-oz. can salmon with liquid
4-oz. can mushrooms, drained
1½ cups bread crumbs
⅓ cup eggbeaters
1 cup shredded fat-free cheese
1 Tbsp. lemon juice
1 Tbsp. minced onion

1. Flake fish in bowl, removing bones. Stir in remaining ingredients. Pour into lightly greased slow cooker.
2. Cover. Cook on Low 2½–3½ hours.

Per Serving: 150 calories (40 calories from fat), 4g total fat (1g saturated, 0g trans), 70mg cholesterol, 650mg sodium, 9g total carbohydrate (1g fiber, 1g sugar), 19g protein, 0%DV vitamin A, 0%DV vitamin C, 20%DV calcium, 6%DV iron.

Salmon Soufflé

Betty B. Dennison Grove City, PA • *Anne Townsend* Albuquerque, NM

MAKES: **4 SERVINGS**
PREP. TIME: **5 MINUTES**
COOKING TIME: **2–3 HOURS**
IDEAL SLOW COOKER SIZE: **2–3-QUART**

15-oz. can salmon, drained and flaked
2 eggs, beaten well
2 cups seasoned croutons
1 cup shredded cheddar cheese
2 chicken bouillon cubes
1 cup boiling water
¼ tsp. dry mustard, *optional*

1. Grease the interior of your cooker with nonstick cooking spray.
2. Combine salmon, eggs, croutons, and cheese in the slow cooker.
3. Dissolve bouillon cubes in boiling water in a small bowl. Add mustard, if you wish, and stir. Pour over salmon mixture and stir together lightly.
4. Cover and cook on High 2–3 hours, or until mixture appears to be set. Allow to stand 15 minutes before serving.

Asian-Style Tuna

Lizzie Ann Yoder Hartville, OH

PICTURED
ON PAGE
167

MAKES: **3 SERVINGS**
PREP. TIME: **15 MINUTES**
COOKING TIME: **1 HOUR**
IDEAL SLOW COOKER SIZE: **2-QUART**

half a green bell pepper, cut in ¼-inch strips

1 small onion, thinly sliced

2 tsp. olive oil

⅓ cup unsweetened pineapple juice

1½ tsp. cornstarch

⅔ cup canned unsweetened pineapple chunks, drained

1 Tbsp. sugar (scant)

1 Tbsp. vinegar

6-oz. can solid, water-packed tuna, drained and flaked

⅛ tsp. black pepper

dash of Tabasco sauce

1. Cook green pepper and onion with oil in a skillet over medium heat, leaving the vegetables slightly crisp.
2. Mix pineapple juice with cornstarch. Add to green pepper mixture.
3. Cook, stirring gently until thickened.
4. Add remaining ingredients. Pour into slow cooker.
5. Cover. Cook on Low 1 hour.

Per Serving: 170 calories (35 calories from fat), 3.5g total fat (0.5g saturated, 0g trans), 20mg cholesterol, 210mg sodium, 18g total carbohydrate (2g fiber, 15g sugar), 17g protein, 0%DV vitamin A, 20%DV vitamin C, 2%DV calcium, 8%DV iron.

Tip: *This is tasty served over brown rice.*

Tuna Barbecue

Esther Martin Ephrata, PA

MAKES: **4 SERVINGS**
PREP. TIME: **10 MINUTES**
COOKING TIME: **4–10 HOURS**
IDEAL SLOW COOKER SIZE: **3–4-QUART**

12-oz. can tuna, drained

2 cups tomato juice

1 medium green pepper, finely chopped

2 Tbsp. onion flakes

2 Tbsp. Worcestershire sauce

3 Tbsp. vinegar

2 Tbsp. sugar

1 Tbsp. prepared mustard

1 rib celery, chopped

dash chili powder

½ tsp. cinnamon

dash of hot sauce, *optional*

1. Combine all ingredients in slow cooker.
2. Cover. Cook on Low 8–10 hours, or on High 4–5 hours. If mixture becomes too dry while cooking, add ½ cup tomato juice.
3. Serve on buns.

Tuna Salad Casserole

Charlotte Fry St. Charles, MO • *Esther Becker* Gordonville, PA

MAKES: **4 SERVINGS**
PREP. TIME: **10 MINUTES**
COOKING TIME: **5–8 HOURS**
IDEAL SLOW COOKER SIZE: **4-QUART**

2 7-oz. cans tuna

10¾-oz. can cream of celery soup

3 hard-boiled eggs, chopped

½ to 1½ cups diced celery

½ cup diced onions

½ cup mayonnaise

¼ tsp. ground pepper

1½ cups crushed potato chips

1. Combine all ingredients except ¼ cup potato chips in slow cooker. Top with remaining chips.
2. Cover. Cook on Low 5–8 hours.

Tuna and Vegetables Noodle Casserole

Leona Miller Millersburg, OH

MAKES: **6 SERVINGS**
PREP. TIME: **20 MINUTES**
COOKING TIME: **3–9 HOURS**
IDEAL SLOW COOKER SIZE: **4-QUART**

2 6½-oz. cans water-packed tuna, drained

2 10½-oz. cans cream of mushroom soup

1 cup milk

2 Tbsp. dried parsley

10-oz. pkg. frozen mixed vegetables, thawed

10-oz. pkg. noodles, cooked and drained

½ cup toasted sliced almonds

1. Combine tuna, soup, milk, parsley, and vegetables. Fold in noodles. Pour into greased slow cooker. Top with almonds.
2. Cover. Cook on Low 7–9 hours, or on High 3–4 hours.

Some new slow cookers cook hotter and faster than older models. So get to know your slow cooker. I suggest a range of cooking times for many of the recipes since cookers vary. When you've found the right length of time for a recipe done in your cooker, note that in your cookbook.

Tuna Noodle Casserole

Ruth Hofstetter   Versailles, Missouri

MAKES: **8 SERVINGS**
PREP. TIME: **10 MINUTES**
COOKING TIME: **2–8 HOURS**
IDEAL SLOW COOKER SIZE: **4-QUART**

2½ cups dry noodles

1 tsp. salt

½ cup finely chopped onion

6- or 12-oz. can tuna, according to your taste preference

10¾-oz. can cream of mushroom soup

half a soup can of water

¼ cup almonds, *optional*

½ cup shredded Swiss *or* sharp cheddar cheese

1 cup frozen peas

1. Combine all ingredients in slow cooker, except peas.
2. Cover. Cook on High 2–3 hours, or on Low 6–8 hours, stirring occasionally.
3. Twenty minutes before end of cooking time, stir in peas and reduce heat to Low if cooking on High.

Tuna Loaf

Tina Goss   Duenweg, MO

MAKES: **4 SERVINGS**
PREP. TIME: **5 MINUTES**
COOKING TIME: **1 HOUR**
IDEAL SLOW COOKER SIZE: **2-QUART**

10¾-oz. can cream of mushroom soup, *divided*

¾ cup milk, *divided*

2 eggs, beaten

2 cups dry stuffing mix

12-oz. can tuna, drained and flaked

1. Place ⅔ of the undiluted soup and ½ cup of the milk in a small saucepan. Blend together; then set aside.
2. Grease the interior of the slow cooker with nonstick cooking spray. Mix the rest of the ingredients together in the slow cooker.
3. Cover and cook on High for 1 hour. Allow to stand for 15 minutes before serving.
4. Meanwhile, heat the reserved soup and milk in the saucepan. Serve over the cooked tuna as a sauce.

Variation: *Add ½ tsp. salt and ¼ tsp. pepper to Step 2.*

Pasta, Meatless, and Other Main Dishes

Convenient Slow Cooker Lasagna

Rachel Yoder Middlebury, IN

MAKES: **6–8 SERVINGS**
PREP. TIME: **30–45 MINUTES**
COOKING TIME: **4 HOURS**
IDEAL SLOW COOKER SIZE: **6-QUART**

PICTURED
ON PAGE
501

1 lb. ground beef

2 29-oz. cans tomato sauce

8-oz. pkg. lasagna noodles, uncooked

4 cups shredded mozzarella cheese

1½ cups cottage cheese

1. Spray the interior of the cooker with nonstick cooking spray.
2. Brown the ground beef in a large nonstick skillet. Drain off drippings.
3. Stir in tomato sauce. Mix well.
4. Spread one-fourth of the meat sauce on the bottom of the slow cooker.
5. Arrange one-third of the uncooked noodles over the sauce. (I usually break them up so they fit better.)
6. Combine the cheeses in a bowl. Spoon one-third of the cheeses over the noodles.
7. Repeat these layers twice.
8. Top with remaining sauce.
9. Cover and cook on Low 4 hours.

Variations:

1. Add 1 chopped onion to the ground beef in Step 2.

2. Add 1 tsp. salt to the tomato sauce and beef in Step 3.

3. Add ½ cup grated Parmesan cheese to the mozzarella and cottage cheeses in Step 6.

4. Add ½ cup additional shredded mozzarella cheese to the top of the lasagna 5 minutes before serving.

Spicy Lasagna

Kathy Hertzler Lancaster, PA • *L. Jean Moore* Pendleton, IN
Mary Ellen Musser Reinholds, PA

MAKES: **6 SERVINGS**
PREP. TIME: **20 MINUTES**
COOKING TIME: **3–9 HOURS**
IDEAL SLOW COOKER SIZE: **4–5-QUART**

10-oz. pkg. lasagna noodles, broken into bite-sized
   pieces, cooked
1 lb. ground beef, browned
½ lb. Italian sausage, sliced and browned
1 onion, chopped
1 clove garlic, minced
12 oz. mozzarella cheese, shredded
12 oz. cottage *or* ricotta cheese
16-oz. can tomato sauce
1 tsp. dried basil
½ tsp. dried oregano
1½ Tbsp. dried parsley flakes
½ tsp. pepper
1½ tsp. salt

1. Combine all ingredients in greased slow
   cooker.
2. Cover. Cook on Low 7–9 hours, or on High
   3–5 hours.

Variation: *Replace mix of ground beef and
sausage with 1½ lbs. ground beef.*

Lasagna with Mushrooms

Violette Harris Denney Carrollton, GA

MAKES: **8 SERVINGS**
PREP. TIME: **20 MINUTES**
COOKING TIME: **5 HOURS**
IDEAL SLOW COOKER SIZE: **4–5-QUART**

8 lasagna noodles, uncooked
1 lb. ground beef
1 tsp. Italian seasoning
28-oz. jar spaghetti sauce
⅓ cup water
4-oz. can sliced mushrooms
15 oz. ricotta cheese
2 cups shredded mozzarella cheese

1. Break noodles. Place half in bottom of
   greased slow cooker.
2. Brown ground beef in saucepan. Drain.
   Stir in Italian seasoning. Spread half over
   noodles in slow cooker.
3. Layer half of sauce and water, half of
   mushrooms, half of ricotta cheese, and
   half of mozzarella cheese over beef. Repeat
   layers.
4. Cover. Cook on Low 5 hours.

Pasta, Meatless, and Other Main Dishes

Egg Noodle Lasagna

Anna Stoltzfus Honey Brook, PA

MAKES: **12–16 SERVINGS**
PREP. TIME: **25 MINUTES**
COOKING TIME: **4 HOURS**
IDEAL SLOW COOKER SIZE: **5-QUART**

6½ cups wide egg noodles, cooked

3 Tbsp. butter *or* margarine

2¼ cups spaghetti sauce

1½ lbs. ground beef, browned

6 ozs. Velveeta cheese, cubed

3 cups shredded mozzarella cheese

1. Toss butter with hot noodles.
2. Spread one-fourth of spaghetti sauce in slow cooker. Layer with one-third of noodles, beef, and cheeses. Repeat layers 2 more times.
3. Cover. Cook on Low 4 hours, or until cheese is melted.

Meat-Free Lasagna

Rosemarie Fitzgerald Gibsonia, PA

MAKES: **8 SERVINGS**
PREP. TIME: **15 MINUTES**
COOKING TIME: **5 HOURS**
IDEAL SLOW COOKER SIZE: **4–5-QUART**

4½ cups fat-free, low-sodium meatless spaghetti sauce

½ cup water

16-oz. container fat-free ricotta cheese

2 cups shredded part-skim mozzarella cheese, *divided*

¾ cup grated Parmesan cheese, *divided*

1 egg

2 tsp. minced garlic

1 tsp. Italian seasoning

8-oz. box no-cook lasagna noodles

1. Mix spaghetti sauce and ½ cup water in a bowl.
2. In a separate bowl, mix ricotta, 1½ cups mozzarella cheese, ½ cup Parmesan cheese, egg, garlic, and seasoning.
3. Spread ¼ of the sauce mixture in bottom of slow cooker. Top with ⅓ of the noodles, breaking if needed to fit.
4. Spread with ⅓ of the cheese mixture, making sure noodles are covered.
5. Repeat layers twice more.
6. Spread with remaining sauce.
7. Cover. Cook on Low 5 hours.
8. Sprinkle with remaining cheeses. Cover. Let stand 10 minutes to allow cheeses to melt.

Per Serving: 360 calories (90 calories from fat),10g total fat (4.5g saturated, 0g trans), 40mg cholesterol, 870mg sodium, 39g total carbohydrate (6g fiber, 10g sugar), 25g protein, 0%DV vitamin A, 0%DV vitamin C, 50%DV calcium, 10%DV iron.

Slow Cooker Almost Lasagna

Jeanette Oberholtzer Manheim, PA

MAKES: **8–10 SERVINGS**
PREP. TIME: **40 MINUTES**
COOKING TIME: **4–6 HOURS**
IDEAL SLOW COOKER SIZE: **6-QUART**

1 box rotini *or* ziti, cooked

2 Tbsp. olive oil

2 28-oz. jars pasta sauce with tomato chunks

2 cups tomato juice

½ lb. ground beef

½ lb. bulk sausage, crumbled, *or* links cut into ¼-inch slices

1 cup Parmesan cheese

½ cup Italian bread crumbs

1 egg

2 cups mozzarella cheese, *divided*

2 cups ricotta cheese

2 eggs

1 cup Parmesan cheese

1½ tsp. parsley flakes

¾ tsp. salt

¼ tsp. pepper

1. In large bowl, toss pasta with olive oil. Add pasta sauce and tomato juice and mix well. Set aside.
2. Brown beef and sausage together in skillet. Drain.
3. Add 1 cup Parmesan cheese, bread crumbs, 1 egg, and 1 cup mozzarella cheese to meat. Set aside.
4. In separate bowl, beat together ricotta cheese, 2 eggs, 1 cup Parmesan cheese, parsley, salt, and pepper. Set aside.
5. Pour half of pasta-sauce mixture into slow cooker. Spread entire ricotta mixture over pasta. Top with entire meat-cheese mixture. Cover with remaining pasta-sauce mixture. Sprinkle with remaining 1 cup mozzarella cheese.
6. Cover. Cook on Low 4–6 hours.

Slow Cooker Spaghetti Sauce

Lucille Amos Greensboro, NC • *Julia Lapp* New Holland, PA

MAKES: **6–8 SERVINGS**
PREP. TIME: **15 MINUTES**
COOKING TIME: **7 HOURS**
IDEAL SLOW COOKER SIZE: **4-QUART**

1 lb. ground beef

1 medium onion, chopped

2 14-oz. cans diced tomatoes, with juice

6-oz. can tomato paste

8-oz. can tomato sauce

1 bay leaf

4 garlic cloves, minced

2 tsp. dried oregano

1 tsp. salt

2 tsp. dried basil

1 Tbsp. brown sugar

½–1 tsp. dried thyme

1. Brown meat and onion in saucepan. Drain well. Transfer to slow cooker.
2. Add remaining ingredients.
3. Cover. Cook on Low 7 hours. If the sauce seems too runny, remove lid during last hour of cooking.

Make an alphabetical list of all the spices in your cupboard and tape it inside your cupboard door for easy reference. Arrange your spices in alphabetical order so you can easily locate them.

Easy-Does-It Spaghetti

Rachel Kauffman Alto, MI • *Lois Stoltzfus* Honey Brook, PA
Deb Unternahrer Wayland, IA

MAKES: **8 SERVINGS**
PREP. TIME: **15 MINUTES**
COOKING TIME: **3¼–8¼ HOURS**
IDEAL SLOW COOKER SIZE: **4-QUART**

2 lbs. ground chuck, browned and drained

1 cup chopped onions

2 cloves garlic, minced

2 15-oz. cans tomato sauce

2–3 tsp. Italian seasoning

1½ tsp. salt

¼ tsp. pepper

2 4-oz. cans sliced mushrooms, drained

6 cups tomato juice

16-oz. dry spaghetti, broken into 4–5-inch pieces

grated Parmesan cheese

1. Combine all ingredients except spaghetti and cheese in 4-quart (or larger) slow cooker.
2. Cover. Cook on Low 6–8 hours, or on High 3–5 hours. Turn to High during last 30 minutes and stir in dry spaghetti. (If spaghetti is not fully cooked, continue cooking another 10 minutes, checking to make sure it is not becoming overcooked.)
3. Sprinkle individual servings with Parmesan cheese.

Variation: *Add 1 tsp. dry mustard and ½ tsp. allspice in Step 1.*

Kathy Hertzler Lancaster, PA

Fresh Mushrooms, Spaghetti, and Meat Sauce

Dawn Day Westminster, CA

MAKES: **6–8 SERVINGS**
PREP. TIME: **30 MINUTES**
COOKING TIME: **6 HOURS**
IDEAL SLOW COOKER SIZE: **4-QUART**

1 lb. ground beef

1 Tbsp. oil, if needed

½ lb. mushrooms, sliced

1 medium onion, chopped

3 garlic cloves, minced

½ tsp. dried oregano

½ tsp. salt

¼ cup grated Parmesan *or* Romano cheese

6-oz. can tomato paste

2 15-oz. cans tomato sauce

15-oz. can chopped or crushed tomatoes

1. Brown ground beef in skillet, in oil if needed. Reserve drippings and transfer meat to slow cooker.
2. Sauté mushrooms, onion, and garlic until onions are transparent. Add to slow cooker.
3. Add remaining ingredients to cooker. Mix well.
4. Cover. Cook on Low 6 hours.
5. Serve with pasta and garlic bread.

Note: *This recipe freezes well.*

Chunky Spaghetti Sauce

Patti Boston   Newark, OH

MAKES: **6 CUPS**
PREP. TIME: **15–20 MINUTES**
COOKING TIME: **3½–8 HOURS**
IDEAL SLOW COOKER SIZE: **4-QUART**

1 lb. ground beef, browned and drained
½ lb. bulk sausage, browned and drained
14½-oz. can Italian tomatoes with basil
15-oz. can Italian tomato sauce
1 medium onion, chopped
1 green pepper, chopped
8-oz. can sliced mushrooms
½ cup dry red wine
2 tsp. sugar
1 tsp. minced garlic

1. Combine all ingredients in slow cooker.
2. Cover. Cook on High 3½–4 hours, or on Low 7–8 hours.

Variations:

1. For added texture and zest, add 3 fresh, medium tomatoes, chopped, and 4 large fresh basil leaves, torn. Stir in 1 tsp. salt and ½ tsp. pepper.

2. To any leftover sauce, add chickpeas or kidney beans and serve chili!

Keep hot dishwater in the sink so you can clean up the kitchen as you go and while the food is baking or cooking.

Pasta Sauce with Meat and Veggies

Marla Folkerts   Holland, OH

MAKES: **6 SERVINGS**
PREP. TIME: **10 MINUTES**
COOKING TIME: **7–8 HOURS**
IDEAL SLOW COOKER SIZE: **4-QUART**

½ lb. ground turkey
½ lb. ground beef
1 rib celery, chopped
2 medium carrots, chopped
1 garlic clove, minced
1 medium onion, chopped
28-oz. can diced tomatoes with juice
½ tsp. salt
¼ tsp. dried thyme
6-oz. can tomato paste
⅛ tsp. pepper

1. Combine turkey, beef, celery, carrots, garlic, and onion in slow cooker.
2. Add remaining ingredients. Mix well.
3. Cover. Cook on Low 7–8 hours.
4. Serve over pasta or rice.

Slimmed-Down Spaghetti Sauce

Light *MEATLESS*

Andrea Cunningham Arlington, KS

MAKES: **8 SERVINGS**
PREP. TIME: **15 MINUTES**
COOKING TIME: **6–8 HOURS**
IDEAL SLOW COOKER SIZE: **4-QUART**

2 tsp. olive oil

1 medium onion, finely chopped

6 cloves garlic, minced

56-oz. can low-sodium crushed tomatoes, *or* 7 cups
    fresh, peeled, diced tomatoes

6-oz. can low-sodium tomato paste

2 tsp. dried basil

½ tsp. dried oregano

1 tsp. salt

½ tsp. black pepper

1 Tbsp. sugar

2 Tbsp. chopped fresh parsley

1. Heat oil in a saucepan over medium heat. Add onion and garlic. Sauté until onion becomes very soft (about 10 minutes).
2. Combine all ingredients except parsley in slow cooker.
3. Cover. Cook on Low 6–8 hours.
4. Add parsley. Cook an additional 30 minutes.
5. Serve over cooked noodles.

Per Serving: 110 calories (15 calories from fat), 2g total fat (0g saturated, 0g trans), 0mg cholesterol, 570mg sodium, 22g total carbohydrate (5g fiber, 3g sugar), 4g protein, 30%DV vitamin A, 20%DV vitamin C, 10%DV calcium, 20%DV iron.

Italian Vegetable Pasta Sauce

MEATLESS

Sherril Bieberly Salina, KS

MAKES: **2½ QUARTS SAUCE**
PREP. TIME: **25 MINUTES**
COOKING TIME: **5–18 HOURS**
IDEAL SLOW COOKER SIZE: **4–5-QUART**

3 Tbsp. olive oil

1 cup packed chopped fresh parsley

3 ribs celery, chopped

1 medium onion, chopped

2 garlic cloves, minced

2-inch sprig fresh rosemary, *or* ½ tsp. dried rosemary

2 small fresh sage leaves, *or* ½ tsp. dried sage

32-oz. can tomato sauce

32-oz. can chopped tomatoes

1 small dried hot chili pepper

¼ lb. fresh mushrooms, sliced, *or* 8-oz. can sliced
    mushrooms, drained

1½ tsp. salt

1. Heat oil in skillet. Add parsley, celery, onion, garlic, rosemary, and sage. Sauté until vegetables are tender. Place in slow cooker.
2. Add tomatoes, chili pepper, mushrooms, and salt.
3. Cover. Cook on Low 12–18 hours, or on High 5–6 hours.

Variation: *Add 2 lbs. browned ground beef to olive oil and sautéed vegetables. Continue with recipe.*

Creamy Spaghetti

Kendra Dreps   Liberty, PA

MAKES: **10–12 SERVINGS**
PREP. TIME: **30 MINUTES**
COOKING TIME: **2–4 HOURS**
IDEAL SLOW COOKER SIZE: **4–5-QUART**

1 lb. dry spaghetti

1 lb. ground beef *or* **loose sausage**

1 lb. 10-oz. jar spaghetti sauce, your favorite flavor

1 lb. Velveeta cheese, cubed

10¾-oz. can cream of mushroom soup

1. Cook spaghetti according to package directions. Drain. Then place in a large mixing bowl.
2. In a nonstick skillet, brown ground beef or sausage. Drain off drippings. Then add to cooked spaghetti in the large bowl.
3. Stir remaining ingredients into bowl. Mix together well, and then place in slow cooker.
4. Cook on Low 2-4 hours, or until heated through.

Creamy Spaghetti with Beef and Veggies

Dale Peterson   Rapid City, SD

MAKES: **6 SERVINGS**
PREP. TIME: **25 MINUTES**
COOKING TIME: **4–6 HOURS**
IDEAL SLOW COOKER SIZE: **5-QUART**

1 cup chopped onions

1 cup chopped green peppers

1 Tbsp. butter

28-oz. can tomatoes with juice

4-oz. can mushrooms, chopped and drained

2¼-oz. can sliced ripe olives, drained

2 tsp. dried oregano

1 lb. ground beef, browned and drained

12 oz. spaghetti, cooked and drained

10¾-oz. can cream of mushroom soup

½ cup water

2 cups (8 oz.) shredded cheddar cheese

¼ cup grated Parmesan cheese

1. Sauté onions and green peppers in butter in skillet until tender. Add tomatoes, mushrooms, olives, oregano, and beef. Simmer for 10 minutes. Transfer to slow cooker.
2. Add spaghetti. Mix well.
3. Combine soup and water. Pour over casserole. Sprinkle with cheeses.
4. Cover. Cook on Low 4-6 hours.

Add 3 Tbsp. oil to water before cooking pasta. It keeps it from sticking together.

Pizza in a Pot

Marianne J. Troyer Millersburg, OH

MAKES: **6–8 SERVINGS**
PREP. TIME: **20 MINUTES**
COOKING TIME: **8–9 HOURS**
IDEAL SLOW COOKER SIZE: **4-QUART**

1 lb. bulk Italian sausage, browned and drained

28-oz. can crushed tomatoes

15½-oz. can chili beans

2¼-oz. can sliced black olives, drained

1 medium onion, chopped

1 small green pepper, chopped

2 garlic cloves, minced

¼ cup grated Parmesan cheese

1 Tbsp. quick-cooking tapioca

1 Tbsp. dried basil

1 bay leaf

1 tsp. salt

1. Combine all ingredients in slow cooker except pasta and mozzarella cheese.
2. Cover. Cook on Low 8–9 hours.
3. Discard bay leaf. Stir well.
4. Serve over pasta. Top with mozzarella cheese.

Cheesy Slow Cooker Pizza

Marla Folkerts Holland, OH • *Ruth Ann Swartzendruber* Hydro, OK
Arlene Wiens Newton, KS

MAKES: **6–8 SERVINGS**
PREP. TIME: **20 MINUTES**
COOKING TIME: **3–4 HOURS**
IDEAL SLOW COOKER SIZE: **4-QUART**

1½ lbs. ground beef *or* bulk Italian sausage

1 medium onion, chopped

1 green pepper, chopped

half a box rigatoni, cooked

7-oz. jar sliced mushrooms, drained

3 oz. sliced pepperoni

16-oz. jar pizza sauce

10 oz. mozzarella cheese, shredded

10 oz. cheddar cheese, shredded

1. Brown ground beef and onions in saucepan. Drain.
2. Layer half of each of the following, in the order given, in slow cooker: ground beef and onions, green pepper, noodles, mushrooms, pepperoni, pizza sauce, cheddar cheese, and mozzarella cheese. Repeat layers.
3. Cover. Cook on Low 3–4 hours.

Tip: *Keep rigatoni covered with sauce so they don't become dry and crunchy.*

Variation: *Add a 10¾-oz. can cream of mushroom soup to the mix, putting half of it in as a layer after the first time the noodles appear, and the other half after the second layer of noodles.*

Dorothy Horst Tiskilwa, IL

Herby Slow Cooker Pizza

Wilma J. Haberkamp Fairbank, IA

MAKES: **8 SERVINGS**
PREP. TIME: **20 MINUTES**
COOKING TIME: **1–2½ HOURS**
IDEAL SLOW COOKER SIZE: **6-QUART**

1 lb. extra-lean ground beef

2 small onions, chopped

14-oz. can fat-free pizza sauce

14-oz. can low-fat, low-sodium spaghetti sauce

1 tsp. garlic powder

1¼ tsp. black pepper

1 tsp. dried oregano

¼ tsp. rubbed sage

12 ozs. dry kluski noodles

1. Brown ground beef and onions in nonstick skillet.
2. In skillet, or in a large bowl, mix together browned meat and onions, pizza sauce, spaghetti sauce, and seasonings and herbs.
3. Boil noodles according to directions on package until tender. Drain.
4. Layer half of beef sauce in bottom of cooker. Spoon in noodles. Top with remaining beef sauce.
5. Cook on Low 1–1½ hours if ingredients are hot when placed in cooker. If the sauce and noodles are at room temperature or have just been refrigerated, cook on High for 2–2½ hours.

Per Serving: 320 calories (70 calories from fat), 8g total fat (2.5g saturated, 0g trans), 65mg cholesterol, 610mg sodium, 42g total carbohydrate (3g fiber, 6g sugar), 20g protein, 8%DV vitamin A, 10%DV vitamin C, 4%DV calcium, 20%DV iron.

Macaroni and Cheese

Cynthia Morris Grottoes, VA
Audrey L. Kneer Williamsfield, IL
Jennifer A. Crouse Mt. Crawford, VA
Esther S. Martin Ephrata, PA • *Virginia Eberly* Loysville, PA

MAKES: **4–5 SERVINGS**
PREP. TIME: **5 MINUTES**
COOKING TIME: **3 HOURS**
IDEAL SLOW COOKER SIZE: **3-QUART**

1–3 Tbsp. butter, melted, depending upon how rich you'd like the dish to be

1½ cups macaroni, uncooked

1 quart milk

8–12 ozs. shredded sharp cheddar cheese, *or* cubed Velveeta cheese (not the low-fat variety)

½–1 tsp. salt, depending upon your taste and dietary preferences

¼ tsp. pepper

1. Stir all ingredients together in slow cooker.
2. Cover and cook on Low 3 hours.

Variations:

1. Add 2–3 Tbsp. onion, finely chopped, and 1 tsp. salt to Step 1.

Dale Peterson Rapid City, SD

2. Instead of macaroni, use ½ lb. uncooked medium noodles.

Vera Martin East Earl, PA • *Lucille Martin* Barnett, MO

Lotsa-Cheese Macaroni and Cheese

Renee Baum Chambersburg, PA

MAKES: **10 SERVINGS**
PREP. TIME: **15 MINUTES**
COOKING TIME: **3 HOURS**
IDEAL SLOW COOKER SIZE: **3-QUART**

1 lb. dry macaroni

1 lb. Velveeta cheese, cubed

8 ozs. extra-sharp cheddar cheese, shredded

1 quart milk

1 stick (½ cup) butter, cut into small chunks

1. Follow package instructions for preparing the macaroni, but cook the macaroni only half the amount of time as called for. Drain. Pour macaroni into slow cooker.
2. Add remaining ingredients and stir together well.
3. Cover and cook on High 3 hours, stirring occasionally.

Macaroni and Cheddar/ Parmesan Cheese

Sherry L. Lapp Lancaster, PA

MAKES: **8 SERVINGS**
PREP. TIME: **15 MINUTES**
COOKING TIME: **3 HOURS**
IDEAL SLOW COOKER SIZE: **4-QUART**

8-oz. pkg. elbow macaroni, cooked al dente

13-oz. can fat-free evaporated milk

1 cup fat-free milk

2 large eggs, slightly beaten

4 cups shredded fat-free sharp cheddar cheese, *divided*

¼ tsp. salt

⅛ tsp. white pepper

¼ cup grated fat-free Parmesan cheese

1. Spray inside of cooker with nonfat cooking spray. Then, in cooker, combine lightly cooked macaroni, evaporated milk, milk, eggs, 3 cups cheddar cheese, salt, and pepper.
2. Top with remaining cheddar and Parmesan cheeses.
3. Cover. Cook on Low 3 hours.

Per Serving: 190 calories (15 calories from fat), 1.5g total fat (0g saturated, 0g trans), 60mg cholesterol, 740mg sodium, 17g total carbohydrate (0g fiber, 7g sugar), 26g protein, 10%DV vitamin A, 0%DV vitamin C, 70%DV calcium, 2%DV iron.

Allow cooked pasta dishes, especially those with cheese, as well as egg dishes, to stand for 10–15 minutes before serving, so that they can absorb their juices and firm up.

Two-Cheeses Macaroni

Mary Stauffer Ephrata, PA
Ruth Ann Bender Cochranville, PA
Esther Burkholder Millerstown, PA

MAKES: **6 SERVINGS**
PREP. TIME: **8–10 MINUTES**
COOKING TIME: **2½ HOURS**
IDEAL SLOW COOKER SIZE: **4–5-QUART**

1 stick (½ cup) butter, cut in pieces
2 cups macaroni, uncooked
2 cups shredded sharp cheese, *divided*
24 ozs. small-curd cottage cheese
2½ cups boiling water

1. Place butter in bottom of slow cooker. Add uncooked macaroni, 1½ cups shredded cheese, and cottage cheese. Stir together until well mixed.
2. Pour boiling water over everything. Do not stir.
3. Cover and cook on High for 2 hours.
4. Stir. Sprinkle with remaining ½ cup shredded cheese.
5. Allow dish to stand for 10–15 minutes before serving to allow sauce to thicken.

Cottage Cheese Casserole

Melani Guengerich Novinger Austin, TX

MAKES: **6 SERVINGS**
PREP. TIME: **20 MINUTES**
COOKING TIME: **4–5 HOURS**
IDEAL SLOW COOKER SIZE: **3-QUART**

2½ tsp. margarine
½ cup fresh mushrooms, chopped
½ cup onions, chopped
½ cup celery, chopped
1 clove garlic, minced
½ tsp. dried marjoram
¾ cup low-sodium tomato paste
4 cups macaroni, cooked
1¼ cups water
2 tsp. salt
1 tsp. sugar
¼ cup parsley, chopped
2 cups low-fat, low-sodium cottage cheese
⅓ cup grated Parmesan cheese

1. Sauté mushrooms, onions, celery, and garlic in margarine in a skillet over medium heat.
2. Combine sautéed vegetables, marjoram, tomato paste, macaroni, water, salt, and sugar.
3. Put half of macaroni mixture in slow cooker.
4. Top with 1 cup cottage cheese, half of Parmesan cheese, and parsley.
5. Repeat layers.
6. Cover. Cook on High 4–5 hours.

Per Serving: 270 calories (40 calories from fat), 4.5g total fat (1.5g saturated, 0g trans), 5mg cholesterol, 930mg sodium, 40g total carbohydrate (4g fiber, 6g sugar), 18g protein, 15%DV vitamin A, 20%DV vitamin C, 20%DV calcium, 20%DV iron.

Variation: *If you enjoy a tomatoey flavor, and your diet allows, you could add an 8-oz. can of low-sodium tomato sauce to Step 2 and reduce the water to ¾ cup.*

Pasta, Meatless, and Other Main Dishes

Convenient Slow Cooker Lasagna, page 489

Marinated Chinese Chicken Salad, page 397

Chocolate Fondue, page 609

503

Lemon Poppy Seed Upside-Down Cake,
page 618

Slow and Easy Macaroni and Cheese

Janice Muller   Derwood, MD

MEATLESS

MAKES: **6–8 SERVINGS**
PREP. TIME: **20 MINUTES**
COOKING TIME: **4¼ HOURS**
IDEAL SLOW COOKER SIZE: **3½-QUART**

1 lb. dry macaroni

½ cup butter

2 eggs

12-oz. can evaporated milk

10¾-oz. can cheddar cheese soup

1 cup milk

4 cups shredded cheddar cheese, *divided*

⅛ tsp. paprika

1. Cook macaroni al dente. Drain and pour hot macaroni into slow cooker.
2. Slice butter into chunks and add to macaroni. Stir until melted.
3. Combine, eggs, evaporated milk, soup, and milk. Add 3 cups cheese. Pour over macaroni and mix well.
4. Cover. Cook on Low 4 hours. Sprinkle with remaining cheese. Cook 15 minutes until cheese melts.
5. Sprinkle with paprika before serving.

Variation: *Add 12-oz. can drained tuna to Step 3.*

Creamy Cooker Dinner

Anna Musser   Manheim, PA

MAKES: **6 SERVINGS**
PREP. TIME: **7 MINUTES**
COOKING TIME: **2½–3 HOURS**
IDEAL SLOW COOKER SIZE: **5-QUART**

2 cups shredded cheese, your choice

2 cups macaroni, uncooked

3 cups milk

2 10¾-oz. cans cream of mushroom soup

2 cups cooked ham, *or* sliced hot dogs, *or* cooked, cubed chicken, *or* cooked ground beef

1. Place all ingredients in slow cooker. Mix together gently, but until well blended.
2. Cover and cook on High 2½–3 hours, or until macaroni is cooked but not overdone.

Easy Stuffed Shells

Rebecca Plank Leichty   Harrisonburg, VA

MAKES: **4–6 SERVINGS**
PREP. TIME: **5 MINUTES**
COOKING TIME: **3–8 HOURS**
IDEAL SLOW COOKER SIZE: **3½–4-QUART**

20-oz. bag frozen stuffed shells

15-oz. can marinara *or* spaghetti sauce

15-oz. can green beans, drained

1. Place shells around edge of greased slow cooker.
2. Cover with marinara sauce.
3. Pour green beans in center.
4. Cover. Cook on Low 8 hours, or on High 3 hours.
5. Serve with garlic toast and salad.

Variation: *Reverse Steps 2 and 3. Double the amount of marinara sauce and pour over both the shells and the beans.*

Tortellini with Broccoli

Susan Kasting Jenks, OK

MAKES: **4 SERVINGS**
PREP. TIME: **10 MINUTES**
COOKING TIME: **2½–3 HOURS**
IDEAL SLOW COOKER SIZE: **4-QUART**

½ cup water
26-oz. jar pasta sauce, your favorite, *divided*
1 Tbsp. Italian seasoning
9-oz. pkg. frozen spinach and cheese tortellini
16-oz. pkg. frozen broccoli florets

1. In a bowl, mix water, pasta sauce, and seasoning together.
2. Pour one-third of sauce into bottom of slow cooker. Top with all the tortellini.
3. Pour one-third of sauce over tortellini. Top with broccoli.
4. Pour remaining sauce over broccoli.
5. Cook on High 2½–3 hours, or until broccoli and pasta are tender but not mushy.

Chicken Broccoli Alfredo

Mrs. Mahlon Miller Hutchinson, KS

MAKES: **4 SERVINGS**
PREP. TIME: **30 MINUTES**
COOKING TIME: **1–2 HOURS**
IDEAL SLOW COOKER SIZE: **3-QUART**

8-oz. pkg. noodles *or* spaghetti (half a 16-oz. pkg.)
1½ cups fresh *or* frozen broccoli
1 lb. uncooked boneless, skinless chicken breasts, cubed
10¾-oz. can cream of mushroom soup
½ cup shredded mild cheddar cheese

1. Cook noodles according to package directions, adding broccoli during the last 4 minutes of the cooking time. Drain.
2. Sauté the chicken in a nonstick skillet, or in the microwave, until no longer pink in the center.
3. Combine all ingredients in slow cooker.
4. Cover and cook on Low 1–2 hours, or until heated through and until cheese is melted.

Garden-Fresh Chili Sauce

Dianna Milhizer Brighton, MI

MAKES: **4 QUARTS, OR 16 SERVINGS**
PREP. TIME: **25 MINUTES**
COOKING TIME: **4 HOURS**
IDEAL SLOW COOKER SIZE: **6-QUART**

1½ cups tomato juice
12 dried red (hot chili) peppers, chopped, or enough to make 2 cups-worth
4 quarts fresh tomatoes, peeled and chopped
2 cups onions, chopped
2 cups red sweet peppers, chopped
1 tsp. ground ginger
1 tsp. ground nutmeg
1 tsp. whole cloves
1 bay leaf
2 tsp. ground cinnamon
2 tsp. salt
4 cups white vinegar
1 tsp. whole peppercorns

1. Bring 1½ cups tomato juice to a boil. Place dried peppers in hot juice and allow to steep and soften for 5 minutes. Cover your hands with plastic gloves. Remove stems from dried peppers, and then puree the peppers in your food processor.
2. Combine all ingredients in large slow cooker.
3. Cover. Cook on High 4 hours.
4. Remove bay leaf.
5. Freeze or can in pint jars.

Per Serving: 80 calories (5 calories from fat), 1g total fat (0g saturated, 0g trans), 0mg cholesterol, 310mg sodium, 16g total carbohydrate (3g fiber, 7g sugar), 2g protein, 40%DV vitamin A, 100%DV vitamin C, 2%DV calcium, 6%DV iron.

Tips:

1. If you prefer a smoother sauce you may puree it in a blender.

2. This is an excellent side dish for Mexican recipes and can be used as a flavoring when cooking pork, chicken, or beef. A little bit goes a long way! You may reduce the amount of chili peppers but then the sauce isn't as pungent. It makes a great last-minute, end-of-the-garden-season use for your tomatoes and peppers.

Marinara Sauce

Dorothy VanDeest Memphis, TN

MAKES: **12 SERVINGS**
PREP. TIME: **15 MINUTES**
COOKING TIME: **6–10 HOURS**
IDEAL SLOW COOKER SIZE: **4-QUART**

2 28-oz. cans low-sodium whole tomatoes
1 onion, finely chopped
2 carrots, pared and finely chopped
1 clove garlic, chopped
2 Tbsp. vegetable oil
1 Tbsp. brown sugar
½ tsp. salt

1. Puree tomatoes in blender or food processor.
2. In a skillet, sauté onions, carrots, and garlic in oil until tender. Do not brown.
3. Combine all ingredients in slow cooker. Stir well.
4. Cover. Cook on Low 6–10 hours.
5. Remove cover. Stir well.
6. Cook on High uncovered for 1 hour for a thicker marinara sauce.

Per Serving: 50 calories (25 calories from fat), 2.5g total fat (0g saturated, 0g trans), 0mg cholesterol, 15mg sodium, 8g total carbohydrate (2g fiber, 4g sugar), 1g protein, 50%DV vitamin A, 20%DV vitamin C, 4%DV calcium, 4%DV iron.

Tip: *You can make this in advance of needing it and then freeze it in handy serving-size containers.*

Pasta with Lentil Sauce

Joy Sutter Iowa City, IA

MAKES: **4–6 SERVINGS**
PREP. TIME: **15 MINUTES**
COOKING TIME: **3–10 HOURS**
IDEAL SLOW COOKER SIZE: **4–5-QUART**

½ cup chopped onions
½ cup chopped carrots
½ cup chopped celery
2 cups diced tomatoes in liquid
1 cup tomato sauce
3–4 ozs. dried lentils, rinsed and drained
½ tsp. dried oregano
½ tsp. dried basil
½ tsp. garlic powder
¼ tsp. crushed red pepper flakes
4 cups angel-hair pasta, hot, cooked

1. Mix all ingredients except pasta in slow cooker.
2. Cover. Cook on Low 8–10 hours, or on High 3–5 hours.
3. Cook pasta according to package directions.
4. Place cooked pasta in large serving bowl and pour lentil sauce over top. Toss to combine.

Per Serving: 230 calories (10 calories from fat), 1g total fat (0g saturated, 0g trans), 0mg cholesterol, 360mg sodium, 46g total carbohydrate (8g fiber, 8g sugar), 10g protein, 50%DV vitamin A, 15%DV vitamin C, 6%DV calcium, 25%DV iron.

Red Beans and Pasta

Naomi E. Fast Hesston, KS

MAKES: **6–8 SERVINGS**
PREP. TIME: **10–15 MINUTES**
COOKING TIME: **3½–4½ HOURS**
IDEAL SLOW COOKER SIZE: **5-QUART**

PICTURED
ON PAGE
236

MEATLESS

3 15-oz. cans chicken *or* vegetable broth

½ tsp. ground cumin

1 Tbsp. chili powder

1 garlic clove, minced

8 ozs. spiral pasta, uncooked

half a large green pepper, diced

half a large red pepper, diced

1 medium onion, diced

15-oz. can red beans, rinsed and drained

chopped fresh parsley

chopped fresh cilantro

1. Combine broth, cumin, chili powder, and garlic in slow cooker.
2. Cover. Cook on High until mixture comes to boil.
3. Add pasta, vegetables, and beans. Stir together well.
4. Cover. Cook on Low 3–4 hours.
5. Add parsley or cilantro before serving.

To get the most flavor from herbs and spices when using them in a slow cooker, use whole fresh herbs rather than ground or crushed.

Minestra di Ceci

Jeanette Oberholtzer Manheim, PA

MAKES: **4–6 SERVINGS**
PREP. TIME: **25 MINUTES**
SOAKING TIME: **8 HOURS**
COOKING TIME: **5½–6 HOURS**
IDEAL SLOW COOKER SIZE: **4-QUART**

1 lb. dry chickpeas

1 sprig fresh rosemary

10 leaves fresh sage

2 Tbsp. salt

1–2 large garlic cloves, minced

olive oil

1 cup small dry pasta, your choice of shape, *or* dry penne

1. Wash chickpeas. Place in slow cooker. Soak for 8 hours in full pot of water, along with rosemary, sage, and salt.
2. Drain water. Remove herbs.
3. Refill slow cooker with water to 1 inch above peas.
4. Cover. Cook on Low 5 hours.
5. Sauté garlic in olive oil in skillet until clear.
6. Puree half of peas, along with several cups of broth from cooker, in blender. Return puree to slow cooker. Add garlic and oil.
7. Boil pasta in saucepan until al dente, about 5 minutes. Drain. Add to beans.
8. Cover. Cook on High 30–60 minutes, or until pasta is tender and heated through, but not mushy.

Variation: *Add ½ tsp. black pepper to Step 1, if you like.*

Pasta, Meatless, and Other Main Dishes

Easy Wheatberries

Elaine Vigoda   Rochester, NY

MAKES: **4–6 SERVINGS**
PREP. TIME: **10 MINUTES**
SOAKING TIME: **2 HOURS**
COOKING TIME: **2 HOURS**
IDEAL SLOW COOKER SIZE: **4-QUART**

1 cup wheatberries

1 cup couscous *or* **small pasta like orzo**

14½-oz. can broth

½–1 broth can of water

½ cup dried craisins *or* **raisins**

1. Cover wheatberries with water and soak 2 hours before cooking. Drain. Spoon wheatberries into slow cooker.
2. Combine with remaining ingredients in slow cooker.
3. Cover. Cook on Low until liquid is absorbed and berries are soft, about 2 hours.

Tip: *This is a satisfying vegetarian main dish, if you use vegetable broth.*

Flavorful Cheese Soufflé Casserole

Vicki Dinkel   Sharon Spring, KS

MAKES: **4 SERVINGS**
PREP. TIME: **15 MINUTES**
COOKING TIME: **4–6 HOURS**
IDEAL SLOW COOKER SIZE: **5-QUART**

14 slices fresh bread, crusts removed, *divided*

3 cups shredded sharp cheese, *divided*

2 Tbsp. butter, melted, *divided*

6 eggs

3 cups milk, scalded

2 tsp. Worcestershire sauce

½ tsp. salt

paprika

1. Tear bread into small pieces. Place half in well-greased slow cooker. Add half the shredded cheese and half the butter. Repeat layers.
2. Beat together eggs, milk, Worcestershire sauce, and salt. Pour over bread and cheese. Sprinkle top with paprika.
3. Cover. Cook on Low 4–6 hours.

Arroz con Queso

Nadine L. Martinitz Salina, KS

MAKES: **6–8 SERVINGS**
PREP. TIME: **15 MINUTES**
COOKING TIME: **6–9 HOURS**
IDEAL SLOW COOKER SIZE: **4-QUART**

14½-oz. can whole tomatoes, mashed

15-oz. can Mexican style beans, undrained

1½ cups long-grain rice, uncooked

1 cup shredded Monterey Jack cheese

1 large onion, finely chopped

1 cup cottage cheese

4¼-oz. can chopped green chili peppers, drained

1 Tbsp. oil

3 garlic cloves, minced

1 tsp. salt

1 cup shredded Monterey Jack cheese

1. Combine all ingredients except final cup of cheese. Pour into well greased slow cooker.
2. Cover. Cook on Low 6–9 hours.
3. Sprinkle with remaining cheese before serving.
4. Serve with salsa.

In recipes calling for rice, don't use minute or quick-cooking rice unless specifically designated.

Red Beans and Rice

Lavina Hochstedler Grand Blanc, MI

MAKES: **8 SERVINGS**
PREP. TIME: **15 MINUTES**
COOKING TIME: **5–6 HOURS**
IDEAL SLOW COOKER SIZE: **3½–4-QUART**

1 medium onion, chopped

½ cup green bell peppers, chopped

2 cloves garlic, minced

2 Tbsp. olive oil *or* canola oil

⅓ cup fresh cilantro *or* parsley, minced

3 16-oz. cans red beans, rinsed and drained

¾ cup water

½ tsp. salt

1 tsp. ground cumin

¼ tsp. black pepper

1. In a large skillet, sauté onion, green pepper, and garlic in oil until tender. Or wilt the onion, pepper, and garlic in the microwave for 2 minutes on High.
2. Add cilantro. Stir in beans, water, salt, cumin, and pepper. Transfer to slow cooker.
3. Cover. Cook on Low 5-6 hours.

Per Serving: 320 calories (40 calories from fat), 4.5g total fat (0.5g saturated, 0g trans), 0mg cholesterol, 150mg sodium, 56g total carbohydrate (16g fiber, 4g sugar), 14g protein, 4%DV vitamin A, 10%DV vitamin C, 2%DV calcium, 6%DV iron.

Tips:

1. If beans are watery as they near the end of the cooking time, remove the lid for the last hour of cooking.

2. Serve over hot, cooked rice.

3. If diets allow, you can serve the dish with shredded cheese for each diner to add to his/her individual serving.

Tastes-Like-Chili-Rellenos

Roseann Wilson Albuquerque, NM

MAKES: **6 SERVINGS**
PREP. TIME: **10 MINUTES**
COOKING TIME: **2–3 HOURS**
IDEAL SLOW COOKER SIZE: **4–5-QUART**

2 4-oz. cans whole green chilies
½ lb. fat-free cheddar cheese, shredded
½ lb. fat-free Monterey Jack cheese, shredded
14½-oz. can low-sodium stewed tomatoes
4 eggs
2 Tbsp. flour
¾ cup fat-free evaporated milk

1. Spray sides and bottom of slow cooker with nonfat cooking spray.
2. Cut chilies into strips. Layer chilies and cheeses in slow cooker. Pour in stewed tomatoes.
3. Combine eggs, flour, and milk. Pour into slow cooker.
4. Cover. Cook on High 2–3 hours.

Per Serving: 230 calories (40 calories from fat), 4.5g total fat (1.5g saturated, 0g trans), 135mg cholesterol, 920mg sodium, 15g total carbohydrate (2g fiber, 9g sugar), 28g protein, 20%DV vitamin A, 10%DV vitamin C, 100%DV calcium, 8%DV iron.

Fruit and Vegetable Curry

Melani Guengerich Novinger Austin, TX

MAKES: **6 SERVINGS**
PREP. TIME: **20 MINUTES**
COOKING TIME: **5–12 HOURS**
IDEAL SLOW COOKER SIZE: **4-QUART**

4 onions, coarsely chopped
2 Tbsp. vegetable oil
2 cloves garlic, minced
1 tsp. gingerroot, grated
1½ Tbsp. ground cumin
½ tsp. cayenne pepper
1½ Tbsp. ground coriander
¼ tsp. ground cardamom
¼ tsp. ground cloves
1 tsp. ground turmeric
2 medium zucchini, quartered lengthwise and sliced
¾ cup water
1 cup green beans, cut
2 firm, tart apples, cored and cubed
half a red bell pepper, chopped
1 cup dried apricots, chopped
½ cup currants *or* raisins
½ cup apricot conserve (or smashed halves and juice)

1. Sauté the onions in oil for 10 minutes. Stir in garlic, gingerroot, and spices. Continue to sauté, stirring constantly for about 3 minutes.
2. Transfer to slow cooker. Add zucchini, water, green beans, apples, red bell pepper, and dried apricots.
3. Cover. Cook on High 5–6 hours, or on Low 10–12 hours.
4. Stir in raisins and apricot conserve just before serving.

Per Serving: 300 calories (50 calories from fat), 6g total fat (1g saturated, 0g trans), 0mg cholesterol, 20mg sodium, 63g total carbohydrate (7g fiber, 48g sugar), 4g protein, 20%DV vitamin A, 30%DV vitamin C, 8%DV calcium, 15%DV iron.

Tip: *This is tasty served over brown rice and topped with peanuts and chopped or sliced bananas.*

Tempeh-Stuffed Peppers

Sara Harter Fredette   Williamsburg, MA

MAKES: **4 SERVINGS**
PREP. TIME: **20 MINUTES**
COOKING TIME: **3–8 HOURS**
IDEAL SLOW COOKER SIZE: **4-QUART**

4 oz. tempeh, cubed

1 garlic clove, minced

28-oz. can crushed tomatoes

2 tsp. soy sauce

¼ cup chopped onions

1½ cups rice, cooked

1½ cups shredded cheese

Tabasco sauce, *optional*

4 green, red, *or* yellow bell peppers, tops removed and seeded

¼ cup shredded cheese

1. Steam tempeh 10 minutes in saucepan. Mash in bowl with the garlic, half the tomatoes, and soy sauce.
2. Stir in onions, rice, 1½ cups cheese, and Tabasco sauce. Stuff into peppers.
3. Place peppers in slow cooker, 3 on the bottom and one on top. Pour remaining half of tomatoes over peppers.
4. Cover. Cook on Low 6–8 hours, or on High 3–4 hours. Top with remaining cheese in last 30 minutes.

Vegetable-Stuffed Peppers

Shirley Hinh   Wayland, IA

MAKES: **8 SERVINGS**
PREP. TIME: **15 MINUTES**
COOKING TIME: **6–8 HOURS**
IDEAL SLOW COOKER SIZE: **6-QUART OVAL, SO THE PEPPERS CAN EACH SIT ON THE BOTTOM OF THE COOKER**

4 large green, red, *or* yellow bell peppers

½ cup quick-cooking rice

¼ cup minced onions

¼ cup sliced black olives

2 tsp. lite soy sauce

¼ tsp. black pepper

1 clove garlic, minced

28-oz. can low-sodium whole tomatoes

6-oz. can low-sodium tomato paste

15¼-oz. can corn *or* kidney beans, drained

1. Cut tops off peppers (reserve) and remove seeds. Stand peppers up in slow cooker.
2. Mix remaining ingredients in a bowl. Stuff peppers.
3. Place pepper tops back on the peppers. Pour remaining ingredients over the stuffed peppers and work down in between the peppers.
4. Cover. Cook on Low 6–8 hours, or until the peppers are done to your liking.
5. If you prefer, you may add ½ cup tomato juice if recipe is too dry.
6. Cut peppers in half and serve.

Per Serving: 100 calories (20 calories from fat), 2g total fat (0g saturated, 0g trans), 0mg cholesterol, 420mg sodium, 22g total carbohydrate (3g fiber, 6g sugar), 3g protein, 10%DV vitamin A, 60%DV vitamin C, 4%DV calcium, 8%DV iron.

Barbecued Lentils

Sue Hamilton   Minooka, IL

MAKES: **8 SERVINGS**
PREP. TIME: **5 MINUTES**
COOKING TIME: **6–8 HOURS**
IDEAL SLOW COOKER SIZE: **4-QUART**

2 cups barbecue sauce

3½ cups water

1 lb. dry lentils

1 pkg. vegetarian hot dogs, sliced

1. Combine all ingredients in slow cooker.
2. Cover. Cook on Low 6–8 hours.

Carrot-Lentil Casserole

Pat Bishop   Bedminster, PA

MAKES: **6 SERVINGS**
PREP. TIME: **15 MINUTES**
COOKING TIME: **4–5 HOURS**
IDEAL SLOW COOKER SIZE: **4–5-QUART**

1 large onion, chopped
1 cup carrots, finely chopped
¾ cup dry lentils
¾ cup brown rice, uncooked
¾ cup low-fat cheese
½ cup chopped green bell pepper
½ tsp. dried thyme
½ tsp. dried basil
½ tsp. dried oregano
¼ tsp. salt
¼ tsp. sage
¼ tsp. garlic powder
1 cup low-sodium canned tomatoes, undrained
1 cup low-fat, low-sodium chicken broth

1. Combine all ingredients in slow cooker.
2. Cover. Cook on High 4–5 hours.

Per Serving: 230 calories (20 calories from fat), 2g total fat (1g saturated, 0g trans), 5mg cholesterol, 260mg sodium, 39g total carbohydrate (10g fiber, 6g sugar), 15g protein, 80%DV vitamin A, 20%DV vitamin C, 20%DV calcium, 20%DV iron.

Lentil and Rice Pilaf

Andrea Cunningham   Arlington, KS

MAKES: **8–10 SERVINGS**
PREP. TIME: **15 MINUTES**
COOKING TIME: **6–8 HOURS**
IDEAL SLOW COOKER SIZE: **4–5-QUART**

2–5 large onions, depending on your taste preference
2 Tbsp. olive oil
6 cups water
1¾ cups lentils, sorted, washed, and drained
2 cups brown rice, washed and drained

1. Slice onions into ½-inch circles. Place in nonstick skillet with olive oil. Sauté over medium heat until onions are golden brown.
2. Remove about 1-onion's-worth from skillet and place on paper towel to drain.
3. Place remaining onions and drippings in slow cooker. Combine with water, lentils, and brown rice.
4. Cover. Cook on Low 6–8 hours.
5. Serve hot or cold. Garnish with crisp brown onions.

Per Serving: 350 calories (30 calories from fat), 3.5g total fat (0.5g saturated, 0g trans), 0mg cholesterol, 15mg sodium, 66g total carbohydrate (16g fiber, 7g sugar), 16g protein, 0%DV vitamin A, 0%DV vitamin C, 4%DV calcium, 25%DV iron.

Tip: *This is good to dip into with pita triangles. It is also good served as a main dish with a basic green salad topped with herbal vinaigrette dressing.*

Variations:

1. If your diet allows, you may want to add 1 tsp. salt to Step 3.

2. If you like some bite to lentils and rice, add ¼–½ tsp. freshly ground pepper to Step 3.

BBQ Veggie Joes

Andrea Cunningham   Arlington, KS

MAKES: **10 SERVINGS**
PREP. TIME: **20 MINUTES**
COOKING TIME: **4–5 HOURS**
IDEAL SLOW COOKER SIZE: **3-QUART**

1 cup dried lentils, rinsed and sorted

2 cups water

1½ cups chopped celery

1½ cups chopped carrots

1 cup chopped onions

¾ cup ketchup

2 Tbsp. dark brown sugar

2 Tbsp. Worcestershire sauce

2 Tbsp. cider vinegar

1. In a medium saucepan, combine lentils and water. Bring to a boil. Reduce heat. Cover and simmer 10 minutes.
2. Combine celery, carrots, onions, ketchup, brown sugar, Worcestershire sauce, and lentils with water in slow cooker. Mix well.
3. Cover. Cook on Low 8–10 hours, or until lentils are soft.
4. Stir in vinegar just before serving.
5. Allow ½ cup filling for each sandwich.

Per Serving: 230 calories (20 calories from fat), 2.5g total fat (0g saturated, 0g trans), 0mg cholesterol, 480mg sodium, 45g total carbohydrate (9g fiber, 10g sugar), 10g protein, 100%DV vitamin A, 0%DV vitamin C, 8%DV calcium, 20%DV iron.

Fill the cooker no more than ⅔ full and no less than half full.

Lentil Tacos

Judy Buller   Bluffton, OH

MAKES: **6 SERVINGS**
PREP. TIME: **15 MINUTES**
COOKING TIME: **3–6 HOURS**
IDEAL SLOW COOKER SIZE: **4-QUART**

¾ cup finely chopped onions

⅛ tsp. garlic powder

1 tsp. canola oil

½ lb. dry lentils, picked clean of stones and floaters

1 Tbsp. chili powder

2 tsp. ground cumin

1 tsp. dried oregano

2 cups fat-free, low-sodium chicken broth

1 cup salsa

12 taco shells

shredded lettuce

chopped tomatoes

shredded, reduced-fat cheddar cheese

fat-free sour cream

taco sauce

1. Sprinkle garlic powder over onions and sauté in oil in skillet until tender. Add lentils and spices. Cook and stir for 1 minute.
2. Place lentil mixture and broth in slow cooker.
3. Cover. Cook on Low 3 hours for somewhat-crunchy lentils, or on Low 6 hours for soft lentils.
4. Add salsa.
5. Spoon about ¼ cup into each taco shell. Top with lettuce, tomatoes, cheese, sour cream, and taco sauce.

Per Serving: 340 calories (100 calories from fat), 11g total fat (3.5g saturated, 2g trans), 15mg cholesterol, 600mg sodium, 42g total carbohydrate (5g fiber, 12g sugar), 19g protein, 40%DV vitamin A, 20%DV vitamin C, 50%DV calcium, 15%DV iron.

Tip: *This mixture is also tasty served over rice.*

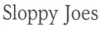

Sloppy Joes

Darla Sathre Baxter, MN

MAKES: **8 SERVINGS**
PREP. TIME: **15 MINUTES**
COOKING TIME: **8–9 HOURS**
IDEAL SLOW COOKER SIZE: **3–4-QUART**

1 onion
1 green bell pepper
4 cloves garlic
2 carrots
8-oz. pkg. tempeh (we like 5-grain)
2 Tbsp. olive oil
1 envelope dry onion soup mix
¼ tsp. ground cumin
16-oz. can pinto beans, drained
16-oz. can fat-free refried beans
½ cup barbecue sauce

1. Dice the onion, green pepper, garlic, carrots, and tempeh. Sauté briefly in olive oil in skillet.
2. Combine with onion soup mix, cumin, beans, and barbecue sauce in slow cooker. You may want to slightly mash the pinto beans.
3. Cook on Low 8–9 hours.
4. Serve on buns. Open-faced is less sloppy!

———————————

Per Serving: 340 calories (70 calories from fat), 8g total fat (1g saturated, 0g trans), 0mg cholesterol, 890mg sodium, 56g total carbohydrate (12g fiber, 9g sugar), 16g protein, 50%DV vitamin A, 20%DV vitamin C, 10%DV calcium, 25%DV iron.

Variation: *You may want to increase the cumin to ½ tsp., if you prefer more bite. You may serve this over pasta or rice, or just-as-is as a side dish.*

Pizza Sloppy Joe

Sue Hamilton Minooka, IL

MAKES: **6 SERVINGS**
PREP. TIME: **5 MINUTES**
COOKING TIME: **6–8 HOURS**
IDEAL SLOW COOKER SIZE: **4-QUART**

1 cup textured vegetable protein (T.V.P., soy)
7-oz. can mushrooms, undrained
15-oz. can low-sodium tomato sauce
14½-oz. can low-sodium Italian diced tomatoes with basil, garlic, and oregano
½ tsp. fennel seeds
½ tsp. crushed red peppers
1 tsp. Italian seasoning
1 tsp. minced roasted garlic
½ tsp. salt

1. Combine all ingredients in slow cooker.
2. Cover. Cook on Low 6–8 hours.

———————————

Per Serving: 90 calories (10 calories from fat), 1g total fat (0g saturated, 0g trans), 0mg cholesterol, 1060mg sodium, 15g total carbohydrate (5g fiber, 7g sugar), 9g protein, 10%DV vitamin A, 10%DV vitamin C, 10%DV calcium, 15%DV iron.

Lamb Stew

Dottie Schmidt   Kansas City, MO

MAKES: **6 SERVINGS**
PREP. TIME: **35 MINUTES**
COOKING TIME: **8–10 HOURS**
IDEAL SLOW COOKER SIZE: **6-QUART**

2 lbs. lean lamb, cubed

½ tsp. sugar

2 Tbsp. canola oil

1½ tsp. salt

¼ tsp. black pepper

¼ cup flour

2 cups water

¾ cup red cooking wine

¼ tsp. garlic powder

2 tsp. Worcestershire sauce

6–8 carrots, sliced

4 small onions, quartered

4 ribs celery, sliced

3 medium potatoes, diced

1. Sprinkle lamb with sugar. Brown in oil in skillet.
2. Remove lamb and place in cooker, reserving drippings. Stir salt, pepper, and flour into drippings in skillet until smooth. Stir in water and wine until smooth, stirring loose the meat drippings. Continue cooking and stirring occasionally until broth simmers and thickens.
3. Pour into cooker. Add remaining ingredients and stir until well mixed.
4. Cover. Cook on Low 8–10 hours.

Per Serving: 440 calories (130 calories from fat), 15g total fat (5g saturated, 0g trans), 90mg cholesterol, 940mg sodium, 39g total carbohydrate (7g fiber, 11g sugar), 32g protein, 400%DV vitamin A, 20%DV vitamin C, 8%DV calcium, 25%DV iron.

"Baked" Lamb Shanks

Irma H. Schoen   Windsor, CT

MAKES: **4–6 SERVINGS**
PREP. TIME: **10 MINUTES**
COOKING TIME: **4–10 HOURS**
IDEAL SLOW COOKER SIZE: **4-QUART**

1 medium onion, thinly sliced

2 small carrots, cut in thin strips

1 rib celery, chopped

3 lamb shanks, cracked

1–2 cloves garlic, split

1½ tsp. salt

¼ tsp. pepper

1 tsp. dried oregano

1 tsp. dried thyme

2 bay leaves, crumbled

½ cup dry white wine

8-oz. can tomato sauce

1. Place onions, carrots, and celery in slow cooker.
2. Rub lamb with garlic and season with salt and pepper. Add to slow cooker.
3. Mix remaining ingredients together in separate bowl and add to meat and vegetables.
4. Cover. Cook on Low 8–10 hours, or on High 4–6 hours.

Roasting bags work well in the slow cooker. Simply fill with meat and vegetables and cook as directed in slow cooker recipes. Follow manufacturer's directions for filling and sealing bags.

Lamb Chops

Shirley Sears Tiskilwa, IL

MAKES: **6–8 SERVINGS**
PREP. TIME: **10 MINUTES**
COOKING TIME: **4–6 HOURS**
IDEAL SLOW COOKER SIZE: **5-QUART**

1 medium onion, sliced

1 tsp. dried oregano

½ tsp. dried thyme

½ tsp. garlic powder

¼ tsp. salt

⅛ tsp. pepper

8 loin lamb chops (1¾–2 lbs.)

2 garlic cloves, minced

¼ cup water

1. Place onion in slow cooker.
2. Combine oregano, thyme, garlic powder, salt, and pepper. Rub over lamb chops. Place in slow cooker. Top with garlic. Pour water down alongside of cooker, so as not to disturb the rub on the chops.
3. Cover. Cook on Low 4–6 hours.

Venison Roast

Colleen Heatwole Burton, MI

MAKES: **6–8 SERVINGS**
PREP. TIME: **15 MINUTES**
MARINATING TIME: **AT LEAST 8 HOURS**
COOKING TIME: **10–12 HOURS**
IDEAL SLOW COOKER SIZE: **5-QUART**

3–4-lb. venison roast

¼ cup vinegar

2 garlic cloves, minced

2 Tbsp. salt

½ cup chopped onions

15-oz. can tomato sauce

1 Tbsp. ground mustard

1 pkg. brown gravy mix

½ tsp. salt

¼ cup water

1. Place venison in deep bowl. Combine vinegar, garlic, and salt. Pour over venison. Add enough cold water to cover venison. Marinate for at least 8 hours in refrigerator.
2. Rinse and drain venison. Place in slow cooker.
3. Combine remaining ingredients and pour over venison.
4. Cover. Cook on Low 10–12 hours.
5. Serve with a green salad, potatoes, and rolls to make a complete meal.

Tips:

1. This is an easy meal to have for a Saturday dinner with guests or extended family. There is usually a lot of sauce, so make plenty of potatoes, noodles, or rice.

2. The sauce on this roast works well for any meat.

Venison in Sauce

Anona M. Teel   Bangar, PA

MAKES: **12 SANDWICHES**
PREP. TIME: **20 MINUTES**
MARINATING TIME: **6–8 HOURS**
COOKING TIME: **8–10 HOURS**
IDEAL SLOW COOKER SIZE: **4-QUART**

3–4-lb. venison roast

½ cup vinegar

2 garlic cloves, minced

2 Tbsp. salt

cold water

oil

large onion, sliced

half a green pepper, sliced

2 ribs celery, sliced

1–2 garlic cloves, minced

1½–2 tsp. salt

¼ tsp. pepper

½ tsp. dried oregano

¼ cup ketchup

1 cup tomato juice

1. Combine vinegar, garlic cloves, and 2 Tbsp. salt. Pour over venison. Add water until meat is covered. Marinate 6–8 hours.
2. Cut meat into pieces. Brown in oil in skillet. Place in slow cooker.
3. Mix remaining ingredients together; then pour into cooker. Stir in meat.
4. Cover. Cook on Low 8–10 hours.
5. Using two forks, pull the meat apart and then stir it through the sauce.
6. Serve on sandwich rolls, or over rice or pasta.

Pot-Roasted Rabbit

Donna Treloar   Gaston, IN

MAKES: **4 SERVINGS**
PREP. TIME: **5–10 MINUTES**
COOKING TIME: **10–12 HOURS**
IDEAL SLOW COOKER SIZE: **4-QUART**

2 onions, sliced

4–5-lb. roasting rabbit

salt to taste

pepper to taste

1 garlic clove, sliced

2 bay leaves

1 whole clove

1 cup hot water

2 Tbsp. soy sauce

2 Tbsp. flour

½ cup cold water

1. Place onion in bottom of slow cooker.
2. Rub rabbit with salt and pepper. Insert garlic in cavity. Place rabbit in slow cooker.
3. Add bay leaves, clove, hot water, and soy sauce.
4. Cover. Cook on Low 10–12 hours.
5. Remove rabbit and thicken gravy by stirring 2 Tbsp. flour blended into ½ cup water into simmering juices in cooker. Continue stirring until gravy thickens. Cut rabbit into serving-size pieces and serve with gravy.

Pasta, Meatless, and Other Main Dishes

Vegetables

Vegetable Medley

Deborah Santiago Lancaster, PA
Judi Manos West Islip, NY

MAKES: **8 SERVINGS**
PREP. TIME: **15 MINUTES**
COOKING TIME: **5–6 HOURS**
IDEAL SLOW COOKER SIZE: **4-QUART**

4 cups potatoes, diced and peeled
1½ cups frozen whole-kernel corn
4 medium tomatoes, seeded and diced
1 cup carrots, sliced
½ cup onions, chopped
¾ tsp. salt
½ tsp. sugar
¾ tsp. dill weed
¼ tsp. black pepper
½ tsp. dried basil
¼ tsp. dried rosemary

1. Combine all ingredients in slow cooker.
2. Cover. Cook on Low 5–6 hours, or until vegetables are tender.

Per Serving: 120 calories (5 calories from fat), 0.5g total fat (0g saturated, 0g trans), 0mg cholesterol, 240mg sodium, 27g total carbohydrate (4g fiber, 5g sugar), 4g protein, 80%DV vitamin A, 20%DV vitamin C, 2%DV calcium, 6%DV iron.

Vegetables tend not to overcook as they do when boiled on your range. Therefore, everything can go into the cooker at one time, with the exception of milk, sour cream, and cream, which should be added during the last hour.

Vegetables with Pasta

Donna Lantgen Rapid City, SD

MAKES: **6 SERVINGS**
PREP. TIME: **20 MINUTES**
COOKING TIME: **6 HOURS**
IDEAL SLOW COOKER SIZE: **3½–4-QUART**

2 cups chopped zucchini

½ cup cherry tomatoes, cut in half

half green *or* red bell pepper, sliced

half medium onion, sliced

½ cup sliced fresh mushrooms

4 cloves garlic, minced

1 Tbsp. olive oil

1 Tbsp. Italian seasoning

8-oz. can tomato sauce

1. Combine all ingredients in slow cooker.
2. Cook on Low 6 hours, or until vegetables are tender.

Per Serving: 80 calories (25 calories from fat), 3g total fat (0g saturated, 0g trans), 0mg cholesterol, 580mg sodium, 12g total carbohydrate (2g fiber, 6g sugar), 4g protein, 20%DV vitamin A, 30%DV vitamin C, 2%DV calcium, 6%DV iron.

Tip: *Serve with your favorite cooked pasta and top with grated low-fat Parmesan or mozzarella cheese.*

Be sure vegetables are thinly sliced or chopped because they cook slowly in a slow cooker.

Vegetable Curry

Sheryl Shenk Harrisonburg, VA

MAKES: **8–10 SERVINGS**
PREP. TIME: **15 MINUTES**
COOKING TIME: **3–10 HOURS**
IDEAL SLOW COOKER SIZE: **4–5-QUART**

16-oz. pkg. baby carrots

3 medium potatoes, cubed

1 lb. fresh *or* frozen green beans, cut in 2-inch pieces

1 green pepper, chopped

1 onion, chopped

1–2 cloves garlic, minced

15-oz. can garbanzo beans, drained

28-oz. can crushed tomatoes

3 Tbsp. minute tapioca

3 tsp. curry powder

2 tsp. salt

1¾ cups boiling water

2 tsp. chicken bouillon granules, *or* 2 chicken bouillon cubes

1. Combine carrots, potatoes, green beans, pepper, onion, garlic, garbanzo beans, and crushed tomatoes in large bowl.
2. Stir in tapioca, curry powder, and salt.
3. Dissolve bouillon in boiling water. Pour over vegetables. Mix well. Spoon into large cooker, or two medium-sized ones.
4. Cover. Cook on Low 8–10 hours, or on High 3–4 hours. Serve with cooked rice.

Variation: *Substitute canned green beans for fresh beans but add toward the end of the cooking time.*

Garden Vegetables

Esther Gingerich   Parnell, IA

Judy A. and Sharon Wantland   Menomonee Falls, WI

MAKES: **6 SERVINGS**
PREP. TIME: **15 MINUTES**
COOKING TIME: **2½–4 HOURS**
IDEAL SLOW COOKER SIZE: **3-QUART**

16-oz. pkg. frozen vegetables, thawed (combination of broccoli, carrots, cauliflower, etc.)
10¾-oz. can cream of mushroom soup
half a soup can water
⅓ cup sour cream
1–2 cups shredded Swiss *or* mozzarella cheese, *divided*
6-oz. can French-fried onions, *divided*

1. In slow cooker, combine thawed vegetables, soup, water, sour cream, half the cheese, and half the onions.
2. Cover and cook on Low 2½–4 hours, or until vegetables are as soft as you like them.
3. Fifteen minutes before the end of the cooking time, sprinkle remaining cheese and onions on top.

Zippy Vegetable Medley

Gloria Frey   Lebanon, PA

MAKES: **4–5 SERVINGS**
PREP. TIME: **10–15 MINUTES**
COOKING TIME: **2½ HOURS**
IDEAL SLOW COOKER SIZE: **2-QUART**

16-oz. pkg. frozen broccoli, cauliflower, and carrots
16-oz. pkg. frozen corn
2 10½-oz. cans fiesta nacho cheese soup
½ cup milk

1. Combine broccoli mixture and corn in slow cooker.
2. Combine soups and milk in a microwave-safe bowl. Microwave for 1 minute on High, or just enough to mix well. When blended, pour over vegetables.
3. Cover and cook on High 2½ hours, or until hot and bubbly and vegetables are done to your liking.

Variation: *If you'd like a milder dish, replace the one can of fiesta nacho cheese soup with one can of cheddar cheese soup.*

Yvonne Boettger   Harrisonburg, VA

"Stir-Fry" Veggies

Shari and Dale Mast Harrisonburg, VA

MAKES: **8 SERVINGS**
PREP. TIME: **20 MINUTES**
COOKING TIME: **8–10 HOURS**
IDEAL SLOW COOKER SIZE: **6-QUART**

16-oz. bag baby carrots

4 ribs celery, chunked

1 medium onion, diced

14½-oz. can low-sodium Italian-style stewed tomatoes

½ tsp. dried basil

½ tsp. dried oregano

½ tsp. salt

1 large red *or* yellow bell pepper, diced

1 small head cabbage, cut up

1 lb. raw broccoli, cut up

1. Combine carrots, celery, onion, tomatoes, basil, oregano, and salt in slow cooker.
2. Cover. Cook on High 3–4 hours, or on Low 6–8 hours, stirring occasionally.
3. Stir in pepper, cabbage, and broccoli.
4. Cook 1 hour more on High, or 2 hours more on Low, stirring occasionally. You may need to add a little water if there is not liquid left on the veggies.

Per Serving: 90 calories (10 calories from fat), 1g total fat (0g saturated, 0g trans), 0mg cholesterol, 220mg sodium, 19g total carbohydrate (7g fiber, 10g sugar), 4g protein, 200%DV vitamin A, 100%DV vitamin C, 10%DV calcium, 15%DV iron.

Tip: *Serve this as a side dish, or as a main dish over hot cooked rice, garnished with Parmesan cheese.*

Tofu and Vegetables

Donna Lantgen Rapid City, SD

MAKES: **6 SERVINGS**
PREP. TIME: **20 MINUTES**
COOKING TIME: **6 HOURS**
IDEAL SLOW COOKER SIZE: **4–5-QUART**

16 ozs. firm tofu, drained and crumbled

½ cup onion, chopped

½ cup celery, chopped

2 cups bok choy, chopped

2 cups napa cabbage, chopped

½ cup pea pods, cut in half

1. Combine all ingredients in slow cooker.
2. Cook on Low 6 hours.

Per Serving: 60 calories (25 calories from fat), 3g total fat (0g saturated, 0g trans), 0mg cholesterol, 25mg sodium, 4g total carbohydrate (1g fiber, 2g sugar), 6g protein, 10%DV vitamin A, 10%DV vitamin C, 10%DV calcium, 8%DV iron.

Note: *I like to serve this with soy sauce on a bed of rice.*

Chinese Vegetables

Rebecca Leichty Harrisonburg, VA

MAKES: **6 SERVINGS**
PREP. TIME: **10 MINUTES**
COOKING TIME: **3–6 HOURS**
IDEAL SLOW COOKER SIZE: **5–6-QUART**

1 bunch celery, sliced on the diagonal

1 large onion, sliced

1-lb. can bean sprouts, drained

12-oz. pkg. chop-suey vegetables

8-oz. can water chestnuts, drained

2 4-oz. cans sliced mushrooms, drained

1 Tbsp. sugar

3 Tbsp. low-sodium soy sauce

¾ cup water

¼ tsp. black pepper, or to taste

1. Spray slow cooker with fat-free cooking spray.
2. Combine all ingredients in slow cooker.
3. Cover. Cook on Low 3–6 hours, depending upon how soft or crunchy you like your vegetables.

Per Serving: 120 calories (0 calories from fat), 0g total fat (0g saturated, 0g trans), 0mg cholesterol, 135mg sodium, 28g total carbohydrate (5g fiber, 5g sugar), 4g protein, 4%DV vitamin A, 40%DV vitamin C, 8%DV calcium, 8%DV iron.

Corn on the Cob

Donna Conto   Saylorsburg, PA

MAKES: **3–4 SERVINGS**
PREP. TIME: **10 MINUTES**
COOKING TIME: **2–3 HOURS**
IDEAL SLOW COOKER SIZE: **5–6-QUART**

6–8 ears of corn (in husk)
½ cup water

1. Remove silk from corn, as much as possible, but leave husks on.
2. Cut off ends of corn so ears can stand in the cooker.
3. Add water.
4. Cover. Cook on Low 2–3 hours.

Cook according to the season. Focus on the vegetables and fruits that are ripe for the month you're in. Visit a local farmer's market for inspiration.

Cheesy Corn

Tina Snyder   Manheim, PA   •   *Jeannine Janzen*   Elbing, KS
Nadine Martinitz   Salina, KS

MAKES: **10 SERVINGS**
PREP. TIME: **5–7 MINUTES**
COOKING TIME: **4 HOURS**
IDEAL SLOW COOKER SIZE: **4-QUART**

3 16-oz. pkgs. frozen corn
8-oz. pkg. cream cheese, cubed
¼ cup butter, cubed
3 Tbsp. water
3 Tbsp. milk
2 Tbsp. sugar
6 slices American cheese, cut into squares

1. Combine all ingredients in slow cooker. Mix well.
2. Cover. Cook on Low 4 hours, or until heated through and the cheese is melted.

"Baked" Corn

Velma Stauffer Akron, PA

Light

MAKES: **8 SERVINGS**
PREP. TIME: **5 MINUTES**
COOKING TIME: **3 HOURS**
IDEAL SLOW COOKER SIZE: **3-QUART**

1 quart corn (be sure to thaw and drain if using frozen corn)

2 eggs, beaten

1 tsp. salt

1 cup fat-free milk

⅛ tsp. black pepper

2 tsp. oil

2 Tbsp. sugar

3 Tbsp. flour

1. Combine all ingredients well. Pour into slow cooker sprayed with fat-free cooking spray.
2. Cover. Cook on High 3 hours.

———————

Per Serving: 140 calories (25 calories from fat), 3g total fat (0.5g saturated, 0g trans), 45mg cholesterol, 320mg sodium, 25g total carbohydrate (2g fiber, 6g sugar), 5g protein, 0%DV vitamin A, 0%DV vitamin C, 4%DV calcium, 4%DV iron.

Beginner cooks should always measure carefully. With more experience you learn to adjust recipes.

Dried Corn

Mary B. Sensenig New Holland, PA

MAKES: **4 SERVINGS**
PREP. TIME: **3–5 MINUTES**
COOKING TIME: **4 HOURS**
IDEAL SLOW COOKER SIZE: **3-QUART**

15-oz. can dried corn

2 Tbsp. sugar

3 Tbsp. butter, softened

1 tsp. salt

1 cup half-and-half

2 Tbsp. water

1. Place all ingredients in slow cooker. Mix together well.
2. Cover and cook on Low 4 hours. If you're able, check after cooking 3 hours to make sure the corn isn't cooking dry. If it appears to be, stir in an additional ¼–½ cup half-and-half. Cover and continue cooking.

Scalloped Corn

Rebecca Plank Leichty Harrisonburg, VA

MAKES: **6 SERVINGS**
PREP. TIME: **10 MINUTES**
COOKING TIME: **3–6 HOURS**
IDEAL SLOW COOKER SIZE: **2-QUART**

2 eggs

10¾-oz. can cream of celery soup

⅔ cup unseasoned bread crumbs

2 cups whole-kernel corn, drained, *or* cream-style corn

1 tsp. minced onion

¼–½ tsp. salt, according to your taste preference

⅛ tsp. pepper

1 Tbsp. sugar

2 Tbsp. butter, melted

1. Beat eggs with fork. Add soup and bread crumbs. Mix well.
2. Add remaining ingredients and mix thoroughly. Pour into greased slow cooker.
3. Cover. Cook on High 3 hours, or on Low 6 hours.

"Baked" Corn and Noodles

Ruth Hershey   Paradise, PA

MAKES: **6 SERVINGS**
PREP. TIME: **20 MINUTES**
COOKING TIME: **3–8 HOURS**
IDEAL SLOW COOKER SIZE: **3-QUART**

3 cups noodles, cooked al dente
2 cups fresh *or* frozen corn, thawed
¾ cup shredded cheddar cheese *or* cubed Velveeta cheese
1 egg, beaten
½ cup butter, melted
½ tsp. salt

1. Combine all ingredients in slow cooker.
2. Cover. Cook on Low 6–8 hours, or on High 3–4 hours.

Mexican Corn

Betty K. Drescher   Quakertown, PA

MAKES: **8–10 SERVINGS**
PREP. TIME: **10 MINUTES**
COOKING TIME: **2¾–4¾ HOURS**
IDEAL SLOW COOKER SIZE: **2-QUART**

2 10-oz. pkgs. frozen corn, partially thawed
4-oz. jar chopped pimentos
⅓ cup chopped green peppers
⅓ cup water
1 tsp. salt
¼ tsp. pepper
½ tsp. paprika
½ tsp. chili powder

1. Combine all ingredients in slow cooker.
2. Cover. Cook on High 45 minutes, then on Low 2–4 hours. Stir occasionally.

Variation: *For more fire, add ⅓ cup salsa to the ingredients, and increase the amounts of pepper, paprika, and chili powder to match your taste.*

Cheesy Hominy from Scratch

Michelle Showalter Bridgewater, VA

MAKES: **12–14 SERVINGS**
PREP. TIME: **10 MINUTES**
COOKING TIME: **4–9 HOURS**
IDEAL SLOW COOKER SIZE: **5–6-QUART**

2 cups cracked hominy

6 cups water

2 Tbsp. flour

1½ cups milk

4 cups shredded sharp cheddar cheese

1–2 tsp. salt

¼ tsp. pepper

4 Tbsp. butter

1. Combine hominy and water in 5–6 quart slow cooker.
2. Cover. Cook on High 3–4 hours, or on Low 6–8 hours.
3. Stir in remaining ingredients.
4. Cover. Cook 30–60 minutes.

Tip: *Cheesy Hominy is a nice change if you're tired of the same old thing. It's wonderful with ham, slices of bacon, or meatballs. Add a green vegetable and you have a lovely meal. Hominy is available at bulk-food stores.*

Southwest Posole

Becky Harder Monument, CO

MAKES: **6 SERVINGS**
PREP. TIME: **5–10 MINUTES**
SOAKING TIME: **4–8 HOURS**
COOKING TIME: **5 HOURS**
IDEAL SLOW COOKER SIZE: **4-QUART**

2 12-oz. pkgs. dry posole

1 garlic clove, minced

2 14-oz. cans vegetable *or* chicken broth

2 10-oz. cans Rotel Mexican diced tomatoes

4-oz. can diced green chilies, *optional*

salt to taste

1. Soak posole for 4–8 hours. Drain water.
2. Combine ingredients in slow cooker.
3. Cover. Cook on High 3 hours; then turn to Low for 2 hours.
4. Serve with enchiladas, black beans, Spanish rice, and chopped lettuce with black olives and tomatoes.

Variation: *Dry posole can be found in the Mexican food department of the grocery store. If you cannot find dry posole, you can used canned hominy and skip to Step 2.*

Hominy and Ham

Reita Yoder   Carlsbad, NM

MAKES: **12–14 SERVINGS**
PREP. TIME: **10 MINUTES**
COOKING TIME: **1½–3 HOURS**
IDEAL SLOW COOKER SIZE: **3–4-QUART**

3 29-oz. cans hominy, drained

10¾-oz. can cream of chicken soup

½ lb. cheddar cheese, shredded or cubed

1 lb. cubed cooked ham

2 2¼-oz. cans green chilies, undrained

1. Mix all ingredients together in slow cooker.
2. Cover and cook on High for 1½ hours, or on Low for 2–3 hours, or until bubbly and cheese is melted.

Tip: *Serve with fresh salsa.*

Mexican Hominy

Janie Steele   Moore, OK

MAKES: **6–8 SERVINGS**
PREP. TIME: **10 MINUTES**
COOKING TIME: **1 HOUR**
IDEAL SLOW COOKER SIZE: **3–4-QUART**

2 29-oz. cans hominy, drained

4-oz. can chopped green chilies, mild or hot

1 cup sour cream

8-oz. jar Cheez Whiz

1. Combine ingredients in slow cooker.
2. Cover and heat on Low for 1 hour, or until cheese is melted and dish is thoroughly hot.

Easy Olive Bake

Jean Robinson   Cinnaminson, NJ

MAKES: **8 SERVINGS**
PREP. TIME: **15 MINUTES**
COOKING TIME: **3 HOURS**
IDEAL SLOW COOKER SIZE: **3½-QUART**

1 cup rice, uncooked

2 medium onions, chopped

½ cup butter, melted

2 cups stewed tomatoes

2 cups water

1 cup black olives, quartered

½–¾ tsp. salt

½ tsp. chili powder

1 Tbsp. Worcestershire sauce

4-oz. can mushrooms with juice

½ cup shredded cheese

1. Wash and drain rice. Place in slow cooker.
2. Add remaining ingredients except cheese. Mix well.
3. Cook on High 1 hour, then on Low 2 hours, or until rice is tender but not mushy.
4. Add cheese before serving.
5. This is a good accompaniment to baked ham.

Fruited Wild Rice with Pecans

Dottie Schmidt   Kansas City, MO

MAKES: **4 SERVINGS**
PREP. TIME: **15 MINUTES**
COOKING TIME: **2–2½ HOURS**
IDEAL SLOW COOKER SIZE: **3-QUART**

½ cup chopped onions

2 Tbsp. butter

6-oz. pkg. long-grain and wild rice

seasoning packet from wild rice pkg.

1½ cups hot water

⅔ cup apple juice

1 large tart apple, chopped

¼ cup raisins

¼ cup coarsely chopped pecans

1. Combine all ingredients except pecans in greased slow cooker.
2. Cover. Cook on High 2–2½ hours.
3. Stir in pecans. Serve.

Mjeddrah

Dianna Milhizer   Brighton, MI

MAKES: **20–24 SERVINGS**
PREP. TIME: **10 MINUTES**
COOKING TIME: **10 HOURS**
IDEAL SLOW COOKER SIZE: **6-QUART**

10 cups water

4 cups dried lentils, rinsed

2 cups brown rice, uncooked

¼ cup olive oil

2 tsp. salt

1. Combine ingredients in large slow cooker.
2. Cover. Cook on High 8 hours, then on Low 2 hours. Add 2 more cups water, if needed, to allow rice to cook and to prevent dish from drying out.

3. This is traditionally eaten with a salad with an oil-and-vinegar dressing over the lentil-rice mixture, similar to a tostada without the tortilla.

Quick Broccoli Fix

Willard E. Roth   Elkhart, IN

MAKES: **6 SERVINGS**
PREP. TIME: **15 MINUTES**
COOKING TIME: **5–6 HOURS**
IDEAL SLOW COOKER SIZE: **3½-QUART**

1 lb. fresh *or* frozen broccoli, cut up

10¾-oz. can cream of mushroom soup

½ cup mayonnaise

½ cup plain yogurt

½ lb. sliced fresh mushrooms

1 cup shredded cheddar cheese, *divided*

1 cup crushed saltine crackers

sliced almonds, *optional*

1. Microwave broccoli for 3 minutes. Place in greased slow cooker.
2. Combine soup, mayonnaise, yogurt, mushrooms, and ½ cup cheese. Pour over broccoli.
3. Cover. Cook on Low 5–6 hours.
4. Top with remaining cheese and crackers for last half hour of cooking time.
5. Top with sliced almonds, for a special touch, before serving.

Broccoli and Rice Casserole

Deborah Swartz   Grottoes, VA

MAKES: **4–6 SERVINGS**
PREP. TIME: **15–20 MINUTES**
COOKING TIME: **3–4 HOURS**
IDEAL SLOW COOKER SIZE: **3½-QUART**

1 lb. chopped broccoli, fresh *or* frozen, thawed

1 medium onion, chopped

¼ cup butter

1 cup minute rice, *or* 1½ cups rice, cooked

10¾-oz. can cream of chicken *or* mushroom soup

¼ cup milk

1⅓ cups Velveeta cheese, cubed, *or* cheddar cheese, shredded

1 tsp. salt

1. Cook broccoli for 5 minutes in saucepan in boiling water. Drain and set aside.
2. Sauté onion in butter in saucepan until tender. Add to broccoli.
3. Combine remaining ingredients. Add to broccoli mixture. Pour into greased slow cooker.
4. Cover. Cook on Low 3–4 hours.

Broccoli Casserole

Dorothy Van Deest   Memphis, TN

MAKES: **6 SERVINGS**
PREP. TIME: **10 MINUTES**
COOKING TIME: **3–5 HOURS**
IDEAL SLOW COOKER SIZE: **3-QUART**

10-oz. pkg. frozen chopped broccoli

6 eggs, beaten

24-oz. carton fat-free small-curd cottage cheese

6 Tbsp. flour

8 ozs. fat-free mild cheese of your choice, diced

2 green onions, chopped

½ tsp. salt

1. Place frozen broccoli in colander. Run cold water over it until it thaws. Separate into pieces. Drain well.
2. Combine remaining ingredients in large bowl and mix until well blended. Stir in broccoli. Pour into slow cooker sprayed with fat-free cooking spray.
3. Cover. Cook on High 1 hour. Stir well, then resume cooking on Low 2–4 hours.

Per Serving: 250 calories (40 calories from fat), 4.5g total fat (1.5g saturated, 0g trans), 200mg cholesterol, 980mg sodium, 20g total carbohydrate (4g fiber, 8g sugar), 32g protein, 20%DV vitamin A, 20%DV vitamin C, 35%DV calcium, 8%DV iron.

Variation: *You can use fresh broccoli instead of frozen.*

To get the best flavor, saute vegetables or brown meat before placing in cooker to cook.

Asian-Style Broccoli

Frieda Weisz Aberdeen, SD

MAKES: **8 SERVINGS**
PREP. TIME: **15 MINUTES**
COOKING TIME: **6 HOURS**
IDEAL SLOW COOKER SIZE: **3½–4-QUART**

2 lbs. fresh broccoli, trimmed and chopped into bite-
    size pieces
1 clove garlic, minced
1 green *or* red bell pepper, cut into thin slices
1 onion, cut into slices
4 Tbsp. light soy sauce
½ tsp. salt
dash of black pepper
1 Tbsp. sesame seeds as garnish, *optional*

1. Combine all ingredients except sesame seeds
   in slow cooker.
2. Cook on Low for 6 hours. Top with sesame
   seeds.
3. Serve on brown rice.

———————————

Per Serving: 50 calories (10 calories from fat), 1 total fat (0g
saturated, 0g trans), 0mg cholesterol, 300mg sodium, 9g total
carbohydrate (4g fiber, 3g sugar), 4g protein, 50%DV vitamin A,
150%DV vitamin C, 6%DV calcium, 15%DV iron.

Broccoli Delight

Nancy Wagner Graves Manhattan, KS

MAKES: **4–6 SERVINGS**
PREP. TIME: **15 MINUTES**
COOKING TIME: **2–6 HOURS**
IDEAL SLOW COOKER SIZE: **3½–4-QUART**

1–2 lbs. broccoli, chopped
2 cups cauliflower, chopped
10¾-oz. can 98% fat-free cream of celery soup
½ tsp. salt
¼ tsp. black pepper
1 medium onion, diced
2–4 garlic cloves, crushed, according to your taste
    preference
½ cup vegetable broth

1. Combine all ingredients in slow cooker.
2. Cook on Low 4–6 hours, or on High 2–3
   hours.

———————————

Per Serving: 110 calories (20 calories from fat), 2.5 total fat (0.5g
saturated, 0.5g trans), 5mg cholesterol, 740mg sodium, 19g total
carbohydrate (5g fiber, 5g sugar), 6g protein, 300%DV vitamin A,
100%DV vitamin C, 10%DV calcium, 10%DV iron.

Golden Cauliflower

Rosalie D. Miller Mifflintown, PA • *Dede Peterson* Rapid City, SD

MAKES: **4–6 SERVINGS**
PREP. TIME: **5–10 MINUTES**
COOKING TIME: **1½–5 HOURS**
IDEAL SLOW COOKER SIZE: **3-QUART**

2 10-oz. pkgs. frozen cauliflower, thawed
salt and pepper
10¾-oz. can condensed cheddar cheese soup
4 slices bacon, crisply fried and crumbled

1. Place cauliflower in slow cooker. Season with
   salt and pepper.

2. Spoon soup over top. Sprinkle with bacon.
3. Cover and cook on High 1½ hours, or on Low 4–5 hours, or until cauliflower is tender.

Tip: *If you forgot to thaw the cauliflower, cook it 30 minutes longer.*

Golden Carrots

Jan Mast Lancaster, PA

MAKES: **6 SERVINGS**
PREP. TIME: **5 MINUTES**
COOKING TIME: **3–4 HOURS**
IDEAL SLOW COOKER SIZE: **2-QUART**

PICTURED
ON PAGE
97

2-lb. pkg. baby carrots
½ cup golden raisins
1 stick (½ cup) butter, melted or softened
⅓ cup honey
2 Tbsp. lemon juice
½ tsp. ground ginger, *optional*

1. Combine all ingredients in slow cooker.
2. Cover and cook on Low 3–4 hours, or until carrots are tender-crisp.

Variation: *To use whole carrots, cut into 1-inch-long chunks. If the carrots are thick, you may need to cook them 5–6 hours until they become tender-crisp.*

To clear honey out of your measuring cup easily, first spray the measuring cup with cooking spray.

Apricot-Glazed Carrots

Marcia S. Myer Manheim, PA

MAKES: **8 SERVINGS**
PREP. TIME: **5 MINUTES**
COOKING TIME: **9¼ HOURS**
IDEAL SLOW COOKER SIZE: **4-QUART**

2 lbs. baby carrots
1 onion, chopped
½ cup water
⅓ cup honey
⅓ cup apricot preserves
2 Tbsp. chopped fresh parsley

1. Place carrots and onions in slow cooker. Add water.
2. Cover and cook on Low 9 hours.
3. Drain liquid from slow cooker.
4. In a small bowl, mix honey and preserves together. Pour over carrots.
5. Cover and cook on High 10–15 minutes.
6. Sprinkle with parsley before serving.

Apple-Glazed Carrots

Gloria Frey Lebanon, PA

MAKES: **4 SERVINGS**
PREP. TIME: **10–15 MINUTES**
COOKING TIME: **2½–3½ HOURS**
IDEAL SLOW COOKER SIZE: **2-QUART**

16-oz. pkg. frozen baby carrots
¼ cup apple cider *or* apple juice
¼ cup apple jelly
1½ tsp. Dijon mustard

1. Put carrots and apple juice in slow cooker.
2. Cover and cook on High 2–3 hours, until carrots are tender.
3. Blend jelly and mustard together in a small bowl.
4. During the last 45 minutes of cooking time, after carrots are tender, stir in blended apple jelly and mustard. Continue to heat until steaming hot.

Orange-Glazed Carrots

Cyndie Marrara Port Matilda, PA

MAKES: **6–8 SERVINGS**
PREP. TIME: **10 MINUTES**
COOKING TIME: **4–6 HOURS**
IDEAL SLOW COOKER SIZE: **3½-QUART**

32-oz. pkg. baby carrots
¼ cup packed brown sugar
½ cup orange juice
1 Tbsp. butter
½–¾ tsp. ground cinnamon, according to your taste preference
¼ tsp. ground nutmeg
2 Tbsp. cornstarch
¼ cup water

1. Combine all ingredients except cornstarch and water in slow cooker.
2. Cover. Cook on Low 4–6 hours, or until carrots are done to your liking.
3. Put carrots in serving dish and keep warm, reserving cooking juices. Put reserved juices in small saucepan. Bring to boil.
4. Mix cornstarch and water in small bowl until blended. Add to juices. Boil one minute or until thickened, stirring constantly.
5. Pour over carrots and serve.

Per Serving: 130 calories (25 calories from fat), 3g total fat (1.5g saturated, 0g trans), 5mg cholesterol, 60mg sodium, 26g total carbohydrate (3g fiber, 18g sugar), 1g protein, 300%DV vitamin A, 20%DV vitamin C, 4%DV calcium, 8%DV iron.

Use light brown sugar for a caramel flavor. Use dark brown sugar when you prefer a molasses flavor and color.

Carrot Casserole

Janessa Hochstedler   East Earl, PA

MAKES: **4–5 SERVINGS**
PREP. TIME: **20 MINUTES**
COOKING TIME: **4–5 HOURS**
IDEAL SLOW COOKER SIZE: **2-QUART**

4 cups sliced carrots

1 medium onion, chopped

10¾-oz. can cream of celery soup

½ cup Velveeta cheese, cubed

¼–½ tsp. salt

1. Mix all ingredients in slow cooker.
2. Cover and cook on Low 4–5 hours, or until carrots are tender but not mushy.

Glazed Root Vegetable Medley

Teena Wagner   Waterloo, ON

MAKES: **6 SERVINGS**
PREP. TIME: **20 MINUTES**
COOKING TIME: **3 HOURS**
IDEAL SLOW COOKER SIZE: **4-QUART**

2 medium parsnips

4 medium carrots

1 turnip, about 4½ inches around

½ cup water

1 tsp. salt

½ cup sugar

3 Tbsp. butter

½ tsp. salt

1. Clean and peel vegetables. Cut in 1-inch pieces.
2. Dissolve salt in water in saucepan. Add vegetables and boil for 10 minutes. Drain, reserving ½ cup liquid.
3. Place vegetables in slow cooker. Add liquid.
4. Stir in sugar, butter, and salt.
5. Cover. Cook on Low 3 hours.

Brussels Sprouts with Pimentos

Donna Lantgon   Rapid City, SD

MAKES: **8 SERVINGS**
PREP. TIME: **5 MINUTES**
COOKING TIME: **6 HOURS**
IDEAL SLOW COOKER SIZE: **3½–4-QUART**

2 lbs. brussels sprouts

¼ tsp. dried oregano

½ tsp. dried basil

2-oz. jar pimentos, drained

¼ cup, *or* 1 small can, sliced black olives, drained

1 Tbsp. olive oil

½ cup water

1. Combine all ingredients in slow cooker.
2. Cook on Low 6 hours.

Per Serving: 70 calories (20 calories from fat), 2.5g total fat (0g saturated, 0g trans), 0mg cholesterol, 25mg sodium, 11g total carbohydrate (3g fiber, 5g sugar), 3g protein, 20%DV vitamin A, 100%DV vitamin C, 4%DV calcium, 10%DV iron.

Sweet-Sour Cabbage

Irma H. Schoen   Windsor, CT

MAKES: **6 SERVINGS**
PREP. TIME: **20 MINUTES**
COOKING TIME: **3–5 HOURS**
IDEAL SLOW COOKER SIZE: **4-QUART**

1 medium head red *or* green cabbage, shredded

2 onions, chopped

4 tart apples, pared, quartered

½ cup raisins

¼ cup lemon juice

¼ cup cider, *or* apple juice

3 Tbsp. honey

1 Tbsp. caraway seeds

⅛ tsp. allspice

½ tsp. salt

1. Combine all ingredients in slow cooker.
2. Cook on High 3–5 hours, depending upon how crunchy or soft you want the cabbage and onions.

Bavarian Cabbage

Joyce Shackelford   Green Bay, WI

MAKES: **4–8 SERVINGS, DEPENDING UPON THE SIZE OF THE CABBAGE HEAD**
PREP. TIME: **10 MINUTES**
COOKING TIME: **3–8 HOURS**
IDEAL SLOW COOKER SIZE: **4-QUART**

1 small head red cabbage, sliced

1 medium onion, chopped

3 tart apples, cored and quartered

2 tsp. salt

1 cup hot water

2 Tbsp. sugar

⅓ cup vinegar

3 Tbsp. bacon drippings

1. Place all ingredients in slow cooker in order listed.
2. Cover. Cook on Low 8 hours, or on High 3 hours. Stir well before serving.

Variation: *Add 6 slices bacon, browned until crisp and crumbled.*

Jean M. Butzer   Batavia, NY

Cabbage Casserole

Edwina Stoltzfus   Narvon, PA

MAKES: **6 SERVINGS**
PREP. TIME: **20 MINUTES**
COOKING TIME: **4–5 HOURS**
IDEAL SLOW COOKER SIZE: **4-QUART**

1 large head cabbage, chopped

2 cups water

1 Tbsp. salt

⅓ cup butter

¼ cup flour

½–1 tsp. salt

¼ tsp. pepper

1⅓ cups milk

1⅓ cups shredded cheddar

1. Cook cabbage in saucepan in boiling water and salt for 5 minutes. Drain. Place in slow cooker.
2. In saucepan, melt butter. Stir in flour, salt, and pepper. Add milk, stirring constantly on low heat for 5 minutes. Remove from heat. Stir in cheese. Pour over cabbage.
3. Cover. Cook on Low 4–5 hours.

Variation: *Replace cabbage with cauliflower.*

"Baked" Tomatoes

Lizzie Ann Yoder   Hartville, OH

MAKES: **4 SERVINGS**
PREP. TIME: **5 MINUTES**
COOKING TIME: **¾–1 HOURS**
IDEAL SLOW COOKER SIZE: **2½–3-QUART**

2 tomatoes, each cut in half
½ Tbsp. olive oil
½ tsp. parsley, chopped, *or* ¼ tsp. dry parsley flakes
¼ tsp. dried oregano
¼ tsp. dried basil

1. Place tomato halves in slow cooker sprayed with non-fat cooking spray.
2. Drizzle oil over tomatoes. Sprinkle with remaining ingredients.
3. Cover. Cook on High 45 minutes–1 hour.

Per Serving: 30 calories (20 calories from fat), 2g total fat (0g saturated, 0g trans), 0mg cholesterol, 5mg sodium, 4g total carbohydrate (0.5g fiber, 2g sugar), 1g protein, 4%DV vitamin A, 10%DV vitamin C, 0%DV calcium, 2%DV iron.

Stewed Tomatoes

Michelle Showalter   Bridgewater, VA

MAKES: **12 SERVINGS**
PREP. TIME: **10 MINUTES**
COOKING TIME: **3–4 HOURS**
IDEAL SLOW COOKER SIZE: **4-QUART**

2 quarts low-sodium canned tomatoes
¼ cup sugar
1 tsp. salt
dash of black pepper
2 Tbsp. butter
2 cups bread cubes

1. Place tomatoes in slow cooker.
2. Sprinkle with sugar, salt, and pepper.
3. Lightly toast bread cubes in melted butter in skillet on top of stove. Spread over tomatoes.
4. Cover. Cook on High 3–4 hours

Per Serving: 90 calories (20 calories from fat), 2.5g total fat (1.5g saturated, 0g trans), 5mg cholesterol, 650mg sodium, 15g total carbohydrate (2g fiber, 9g sugar), 2g protein, 10%DV vitamin A, 10%DV vitamin C, 10%DV calcium, 4%DV iron.

Variation: *If you prefer bread that is less moist and soft, add bread cubes 15 minutes before serving and continue cooking without the lid.*

A little sugar brings out the flavor of most foods. Brown sugar cuts the acid in tomato dishes.

Cranberry-Orange Beets

Jean Butzer Batavia, NY

MAKES: **6 SERVINGS**
PREP. TIME: **15 MINUTES**
COOKING TIME: **3½–7½ HOURS**
IDEAL SLOW COOKER SIZE: **6-QUART**

2 lbs. medium beets, peeled and quartered

½ tsp. ground nutmeg

1 cup cranberry juice

1 tsp. orange peel, finely shredded, *optional*

2 Tbsp. butter

2 Tbsp. sugar

4 tsp. cornstarch

1. Place beets in slow cooker. Sprinkle with nutmeg.
2. Add cranberry juice and orange peel. Dot with butter.
3. Cover. Cook on Low 6–7 hours, or on High 3–3½ hours.
4. In small bowl, combine sugar and cornstarch.
5. Remove ½ cup of cooking liquid and stir into cornstarch.
6. Stir mixture into slow cooker.
7. Cover. Cook on High 15–30 minutes.

Per Serving: 150 calories (35 calories from fat), 4g total fat (2.5g saturated, 0g trans), 10mg cholesterol, 120mg sodium, 26g total carbohydrate (4g fiber, 19g sugar), 2g protein, 4%DV vitamin A, 20%DV vitamin C, 2%DV calcium, 8%DV iron.

One hour on High equals about 2 to 2½ hours on Low.

Harvard Beets

Marjorie Yoder Guengerich Harrisonburg, VA

MAKES: **6 SERVINGS**
PREP. TIME: **5 MINUTES**
COOKING TIME: **1 HOUR**
IDEAL SLOW COOKER SIZE: **3-QUART**

⅓ cup sugar

2 Tbsp. flour

¼ cup beet juice *or* water

¼ cup vinegar

2 16-oz. cans sliced beets, drained

1. Mix sugar and flour. Stir in beet juice and vinegar. Mix well.
2. Place beets in slow cooker. Pour sugar and vinegar mixture over beets. Stir to coat.
3. Cover. Cook on High 1 hour. Turn to Low until ready to serve.

Per Serving: 100 calories (0 calories from fat), 0g total fat (0g saturated, 0g trans), 0mg cholesterol, 75mg sodium, 24g total carbohydrate (3g fiber, 17g sugar), 2g protein, 0%DV vitamin A, 0%DV vitamin C, 0%DV calcium, 8%DV iron.

Mushrooms in Red Wine

Donna Lantgen Rapid City, SD

MAKES: **4 SERVINGS**
PREP. TIME: **5 MINUTES**
COOKING TIME: **6 HOURS**
IDEAL SLOW COOKER SIZE: **2–3-QUART**

1 lb. fresh mushrooms, stemmed, trimmed, and cleaned

4 cloves garlic, minced

¼ cup onion

1 Tbsp. olive oil

1 cup red wine

1. Combine all ingredients in slow cooker.
2. Cook on Low 6 hours.

Per Serving: 110 calories (35 calories from fat), 4g total fat (0.5g saturated, 0g trans), 0mg cholesterol, 10mg sodium, 7g total carbohydrate (2g fiber, 2g sugar), 4g protein, 0%DV vitamin A, 6%DV vitamin C, 2%DV calcium, 8%DV iron.

Tip: *You can serve this as a side dish or as a condiment.*

Variations:

1. You can use this as the base for a sauce to which you could add steak tips or ground beef, as well as 2 cups chopped onions, 2 tsp. dried oregano, 1½ tsp. salt, ½ tsp. black pepper, and 4 cloves minced garlic.

2. You could add a quart of spaghetti sauce and serve the mixture over a pound of your favorite pasta.

Wild Mushrooms Italian

Connie Johnson Loudon, NH

MAKES: **5–7 SERVINGS**
PREP. TIME: **20 MINUTES**
COOKING TIME: **6–8 HOURS**
IDEAL SLOW COOKER SIZE: **5-QUART**

2 large onions, chopped

3 large red bell peppers, chopped

3 large green bell peppers, chopped

2 Tbsp. oil

12-oz. pkg. oyster mushrooms, cleaned and chopped

4 garlic cloves, minced

3 fresh bay leaves

10 fresh basil leaves, chopped

1½ tsp. salt

1½ tsp. black pepper

28-oz. can low-sodium Italian plum tomatoes, crushed or chopped

1. Sauté onions and peppers in oil in skillet until soft. Stir in mushrooms and garlic. Sauté just until mushrooms begin to turn brown. Pour into slow cooker.
2. Add remaining ingredients. Stir well.
3. Cover. Cook on Low 6–8 hours.

Per Serving: 180 calories (60 calories from fat), 7g total fat (1g saturated, 0g trans), 0mg cholesterol, 1040mg sodium, 29g total carbohydrate (8g fiber, 6g sugar), 7g protein, 50%DV vitamin A, 150%DV vitamin C, 8%DV calcium, 25%DV iron.

Tip: *This dish is good as an appetizer or on pita bread, or served over rice or pasta for a main dish.*

Vegetables

Stuffed Mushrooms

Melanie L. Thrower   McPherson, KS

MAKES: **4–6 SERVINGS**
PREP. TIME: **20–30 MINUTES**
COOKING TIME: **2–4 HOURS**
IDEAL SLOW COOKER SIZE: **3-QUART**

8–10 large mushrooms
¼ tsp. minced garlic
1 Tbsp. oil
dash of salt
dash of pepper
dash of cayenne pepper, *optional*
¼ cup shredded Monterey Jack cheese

1. Remove stems from mushrooms and dice.
2. Heat oil in skillet. Sauté diced stems with garlic until softened. Remove skillet from heat.
3. Stir in seasonings and cheese. Stuff into mushroom shells. Place in slow cooker.
4. Cover. Heat on Low 2–4 hours.

Variations:

1. Add 1 Tbsp. minced onion to Step 2.
2. Use Monterey Jack cheese with jalapeños.

Very Special Spinach

Jeanette Oberholtzer   Manheim, PA

MAKES: **8 SERVINGS**
PREP. TIME: **10 MINUTES**
COOKING TIME: **5 HOURS**
IDEAL SLOW COOKER SIZE: **4-QUART**

3 10-oz. boxes frozen spinach, thawed and drained
2 cups cottage cheese
1½ cups shredded cheddar cheese
3 eggs
¼ cup flour
1 tsp. salt
½ cup butter, *or* margarine, melted

1. Mix together all ingredients.
2. Pour into slow cooker.
3. Cook on High 1 hour. Reduce heat to Low and cook 4 more hours.

Caramelized Onions

Mrs. J.E. Barthold   Bethlehem, PA

MAKES: **6–8 SERVINGS**
PREP. TIME: **10 MINUTES**
COOKING TIME: **12 HOURS**
IDEAL SLOW COOKER SIZE: **4-QUART**

6–8 large Vidalia *or* other sweet onions
4 Tbsp. butter, *or* margarine
10-oz. can chicken *or* vegetable broth

1. Peel onions. Remove stems and root ends. Place in slow cooker.
2. Pour butter and broth over.
3. Cook on Low 12 hours.

Tip: *Serve as a side dish, or use onions and liquid to flavor soups or stews, or as topping for pizza.*

Cheesy Onions

Janessa Hochstedler East Earl, PA

MAKES: **6–8 SERVINGS**
PREP. TIME: **10–20 MINUTES**
COOKING TIME: **2–4 HOURS**
IDEAL SLOW COOKER SIZE: **2-QUART**

1½ lbs. small onions

4 slices bacon, cooked and crumbled

10½-oz. can cheddar cheese soup

½ cup milk

¼ cup grated Parmesan cheese

1. Peel onions, but leave whole. Place in slow cooker.
2. Mix remaining ingredients together in a bowl.
3. Pour into slow cooker. Gently mix in onions.
4. Cook on High 2 hours, or on Low 4 hours, or until onions are fully tender.

Freeze extra onions and celery rather than letting them spoil in the refrigerator. You can use them later in chili, soups, or barbecue.

Swiss-Irish Hot Sauce

Jo Haberkamp Fairbank, IA

MAKES: **6–8 SERVINGS**
PREP. TIME: **15 MINUTES**
COOKING TIME: **4 HOURS**
IDEAL SLOW COOKER SIZE: **3-QUART**

2 medium onions, diced

5 garlic cloves, minced

¼ cup oil

1-lb. can tomatoes, pureed

15-oz. can tomato sauce

12-oz. can tomato paste

2 Tbsp. parsley, fresh or dried

½ tsp. red pepper

½ tsp. black pepper

1 tsp. chili powder

1 tsp. dried basil

2 tsp. Worcestershire sauce

2 tsp. Tabasco sauce

¼ cup red wine

1. Sauté onions and garlic in oil in skillet.
2. Combine all ingredients in slow cooker.
3. Cover. Cook on Low 4 hours.
4. This is a flavorful sauce for eating over pasta or baked potatoes. Serve with French bread and a tossed salad.

Slow Cooker Ratatouille

Nanci Keatley Salem, OR

MAKES: **6 SERVINGS**
PREP. TIME: **20 MINUTES**
COOKING TIME: **4–7 HOURS**
IDEAL SLOW COOKER SIZE: **5–6-QUART**

1 Tbsp. olive oil

1 large onion, chopped

6 large garlic cloves, minced

1 green bell pepper, cut into strips

1 red bell pepper, cut into strips

1 medium eggplant, cubed

2 cups thickly sliced mushrooms

4 tomatoes, cubed

1 cup low-sodium tomato puree

¼ cup dry red wine *or* wine vinegar

1 Tbsp. lemon juice

2 tsp. dried thyme

1 tsp. dried oregano

1 tsp. ground cumin

½–1 tsp. salt

¼–½ tsp. black pepper

4 Tbsp. minced fresh basil

¼ cup chopped fresh parsley

1. Turn slow cooker on High for 2 minutes.
2. Pour oil into slow cooker and add remaining ingredients except parsley and fresh basil.
3. Cover. Cook on High 2 hours, then on Low 4–5 hours.
4. Stir in fresh basil. Sprinkle with parsley. Serve.

———————————

Per Serving: 120 calories (30 calories from fat), 3g total fat (0g saturated, 0g trans), 0mg cholesterol, 30mg sodium, 20g total carbohydrate (6g fiber, 10g sugar), 4g protein, 30%DV vitamin A, 50%DV vitamin C, 6%DV calcium, 15%DV iron.

Tip: *This is delicious over whole wheat pasta or brown rice! It also makes great pizza topping.*

Variation *You may substitute 1 rounded Tbsp. dried basil for the fresh basil. If you do that, then add the basil to Step 2.*

Mediterranean Eggplant

Willard E. Roth Elkhart, IN

MAKES: **8 SERVINGS**
PREP. TIME: **20 MINUTES**
COOKING TIME: **5–6 HOURS**
IDEAL SLOW COOKER SIZE: **5-QUART**

1 medium red onion, chopped

2 cloves garlic, crushed

1 cup fresh mushrooms, sliced

2 Tbsp. olive oil

1 eggplant, unpeeled, cubed

2 green bell peppers, coarsely chopped

28-oz. can crushed tomatoes

28-oz. can garbanzo beans, drained and rinsed

2 Tbsp. fresh rosemary

1 cup chopped fresh parsley

½ cup kalamata olives, pitted and sliced

1. Sauté onion, garlic, and mushrooms in olive oil in a skillet over medium heat. Transfer to slow cooker coated with non-fat cooking spray.
2. Add eggplant, peppers, tomatoes, garbanzo beans, rosemary, and parsley.
3. Cover. Cook on Low 5–6 hours.
4. Stir in olives just before serving.
5. Serve with couscous or polenta.

———————————

Per Serving: 250 calories (70 calories from fat), 8g total fat (1g saturated, 0g trans), 0mg cholesterol, 370mg sodium, 38g total carbohydrate (9g fiber, 8g sugar), 11g protein, 10%DV vitamin A, 40%DV vitamin C, 15%DV calcium, 30%DV iron.

Vegetables

Caponata

Katrine Rose Woodbridge, VA

MAKES: **10 SERVINGS**
PREP. TIME: **15 MINUTES**
COOKING TIME: **7–8 HOURS**
IDEAL SLOW COOKER SIZE: **4-QUART**

1 medium eggplant, peeled and cut into ½-inch cubes

14-oz. can low-sodium diced tomatoes

1 medium onion, chopped

1 red bell pepper, cut into ½-inch pieces

¾ cup low-sodium salsa

¼ cup olive oil

2 Tbsp. capers, drained

3 Tbsp. balsamic vinegar

3 garlic cloves, minced

1¼ tsp. dried oregano

⅓ cup chopped fresh basil

1. Combine all ingredients except basil and bread in slow cooker.
2. Cover. Cook on Low 7–8 hours, or until vegetables are tender.
3. Stir in basil. Serve over slices of toasted French bread.

Per Serving: 340 calories (70 calories from fat), 8g total fat (1.5g saturated, 0.5g trans), 0mg cholesterol, 830mg sodium, 58g total carbohydrate (5g fiber, 5g sugar), 10g protein, 2%DV vitamin A, 10%DV vitamin C, 10%DV calcium, 15%DV iron.

Cooked pasta and rice should be added during the last 1–1½ hours of cooking time to prevent them from disintegrating.

Eggplant Italian

Melanie Thrower McPherson, KS

MAKES: **6–8 SERVINGS**
PREP. TIME: **20 MINUTES**
COOKING TIME: **4 HOURS**
IDEAL SLOW COOKER SIZE: **4–5-QUART; AN OVAL COOKER WORKS BEST!**

2 eggplants

¼ cup eggbeaters

24 ozs. fat-free cottage cheese

¼ tsp. salt

black pepper to taste

14-oz. can tomato sauce

2–4 Tbsp. Italian seasoning, according to your taste preference

1. Peel eggplants and cut in ½-inch-thick slices. Soak in salt-water for about 5 minutes to remove bitterness. Drain well.
2. Spray slow cooker with fat-free cooking spray.
3. Mix eggbeaters, cottage cheese, salt, and pepper together in bowl.
4. Mix tomato sauce and Italian seasoning together in another bowl.
5. Spoon a thin layer of tomato sauce into bottom of slow cooker. Top with about one-third of the eggplant slices, and then one-third of the egg-cheese mixture, and finally one-third of the remaining tomato sauce mixture.
6. Repeat those layers twice, ending with seasoned tomato sauce.
7. Cover. Cook on High 4 hours. Allow to rest 15 minutes before serving.

Per Serving: 120 calories (10 calories from fat), 1g total fat (0g saturated, 0g trans), 30mg cholesterol, 940mg sodium, 17g total carbohydrate (4g fiber, 11g sugar), 11g protein, 15%DV vitamin A, 4%DV vitamin C, 8%DV calcium, 4%DV iron.

Variation: *For more spice, add red pepper seasoning to taste in Step 4.*

Eggplant & Zucchini Casserole

Jennifer Dzialowski Brighton, MI

MAKES: **6 SERVINGS**
PREP. TIME: **20 MINUTES**
COOKING TIME: **5–6 HOURS**
IDEAL SLOW COOKER SIZE: **5-QUART**

2 egg whites

1 medium eggplant

1 medium zucchini

1½ cups bread crumbs

1 tsp. garlic powder

1 tsp. low-sodium Italian seasoning

48-oz. jar fat-free, low-sodium spaghetti sauce

8-oz. bag low-fat shredded mozzarella cheese

1. Beat egg whites in small bowl.
2. Slice eggplant and zucchini. Place in separate bowl.
3. Combine in another bowl bread crumbs, garlic powder, and Italian seasoning.
4. Dip sliced veggies in egg white and then in bread crumbs. Layer in slow cooker, pouring sauce and sprinkling cheese over each layer. (Reserve ½ cup cheese). Top with sauce.
5. Cover. Cook on Low 5–6 hours, or until vegetables are tender.
6. Top with remaining cheese during last 15 minutes of cooking.

Per Serving: 280 calories (100 calories from fat), 11g total fat (4.5g saturated, 0g trans), 20mg cholesterol, 1380mg sodium, 30g total carbohydrate (6g fiber, 15g sugar), 15g protein, 20%DV vitamin A, 20%DV vitamin C, 30%DV calcium, 15%DV iron.

Variation: *For added flavoring, sprinkle chopped onions and minced garlic over each layer of vegetables.*

Squash Medley

Evelyn Page Riverton, WY

MAKES: **8 SERVINGS**
PREP. TIME: **20 MINUTES**
COOKING TIME: **4–6 HOURS**
IDEAL SLOW COOKER SIZE: **3½-QUART**

8 summer squash, each about 4-inches long, thinly sliced

½ tsp. salt

2 tomatoes, peeled and chopped

¼ cup sliced green onions

half a small sweet green pepper, chopped

1 chicken bouillon cube

¼ cup hot water

4 slices bacon, fried and crumbled

¼ cup fine dry bread crumbs

1. Sprinkle squash with salt.
2. In slow cooker, layer half the squash, tomatoes, onions, and pepper. Repeat layers.
3. Dissolve bouillon in hot water. Pour into slow cooker.
4. Top with bacon. Sprinkle bread crumbs over top.
5. Cover. Cook on Low 4–6 hours.

Variation: *For a sweeter touch, sprinkle 1 Tbsp. brown sugar over half the layered vegetables. Repeat over second half of layered vegetables.*

Keep a Ziplock bag in the freezer to collect the unused ends of bread loaves. When the bag is full, whirl in food processor. Return to bag and freeze — you'll always have fresh bread crumbs at your fingertips.

Zucchini Casserole

Rebecca Leichty Harrisonburg, VA

MAKES: **6 SERVINGS**
PREP. TIME: **20 MINUTES**
COOKING TIME: **4–6 HOURS**
IDEAL SLOW COOKER SIZE: **3-QUART**

2–3 cups thinly sliced zucchini

1 medium onion, diced

2 large carrots, shredded (enough to make 1 cup)

10¾-oz. can 98% fat free cream of celery soup

10¾-oz. can condensed cream of chicken soup

¼ tsp. salt

dash of black pepper

dash of ground cumin, if you like

1. Spray slow cooker with fat-free cooking spray. Mix vegetables, soups, and salt together gently in slow cooker. Cover.
2. Cook on High 4–6 hours, or until vegetables are as crunchy or as soft as you like.

Per Serving: 100 calories (40 calories from fat), 4.5g total fat (1.5g saturated, 0.5g trans), 5mg cholesterol, 760mg sodium, 12g total carbohydrate (2g fiber, 4g sugar), 3g protein, 100%DV vitamin A, 6%DV vitamin C, 4%DV calcium, 4%DV iron.

Zucchini in Sour Cream

Lizzie Ann Yoder Hartville, OH

MAKES: **6 SERVINGS**
PREP. TIME: **10 MINUTES**
COOKING TIME: **1–1½ HOURS**
IDEAL SLOW COOKER SIZE: **3–4-QUART**

4 cups unpeeled, sliced zucchini

1 cup fat-free sour cream

¼ cup skim milk

1 cup chopped onions

1 tsp. salt

1 cup shredded low-fat sharp cheddar cheese

1. Parboil zucchini in microwave for 2–3 minutes. Turn into slow cooker sprayed with non-fat cooking spray.
2. Combine sour cream, milk, onions, and salt. Pour over zucchini and stir gently.
3. Cover. Cook on Low 1–1½ hours.
4. Sprinkle cheese over vegetables 30 minutes before serving.

Per Serving: 100 calories (20 calories from fat), 2g total fat (1g saturated, 0g trans), 10mg cholesterol, 430mg sodium, 12g total carbohydrate (1g fiber, 7g sugar), 8g protein, 10%DV vitamin A, 0%DV vitamin C, 20%DV calcium, 4%DV iron.

Squash Casserole

Sharon Anders Alburtis, PA

MAKES: **4–6 SERVINGS**
PREP. TIME: **15 MINUTES**
COOKING TIME: **7–9 HOURS**
IDEAL SLOW COOKER SIZE: **4-QUART**

2 lbs. yellow summer squash *or* zucchini thinly sliced (about 6 cups)

half a medium onion, chopped

1 cup peeled, shredded carrot

10¾-oz. can condensed cream of chicken soup

1 cup sour cream

¼ cup flour

8-oz. pkg. seasoned stuffing crumbs

½ cup butter, melted

1. Combine squash, onion, carrots, and soup.
2. Mix together sour cream and flour. Stir into vegetables.
3. Toss stuffing mix with butter. Spread half in bottom of slow cooker. Add vegetable mixture. Top with remaining crumbs.
4. Cover. Cook on Low 7–9 hours.

Acorn Squash

Janet L. Roggie Lowville, NY • Mary Stauffer Ephrata, PA
Leona Yoder Hartville, OH • June S. Groff Denver, PA
Trudy Kutter Corfu, NY

MAKES: **4–6 SERVINGS**
PREP. TIME: **5 MINUTES**
COOKING TIME: **7–8 HOURS**
IDEAL SLOW COOKER SIZE: **4–5-QUART, DEPENDING ON THE
    SIZE OF THE SQUASH**

whole acorn squash

water

salt

cinnamon

butter

brown sugar *or* maple syrup, *optional*

1. Wash squash. Cut off stem. Place whole
   squash in slow cooker. Add water to a depth
   of about 1 inch.
2. Cover and cook on Low 7–8 hours,
   depending on the size of the squash. Jag
   with a sharp fork to see if it's tender. Cook
   longer if it isn't. Check every 2 hours during
   cooking time, if you can, to make sure the
   squash isn't cooking dry. Add water if it
   drops below 1-inch deep.
3. Remove squash from cooker and allow to
   cool until you can handle it.
4. Cut in half with a long-bladed knife. Scoop
   seeds out of both halves.
5. To serve, sprinkle flesh with salt and
   cinnamon. Dot with butter. Drizzle with
   brown sugar or maple syrup, if you wish.
   Or scoop out the flesh with a spoon into a
   mixing bowl. Add remaining ingredients
   and mash together until well blended and
   smooth.

Variation: *Cut the squash in half before placing
in cooker. Scoop out seeds. Wrap each half in
foil and place in cooker. Add water to a depth of
1-inch.*

*Continue with Step 2 above, but skip Steps 3
and 4.*

Alice Rush Quakertown, PA

Squash and Apples

Sharon Miller Holmesville, OH

MAKES: **6 SERVINGS**
PREP. TIME: **25 MINUTES**
COOKING TIME: **6–8 HOURS**
IDEAL SLOW COOKER SIZE: **6-QUART**

**1 large butternut squash, peeled, seeded, and cut into
    ¼-inch slices**

**2 medium cooking apples, cored and cut into ¼-inch
    slices**

3 Tbsp. raisins, *optional*

3 Tbsp. reduced-calorie pancake syrup

dash of ground cinnamon *and/or* nutmeg

¼ cup apple cider *or* apple juice

1. Layer half of the following ingredients in
   slow cooker: squash, apples, and raisins.
2. Drizzle with half the syrup.
3. Repeat layers.
4. Pour cider over the top.
5. Cook on Low 6–8 hours, or until squash is
   tender.

Per Serving: 130 calories (0 calories from fat), 0g total fat (0g
saturated, 0g trans), 0mg cholesterol, 10mg sodium, 34g total
carbohydrate (8g fiber, 15g sugar), 2g protein, 200%DV vitamin A,
20%DV vitamin C, 10%DV calcium, 8%DV iron.

Vegetables

Stuffed Peppers with Beef

Eleanor J. Ferreira   N. Chelmsford, MA

MAKES: **6–8 SERVINGS**
PREP. TIME: **15 MINUTES**
COOKING TIME: **4–12 HOURS**
IDEAL SLOW COOKER SIZE: **6-QUART**

6–8 green peppers

1–2 lbs. ground beef

1 onion, chopped

¼ tsp. salt

¼ tsp. pepper

1 egg

1 slice white bread

28-oz. can whole *or* stewed tomatoes

1. Cut peppers in half and remove seeds.
2. Combine ground beef, onion, salt, pepper, and egg. Tear bread into small pieces. Add to ground beef mixture. Stuff into peppers.
3. Form remaining meat into oblong shape. Place meatloaf and peppers into slow cooker. Pour in tomatoes.
4. Cover. Cook on Low 6–12 hours, or on High 4–5 hours.

Purely Artichokes

Gertrude Dutcher   Hartville, OH

MAKES: **4–6 SERVINGS**
PREP. TIME: **15 MINUTES**
COOKING TIME: **6–8 HOURS**
IDEAL SLOW COOKER SIZE: **4-QUART**

4–6 artichokes

1–1½ tsp. salt

1 cup lemon juice, *divided*

2 cups hot water

1 stick (½ cup) butter, melted

1. Wash and trim artichokes. Cut off about 1 inch from top. If you wish, trim tips of leaves. Stand chokes upright in slow cooker.
2. Sprinkle each choke with ¼ tsp. salt and 2 Tbsp. lemon juice.
3. Pour 2 cups hot water around the base of the artichokes.
4. Cover and cook on Low 6–8 hours.
5. Serve with melted butter and lemon juice for dipping.

Easy Flavor-Filled Green Beans

Paula Showalter   Weyers Cave, VA

MAKES: **10 SERVINGS**
PREP. TIME: **5–10 MINUTES**
COOKING TIME: **3–4 HOURS**
IDEAL SLOW COOKER SIZE: **3–3½-QUART**

2 quarts green beans, drained

⅓ cup chopped onions

4-oz. can mushrooms, drained

2 Tbsp. brown sugar

3 Tbsp. butter

pepper to taste

1. Combine beans, onions, and mushrooms in slow cooker.
2. Sprinkle with brown sugar.
3. Dot with butter.
4. Sprinkle with pepper.
5. Cover. Cook on High 3–4 hours. Stir just before serving.

Green Beans with Dill

Rebecca Leichty   Harrisonburg, VA

MAKES: **8 SERVINGS**
PREP. TIME: **5 MINUTES**
COOKING TIME: **3–4 HOURS**
IDEAL SLOW COOKER SIZE: **3½–4-QUART**

Light

**2 quarts cut green beans, or 4 14½-oz. cans cut green
     beans**

2 tsp. beef bouillon granules

½ tsp dill seed

¼ cup water

1. Spray slow cooker with fat-free cooking spray.
2. Add all ingredients and mix well.
3. Cook on High 3–4 hours.

Per Serving: 35 calories (0 calories from fat), 0g total fat (0g
saturated, 0g trans), 0mg cholesterol, 310mg sodium, 8g total
carbohydrate (4g fiber, 3g sugar), 2g protein, 15%DV vitamin A,
20%DV vitamin C, 4%DV calcium, 6%DV iron.

Variations:

*1. If you like, add 2 Tbsp. minced onions to
Step 2.*

*2. If your sodium counter allows, you may want
to add 1 tsp. garlic salt to Step 2.*

Green Beans au Gratin

Donna Lantgen   Chadron, NE

MAKES: **12–14 SERVINGS**
PREP. TIME: **10 MINUTES**
COOKING TIME: **5–6 HOURS**
IDEAL SLOW COOKER SIZE: **4-QUART**

2 lbs. frozen green beans, or 4 14½-oz. cans, drained

**1–2 cups cubed Velveeta cheese, depending upon how
     much you like cheese**

½ cup chopped onion

½ cup milk

1 Tbsp. flour

1. Place beans, cheese, and onion in slow
   cooker. Stir together well.
2. Place milk first, and then flour, in a jar
   with a tight-fitting lid. Shake together
   until smooth. Or mix together in a small
   bowl until smooth. Then stir into other
   ingredients.
3. Cover and cook on Low 5–6 hours, or until
   beans are fully cooked and heated through.

Green Bean Casserole

Vicki Dinkel   Sharon Springs, KS

PICTURED
ON PAGE
603

MAKES: **9–11 SERVINGS**
PREP. TIME: **10 MINUTES**
COOKING TIME: **3–10 HOURS**
IDEAL SLOW COOKER SIZE: **3½–4-QUART**

3 10-oz. pkgs. frozen, cut green beans

2 10½-oz. cans cheddar cheese soup

½ cup water

¼ cup chopped green onions

4-oz. can sliced mushrooms, drained

8-oz. can water chestnuts, drained and sliced, *optional*

½ cup slivered almonds

1 tsp. salt

¼ tsp. pepper

1. Combine all ingredients in lightly greased
   slow cooker. Mix well.
2. Cover. Cook on Low 8–10 hours, or on High
   3–4 hours.

Special Green Beans

Sara Kinsinger Stuarts Draft, VA

MAKES: **12–14 SERVINGS**
PREP. TIME: **30–45 MINUTES**
COOKING TIME: **1–2 HOURS**
IDEAL SLOW COOKER SIZE: **4-QUART**

4 14½-oz. cans green beans, drained

10¾-oz. can cream of mushroom soup

14½-oz. can chicken broth

1 cup tater tots

3-oz. can French-fried onion rings

1. Put green beans in slow cooker.
2. In a bowl, mix soup and broth together. Spread over beans.
3. Spoon tater tots over all. Top with onion rings.
4. Cover and bake on High 1–2 hours, or until heated through and potatoes are cooked.

Creole Green Beans

Jan Mast Lancaster, PA

MAKES: **4–6 SERVINGS**
PREP. TIME: **10 MINUTES**
COOKING TIME: **3–4 HOURS**
IDEAL SLOW COOKER SIZE: **2-QUART**

2 small onions, chopped

half a stick (¼ cup) butter

4 cups green beans, fresh *or* frozen

½ cup salsa

2–3 Tbsp. brown sugar

½ tsp. garlic salt, *optional*

1. Sauté onions in butter in a saucepan.
2. Combine with remaining ingredients in slow cooker.
3. Cover and cook on Low 3–4 hours, or longer, depending upon how soft or crunchy you like your beans.

Greek-Style Green Beans

Diann J. Dunham State College, PA

MAKES: **6 SERVINGS**
PREP. TIME: **5 MINUTES**
COOKING TIME: **2–5 HOURS**
IDEAL SLOW COOKER SIZE: **4-QUART**

20 ozs. whole or cut-up frozen beans (not French cut)

2 cups tomato sauce

2 tsp. dried onion flakes, *optional*

pinch of dried marjoram *or* oregano

pinch of ground nutmeg

pinch of cinnamon

1. Combine all ingredients in slow cooker, mixing together thoroughly.
2. Cover and cook on Low 2–4 hours if the beans are defrosted, or 3–5 hours on Low if the beans are frozen, or until the beans are done to your liking.

Barbecued Green Beans

Arlene Wengerd   Millersburg, OH

MAKES: **4–6 SERVINGS**
PREP. TIME: **20 MINUTES**
COOKING TIME: **3–8 HOURS**
IDEAL SLOW COOKER SIZE: **3–4-QUART**

1 lb. bacon
¼ cup chopped onions
¾ cup ketchup
½ cup brown sugar
3 tsp. Worcestershire sauce
¾ tsp. salt
4 cups green beans

1. Brown bacon in skillet until crisp and then break into pieces. Reserve 2 Tbsp. bacon drippings.
2. Sauté onions in bacon drippings.
3. Combine ketchup, brown sugar, Worcestershire sauce, and salt. Stir into bacon and onions.
4. Pour mixture over green beans and mix lightly.
5. Pour into slow cooker and cook on High 3–4 hours, or on Low 6–8 hours.

Dutch Green Beans

Edwina Stoltzfus   Narvon, PA

MAKES: **4–6 SERVINGS**
PREP. TIME: **20 MINUTES**
COOKING TIME: **4½ HOURS**
IDEAL SLOW COOKER SIZE: **4–5-QUART**

½ lb. bacon
4 medium onions, sliced
2 quarts fresh, frozen, *or* canned green beans
4 cups canned stewed tomatoes *or* diced fresh tomatoes
½–¾ tsp. salt
¼ tsp. pepper

1. Brown bacon until crisp in skillet. Drain, reserving 2 Tbsp. drippings. Crumble bacon into small pieces.
2. Sauté onions in bacon drippings.
3. Combine all ingredients in slow cooker.
4. Cover. Cook on Low 4½ hours.

Super Green Beans

Esther J. Yoder   Hartville, OH

MAKES: **5 SERVINGS**
PREP. TIME: **15 MINUTES**
COOKING TIME: **1–2 HOURS**
IDEAL SLOW COOKER SIZE: **3-QUART**

2 14½-oz. cans green beans, undrained
1 cup cooked cubed ham
⅓ cup finely chopped onion
1 Tbsp. butter, melted, *or* bacon drippings

1. Place undrained beans in cooker. Add remaining ingredients and mix well.
2. Cook on High 1–2 hours, or until steaming hot.

Vegetables

Easy Baked Beans

Alma Weaver   Ephrata, PA

MAKES: **8 SERVINGS**
PREP. TIME: **10 MINUTES**
COOKING TIME: **2 HOURS**
IDEAL SLOW COOKER SIZE: **2½-QUART**

2 16-oz. cans baked beans

¼ cup brown sugar

½ tsp. dried mustard

½ cup ketchup

2 small onions, chopped

1 tsp. Worcestershire sauce

1. Combine all ingredients in slow cooker.
2. Cover. Cook on High 2 hours.

Per Serving: 180 calories (15 calories from fat), 1.5g total fat (0g saturated, 0g trans), 5mg cholesterol, 610mg sodium, 38g total carbohydrate (8g fiber, 17g sugar), 6g protein, 10%DV vitamin A, 2%DV vitamin C, 6%DV calcium, 8%DV iron.

Tip: *You can reduce the amount of brown sugar without harming the dish, if you prefer a less-sweet outcome.*

Barbecued Baked Beans

Mary Ann Bowman   East Earl, PA

MAKES: **8–10 SERVINGS**
PREP. TIME: **10 MINUTES**
COOKING TIME: **3–4 HOURS**
IDEAL SLOW COOKER SIZE: **4-QUART**

2 16-oz. cans baked beans, your choice of variety

2 15-oz. cans kidney *or* pinto beans, *or* one of each, drained

½ cup brown sugar

1 cup ketchup

1 onion, chopped

1. Combine all ingredients in slow cooker. Mix well.
2. Cover and cook on Low 3–4 hours, or until heated through.

Mac's Beans

Wilma Haberkamp   Fairbank, IA   •   *Mabel Shirk*   Mount Crawford, VA

MAKES: **6–8 SERVINGS**
PREP. TIME: **20 MINUTES**
COOKING TIME: **4 HOURS**
IDEAL SLOW COOKER SIZE: **3–4-QUART**

4 slices bacon

3 15-oz. cans kidney beans, drained, *or* other beans of your choice

1 cup chili sauce

½ cup sliced green *or* red onions

⅓ cup brown sugar

1. In a small nonstick skillet, brown bacon until crisp. Reserve drippings. Crumble the bacon.
2. Combine all ingredients except brown sugar in slow cooker. Sprinkle brown sugar over the top.
3. Cover and cook on Low 4 hours.
4. Serve the beans directly from your slow cooker.

Variations:
1. *Use regular onions instead of green onions.*
2. *Used canned lima beans instead of kidney beans.*

I fry several pounds of bacon and then freeze it for quick access when I need it for a recipe.

Barbecued Beans and Beef

Joan Miller   Wayland, IA

MAKES: **6 SERVINGS**
PREP. TIME: **20–25 MINUTES**
COOKING TIME: **9–11 HOURS**
IDEAL SLOW COOKER SIZE: **3½–4-QUART**

1 medium onion, chopped

3 slices bacon, cut into squares

1½ lbs. boneless beef chuck roast *or* ribs

½ cup barbecue sauce

3 16-oz. cans baked beans (not pork and beans!)

1. Mix onion and bacon together in slow cooker.
2. Top with beef. Pour barbecue sauce over beef.
3. Cover and cook on Low 8–10 hours, or until beef is tender but not dried out.
4. Remove beef from slow cooker and place on cutting board. Cut beef into ½-inch pieces.
5. Pour juices from slow cooker through a strainer into a small bowl. Reserve the onion, bacon and only ½ cup of cooking juices.
6. Return cut-up beef, onions, and bacon and reserved ½ cup juices to slow cooker. Stir in baked beans.
7. Cover and cook on High 40–50 minutes, or until heated throughout.

Makes-A-Meal Baked Beans

Ruth Fisher   Leicester, NY

MAKES: **6–8 SERVINGS**
PREP. TIME: **15 MINUTES**
COOKING TIME: **3 HOURS**
IDEAL SLOW COOKER SIZE: **3-QUART**

1 lb. ground beef

½ cup chopped onions

½ tsp. taco seasoning, or more

1 or 2 15-oz. cans pork and beans

¾ cup barbecue sauce

1. Brown ground beef and onions in a nonstick skillet. Drain.
2. Stir all ingredients together in the slow cooker, including the browned ground beef and onions.
3. Cover and cook on Low 3 hours.

Full Meal Deal Beans

Reita Yoder   Carlsbad, NM

MAKES: **10–12 SERVINGS**
PREP. TIME: **25 MINUTES**
SOAKING TIME: **8 HOURS, OR OVERNIGHT**
COOKING TIME: **7–8 HOURS**
IDEAL SLOW COOKER SIZE: **2-QUART**

3 cups dry pinto beans, sorted and washed

3 quarts water

1 ham bone with lots of ham still hanging on!

1 bunch green onions, chopped

1 Tbsp. ground cumin, *optional*

5½ cups water

10¾-oz. can Rotel chili and tomatoes

salt to taste, *optional*

1. Place dry beans in a large soup kettle and cover with 3 quarts water. Cover and allow to stand overnight or for 8 hours. Or for a quicker method, follow the same directions, but instead of standing for 8 hours, bring to a boil and cook for 2 minutes. Keep beans covered, remove from heat, and allow to stand for 1 hour. Drain beans.
2. Place ham bone, green onions, and cumin in the bottom of the slow cooker.
3. Put drained beans on top. Add 5½ cups fresh water and tomatoes.
4. Cover and cook on High 7–8 hours, or until beans are soft.
5. Stir in salt if you wish. Let stand 15 minutes before serving.

Scandinavian Beans

Virginia Bender   Dover, DE

MAKES: **8 SERVINGS**
PREP. TIME: **1½–2 HOURS**
SOAKING TIME: **8 HOURS**
COOKING TIME: **5–6 HOURS**
IDEAL SLOW COOKER SIZE: **4–5-QUART**

1 lb. dried pinto beans

6 cups water

12 ozs. bacon, *or* 1 ham hock

1 onion, chopped

2–3 garlic cloves, minced

¼ tsp. pepper

1 tsp. salt

¼ cup molasses

1 cup ketchup

Tabasco to taste

1 tsp. Worcestershire sauce

¾ cup brown sugar

½ cup cider vinegar

¼ tsp. dry mustard

1. Soak beans in water in soup pot for 8 hours. Bring beans to boil and cook 1½–2 hours, or until soft. Drain, reserving liquid.
2. Combine all ingredients in slow cooker, using just enough bean liquid to cover everything. Cook on Low 5–6 hours. If using ham hock, debone, cut ham into bite-sized pieces, and mix into beans.

Adding salt to dry beans before they are cooked soft will prevent them from getting soft.

Refried Beans with Bacon

Arlene Wengerd   Millersburg, OH

MAKES: **8 SERVINGS**
PREP. TIME: **5 MINUTES**
COOKING TIME: **5 HOURS**
IDEAL SLOW COOKER SIZE: **4-QUART**

2 cups dried red *or* pinto beans

6 cups water

2 garlic cloves, minced

1 large tomato, peeled, seeded, and chopped, *or* 1 pint tomato juice

1 tsp. salt

½ lb. bacon

shredded cheese

1. Combine beans, water, garlic, tomato, and salt in slow cooker.
2. Cover. Cook on High 5 hours, stirring occasionally. When the beans become soft, drain off some liquid.
3. While the beans cook, brown bacon in skillet. Drain, reserving drippings. Crumble bacon. Add half of bacon and 3 Tbsp. drippings to beans. Stir.
4. Mash or puree beans with a food processor. Fry the mashed bean mixture in the remaining bacon drippings. Add more salt to taste.
5. To serve, sprinkle the remaining bacon and shredded cheese on top of beans.

Variations:

1. Instead of draining off liquid, add ⅓ cup dry minute rice and continue cooking about 20 minutes. Add a dash of hot sauce and a dollop of sour cream to individual servings.

2. Instead of frying the mashed bean mixture, place several spoonfuls on flour tortillas, roll up, and serve.

Susan McClure   Dayton, VA

Red Beans with Pork and Rice

Margaret A. Moffitt   Bartlett, TN

MAKES: **8–10 SERVINGS**
PREP. TIME: **5 MINUTES**
SOAKING TIME: **8 HOURS, OR OVERNIGHT**
COOKING TIME: **10–12 HOURS**
IDEAL SLOW COOKER SIZE: **4–5-QUART**

1-lb. pkg. dried red beans water

salt pork, ham hocks, *or* sausage, cut into small chunks

2 tsp. salt

1 tsp. pepper

3–4 cups water

6-oz. can tomato paste

8-oz. can tomato sauce

4 garlic cloves, minced

1. Soak beans for 8 hours or overnight. Drain. Discard soaking water.
2. Mix together all ingredients in slow cooker.
3. Cover. Cook on Low 10–12 hours, or until beans are soft. Serve over rice.

Tip: *These beans freeze well.*

Variation: *Use canned red kidney beans. Cook 1 hour on High, and then 3 hours on Low.*

No-Meat Baked Beans

Esther Becker   Gordonville, PA

MAKES: **8–10 SERVINGS**
PREP. TIME: **5 MINUTES**
SOAKING TIME: **8 HOURS, OR OVERNIGHT**
COOKING TIME: **6½–9½ HOURS**
IDEAL SLOW COOKER SIZE: **3½-QUART**

1 lb. dried navy beans

6 cups water

1 small onion, chopped

¾ cup ketchup

½ cup brown sugar

¾ cup water

1 tsp. dry mustard

3 Tbsp. dark molasses

1 tsp. salt

1. Soak beans in water overnight in large soup kettle. Cook beans in water until soft, about 1½ hours. Drain, discarding bean water.
2. Stir together all ingredients in slow cooker. Mix well.
3. Cover. Cook on Low 5–8 hours, or until beans are well flavored but not breaking down.

Per Serving: 290 calories (10 calories from fat), 1g total fat (0g saturated, 0g trans), 0mg cholesterol, 580mg sodium, 60g total carbohydrate (14g fiber, 25g sugar), 13g protein, 0%DV vitamin A, 0%DV vitamin C, 15%DV calcium, 30%DV iron.

If there is too much liquid in your cooker, stick a toothpick under the edge of the lid to tilt it slightly and to allow the steam to escape.

Vegetables

From-Scratch Baked Beans

Wanda Roth Napoleon, OH

MAKES: **6 SERVINGS**
PREP. TIME: **5 MINUTES**
PRE-COOKING TIME: **8 HOURS, OR OVERNIGHT**
COOKING TIME: **6 HOURS**
IDEAL SLOW COOKER SIZE: **3½–4-QUART**

2½ cups Great Northern dried beans

4 cups water

1½ cups tomato sauce

½ cup brown sugar

2 tsp. salt

1 small onion, chopped

½ tsp. chili powder

1. Wash and drain dry beans. Combine beans and water in slow cooker. Cook on Low 8 hours, or overnight.
2. Stir in remaining ingredients. Cook on Low 6 hours. If the beans look too watery as they near the end of their cooking time, you can remove the lid during the last 30–60 minutes.

Per Serving: 350 calories (10 calories from fat), 1g total fat (0g saturated, 0g trans), 0mg cholesterol, 1170mg sodium, 71g total carbohydrate (17g fiber, 26g sugar), 18g protein, 0%DV vitamin A, 4%DV vitamin C, 15%DV calcium, 30%DV iron.

Barbecued Lima Beans

Carol Findling Princeton, IL

MAKES: **6 SERVINGS**
PREP. TIME: **5 MINUTES**
SOAKING TIME: **8 HOURS, OR OVERNIGHT**
COOKING TIME: **8–10 HOURS**
IDEAL SLOW COOKER SIZE: **3½-QUART**

1¼ cups dried lima beans

half a medium onion, chopped in large pieces

½ tsp. salt

½ tsp. dry mustard

1 tsp. cider vinegar

2 Tbsp. molasses

¼ cup chili sauce *or* medium salsa

several drops Tabasco sauce

1. Place beans in bowl and cover with water. Let beans soak overnight. Drain, reserving 1 cup liquid from beans.
2. Combine all ingredients in slow cooker, including 1 cup bean liquid.
3. Cook on Low 8–10 hours.

Per Serving: 180 calories (5 calories from fat), 0.5g total fat (0g saturated, 0g trans), 0mg cholesterol, 330mg sodium, 35g total carbohydrate (9g fiber, 11g sugar), 9g protein, 0%DV vitamin A, 0%DV vitamin C, 6%DV calcium, 15%DV iron.

Variation: *The recipe as noted above has almost no fat. For added flavor, and if your diet allows, add ¼ lb. lean ham, smoked, or Cajun turkey, or soy-bacon during the last hour.*

Hot Bean Dish without Meat

Jeannme Janzen Elbing, KS

MAKES: **8–10 SERVINGS**
PREP. TIME: **10 MINUTES**
COOKING TIME: **3–4 HOURS**
IDEAL SLOW COOKER SIZE: **4-QUART**

16-oz. can kidney beans, drained
15-oz. can lima beans, drained
¼ cup vinegar
2 Tbsp. molasses
2 heaping Tbsp. brown sugar
2 Tbsp. minced onion
mustard to taste
Tabasco sauce to taste

1. Place beans in slow cooker.
2. Combine remaining ingredients. Pour over beans.
3. Cover. Cook on Low 3–4 hours.

Variation: *Add 1 lb. browned ground beef to make this a meaty main dish.*

Four Zesty Beans

Ann Van Doren Lady Lake, FL

MAKES: **10 SERVINGS**
PREP. TIME: **5 MINUTES**
COOKING TIME: **2–2½ HOURS**
IDEAL SLOW COOKER SIZE: **4–5-QUART**

2 15½-oz. cans Great Northern beans, rinsed and drained
2 15-oz. cans black beans, rinsed and drained
15-oz. can butter beans, rinsed and drained
15-oz. can baked beans, undrained
2 cups salsa
½ cup brown sugar

1. In slow cooker combine Great Northern beans, black beans, butter beans, and baked beans.

2. Stir in salsa and brown sugar.
3. Cover. Cook on Low 2–2½ hours.

Per Serving: 300 calories (10 calories from fat), 1.5g total fat (0g saturated, 0g trans), 0mg cholesterol, 840mg sodium, 60g total carbohydrate (14g fiber, 16g sugar), 16g protein, 10%DV vitamin A, 8%DV vitamin C, 10%DV calcium, 25%DV iron.

Barbecued Black Beans with Sweet Potatoes

Barbara Jean Fabel Wausau, WI

MAKES: **4–6 SERVINGS**
PREP. TIME: **15 MINUTES**
COOKING TIME: **2–4 HOURS**
IDEAL SLOW COOKER SIZE: **3-QUART**

4 large sweet potatoes, peeled and cut into 8 chunks *each*
15-oz. can black beans, rinsed and drained
1 medium onion, diced
2 ribs celery, sliced
9 ozs. Sweet Baby Ray's Barbecue Sauce

1. Place sweet potatoes in slow cooker.
2. Combine remaining ingredients. Pour over sweet potatoes.
3. Cover. Cook on High 2–3 hours, or on Low 4 hours.

Slow Cooker Kidney Beans

Jeanette Oberholtzer   Manheim, PA

MAKES: **12 SERVINGS**
PREP. TIME: **10–15 MINUTES**
COOKING TIME: **6–7 HOURS**
IDEAL SLOW COOKER SIZE: **5-QUART**

2 30-oz. cans kidney beans, rinsed and drained

28-oz. can diced tomatoes, drained

2 medium red bell peppers, chopped

1 cup ketchup

½ cup brown sugar

¼ cup honey

¼ cup molasses

1 Tbsp. Worcestershire sauce

1 tsp. dry mustard

2 medium red apples, cored, cut into pieces

1. Combine all ingredients, except apples, in slow cooker.
2. Cover. Cook on Low 4–5 hours.
3. Stir in apples.
4. Cover. Cook 2 more hours.

Note: *Tasty, meatless eating!*

Cowboy Beans

Sharon Timpe   Mequon, WI

MAKES: **10–12 SERVINGS**
PREP. TIME: **15–20 MINUTES**
COOKING TIME: **3–7 HOURS**
IDEAL SLOW COOKER SIZE: **3½-QUART**

6 slices bacon, cut in pieces

½ cup onions, chopped

1 garlic clove, minced

16-oz. can baked beans

16-oz. can kidney beans, drained

15-oz. can butter beans *or* pinto beans, drained

2 Tbsp. dill pickle relish *or* chopped dill pickles

⅓ cup chili sauce *or* ketchup

2 tsp. Worcestershire sauce

½ cup brown sugar

⅛ tsp. hot pepper sauce, *optional*

1. Lightly brown bacon, onions, and garlic in skillet. Drain.
2. Combine all ingredients in slow cooker. Mix well.
3. Cover. Cook on Low 5–7 hours, or on High 3–4 hours.

Write in your cookbook the date when you tried a particular recipe and whether or not you liked it. Develop a rating system for each recipe you try (Excellent, Good, Yummy, Okay). Write notes about what might be a good addition or deletion the next time you make it.

Sweet-Sour Bean Trio

Barbara Walker Sturgis, SD

MAKES: **8 SERVINGS**
PREP. TIME: **10 MINUTES**
COOKING TIME: **6–8 HOURS**
IDEAL SLOW COOKER SIZE: **3½-QUART**

4 slices lean bacon

1 onion, chopped

¼ cup brown sugar

1 tsp. prepared mustard

1 clove garlic, crushed

½ tsp. salt

¼ cup vinegar

16-oz. can low-sodium lima beans, drained

16-oz. can low-sodium baked beans, undrained

16-oz. can low-sodium kidney beans, drained

1. Brown bacon in a nonstick skillet. Crumble. Combine bacon, 2 Tbsp. drippings from bacon, onion, brown sugar, mustard, garlic, salt, and vinegar.
2. Mix with beans in slow cooker.
3. Cover. Cook on Low 6–8 hours.

Per Serving: 210 calories (20 calories from fat), 2g total fat (0.5g saturated, 0g trans), 5mg cholesterol, 570mg sodium, 40g total carbohydrate (9g fiber, 15g sugar), 11g protein, 4%DV vitamin A, 4%DV vitamin C, 6%DV calcium, 10%DV iron.

Tip: *These beans are a good side dish or are good served over rice.*

Five Baked Beans

Betty B. Dennison Grove City, PA

MAKES: **12 SERVINGS**
PREP. TIME: **10 MINUTES**
COOKING TIME: **4–12 HOURS**
IDEAL SLOW COOKER SIZE: **4–5-QUART**

6 slices turkey bacon

1 cup onions, chopped

1 clove garlic, minced

16-oz. can low-sodium lima beans, drained

16-oz. can low-sodium beans with tomato sauce, undrained

15½-oz. can low-sodium red kidney beans, drained

15-oz. can low-sodium butter beans, drained

15-oz. can low-sodium garbanzo beans, drained

¾ cup ketchup

½ cup unsulfured molasses

¼ cup brown sugar

1 Tbsp. prepared mustard

1 Tbsp. Worcestershire sauce

1 onion sliced and cut into rings, *optional*

1. In a nonstick skillet, cook bacon until browned.
2. Combine chopped onions, bacon, garlic, lima beans, beans with tomato sauce, kidney beans, butter beans, garbanzo beans, ketchup, molasses, brown sugar, mustard, and Worcestershire sauce in slow cooker.
3. Top with onions if desired.
4. Cover. Cook on Low 10–12 hours, or on High 4–5 hours.

Per Serving: 200 calories (20 calories from fat), 2g total fat (0.5g saturated, 0g trans), 5mg cholesterol, 600mg sodium, 40g total carbohydrate (7g fiber, 16g sugar), 8g protein, 4%DV vitamin A, 4%DV vitamin C, 8%DV calcium, 20%DV iron.

Variation: *If you prefer less sweet beans, leave out the molasses and add the liquid from all the canned beans.*

Vegetables

Partytime Beans

Beatrice Martin   Goshen, IN

MAKES: **14–16 SERVINGS**
PREP. TIME: **15–20 MINUTES**
COOKING TIME: **5–7 HOURS**
IDEAL SLOW COOKER SIZE: **4-QUART**

1½ cups ketchup

1 onion, chopped

1 green pepper, chopped

1 sweet red pepper, chopped

½ cup water

½ cup packed brown sugar

2 bay leaves

2–3 tsp. cider vinegar

1 tsp. ground mustard

⅛ tsp. pepper

16-oz. can kidney beans, rinsed and drained

15½-oz. can Great Northern beans, rinsed and drained

15-oz. can lima beans, rinsed and drained

15-oz. can black beans, rinsed and drained

15½-oz. can black-eyed peas, rinsed and drained

1. Combine first 10 ingredients in slow cooker. Mix well.
2. Add remaining ingredients. Mix well.
3. Cover. Cook on Low 5–7 hours, or until onion and peppers are tender.
4. Remove bay leaves before serving.
5. Serve with grilled hamburgers, tossed salad or veggie tray, chips, fruit, and cookies.

Cheesy Baked Beans

Linda Sluiter   Schererville, IN

MAKES: **12 SERVINGS**
PREP. TIME: **10 MINUTES**
COOKING TIME: **6 HOURS**
IDEAL SLOW COOKER SIZE: **4-QUART**

16-oz. can red kidney beans, drained

15½-oz. can butter beans, drained

18-oz. jar B&M beans

¼ lb. Velveeta cheese, cubed

½ lb. bacon, diced

½ cup brown sugar

⅓ cup sugar

2 dashes Worcestershire sauce

1. Combine all ingredients in slow cooker.
2. Cover. Cook on Low 6 hours. Do not stir until nearly finished cooking.

Lotsa-Beans Pot

Dorothy Van Deest Memphis, TN

MAKES: **15–20 SERVINGS**
PREP. TIME: **30 MINUTES**
COOKING TIME: **3–4 HOURS**
IDEAL SLOW COOKER SIZE: **5-QUART**

8 bacon strips, diced
2 onions, thinly sliced
1 cup packed brown sugar
½ cup cider vinegar
1 tsp. salt
1 tsp. ground mustard
½ tsp. garlic powder
28-oz. can baked beans
16-oz. can kidney beans, rinsed and drained
15½-oz. can pinto beans, rinsed and drained
15-oz. can lima beans, rinsed and drained
15½-oz. can black-eyed peas, rinsed and drained

1. Cook bacon in skillet until crisp. Remove to paper towels.
2. Drain, reserving 2 Tbsp. drippings.
3. Sauté onions in drippings until tender.
4. Add brown sugar, vinegar, salt, mustard, and garlic powder to skillet. Bring to boil.
5. Combine beans and peas in slow cooker. Add onion mixture and bacon. Mix well.
6. Cover. Cook on High 3-4 hours.

Note: *This hearty bean concoction tastes especially yummy when the gang comes in from a Saturday afternoon of raking leaves. Keep it warm to hot and serve it from the pot.*

Auntie Ginny's Baked Beans

Becky Harder Monument, CO

MAKES: **8 SERVINGS**
PREP. TIME: **15 MINUTES**
COOKING TIME: **4–5 HOURS**
IDEAL SLOW COOKER SIZE: **3-QUART**

4 slices bacon, diced
28-oz. can pork and beans
1 tsp. dark molasses
1 Tbsp. brown sugar
1 cup dates, cut up
1 medium onion, chopped

1. Partially fry bacon. Drain.
2. Combine ingredients in slow cooker.
3. Cover. Cook on Low 4–5 hours.

Note: *Written down at the bottom of this recipe was this note: "Harder picnic—1974." Notations such as that one help us remember special family get-togethers or reunions.*

This recipe was shared almost 20 years ago as we gathered cousins and aunts together in our hometown. Today no one from our family lives in the hometown and we cousins are scattered over six states, but one way to enjoy fond memories is to record dates or events on recipes we share with each other.

Tip: *There are many varieties of canned baked beans available. Choose a flavor that fits your guests—from vegetarian (you'll want to leave out the bacon above if this is important to your diners) to country-style to onion.*

"Lean" Cowboy Beans

John D. Allen   Rye, CO

MAKES: **8 SERVINGS**
PREP. TIME: **15 MINUTES**
COOKING TIME: **1–2 HOURS**
IDEAL SLOW COOKER SIZE: **4-QUART**

1 lb. ground turkey

16-oz. can baked beans, undrained

16-oz. can kidney beans, drained

2 cups onions, chopped

¾ cup brown sugar

1 cup ketchup

2 Tbsp. dry mustard

¼ tsp. salt

2 tsp. cider vinegar

1. Brown turkey in nonstick skillet over medium heat.
2. Combine all ingredients in slow cooker sprayed with non-fat cooking spray.
3. Cover. Cook on High 1–2 hours.

Per Serving: 320 calories (50 calories from fat), 5g total fat (1g saturated, 0g trans), 35mg cholesterol, 880mg sodium, 53g total carbohydrate (7g fiber, 30g sugar), 18g protein, 10%DV vitamin A, 8%DV vitamin C, 6%DV calcium, 15%DV iron.

Variation: *For a milder taste, sauté the chopped onions with the turkey in Step 1. You may also decrease the dry mustard to 1 Tbsp., or according to your taste.*

Most slow cookers perform best when more than half full.

Mixed Slow Cooker Beans

Carol Peachey   Lancaster, PA

MAKES: **6 SERVINGS**
PREP. TIME: **10 MINUTES**
COOKING TIME: **4–5 HOURS**
IDEAL SLOW COOKER SIZE: **3½–4-QUART**

16-oz. can kidney beans, drained

15½-oz. can baked beans, undrained

1 pint home-frozen, or 1-lb. pkg. frozen, lima beans

1 pint home-frozen, or 1-lb. pkg. frozen, green beans

4 slices lean turkey bacon, browned and crumbled

½ cup ketchup

⅓ cup sugar

⅓ cup brown sugar

2 Tbsp. vinegar

½ tsp. salt

1. Combine beans and bacon in slow cooker.
2. Stir together remaining ingredients. Add to beans and mix well.
3. Cover. Cook on Low 4–5 hours.

Per Serving: 360 calories (30 calories from fat), 3.5g total fat (0.5g saturated, 0g trans), 10mg cholesterol, 1100mg sodium, 71g total carbohydrate (12g fiber, 33g sugar), 14g protein, 10%DV vitamin A, 0%DV vitamin C, 10%DV calcium, 20%DV iron.

Four Beans and Sausage

Mary Seielstad Sparks, NV

MAKES: **8 SERVINGS**
PREP. TIME: **10 MINUTES**
COOKING TIME: **4–10 HOURS**
IDEAL SLOW COOKER SIZE: **5-QUART**

15-oz. can Great Northern beans, drained

15½-oz. can black beans, rinsed and drained

16-oz. can red kidney beans, drained

15-oz. can butter beans, drained

1½ cups ketchup

½ cup chopped onions

1 green pepper, chopped

1 lb. smoked sausage, cooked and cut into ½-inch slices

¼ cup brown sugar

2 garlic cloves, minced

1 tsp. Worcestershire sauce

½ tsp. dry mustard

½ tsp. Tabasco sauce

1. Combine all ingredients in slow cooker.
2. Cover. Cook on Low 9–10 hours, or on High 4–5 hours.

Creole Black Beans

Joyce Kaut Rochester, NY

MAKES: **6–8 SERVINGS**
PREP. TIME: **15 MINUTES**
COOKING TIME: **8 HOURS**
IDEAL SLOW COOKER SIZE: **4-QUART**

¾ lb. lean smoked sausage, sliced in ¼-inch pieces and browned

3 15-oz. cans black beans, drained

1½ cups chopped onions

1½ cups chopped green bell peppers

1½ cups chopped celery

4 garlic cloves, minced

2 tsp. dried thyme

1½ tsp. dried oregano

1½ tsp. black pepper

1 chicken bouillon cube

3 bay leaves

8-oz. can tomato sauce

1 cup water

1. Combine all ingredients in slow cooker.
2. Cover. Cook on Low 8 hours, or on High 4 hours.
3. Remove bay leaves before serving.

Per Serving: 250 calories (80 calories from fat), 9g total fat (3g saturated, 0g trans), 15mg cholesterol, 1080mg sodium, 34g total carbohydrate (11g fiber, 6g sugar), 13g protein, 0%DV vitamin A, 30%DV vitamin C, 10%DV calcium, 20%DV iron.

Variation: *For a different consistency, you may substitute a 14½-oz. can of low-sodium stewed tomatoes for the tomato sauce. This is tasty served over steamed rice.*

Vegetables

Pizza Beans

Kelly Evenson Pittsboro, NC

MAKES: **6 SERVINGS**
PREP. TIME: **30 MINUTES**
COOKING TIME: **7–9 HOURS**
IDEAL SLOW COOKER SIZE: **4-QUART**

16-oz. can pinto beans, drained

16-oz. can kidney beans, drained

2¼-oz. can ripe olives sliced, drained

28-oz. can stewed or whole tomatoes

¾ lb. bulk Italian sausage

1 Tbsp. oil

1 green pepper, chopped

1 medium onion, chopped

1 garlic clove, minced

1 tsp. salt

1 tsp. dried oregano

1 tsp. dried basil

Parmesan cheese

1. Combine beans, olives, and tomatoes in slow cooker.
2. Brown sausage in oil in skillet. Drain, reserving drippings. Transfer sausage to slow cooker.
3. Sauté green pepper in drippings 1 minute, stirring constantly. Add onions and continue stirring until onions start to become translucent. Add garlic and cook 1 more minute. Transfer to slow cooker.
4. Stir in seasonings.
5. Cover. Cook on Low 7–9 hours.
6. To serve, sprinkle with Parmesan cheese.

Variation: *For a thicker soup, 20 minutes before serving remove ¼ cup liquid from cooker and add 1 Tbsp. cornstarch. Stir until dissolved. Return to soup. Cook on High for 15 minutes, or until thickened.*

Cajun Sausage and Beans

Melanie Thrower McPherson, KS

MAKES: **4–6 SERVINGS**
PREP. TIME: **10 MINUTES**
COOKING TIME: **8 HOURS**
IDEAL SLOW COOKER SIZE: **4-QUART**

1 lb. smoked sausage, sliced into ¼-inch pieces

16-oz. can red beans

16-oz. can crushed tomatoes with green chilies

1 cup chopped celery

half an onion, chopped

2 Tbsp. Italian seasoning

Tabasco sauce to taste

1. Combine all ingredients in slow cooker.
2. Cover. Cook on Low 8 hours.
3. Serve over rice or as a thick zesty soup.

Sausage Bean Quickie

Ellen Ranck Gap, PA

MAKES: **4 SERVINGS**
PREP. TIME: **10 MINUTES**
COOKING TIME: **1–10 HOURS**
IDEAL SLOW COOKER SIZE: **3–4-QUART**

4–6 cooked brown 'n serve sausage links, cut into
    1-inch pieces

2 tsp. cider vinegar

2 16-oz. cans red kidney *or* baked beans, drained

7-oz. can pineapple chunks, undrained

2 tsp. brown sugar

3 Tbsp. flour

1. Combine sausage, vinegar, beans, and pineapple in slow cooker.
2. Combine brown sugar with flour. Add to slow cooker. Stir well.
3. Cover. Cook on Low 5–10 hours, or on High 1–2 hours.

"Famous" Baked Beans

Katrine Rose   Woodbridge, VA

MAKES: **10 SERVINGS**
PREP. TIME: **20 MINUTES**
COOKING TIME: **3–6 HOURS**
IDEAL SLOW COOKER SIZE: **4-QUART**

1 lb. ground beef

¼ cup minced onions

1 cup ketchup

4 15-oz. cans pork and beans

1 cup brown sugar

2 Tbsp. liquid smoke

1 Tbsp. Worcestershire sauce

1. Brown beef and onions in skillet. Drain. Spoon meat and onions into slow cooker.
2. Add remaining ingredients and stir well.
3. Cover. Cook on High 3 hours, or on Low 5–6 hours.

Note: *There are many worthy baked bean recipes, but this one is both easy and absolutely delicious. The secret to this recipe is the liquid smoke. I get many requests for this recipe, and some friends have added the word "famous" to its name.*

Hearty Barbecued Beans

Esther J. Yoder   Hartville, OH

MAKES: **10 SERVINGS**
PREP. TIME: **20 MINUTES**
COOKING TIME: **2–3 HOURS**
IDEAL SLOW COOKER SIZE: **3-QUART**

1 lb. ground beef

½ cup chopped onions

½ tsp. salt

¼ tsp. pepper

28-oz. can pork and beans (your favorite variety)

½ cup ketchup

1 Tbsp. Worcestershire sauce

1 Tbsp. vinegar

¼ tsp. Tabasco sauce

1. Brown beef and onions together in skillet. Drain.
2. Combine all ingredients in slow cooker.
3. Cover. Cook on High 2–3 hours, stirring once or twice.
4. Serve with fresh raw vegetables and canned peaches.

Note: *These beans' flavor gets better on the second and third days.*

In place of ground meat in a recipe, use vegetarian burgers. Cut them up, and you won't need to brown the meat.

Calico Beans with Corn

Betty Lahman   Elkton, VA

MAKES: **6–8 SERVINGS**
PREP. TIME: **15 MINUTES**
COOKING TIME: **3–4 HOURS**
IDEAL SLOW COOKER SIZE: **4-QUART**

1 lb. ground beef, browned and drained

14¾-oz. can lima beans

15½-oz. can pinto beans

15¼-oz. can corn

¼ cup brown sugar

1 cup ketchup

1 Tbsp. vinegar

2 tsp. prepared mustard

1 medium onion, chopped

1. Combine all ingredients in slow cooker.
2. Cover. Cook on High 3–4 hours.

Casey's Beans

Cheryl Bartel   Hillsboro, KS

MAKES: **10–12 SERVINGS**
PREP. TIME: **20 MINUTES**
COOKING TIME: **5–6 HOURS**
IDEAL SLOW COOKER SIZE: **5–6-QUART**

½ lb. ground beef

10 slices bacon, diced

½ cup chopped onions

⅓ cup brown sugar

⅓ cup sugar, *optional*

¼ cup ketchup

¼ cup barbecue sauce

2 Tbsp. prepared mustard

2 Tbsp. molasses

½ tsp. salt

½ tsp. chili powder

½ tsp. pepper

1-lb. can kidney beans, drained

1-lb. can butter beans, drained

1-lb. can black beans, drained

1-lb. can pork and beans

1. Brown ground beef, bacon, and onion in deep saucepan. Drain.
2. Stir in remaining ingredients, except beans. Mix well. Stir in beans. Pour into slow cooker.
3. Cover. Cook on Low 5–6 hours.

Bacon and Beef Calico Beans

LeAnne Nolt   Leola, PA

MAKES: **10 SERVINGS**
PREP. TIME: **20 MINUTES**
COOKING TIME: **2–6 HOURS**
IDEAL SLOW COOKER SIZE: **4–5-QUART**

¼-½ lb. bacon

1 lb. ground beef

1 medium onion, chopped

2-lb. can pork and beans

1-lb. can Great Northern beans, drained

14½-oz. can French-style green beans, drained

½ cup brown sugar

½ cup ketchup

½ tsp. salt

2 Tbsp. cider vinegar

1 Tbsp. prepared mustard

1. Brown bacon, ground beef, and onion in skillet until soft. Drain.
2. Combine all ingredients in slow cooker.
3. Cover Cook on Low 5–6 hours, or on High 2–3 hours.

Smoky Beans

John D. Allen Rye, CO

MAKES: **10–12 SERVINGS**
PREP. TIME: **20 MINUTES**
COOKING TIME: **4–6 HOURS**
IDEAL SLOW COOKER SIZE: **5-QUART**

1 large onion, chopped

1 lb. ground beef, browned

15-oz. can pork and beans

15-oz. can ranch-style beans, drained

16-oz. can kidney beans, drained

1 cup ketchup

1 tsp. salt

1 Tbsp. prepared mustard

2 Tbsp. brown sugar

2 Tbsp. hickory-flavored barbecue sauce

½–1 lb. small smoky link sausages, *optional*

1. Brown ground beef and onion in skillet. Drain. Transfer to slow cooker set on High.
2. Add remaining ingredients. Mix well.
3. Reduce heat to Low and cook 4–6 hours. Use a paper towel to absorb oil that's risen to the top before stirring and serving.

Pineapple Baked Beans

Sue Pennington Bridgewater, VA

MAKES: **6–8 MAIN-DISH SERVINGS, OR 12–16 SIDE-DISH SERVINGS**
PREP. TIME: **15 MINUTES**
COOKING TIME: **4–8 HOURS**
IDEAL SLOW COOKER SIZE: **4-QUART**

1 lb. ground beef

28-oz. can baked beans

8-oz. can pineapple tidbits, drained

4½-oz can sliced mushrooms, drained

1 large onion, chopped

1 large green pepper, chopped

½ cup barbecue sauce

2 Tbsp. soy sauce

1 clove garlic, minced

½ tsp. salt

¼ tsp. pepper

1. Brown ground beef in skillet. Drain. Place in slow cooker.
2. Stir in remaining ingredients. Mix well.
3. Cover Cook on Low 4–8 hours, or until bubbly. Serve in soup bowls.

Wrap cut-up onions or peppers in a paper towel before placing them in a Ziplock bag and refrigerating. The paper towel absorbs moisture and delays spoiling.

Apple Bean Bake

Barbara A. Yoder   Goshen, IN

MAKES: **10–12 SERVINGS**
PREP. TIME: **20 MINUTES**
COOKING TIME: **2–4 HOURS**
IDEAL SLOW COOKER SIZE: **4–5-QUART**

4 Tbsp. buffer
2 large Granny Smith apples, cubed
½ cup brown sugar
¼ cup sugar
½ cup ketchup
1 tsp. cinnamon
1 Tbsp. molasses
1 tsp. salt
24-oz. can Great Northern beans, undrained
24-oz. can pinto beans, undrained
ham chunks, *optional*

1. Melt butter in skillet. Add apples and cook until tender.
2. Stir in brown sugar and sugar. Cook until they melt. Stir in ketchup, cinnamon, molasses, and salt.
3. Add beans and ham chunks. Mix well. Pour into slow cooker.
4. Cover. Cook on High 2–4 hours.

Apple Bean Pot

Charlotte Bull   Cassville, MO

MAKES: **12 SERVINGS**
PREP. TIME: **15 MINUTES**
COOKING TIME: **3½–4½ HOURS**
IDEAL SLOW COOKER SIZE: **4-QUART**

53-oz. can baked beans, well drained
1 large onion, chopped
3 tart apples, peeled and chopped
½ cup ketchup *or* **barbecue sauce**
½ cup firmly packed brown sugar

1 pkg. smoky cocktail sausages, *or* **chopped hot dogs,** *or* **chopped ham chunks,** *optional*

1. Place beans in slow cooker.
2. Add onions and apples. Mix well.
3. Stir in ketchup or barbecue sauce, brown sugar, and meat. Mix.
4. Cover. Heat on Low 3–4 hours, and then on High 30 minutes.

Chili Boston Baked Beans

Ann Driscoll   Albuquerque, MN

MAKES: **20 SERVINGS**
PREP. TIME: **15 MINUTES**
COOKING TIME: **6–8 HOURS**
IDEAL SLOW COOKER SIZE: **4–5-QUART**

1 cup raisins
2 small onions, diced
2 tart apples, diced
1 cup chili sauce
1 cup chopped ham *or* **crumbled bacon**
2 1-lb., 15-oz. cans baked beans
3 tsp. dry mustard
½ cup sweet pickle relish

1. Mix together all ingredients.
2. Cover. Cook on Low 6–8 hours.

Company Mashed Potatoes

Eileen Eash   Carlsbad, NM

MAKES: **12 SERVINGS**
PREP. TIME: **20 MINUTES**
COOKING TIME: **12–16 HOURS**
IDEAL SLOW COOKER SIZE: **6-QUART**

15 medium potatoes

1 cup sour cream

1 small onion, diced fine

1 tsp. salt

⅛–¼ tsp. pepper, according to your taste preference

1–2 cups buttermilk

1 cup fresh, chopped spinach, *optional*

1 cup shredded Colby *or* cheddar cheese, *optional*

1. Peel and quarter potatoes. Place in slow cooker. Barely cover with water.
2. Cover. Cook on Low 8–10 hours. Drain water.
3. Mash potatoes. Add remaining ingredients except cheese.
4. Cover. Heat on Low 4–6 hours.
5. Sprinkle with cheese 5 minutes before serving.

Note: *Buttermilk gives mashed potatoes a unique flavor that most people enjoy. I often serve variations of this recipe for guests and they always ask what I put in the potatoes.*

Tips:
1. Save the water drained from cooking the potatoes and use it to make gravy or a soup base.
2. Small amounts of leftovers from this recipe add a special flavor to vegetable or noodle soup for another meal.

Refrigerator Mashed Potatoes

Deborah Swartz   Grottoes, VA

MAKES: **8–10 SERVINGS**
PREP. TIME: **30 MINUTES**
COOKING TIME: **2 HOURS**
IDEAL SLOW COOKER SIZE: **6-QUART**

5 lbs. potatoes

8-oz. pkg. cream cheese, softened

1 cup sour cream

1 tsp. salt

¼ tsp. pepper

¼ cup crisp bacon, crumbled

2 Tbsp. butter

1. Cook and mash potatoes.
2. Add remaining ingredients except butter. Put in slow cooker. Dot with butter.
3. Cover. Cook on Low 2 hours.

Variations:
1. These potatoes can be made several days ahead and refrigerated. Cook refrigerated potatoes on Low for 5 hours.
2. If you wish, sprinkle 1 cup cheddar cheese over the top of the potatoes during their last half hour in slow cooker.
3. Substitute chopped ham for the bacon.
4. Add 2 Tbsp. chopped fresh chives to Step 2.

Vegetables

Do-Ahead Mashed Potatoes

Shari and Dale Mast   Harrisonburg, VA

MAKES: **8 SERVINGS**
PREP. TIME: **45 MINUTES**
COOKING TIME: **3–4 HOURS**
IDEAL SLOW COOKER SIZE: **6-QUART**

12 medium potatoes, washed, peeled, and quartered

1 small *or* medium onion, chopped

4 ozs. Neufchatel *or* fat-free cream cheese

1 tsp. salt

¼ tsp. black pepper

1 cup skim milk

1. In a saucepan, cover potatoes and onion with water. Bring to a boil, and then simmer over medium-low heat for 30 minutes or so, until fully softened. Drain.
2. Mash potatoes and onion with a potato masher to remove chunks.
3. In a large mixing bowl, combine partially mashed potatoes, cream cheese, salt, pepper, and milk. Whip together on High for 3 minutes.
4. Transfer potatoes into slow cooker. Cover and refrigerate overnight.
5. Cook on Low 3–4 hours.

Per Serving: 280 calories (5 calories from fat), 0.5g total fat (0g saturated, 0g trans), 0mg cholesterol, 400mg sodium, 59g total carbohydrate (7g fiber, 5g sugar), 10g protein, 0%DV vitamin A, 60%DV vitamin C, 10%DV calcium, 15%DV iron.

Variation: *If your diet allows, you may want to increase the salt to 1¼ or 1½ tsp. in Step 3.*

Cheddar Mashed Potatoes

Gloria Good   Harrisonburg, VA

MAKES: **5–6 SERVINGS**
PREP. TIME: **10 MINUTES**
COOKING TIME: **3–5 HOURS**
IDEAL SLOW COOKER SIZE: **2-QUART**

10¾-oz. condensed cheddar cheese soup

½ cup sour cream

2 Tbsp. chopped green onions

dash of pepper

3 cups leftover, or stiff, seasoned mashed potatoes

1. Spray interior of slow cooker with nonstick cooking spray.
2. Mix all ingredients together in slow cooker.
3. Cover and cook on High 3 hours, or on Low 5 hours, or until potatoes are thoroughly hot.

Garlic Mashed Potatoes

Katrine Rose   Woodbridge, VA

MAKES: **6 SERVINGS**
PREP. TIME: **20 MINUTES**
COOKING TIME: **4–7 HOURS**
IDEAL SLOW COOKER SIZE: **4-QUART**

2 lbs. baking potatoes, unpeeled and cut into ½-inch
  cubes
¼ cup water
3 Tbsp. butter, sliced
1 tsp. salt
¾ tsp. garlic powder
¼ tsp. black pepper
1 cup milk

1. Combine all ingredients, except milk, in slow
   cooker. Toss to combine.
2. Cover. Cook on Low 7 hours, or on High
   4 hours.
3. Add milk to potatoes during last 30 minutes
   of cooking time.
4. Mash potatoes with potato masher or
   electric mixer until fairly smooth.
5. Serve immediately, or if making ahead,
   allow to cool and chill in fridge.
6. Place in slow cooker 2 hours before serving.
   Cover. Set cooker on Low.
7. Stir before serving.

Note: *These potatoes will taste freshly mashed,
and they will spare you last-minute work.*

*Always use big bowls and big utensils
when cooking. You have to wash them
anyway. Bowls and pans that are too small
make for frustration.*

Creamy Mashed Potatoes

Brenda S. Burkholder   Port Republic, VA

MAKES: **10–12 SERVINGS**
PREP. TIME: **10–15 MINUTES**
COOKING TIME: **3–5 HOURS**
IDEAL SLOW COOKER SIZE: **6-QUART**

2 tsp. salt
6 Tbsp. (¾ stick) butter, melted
2¼ cups milk
6⅞ cups potato flakes
6 cups water
1 cup sour cream
4–5 ozs. (approximately half of a large pkg.) cream
  cheese, softened

1. Combine first five ingredients as directed on
   potato box.
2. Whip cream cheese with electric mixer until
   creamy. Blend in sour cream.
3. Fold potatoes into cheese and sour cream.
   Beat well. Place in slow cooker.
4. Cover. Cook on Low 3–5 hours.

Potato Cheese Puff

Mary Sommerfeld   Lancaster, PA

MAKES: **10 SERVINGS**
PREP. TIME: **45 MINUTES**
COOKING TIME: **2½–4 HOURS**
IDEAL SLOW COOKER SIZE: **4–5-QUART**

12 medium potatoes, boiled and mashed
1 cup milk
6 Tbsp. butter
¾ tsp. salt
2¼ cups Velveeta cheese, cubed
2 eggs, beaten

1. Combine all ingredients. Pour into slow cooker.
2. Cover. Cook on High 2½ hours, or on Low
   3–4 hours.

Vegetables

"Baked" Potatoes

Valerie Hertzler Weyers Cave, VA • *Carol Peachey* Lancaster, PA
Janet L. Roggie Lowville, NY

MAKES: **AS MANY SERVINGS AS YOU NEED!**
PREP. TIME: **5 MINUTES**
COOKING TIME: **2½–10 HOURS**
IDEAL SLOW COOKER SIZE: **LARGE ENOUGH TO HOLD THE POTATOES!**

potatoes

1. Prick potatoes with fork and wrap in foil.
2. Cover. Do not add water. Cook on High 2½–4 hours, or on Low 8–10 hours.

Seasoned "Baked" Potatoes

Donna Conto Saylorsburg, PA

MAKES: **AS MANY SERVINGS AS YOU NEED!**
PREP. TIME: **5 MINUTES**
COOKING TIME: **4–10 HOURS**
IDEAL SLOW COOKER SIZE: **LARGE ENOUGH TO HOLD THE POTATOES!**

potatoes
olive *or* vegetable oil
Season-All, *or* your choice of favorite dry seasonings

1. Wash and scrub potatoes. Rub each unpeeled potato with oil.
2. Put about 1 tsp. seasoning per potato in a mixing bowl or a plastic bag. Add potatoes one at a time and coat with seasonings.
3. Place potatoes in slow cooker as you finish coating them.
4. Cover and cook on High 4 hours, or on Low 8–10 hours, or until potatoes are tender when jagged.

Stress-Free "Baked" Potatoes

Leona Yoder Hartville, OH

MAKES: **12 SERVINGS**
PREP. TIME: **10 MINUTES**
COOKING TIME: **4–10 HOURS**
IDEAL SLOW COOKER SIZE: **4–5-QUART**

12 potatoes
butter, softened

1. Spray slow cooker with nonstick cooking spray.
2. Rub butter over unpeeled whole potatoes. Place in slow cooker.
3. Cover and cook on High 4–5 hours, or on Low 8–10 hours, or until potatoes are tender when jagged.

Tip: *Mix 1 Tbsp. pesto into ½ cup sour cream for a luscious baked potato topping.*

Cornflake Cooker Potatoes

Anne Nolt Thompsontown, PA

MAKES: **4–6 SERVINGS**
PREP. TIME: **15 MINUTES**
COOKING TIME: **4 HOURS**
IDEAL SLOW COOKER SIZE: **3-QUART**

6–8 potatoes, peeled
2 tsp. salt
2–3 Tbsp. butter
1 cup cornflakes, slightly crushed

1. Place potatoes in slow cooker.
2. Fill cooker with hot water. Sprinkle with salt.
3. Cover and cook on High 4 hours, or until potatoes are tender.
4. While potatoes are cooking, melt butter. Continue melting until butter browns, but does not burn. (Watch carefully!) Stir in cornflakes. Set aside.
5. Drain potatoes. Spoon buttered cornflakes over potatoes. Or mash potatoes and then top with buttered cornflakes.

Creamy Scalloped Potatoes

Sara Kinsinger Stuarts Draft, VA

MAKES: **6 SERVINGS**
PREP. TIME: **15 MINUTES**
COOKING TIME: **3–9 HOURS**
IDEAL SLOW COOKER SIZE: **4-QUART**

6 large potatoes, peeled and thinly sliced
1 small onion, thinly sliced
¼ cup flour
1 tsp. salt
¼ tsp. pepper
2 Tbsp. butter, melted
¼ cup milk
10¾-oz. can cream of mushroom soup
4 slices American cheese, *or* 1 cup shredded cheddar cheese

1. Place half of potatoes in slow cooker. Top with half of onion, flour, salt, and pepper. Repeat layers.
2. Mix together butter, milk, and soup. Pour over potato layers.
3. Cover. Cook on Low 6–9 hours, or on High 3–4 hours, or until potatoes are soft.
4. Add cheese 30 minutes before serving.

Variation: *Eliminate ¼ cup milk. Simply top seasoned and layered vegetables with chunks of butter and then pour soup over top.*

Note: *I make this recipe often when I'm having company for lunch after church. (For that, I cook the dish on High.) Using a slow cooker for the potatoes allows you to have more room in your oven for other dishes on the menu.*

Ruth Hershey Paradise, PA

Cheesy Scalloped Potatoes

Nancy Wagner Graves Manhattan, KS

MAKES: **8–10 SERVINGS**
PREP. TIME: **5–15 MINUTES, DEPENDING UPON THE KIND OF
    POTATOES YOU USE**
COOKING TIME: **3–4 HOURS FOR FRESH POTATOES; 2–5
    HOURS FOR FROZEN HASH BROWNS**
IDEAL SLOW COOKER SIZE: **4–5-QUART**

2 Tbsp. dried minced onion

1 medium clove garlic, minced

1 tsp. salt

8–10 medium fresh potatoes, sliced, *or* 30-oz. bag
    frozen hash browns, *divided*

8-oz. pkg. cream cheese, cubed, *divided*

½ cup shredded cheddar cheese, *optional*

1. Spray interior of slow cooker with nonstick
   cooking spray.
2. In a small bowl, combine onion, garlic, and
   salt.
3. Layer about one-fourth of the potatoes into
   the slow cooker.
4. Sprinkle one-fourth of onion-garlic mixture
   over potatoes.
5. Spoon about one-third of cream cheese
   cubes over top.
6. Repeat layers, ending with the seasoning.
7. If using fresh potatoes, cook on High 3–4
   hours, or until potatoes are tender. If using
   frozen hash browns, cook on High 2 hours,
   or on Low 4–5 hours, or until potatoes are
   tender and cooked through.
8. Stir potatoes to spread out the cream cheese.
   If you wish, you can mash the potatoes at
   this point.
9. If you like, sprinkle shredded cheese over
   top of the sliced or mashed potatoes.
10. Cover and cook an additional 10 minutes,
    or until the cheese is melted.

Simply Scalloped Potatoes

Ruth Ann Penner Hillsboro, KS

MAKES: **3–4 SERVINGS**
PREP. TIME: **10 MINUTES**
COOKING TIME: **2 HOURS**
IDEAL SLOW COOKER SIZE: **3-QUART**

2 cups thinly sliced raw potatoes, *divided*

1 Tbsp. flour

1 tsp. salt

pepper

1 cup milk

1 Tbsp. butter

1. Spray slow cooker with nonstick cooking
   spray.
2. Put half of thinly sliced potatoes in bottom
   of slow cooker.
3. In a small bowl, mix together flour, salt, and
   pepper. Sprinkle half over top of potatoes.
4. Repeat layering.
5. Pour milk over all. Dot with butter.
6. Cover and cook on High 2 hours.

Tips:

*1. Pour milk over all as soon as possible to
avoid having potatoes turn dark.*

2. Top with shredded cheese, if you wish.

Variation: *A cup of fully cooked ham cubes
could be stirred in before serving.*

*Using a wide blade peeler makes peeling
potatoes a breeze.*

Rustic Potatoes au Gratin

Nancy Savage Factoryville, PA

MAKES: **6 SERVINGS**
PREP. TIME: **10 MINUTES**
COOKING TIME: **6–8 HOURS**
IDEAL SLOW COOKER SIZE: **5-QUART**

½ cup skim milk

10¾-oz. can light condensed cheddar cheese soup

8-oz. pkg. fat-free cream cheese, softened

1 clove garlic, minced

¼ tsp. ground nutmeg

¼ tsp. black pepper

2 lbs. baking potatoes (about 7) cut into ¼-inch-thick
  slices

1 small onion, thinly sliced

paprika

1. Heat milk in small saucepan over medium
   heat until small bubbles form around edge of
   pan. Remove from heat.
2. Add soup, cream cheese, garlic, nutmeg, and
   pepper to pan. Stir until smooth.
3. Spray inside of slow cooker with nonfat
   cooking spray. Layer one-quarter of potatoes
   and onions on bottom of slow cooker.
4. Top with one-quarter of soup mixture.
   Repeat layers 3 times.
5. Cover. Cook on Low 6–8 hours, or until
   potatoes are tender and most of liquid is
   absorbed.
6. Sprinkle with paprika before serving.

Per Serving: 210 calories (35 calories from fat), 4g total fat (1.5g
saturated, 1g trans), 10mg cholesterol, 620mg sodium, 36g total
carbohydrate (4g fiber, 4g sugar), 11g protein, 10%DV vitamin A,
20%DV vitamin C, 10%DV calcium, 8%DV iron.

Potatoes Perfect

Naomi Ressler Harrisonburg, VA

MAKES: **4–6 SERVINGS**
PREP. TIME: **15 MINUTES**
COOKING TIME: **3–10 HOURS**
IDEAL SLOW COOKER SIZE: **3½-QUART**

¼ lb. bacon, diced and browned until crisp

2 medium onions, thinly sliced

6–8 medium potatoes, thinly sliced

½ lb. cheddar cheese, thinly sliced

salt to taste

pepper to taste

2–4 Tbsp. butter

1. Layer half of bacon, onions, potatoes, and
   cheese in greased slow cooker. Season to
   taste.
2. Dot with butter. Repeat layers.
3. Cover. Cook on Low 8–10 hours, or on High
   3–4 hours, or until potatoes are soft.

Uptown Scalloped Potatoes

Dede Peterson   Rapid City, SD

MAKES: **8–10 SERVINGS**
PREP. TIME: **15 MINUTES**
COOKING TIME: **6–7 HOURS**
IDEAL SLOW COOKER SIZE: **6-QUART**

5 lbs. red potatoes, peeled and sliced

2 cups water

1 tsp. cream of tartar

¼ lb. bacon, cut in 1-inch squares, browned until crisp,
   and drained

dash of salt

½ pint whipping cream

1 pint half-and-half

1. Toss potatoes in water and cream of tartar. Drain.
2. Layer potatoes and bacon in large slow cooker. Sprinkle with salt.
3. Mix whipping cream and half-and-half. Pour over.
4. Cover. Cook on Low 6–7 hours.

Variation: *For added flavor, cut one large onion into thin rings. Sauté in bacon drippings; then layer onion along with potatoes and bacon. Sprinkle each layer of potatoes with salt and pepper. Continue with Step 3.*

Mustard Potatoes

Frances Musser   Newmanstown, PA

MAKES: **6 SERVINGS**
PREP. TIME: **5 MINUTES**
COOKING TIME: **2–4 HOURS**
IDEAL SLOW COOKER SIZE: **4-QUART**

½ cup onions, chopped

1 Tbsp. butter

1½ tsp. prepared mustard

1 tsp. salt

¼ tsp. black pepper

½ cup fat-free *or* 2% milk

¼ lb. low-fat cheese, shredded

6 medium potatoes, cooked and grated

1. Sauté onion in butter in skillet. Add mustard, salt, pepper, milk, and cheese.
2. Place potatoes in slow cooker. Do not press down.
3. Pour mixture over potatoes.
4. Cover. Cook on Low 3–4 hours.
5. Toss potatoes with a large spoon when ready to serve.

Per Serving: 230 calories (30 calories from fat), 3.5g total fat (2g saturated, 0g trans), 10mg cholesterol, 430mg sodium, 40g total carbohydrate (5g fiber, 4g sugar), 10g protein, 4%DV vitamin A, 30%DV vitamin C, 20%DV calcium, 10%DV iron.

Variation: *If you like an unmistakable mustardy taste, and your diet allows, you can double the amount of mustard.*

Cook potatoes ahead of time while doing other things — then they will be ready when you want them.

Cheese Potatoes and Croutons

Joyce Shackelford   Green Bay, WI

MAKES: **10 SERVINGS**
PREP. TIME: **10–15 MINUTES**
COOKING TIME: **8¼ HOURS**
IDEAL SLOW COOKER SIZE: **5-QUART**

6 potatoes, peeled and cut into ¼-inch strips
2 cups sharp cheddar cheese, shredded
10¾-oz. can cream of chicken soup
1 small onion, chopped
4 Tbsp. butter, melted
1 tsp. salt
1 tsp. pepper
1 cup sour cream
2 cups seasoned stuffing cubes
3 Tbsp. butter, melted

1. Toss together potatoes and cheese. Place in slow cooker.
2. Combine soup, onion, 4 Tbsp. butter, salt, and pepper. Pour over potatoes.
3. Cover. Cook on Low 8 hours.
4. Stir in sour cream. Cover and heat for 10 more minutes.
5. Meanwhile, toss together stuffing cubes and 3 Tbsp. butter. Sprinkle over potatoes just before serving.

In order to prevent peeled potatoes from discoloring, drop them into a cup of cold water with ½ teaspoon cream of tartar dissolved in it. Drain the potatoes when you're ready to use them.

Creamy Red Potatoes

Mrs. J.E. Barthold   Bethlehem, PA

MAKES: **4–6 SERVINGS**
PREP. TIME: **10 MINUTES**
COOKING TIME: **8 HOURS**
IDEAL SLOW COOKER SIZE: **4-QUART**

2 lbs. small red potatoes, quartered
8-oz. pkg. cream cheese, softened
10¾-oz. can cream of potato soup
1 envelope dry Ranch salad dressing mix

1. Place potatoes in slow cooker.
2. Beat together cream cheese, soup, and salad dressing mix. Stir into potatoes.
3. Cover. Cook on Low 8 hours, or until potatoes are tender.

Creamy Hash Browns

Starla Kreider   Mohrsville, PA

MAKES: **14 SERVINGS**
PREP. TIME: **10 MINUTES**
COOKING TIME: **4–5 HOURS**
IDEAL SLOW COOKER SIZE: **5-QUART**

30-oz. package frozen, diced hash browns
2 cups cubed or shredded cheese of your choice
2 cups sour cream
2 10¾-oz. cans cream of chicken soup
half a stick (¼ cup) butter, melted

1. Place hash browns in an ungreased slow cooker.
2. Combine remaining ingredients and pour over the potatoes. Mix well.
3. Cover and cook on Low 4–5 hours, or until potatoes are tender and heated through.

Cheesy Hash Brown Potatoes

Clarice Williams Fairbank, IA

MAKES: **6–8 SERVINGS**
PREP. TIME: **10 MINUTES**
COOKING TIME: **4–4½ HOURS**
IDEAL SLOW COOKER SIZE: **4-QUART**

2 10¾-oz. cans cheddar cheese soup

1⅓ cups buttermilk

2 Tbsp. butter, melted

½ tsp. seasoned salt

¼ tsp. garlic powder

¼ tsp. pepper

2-lb. pkg. frozen, cubed hash brown potatoes

¼ cup grated Parmesan cheese

1 tsp. paprika

1. Combine soup, buttermilk, butter, seasoned salt, garlic powder, and pepper in slow cooker. Mix well.
2. Stir in hash browns. Sprinkle with Parmesan cheese and paprika.
3. Cover. Cook on Low 4–4½ hours, or until potatoes are tender.

Garlicky Potatoes

Donna Lantgen Rapid City, SD

MAKES: **6 SERVINGS**
PREP. TIME: **10 MINUTES**
COOKING TIME: **5–6 HOURS**
IDEAL SLOW COOKER SIZE: **3½-QUART**

6 potatoes, peeled and cubed

6 garlic cloves, minced

¼ cup dried onion, *or* 1 medium onion, chopped

2 Tbsp. olive oil

1. Combine all ingredients in slow cooker.
2. Cook on Low 5–6 hours, or until potatoes are soft but not turning brown.

———————

Per Serving: 220 calories (40 calories from fat), 4.5 total fat (0.5g saturated, 0g trans), 0mg cholesterol, 15mg sodium, 40g total carbohydrate (5g fiber, 3g sugar), 5g protein, 0%DV vitamin A, 30%DV vitamin C, 4%DV calcium, 10%DV iron.

Variation: *For added flavor, stir in ¼ tsp. dill weed and/or ¼ tsp. dried basil as part of Step 1.*

Herbed Potatoes

Jo Haberkamp   Fairbank, IA

MAKES: **6 SERVINGS**
PREP. TIME: **10 MINUTES**
COOKING TIME: **2½–3 HOURS**
IDEAL SLOW COOKER SIZE: **3-QUART**

1½ lbs. small new potatoes
¼ cup water
¼ cup butter, melted
3 Tbsp. chopped fresh parsley
1 Tbsp. lemon juice
1 Tbsp. chopped fresh chives
1 Tbsp. dill weed
¼–½ tsp. salt, according to your taste preference
⅛–¼ tsp. pepper, according to your taste preference

1. Wash potatoes. Peel a strip around the center of each potato. Place in slow cooker.
2. Add water.
3. Cover. Cook on High 2½–3 hours. Drain well.
4. In saucepan, heat butter, parsley, lemon juice, chives, dill, salt, and pepper. Pour over potatoes.
5. Serve with ham or any meat dish that does not make gravy.

Rosemary New Potatoes

Carol Shirk   Leola, PA

MAKES: **4–5 SERVINGS**
PREP. TIME: **15 MINUTES**
COOKING TIME: **2–6 HOURS**
IDEAL SLOW COOKER SIZE: **3–4-QUART**

1½ lbs. new red potatoes, unpeeled
1 Tbsp. olive oil
1 Tbsp. fresh chopped rosemary, or 1 tsp. dried rosemary
1 tsp. garlic and pepper seasoning, or 1 large clove garlic, minced, plus ½ tsp. salt, and ¼ tsp. pepper

1. If the potatoes are larger than golf balls, cut them in half or in quarters.
2. In a bowl or plastic bag, toss potatoes with olive oil, coating well.
3. Add rosemary and garlic and pepper seasoning (or the minced garlic, salt, and pepper). Toss again until the potatoes are well coated.
4. Place potatoes in slow cooker. Cook on High 2–3 hours, or on Low 5–6 hours, or until potatoes are tender but not mushy or dry.

If your recipe calls for 3 Tablespoons of fresh basil, and you have only dried basil, use 1 Tablespoon of dried basil. In other words, 1 portion of dried herbs can be substituted for 3 portions of fresh herbs. And vice versa.

Vegetables

Parmesan Potato Wedges

Carol and John Ambrose   McMinnville, OR

MAKES: **6 SERVINGS**
PREP. TIME: **15 MINUTES**
COOKING TIME: **4 HOURS**
IDEAL SLOW COOKER SIZE: **3-QUART**

2 lbs. red potatoes, cut into ½-inch wedges or strips
¼ cup chopped onion
2 Tbsp. butter, cut into pieces
1½ tsp. dried oregano
¼ cup grated Parmesan cheese

1. Layer potatoes, onion, butter, and oregano in slow cooker.
2. Cover and cook on High 4 hours, or until potatoes are tender but not dry or mushy.
3. Spoon into serving dish and sprinkle with cheese.

Lemon Red Potatoes

Joyce Shackelford   Green Bay, WI

MAKES: **6 SERVINGS**
PREP. TIME: **10 MINUTES**
COOKING TIME: **2½–3 HOURS**
IDEAL SLOW COOKER SIZE: **4-QUART**

1½ lbs. medium red potatoes
¼ cup water
2 Tbsp. butter, melted
1 Tbsp. lemon juice
3 Tbsp. fresh chives, snipped
chopped fresh parsley
1 tsp. salt
½ tsp. black pepper

1. Cut a strip of peel from around the middle of each potato. Place potatoes and water in slow cooker.
2. Cover. Cook on High 2½–3 hours.
3. Drain.
4. Combine butter, lemon juice, chives, and parsley. Pour over potatoes. Toss to coat.
5. Season with salt and pepper.

Per Serving: 120 calories (35 calories from fat), 4g total fat (2.5g saturated, 0g trans), 10mg cholesterol, 400mg sodium, 18g total carbohydrate (2g fiber, 1g sugar), 2g protein, 0%DV vitamin A, 20%DV vitamin C, 2%DV calcium, 6%DV iron.

Onion Potatoes

Donna Lantgen   Chadron, NE

MAKES: **6 SERVINGS**
PREP. TIME: **20–30 MINUTES**
COOKING TIME: **5–6 HOURS**
IDEAL SLOW COOKER SIZE: **4-QUART**

6 medium potatoes, diced

⅓ cup olive oil

1 envelope dry onion soup mix

1. Combine potatoes and olive oil in plastic bag. Shake well.
2. Add onion soup mix. Shake well.
3. Pour into slow cooker.
4. Cover and cook on Low 5-6 hours.

Pizza Potatoes

Margaret Wenger Johnson   Keezletown, VA

MAKES: **4–6 SERVINGS**
PREP. TIME: **15 MINUTES**
COOKING TIME: **6–10 HOURS**
IDEAL SLOW COOKER SIZE: **4-QUART**

6 medium potatoes, sliced

1 large onion, thinly sliced

2 Tbsp. olive oil

2 cups shredded mozzarella cheese

2 oz. sliced pepperoni

1 tsp. salt

8-oz. can pizza sauce

1. Sauté potato and onion slices in oil in skillet until onions appear transparent. Drain well.
2. In slow cooker, combine potatoes, onions, cheese, pepperoni, and salt.
3. Pour pizza sauce over top.
4. Cover. Cook on Low 6-10 hours, or until potatoes are soft.

Potatoes O'Brien

Rebecca Meyerkorth   Wamego, KS

MAKES: **6 SERVINGS**
PREP. TIME: **10 MINUTES**
COOKING TIME: **4–5 HOURS**
IDEAL SLOW COOKER SIZE: **4-QUART**

32-oz. pkg. shredded potatoes

¼ cup chopped onions

¼ cup chopped green peppers

2 Tbsp. chopped pimento

1 cup chopped ham

¾ tsp. salt

¼ tsp. pepper

3 Tbsp. butter

3 Tbsp. flour

½ cup milk

10¾-oz. can cream of mushroom soup

1 cup shredded cheddar cheese, *divided*

1. Place potatoes, onions, green peppers, pimento, and ham in slow cooker. Sprinkle with salt and pepper.
2. Melt butter in saucepan. Stir in flour; then add half of milk. Stir rapidly to remove all lumps. Stir in remaining milk. Stir in mushroom soup and ½ cup cheese. Pour over potatoes.
3. Cover. Cook on Low 4-5 hours. Sprinkle remaining cheese on top about ½ hour before serving.

I like to keep cooked, peeled sweet potatoes in the freezer. I also keep cooked meats frozen in bags to quickly fix casseroles. I have frozen cooked grated white potatoes as well.

Hot German Potato Salad

Char Hagner Montague, MI

Penny Blosser Beavercreek, OH

MAKES: **8 SERVINGS**
PREP. TIME: **20 MINUTES**
COOKING TIME: **3–8 HOURS**
IDEAL SLOW COOKER SIZE: **3½–4-QUART**

6–7 cups potatoes, sliced

1 cup onions, chopped

1 cup celery, chopped

1 cup water

⅓ cup vinegar

¼ cup sugar

2 Tbsp. quick-cooking tapioca

1 tsp. salt

1 tsp. celery seed

¼ tsp. black pepper

6 slices lean turkey bacon, cooked and crumbled

¼ cup fresh parsley

1. Combine potatoes, onions, and celery in slow cooker.
2. In a bowl, combine water, vinegar, sugar, tapioca, salt, celery seed, and black pepper.
3. Pour over potatoes. Mix together gently.
4. Cover. Cook on Low 6–8 hours, or on High 3–4 hours.
5. Stir in bacon and parsley just before serving.

Per Serving: 170 calories (20 calories from fat), 2.5g total fat (0.5g saturated, 0g trans), 10mg cholesterol, 440mg sodium, 32g total carbohydrate (3g fiber, 8g sugar), 4g protein, 0%DV vitamin A, 25%DV vitamin C, 4%DV calcium, 8%DV iron.

Potato-Stuffed Cabbage

Jeanette Oberholtzer Manheim, PA

MAKES: **10 SERVINGS**
PREP. TIME: **20 MINUTES**
COOKING TIME: **4–6 HOURS**
IDEAL SLOW COOKER SIZE: **6-QUART**

half a large head cabbage, thinly sliced

2½ lbs. potatoes (6 or 7 medium), peeled and grated

1 onion, sliced

¼ cup rice, uncooked

1 apple, peeled and sliced

½–1 tsp. dried dill, according to your taste preference

¼–½ tsp. black pepper, according to your taste preference

¼ tsp. ground ginger

1 egg white

14¼-oz. can tomatoes

1. Spray inside of cooker with nonfat cooking spray. Then begin layering vegetables into cooker. Place one-third of the cabbage, one-third of the potatoes, one-third of the onion, one-third of the rice, one-third of the apple, and one-third of the spices and seasonings into the cooker.
2. Repeat twice.
3. Beat egg white until frothy. Fold into tomatoes. Spoon over top of vegetables.
4. Cover. Cook on Low 4–6 hours, or until vegetables jag tender.

Per Serving: 120 calories (0 calories from fat), 0g total fat (0g saturated, 0g trans), 0mg cholesterol, 135mg sodium, 28g total carbohydrate (5g fiber, 5g sugar), 4g protein, 4%DV vitamin A, 40%DV vitamin C, 8%DV calcium, 8%DV iron.

"Baked" Sweet Potatoes

Shari Mast   Harrisonburg, VA

MAKES: **6–8 SERVINGS**
PREP. TIME: **10 MINUTES**
COOKING TIME: **4–8 HOURS**
IDEAL SLOW COOKER SIZE: **5-QUART**

6–8 medium sweet potatoes

1. Scrub and prick sweet potatoes with fork. Wrap each in tin foil and arrange in slow cooker.
2. Cover. Cook on Low 6–8 hours, or on High 4–5 hours, or until each potato is soft.
3. Remove from foil and serve with butter and salt.

Simply Sweet Potatoes

Leona Yoder   Hartville, OH

MAKES: **4 SERVINGS**
PREP. TIME: **5 MINUTES**
COOKING TIME: **6–9 HOURS**
IDEAL SLOW COOKER SIZE: **2–3-QUART**

3 large sweet potatoes
¼ cup water

1. Place unpeeled sweet potatoes into slow cooker.
2. Add ¼ cup water.
3. Cover and cook on High 1 hour. Then turn to Low and cook for 5–8 hours, or until potatoes are tender.

Fruity Sweet Potatoes

Jean Butzer   Batavia, NY   •   *Evelyn Page*   Lance Creek, WY

MAKES: **6 SERVINGS**
PREP. TIME: **15 MINUTES**
COOKING TIME: **6–8 HOURS**
IDEAL SLOW COOKER SIZE: **3–4-QUART**

2 lbs. (about 6 medium) sweet potatoes *or* yams
1½ cups applesauce
⅔ cup brown sugar
3 Tbsp. butter, melted
1 tsp. cinnamon
chopped nuts, *optional*

1. Peel sweet potatoes if you wish. Cut into cubes or slices. Place in slow cooker.
2. In a bowl, mix together applesauce, brown sugar, butter, and cinnamon. Spoon over potatoes.
3. Cover and cook on Low 6–8 hours, or until potatoes are tender.
4. Mash potatoes and sauce together if you wish with a large spoon—or spoon potatoes into serving dish and top with the sauce.
5. Sprinkle with nuts, if you want.

Variation: *Instead of raw sweet potatoes, substitute a 40-oz. can of cut-up sweet potatoes, drained. Then cook on Low for only 3–4 hours.*
Shelia Heil   Lancaster, PA

Sweet Potatoes and Apples

Bernita Boyts   Shawnee Mission, KS

MAKES: **8–10 SERVINGS**
PREP. TIME: **10–15 MINUTES**
COOKING TIME: **6–8 HOURS**
IDEAL SLOW COOKER SIZE: **3-QUART**

3 large sweet potatoes, peeled and cubed

3 large tart and firm apples, peeled and sliced

½–¾ tsp. salt

⅛–¼ tsp. pepper

1 tsp. sage

1 tsp. ground cinnamon

4 Tbsp. (½ stick) butter, melted

¼ cup maple syrup

toasted sliced almonds *or* chopped pecans, *optional*

1. Place half the sweet potatoes in slow cooker. Layer in half the apple slices.
2. Mix together seasonings. Sprinkle half over apples.
3. Mix together butter and maple syrup. Spoon half over seasonings.
4. Repeat layers.
5. Cover. Cook on Low 6–8 hours or until potatoes are soft, stirring occasionally.
6. To add a bit of crunch, sprinkle with toasted almonds or pecans when serving.
7. Serve with pork or poultry.

Sweet Potato, Fruit Compote

Ilene Bontrager   Arlington, KS

MAKES: **8 SERVINGS**
PREP. TIME: **20 MINUTES**
COOKING TIME: **5–6 HOURS**
IDEAL SLOW COOKER SIZE: **3½-QUART**

4 cups sweet potatoes, peeled and cubed

3 tart cooking apples, peeled and diced

20-oz. can unsweetened pineapple chunks, undrained

¼ cup brown sugar

1 cup miniature marshmallows, *divided*

1. Cook sweet potatoes in a small amount of water in a saucepan until almost soft. Drain.
2. Combine sweet potatoes, apples, and pineapples in slow cooker.
3. Sprinkle with brown sugar and ⅔ cup marshmallows.
4. Cover. Cook on Low 5–6 hours.
5. Thirty minutes before serving, top potatoes and fruit with remaining ⅓ cup marshmallows. Cover and continue cooking.

Per Serving: 200 calories (0 calories from fat), 0g total fat (0g saturated, 0g trans), 0mg cholesterol, 15mg sodium, 49g total carbohydrate (4g fiber, 31g sugar), 2g protein, 400%DV vitamin A, 20%DV vitamin C, 4%DV calcium, 6%DV iron.

Invest in good quality knives. They make preparation much easier.

Pineapple Sweet Potatoes

Annabelle Unternahrer   Shipshewana, IN

MAKES: **10 SERVINGS**
PREP. TIME: **5 MINUTES**
COOKING TIME: **2–4 HOURS**
IDEAL SLOW COOKER SIZE: **4-QUART**

10-oz. can unsweetened crushed pineapple, drained
2 Tbsp. dark brown sugar
40-oz. can unsweetened yams, drained

1. Mix crushed pineapples with brown sugar.
2. Combine with yams in slow cooker sprayed with cooking spray.
3. Cover. Cook on Low 2–4 hours, or until heated through.

Per Serving: 130 calories (0 calories from fat), 0g total fat (0g saturated, 0g trans), 0mg cholesterol, 85mg sodium, 31g total carbohydrate (2g fiber, 23g sugar), 2g protein, 300%DV vitamin A, 10%DV vitamin C, 4%DV calcium, 10%DV iron.

Tip: *This recipe can be doubled easily. Just remember to allow extra time for it to heat; perhaps an additional hour.*

Glazed Sweet Potatoes

Jan Mast   Lancaster, PA

MAKES: **8–10 SERVINGS**
PREP. TIME: **20 MINUTES**
COOKING TIME: **3–4 HOURS**
IDEAL SLOW COOKER SIZE: **2-QUART**

8–10 medium sweet potatoes
½ tsp. salt
¾ cup brown sugar
2 Tbsp. butter
1 Tbsp. flour
¼ cup water

1. Cook sweet potatoes in 2–3-inches water in a large saucepan until barely soft. Drain. When cool enough to handle, peel and slice into slow cooker.
2. While potatoes are cooking in the saucepan, combine remaining ingredients in a microwave-safe bowl.
3. Microwave on High for 1½ minutes. Stir. Repeat until glaze thickens slightly.
4. Pour glaze over peeled, cooked sweet potatoes in slow cooker.
5. Cover and cook on High 3–4 hours.

Be careful about adding liquids to food in a slow cooker. Foods have natural juices in them, and unlike oven cooking which is dry, food juices remain in the slow cooker as the food cooks.

Vegetables

Glazed Maple Sweet Potatoes

Jeannine Janzen   Elbing, KS

MAKES: **5 SERVINGS**
PREP. TIME: **5–10 MINUTES**
COOKING TIME: **7–9 HOURS**
IDEAL SLOW COOKER SIZE: **4-QUART**

5 medium sweet potatoes, cut in ½-inch-thick slices
¼ cup brown sugar, packed
¼ cup pure maple syrup
¼ cup apple cider
2 Tbsp. butter

1. Place potatoes in slow cooker.
2. In a small bowl, combine brown sugar, maple syrup, and apple cider. Mix well. Pour over potatoes. Stir until all potato slices are covered.
3. Cover and cook on Low 7–9 hours, or until potatoes are tender.
4. Stir in butter before serving.

Orange Yams

Gladys Longacre   Susquehanna, PA

MAKES: **6–8 SERVINGS**
PREP. TIME: **15 MINUTES**
COOKING TIME: **3 HOURS**
IDEAL SLOW COOKER SIZE: **3½-QUART**

40-oz. can yams, drained
2 apples, cored, peeled, thinly sliced
3 Tbsp. butter, melted
2 tsp. orange zest
1 cup orange juice
2 Tbsp. cornstarch
½ cup brown sugar
1 tsp. salt
dash of ground cinnamon *and/or* nutmeg

1. Place yams and apples in slow cooker.
2. Add butter and orange zest.
3. Combine remaining ingredients and pour over yams.
4. Cover. Cook on High 1 hour and on Low 2 hours, or until apples are tender.

Variation: *Substitute 6–8 medium cooked sweet potatoes, or approximately 4 cups cubed butternut squash, for yams.*

Sweet Potato Casserole

Jean Butzer Batavia, NY

MAKES: **8 SERVINGS**
PREP. TIME: **10 MINUTES**
COOKING TIME: **3–4 HOURS**
IDEAL SLOW COOKER SIZE: **3½-QUART**

2 29-oz. cans sweet potatoes, drained and mashed

2 Tbsp. brown sugar

1 Tbsp. orange juice

2 eggs, beaten

½ cup fat-free milk

⅓ cup chopped pecans

⅓ cup brown sugar

2 Tbsp. flour

2 tsp. butter, melted

1. Combine sweet potatoes and 2 Tbsp. brown sugar.
2. Stir in orange juice, eggs, and milk. Transfer to greased slow cooker.
3. Combine pecans, ⅓ cup brown sugar, flour, and butter. Spread over sweet potatoes.
4. Cover. Cook on High 3–4 hours.

Per Serving: 330 calories (50 calories from fat), 6g total fat (1.5g saturated, 0g trans), 50mg cholesterol, 180mg sodium, 63g total carbohydrate (4g fiber, 46g sugar), 7g protein, 500%DV vitamin A, 0%DV vitamin C, 10%DV calcium, 20%DV iron.

Rosy Sweet Potatoes

Evelyn L. Ward Greeley, CO

MAKES: **8 SERVINGS**
PREP. TIME: **5 MINUTES**
COOKING TIME: **3–4 HOURS**
IDEAL SLOW COOKER SIZE: **3½–4-QUART**

40-oz. can unsweetened sweet potato chunks, drained

21-oz. can lite apple pie filling

⅓ cup brown sugar

⅓ cup red hots

1 tsp. ground cinnamon

1. Combine all ingredients in a large bowl. Pour into slow cooker sprayed with non-fat cooking spray.
2. Cover. Cook on Low 3–4 hours.

Per Serving: 280 calories (25 calories from fat), 3g total fat (1g saturated, 0g trans), 5mg cholesterol, 220mg sodium, 62g total carbohydrate (3g fiber, 46g sugar), 4g protein, 400%DV vitamin A, 2%DV vitamin C, 6%DV calcium, 15%DV iron.

Never Fail Rice

Mary E. Wheatley   Mashpee, MA

MAKES: **6 SERVINGS**
PREP. TIME: **5 MINUTES**
COOKING TIME: **2–6 HOURS**
IDEAL SLOW COOKER SIZE: **1–2-QUART**

1 cup long-grain rice, uncooked
2 cups water
½ tsp. salt
½ Tbsp. butter

1. Combine all ingredients in small slow cooker.
2. Cover. Cook on Low 4–6 hours, or on High 2–3 hours, or until rice is just fully cooked.
3. Fluff with a fork. Serve.

Per Serving: 120 calories (10 calories from fat), 1g total fat (0.5g saturated, 0g trans), 5mg cholesterol, 200mg sodium, 25g total carbohydrate (0g fiber, 0g sugar), 2g protein, 0%DV vitamin A, 0%DV vitamin C, 2%DV calcium, 8%DV iron.

Don't peek. It takes 15–20 minutes for the cooker to regain lost steam and return to the right temperature.

Herb Rice

Frieda Weisz   Aberdeen, SD

MAKES: **6 SERVINGS**
PREP. TIME: **5 MINUTES**
COOKING TIME: **4–6 HOURS**
IDEAL SLOW COOKER SIZE: **3½-QUART**

3 chicken bouillon cubes
3 cups water
1½ cups long-grain rice, uncooked
1 tsp. dried rosemary
½ tsp. dried marjoram
¼ cup dried parsley, chopped
1 Tbsp. butter *or* margarine
¼ cup onions, diced
½ cup slivered almonds, *optional*

1. Mix together chicken bouillon cubes and water.
2. Combine all ingredients in slow cooker.
3. Cook on Low 4–6 hours, or until rice is fully cooked.

Per Serving: 70 calories (20 calories from fat), 2g total fat (1g saturated, 0g trans), 5mg cholesterol, 610mg sodium, 10g total carbohydrate (0.5g fiber, 1g sugar), 1g protein, 4%DV vitamin A, 2%DV vitamin C, 2%DV calcium, 6%DV iron.

Variation: *If you prefer, you may use 24 ozs. (or 3 cups) fat-free low-sodium chicken broth instead of the bouillon cubes and water*

Wild Rice

Ruth S. Weaver   Reinholds, PA

MAKES: **5 SERVINGS**
PREP. TIME: **10 MINUTES**
COOKING TIME: **2½–3 HOURS**
IDEAL SLOW COOKER SIZE: **3-QUART**

1 cup wild rice *or* wild rice mixture, uncooked
½ cup sliced fresh mushrooms
½ cup diced onions
½ cup diced green *or* red bell peppers
1 Tbsp. oil
½ tsp. salt
¼ tsp. black pepper
2½ cups fat-free, low-sodium chicken broth

1. Layer rice and vegetables in slow cooker. Pour oil, salt, and pepper over vegetables. Stir.
2. Heat chicken broth. Pour over ingredients in slow cooker.
3. Cover. Cook on High 2½–3 hours, or until rice is soft and liquid is absorbed.

Per Serving: 180 calories (30 calories from fat), 3.5g total fat (0g saturated, 0g trans), 0mg cholesterol, 300mg sodium, 31g total carbohydrate (3g fiber, 2g sugar), 9g protein, 0%DV vitamin A, 10%DV vitamin C, 2%DV calcium, 10%DV iron.

Risi Bisi (Peas and Rice)

Cyndie Marrara   Port Matilda, PA

MAKES: **6 SERVINGS**
PREP. TIME: **10–15 MINUTES**
COOKING TIME: **2½–3½ HOURS**
IDEAL SLOW COOKER SIZE: **4-QUART**

1½ cups converted long-grain white rice, uncooked
¾ cup chopped onions
2 garlic cloves, minced
2 14½-oz. cans reduced-sodium chicken broth
⅓ cup water
¾ tsp. Italian seasoning
½ tsp. dried basil leaves
½ cup frozen baby peas, thawed
¼ cup grated Parmesan cheese

1. Combine rice, onions, and garlic in slow cooker.
2. In saucepan, mix together chicken broth and water. Bring to boil. Add Italian seasoning and basil leaves. Stir into rice mixture.
3. Cover. Cook on Low 2–3 hours, or until liquid is absorbed.
4. Stir in peas. Cover. Cook 30 minutes. Stir in cheese.

Slow cookers fit any season. When it's hot outside, they don't heat up your kitchen. So turn on your cooker before heading to the pool or the beach — or the garden. Or put your dinner in the slow cooker, and then go play or watch your favorite sport.

Hometown Spanish Rice

Beverly Flatt-Getz   Warriors Mark, PA

MAKES: **6–8 SERVINGS**
PREP. TIME: **20 MINUTES**
COOKING TIME: **2–4 HOURS**
IDEAL SLOW COOKER SIZE: **4-QUART**

1 large onion, chopped

1 bell pepper, chopped

1 lb. bacon, cooked, and broken into bite-size pieces

2 cups long-grain rice, cooked

28-oz. can stewed tomatoes with juice

grated Parmesan cheese, *optional*

1. Sauté onion and pepper in a small nonstick frying pan until tender.
2. Spray interior of slow cooker with nonstick cooking spray.
3. Combine all ingredients in the slow cooker.
4. Cover and cook on Low 4 hours, or on High 2 hours, or until heated through.
5. Sprinkle with Parmesan cheese just before serving, if you wish.

Rice 'n Beans 'n Salsa

Heather Horst   Lebanon, PA

MAKES: **6–8 SERVINGS**
PREP. TIME: **7 MINUTES**
COOKING TIME: **4–10 HOURS**
IDEAL SLOW COOKER SIZE: **3–5-QUART**

2 16-oz. cans black *or* **navy beans, drained**

14-oz. can chicken broth

1 cup long-grain white *or* **brown rice, uncooked**

1 quart salsa, your choice of heat

1 cup water

½ tsp. garlic powder

1. Combine all ingredients in slow cooker. Stir well.
2. Cover and cook on Low 8–10 hours, or on High 4 hours.

Red Bean and Brown Rice Stew

Barbara Gautcher   Harrisonburg, VA

MAKES: **6 SERVINGS**
PREP. TIME: **15 MINUTES**
SOAKING TIME: **8 HOURS, OR OVERNIGHT**
COOKING TIME: **6 HOURS**
IDEAL SLOW COOKER SIZE: **6-QUART**

2 cups dried red beans

water

¾ cup brown rice, uncooked

4 cups water

6 carrots, peeled if you wish, and cut into chunks

1 large onion, cut into chunks

1 Tbsp. cumin

1. Place dried beans in slow cooker and cover with water. Allow to soak for 8 hours or overnight. Drain. Discard soaking water.
2. Return soaked beans to cooker. Stir in all remaining ingredients.
3. Cover and cook on Low 6 hours, or until all vegetables are tender.

Variation: *Add 1 tsp. salt to Step 2.*

Broccoli-Rice Casserole

Liz Rugg   Wayland, IA

MAKES: **6 SERVINGS**
PREP. TIME: **5 MINUTES**
COOKING TIME: **3–4 HOURS**
IDEAL SLOW COOKER SIZE: **3–4-QUART**

1 cup minute rice, uncooked

1-lb. pkg. frozen chopped broccoli

8-oz. jar processed cheese spread

10¾-oz. can cream of mushroom soup

1. Mix all ingredients together in slow cooker.

2. Cover and cook on High 3–4 hours, or until rice and broccoli are tender but not mushy or dry.

Wild Rice Pilaf

Judi Manos   West Islip, NY

MAKES: **6 SERVINGS**
PREP. TIME: **10 MINUTES**
COOKING TIME: **3½–5 HOURS**
IDEAL SLOW COOKER SIZE: **3–4-QUART**

1½ cups wild rice, uncooked

½ cup finely chopped onion

14-oz. can chicken broth

2 cups water

4-oz. can sliced mushrooms, drained

½ tsp. dried thyme leaves

1. Spray slow cooker with nonstick cooking spray.
2. Rinse rice and drain well.
3. Combine rice, onion, chicken broth, and water in slow cooker. Mix well.
4. Cover and cook on High 3–4 hours.
5. Add mushrooms and thyme and stir gently.
6. Cover and cook on Low 30–60 minutes longer, or until wild rice pops and is tender.

Variation: *Add ¾ tsp. salt in Step 3.*

Flavorful Fruited Rice

Sandra Haverstraw Hummelstown, PA

MAKES: **4 SERVINGS**
PREP. TIME: **7 MINUTES**
COOKING TIME: **2 HOURS**
IDEAL SLOW COOKER SIZE: **2–3½-QUART**

⅓ cup chopped onion

6-oz. pkg. long-grain and wild rice mix

2 cups chicken broth

¼ cup dried cranberries

¼ cup chopped dried apricots

1. Spray small frying pan with nonstick cooking spray. Add chopped onions and cook on medium heat about 5 minutes, or until onions begin to brown.
2. Place onions and remaining ingredients in the slow cooker, including the seasonings in the rice package. Stir well to dissolve seasonings.
3. Cover and cook on High 2 hours. Fluff with fork to serve.

Variations:

1. Just before serving sprinkle dish with ½ cup toasted pecans, or other nuts.

2. Use other dried fruits instead of the cranberries, such as raisins or dried cherries.

Chopping dried fruit can be difficult. Make it easier by spraying your kitchen scissors with nonstick cooking spray before chopping. Fruits won't stick to the blade.

Cheddar Rice

Natalia Showalter Mt. Solon, VA

MAKES: **8–10 SERVINGS**
PREP. TIME: **10–15 MINUTES**
COOKING TIME: **2–3 HOURS**
IDEAL SLOW COOKER SIZE: **3-QUART**

2 cups brown rice, uncooked

3 Tbsp. butter

½ cup thinly sliced green onions *or* shallots

1 tsp. salt

5 cups water

½ tsp. pepper

2 cups shredded cheddar cheese

1 cup slivered almonds, *optional*

1. Combine rice, butter, green onion, and salt in slow cooker.
2. Bring water to boil and pour over rice mixture.
3. Cover and cook on High 2–3 hours, or until rice is tender and liquid is absorbed.
4. Five minutes before serving stir in pepper and cheese.
5. Garnish with slivered almonds, if you wish.

Herbed Lentils and Rice

Sharon Miller   Holmesville, OH

MAKES: **4 SERVINGS**
PREP. TIME: **10 MINUTES**
COOKING TIME: **6–8 HOURS**
IDEAL SLOW COOKER SIZE: **3-QUART**

2¾ cups reduced-sodium fat-free chicken broth
¾ cup water
¾ cup dry lentils, rinsed
¾ cup onions, chopped
½ cup dry wild rice
½ tsp. dried basil
¼ tsp. dried oregano
¼ tsp. dried thyme
⅛ tsp. garlic powder
½ tsp. salt
¼ tsp. black pepper
1 cup shredded reduced-fat Swiss cheese

1. Spray slow cooker with fat-free cooking spray.
2. Combine all ingredients except cheese in slow cooker.
3. Cook on Low 6–8 hours, or until lentils and rice are tender. Do not remove lid until it has cooked at least 6 hours.
4. Stir in shredded cheese 5–10 minutes before serving.

Per Serving: 420 calories (130 calories from fat), 14g total fat (9g saturated, 0g trans), 35mg cholesterol, 500mg sodium, 41g total carbohydrate (10g fiber, 3g sugar), 33g protein, 15%DV vitamin A, 2%DV vitamin C, 60%DV calcium, 30%DV iron.

Vegetable Rice Casserole

Esther Martin   Ephrata, PA

MAKES: **8 SERVINGS**
PREP. TIME: **10 MINUTES**
COOKING TIME: **3–4 HOURS**
IDEAL SLOW COOKER SIZE: **6-QUART**

¼ cup rice, uncooked
1 lb. zucchini, sliced
1 lb. yellow summer squash, sliced
1 large onion, sliced
1 Tbsp. dried basil, *divided*
1 medium green bell pepper, julienned
4 celery ribs with leaves, chopped
2 large tomatoes, sliced
¼ cup packed brown sugar
½ tsp. salt
¼ tsp. black pepper
2 Tbsp. olive oil

1. Spread rice in slow cooker that has been coated with fat-free cooking spray.
2. Layer in zucchini, yellow squash, onion, and half the basil.
3. Top with green pepper, celery, and tomatoes.
4. Combine brown sugar, salt, and pepper. Sprinkle over vegetables. Drizzle with oil.
5. Cover. Cook on High 3–4 hours, or until the vegetables reach the degree of "doneness" that you prefer.
6. Sprinkle with remaining basil when finished.

Per Serving: 100 calories (35 calories from fat), 4g total fat (0.5g saturated, 0g trans), 0mg cholesterol, 170mg sodium, 16g total carbohydrate (3g fiber, 11g sugar), 2g protein, 10%DV vitamin A, 30%DV vitamin C, 4%DV calcium, 6%DV iron.

Variations:

1. If your diet allows, and if you prefer a less juicy dish, increase the amount of rice to ½ cup.

2. If you want to use fresh basil instead of dried, stir in 3 Tbsp. just before serving the dish.

Vegetables

Moist Poultry Dressing

Virginia Bender Dover, DE • *Josie Boilman* Maumee, OH
Sharon Brubaker Myerstown, PA • *Joette Droz* Kalona, IA
Jacqueline Stefl E. Bethany, NY

MAKES: **14 SERVINGS**
PREP. TIME: **25 MINUTES**
COOKING TIME: **5 HOURS**
IDEAL SLOW COOKER SIZE: **5-QUART**

2 4½-oz. cans sliced mushrooms, drained

4 celery ribs, chopped (about 2 cups)

2 medium onions, chopped

¼ cup minced fresh parsley

¼–¾ cup butter (enough to flavor bread)

13 cups cubed day-old bread

1½ tsp. salt

1½ tsp. sage

1 tsp. poultry seasoning

1 tsp. dried thyme

½ tsp. pepper

2 eggs

1 or 2 14½-oz. cans chicken broth (enough to moisten bread)

1. In large skillet, sauté mushrooms, celery, onions, and parsley in margarine until vegetables are tender.
2. Toss together bread cubes, salt, sage, poultry seasoning, thyme, and pepper. Add mushroom mixture.
3. Combine eggs and broth and add to bread mixture. Mix well.
4. Pour into greased slow cooker. Cook on Low 5 hours, or until meat thermometer reaches 160°.

Tip: *This is a good way to free up the oven when you're making a turkey.*

Variations:

1. Use 2 bags bread cubes for stuffing. Make one mixed bread (white and wheat) and the other cornbread cubes.

2. Add ½ tsp. dried marjoram to Step 2.

Arlene Miller Hutchinson, KS

Fresh Herb Stuffing

Barbara J. Fabel Wausau, WI

MAKES: **8 SERVINGS**
PREP. TIME: **25 MINUTES**
COOKING TIME: **4–5 HOURS**
IDEAL SLOW COOKER SIZE: **6-QUART**

3 Tbsp. butter

3 onions, chopped

4 celery ribs, chopped

½ cup chopped fresh parsley

1 Tbsp. chopped fresh rosemary

1 Tbsp. chopped fresh thyme

1 Tbsp. chopped fresh marjoram

1 Tbsp. chopped fresh sage

1 tsp. salt

½ tsp. freshly-ground black pepper

1 loaf stale low-fat sourdough bread, cut in 1-inch cubes

2 cups fat-free chicken broth

1. Sauté onions and celery in butter in skillet until transparent. Remove from heat and stir in fresh herbs and seasonings.
2. Place bread cubes in large bowl. Add onion/herb mixture. Add enough broth to moisten. Mix well but gently. Turn into greased slow cooker.
3. Cover. Cook on High 1 hour. Reduce heat to Low and continue cooking 3–4 hours.

Per Serving: 100 calories (45 calories from fat), 5g total fat (3g saturated, 0g trans), 10mg cholesterol, 420mg sodium, 11g total carbohydrate (2g fiber, 3g sugar), 3g protein, 6%DV vitamin A, 6%DV vitamin C, 4%DV calcium, 8%DV iron.

Potato Filling

Miriam Nolt   New Holland, PA

MAKES: **20 SERVINGS**
PREP. TIME: **40 MINUTES**
COOKING TIME: **3 HOURS**
IDEAL SLOW COOKER SIZE: **2 5-QUART COOKERS**

1 cup celery, chopped fine

1 medium onion, minced

½ cup butter

2 15-oz. pkgs. low-fat bread cubes

6 eggs, beaten

1 quart fat-free milk

1 quart mashed potatoes

3 tsp. salt

2 pinches saffron

1 cup boiling water

1 tsp. black pepper

1. Sauté celery and onion in butter in skillet until transparent.
2. Combine sautéed mixture with bread cubes. Stir in remaining ingredients. Add more milk if mixture isn't very moist.
3. Pour into large, or several medium-sized, slow cookers. Cook on High 3 hours, stirring up from bottom every hour or so to make sure the filling isn't sticking.

———————————

Per Serving: 260 calories (45 calories from fat), 5g total fat (2.5g saturated, 0g trans), 65mg cholesterol, 510mg sodium, 70g total carbohydrate (4g fiber, 4g sugar), 10g protein, 0%DV vitamin A, 10%DV vitamin C, 10%DV calcium, 20%DV iron.

Tip: *This recipe can be cut in half successfully.*

Slow Cooker Stuffing with Poultry

Pat Unternahrer   Wayland, IA

MAKES: **18 SERVINGS**
PREP. TIME: **15 MINUTES**
COOKING TIME: **7–9 HOURS**
IDEAL SLOW COOKER SIZE: **6–7-QUART, OR 2 4-QUART COOKERS**

1 large loaf dried low-fat bread, cubed

2 cups chopped, cooked turkey *or* chicken, skin removed

1 large onion, chopped

3 ribs celery with leaves, chopped

¼ cup butter, melted

4 cups fat-free chicken broth

1 Tbsp. poultry seasoning

1 tsp. salt

4 eggs, beaten

½ tsp. black pepper

1. Mix together all ingredients. Pour into slow cooker.
2. Cover and cook on High 1 hour, then reduce to Low 6–8 hours.

———————————

Per Serving: 110 calories (40 calories from fat), 4.5g total fat (1.5g saturated, 0g trans), 60mg cholesterol, 270mg sodium, 12g total carbohydrate (4g fiber, 1g sugar), 10g protein, 0%DV vitamin A, 0%DV vitamin C, 6%DV calcium, 10%DV iron.

Slow Cooker Stuffing with Sausage

Dede Peterson   Rapid City, SD

MAKES: **10 SERVINGS**
PREP. TIME: **35–40 MINUTES**
COOKING TIME: **4 HOURS**
IDEAL SLOW COOKER SIZE: **6-QUART**

12 cups toasted bread crumbs *or* dressing mix

1 lb. bulk sausage, browned and drained

¼–1 cup butter (enough to flavor bread)

1 cup or more finely chopped onions

1 cup or more finely chopped celery

8-oz. can sliced mushrooms, with liquid

¼ cup chopped fresh parsley

2 tsp. poultry seasoning (omit if using dressing mix)

dash of pepper

½ tsp. salt

2 eggs, beaten

4 cups chicken stock

1. Combine bread crumbs and sausage.
2. Melt butter in skillet. Add onions and celery and sauté until tender. Stir in mushrooms and parsley. Add seasonings. Pour over bread crumbs and mix well.
3. Stir in eggs and chicken stock.
4. Pour into slow cooker and bake on High 1 hour, and on Low an additional 3 hours.

Variations:

1. For a drier stuffing, reduce the chicken stock to 1½ cups (or 14½-oz. can chicken broth) and eliminate the sausage.

2. For a less spicy stuffing, reduce the poultry seasoning to ½ tsp.

Dolores Metzler   Mechanicsburg, PA

3. Substitute 3½–4½ cups cooked and diced giblets in place of sausage. Add another can mushrooms and 2 tsp. sage in Step 2.

Mrs. Don Martins   Fairbank, IA

Slow Cooker Dressing

Marie Shank   Harrisonburg, VA

MAKES: **16 SERVINGS**
PREP. TIME: **10 MINUTES, PLUS BAKING TIME FOR CORNBREAD**
COOKING TIME: **2–8 HOURS**
IDEAL SLOW COOKER SIZE: **6-QUART**

2 boxes Jiffy Cornbread mix

8 slices day-old bread

4 eggs

1 onion, chopped

½ cup chopped celery

2 10¾-oz. cans cream of chicken soup

2 cups chicken broth

1 tsp. salt

½ tsp. pepper

1½ Tbsp. sage *or* poultry seasoning

½–¾ cup butter

1. Prepare cornbread according to package instructions.
2. Crumble cornbread and bread together.
3. In large bowl combine all ingredients except butter and spoon into 6-quart greased slow cooker, or 2 smaller cookers. Dot top with butter.
4. Cover. Cook on High 2–4 hours, or on Low 3–8 hours.

Variations:

1. Prepare your favorite cornbread recipe in an 8-inch-square baking pan instead of using the cornbread mix.

2. For a more moist dressing, use 2 14½-oz. cans chicken broth instead of 2 cups chicken broth.

3. You may reduce the butter to 2 Tbsp. Serve with roast chicken or turkey drumsticks.

Helen Kenagy   Carlsbad, NM

Apple Stuffing

Judi Manos West Islip, NY • *Jeanette Oberholtzer* Manheim, PA

MAKES: **4–5 SERVINGS**
PREP. TIME: **20 MINUTES**
COOKING TIME: **4–5 HOURS**
IDEAL SLOW COOKER SIZE: **4–6-QUART**

1 stick (½ cup) butter, *divided*

1 cup chopped walnuts

2 onions, chopped

14-oz. pkg. dry herb-seasoned stuffing mix

1½ cups applesauce

water, *optional*

1. In nonstick skillet, melt 2 Tbsp. of butter. Sauté walnuts over medium heat until toasted, about 5 minutes, stirring frequently. Remove from skillet and set aside.
2. Melt remaining butter in skillet. Add onions and cook 3–4 minutes, or until almost tender. Set aside.
3. Spray slow cooker with nonstick cooking spray. Place dry stuffing mix in slow cooker.
4. Add onion-butter mixture and stir. Add applesauce and stir.
5. Cover and cook on Low 4–5 hours, or until heated through. Check after Stuffing has cooked for 3½ hours. If it's sticking to the cooker, drying out, or becoming too brown on the edges, stir in ½–1 cup water. Continue cooking.
6. Sprinkle with walnuts before serving.

Keep nuts, coconut, and whole wheat flour in airtight containers in the freezer in order to retain their freshness and flavor.

Sweet Potato Stuffing

Tina Snyder Manheim, PA

MAKES: **8 SERVINGS**
PREP. TIME: **15 MINUTES**
COOKING TIME: **4 HOURS**
IDEAL SLOW COOKER SIZE: **4-QUART**

½ cup chopped celery

½ cup chopped onions

¼ cup butter

6 cups dry bread cubes

1 large sweet potato, cooked, peeled, and cubed

½ cup chicken broth

¼ cup chopped pecans

½ tsp. poultry seasoning

½ tsp. rubbed sage

½ tsp. salt

¼ tsp. pepper

1. Sauté celery and onion in skillet in butter until tender. Pour into greased slow cooker.
2. Add remaining ingredients. Toss gently.
3. Cover. Cook on Low 4 hours.

Desserts and Sweets

Cherry Cobbler

Michele Ruvola Selden, NY

PICTURED
ON PAGE
233

MAKES: **6–8 SERVINGS**
PREP. TIME: **5 MINUTES**
COOKING TIME: **2½–5½ HOURS**
IDEAL SLOW COOKER SIZE: **3-QUART**

21-oz. can cherry pie filling
1¾ cups dry cake mix of your choice
1 egg
3 Tbsp. evaporated milk
½ tsp. cinnamon

1. Lightly spray the slow cooker with nonstick cooking spray.
2. Place pie filling in slow cooker and cook on High 30 minutes.
3. Meanwhile, mix together remaining ingredients in bowl until crumbly. Spoon onto hot pie filling.
4. Cover and cook on Low 2–5 hours, or until a toothpick inserted into center of topping comes out dry.
5. Serve warm or cooled.

A slow cooker is great for taking food to a potluck supper, even if you didn't prepare it in the cooker.

Just Peachy

Betty B. Dennison   Grove City, PA

MAKES: **4–6 SERVINGS**
PREP. TIME: **2–3 MINUTES**
COOKING TIME: **4–5 HOURS**
IDEAL SLOW COOKER SIZE: **3-QUART**

4 cups sliced peaches, fresh *or* canned (if using canned
  peaches, reserve the juice)

⅔ cup rolled dry oats

⅓ cup all-purpose baking mix

½ cup sugar

½ cup brown sugar

½ tsp. cinnamon, *optional*

½ cup water *or* reserved peach juice

1. Spray inside of slow cooker with nonstick cooking spray.
2. Place peaches in slow cooker.
3. In a bowl, mix together all dry ingredients. When blended, stir in water or juice until well mixed.
4. Spoon batter into cooker and stir into peaches, just until blended.
5. Cover and cook on Low 4–5 hours.
6. Serve warm with vanilla ice cream or frozen yogurt.

Black and Blue Cobbler

Renee Shirk   Mount Joy, PA

MAKES: **6 SERVINGS**
PREP. TIME: **20 MINUTES**
COOKING TIME: **2–2½ HOURS**
IDEAL SLOW COOKER SIZE: **5-QUART**

1 cup flour

¾ cup sugar

1 tsp. baking powder

¼ tsp. salt

¼ tsp. ground cinnamon

¼ tsp. ground nutmeg

2 eggs, beaten

2 Tbsp. milk

2 Tbsp. vegetable oil

2 cups fresh *or* frozen blueberries

2 cups fresh *or* frozen blackberries

¾ cup water

1 tsp. grated orange peel

¾ cup sugar

whipped topping *or* ice cream, *optional*

1. Combine flour, ¾ cup sugar, baking powder, salt, cinnamon, and nutmeg.
2. Combine eggs, milk, and oil. Stir into dry ingredients until moistened.
3. Spread the batter evenly over bottom of greased 5-quart slow cooker.
4. In saucepan, combine berries, water, orange peel, and ¾ cup sugar. Bring to boil. Remove from heat and pour over batter. Cover.
5. Cook on High 2–2½ hours, or until toothpick inserted into batter comes out clean. Turn off cooker.
6. Uncover and let stand 30 minutes before serving. Spoon from cooker and serve with whipped topping or ice cream, if desired.

Cranberry Pudding

Margaret Wheeler   North Bend, OR

MAKES: **8–10 SERVINGS**
PREP. TIME: **20 MINUTES**
COOKING TIME: **3–4 HOURS**
IDEAL SLOW COOKER SIZE: **4–5-QUART**

Pudding:
1⅓ cups flour
½ tsp. salt
2 tsp. baking soda
⅓ cup boiling water
½ cup dark molasses
2 cups whole cranberries
½ cup chopped nuts
½ cup water

Butter Sauce:
1 cup confectioners sugar
½ cup heavy cream *or* evaporated milk
½ cup butter
1 tsp. vanilla

1. Mix together flour and salt.
2. Dissolve soda in boiling water. Add to flour and salt.
3. Stir in molasses. Blend well.
4. Fold in cranberries and nuts.
5. Pour into well greased and floured bread or cake pan that will sit in your cooker. Cover with greased foil.
6. Pour ½ cup water into cooker. Place foil-covered pan in cooker. Cover with cooker lid and steam on High 3 to 4 hours, or until pudding tests done with a wooden pick.
7. Remove pan and uncover. Let stand 5 minutes, then unmold.
8. To make butter sauce, mix together all ingredients in saucepan. Cook, stirring over medium heat until sugar dissolves.
9. Serve warm butter sauce over warm cranberry pudding.

Pumpkin Pie Pudding

Sue Hamilton   Minooka, IL

MAKES: **8 SERVINGS**
PREP. TIME: **10 MINUTES**
COOKING TIME: **3 HOURS**
IDEAL SLOW COOKER SIZE: **3-QUART**

15-oz. can pumpkin
12-oz. can evaporated skim milk
¾ cup Splenda
½ cup low-fat buttermilk baking mix
2 eggs, beaten, *or* 6 egg whites
2 tsp. pumpkin pie spice
1 tsp. lemon zest

1. Combine all ingredients in slow cooker sprayed with cooking spray. Stir until lumps disappear.
2. Cover. Cook on Low 3 hours.
3. Serve warm or cold.

Per Serving: 140 calories (30 calories from fat), 3.5g total fat (1g saturated, 0g trans), 50mg cholesterol, 220mg sodium, 21g total carbohydrate (2g fiber, 7g sugar), 7g protein, 200%DV vitamin A, 2%DV vitamin C, 15%DV calcium, 8%DV iron.

Tip: *If you like, and your diet permits, add a spoonful of low-fat whipped topping to each serving.*

You've decided to cook pumpkin from scratch, and the shell is too hard to peel? Cut the pumpkin in half and scoop out the seeds. Place the 2 halves, cut-side down, in a large baking dish or on a baking sheet. Bake at 350° for about 1½ hours, or until tender. Spoon the cooked pumpkin out of the shell.

Bread Pudding

Winifred Ewy Newton, KS • *Helen King* Fairbank, IA
Elaine Patton West Middletown, PA

MAKES: **6 SERVINGS**
PREP. TIME: **20 MINUTES**
COOKING TIME: **4–5 HOURS**
IDEAL SLOW COOKER SIZE: **4-QUART**

8 slices bread (raisin bread is especially good), cubed
4 eggs
2 cups milk
¼ cup sugar
¼ cup butter, melted
½ cup raisins (use only ¼ cup if using raisin bread)
½ tsp. cinnamon

Sauce:
2 Tbsp. butter
2 Tbsp. flour
1 cup water
¾ cup sugar
1 tsp. vanilla

1. Place bread cubes in greased slow cooker.
2. Beat together eggs and milk. Stir in sugar, butter, raisins, and cinnamon. Pour over bread and stir.
3. Cover and cook on High 1 hour. Reduce heat to Low and cook 3–4 hours, or until thermometer reaches 160°.
4. Make sauce just before pudding is done baking. Begin by melting butter in saucepan. Stir in flour until smooth. Gradually add water, sugar, and vanilla. Bring to boil. Cook, stirring constantly for 2 minutes, or until thickened.
5. Serve sauce over warm bread pudding.

Variations:
1. Use dried cherries instead of raisins. Use cherry flavoring in sauce instead of vanilla.
Char Hagnes Montague, MI

2. Use ¼ tsp. ground cinnamon and ¼ tsp. ground nutmeg, instead of ½ tsp. ground cinnamon in pudding.

3. Use 8 cups day-old unfrosted cinnamon rolls instead of the bread.
Beatrice Orgist Richardson, TX

4. Use ½ tsp. vanilla and ¼ tsp. ground nutmeg instead of ½ tsp. cinnamon.
Nanci Keatley Salem, OR

Apple-Nut Bread Pudding

Ruth Ann Hoover New Holland, PA

MAKES: **6–8 SERVINGS**
PREP. TIME: **15 MINUTES**
COOKING TIME: **3–4 HOURS**
IDEAL SLOW COOKER SIZE: **4-QUART**

8 slices raisin bread, cubed
2–3 medium tart apples, peeled and sliced
1 cup chopped pecans, toasted
1 cup sugar
1 tsp. ground cinnamon
½ tsp. ground nutmeg
3 eggs, lightly beaten
2 cups half-and-half
¼ cup apple juice
¼ cup butter, melted

1. Place bread cubes, apples, and pecans in greased slow cooker and mix together gently.
2. Combine sugar, cinnamon, and nutmeg. Add remaining ingredients. Mix well. Pour over bread mixture.
3. Cover. Cook on Low 3–4 hours, or until knife inserted in center comes out clean.
4. Serve with ice cream.

Desserts and Sweets

Caramel Apples on Sticks, page 631

601

Christmas Wassail, page 647

Green Bean Casserole,
page 548

Hot Fudge Cake, page 612

Pumpkin Pie Dessert

Bonnie Whaling   Clearfield, PA

MAKES: **4–6 SERVINGS**
PREP. TIME: **15–20 MINUTES**
COOKING TIME: **3–4 HOURS**
IDEAL SLOW COOKER SIZE: **5–6-QUART**

19-oz. can pumpkin pie filling

12-oz. can evaporated milk

2 eggs, lightly beaten

boiling water

1 cup gingersnap cookie crumbs

1. In a large mixing bowl, stir together pie filling, milk, and eggs until thoroughly mixed.
2. Pour into an ungreased baking insert designed to fit into your slow cooker. (See Tip on page 611.)
3. Place filled baking insert into slow cooker. Cover the insert with its lid, or with 8 paper towels.
4. Carefully pour boiling water into cooker around the baking insert, to a depth of one inch.
5. Cover cooker. Cook on High 3–4 hours, or until a tester inserted in center of custard comes out clean.
6. Remove baking insert from slow cooker. Remove its lid. Sprinkle dessert with cookie crumbs. Serve warm from baking insert.

"Baked" Custard

Barbara Smith   Bedford, PA

MAKES: **5–6 SERVINGS**
PREP. TIME: **10–15 MINUTES**
COOKING TIME: **2–3 HOURS**
IDEAL SLOW COOKER SIZE: **4–5-QUART**

2 cups whole milk

3 eggs, slightly beaten

⅓ cup, plus ½ tsp., sugar, *divided*

1 tsp. vanilla

¼ tsp. cinnamon

1. Heat milk in a small uncovered saucepan until a skin forms on top. Remove from heat and let cool slightly.
2. Meanwhile, in a large mixing bowl combine eggs, ⅓ cup sugar, and vanilla.
3. Slowly stir cooled milk into egg-sugar mixture.
4. Pour into a greased 1-quart baking dish which will fit into your slow cooker, or into a baking insert designed for your slow cooker. (See Tip on page 611.)
5. Mix cinnamon and ½ tsp. reserved sugar in a small bowl. Sprinkle over custard mixture.
6. Cover baking dish or insert with foil. Set container on a metal rack or trivet in slow cooker. Pour hot water around dish to a depth of 1 inch.
7. Cover cooker. Cook on High 2–3 hours, or until custard is set. (When blade of a knife inserted in center of custard comes out clean, custard is set.)
8. Serve warm from baking dish or insert.

Variations: *Instead of the cinnamon, use ¼ tsp. nutmeg or 1–2 Tbsp. grated coconut.*

Jean Butzer   Batavia, NY

Tapioca

Ruth Ann Hoover New Holland, PA • *Sharon Anders* Alburtis, PA
Pat Unternahrer Wayland, IA

MAKES: **10–12 SERVINGS**
PREP. TIME: **5–10 MINUTES**
COOKING TIME: **3½ HOURS**
CHILLING TIME: **4–5 HOURS**
IDEAL SLOW COOKER SIZE: **3-QUART**

2 quarts whole milk

1¼ cups sugar

1 cup dry small pearl tapioca

4 eggs

1 tsp. vanilla

whipped topping, *optional*

1. Combine milk and sugar in slow cooker, stirring until sugar is dissolved as well as possible. Stir in tapioca.
2. Cover and cook on High 3 hours.
3. In a small mixing bowl, beat eggs slightly. Beat in vanilla and about 1 cup hot milk from slow cooker. When well mixed, stir into slow cooker.
4. Cover and cook on High 20 more minutes.
5. Chill for several hours. Serve with whipped topping if you wish.

Variations:

1. For a less stiff pudding, use only 3 eggs and/ or only ¾ cup small pearl tapioca.

Susan Kasting Jenks, OK • *Karen Stoltzfus* Alto, MI

2. For an airier pudding, beat chilled pudding with a rotary beater until fluffy. Fold in an 8-oz. container of whipped topping.

Evelyn Page Lance Creek, WY

3. Top chilled pudding with a crushed or broken chocolate candy bar. Or serve the tapioca warm without any topping.

Karen Stoltzfus Alto, MI

4. Top chilled pudding with cut-up fruit or berries of your choice (peaches, strawberries, or blueberries are especially good).

Virginia Eberly Loysville, PA

Pineapple Tapioca

Janessa K. Hochstedler East Earl, PA

MAKES: **4–6 SERVINGS**
PREP. TIME: **15 MINUTES**
COOKING TIME: **3 HOURS**
CHILLING TIME: **2–3 HOURS**
IDEAL SLOW COOKER SIZE: **3-QUART**

2½ cups water

2½ cups pineapple juice

½ cup dry small pearl tapioca

¾–1 cup sugar

15-oz. can crushed pineapple, undrained

1. Mix first four ingredients together in slow cooker.
2. Cover and cook on High 3 hours.
3. Stir in crushed pineapple. Chill for several hours.

Blushing Apple Tapioca

Julie Weaver   Reinholds, PA

MAKES: **8–10 SERVINGS**
PREP. TIME: **15–20 MINUTES**
COOKING TIME: **3–4 HOURS**
IDEAL SLOW COOKER SIZE: **4-QUART**

8–10 tart apples
½ cup sugar
4 Tbsp. minute tapioca
4 Tbsp. red cinnamon candy
½ cup water
whipped topping, *optional*

1. Pare and core apples. Cut into eighths lengthwise and place in slow cooker.
2. Mix together sugar, tapioca, candy, and water. Pour over apples.
3. Cook on High 3–4 hours.
4. Serve hot or cold. Top with whipped cream.

Old-Fashioned Rice Pudding

Ann Bender   Fort Defiance, VA   •   *Gladys M. High*   Ephrata, PA
Mrs. Don Martins   Fairbank, IA

MAKES: **6 SERVINGS**
PREP. TIME: **10 MINUTES**
COOKING TIME: **2–6 HOURS**
IDEAL SLOW COOKER SIZE: **4-QUART**

2½ cups rice, cooked
1½ cups evaporated milk *or* scalded milk
⅔ cup brown *or* white sugar
1 Tbsp. soft butter
2 tsp. vanilla
½–1 tsp. nutmeg
1 eggs, beaten
½–1 cup raisins

1. Mix together all ingredients. Pour into lightly greased slow cooker.

2. Cover and cook on High 2 hours, or on Low 4–6 hours. Stir after first hour.
3. Serve warm or cold.

Mama's Rice Pudding

Donna Barnitz   Jenks, OK   •   *Shari Jensen*   Fountain, CO

MAKES: **4–6 SERVINGS**
PREP. TIME: **5 MINUTES**
COOKING TIME: **6–7 HOURS**
CHILLING TIME: **2–3 HOURS**
IDEAL SLOW COOKER SIZE: **4-QUART**

½ cup white rice, uncooked
½ cup sugar
1 tsp. vanilla
1 tsp. lemon extract
1 cup plus 2 Tbsp. milk
1 tsp. butter
2 eggs, beaten
1 tsp. cinnamon
½ cup raisins
1 cup whipping cream, whipped
nutmeg

1. Combine all ingredients except whipped cream and nutmeg in slow cooker. Stir well.
2. Cover pot. Cook on Low 6–7 hours, until rice is tender and milk absorbed. Be sure to stir once every 2 hours during cooking.
3. Pour into bowl. Cover with plastic wrap and chill several hours.
4. Before serving, fold in whipped cream and sprinkle with nutmeg.

I like to slightly under-bake cookies to keep them soft.

Vanilla Bean Rice Pudding

Michele Ruvola Selden, NY

MAKES: **12 SERVINGS**
PREP. TIME: **10 MINUTES**
COOKING TIME: **2½–4 HOURS**
IDEAL SLOW COOKER SIZE: **4-QUART**

6 cups fat-free milk

1½ cups converted rice, uncooked

1 cup sugar

1 cup raisins

1 Tbsp. butter *or* margarine, melted

½ tsp. salt

1 vanilla bean, split

1 large egg

½ tsp. ground cinnamon

8-oz. carton fat-free sour cream

1. Combine milk, rice, sugar, raisins, butter, and salt in slow cooker. Stir well.
2. Scrape seeds from vanilla bean. Add seeds and bean to milk mixture.
3. Cover with lid and cook on High 2½–4 hours, or just until rice is tender and most of liquid is absorbed.
4. Place egg in small bowl. Stir well with a whisk and gradually add ½ cup hot rice mixture to egg.
5. Return egg mixture to slow cooker, stirring constantly with whisk. Cook 1 minute while stirring. Remove inner vessel from slow cooker.
6. Let stand 5 minutes. Mix in cinnamon and sour cream. Discard vanilla bean.
7. Serve warm, not hot, or refrigerate until fully chilled.

Per Serving: 270 calories (15 calories from fat), 2g total fat (1g saturated, 0g trans), 20mg cholesterol, 180mg sodium, 55g total carbohydrate (0.5g fiber, 33g sugar), 8g protein, 8%DV vitamin A, 2%DV vitamin C, 20%DV calcium, 8%DV iron.

Tip: *If your diet permits, you may top individual servings with light, or fat-free, vanilla-flavored whipped topping.*

Chocolate Rice Pudding

Michele Ruvola Selden, NY

MAKES: **4 SERVINGS**
PREP. TIME: **10 MINUTES**
COOKING TIME: **2½–3½ HOURS**
IDEAL SLOW COOKER SIZE: **3-QUART**

4 cups white rice, cooked

¾ cup sugar

¼ cup baking cocoa powder

3 Tbsp. butter, melted

1 tsp. vanilla

2 12-oz. cans evaporated milk

whipped cream

sliced toasted almonds

maraschino cherries

1. Combine first 6 ingredients in greased slow cooker.
2. Cover. Cook on Low 2½–3½ hours, or until liquid is absorbed.
3. Serve warm or chilled. Top individual servings with a dollop of whipped cream, sliced toasted almonds, and a maraschino cherry.

Before whipping heavy cream, stick the mixing bowl and beaters in the freezer for 10 minutes or more. The cold utensils will speed up the whipping process.

Chocolate Fondue

Diann J. Dunham   State College, PA

MAKES: **2½–3 CUPS**
PREP. TIME: **5 MINUTES**
COOKING TIME: **2½ HOURS**
IDEAL SLOW COOKER SIZE: **2-QUART**

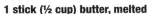

PICTURED
ON PAGE
503

1 stick (½ cup) butter, melted
1½ cups sugar
¼ cup whipping cream
3 Tbsp. creme de cocoa, rum, *or* orange-flavored liqueur
  (*or* 1 tsp. orange, rum, *or* vanilla flavoring)
6 1-oz. squares unsweetened chocolate

1. Combine butter and sugar in the slow cooker until well mixed.
2. Stir in whipping cream until well blended. Stir in liqueur or flavoring until well blended.
3. Stir in squares of chocolate.
4. Cover and cook on High 30 minutes.
5. Stir well, turn cooker to Low, and cook 2 hours.
6. Serve warm from the cooker with angel food or pound cake cut into bite-sized pieces, marshmallows, apple slices, banana chunks, and strawberries, whole or halved.

Tip: *As long as an inch or more of the fondue remains in the cooker, you can keep the cooker turned on Low for up to 6 hours. Stir occasionally.*

Freeze over-ripe bananas. Use them for smoothies or in banana bread.

Dessert Fondue

Sara Kinsinger   Stuarts Draft, VA
Bonita Ensenberger   Albuquerque, NM

MAKES: **ABOUT 3 CUPS**
PREP. TIME: **10–15 MINUTES**
COOKING TIME: **2 HOURS**
IDEAL SLOW COOKER SIZE: **4-QUART**

1 Tbsp. butter
16 1-oz. candy bars, half milk chocolate; half semi-
  sweet chocolate, broken
30 large marshmallows
⅓ cup milk
1 cup whipping cream

1. Grease slow cooker with butter. Turn to High for 10 minutes.
2. Meanwhile, mix broken candy bars, marshmallows, and milk together in a bowl.
3. Put candy-milk mixture into slow cooker.
4. Cover and cook on Low for 30 minutes. Stir. Cover and cook another 30 minutes. Stir.
5. Gradually stir in whipping cream. Cover and cook on Low another hour.
6. Serve the fondue warm from the cooker with pieces of pound cake, angel-food cake, bananas, and pretzels for dipping.

Cherry Chocolate Fondue

Eleanor J. Ferriera North Chelmsford, MA

MAKES: **6 SERVINGS**
PREP. TIME: **5 MINUTES**
COOKING TIME: **1–3 HOURS**
IDEAL SLOW COOKER SIZE: **3-QUART**

1 pkg. (8 squares) semisweet chocolate

4-oz. pkg. sweet cooking chocolate

¾ cup sweetened condensed milk

¼ cup sugar

2 Tbsp. kirsch

fresh cherries with stems

squares of sponge cake

1. Break both chocolates into pieces and place in cooker. Set cooker to High and stir chocolate constantly until it melts.
2. Turn cooker to Low and stir in milk and sugar. Stir until thoroughly blended.
3. Stir in kirsch. Cover and cook on Low until fondue comes to a very gentle simmer.
4. Bring fondue to table, along with cherries and sponge cake squares to dip into it.

Upside-Down Chocolate Pudding Cake

Sarah Herr Goshen, IN

MAKES: **8 SERVINGS**
PREP. TIME: **15 MINUTES**
COOKING TIME: **2–3 HOURS**
IDEAL SLOW COOKER SIZE: **3½-QUART**

1 cup dry all-purpose baking mix

1 cup sugar, *divided*

3 Tbsp. unsweetened cocoa powder, plus ⅓ cup, *divided*

½ cup milk

1 tsp. vanilla

1⅔ cups hot water

1. Spray inside of slow cooker with nonstick cooking spray.
2. In a bowl, mix together baking mix, ½ cup sugar, 3 Tbsp. cocoa powder, milk, and vanilla. Spoon batter evenly into slow cooker.
3. In a clean bowl, mix remaining ½ cup sugar, ⅓ cup cocoa powder, and hot water together. Pour over batter in slow cooker. Do not stir.
4. Cover and cook on High 2–3 hours, or until toothpick inserted in center of cake-y part comes out clean.

Note: *The batter will rise to the top and turn into cake. Underneath will be a rich chocolate pudding.*

Desserts and Sweets

Chocolate Soufflé Cake

Rachel Yoder Middlebury, IN

MAKES: **10–12 SERVINGS**
PREP. TIME: **5 MINUTES**
COOKING TIME: **6 HOURS**
IDEAL SLOW COOKER SIZE: **6-QUART**

18¼-oz. pkg. chocolate cake mix

½ cup vegetable oil

2 cups sour cream

4 eggs, beaten

3-oz. box instant chocolate pudding mix

1 cup chocolate chips, *optional*

1. Combine all ingredients in a large mixing bowl.
2. Spray interior of slow cooker with nonstick cooking spray. Pour soufflé mixture into cooker.
3. Cover and cook on Low 6 hours. (Do not lift the lid until the end of the cooking time!)
4. Insert toothpick into center of cake to see if it comes out clean. If it does, the soufflé is finished. If it doesn't, continue cooking another 15 minutes. Check again. Repeat until it's finished cooking.
5. Serve warm from the cooker with ice cream or frozen yogurt.

Don't measure ingredients over the bowl in which you are mixing or baking the recipe, in case more than you need comes tumbling out.

Chocolate Peanut Butter Cake

Esther Hartzler Carlsbad, NM

MAKES: **8–10 SERVINGS**
PREP. TIME: **7 MINUTES**
COOKING TIME: **2–2½ HOURS**
IDEAL SLOW COOKER SIZE: **5–6-QUART**

2 cups dry milk chocolate cake mix

½ cup water

6 Tbsp. peanut butter

2 eggs

½ cup chopped nuts

1. Combine all ingredients in electric mixer bowl. Beat for 2 minutes.
2. Spray interior of a baking insert, designed to fit into your slow cooker. (See Tip below.) Flour interior of greased insert. Pour batter into insert. Place insert in slow cooker.
3. Cover insert with 8 paper towels.
4. Cover cooker. Cook on High 2–2½ hours, or until toothpick inserted into center of cake comes out clean.
5. Allow cake to cool. Then invert onto a serving plate, cut, and serve.

Tip: *Need a baking insert for your slow cooker? Check the manufacturer's website to order one. Or check the pamphlets that were included in the box that your slow cooker was packaged in. An order form is usually included among those items.*

Peanut Butter and Hot Fudge Pudding Cake

Sara Wilson   Blairstown, MO

MAKES: **6 SERVINGS**
PREP. TIME: **10 MINUTES**
COOKING TIME: **2–3 HOURS**
IDEAL SLOW COOKER SIZE: **4-QUART**

½ cup flour

¼ cup sugar

¾ tsp. baking powder

⅓ cup milk

1 Tbsp. oil

½ tsp. vanilla

¼ cup peanut butter

½ cup sugar

3 Tbsp. unsweetened cocoa powder

1 cup boiling water

vanilla ice cream

1. Combine flour, ¼ cup sugar, and baking powder. Add milk, oil, and vanilla. Mix until smooth. Stir in peanut butter. Pour into slow cooker.
2. Mix together ½ cup sugar and cocoa powder. Gradually stir in boiling water. Pour mixture over batter in slow cooker. Do not stir.
3. Cover and cook on High 2–3 hours, or until toothpick inserted comes out clean.
4. Serve warm with ice cream.

Hot Fudge Cake

Evelyn L. Ward   Greeley, CO

PICTURED
ON PAGE
604

Light

MAKES: **8 SERVINGS**
PREP. TIME: **10 MINUTES**
COOKING TIME: **1½–1¾ HOURS**
IDEAL SLOW COOKER SIZE: **3½-QUART**

1¾ cups brown sugar, *divided*

1 cup flour

3 Tbsp., plus ¼ cup, unsweetened cocoa, *divided*

1½ tsp. baking powder

½ tsp. salt

½ cup skim milk

2 Tbsp. butter, melted

½ tsp. vanilla

1¾ cups boiling water

1. In a mixing bowl, mix together 1 cup brown sugar, flour, 3 Tbsp. cocoa, baking powder, and salt.
2. Stir in milk, butter, and vanilla.
3. Pour into slow cooker sprayed with non-fat cooking spray.
4. In a separate bowl, mix together ¾ cup brown sugar and ¼ cup cocoa. Sprinkle over batter in the slow cooker. Do not stir.
5. Pour boiling water over mixture. Do not stir.
6. Cover. Cook on High 1½–1¾ hours, or until toothpick inserted into cake comes out clean.

Per Serving: 280 calories (35 calories from fat), 3.5g total fat (2g saturated, 0g trans), 10mg cholesterol, 180mg sodium, 63g total carbohydrate (2g fiber, 48g sugar), 3g protein, 0%DV vitamin A, 0%DV vitamin C, 10%DV calcium, 15%DV iron.

Tip: *Serve with low-fat ice cream or fat-free whipped topping if you wish, and if diets allow.*

Self-Frosting Fudge Cake

Mary Puterbaugh Elwood, IN

MAKES: **8–10 SERVINGS**
PREP. TIME: **10 MINUTES**
COOKING TIME: **2–3 HOURS**
IDEAL SLOW COOKER SIZE: **4–5-QUART**

2½ cups of 18½-oz. pkg. chocolate fudge pudding cake mix

2 eggs

¾ cup water

3 Tbsp. oil

⅓ cup pecan halves

¼ cup chocolate syrup

¼ cup warm water

3 Tbsp. sugar

1. Combine cake mix, eggs, ¾ cup water, and oil in electric mixer bowl. Beat 2 minutes.
2. Pour into greased and floured bread or cake pan that will fit into your slow cooker.
3. Sprinkle nuts over mixture.
4. Blend together chocolate syrup, ¼ cup water, and sugar. Spoon over batter.
5. Cover. Bake on High 2–3 hours.
6. Serve warm from slow cooker.

Black Forest Cake

Marla Folkerts Holland, OH

MAKES: **8–10 SERVINGS**
PREP. TIME: **10 MINUTES**
COOKING TIME: **2–2½ HOURS**
IDEAL SLOW COOKER SIZE: **4–5-QUART**

20-oz. can cherry pie filling (Lite or regular)

18¼-oz. box chocolate cake mix, butter-style

1. Preheat slow cooker on High for 10 minutes.
2. Meanwhile, spray interior of baking insert, designed to fit into your slow cooker, with nonstick cooking spray. (See Tip on page 611.)
3. In a bowl, stir together pie filling and cake mix until mix is thoroughly moistened. Spoon into insert.
4. Place insert into cooker. Cover insert with 8 paper towels. Cover slow cooker.
5. Cook on High 1¾ hours. Remove paper towels and cooker lid. Continue cooking for another 30 minutes, or until a toothpick inserted in the center of the cake comes out clean.
6. Remove baking insert from cooker. Serve cake warm directly from the insert.

Always cut brownies with a plastic knife. It prevents clumping and ragged edges.

Peanut Butter Cake

Velma Sauder Leola, PA

MAKES: **6 SERVINGS**
PREP. TIME: **5–10 MINUTES**
COOKING TIME: **2–3 HOURS**
IDEAL SLOW COOKER SIZE: **4-QUART**

2 cups yellow cake mix
⅓ cup crunchy peanut butter
½ cup water

1. Combine all ingredients in electric mixer bowl. Beat with electric mixer about 2 minutes.
2. Pour batter into greased and floured baking-pan insert, designed to fit inside your slow cooker. (See Tip on page 611.)
3. Place baking-pan insert into slow cooker. Cover with 8 paper towels.
4. Cover cooker. Cook on High 2–3 hours, or until toothpick inserted into center of cake comes out clean. About 30 minutes before the end of the cooking time, remove the cooker's lid, but keep the paper towels in place.
5. When cake is fully cooked, remove insert from slow cooker. Turn insert upside-down on a serving plate and remove cake.

Fruity Cake

Janice Muller Derwood, MD

MAKES: **10–12 SERVINGS**
PREP. TIME: **15 MINUTES**
COOKING TIME: **3–5 HOURS**
IDEAL SLOW COOKER SIZE: **3½–4-QUART**

1 or 2 21-oz. cans apple, blueberry, *or* peach pie filling
18¼-oz. pkg. yellow cake mix
1 stick (½ cup) butter, melted
⅓ cup chopped walnuts

1. Spray interior of slow cooker with nonstick cooking spray.
2. Place pie filling in slow cooker.
3. In a mixing bowl, combine dry cake mix and butter. Spoon over filling.
4. Drop walnuts over top.
5. Cover and cook on Low 3–5 hours, or until a toothpick inserted into center of topping comes out clean.

Easy Autumn Cake

Janice Muller Derwood, MD

MAKES: **8 SERVINGS**
PREP. TIME: **15 MINUTES**
COOKING TIME: **3–5 HOURS**
IDEAL SLOW COOKER SIZE: **3½–4-QUART**

2 16-oz. cans sliced apples, undrained (not pie filling)
18¼-oz. pkg. spice cake mix
1 stick (½ cup butter), melted
½ cup pecans, chopped

1. Spray interior of slow cooker with nonstick cooking spray.
2. Spoon apples and their juice into slow cooker, spreading evenly over the bottom.
3. Sprinkle with dry spice cake mix.
4. Pour melted butter over dry mix. Top with chopped pecans.
5. Cook on Low 3–5 hours, or until a toothpick inserted into topping comes out dry.
6. Serve warm from cooker.

Carrot Cake

Colleen Heatwole Burton, MI

MAKES: **6–8 SERVINGS**
PREP. TIME: **20 MINUTES**
COOKING TIME: **3–4 HOURS**
IDEAL SLOW COOKER SIZE: **LARGE ENOUGH TO HOLD YOUR BAKING INSERT**

½ cup salad oil

2 eggs

1 Tbsp. hot water

½ cup grated raw carrots

¾ cup flour

¾ cup sugar

½ tsp. baking powder

⅛ tsp. salt

¼ tsp. ground allspice

½ tsp. ground cinnamon

⅛ tsp. ground cloves

½ cup chopped nuts

½ cup raisins *or* chopped dates

2 Tbsp. flour

1. In large bowl, beat oil, eggs, and water for 1 minute.
2. Add carrots. Mix well.
3. Stir together flour, sugar, baking powder, salt, allspice, cinnamon, and cloves. Add to creamed mixture.
4. Toss nuts and raisins in bowl with 2 Tbsp. flour. Add to creamed mixture. Mix well.
5. Pour into greased and floured 3-lb. shortening can or slow cooker baking insert. (See Tip on page 611.) Place can or baking insert in slow cooker.
6. Cover insert with its lid, or cover can with 8 paper towels, folded down over edge of slow cooker to absorb moisture. Cover paper towels with cooker lid. Cook on High 3–4 hours.
7. Remove can or insert from cooker and allow to cool on rack for 10 minutes. Run knife around edge of cake. Invert onto serving plate.

Lemon Pudding Cake

Jean Butzer Batavia, NY

MAKES: **5–6 SERVINGS**
PREP. TIME: **15 MINUTES**
COOKING TIME: **2–3 HOURS**
IDEAL SLOW COOKER SIZE: **3–4-QUART**

3 eggs, whites and yolks separated

1 tsp. grated lemon peel

¼ cup lemon juice

3 Tbsp. butter, melted

1½ cups milk

¾ cup sugar

¼ cup flour

⅛ tsp. salt

1. Beat eggs whites until stiff peaks form. Set aside.
2. Beat eggs yolks. Blend in lemon peel, lemon juice, butter, and milk.
3. In separate bowl, combine sugar, flour, and salt. Add to egg-lemon mixture, beating until smooth.
4. Fold into beaten egg whites.
5. Spoon into slow cooker.
6. Cover and cook on High 2–3 hours.
7. Serve with spoon from cooker.

Warm a lemon to room temperature before squeezing it in order to get more juice from it.

Apple Peanut Crumble

Phyllis Attig Reynolds, IL • *Joan Becker* Dodge City, KS
Pam Hochstedler Kalona, IA

MAKES: **4–5 SERVINGS**
PREP. TIME: **10 MINUTES**
COOKING TIME: **5–6 HOURS**
IDEAL SLOW COOKER SIZE: **4-QUART**

4–5 cooking apples, peeled and sliced
⅔ cup packed brown sugar
½ cup flour
½ cup quick-cooking dry oats
½ tsp. cinnamon
¼-½ tsp. nutmeg
⅓ cup butter, softened
2 Tbsp. peanut butter
ice cream *or* whipped cream

1. Place apple slices in slow cooker.
2. Combine brown sugar, flour, oats, cinnamon, and nutmeg.
3. Cut in butter and peanut butter. Sprinkle over apples.
4. Cover cooker and cook on Low 5–6 hours.
5. Serve warm or cold, plain or with ice cream or whipped cream.

Apple Cake

Esther Becker Gordonville, PA • *Wanda S. Curtin* Bradenton, FL

MAKES: **8–10 SERVINGS**
PREP. TIME: **15 MINUTES**
COOKING TIME: **3½–4 HOURS**
IDEAL SLOW COOKER SIZE: **4–5-QUART**

2 cups sugar
1 cup oil
2 eggs
1 tsp. vanilla
2 cups chopped apples
2 cups flour
1 tsp. salt
1 tsp. baking soda
1 tsp. nutmeg
1 cup chopped walnuts *or* pecans

1. Beat together sugar, oil, and eggs. Add vanilla.
2. Add apples. Mix well.
3. Sift together flour, salt, baking soda, and nutmeg. Add dry ingredients and nuts to apple mixture. Stir well.
4. Pour batter into greased and floured bread or cake pan that fits into your slow cooker. Cover with pan's lid, or greased foil. Place pan in slow cooker. Cover cooker.
5. Bake on High 3½–4 hours. Let cake stand in pan for 5 minutes after removing from slow cooker.
6. Remove cake from pan, slice, and serve.

Variation: *Instead of a baking insert, pour batter into greased and floured 2-lb. coffee can. Cover top of can with 6 to 8 paper towels. Place can in slow cooker. Cover cooker, tilting lid slightly to allow release of extra moisture. Continue with Step 5 above.*

Low-Fat Apple Cake

Sue Hamilton   Minooka, IL

MAKES: **8 SERVINGS**
PREP. TIME: **15 MINUTES**
COOKING TIME: **2½–3 HOURS**
IDEAL SLOW COOKER SIZE: **4-QUART**

1 cup flour
¾ cup sugar
2 tsp. baking powder
1 tsp. ground cinnamon
¼ tsp. salt
4 medium cooking apples, chopped
⅓ cup eggbeaters
2 tsp. vanilla

1. Combine flour, sugar, baking powder, cinnamon, and salt.
2. Add apples, stirring lightly to coat.
3. Combine eggbeaters and vanilla. Add to apple mixture. Stir until just moistened. Spoon into lightly greased slow cooker.
4. Cover. Bake on High 2½–3 hours.
5. Serve warm.

Per Serving: 180 calories (10 calories from fat), 1g total fat (0g saturated, 0g trans), 35mg cholesterol, 85mg sodium, 41g total carbohydrate (2g fiber, 26g sugar), 3g protein, 0%DV vitamin A, 0%DV vitamin C, 6%DV calcium, 6%DV iron.

You can use a 2-lb. coffee can, 2 1-lb. coffee cans, 3 16-oz. vegetable cans, a 6–7 cup mold, or a 1½–2-quart baking dish for "baking" cakes in a slow cooker. Leave the cooker lid slightly open to let extra moisture escape.

Harvey Wallbanger Cake

Roseann Wilson   Albuquerque, NM

MAKES: **8 SERVINGS**
PREP. TIME: **10 MINUTES**
COOKING TIME: **2½–3½ HOURS**
IDEAL SLOW COOKER SIZE: **4–5-QUART**

Cake:

16-oz. pkg. pound cake mix
⅓ cup vanilla instant pudding (reserve rest of pudding from 3-oz. pkg. for glaze)
¼ cup salad oil
3 eggs
2 Tbsp. Galliano liqueur
⅔ cup orange juice

Glaze:

remaining pudding mix
⅔ cup orange juice
1 Tbsp. Galliano liqueur

1. Mix together all ingredients for cake. Beat for 3 minutes. Pour batter into greased and floured bread or cake pan that will fit into your slow cooker. Cover pan.
2. Bake in covered slow cooker on High 2½–3½ hours.
3. Invert cake onto serving platter.
4. Mix together glaze ingredients. Spoon over cake.

Fruity Delight Cake

Janice Muller Derwood, MD

MAKES: **8–10 SERVINGS**
PREP. TIME: **10 MINUTES**
COOKING TIME: **2–3 HOURS**
IDEAL SLOW COOKER SIZE: **3½-QUART**

20-oz. can crushed pineapple

21-oz. can blueberry *or* **cherry pie filling**

18½-oz. pkg. yellow cake mix

cinnamon

½ cup butter

1 cup chopped nuts

1. Grease bottom and sides of slow cooker.
2. Spread layers of pineapple, blueberry pie filling, and dry cake mix. Be careful not to mix the layers.
3. Sprinkle with cinnamon.
4. Top with thin layers of butter chunks and nuts.
5. Cover. Cook on High 2–3 hours.
6. Serve with vanilla ice cream.

   Variation: *Use a pkg. of spice cake mix and apple pie filling.*

Lemon Poppy Seed Upside-Down Cake

Jeanette Oberholtzer Manheim, PA

PICTURED ON PAGE 504

MAKES: **8–10 SERVINGS**
PREP. TIME: **10–15 MINUTES**
COOKING TIME: **2–2½ HOURS**
IDEAL SLOW COOKER SIZE: **2-QUART**

1 pkg. lemon poppy seed bread mix

1 egg

8 ozs. light sour cream

½ cup water

Sauce:

1 Tbsp. butter

¾ cup water

½ cup sugar

¼ cup lemon juice

1. Combine first four ingredients until well moistened. Spread in lightly greased slow cooker.
2. Combine sauce ingredients in small saucepan. Bring to boil. Pour boiling mixture over batter.
3. Cover. Cook on High 2–2½ hours. Edges will be slightly brown. Turn heat off and leave in cooker for 30 minutes with cover slightly ajar.
4. When cool enough to handle, hold a large plate over top of cooker, then invert.
5. Allow to cool before slicing.

Don't be afraid to correct mistakes as you cook. One time I baked a pound cake that fell in the middle. I filled it with fresh berries — it was a hit!

Chocolate Mud Cake

Marci Baum   Annville, PA

Light

MAKES: **8 SERVINGS**
PREP. TIME: **20 MINUTES**
COOKING TIME: **1–2 HOURS**
COOLING TIME: **25 MINUTES**
IDEAL SLOW-COOKER SIZE: **4-QUART**

1 cup flour

2 tsp. baking powder

2 Tbsp. butter

2 ozs. semisweet chocolate *or* ⅓ cup chocolate chips

1 cup sugar, *divided*

3 Tbsp. plus ⅓ cup Dutch-processed cocoa, *divided*

1 Tbsp. vanilla extract

¼ tsp. salt

⅓ cup skim milk

1 egg yolk

⅓ cup brown sugar

1½ cups hot water

1. Coat inside of slow cooker with nonfat cooking spray.
2. In mixing bowl, whisk together flour and baking powder. Set aside.
3. In a large microwave-safe mixing bowl, melt the butter and chocolate in the microwave. Mix well.
4. Whisk in ⅔ cup sugar, 3 Tbsp. cocoa, vanilla, salt, milk, and egg yolk.
5. Add the flour mixture. Stir until thoroughly mixed.
6. Pour batter into slow cooker. Spread evenly.
7. Whisk together remaining sugar, cocoa, and hot water until sugar is dissolved. Pour over batter in slow cooker. Do not stir.
8. Cover. Cook on High 1–2 hours. The cake will be very moist and floating on a layer of molten chocolate when it's done. And you'll know it is done cooking when nearly all the cake is set and its edges begin to pull away from the sides of the pot.
9. Turn off slow cooker and remove lid. Try not to let the condensed steam from the lid drip onto the cake. Let cool for 25 minutes before cutting and spooning onto individual plates.

Per Serving: 370 calories (60 calories from fat), 7g total fat (3.5g saturated, 0g trans), 35mg cholesterol, 150mg sodium, 72g total carbohydrate (2g fiber, 53g sugar), 9g protein, 0%DV vitamin A, 0%DV vitamin C, 25%DV calcium, 8%DV iron.

Note: *If diets permit, serve the cake with low-fat or fat-free frozen yogurt.*

Brownies with Nuts

Dorothy VanDeest Memphis, TN

MAKES: **24 BROWNIES**
PREP. TIME: **10–15 MINUTES**
COOKING TIME: **3 HOURS**
IDEAL SLOW COOKER SIZE: **5-QUART**

half a stick (¼ cup) butter, melted
1 cup chopped nuts, *divided*
23-oz. pkg. brownie mix

1. Pour melted butter into a baking insert designed to fit into your slow cooker. (See Tip on page 611.) Swirl butter around to grease sides of insert.
2. Sprinkle butter with half the nuts.
3. In a bowl, mix brownies according to package directions. Spoon half the batter into the baking insert, trying to cover the nuts evenly.
4. Add remaining half of nuts. Spoon in remaining batter.
5. Place insert in slow cooker. Cover insert with 8 paper towels.
6. Cover cooker. Cook on High 3 hours. Do not check or remove cover until last hour of cooking. Then insert toothpick into center of brownies. If it comes out clean, the brownies are finished. If it doesn't, continue cooking another 15 minutes. Check again. Repeat until pick comes out clean.
7. When finished cooking, uncover cooker and baking insert. Let brownies stand 5 minutes.
8. Invert insert onto serving plate. Cut brownies with a plastic knife (so the crumbs don't drag). Serve warm.

Use a pizza cutter to cut bar cookies into neat squares in half the time.

Graham Cracker Cookies

Cassandra Ly Carlisle, PA

MAKES: **8 DOZEN COOKIES**
PREP. TIME: **10 MINUTES**
COOKING TIME: **1½ HOURS**
IDEAL SLOW COOKER SIZE: **4-QUART**

12-oz. pkg. (2 cups) semi-sweet chocolate chips
2 1-oz. squares unsweetened baking chocolate, shaved
2 14-oz. cans sweetened condensed milk
3¾ cups crushed graham cracker crumbs, *divided*
1 cup finely chopped walnuts

1. Place chocolate in slow cooker.
2. Cover. Cook on High 1 hour, stirring every 15 minutes. Continue to cook on Low, stirring every 15 minutes, or until chocolate is melted (about 30 minutes).
3. Stir milk into melted chocolate.
4. Add 3 cups graham cracker crumbs, 1 cup at a time, stirring after each addition.
5. Stir in nuts. Mixture should be thick but not stiff.
6. Stir in remaining graham cracker crumbs to reach consistency of cookie dough.
7. Drop by heaping teaspoonfuls onto lightly greased cookie sheets. Keep remaining mixture warm by covering and turning the slow cooker to Warm.
8. Bake in oven at 325° for 7–9 minutes, or until tops of cookies begin to crack. Remove from oven. Cool 1–2 minutes before transferring to waxed paper.

Tip: *These cookies freeze well.*

Note: *This delectable fudge-like cookie is a family favorite. The original recipe (from my maternal grandmother) was so involved and yielded so few cookies that my mom and I would get together to make a couple of batches only at*

Christmas-time. Adapting the recipe for using a slow cooker, rather than a double boiler, allows me to prepare a double batch without help.

Seven Layer Bars

Mary W. Stauffer Ephrata, PA

MAKES: **6–8 SERVINGS**
PREP. TIME: **5–10 MINUTES**
COOKING TIME: **2–3 HOURS**
IDEAL SLOW COOKER SIZE: **4–5-QUART**

¼ cup butter, melted
½ cup graham cracker crumbs
½ cup chocolate chips
½ cup butterscotch chips
½ cup flaked coconut
½ cup chopped nuts
½ cup sweetened condensed milk

1. Layer ingredients in a bread or cake pan that fits in your slow cooker, in the order listed. Do not stir.
2. Cover and bake on High 2–3 hours, or until firm. Remove pan and uncover. Let stand 5 minutes.
3. Unmold carefully on plate and cool.

Easy Chocolate Clusters

Marcella Stalter Flanagan, IL

MAKES: **3½ DOZEN CLUSTERS**
PREP. TIME: **5 MINUTES**
COOKING TIME: **2 HOURS**
IDEAL SLOW COOKER SIZE: **4-QUART**

2 lbs. white coating chocolate, broken into small pieces
2 cups (12 oz.) semisweet chocolate chips
4-oz. pkg. sweet German chocolate
24-oz. jar roasted peanuts

1. Combine coating chocolate, chocolate chips, and German chocolate. Cover and cook on High 1 hour. Reduce heat to Low and cook 1 hour longer, or until chocolate is melted, stirring every 15 minutes.
2. Stir in peanuts. Mix well.
3. Drop by teaspoonfuls onto waxed paper. Let stand until set. Store at room temperature.

Chunky Applesauce

Joan Becker Dodge City, KS • *Rosanne Hankins* Stevensville, MD

MAKES: **8–10 SERVINGS**
PREP. TIME: **10 MINUTES**
COOKING TIME: **3–10 HOURS**
IDEAL SLOW COOKER SIZE: **4-QUART**

8 apples, peeled, cored, and cut into chunks or slices (6 cups)
1 tsp. cinnamon
½ cup water
½–1 cup sugar *or* cinnamon red hot candies

1. Combine all ingredients in slow cooker.
2. Cook on Low 8–10 hours, or on High 3–4 hours.

Chunky Cranberry Applesauce

Christie Anne Detamore-Hunsberger Harrisonburg, VA

MAKES: **6 SERVINGS**
PREP. TIME: **15 MINUTES**
COOKING TIME: **3–4 HOURS**
IDEAL SLOW COOKER SIZE: **3-QUART**

6 MacIntosh, *or* Winesap, *or* favorite baking apple,
    peeled or unpeeled, cut into 1-inch cubes
½ cup apple juice
½ cup fresh *or* frozen cranberries
¼ cup sugar
¼ tsp. ground cinnamon, *optional*

1. Combine all ingredients in slow cooker.
2. Cover and cook on Low 3–4 hours, or until apples are as soft as you like them.
3. Serve warm, or refrigerate and serve chilled. Serve the sauce as a side dish during the main course. Or have it for dessert, topping pound cake or ice cream.

Spiced Apples

Shari and Dale Mast Harrisonburg, VA

MAKES: **10–12 SERVINGS**
PREP. TIME: **5 MINUTES**
COOKING TIME: **4–5 HOURS**
IDEAL SLOW COOKER SIZE: **6-QUART**

16 cups sliced apples, peeled or unpeeled, *divided*
½ cup brown sugar, *divided*
3 Tbsp. minute tapioca, *divided*
1 tsp. ground cinnamon, *divided*

1. Layer half of sliced apples, sugar, tapioca, and cinnamon in slow cooker.
2. Repeat, making a second layer using remaining ingredients.

3. Cover. Cook on High 4 hours, or on Low 5 hours.
4. Stir before serving. Delicious hot or cold.

Per Serving: 130 calories (0 calories from fat), 0g total fat (0g saturated, 0g trans), 0mg cholesterol, 0mg sodium, 33g total carbohydrate (3g fiber, 27g sugar), 0g protein, 0%DV vitamin A, 0%DV vitamin C, 2%DV calcium, 2%DV iron.

Apple Appeal

Anne Townsend Albuquerque, NM

MAKES: **6 SERVINGS**
PREP. TIME: **10 MINUTES**
COOKING TIME: **4–5 HOURS**
IDEAL SLOW COOKER SIZE: **3-QUART**

6 baking apples, peeled, cored, and quartered
¼ tsp. nutmeg
2 Tbsp. sugar
¾ tsp. Asian five-spice powder
¼ cup apple juice

1. Place prepared apples in slow cooker.
2. In a small mixing bowl, combine all remaining ingredients.
3. Pour into slow cooker, stirring gently to coat apples.
4. Cover and cook on Low 4–5 hours, or until apples are as tender as you want them.
5. Serve the apples sliced or mashed and warm, cold, or at room-temperature.
6. These versatile apples may be served as a side-dish with ham, scalloped potatoes, green beans amandine, cornbread, pecan tarts, and as a topping for toast!

Zesty Pears

Barbara Walker Sturgis, SD

MAKES: **6 SERVINGS**
PREP. TIME: **15 MINUTES**
COOKING TIME: **4–6 HOURS**
IDEAL SLOW COOKER SIZE: **2–3-QUART**

6 fresh pears

½ cup raisins

¼ cup brown sugar

1 tsp. grated lemon peel

¼ cup brandy

½ cup sauterne wine

½ cup macaroon crumbs

1. Peel and core pears. Cut into thin slices.
2. Combine raisins, sugar, and lemon peel. Layer alternately with pear slices in slow cooker.
3. Pour brandy and wine over top.
4. Cover. Cook on Low 4–6 hours.
5. Spoon into serving dishes. Cool. Sprinkle with macaroons. Serve plain or topped with sour cream.

Carmeled Pears 'n Wine

Sharon Timpe Jackson, WI

MAKES: **6 SERVINGS**
PREP. TIME: **10 MINUTES**
COOKING TIME: **4–6 HOURS**
IDEAL SLOW COOKER SIZE: **6-QUART**

PICTURED ON PAGE 31

6 medium fresh pears with stems

1 cup white wine (sauterne works well)

½ cup sugar

½ cup water

3 Tbsp. lemon juice

2 apple cinnamon sticks, each about 2½–3-inch long

3 whole dried cloves

¼ tsp. ground nutmeg

6 Tbsp. fat-free caramel apple dip

1. Peel pears, leaving whole with stems intact.
2. Place upright in slow cooker. Shave bottom if needed to level fruit.
3. Combine wine, sugar, water, lemon juice, cinnamon, cloves, and nutmeg. Pour over pears.
4. Cook on Low 4–6 hours, or until pears are tender.
5. Cool pears in liquid.
6. Transfer pears to individual serving dishes. Place 2 tsp. cooking liquid in bottom of each dish.
7. Microwave caramel dip for 20 seconds and stir. Repeat until heated through.
8. Drizzle caramel over pears and serve.

Per Serving: 290 calories (25 calories from fat), 2.5 total fat (0g saturated, 0g trans), 0mg cholesterol, 140mg sodium, 62g total carbohydrate (4g fiber, 42g sugar), 2g protein, 0%DV vitamin A, 4%DV vitamin C, 15%DV calcium, 6%DV iron.

Strawberry Rhubarb Sauce

Tina Snyder   Manheim, PA

MAKES: **8 SERVINGS**
PREP. TIME: **10 MINUTES**
COOKING TIME: **6–7 HOURS**
IDEAL SLOW COOKER SIZE: **3½-QUART**

6 cups sliced rhubarb
¾ cup sugar
1 cinnamon stick, *optional*
½ cup white grape juice
2 cups sliced strawberries, unsweetened

1. Place rhubarb in slow cooker. Pour sugar over. Add cinnamon stick, if you wish, and grape juice. Stir well.
2. Cover and cook on Low 5-6 hours, or until rhubarb is tender.
3. Stir in strawberries. Cook 1 hour longer.
4. Remove cinnamon stick if you've used it. Chill.

Per Serving: 120 calories (0 calories from fat), 0g total fat (0g saturated, 0g trans), 0mg cholesterol, 10mg sodium, 29g total carbohydrate (3g fiber, 26g sugar), 1g protein, 0%DV vitamin A, 30%DV vitamin C, 10%DV calcium, 4%DV iron.

Tip: *Serve as is, or, if diets allow, over cake or ice cream.*

To easily crush strawberries, put about a cup into your blender. Using the pulse button, chop them coarsely. Then add more berries and continue to use the pulse button until they are as chunky or as fine as desired.

Rhubarb Sauce

Esther Porter   Minneapolis, MN

MAKES: **6 SERVINGS**
PREP. TIME: **10 MINUTES**
COOKING TIME: **4–5 HOURS**
IDEAL SLOW COOKER SIZE: **4½-QUART**

1½ lbs. rhubarb
⅛ tsp. salt
½ cup water
½ cup sugar
pinch of baking soda

1. Cut rhubarb into ½-inch thick slices.
2. Combine all ingredients except baking soda in slow cooker. Cook on Low 4–5 hours. Stir in baking soda.
3. Serve chilled.

Per Serving: 90 calories (0 calories from fat), 0g total fat (0g saturated, 0g trans), 0mg cholesterol, 55mg sodium, 22g total carbohydrate (2g fiber, 19g sugar), 1g protein, 0%DV vitamin A, 0%DV vitamin C, 10%DV calcium, 2%DV iron.

Desserts and Sweets

Pineapple Sauce

Elizabeth L. Richards   Rapid City, SD

MAKES: **8 SERVINGS**
PREP. TIME: **5 MINUTES**
COOKING TIME: **2 HOURS**
IDEAL SLOW COOKER SIZE: **3-QUART**

4 cups apple juice

15-oz. can light crushed pineapples, undrained

1½ cups golden raisins

½ tsp. ground cinnamon

½ tsp. ground allspice

½ cup sugar

¼ cup cornstarch

1. Combine all ingredients in slow cooker. Mix well.
2. Cover. Cook on High 2 hours.
3. Serve as a topping for dessert, as a topping for baked ham, or as a side dish during the holidays.

Per Serving: 250 calories (0 calories from fat), 0g total fat (0g saturated, 0g trans), 0mg cholesterol, 10mg sodium, 63g total carbohydrate (2g fiber, 53g sugar), 1g protein, 0%DV vitamin A, 60%DV vitamin C, 2%DV calcium, 8%DV iron.

"Bake" cakes in a cake pan set directly on the bottom of your slow cooker. Cover the top with 4–5 layers of paper towels to help absorb the moisture from the top of the cake. Leave the cooker lid open slightly to let extra moisture escape.

Southwest Cranberries

Bernita Boyts   Shawnee Mission, KS

MAKES: **8 SERVINGS**
PREP. TIME: **5 MINUTES**
COOKING TIME: **2–3 HOURS**
IDEAL SLOW COOKER SIZE: **1½–2-QUART**

16-oz. can whole berry cranberry sauce

10½-oz. jar jalapeño jelly

2 Tbsp. chopped fresh cilantro

1. Combine ingredients in slow cooker.
2. Cover. Cook on Low 2–3 hours.
3. Cool. Serve at room temperature.
4. Serve these spicy cranberries as a side dish or as a marinade for poultry or pork.

Curried Fruit

Jane Meiser   Harrisonburg, VA

MAKES: **8–10 SERVINGS**
PREP. TIME: **10 MINUTES**
MARINATING TIME: **2–8 HOURS**
COOKING TIME: **8–10 HOURS**
IDEAL SLOW COOKER SIZE: **3½–4-QUART**

1 can peaches, undrained

1 can apricots, undrained

1 can pears, undrained

1 large can pineapple chunks, undrained

1 can black cherries, undrained

½ cup brown sugar

1 tsp. curry powder

3–4 Tbsp. quick-cooking tapioca, depending upon how thickened you'd like the finished dish to be

butter, *optional*

1. Combine fruit. Let stand for at least 2 hours, or up to 8, to allow flavors to blend. Drain. Place in slow cooker.
2. Add remaining ingredients. Mix well. Top with butter, if you want.
3. Cover. Cook on Low 8–10 hours.
4. Serve warm or at room temperature.

Fruit Dessert Topping

Lavina Hochstedler   Grand Blanc, MI

MAKES: **6 CUPS**
PREP. TIME: **20 MINUTES**
COOKING TIME: **3½–4¾ HOURS**
IDEAL SLOW COOKER SIZE: **3½-QUART**

3 tart apples, peeled and sliced

3 pears, peeled and sliced

1 Tbsp. lemon juice

½ cup packed brown sugar

½ cup maple syrup

¼ cup butter, melted

½ cup chopped pecans

¼ cup raisins

2 cinnamon sticks

1 Tbsp. cornstarch

2 Tbsp. cold water

1. Toss apples and pears in lemon juice in slow cooker.
2. Combine brown sugar, maple syrup, and butter. Pour over fruit.
3. Stir in pecans, raisins, and cinnamon sticks.
4. Cover. Cook on Low 3–4 hours.
5. Combine cornstarch and water until smooth. Gradually stir into slow cooker.
6. Cover. Cook on High 30–40 minutes, or until thickened.
7. Discard cinnamon sticks. Serve over pound cake or ice cream.

Note: *We also like this served along with pancakes or an egg casserole. We always use Fruit Dessert Topping for our breakfasts at church camp.*

Desserts and Sweets

Dried Fruit

Janet Roggie   Lowville, NY

MAKES: **3–4 SERVINGS**
PREP. TIME: **5 MINUTES**
COOKING TIME: **4–8 HOURS**
IDEAL SLOW COOKER SIZE: **1½-QUART**

2 cups mixed dried fruit
¼ cup water

1. Place dried fruit in slow cooker. Add water.
2. Cover. Cook on Low 4–8 hours.
3. Serve warm with a spoonful of sour cream on each individual serving and a dash of ground nutmeg.

Tip: *This is a good alternative to fresh fruit in the wintertime.*

Variation: *To do more than plump the fruit, and to increase juiciness, increase water to ½ cup.*

Scandinavian Fruit Soup

Willard E. Roth   Elkhart, IN

MAKES: **12 SERVINGS**
PREP. TIME: **5 MINUTES**
COOKING TIME: **8 HOURS**
IDEAL SLOW COOKER SIZE: **4-QUART**

1 cup dried apricots
1 cup dried sliced apples
1 cup dried pitted prunes
1 cup canned pitted red cherries
½ cup quick-cooking tapioca
1 cup grape juice *or* red wine
3 cups water, or more
½ cup orange juice
¼ cup lemon juice
1 Tbsp. grated orange peel
½ cup brown sugar

1. Combine apricots, apples, prunes, cherries, tapioca, and grape juice in slow cooker. Cover with water.
2. Cook on Low for at least 8 hours.
3. Before serving, stir in remaining ingredients.
4. Serve warm or cold, as a soup or dessert. Delicious served chilled over vanilla ice cream or frozen yogurt.

Cook your favorite "Plum Pudding" recipe in a can set inside a slow cooker on a metal rack or trivet. Pour about 2 cups warm water around it. The water helps steam the pudding. Cover the can tightly with foil to help keep the cake dry. Cover the cooker with its lid. Cook on High.

Apple Schnitz

Betty Hostetler Allensville, PA

MAKES: **6–8 SERVINGS**
PREP. TIME: **5 MINUTES**
COOKING TIME: **2½–6 HOURS**
IDEAL SLOW COOKER SIZE: **3-QUART**

1 quart dried apples

3 cups water

1 cup sugar

1 tsp. ground cinnamon

1 tsp. salt

1. Combine apples, water, sugar, cinnamon, and salt in slow cooker.
2. Cover. Cook on Low 6 hours, or on High 2½ hours.
3. Serve warm as a side dish with bean soup, or as filling for Half Moon Pies (see below).
4. For pie filling, remove apples from slow cooker. Mash until smooth with potato masher or put through food mill. Cool.

Pie Crust:

4 cups flour

2 tsp. salt

4 Tbsp. shortening

¼ cold water or more

1. Combine flour and salt. Cut in shortening until mixture resembles small peas.
2. Add ¼ cup cold water to dough, adding more by tablespoonfuls as needed to make a soft pie dough.
3. Pinch off small pieces of dough, each about the size of a large walnut. Roll into round pieces, each about 8 inches in diameter.
4. Jag one half of the circle a few times with a sharp fork to create holes for the steam to escape while baking. On the other half place a heaping tablespoon of apple filling.

Fold one-half of dough up over the half holding the pie filling, shaping the pie like a half moon. Press edges of dough together. Cut off remaining dough and crimp edges.

5. Bake at 350° for 30 minutes.

Note: *On a cold winter day, Mother would prepare dried beans to make soup. After the beans were soft, she added milk to the soup pot. She heated the mixture to the boiling point, then added rivels. While the beans were cooking, she cooked dried apples until they were soft. She served these Half Moon Pies as a side dish/dessert with the soup.*

I always keep 1-cup measuring cups in my sugar and flour canisters. That way I can reach in and measure what I need from that one cup.

Desserts and Sweets

Apple Crisp

Michelle Strite   Goshen, IN

MAKES: **6–8 SERVINGS**
PREP. TIME: **5–10 MINUTES**
COOKING TIME: **2–3 HOURS**
IDEAL SLOW COOKER SIZE: **2-QUART**

1 quart canned apple pie filling, *or*

⅔ cup sugar

1¼ cups water

3 Tbsp. cornstarch

4 cups sliced, peeled apples

½ tsp. ground cinnamon

¼ tsp. ground allspice

¾ cup quick oatmeal

½ cup brown sugar

½ cup flour

¼ cup butter, at room temperature

1. Place pie filling in slow cooker. If not using prepared filling, combine ⅔ cup sugar, water, cornstarch, apples, cinnamon, and allspice. Place in cooker.
2. Combine remaining ingredients until crumbly. Sprinkle over apple filling.
3. Cover. Cook on Low 2–3 hours.

Applescotch Crisp

Mary Jane Musser   Manheim, PA

MAKES: **6 SERVINGS**
PREP. TIME: **10–15 MINUTES**
COOKING TIME: **5–6 HOURS**
IDEAL SLOW COOKER SIZE: **3-QUART**

4 cups cooking apples, peeled and sliced

⅔ cup brown sugar

½ cup flour

½ cup quick-cooking oats

3½-oz. pkg. cook-n-serve butterscotch pudding mix

1 tsp. ground cinnamon

½ cup cold butter

1. Place apples in slow cooker.
2. Combine remaining ingredients. Cut in butter until mixture resembles coarse crumbs. Sprinkle over apples.
3. Cover. Cook on Low 5–6 hours.
4. Serve with ice cream.

Variation: *For a less-sweet dish, use only ¼ cup brown sugar.*

"Baked" Stuffed Apples

Miriam Nolt New Holland, PA • *Ruth Hofstetter* Versailles, MO
Sara Kinsinger Stuarts Draft, VA • *Betty Drescher* Quakertown, PA
Dorothy Lingerfelt Stonyford, CA • *Kaye Taylor* Florissant, MO
Dale Peterson Rapid City, SD • *Karen Ceneviva* New Haven, CT

MAKES: **6–8 SERVINGS**
PREP. TIME: **15–30 MINUTES**
COOKING TIME: **2½–5 HOURS**
IDEAL SLOW COOKER SIZE: **5-QUART**

2 Tbsp. raisins

¼ cup sugar

**6–8 medium baking apples, cored but left whole and
    unpeeled**

1 tsp. ground cinnamon

2 Tbsp. butter

½ cup water

1. Mix raisins and sugar together in a small bowl.
2. Stand apples on bottom of slow cooker. Spoon raisin-sugar mixture into centers of apples, dividing evenly among apples.
3. Sprinkle stuffed apples with cinnamon. Dot with butter.
4. Add ½ cup water along the edge of the cooker.
5. Cover and cook on Low 3–5 hours, or on High 2½–3½ hours, or until apples are tender but not collapsing.
6. Serve warm as is, or with ice cream or frozen yogurt.

Variations:

1. Instead of raisins, use chopped walnuts or pecans.

Connie Casteel Mt. Pleasant, IA

2. Instead of keeping the apples whole, core them and cut them in half. Lay them cut-side up and fill the core area. Lay apples in slow cooker with cut- and stuffed-sides up, stacking them if necessary.

Carol Eberly Harrisonburg, VA

3. Instead of granulated sugar, use ¼ cup brown sugar. And instead of cinnamon use apple pie spices, or a mixture of ground allspice, cloves, and cinnamon to equal 1 tsp.

Linda E. Wilcox Blythewood, SC • *Arlene M. Kopp* Lineboro, MD

4. Instead of sugar, use ¼ cup Splenda.

Leona Yoder Hartville, OH

Fruit/Nut "Baked" Apples

Cyndie Marrara Port Matilda, PA

MAKES: **4 SERVINGS**
PREP. TIME: **25 MINUTES**
COOKING TIME: **1½–3 HOURS**
IDEAL SLOW COOKER SIZE: **4-QUART**

4 large firm baking apples

1 Tbsp. lemon juice

⅓ cup chopped dried apricots

⅓ cup chopped walnuts *or* pecans

3 Tbsp. packed brown sugar

½ tsp. cinnamon

2 Tbsp. butter, melted

½ cup water *or* apple juice

4 pecan halves, *optional*

1. Scoop out center of apples creating a cavity 1½ inches wide and stopping ½ inch from the bottom of each. Peel top of each apple down about 1 inch. Brush edges with lemon juice.
2. Mix together apricots, nuts, brown sugar, and cinnamon. Stir in butter. Spoon mixture evenly into apples.

3. Put ½ cup water or juice in bottom of slow cooker. Put 2 apples in bottom, and 2 apples above, but not squarely on top of other apples. Cover and cook on Low 1½–3 hours, or until tender.

4. Serve warm or at room temperature. Top each apple with a pecan half, if desired.

Caramel Apples

Elaine Patton West Middletown, PA • *Renee Shirk* Mount Joy, PA
Rhonda Lee Schmidt Scranton, PA

MAKES: **4 SERVINGS**
PREP. TIME: **15 MINUTES**
COOKING TIME: **4–6 HOURS**
IDEAL SLOW COOKER SIZE: **4-QUART**

4 very large tart apples, cored
½ cup apple juice
8 Tbsp. brown sugar
12 hot cinnamon candies
4 Tbsp. butter
8 caramel candies
¼ tsp. ground cinnamon
whipped cream

1. Remove ½-inch-wide strip of peel off the top of each apple and place apples in slow cooker.

2. Pour apple juice over apples.

3. Fill the center of each apple with 2 Tbsp. brown sugar, 3 hot cinnamon candies, 1 Tbsp. butter, or margarine, and 2 caramel candies. Sprinkle with cinnamon.

4. Cover and cook on Low 4–6 hours, or until tender.

5. Serve hot with whipped cream.

Caramel Apples on Sticks

Becky Harder Monument, CO • *Jeanette Oberholtzer* Manheim, PA

MAKES: **8–10 SERVINGS**
PREP. TIME: **30 MINUTES**
COOKING TIME: **1–1½ HOURS**
IDEAL SLOW COOKER SIZE: **2-QUART**

PICTURED
ON PAGE
601

2 14-oz. bags of caramels
¼ cup water
8–10 medium apples
sticks
waxed paper
granulated sugar

1. Combine caramels and water in slow cooker.

2. Cover. Cook on High for 1–1½ hours, stirring every 5 minutes.

3. Wash and dry apples. Insert a stick into stem end of each apple. Turn cooker to Low. Dip apple into hot caramel, turning to coat entire surface.

4. Holding apple above cooker, scrape off excess accumulation of caramel from bottom of apple.

5. Dip bottom of caramel-coated apple in granulated sugar to keep it from sticking. Place apple on greased waxed paper to cool.

Note: *This is a good recipe for Fall parties. Children won't forget the experience of dipping their own apples. Room mothers can make the mix ahead of time and bring it into the classroom. This recipe is also a fun intergenerational activity.*

As children, my sister and I were rewarded with a store-bought caramel apple, only after our Saturday night baths and our Sunday school lessons had been completed. I remember that the waxed paper wrapped around each apple had colorful clowns printed on it, and they sold for less than 50¢ each.

Becky Harder Monument, CO

Apple Dish

Vera Martin   East Earl, PA

MAKES: **ABOUT 7 CUPS**
PREP. TIME: **15–20 MINUTES**
COOKING TIME: **2–2½ HOURS**
IDEAL SLOW COOKER SIZE: **3–4-QUART**

¾ cup sugar

3 Tbsp. flour

1½ tsp. cinnamon, *optional*

5 large baking apples, pared, cored, and diced into
¾-inch pieces

half a stick (¼ cup) butter, melted

3 Tbsp. water

1. Spray interior of slow cooker with nonstick cooking spray.
2. In a large bowl, mix sugar and flour together, along with cinnamon if you wish. Set aside.
3. Mix apples, butter, and water together in slow cooker. Gently stir in flour mixture until apples are well coated.
4. Cover and cook on High 1½ hours, and then on Low 30–60 minutes, or until apples are done to your liking.
5. Serve with milk poured over top.

Variation: *Add ½ cup dry quick or rolled oats to Step 2, if you wish.*

Deb Herr   Mountaintop, PA

Apple Caramel Dessert

Jeanette Oberholtzer   Manheim, PA

MAKES: **7 SERVINGS**
PREP. TIME: **15 MINUTES**
COOKING TIME: **6 HOURS**
IDEAL SLOW COOKER SIZE: **2-QUART**

2 medium apples, peeled, cored, and cut in wedges

½ cup apple juice

7 ozs. caramel candy

1 tsp. vanilla

⅛ tsp. ground cardamom

½ tsp. ground cinnamon

⅓ cup creamy peanut butter

7 slices angel food cake

1 quart vanilla ice cream

1. Combine apple juice, caramel candies, vanilla, and spices. Place in slow cooker.
2. Drop peanut butter, 1 tsp. at a time, into slow cooker. Stir.
3. Add apple wedges.
4. Cover. Cook on Low 5 hours.
5. Stir well.
6. Cover. Then cook 1 more hour on Low.
7. Serve ⅓ cup warm mixture over each slice of angel food cake and top with ice cream.

Beverages

Home-Style Tomato Juice

Wilma Haberkamp   Fairbank, IA

MAKES: **4 CUPS**
PREP. TIME: **20 MINUTES**
COOKING TIME: **4–6 HOURS**
IDEAL SLOW COOKER SIZE: **3-QUART**

10–12 large ripe tomatoes
1 tsp. salt
1 tsp. seasoned salt
¼ tsp. pepper
1 Tbsp. sugar

1. Wash and drain tomatoes. Remove core and blossom ends.
2. Place the whole tomatoes in your slow cooker. (Do not add water.)
3. Cover and cook on Low 4–6 hours, or until tomatoes are very soft.
4. Press them through a sieve or food mill.
5. Add seasonings. Chill.

Tip: *If you have more than 10–12 tomatoes, you can use a larger slow cooker and double the recipe.*

Buy fruits and vegetables when they are in season. They will be cheaper, and their quality will be greater than those that are out of season and have been shipped long distances.

Spicy Hot Cider

Michelle High   Fredericksburg, PA

MAKES: **16 SERVINGS**
PREP. TIME: **5 MINUTES**
COOKING TIME: **3 HOURS**
IDEAL SLOW COOKER SIZE: **5-QUART**

1 gallon apple cider
4 cinnamon sticks
2 Tbsp. ground allspice
¼–½ cup brown sugar

1. Combine all ingredients in slow cooker. Begin with ¼ cup brown sugar. Stir to dissolve. If you'd like the cider to be sweeter, add more, up to ½ cup total.
2. Cover and cook on Low 3 hours.
3. Serve warm from the cooker.

Red Hot Apple Cider

Allison Ingels   Maynard, IA

MAKES: **16 SERVINGS**
PREP. TIME: **5 MINUTES**
COOKING TIME: **1½–2 HOURS**
IDEAL SLOW COOKER SIZE: **5-QUART**

1 gallon apple cider *or* **apple juice**
1¼ cups red cinnamon hearts
16 4-inch-long cinnamon sticks

1. Combine cider and cinnamon hearts in slow cooker.
2. Cover. Cook on Low 1½–2 hours.
3. Serve hot with a cinnamon stick in each cup.

Note: *Our family enjoys this recipe on cold winter evenings and especially on Christmas Eve. The smell creates a very relaxing atmosphere.*

Hot Apple Cider

Jeannine Janzen   Elbing, KS

MAKES: **4 SERVINGS**
PREP. TIME: **5 MINUTES**
COOKING TIME: **2–3 HOURS**
IDEAL SLOW COOKER SIZE: **3-QUART**

1 quart apple cider
⅛ tsp. nutmeg
½ cup red cinnamon hearts

1. Combine all ingredients in slow cooker.
2. Cover and cook on High 2–3 hours, or until very hot. If you're at home and available, stir the cider occasionally to help dissolve the red candy.
3. Serve warm from the slow cooker.

Citrus-Cinnamon Apple Cider

Dawn Hahn   Lititz, PA

MAKES: **16 SERVINGS**
PREP. TIME: **5 MINUTES**
COOKING TIME: **3–5 HOURS**
IDEAL SLOW COOKER SIZE: **5-QUART**

½ cup red cinnamon hearts
1 gallon apple cider
16 orange slice halves
16 3–4-inch-long cinnamon sticks

1. Pour cinnamon hearts into bottom of slow cooker.
2. Add apple cider.
3. Cook on Low 3–5 hours, or until cider is very hot and candy has melted. If you're able, stir occasionally to help the candy dissolve.
4. Place one orange slice half and one cinnamon stick in each cup. Pour hot cider over top.

Tip: *This is great to serve at a Christmas or Valentine's party.*

Hot Spiced Cider

Elva Evers North English, IA

MAKES: **6 1-CUP SERVINGS**
PREP. TIME: **5 MINUTES**
COOKING TIME: **4 HOURS**
IDEAL SLOW COOKER SIZE: **3–4-QUART**

12-oz. can frozen apple juice
3 3-inch cinnamon sticks
6 whole cloves

1. Combine all ingredients in slow cooker.
2. Cover and simmer on Low 4 hours.
3. Remove cinnamon and cloves before serving.

Variation: *Omit the cinnamon and cloves. Use ¼ cup fresh or dried mint tea leaves instead.*

Great Mulled Cider

Charlotte Shaffer East Earl, PA • *Barbara Sparks* Glen Burnie, MD

MAKES: **8–10 1-CUP SERVINGS**
PREP. TIME: **5 MINUTES**
COOKING TIME: **3 HOURS**
IDEAL SLOW COOKER SIZE: **4-QUART**

2 quarts apple cider
½ cup frozen orange juice concentrate
½ cup brown sugar
½ tsp. ground allspice, *or* 1 tsp. whole allspice
1½ tsp. whole cloves
2 cinnamon sticks
orange slices

1. Tie all whole spices in cheesecloth bag, then combine all ingredients in slow cooker.
2. Cover and simmer on Low 3 hours.

Orange Cider Punch

Naomi Ressler Harrisonburg, VA

MAKES: **9–12 6-OZ. SERVINGS**
PREP. TIME: **5–10 MINUTES**
COOKING TIME: **2–10 HOURS**
IDEAL SLOW COOKER SIZE: **3½-QUART**

1 cup sugar
2 cinnamon sticks
1 tsp. whole nutmeg
2 cups apple cider *or* apple juice
6 cups orange juice
fresh orange

1. Combine all ingredients except the fresh orange in slow cooker.
2. Cover. Cook on Low 4–10 hours, or on High 2–3 hours.
3. Float thin slices of an orange in cooker before serving.

Citrus Cider

Valerie Drobel Carlisle, PA

MAKES: **8–10 SERVINGS**
PREP. TIME: **10 MINUTES**
COOKING TIME: **2–5 HOURS**
IDEAL SLOW COOKER SIZE: **3–5-QUART**

2 quarts apple cider
½ cup packed brown sugar
2 4-inch-long cinnamon sticks
1 tsp. whole cloves
1 orange *or* lemon, sliced

1. Pour cider into slow cooker. Stir in brown sugar.
2. Place cinnamon sticks and cloves in cheesecloth and tie with string to form a bag. Float in slow cooker.
3. Add fruit slices on top.
4. Cover and cook on Low 2-5 hours. Remove spice bag. Stir before serving.

Variations:

1. Add ⅓ tsp. ground ginger to Step 1.

Christie Anne Detamore-Hunsberger Harrisonburg, VA

2. Add 1 tsp. whole allspice to the cheesecloth bag in Step 2.

Mary Stauffer Ephrata, PA

3. Eliminate the brown sugar for a less sweet beverage.

Pauline Morrison St. Marys, ON

Orange Spiced Cider

Carolyn Baer Conrath, WI

MAKES: **8 SERVINGS**
PREP. TIME: **5 MINUTES**
COOKING TIME: **2–3 HOURS**
IDEAL SLOW COOKER SIZE: **2–3-QUART**

4 cups unsweetened apple juice
12-oz. can orange juice concentrate, thawed
½ cup water
1 Tbsp. red cinnamon hearts
½ tsp. ground nutmeg
1 tsp. whole cloves
8 fresh orange slice halves, *optional*
8 3–4-inch-long cinnamon sticks, *optional*

1. Combine first five ingredients in the slow cooker.
2. Place cloves on a piece of cheesecloth. Tie with string to create a bag. Submerge bag in juices in slow cooker.
3. Cover and cook on Low 2–3 hours, or until cider is very hot.
4. Remove bag before serving. Stir cider.
5. If you wish, place a cinnamon stick, topped with an orange slice, in each cup. Pour in hot cider.

Cranberry-Apple Cider

Norma Grieser   Clarksville, MI

MAKES: **20 SERVINGS**
PREP. TIME: **10 MINUTES**
COOKING TIME: **2–3 HOURS**
IDEAL SLOW COOKER SIZE: **8-QUART**

1 gallon cider *or* apple juice

64-oz. can cranberry juice cocktail

½ cup brown sugar

1 cup red cinnamon hearts

2 tsp. cinnamon

1. Pour ingredients together in slow cooker. Stir together well.
2. Cover and heat on High 2–3 hours, or until cider is very hot. If you're home and able to do so, stir occasionally to help the candy dissolve.
3. Serve warm from the cooker.

Fruity Wassail with Oranges

Melissa Warner   Broad Top, PA

MAKES: **10 SERVINGS**
PREP. TIME: **5 MINUTES**
COOKING TIME: **5–9 HOURS**
IDEAL SLOW COOKER SIZE: **3-QUART**

2 quarts apple juice *or* cider

2 cups cranberry juice cocktail

2 4-inch-long sticks cinnamon

1 tsp. whole allspice

10-oz. can mandarin oranges, with juice

1. Place apple juice, or cider, and cranberry juice in slow cooker.
2. Place cinnamon sticks and whole allspice on a piece of cheesecloth. Tie with a string to make a bag. Place in cooker.
3. Cover and cook on High 1 hour, and then on Low 4–8 hours.
4. Add oranges and their juice 15 minutes before serving.
5. Remove cheesecloth bag before serving.

Spiced Cranberry Cider

Esther Burkholder   Millerstown, PA

MAKES: **7 SERVINGS**
PREP. TIME: **5–10 MINUTES**
COOKING TIME: **3–5 HOURS**
IDEAL SLOW COOKER SIZE: **3-QUART**

1 quart apple cider

3 cups cranberry juice cocktail

3 Tbsp. brown sugar

2 3-inch-long cinnamon sticks

¾ tsp. whole cloves

½ lemon, thinly sliced, *optional*

1. Pour apple cider and cranberry juice into slow cooker.
2. Stir in brown sugar.
3. Put spices on a piece of cheesecloth. Tie with a string to create a bag. Place in slow cooker.
4. Stir in lemon slices if you wish.
5. Cover and cook on Low 3–5 hours, or until cider is very hot. If you're able, stir occasionally to be sure brown sugar is dissolving.
6. Remove spice bag, and lemon slices if you've included them, before serving warm from the cooker.

Variation: *Instead of whole cloves, substitute 1 tsp. whole allspice.*

Jean Butzer   Batavia, NY

Cranberry Punch

Betty B. Dennison Grove City, PA

MAKES: **8 SERVINGS**
PREP. TIME: **10 MINUTES**
COOKING TIME: **4 HOURS**
IDEAL SLOW COOKER SIZE: **4-QUART**

8 whole cardamom pods
2 sticks cinnamon
12 whole cloves
4 cups dry red wine
2 6-oz. cans frozen cranberry concentrate
2⅔ cups water
½ cup honey (or to taste)
1 orange sliced into 8 thin crescents

1. Make a spice packet of the following items: Pinch open cardamom pods to release seeds and place them on a piece of cheesecloth or paper coffee filter. Add cinnamon sticks and cloves. Tie with a string to make a bag.
2. Pour wine, cranberry concentrate, water, and honey into slow cooker. Heat on Low.
3. Submerge spice packet in the liquid and heat but do not boil.
4. Let punch steep on Low for up to 4 hours.
5. To serve, remove and discard spice bag. Divide punch among cups. Float an orange slice in each cup. Serve warm.

Per Serving: 240 calories (0 calories from fat), 0g total fat (0g saturated, 0g trans), 0mg cholesterol, 30mg sodium, 40g total carbohydrate (3g fiber, 33g sugar), 2g protein, 4%DV vitamin A, 20%DV vitamin C, 8%DV calcium, 10%DV iron.

Assemble all of your measured ingredients first. Then add as the recipe calls for them.

Fruity Hot Punch

Evelyn L. Ward Greeley, CO

MAKES: **12 SERVINGS**
PREP. TIME: **10 MINUTES**
COOKING TIME: **4 HOURS**
IDEAL SLOW COOKER SIZE: **5-QUART**

2 16-oz. cans cranberry sauce, mashed
4 cups water
1 quart pineapple juice
¾ cup brown sugar
¼ tsp. salt
¼ tsp. ground nutmeg
¾ tsp. ground cloves
½ tsp. ground allspice
12 cinnamon sticks
butter, *optional*

1. Combine all ingredients in slow cooker.
2. Cover. Heat on Low 4 hours.
3. Serve in mugs with cinnamon stick stirrers. Dot each serving with butter if you wish.

Note: *My daughter is a teacher and has served this at faculty meetings when it's her turn to treat.*

Zingy Cranberry Punch

Marianne Troyer Millersburg, OH

MAKES: **13–14 1-CUP SERVINGS**
PREP. TIME: **5–10 MINUTES**
COOKING TIME: **2–3 HOURS**
IDEAL SLOW COOKER SIZE: **4–5-QUART**

2 quarts hot water

1½ cups sugar

1 quart cranberry juice

¾ cup orange juice

¼ cup lemon juice

12 whole cloves, *optional*

½ cup red hot candies

1. Combine water, sugar, and juices. Stir until sugar is dissolved.
2. Place cloves in double thickness of cheesecloth and tie with string. Add to slow cooker.
3. Add cinnamon candies.
4. Cover and Cook on Low 2-3 hours, or until heated thoroughly.
5. Remove spice bag before serving.

Hot Spicy Lemonade Punch

Mary E. Herr The Hermitage Three Rivers, MI

MAKES: **9–10 1-CUP SERVINGS**
PREP. TIME: **5–10 MINUTES**
COOKING TIME: **3–4 HOURS**
IDEAL SLOW COOKER SIZE: **4-QUART**

4 cups cranberry juice

⅓–⅔ cup sugar

12-oz. can lemonade concentrate, thawed

4 cups water

1–2 Tbsp. honey

6 whole cloves

2 cinnamon sticks, broken

1 lemon, sliced

1. Combine juice, sugar, lemonade, water, and honey in slow cooker.
2. Tie cloves and cinnamon in small cheesecloth square. Add spice bag and lemon slices to slow cooker.
3. Cover and cook on Low 3-4 hours. Remove spice bag. Keep hot in slow cooker until ready to serve.

Red Raspberry Fruit Punch

Karen Stoltzfus Alto, MI

MAKES: **10 1-CUP SERVINGS**
PREP. TIME: **5–10 MINUTES**
COOKING TIME: **1 HOUR**
IDEAL SLOW COOKER SIZE: **4-QUART**

1 quart cranberry juice

3 cups water

6-oz. can frozen orange juice concentrate, thawed

10-oz. pkg. frozen red raspberries, thawed

2 oranges, sliced

6 sticks cinnamon

12 whole allspice

1. Combine all ingredients in slow cooker.
2. Heat on High 1 hour, or until hot. Turn to Low while serving.

Pineapple-Cranberry Punch

Kathy Hertzler   Lancaster, PA

MAKES: **12 1-CUP SERVINGS**
PREP. TIME: **5 MINUTES**
COOKING TIME: **6 HOURS**
IDEAL SLOW COOKER SIZE: **4-QUART**

1 tsp. whole cloves

5 cups pineapple juice

5 cups cranberry juice

2¼ cups water

½ cup brown sugar

2 cinnamon sticks

¼ tsp. salt

1. Place cloves in small cheesecloth bag or tea ball.
2. Mix together all ingredients in slow cooker.
3. Cook on Low 6 hours. Remove cloves. Serve hot.

Tropical Cranberry Punch

Barbara Aston   Ashdown, AR

MAKES: **10 1-CUP SERVINGS**
PREP. TIME: **10 MINUTES**
COOKING TIME: **4½–5 HOURS**
IDEAL SLOW COOKER SIZE: **4-QUART**

2 16-oz. cans jellied cranberry sauce

2 quarts water

2 cups frozen orange juice concentrate

1 quart pineapple juice, *optional*

half a stick of butter

¾ cup firmly packed brown sugar

½ tsp. ground cinnamon

½ tsp. ground allspice

¼ tsp. ground cloves

¼ tsp. ground nutmeg

¼ tsp. salt

1. Mix together all ingredients.
2. Heat on High until boiling, then reduce to Low for 4 hours. Serve hot.

Wine Cranberry Punch

C.J. Slagle   Roann, IN

MAKES: **8 1-CUP SERVINGS**
PREP. TIME: **5–10 MINUTES**
COOKING TIME: **1–2 HOURS**
IDEAL SLOW COOKER SIZE: **3–4-QUART**

1 pint cranberry juice cocktail

1 cup water

¾ cup sugar

2 sticks cinnamon

6 whole cloves

⅘ quart burgundy wine

1 lemon, thinly sliced

1. Combine ingredients in slow cooker.
2. Heat on Low 1–2 hours. Strain and serve hot.
3. Keep hot and serve from slow cooker set on lowest setting.

Citrus Mulled Cider / Wine

Mitzi McGlynchey Downingtown, PA

MAKES: **8–10 1-CUP SERVINGS**
PREP. TIME: **5 MINUTES**
COOKING TIME: **3–4 HOURS**
IDEAL SLOW COOKER SIZE: **4-QUART**

½ tsp. whole cloves

½ tsp. whole allspice

½ gallon apple cider *or* red burgundy wine

2 3-inch cinnamon sticks

1 tsp. ground nutmeg

orange slices, *optional*

cinnamon sticks, *optional*

1. Place cloves and allspice in cheesecloth bag or tea ball.
2. Combine spices, apple cider or wine, 2 cinnamon sticks, and nutmeg in slow cooker.
3. Cook on High 1 hour. Reduce heat, and simmer 2–3 hours.
4. Garnish individual servings with orange slices or cinnamon sticks.

Mulled Wine

Julie McKenzie Punxsutawney, PA

MAKES: **8 1-CUP SERVINGS**
PREP. TIME: **5–10 MINUTES**
COOKING TIME: **1 HOUR**
IDEAL SLOW COOKER SIZE: **3–4-QUART**

½ cup sugar

1½ cups boiling water

half a lemon, thinly sliced

3 cinnamon sticks

3 whole cloves

1 bottle red dinner wine (burgundy *or* claret)

1. Dissolve sugar in boiling water in saucepan.

2. Add remaining ingredients.
3. Pour into slow cooker. Heat on Low for at least 1 hour, until wine is hot. Do not boil.
4. Serve from cooker into mugs.

Spiced Apple Cider

Janice Muller Derwood, MD

MAKES: **18–20 SERVINGS**
PREP. TIME: **5–10 MINUTES**
COOKING TIME: **4–6 HOURS**
IDEAL SLOW COOKER SIZE: **6-QUART**

2 sticks cinnamon

1 cup orange juice

1 tsp. cinnamon

1 tsp. ground cloves

¼ cup lemon juice

2 tsp. whole cloves

1 gallon apple cider

2 tsp. ground nutmeg

½ cup pineapple juice

1 tsp. ginger

1 tsp. lemon peel

1 cup sugar

1. Mix all ingredients in 6-quart slow cooker.
2. Simmer on Low 4–6 hours.

Yummy Hot Cider

Char Hagner   Montague, MI

MAKES: **10–11 1-CUP SERVINGS**
PREP. TIME: **5 MINUTES**
COOKING TIME: **2 HOURS**
IDEAL SLOW COOKER SIZE: **4-QUART**

3 3-inch sticks cinnamon

2 tsp. whole cloves

1 tsp. whole nutmeg, *or* **½ tsp. ground nutmeg**

½ gallon apple cider

1 cup sugar

2 cups orange juice

½ cup lemon juice

1. Tie spices in cheesecloth or tea strainer and place in slow cooker.
2. Add apple cider and sugar, stirring well.
3. Cover. Simmer on Low 1 hour. Remove spices and stir in orange juice and lemon juice. Continue heating 1 more hour. Serve cider from cooker, set on Low.

Ginger Hot Cider

Ilene Bontrager   Arlington, KS

MAKES: **18–20 1-CUP SERVINGS**
PREP. TIME: **5 MINUTES**
COOKING TIME: **5–6 HOURS**
IDEAL SLOW COOKER SIZE: **6-QUART**

1 gallon apple cider

1 quart cranberry juice

5–6 cinnamon sticks

2 tsp. whole cloves

½ tsp. ginger

1 whole orange, sliced

1. Combine cider and cranberry juice in slow cooker.

2. Place cinnamon sticks and cloves in cheesecloth bag and add to slow cooker. Stir in ginger.
3. Heat on High 5–6 hours.
4. Float orange slices on top before serving.

Old-Fashioned Cranberry Cider

Kristi See   Weskan, KS

MAKES: **10–12 SERVINGS**
PREP. TIME: **10 MINUTES**
COOKING TIME: **5–9 HOURS**
IDEAL SLOW COOKER SIZE: **4-QUART**

2 quarts apple cider *or* **apple juice**

1 pint cranberry juice

½–¾ cup sugar, according to your taste preference

2 cinnamon sticks

1 tsp. whole allspice

1 orange, studded with whole cloves

1. Put all ingredients in slow cooker.
2. Cover. Cook on High 1 hour, then on Low 4–8 hours. Serve warm.
3. Serve with finger foods.

Tip: *To garnish wassail with an orange, insert 10–12 ½-inch-long whole cloves halfway into orange. Place studded orange in flat baking pan with ¼ cup water. Bake at 325° for 30 minutes. Just before serving, float orange on top of wassail.*

Note: *I come from a family of eight children, and every Christmas we all get together. We eat dinner, and then sit around playing games and drinking Old-Fashioned Cranberry Cider.*

Lime-Cranberry Punch

Sandra Haverstraw   Hummelstown, PA

MAKES: **10–12 SERVINGS**
PREP. TIME: **5 MINUTES**
COOKING TIME: **3–4 HOURS**
IDEAL SLOW COOKER SIZE: **4-QUART**

8 cups cranberry juice cocktail

3 cups water

½ cup fresh lime juice

⅔ cup sugar

3 4-inch-long cinnamon sticks, broken in half

8 half-slices of an orange, *optional*

1. Place all ingredients except oranges slices in slow cooker. Stir until sugar is dissolved.
2. Cover and simmer on Low 3–4 hours, or until very hot.
3. With a slotted spoon, remove cinnamon sticks and discard before serving.
4. If you wish, float a half-slice of orange on each individual serving of hot punch.

Tip: *Refrigerate any leftover punch; then reheat it or enjoy it cold.*

Spicy Autumn Punch

Marlene Bogard   Newton, KS

MAKES: **16 SERVINGS**
PREP. TIME: **35 MINUTES**
COOKING TIME: **3–4 HOURS**
IDEAL SLOW COOKER SIZE: **3½-QUART**

2 oranges

8 whole cloves

6 cups apple juice

1 cinnamon stick

¼ tsp. ground nutmeg

3 Tbsp. lemon juice

¼ cup honey

2¼ cups pineapple juice

1. Press cloves into oranges. Bake at 350° for 30 minutes.
2. Meanwhile, combine apple juice and cinnamon stick in slow cooker.
3. Cover. Cook on High 1 hour.
4. Add remaining ingredients except oranges.
5. Cover. Cook on Low 2–3 hours. Add oranges at end of cooking time, either whole or in quarters.

Don't be afraid to alter recipes to your liking.

Fruit Cider Punch

Becky Frey Lebanon, PA

MAKES: **10–12 SERVINGS**
PREP. TIME: **5–10 MINUTES**
COOKING TIME: **4–10 HOURS**
IDEAL SLOW COOKER SIZE: **3½-QUART**

4 cups apple cider

2 cups cranberry juice

1 cup orange juice

12-oz. can apricot nectar

¼ cup sugar, *optional*

2 4-inch-long sticks cinnamon

1. Combine all ingredients thoroughly in slow cooker.
2. Cover and cook on Low 4–10 hours.
3. Serve warm from the cooker.

Tip: *Taste the punch before adding the sugar to see if you think it's needed.*

Autumn Sipper

Shari Jensen Fountain, CO

MAKES: **8 1-CUP SERVINGS**
PREP. TIME: **5–10 MINUTES**
COOKING TIME: **4 HOURS**
IDEAL SLOW COOKER SIZE: **4-QUART**

1 Tbsp. whole allspice

3 3-inch cinnamon sticks

2 whole cloves

1 piece *each* lemon and orange peel, each about the size of a half dollar

1 piece crystallized ginger, about the size of a quarter

3 cups apricot nectar

5 cups apple juice

cinnamon sticks and orange slices, *optional*

1. Place spices, citrus peels, and ginger in a cheesecloth or coffee filter. Tie securely. Place in bottom of slow cooker.
2. Pour in apple juice and nectar. Cover.
3. Cook on High 1 hour, then on Low 3 hours.
4. Garnish filled glasses with cinnamon sticks and orange slices.

Spiced Apricot Cider

Janet Oberholtzer Ephrata, PA

MAKES: **4–6 SERVINGS**
PREP. TIME: **5 MINUTES**
COOKING TIME: **3–4 HOURS**
IDEAL SLOW COOKER SIZE: **2-QUART**

2 12-oz. cans apricot nectar

¼ cup lemon juice

2 cups water

¼ cup sugar

3 whole cloves

3 3–4-inch-long cinnamon sticks

1. Combine juices, water, and sugar in slow cooker. Mix well.
2. Place whole cloves and cinnamon sticks on a piece of cheesecloth. Tie with a string to create a bag. Submerge in juices in cooker.
3. Cover and cook on Low 3–4 hours, or until cider is very hot.
4. Remove cloves and cinnamon sticks before serving. Serve warm from the cooker.

Peachy Spiced Cider

Joyce Shackelford   Green Bay, WI

MAKES: **8 SMALL SERVINGS**
PREP. TIME: **5 MINUTES**
COOKING TIME: **4–6 HOURS**
IDEAL SLOW COOKER SIZE: **2-QUART**

4 5½-oz. cans peach nectar

2 cups unsweetened apple juice

½ tsp. ground ginger

¼ tsp. ground cinnamon

¼ tsp. ground nutmeg

4 fresh orange slices, cut ¼-inch thick and then halved

1. Combine peach nectar, apple juice, ginger, cinnamon, and nutmeg in slow cooker.
2. Top with orange slices.
3. Cover. Cook on Low 4–6 hours.
4. Remove orange slices and stir before serving.

Per Serving: 180 calories (0 calories from fat), 0g total fat (0g saturated, 0g trans), 0mg cholesterol, 15mg sodium, 44g total carbohydrate (3g fiber, 41g sugar), 1g protein, 6%DV vitamin A, 100%DV vitamin C, 4%DV calcium, 6%DV iron.

Hot Apple Cinnamon Drink

Marla Folkerts   Holland, OH

MAKES: **24 SERVINGS**
PREP. TIME: **5 MINUTES**
COOKING TIME: **3–5 HOURS**
IDEAL SLOW COOKER SIZE: **6-QUART**

1 gallon cider

2 liters diet ginger ale

4 ozs. hard candies—your choice of flavors

cinnamon sticks, *optional*

1. Combine all ingredients in slow cooker.
2. Cover. Simmer on Low 3–5 hours.

Per Serving: 100 calories (0 calories from fat), 0g total fat (0g saturated, 0g trans), 0mg cholesterol, 30mg sodium, 25g total carbohydrate (0g fiber, 20g sugar), 0g protein, 0%DV vitamin A, 0%DV vitamin C, 0%DV calcium, 0%DV iron.

Vanilla Hot Mulled Cider

Shirley Unternahrer Hinh   Wayland, IA

MAKES: **12 SERVINGS**
PREP TIME: **5 MINUTES**
COOKING TIME: **5 HOURS**
IDEAL SLOW COOKER SIZE: **3½-QUART**

2 quarts apple cider

¼–½ cup brown sugar, according to your taste preference

½ tsp. vanilla

1 cinnamon stick

4 cloves

1. Combine ingredients in slow cooker.
2. Cover. Cook on Low 5 hours. Stir.

Note: *Our kids just tried hot mulled cider for the first time this past Christmas. They loved it. It's fun to try new old things.*

Cider Snap

Cathy Boshart   Lebanon, PA

MAKES: **12–16 SERVINGS**
PREP. TIME: **5–10 MINUTES**
COOKING TIME: **2 HOURS**
IDEAL SLOW COOKER SIZE: **3½-QUART**

2 quarts apple cider *or* apple juice
4 Tbsp. red cinnamon candies
at least 16 apple slices
at least 16 cinnamon sticks

1. Combine cider and cinnamon candies in slow cooker.
2. Cover. Cook on High 2 hours until candies dissolve and cider is hot.
3. Ladle into mugs and serve with apple slice floaters and cinnamon stick stirrers.

Note: *This is a cold-winter-night luxury. Make it in the morning and keep it on Low throughout the day so its good fragrance can fill the house.*

Maple Mulled Cider

Leesa Lesenski   Wheately, MA

MAKES: **8–10 SERVINGS**
PREP. TIME: **5–10 MINUTES**
COOKING TIME: **2 HOURS**
IDEAL SLOW COOKER SIZE: **3½-QUART**

½ gallon cider
3–4 cinnamon sticks
2 tsp. whole cloves
2 tsp. whole allspice
1–2 Tbsp. orange juice concentrate, *optional*
1–2 Tbsp. maple syrup, *optional*

1. Combine ingredients in slow cooker.
2. Cover. Heat on Low for 2 hours. Serve warm.

Tip: *Serve at Halloween, Christmas caroling, or sledding parties.*

Deep Red Apple Cider

Judi Manos   West Islip, NY

MAKES: **8–9 SERVINGS**
PREP. TIME: **5–10 MINUTES**
COOKING TIME: **3–4 HOURS**
IDEAL SLOW COOKER SIZE: **3½-QUART**

5 cups apple cider
3 cups dry red wine
¼ cup brown sugar
½ tsp. whole cloves
¼ tsp. whole allspice
1 stick cinnamon

1. Combine all ingredients in slow cooker.
2. Cover. Cook on Low 3–4 hours.
3. Remove cloves, allspice, and cinnamon before serving.

Variation: *You can use 8 cups apple cider and no red wine.*

Hot Spicy Cider for a Crowd

Lydia A. Yoder   London, OH

MAKES: **32 SERVINGS**
PREP. TIME: **5–10 MINUTES**
COOKING TIME: **2–6 HOURS**
IDEAL SLOW COOKER SIZE: **6-QUART**

1 gallon apple cider

1 cup sugar

2 tsp. ground cloves

2 tsp. ground allspice

2 3-inch-long cinnamon sticks

2 oranges studded with cloves

1. Combine all ingredients in slow cooker.
2. Cover. Cook on Low 5-6 hours, or on High 2-3 hours.

Variation: *You can replace apple cider with apple juice, especially if cider is out of season, and ¼ cup orange juice for the oranges.*

Wassail Punch

Marcia S. Myer   Manheim, PA

MAKES: **18 SERVINGS**
PREP. TIME: **5 MINUTES**
COOKING TIME: **2–3 HOURS**
IDEAL SLOW COOKER SIZE: **4-QUART**

2 quarts apple cider

2 cups orange juice

2 cups pineapple juice

½ cup lemon juice

⅓–½ cup sugar, according to your taste preference

12 whole cloves

4 cinnamon sticks

orange slices *or* clove-studded orange slices, *optional*

1. Combine all ingredients in slow cooker. Mix well.

2. Cover. Cook on Low 2-3 hours.
3. Remove cloves and cinnamon sticks before serving.

Per Serving: 140 calories (0 calories from fat), 0g total fat (0g saturated, 0g trans), 0mg cholesterol, 15mg sodium, 34g total carbohydrate (0.5g fiber, 31g sugar), 0g protein, 2%DV vitamin A, 20%DV vitamin C, 2%DV calcium, 2%DV iron.

Christmas Wassail

Linda Sluiter   Schererville, IN

MAKES: **8 SERVINGS**
PREP. TIME: **5 MINUTES**
COOKING TIME: **1–2 HOURS**
IDEAL SLOW COOKER SIZE: **3-QUART**

PICTURED ON PAGE 602

1 quart apple cider

½ cup orange *or* pineapple juice

2 cups water

3 orange pekoe tea bags

¼ cup brown sugar

¼ tsp. ground cinnamon

¼ tsp. ground cloves

oranges

1. Combine all ingredients except oranges in slow cooker.
2. Cover. Cook on High 1-2 hours.
3. Slice oranges to float on top. Serve in mugs.

Per Serving: 160 calories (0 calories from fat), 0g total fat (0g saturated, 0g trans), 0mg cholesterol, 20mg sodium, 45g total carbohydrate (7g fiber, 35g sugar), 1g protein, 2%DV vitamin A, 100%DV vitamin C, 8%DV calcium, 4%DV iron.

Holiday Wassail

Dolores S. Kratz   Souderton, PA

MAKES: **8 1-CUP SERVINGS**
PREP. TIME: **10 MINUTES**
COOKING TIME: **3–4 HOURS**
IDEAL SLOW COOKER SIZE: **4-QUART**

16-oz. can apricot halves, undrained

4 cups unsweetened pineapple juice

2 cups apple cider

1 cup orange juice

18 whole cloves

6 3½-inch cinnamon sticks, broken

1. In blender or food processor, blend apricots and liquid until smooth.
2. Place cloves and cinnamon sticks in cheesecloth bag.
3. Put all ingredients in slow cooker. Cook on Low 3–4 hours. Serve hot.

Hot Wassail Drink

Dale Peterson   Rapid City, SC

MAKES: **24–27 1-CUP SERVINGS**
PREP. TIME: **10 MINUTES**
COOKING TIME: **1–2 HOURS**
IDEAL SLOW COOKER SIZE: **6-QUART**

12-oz. can frozen orange juice

12-oz. can frozen lemonade

2 quarts apple juice

2 cups sugar, or less

3 Tbsp. whole cloves

2 tbsp. ground ginger

4 tsp. ground cinnamon

10 cups hot water

6 cups strong tea

1. Mix juices, sugar, and spices in slow cooker.
2. Add hot water and tea.

3. Heat on High until hot (1–2 hours), then on Low while serving.

Wassail Hot Cider

Ruth Hershey   Paradise, PA

MAKES: **18 6-OZ. SERVINGS**
PREP. TIME: **10–15 MINUTES**
COOKING TIME: **4 HOURS**
IDEAL SLOW COOKER SIZE: **6-QUART**

3 tea bags, your choice of flavors

1 quart boiling water

2 quarts cider

1 quart cranberry juice

2 cups orange juice

½ cup sugar

3 cinnamon sticks

12 whole cloves

thin orange slices, *optional*

1. Steep tea in boiling water for 5 minutes. Remove tea bags and pour tea into cooker.
2. Combine all remaining ingredients in slow cooker.
3. Cover. Cook on Low 4 hours.
4. Float orange slices in cider when ready to serve. Keep warm in cooker while serving.

Fruity Pineapple Wassail

Kelly Evenson Pittsboro, NC

MAKES: **20 CUPS**
PREP. TIME: **10 MINUTES**
COOKING TIME: **1–2 HOURS**
IDEAL SLOW COOKER SIZE: **5-QUART**

6 cups apple cider

1 cinnamon stick

¼ tsp. ground nutmeg

¼ cup honey

3 Tbsp. lemon juice

1 tsp. grated lemon rind

46-oz. can pineapple juice

1. Combine ingredients in slow cooker.
2. Cover. Cook on Low 1–2 hours.
3. Serve warm from slow cooker.

Variation: *Use 3 cups cranberry juice and reduce the amount of pineapple juice by 3 cups, to add more color and to change the flavor of the wassail.*

Spiced Wassail

Virginia Bender Dover, DE

MAKES: **16–18 SERVINGS**
PREP. TIME: **10 MINUTES**
COOKING TIME: **2–8 HOURS**
IDEAL SLOW COOKER SIZE: **6-QUART**

1 gallon cider

6-oz. container orange juice concentrate

6-oz. container lemonade concentrate

½–1 cup brown sugar

1 tsp. whole nutmeg

1 Tbsp. whole cloves

1 Tbsp. whole allspice

orange slices

cinnamon sticks

1. Combine cider, orange juice and lemonade concentrates, and brown sugar. Mix well.
2. Place nutmeg, cloves, and allspice in cheesecloth bag or spice ball. Add to juices in slow cooker.
3. Cover. Cook on Low 2–8 hours.
4. Float orange slices and cinnamon sticks on top. Ladle from slow cooker to serve.

Have one or two "company specials" you can make when friends show up unexpectedly.

Stunner Wassail

John D. Allen Rye, CO • *Susan Yoder Graber* Eureka, IL
Jan Pembleton Arlington, TX

MAKES: 12 1-CUP SERVINGS
PREP. TIME: 5–10 MINUTES
COOKING TIME: 5–9 HOURS
IDEAL SLOW COOKER SIZE: 4-QUART

2 quarts cider

1 pint cranberry juice

⅓–⅔ cup sugar

1 tsp. aromatic bitters

2 sticks cinnamon

1 tsp. whole allspice

1 small orange, studded with whole coves

1 cup rum, *optional*

1. Put all ingredients into cooker. Cover and cook on High 1 hour, then on Low 4–8 hours.
2. Serve warm from cooker.

   Tip: *If the wassail turns out to be too sweet for you, add more cranberry juice until you find the flavor balance to be more pleasing.*

Holiday Spice Punch

Maryland Massey Millington, MD

MAKES: 10 1-CUP SERVINGS
PREP. TIME: 5 MINUTES
COOKING TIME: 2 HOURS
IDEAL SLOW COOKER SIZE: 4-QUART

2 quarts apple cider

2 cups cranberry juice

2 Tbsp. mixed whole spices — allspice, cloves, coriander, and ginger

2 3-inch cinnamon sticks, broken

lemon *or* orange slices studded with whole cloves

1. Pour cider and juice into slow cooker. Place mixed spices in muslin bag or tea ball. Add to juice.
2. Cover and simmer on Low 2 hours.
3. Float cinnamon sticks and fruit slices in individual mugs as you serve.

Apple-Honey Tea

Jeanne Allen Rye, CO

MAKES: 6 1-CUP SERVINGS
PREP. TIME: 5 MINUTES
COOKING TIME: 1–2 HOURS
IDEAL SLOW COOKER SIZE: 3–4-QUART

12-oz. can frozen apple juice/cider concentrate

2 Tbsp. instant tea powder

1 Tbsp. honey

½ tsp. ground cinnamon

1. Reconstitute the apple juice/cider concentrate according to package directions. Pour into slow cooker.
2. Add tea powder, honey, and cinnamon. Stir to blend.
3. Heat on Low 1–2 hours. Stir well before serving since cinnamon tends to settle on bottom.

Hot Mulled Apple Tea

Barbara Tenney   Delta, PA

MAKES: **16 1-CUP SERVINGS**
PREP. TIME: **5–10 MINUTES**
COOKING TIME: **2 HOURS**
IDEAL SLOW COOKER SIZE: **5-QUART**

½ gallon apple cider
½ gallon strong tea
1 sliced lemon
1 sliced orange
3 3-inch cinnamon sticks
1 Tbsp. whole cloves
1 Tbsp. allspice
brown sugar to taste

1. Combine all in slow cooker.
2. Heat on Low 2 hours.

Johnny Appleseed Tea

Sheila Plock   Boalsburg, PA

MAKES: **8–9 CUPS**
PREP. TIME: **15–20 MINUTES**
COOKING TIME: **1–2 HOURS**
IDEAL SLOW COOKER SIZE: **3-QUART**

2 quarts water, *divided*
6 tea bags of your favorite flavor
6 ozs. frozen apple juice, thawed
¼ cup, plus 2 Tbsp., firmly packed
brown sugar

1. Bring 1 quart water to boil. Add tea bags.
   Remove from heat. Cover and let steep
   5 minutes. Pour into slow cooker.
2. Add remaining ingredients and mix well.
3. Cover. Heat on Low until hot. Continue on
   Low while serving from slow cooker.

Note: *I serve this wonderful hot beverage with
cookies at our Open House Tea and Cookies
afternoon, which I host at Christmas-time for
friends and neighbors.*

Spicy Tea

Ruth Retter   Manheim, PA

MAKES: **9–10 SERVINGS**
PREP. TIME: **15 MINUTES**
COOKING TIME: **2–3 HOURS**
IDEAL SLOW COOKER SIZE: **3½-QUART**

6 cups water
6 tea bags, experiment with various flavors, or use your
   favorite
⅓ cup sugar
2 Tbsp. honey
1½ cups orange juice
1½ cups pineapple juice

1. Place water in a saucepan and bring to a boil.
   Add tea bags to boiling water. Let stand 5
   minutes.
2. Remove tea bags. Pour tea into slow cooker.
3. Stir in remaining ingredients.
4. Cover and cook on Low 2–3 hours, until
   very hot.

Tip: *Float half an orange slice on each cup of tea.*

Hot Fruit Tea

Kelly Evenson Pittsboro, NC

MAKES: **20 SERVINGS**
PREP. TIME: **20 MINUTES**
COOKING TIME: **KEEP WARM**
IDEAL SLOW COOKER SIZE: **5-QUART**

5–6 tea bags, fruit flavor of your choice
2 cups boiling water
1¾ cups sugar
2 cinnamon sticks
2½ quarts water
1¼ tsp. vanilla
1¼ tsp. almond extract
juice of 3 lemons
juice of 3 oranges

1. Steep tea bags in boiling water for 5 minutes.
2. Bring tea water, sugar, cinnamon sticks, and 2½ quarts water to boil in saucepan. Remove from heat and add remaining ingredients.
3. Pour tea into slow cooker and keep warm there while serving.

Tip: *Float thinly cut fresh lemon and/or orange slices in tea.*

Delta Tea

Vera F. Schmucker Goshen, IN

MAKES: **6 CUPS**
PREP. TIME: **5 MINUTES**
COOKING TIME: **3–4 HOURS**
IDEAL SLOW COOKER SIZE: **2–3-QUART**

6-oz. can frozen lemonade
5 cups water
1 tsp. vanilla
1 tsp. almond flavoring
3 tsp. dry instant tea

1. Combine all ingredients in slow cooker.
2. Cover and cook on High 3–4 hours, or until very hot.
3. Serve hot from the cooker, or ice it and serve cold.

Hot Buttered Lemonade

Janie Steele Moore, OK

MAKES: **5–6 SERVINGS**
PREP. TIME: **5–10 MINUTES**
COOKING TIME: **2½ HOURS**
IDEAL SLOW COOKER SIZE: **2-QUART**

4½ cups water
¾ cup sugar
1½ tsp. grated lemon peel
¾ cup lemon juice
2 Tbsp. butter
6 cinnamon sticks

1. Combine water, sugar, lemon peel, lemon juice, and butter in slow cooker.
2. Cover. Cook on High for 2½ hours, or until well heated through.
3. Serve very hot with a cinnamon stick in each mug.

Orange-Ginger Tea

Jeanne Heyerly Chenoa, IL

MAKES: **8–10 SERVINGS**
PREP. TIME: **5 MINUTES**
COOKING TIME: **4–6 HOURS**
IDEAL SLOW COOKER SIZE: **2½-QUART**

2 quarts water
3 1-inch-squares fresh gingerroot, sliced
3 Tbsp. brown sugar *or* honey
1 orange, sliced

1. Place water and gingerroot in slow cooker.
2. Cover. Cook on High 2 hours, then on Low 2–4 hours.
3. Add sugar or honey and sliced orange 1 hour before serving.

Per Serving: 20 calories (0 calories from fat), 0g total fat (0g saturated, 0g trans), 0mg cholesterol, 10mg sodium, 6g total carbohydrate (0g fiber, 5g sugar), 0g protein, 0%DV vitamin A, 8%DV vitamin C, 2%DV calcium, 0%DV iron.

Note: *This tea makes cold-sufferers feel better!*

Mint Tea

Leona Miller Millersburg, OH

MAKES: **8 SERVINGS**
PREP. TIME: **5 MINUTES**
COOKING TIME: **2 HOURS**
IDEAL SLOW COOKER SIZE: **3-QUART**

2 quarts hot water
Splenda to taste
8 tea bags
2 drops mint extract

1. Combine water and Splenda in slow cooker. Mix well until Splenda is dissolved.

2. Add the tea bags and mint extract.
3. Cook on High 2 hours.

Per Serving: 0 calories (0 calories from fat), 0g total fat (0g saturated, 0g trans), 0mg cholesterol, 5mg sodium, 0g total carbohydrate (0g fiber, 0g sugar), 0g protein, 0%DV vitamin A, 0%DV vitamin C, 0%DV calcium, 0%DV iron.

Note: *This is nice for hot breakfast buffets.*

Almond Tea

Frances Schrag Newton, KS

MAKES: **10–11 SERVINGS**
PREP. TIME: **5 MINUTES**
COOKING TIME: **1 HOUR**
IDEAL SLOW COOKER SIZE: **4½-QUART**

10 cups boiling water
1 Tbsp. instant tea
⅔ cup lemon juice
6 Tbsp. sugar
1 tsp. vanilla
1 tsp. almond extract

1. Mix together all ingredients in slow cooker.
2. Turn to High and heat thoroughly (about 1 hour). Turn to Low while serving.

Per Serving: 30 calories (0 calories from fat), 0g total fat (0g saturated, 0g trans), 0mg cholesterol, 5mg sodium, 8g total carbohydrate (0g fiber, 7g sugar), 0g protein, 0%DV vitamin A, 0%DV vitamin C, 0%DV calcium, 0%DV iron.

Carolers' Hot Chocolate

Pat Unternahrer Wayland, IA

MAKES: **12–14 1-CUP SERVINGS**
PREP. TIME: **10 MINUTES**
COOKING TIME: **2–2½ HOURS**
IDEAL SLOW COOKER SIZE: **4–5-QUART**

10 cups milk
¾ cup sugar
¾ cup cocoa *or* hot chocolate mix
½ tsp. salt
2 cups hot water
marshmallows

1. Measure milk into slow cooker. Turn on High.
2. Mix together sugar, salt, and cocoa in heavy pan. Add hot water. Stir and boil 3 minutes, stirring often.
3. Pour into milk. Cook on High 2–2½ hours.

Hot Chocolate with Stir-Ins

Stacy Schmucker Stoltzfus Enola, PA

MAKES: **12 6-OZ. SERVINGS**
PREP. TIME: **5 MINUTES**
COOKING TIME: **1–2 HOURS**
IDEAL SLOW COOKER SIZE: **4-QUART**

9½ cups water
1½ cups hot chocolate mix
Stir-ins:
    smooth peanut butter
    chocolate-mint candies, chopped
    candy canes, broken
    assorted flavored syrups: hazelnut, almond, raspberry, Irish creme
    instant coffee granules
    cinnamon
    nutmeg
whipped topping
candy sprinkles

1. Pour water into slow cooker. Heat on High 1–2 hours. (Or heat water in tea kettle and pour into slow cooker.) Turn cooker to Low to keep hot for hours.
2. Stir in hot chocolate mix until blended.
3. Arrange stir-ins in small bowls.
4. Instruct guests to place approximately 1 Tbsp. of desired stir-in in mug before ladling hot chocolate in. Stir well.
5. Top with whipped topping and candy sprinkles.

Crockery Cocoa

Betty Hostetler Allensville, PA

MAKES: **9–12 SERVINGS, DEPENDING ON SIZE OF MUGS**
PREP. TIME: **10 MINUTES**
COOKING TIME: **1–4 HOURS**
IDEAL SLOW COOKER SIZE: **3½-QUART**

½ cup sugar

½ cup unsweetened cocoa powder

2 cups boiling water

3½ cups nonfat dry milk powder

6 cups water

1 tsp. vanilla

marshmallows

1 tsp. ground cinnamon

1. Combine sugar and cocoa powder in slow cooker. Add 2 cups boiling water. Stir well to dissolve.
2. Add dry milk powder, 6 cups water, and vanilla. Stir well to dissolve.
3. Cover. Cook on Low 4 hours, or on High 1–1½ hours.
4. Before serving, beat with rotary beater to make frothy. Ladle into mugs. Top with marshmallows and sprinkle with cinnamon.

Variations:

1. Add ⅛ tsp. ground nutmeg, along with ground cinnamon in Step 4.

2. Mocha-style—Stir ¾ tsp. coffee crystals into each serving in Step 4.

3. Coffee-Cocoa—Pour half-cups of freshly brewed, high quality coffee; top with half-cups of Crockery Cocoa.

Hot Mint Malt

Clarice Williams Fairbank, IA

MAKES: **6 SERVINGS**
PREP. TIME: **5 MINUTES**
COOKING TIME: **2–3 HOURS**
IDEAL SLOW COOKER SIZE: **2–3-QUART**

6 chocolate-covered cream-filled mint patties

5 cups milk

½ cup chocolate malted milk powder

1 tsp. vanilla

whipping cream, whipped stiff

1. In slow cooker, combine mint patties with milk, malted milk powder, and vanilla.
2. Heat on Low 2–3 hours. If you're able, stir occasionally to help melt the patties.
3. When the drink is thoroughly heated, beat with rotary beater until frothy.
4. Pour into cups and top with whipped cream.

Hot Chocolate Malted

Sharon Timpe Jackson, WI

MAKES: **8–10 SERVINGS**
PREP. TIME: **10 MINUTES**
COOKING TIME: **3 HOURS**
IDEAL SLOW COOKER SIZE: **3½-QUART**

1½ cups hot cocoa mix

½ cup chocolate malted milk powder

6 caramels, unwrapped

1 tsp. vanilla

8 cups water *or* milk

whipped topping, *optional*

25–30 miniature marshmallows, *optional*

1. Mix all ingredients except the last 2 optional ones in a slow cooker.
2. Heat on High 3 hours, stirring occasionally if you're home and able to do so.
3. Taste before serving. Depending upon the hot cocoa mix you've used, you may want to add more water or milk. (Heat additional liquid in the microwave before adding to the hot chocolate.)
4. Ladle into cups and top each with a dollop of whipped cream or marshmallows, if you wish.

Creamy Hot Chocolate

Deborah Heatwole Waynesboro, GA

MAKES: **8 SERVINGS**
PREP. TIME: **15 MINUTES**
COOKING TIME: **2–4 HOURS**
IDEAL SLOW COOKER SIZE: **3-QUART**

½ cup dry baking cocoa

14-oz. can sweetened condensed milk

⅛ tsp. salt

7½ cups water

1½ tsp. vanilla

24, or more, miniature marshmallows, *optional*

1. In slow cooker, combine dry cocoa, milk, and salt. Stir until smooth. Add water gradually, stirring until smooth.
2. Cover and cook on High 2 hours, or on Low 4 hours, or until very hot.
3. Just before serving, stir in vanilla.
4. Top each serving with 3 or more marshmallows, if you wish.

Tips:

1. To speed things up, heat the water before adding it to the chocolate mixture.

2. Keep hot chocolate warm on Low up to 4 hours in the slow cooker.

Variation: *Add a mocha flavor by stirring in instant coffee in Step 3.*

Italian Hot Chocolate

Cyndie Marrara Port Matilda, PA

MAKES: **4–6 SMALL SERVINGS**
PREP. TIME: **3–5 MINUTES**
COOKING TIME: **1–2 HOURS**
IDEAL SLOW COOKER SIZE: **1–2-QUART**

2 cups brewed strong coffee

½ cup instant hot chocolate mix

1 4-inch-long cinnamon stick, broken into large pieces

1 cup whipping cream

1 Tbsp. powdered sugar

1. Put coffee, hot chocolate mix, and cinnamon sticks into slow cooker. Stir.
2. Cover and cook on High 1–2 hours, or until very hot. Discard cinnamon pieces.
3. Immediately after you've turned on the cooker, place electric mixer beaters and mixer bowl in the fridge to chill (this makes the cream more likely to whip).
4. Just before serving, pour the whipping cream into the chilled electric mixer bowl. Beat cream on high speed until soft peaks form.
5. Fold sugar into whipped cream. Beat again on high speed until stiff peaks form.
6. Ladle hot chocolate coffee into small cups. Top each with a dollop of whipped cream.

Party Mocha

Barbara Sparks Glen Burnie, MD

MAKES: **10 SERVINGS**
PREP. TIME: **5 MINUTES**
COOKING TIME: **3 HOURS**
IDEAL SLOW COOKER SIZE: **3–4-QUART**

½ cup instant coffee granules

6 envelopes instant cocoa mix

2 quarts hot water

2 cups milk

whipped topping, *optional*

10 4-inch-long cinnamon sticks, *optional*

10 peppermint sticks, *optional*

1. Combine all ingredients, except the last 3 optional ones, in the slow cooker. Stir well.
2. Cover and cook on High 3 hours.
3. Stir and turn to Low to keep warm while serving.
4. To serve, pour mocha into cups. Top each with a dollop of whipped topping, or add a cinnamon stick or peppermint stick to each cup, if you wish.

When you find a recipe that you love, make a notation in the cookbook that it is a great recipe.

Spiced Coffee

Joyce Shackelford Green Bay, WI

MAKES: **8 SERVINGS**
PREP. TIME: **15 MINUTES**
COOKING TIME: **2–3 HOURS**
IDEAL SLOW COOKER SIZE: **3-QUART**

8 cups brewed coffee
⅓ cup sugar
¼ cup low-fat chocolate syrup
½ tsp. anise extract
4 cinnamon sticks, halved
1½ tsp. whole cloves

1. Combine coffee, sugar, chocolate syrup, and anise extract in slow cooker.
2. Place cinnamon sticks and cloves in cheesecloth bag. Place in slow cooker.
3. Cover. Cook on Low 2–3 hours.
4. Discard spice bag.
5. Ladle coffee into mugs. Garnish each with half a cinnamon stick.

Per Serving: 70 calories (10 calories from fat), 1g total fat (0g saturated, 0g trans), 0mg cholesterol, 20mg sodium, 17g total carbohydrate (0.5g fiber, 14g sugar), 0g protein, 6%DV vitamin A, 2%DV vitamin C, 2%DV calcium, 10%DV iron.

French Vanilla Eggnog

Char Hagner Montague, MI

MAKES: **8 SERVINGS**
PREP. TIME: **5 MINUTES**
COOKING TIME: **1–2 HOURS**
IDEAL SLOW COOKER SIZE: **2-QUART**

1 quart low-fat eggnog
1 Tbsp. instant decaf French vanilla coffee granules
¼ cup coffee-flavored liqueur

1. Combine eggnog and coffee granules in slow cooker.
2. Cover. Cook on Low 1–2 hours until mixture is hot and coffee granules dissolve.
3. Add coffee liqueur just before serving.
4. Ladle into mugs.

Per Serving: 170 calories (40 calories from fat), 4.5g total fat (2.5g saturated, 0g trans), 50mg cholesterol, 85mg sodium, 24g total carbohydrate (0g fiber, 22g sugar), 6g protein, 4%DV vitamin A, 0%DV vitamin C, 15%DV calcium, 0%DV iron.

Tip: *If you like, and if your diet allows, you may want to serve the eggnog topped with a spoonful of low-fat whipping cream and a sprinkling of shaved chocolate.*

If you can read a recipe and follow directions, you can cook.

Equivalent Measurements

dash = little less than ⅛ tsp.

3 teaspoons = 1 Tablespoon

2 Tablespoons = 1 oz.

4 Tablespoons = ¼ cup

5 Tablespoons plus 1 tsp. = ⅓ cup

8 Tablespoons = ½ cup

12 Tablespoons = ¾ cup

16 Tablespoons = 1 cup

1 cup = 8 ozs. liquid

2 cups = 1 pint

4 cups = 1 quart

4 quarts = 1 gallon

1 stick butter = ¼ lb.

1 stick butter = ½ cup

1 stick butter = 8 Tbsp.

Beans, 1 lb. dried = 2–2½ cups
(depending upon the size of the beans)

Bell peppers, 1 large = 1 cup chopped

Cheese, hard (for example, cheddar,
Swiss, Monterey Jack, mozzarella),
1 lb. grated = 4 cups

Cheese, cottage, 1 lb. = 2 cups

Chocolate chips, 6-oz. pkg. = 1 scant cup

Crackers (butter, saltines, snack),
20 single crackers = 1 cup crumbs

Herbs, 1 Tbsp. fresh = 1 tsp. dried

Lemon, 1 medium-sized = 2–3 Tbsp. juice

Lemon, 1 medium-sized = 2–3 tsp. grated rind

Mustard, 1 Tbsp. prepared = 1 tsp. dry or
ground mustard

Oatmeal, 1 lb. dry = about 5 cups dry

Onion, 1 medium-sized = ½ cup chopped

Pasta

Macaronis, penne, and other small or
tubular shapes, 1 lb. dry = 4 cups
uncooked

Noodles, 1 lb. dry = 6 cups uncooked

Spaghetti, linguine, fettucine,
1 lb. dry = 4 cups uncooked

Potatoes, white, 1 lb. = 3 medium-sized
potatoes = 2 cups mashed

Potatoes, sweet, 1 lb. = 3 medium-sized
potatoes = 2 cups mashed

Rice, 1 lb. dry = 2 cups uncooked

Sugar, confectioners, 1 lb. = 3½ cups sifted

Whipping cream, 1 cup unwhipped = 2 cups
whipped

Whipped topping, 8-oz. container = 3 cups

Yeast, dry, 1 envelope (¼ oz.) = 1 Tbsp.

Assumptions about Ingredients

flour = unbleached *or* white, and all-purpose

oatmeal or oats = dry, quick *or* rolled (old-fashioned), unless specified

pepper = black, finely ground

rice = regular, long-grain (not minute or instant unless specified)

salt = table salt

shortening = solid, not liquid

sugar = granulated sugar (not brown and not confectioners)

Three Hints

1 If you'd like to cook more at home—without being in a frenzy—go off by yourself with your cookbook some evening and make a week of menus. Then make a grocery list from that. Shop from your grocery list.

2 Thaw frozen food in a bowl in the fridge (not on the counter-top). If you forget to stick the food in the fridge, put it in a microwave-safe bowl and defrost it in the microwave just before you're ready to use it.

3 Let roasted meat, as well as pasta dishes with cheese, rest for 10–20 minutes before slicing or dishing. That will allow the juices to re-distribute themselves throughout the cooked food. You'll have juicier meat, and a better presentation of your pasta dish.

Substitute Ingredients
for when you're in a pinch

For one cup **buttermilk**—use 1 cup plain yogurt; or pour 1⅓ Tbsp. lemon juice or vinegar into a 1-cup measure. Fill the cup with milk. Stir and let stand for 5 minutes. Stir again before using.

For 1 oz. **unsweetened baking chocolate**—stir together 3 Tbsp. unsweetened cocoa powder and 1 Tbsp. butter, softened.

For 1 Tbsp. **cornstarch**—use 2 Tbsp. all-purpose flour; or 4 tsp. minute tapioca.

For 1 **garlic clove**—use ¼ tsp. garlic salt (reduce salt in recipe by ⅛ tsp.); or ⅛ tsp. garlic powder.

For 1 Tbsp. **fresh herbs**—use 1 tsp. dried herbs.

For ½ lb. **fresh mushrooms**—use 1 6-oz. can mushrooms, drained.

For 1 Tbsp. **prepared mustard**—use 1 tsp. dry or ground mustard.

For 1 **medium-sized fresh onion**—use 2 Tbsp. minced dried onion; or 2 tsp. onion salt (reduce salt in recipe by 1 tsp.); or 1 tsp. onion powder. Note: These substitutions will work for meat balls and meat loaf, but not for sautéing.

For 1 cup **sour milk**—use 1 cup plain yogurt; or pour 1 Tbsp. lemon juice or vinegar into a 1-cup measure. Fill with milk. Stir and then let stand for 5 minutes. Stir again before using.

For 2 Tbsp. **tapioca**—use 3 Tbsp. all-purpose flour.

For 1 cup canned **tomatoes**—use 1⅓ cups diced fresh tomatoes, cooked gently for 10 minutes.

For 1 Tbsp. **tomato paste**—use 1 Tbsp. ketchup.

For 1 Tbsp. **vinegar**—use 1 Tbsp. lemon juice.

For 1 cup **heavy cream**—add ⅓ cup melted butter to ¾ cup milk. *Note: This will work for baking and cooking, but not for whipping.*

For 1 cup **whipping cream**—chill thoroughly ⅔ cup evaporated milk, plus the bowl and beaters, then whip; or use 2 cups bought whipped topping.

For ½ cup **wine**—pour 2 Tbsp. wine vinegar into a ½ -cup measure. Fill with broth (chicken, beef, or vegetable). Stir and then let stand for 5 minutes. Stir again before using.

Kitchen Tools and Equipment You Really Ought to Have

1 Make sure you have a little electric vegetable chopper, the size that will handle 1 cup of ingredients at a time.

2 Don't try to cook without a good paring knife that's sharp (and holds its edge) and fits in your hand.

3 Almost as important—a good chef's knife (we always called it a "butcher" knife) with a wide, sharp blade that's about 8 inches long, good for making strong cuts through meats.

4 You really ought to have a good serrated knife with a long blade, perfect for slicing bread.

5 Invest in at least one broad, flexible, heat-resistant spatula. And also a narrow one.

6 You ought to have a minimum of 2 wooden spoons, each with a 10-12 inch-long handle. They're perfect for stirring without scratching.

7 Get a washable cutting board. You'll still need it, even though you have an electric vegetable chopper (#1 above).

8 A medium-sized whisk takes care of persistent lumps in batters, gravies, and sauces when there aren't supposed to be any.

9 Get yourself a salad spinner.

Index

Chicken with Broccoli Rice, 344
Cream of Broccoli and Mushroom Soup,
 186
Dawn's Quick & Healthy Vegetable Soup,
 180
Egg and Broccoli Casserole, 67
Garden Vegetables, 521
Ham-Broccoli Casserole, 451
Ham 'n Cheese Soup, 169
Hearty Broccoli-Beef Dip, 13
Hot Broccoli Dip, 44
Quick Broccoli Fix, 528
Savory Slow Cooker Chicken, 348
Soup to Get Thin On, 177
"Stir-Fry" Veggies, 522
Swiss Cheese and Veggie Soup, 184
Szechwan-Style Chicken and Broccoli, 350
Tortellini with Broccoli, 506
Zippy Vegetable Medley, 521
Broccoli and Rice Casserole, 529
Broccoli Casserole, 529
Broccoli-Cheese Dip, 43
Broccoli-Cheese Soup, 187
Broccoli-Cheese with Noodles Soup, 187
Broccoli Cornbread, 79
Broccoli Delight, 530
Broccoli, Potato, and Cheese Soup, 186
Broccoli-Rice Casserole, 590
Broccoli Soup, 185
Broccoli-Turkey Supreme, 410
Brownies with Nuts, 620
Brown-Sugar Chili, 124
Brown-Sugar Pear Butter, 59
Brunswick Soup Mix, 162
Brussels Sprouts with Pimentos, 533
Brussels Sprouts
 Brussels Sprouts with Pimentos, 533
Buffalo Chicken Wing Soup, 139
Buffet Beef , 230
Burgundy Pot Roast, 240
Burgundy Roast, 239
Busy Cook's Stew, 86
Butter Beans *See Beans, Butter*
Butternut Squash Soup, 195
Butterscotch Dip, 59
Butterscotch Haystacks, 60
Butterscotch
 Butterscotch Dip, 59
 Butterscotch Haystacks, 60
 Seven Layer Bars, 621

C

Cabbage and Corned Beef, 212
Cabbage Casserole, 534
Cabbage Joe, 415
Cabbage-Sausage Soup, 172
Cabbage
 Barley-Cabbage Soup, 178
 Bavarian Cabbage, 534
 Beef-Vegetable Casserole, 265
 Best Everyday Stew, 256
 Bratwurst Stew, 468
 Cabbage and Corned Beef, 212
 Cabbage Casserole, 534
 Cabbage Joe, 415
 Cabbage-Sausage Soup, 172
 Cedric's Casserole, 267
 Chicken Vegetable Gala, 352
 Corned Beef Dinner, 213
 Flavor-Filled Pork and Sauerkraut, 428
 Fruity Corned Beef and Cabbage, 212
 German Potato Soup, 164
 Grace's Minestrone Soup, 182
 Ham and Cabbage, 450
 Hearty Bean and Vegetable Soup, 116
 Jeanne's Vegetable-Beef Borscht, 84
 Kielbasa and Cabbage, 465
 Lilli's Vegetable-Beef Soup, 84
 Low-Calorie Soup, 177
 Minestrone, 176
 Nutritious Meat Loaf, 313
 Pork and Cabbage Dinner, 438
 Potato-Stuffed Cabbage, 581
 Soup to Get Thin On, 177
 "Stir-Fry" Veggies, 522
 Stuffed Cabbage, 266
 Stuffed Ground Beef, 266
 Sweet-Sour Cabbage, 534
 Tofu and Vegetables, 522
Cacciatore
 Chicken and Sausage Cacciatore, 373
 Chicken Cacciatore with Spaghetti, 372
 Low-Fat Chicken Cacciatore, 372
Cajun Sausage and Beans, 563
Cake
 Apple Cake, 616
 Black Forest Cake, 613
 Carrot Cake, 615
 Chocolate Mud Cake, 619
 Chocolate Peanut Butter Cake, 611

Chocolate Soufflé Cake, 611
 Easy Autumn Cake, 614
 Fruity Cake, 614
 Fruity Delight Cake, 618
 Harvey Wallbanger Cake, 617
 Hot Fudge Cake, 612
 Lemon Poppy Seed Upside-Down Cake,
 618
 Lemon Pudding Cake, 615
 Low-Fat Apple Cake, 617
 Peanut Butter and Hot Fudge Pudding
 Cake, 612
 Peanut Butter Cake, 614
 Self-Frosting Fudge Cake, 613
 Streusel Cake, 74
 Upside-Down Chocolate Pudding Cake,
 610
Calico Beans with Corn, 565
California Chicken, 385
Can-You-Believe-It's-So-Simple Salsa
 Chicken, 375
Candies
 Slow Cooker Candy, 60
Cannellini Beans *See Beans, Cannellini*
Cape Breton Chicken, 346
Caponata, 541
Caramel Apples, 631
Caramel Apples on Sticks, 631
Caramelized Onions, 538
Caribbean-Style Black Bean Soup, 108
Carmeled Pears 'n Wine, 623
Carolers' Hot Chocolate, 654
Carolina Pot Roast, 424
Carrot Cake, 615
Carrot Casserole, 533
Carrot-Lentil Casserole, 513
Carrots
 Apple-Glazed Carrots, 532
 Apricot-Glazed Carrots, 531
 Carrot Cake, 615
 Carrot Casserole, 533
 Carrot-Lentil Casserole, 513
 Golden Carrots, 531
 Orange-Glazed Carrots, 532
Casey's Beans, 565
Cashews
 Asian Chicken Cashew Dish, 366
 Norma's Vegetarian Chili, 117
Casserole Verde, 288
Cassoulet Chowder, 146

Index

About the Author

Phyllis Pellman Good is a *New York Times* bestselling author whose books have sold nearly 10 million copies.

Good authored the national #1 bestselling cookbook ***Fix-It and Forget-It Cookbook: Feasting with Your Slow Cooker*** (with Dawn J. Ranck), which appeared on *The New York Times* bestseller list, as well as the bestseller lists of *USA Today*, *Publishers Weekly*, and *Book Sense*. And she is the author of ***Fix-It and Forget-It Lightly: Healthy, Low-Fat Recipes for Your Slow Cooker***, which has also appeared on *The New York Times* bestseller list. In addition, Good authored ***Fix-It and Forget-It 5-Ingredient Favorites: Comforting Slow-Cooker Recipes***; ***Fix-It and Forget-It Recipes for Entertaining: Slow-Cooker Favorites for all the Year Round*** (with Ranck); and ***Fix-It and Forget-It Diabetic Cookbook: Slow-Cooker Favorites to Include Everyone*** (with the American Diabetes Association), all in the series.

Good is also the author of the *Fix-It and Enjoy-It* series, a "cousin" series to the phenomenally successful *Fix-It and Forget-It* cookbooks. There are currently three books in that series: the flagship book, ***Fix-It and Enjoy-It Cookbook: All-Purpose, Welcome-Home Recipes***, which appeared on *The New York Times* bestseller list; ***Fix-It and Enjoy-It 5-Ingredient Recipes: Quick and Easy—for Stove-Top and Oven!***; and ***Fix-It and Enjoy-It Diabetic Cookbook: Stove-Top and Oven Recipes—for Everyone!*** (with the American Diabetes Association). Forthcoming is ***Fix-It and Enjoy-It Healthy Cookbook: 400 Great Stove-Top and Oven Recipes*** (with nutritional expertise from Mayo Clinic).

Good's other cookbooks include ***Favorite Recipes with Herbs***, ***The Best of Amish Cooking***, and ***The Central Market Cookbook***.

Phyllis Pellman Good is Executive Editor at Good Books. (Good Books has published hundreds of titles by more than 135 authors.) She received her B.A. and M.A. in English from New York University. She and her husband, Merle, live in Lancaster, Pennsylvania. They are the parents of two young-adult daughters.

For a complete listing of books by Phyllis Pellman Good, as well as excerpts and reviews, visit www.Fix-ItandForget-It.com or www.GoodBooks.com.

National Bestsellers!

More than 8.9 million copies sold!

New York Times bestselling author
Phyllis Pellman Good

⇨ *For slow cookers:*

*Fix-It and Forget-It
5-ingredient Favorites*

*Fix-It and Forget-It
Cookbook*

*Fix-It and Forget-It
Lightly*

*Fix-It and Forget-It
Recipes for Entertaining*

*Fix-It and Forget-It
Diabetic Cookbook*

⇨ *For stove-top and oven:*

*Fix-It and Enjoy-It!
Cookbook*

*Fix-It and Enjoy-It!
Diabetic Cookbook*

*Fix-It and Enjoy-It!
5-Ingredient Recipes*

*Fix-It and Enjoy-It!
Healthy Cookbook*

*"Little fuss.
Lots of flavor.
We busy people
love that!"
– Phyllis*